Classical Japanese Prose

Classical Japanese Prose

An Anthology

Compiled and Edited by

Helen Craig McCullough

Stanford University Press
Stanford, California

Stanford University Press
Stanford, California

© 1990 by the Board of Trustees of the
Leland Stanford Junior University
Printed in the United States of America

Original printing 1990
Last figure below indicates year of this printing:

00 99 98 97 96 95 94 93 92 91

CIP data appear at the end of the book

For Duncan

Preface

With the exceptions that follow, the translations in this volume are based on *Nihon koten bungaku taikei* texts. *The Gossamer Journal* is based on Kakimoto Tsutomu, ed., *Kagerō nikki zenchūshaku*, 2 vols. (1966); *The Pillow Book of Sei Shōnagon* on Matsuo Satoshi and Nagai Kazuko, eds., *Makura no sōshi*, vol. 11 of Shōgakkan, *Nihon koten bungaku zenshū* (1974); *The Confessions of Lady Nijō* on Tsugita Kasumi, ed., *Towazugatari*, vol. 62 of Asahi Shinbunsha, *Nihon koten zensho* (1966); *An Account of a Journey to the East* on Tamai Kōsuke, ed., *Tōkan kikō*, in vol. 64 of *Nihon koten zensho* (1957); and *The Journal of the Sixteenth-Night Moon* on Ishida Yoshisada, ed., *Izayoi nikki*, in vol. 64 of *Nihon koten zensho*. Translations are mine unless otherwise indicated.

Ages mentioned in the texts are calculated in the Japanese manner, according to the number of calendar years during which a person lives. Those mentioned elsewhere are calculated in the Western manner.

Because the Japanese calendar was divided into twelve months approximately equivalent to the lunations, they did not correspond to their numerical equivalents in the Western calendar. The Seventh Month, for example, always included part of August, and in a given year might fall as late as the latter half of August and the first half of September. The four seasons were regarded as consisting of four months each, with spring beginning on the First Day of the First Month, summer on the First Day of the Fourth Month, and so on.

A brief discussion of classical verse and its conventions is provided in Appendix B, "Classical Japanese Poetry"; background information concerning other important aspects of court life, in Appendix A, "Offices, Ranks, and the Imperial Palace." Information on historical and mythical figures, place-names, and events appears in the Glossary; and where pertinent, the principal characters who figure in a selection are identified in separate lists at the ends of the introductory sections.

I am grateful to Stanford University Press for permission to use copyrighted materials; to Special Collections, Brigham Young University Library, for permission to reproduce a picture of Sei Shōnagon from *Wakoku Tamakazura*; to the East Asiatic Library, University of California at Berkeley, for permission to reproduce xylograph prints from its collection; to the Center for Japanese Studies, University of California at Berkeley, for financial assistance; to William McCullough for reading the Introduction and offering helpful advice; to Steven D. Carter for editorial advice and extensive computer assistance; and to an anonymous reader for valuable suggestions and corrections. It is a special pleasure to thank three associate translators: Robert L. Backus, for agreeing to the use of selections from *The Riverside Counselor's Stories* (Stanford, Calif., 1985); Steven D. Carter, for preparing the selections from *Essays in Idleness*; and George Perkins, for making available portions of his unpublished dissertation, "A Study and Partial Translation of *Masukagami*" (Stanford University, 1977).

The following abbreviations have been used:

1. Imperial poetic anthologies. Numbers following these abbreviations are those in Matsushita Daizaburō and Watanabe Fumio, eds., *Kokka taikan*, vol. 1 (Kyōbunsha, 1903).

GSIS	*Goshūishū* (Later Collection of Gleanings, 1086)
GSS	*Gosenshū* (Later Collection, ca. 951)
KKS	*Kokinshū* (Collection of Early and Modern Poetry, ca. 905)
KYS	*Kin'yōshū* (Collection of Golden Leaves, 1124–27)
MYS	*Man'yōshū* (Collection for a Myriad Ages, after 759)
SCSS	*Shin chokusenshū* (New Imperial Collection, 1234)
ShokuGSS	*Shoku gosenshū* (Later Collection Continued, 1251)
SIS	*Shūishū* (Collection of Gleanings, ca. 1006)
SKKS	*Shin kokinshū* (New Collection of Early and Modern Poetry, 1206)
SZS	*Senzaishū* (Collection for a Thousand Years, 1188)

2. Other

WKRES   *Wakan rōeishū* (Collection of Japanese and Chinese *Rōei* Songs, ca. 1011). In Kawaguchi Hisao and Shida Engi, eds., *Wakan rōeishū, Ryōjin hishō,* vol. 73 of *Nihon koten bungaku taikei.*

H.C.M.

Contents

Maps

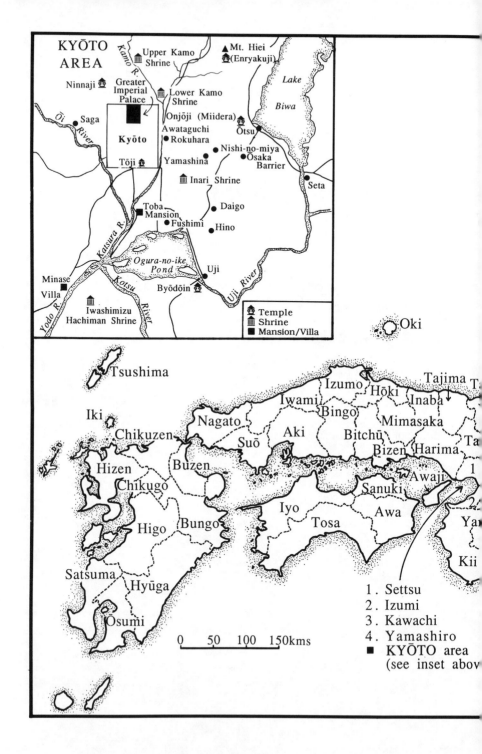

KYŌTO AREA

Upper Kamo Shrine
Mt. Hiei (Enryakuji)
Ninnaji
Greater Imperial Palace
Lower Kamo Shrine
Lake Biwa
Ōi River
Saga
Onjōji (Miidera)
Awataguchi
Ōtsu
Kyōto
Rokuhara
Nishi-no-miya
Ōsaka Barrier
Tōji
Yamashina
Inari Shrine
Seta
Toba Mansion
Daigo
Fushimi
Hino
Katsura R.
Ogura-no-ike Pond
Uji
Minase Villa
Kotsu
Byōdōin
Uji River
Iwashimizu Hachiman Shrine
Yodo R.

☯ Temple
🏛 Shrine
■ Mansion/Villa

Oki
Tsushima
Tajima
Izumo Hōki
Iwami
Inaba
Iki
Nagato
Bingo
Mimasaka
Chikuzen
Aki
Bitchū
Bizen Harima
Hizen
Buzen
Awaji
Chikugo
Sanuki
Iyo
Awa
Higo
Bungo
Tosa
Kii
Satsuma
Hyūga
Osumi

0   50   100   150kms

1. Settsu
2. Izumi
3. Kawachi
4. Yamashiro
■ KYŌTO area (see inset abov

SEA OF JAPAN

Mutsu

Dewa

Sado

Noto

Echigo

Kaga Etchū

hizen
akasa Hida Kōzuke

Shinano Shimotsuke

Mino Musashi

Owari Kai Hitachi

Mikawa Suruga Sagami Shimōsa

Tōtōmi Izu Kazusa

Shima Awa

PACIFIC OCEAN

C. Semans '88

Japan in the classical age

Classical Japanese Prose

Introduction

This volume contains a selection of Japanese prose literature dating from the classical age, the centuries during which the preeminent cultural and aesthetic values were those of the Heian court. The age may be said to have begun in the ninth century, shortly before the birth of our earliest known author, Ki no Tsurayuki (ca. 872–945), and to have ended around the seventeenth century, when new social conditions gave rise to the altered perspective and literary innovations of Ihara Saikaku (1642–93) and later writers. Matsuo Bashō (1644–94), the last major figure to found his practice on the old tradition, is the last author represented.[1]

During the early centuries of the classical age, the imperial seat at Heian (modern Kyōto) was both the cultural capital of Japan and the locus of power. Wealth from the provinces supported a tiny hereditary aristocracy of perhaps 400 or 500 persons, whose male members monopolized the positions in a Chinese-style bureaucracy and whose female members occupied themselves with men, pregnancies, deliveries, polite accomplishments, the sewing and perfuming of the elaborate costumes worn by both sexes, and related concerns. Thanks in part to accidents of geography, the aristocratic class enjoyed centuries of peaceful dominance, unthreatened by the kind of internal and external challenges that

1. The anthology seeks to bring together noteworthy works in convenient, affordable form, and to present them either complete or in excerpts long enough to give an adequate impression of the originals. Because of space limitations, I have had to omit the two long masterpieces of the age, *The Tale of Genji* and *The Tale of the Heike*, which deserve to be read in their entirety, and which are readily available in paperback English translations.

made warfare a way of life for its counterparts in other times and places. It was not military prowess that won a man social prominence and political influence, but rather birth; skill in the establishment and maintenance of patronage relationships, including the forging of advantageous marital alliances; expertise in the rituals and ceremonies that governed the conduct of official and private life; and—not the least important—the ability to hold his own as a poet, musician, and calligrapher.

Ultimately of Chinese origin but thoroughly naturalized, the emphasis on the arts was one of the more striking aspects of Heian civilization. In a society where poetry and music were integral components of formal and informal social occasions and private life, an apt verse might win a promotion in office or thaw an unresponsive heart, and moral turpitude was scarcely more reprehensible than a clumsy hand. In Heian eyes, the truly admirable personal qualities included those that reflected aesthetic values. The "good" man was apt to be someone with rarified tastes whose immersion in Chinese history and literature, Japanese poetry, and Buddhist doctrine had made him sensitive to the feelings of others, responsive to nature in all its manifestations, and acutely conscious of the vulnerability of beauty, the ephemerality of worldly things, and the pathos of the human condition. By definition, he belonged to the aristocracy, the only class consistently capable of refined feeling. Such a man was said to have "heart" (*kokoro*) and to understand the "sadness of things" (*mono no aware*). An aristocratic woman was expected to possess the same qualities, partly as a birthright and partly through education—which, however, did not include Chinese learning. It was people of that kind who constituted the chief producers, consumers, and patrons of literature in Japan between the ninth and the late twelfth centuries, a subdivision of the classical age that is referred to in this volume as the Heian period.

A crucial development of the Heian period was the emergence, around the middle of the ninth century, of a forerunner of the modern hiragana syllabary. After the importation of the Chinese writing system, male Japanese aristocrats had begun to write poetry and "serious" (i.e., nonfictional) belletristic prose in Chinese.[2] A large collection of poetry

2. Chinese characters were introduced around the fourth century A.D., but their initial use was limited to Chinese and Korean immigrants. It is not clear exactly when Japanese males became literate.

in Japanese, composed by both men and women, had also been committed to writing around the middle of the eighth century, albeit with difficulty, by means of Chinese characters used for their phonetic and semantic values. But there had been no satisfactory medium in which to record the vernacular language, and no way for women to achieve literacy, discouraged as they were from the study of Chinese. The new syllabary, by making it easier for people to exchange the formal and informal poems demanded on social occasions, played a vital role in creating and nurturing the literary atmosphere that was to become characteristic of the society. In providing a simple means of recording vernacular prose, it also paved the way for the appearance of a remarkable group of feminine authors. Of six individual titles (as opposed to collections) represented in the Heian portion of this anthology, two are known to have been written by women and a third can almost certainly be ascribed to a feminine hand. The author of the greatest single classical work, *The Tale of Genji* (Genji monogatari, 11th c.), was a woman, as were the authors of *The Diary of Murasaki Shikibu* (Murasaki shikibu nikki, 11th c.) and *The Sarashina Diary* (Sarashina nikki, 11th c.), the only other major Heian works by identifiable authors not included here.

At the Heian court, where the ability to turn a passable verse was a social skill acquired through familiarity with well-established conventions, a true literary gift appears to have been no more common than in other societies. Of the talented few, most belonged to the provincial Governor class, the lower stratum of the aristocracy. Many of the male writers were quasi-professional poets who were well represented in imperial anthologies, participated in poetry contests sponsored by the great, and composed verses on commission for folding screens; others were scholars admired for their ability to write poetry, essays, memorials, and Buddhist petitions in Chinese; and still others were anonymous authors of histories and tales in Japanese.

Histories and tales in the vernacular enjoyed little prestige, partly because vernacular prose was still very much an upstart as late as the tenth century, partly because of the traditional Confucian hostility to fiction. Most men considered such writing a frivolous waste of time. For women, however, Japanese was the sole medium available for sustained literary expression, and thus it was largely women who first demonstrated the superiority of the language to Chinese as a means of dealing in significant and memorable fashion with the realities of contemporary life. A number of Heian women were excellent poets, but those who turned to prose were the ones who produced an impressive proportion of the enduring monuments of Japanese literature.

The mere existence of the kana syllabary was insufficient in itself to inspire an outpouring of feminine literature such as the Heian period witnessed. At the very least, a woman also needed leisure, access to paper (a precious commodity), and the kind of experiences and social environment that would stimulate the creative impulse. For a provincial Governor's talented daughter, service as a lady-in-waiting in an exalted household provided just such conditions.

The typical daughter of a high court noble—a Minister of State or a Regent—spent a good deal of time in pursuits related to literature. She studied the poetry of the past, composed innumerable verses of her own, and took a lively interest in romances. If she was very young or found herself in a situation requiring an exceptional performance, she might call on a lady-in-waiting to act as a surrogate poet; when she obtained the loan of an interesting story, she might ask a lady to copy it; when she wished to amuse herself with a romance, she might command a lady to read it aloud while she herself gazed at an illustrated version of the same tale. She might call on all her attendants to stage a contest pitting old tales against new ones. And she was highly appreciative of anyone who supplied her with original reading matter.

If such a high-born lady happened to become an imperial consort, the engagement of literary women to serve in her entourage became a matter of political concern. During the first two-thirds of the Heian period, power at court was exercised almost exclusively by a single great clan, the Fujiwara, whose male leaders married their sisters and daughters to Crown Princes and Emperors, pulled strings to ensure the succession of the resultant sons (there being no rule of primogeniture), and dominated young sovereigns as maternal uncles and grandfathers. Intra-clan rivalries and polygyny led to the presence of multiple imperial consorts, each supported by a father dedicated to the advancement of her career, and each eager to make her apartments more attractive than those of her competitors.

Any consort would, of course, have been schooled in the approved accomplishments long before her presentation, and her father would have provided her with a sumptuous wardrobe and luxurious furnishings for her palace residence. Of equal importance, if she hoped to interest a cultivated young Emperor and his gentlemen, was a troupe of pretty, clever ladies-in-waiting. The contribution of such women to the ambience of a successful salon is illustrated with especial clarity in *The Pillow Book of Sei Shōnagon* (Makura no sōshi, ca. 1000–1010). Amusing stories and quips; elegant contests matching pictures, fans, or singing insects, with accompanying poems; witty literary allusions; deft poetic repartee—all invited the Emperor to linger at the consort's side. Sei Shōnagon herself, a born raconteur and a writer of rare sensibility, was the star of one such salon, even though she was somewhat old for a court lady-in-waiting.

Not all Heian women authors served imperial consorts, but almost all the important ones of whom we have knowledge either possessed or acquired court connections. Sei Shōnagon and her contemporary Murasaki Shikibu, the two great feminine luminaries of the period, were both provincial Governors' daughters whose literary powers won them appointments as Empresses' ladies-in-waiting in the day of Fujiwara no Michinaga (966–1027), when Heian society was at the peak of its brilliance.

Abundant economic resources and demonstrable practical utility had been the supports sustaining magnificent establishments like those of Empresses Teishi and Shōshi, the rival consorts whom Sei Shōnagon and Murasaki Shikibu served. In the second half of the eleventh century, the Fujiwara hegemony was challenged successfully by an energetic former sovereign's creation of an alternative power center, the Retired Emperor's Office. A diminution of the role of the imperial consort followed, and literary ladies tended thenceforth to gravitate to the households of members of the imperial clan, such as Princesses and the Retired Emperors themselves.

During and after the twelfth century, even more significant changes occurred. The aristocracy, which had grown increasingly lax in its control over the provinces, began to lose economic and political power to a rising class of provincial warriors. In the 1180's, after some preliminary rumbles, a major war was fought between two great military clans, the Taira (also called Heike) and the Minamoto (also called Genji). The establishment by the victorious Minamoto chieftain, Yoritomo, of a military government, the Kamakura shogunate, left the Retired Emperor of the day, Go-Toba (1180–1239; r. 1183–97), with only nominal authority; and an abortive attempt to overthrow the shogunate in

1221 resulted in Go-Toba's exile to Oki Island, where he remained until his death.

In 1333, an enfeebled shogunate was brought down by Emperor Go-Daigo (1288–1339; r. 1318–39), but he was little more than the puppet of ambitious warriors, and his brief "restoration" ended three years later with the creation of a new military government, the Ashikaga shogunate, in the Muromachi district of the capital. That event led, in turn, to more strife among power-hungry warriors—a long period of civil discord ending only with the establishment of the Tokugawa shogunate at Edo (modern Tōkyō) in 1603.

Meanwhile, the aristocracy was reduced to desperate straits. Revenues from the provinces dried up; the terrible Ōnin Wars of 1467–77 destroyed more than half the capital; and the citizens were terrorized by huge outlaw gangs, armies of militant monks, arsonists, and debtors rioting against the shogunate. Living in makeshift dwellings and scrambling to keep body and soul together, the court nobles of the fifteenth century were in no position to supply their daughters with ladies-in-waiting of the old kind, or to extend the patronage that had supported the male poets and scholars of an earlier era. The women retreated to the obscurity of the home, and many of the male literati joined others of the minor aristocracy in taking Buddhist vows, unable to maintain themselves as members of society.

Literary activity continued because the cultural values established in the Heian period were not seriously questioned, but leading members of the military class took over the sponsorship of ambitious public events like noh performances and large-scale linked-verse sessions. Readers and audiences, a more heterogeneous group than before, included warriors and some commoners; and a significant number of the best prose works, as well as of the best poems, were produced by reclusive Buddhist monks, men who had renounced the world to devote their lives to religion and the arts. That era of changing sponsors, consumers, and producers of literature, which extended roughly from the thirteenth through the sixteenth century, will be designated below as the medieval period.

In surveying the prose literature of the classical age, we will need to depart from familiar concepts. Western readers have usually regarded belletristic prose as consisting of two main types of narrative fiction, the novel and the short story, supplemented by lesser fiction, certain essays, and a few distinguished examples of historical, biographical, and auto-biographical writing. In Heian and medieval Japan, where fiction was, by definition, beneath serious consideration, there was a strong incentive for an author to assert that he was telling a true story. Even a romance like *The Tale of the Bamboo Cutter* (Taketori monogatari, late 9th c.?) borrowed the names of historical figures for some of its moon maiden's suitors; even an improbable yarn in a collection of anecdotes strove for verisimilitude by mentioning dates and places. And many writers purported to eschew fiction altogether, presenting their works as factual descriptions of real persons and events, and themselves as historians, record keepers, and memoirists. The desire of readers to hear about believable people in believable situations makes such authorial stances common in all societies. But we are faced with a difficulty if we try to associate the usual Western concept of a diary with an autobiographical work like *The Gossamer Journal*, which exhibits some diary-like features but shifts between first- and third-person narration and suppresses material irrelevant to a clearly defined central theme, or if we accept the term history for *The Tale of the Heike* (Heike monogatari, 13th–14th c.), a basically true but highly colored account of the rise and fall of the Taira clan, which was pigeonholed uneasily by some early Westerners as a historical romance and by others as an epic. Unfortunately, no satisfactory classification system for such works has been devised, either by modern Japanese scholars or by their Western counterparts. Purely as a matter of convenience, we shall here consider all classical belletristic prose as falling into two overlapping general categories: Tales and Memoirs.

The oldest surviving Japanese tales are myths, legends, folktales, and anecdotes preserved in eighth-century sources. Those stories and later ones of the same kind are known to literary historians as *setsuwa*, a term translatable as "explanatory talk," "informative narration," or simply "telling." Setsuwa have in common brevity; an uncomplicated plot unfolded in plain, direct language; character delineation through dialogue and action rather than through description and psychological analysis; and a predilection for amusing, startling, dramatic, or marvelous subject matter. Their characters belong to every walk of life, their settings range from the mansions of the upper classes to the rural countryside, and their narrators are as likely to commend resourcefulness and ingenuity, even when exercised in the pursuit of dubious ends, as to describe and applaud courtly sensibility. Almost all are of ultimately oral provenance, all claim factuality, and a very high percentage convey Buddhist messages, relating instances of karmic retribution, recording miraculous events in the lives of eminent monks, and the like. Many hundreds have been preserved in anonymous collections dating from the Heian and early medieval periods, and great numbers have also been incorporated into a remarkably wide variety of other classical works.

The setsuwa dropped out of sight after the early fourteenth century, but many of its characteristics persisted in a similar genre, the "companion booklet" (*otogi zōshi*), which became one of the principal short prose forms of the fifteenth and sixteenth centuries. Some 400 to 500 companion booklets survive, all in illustrated versions and all showing oral influence in their narrative techniques. They deal in straightforward, brisk fashion with love, poetry, cruel stepmothers, military heroes, monks, ghosts, talking animals, and many other topics and themes reflective of traditional aristocratic concerns, of armed conflict with its social and religious effects, and of the abiding fascination of the supernatural.

Another type of brief story related to the setsuwa, the poem tale (*uta monogatari*), survives mainly in three anonymous collections dating from around the middle of the tenth century. Poem tales, as the name implies, are anecdotes and legends centering on poetry.[3] The prose portion of such a tale may consist of only one or two introductory sentences explaining the circumstances under which the poem was composed, or it may run on at greater length, as in some of the selections in this anthology from *Tales of Ise* (Ise monogatari), the earliest and classic example of the genre. *Tales of Ise* shows traces of oral genesis, such as the stylized "Once a man" with which many of its tales begin, but it differs in two significant respects from the setsuwa per se. First, the subject matter is firmly grounded in the life of the aristocracy, with emphasis on demonstrations of courtly sensibility, especially as concerns relations between the sexes. And second, although the narrative style lacks the complexity and richness of the high Heian period, it nevertheless achieves a simple elegance rarely encountered in the setsuwa. *Tales of Ise* represents one of the first serious explorations of the possibilities of Japanese prose as a literary medium.

3. The term *uta monogatari* can also refer to a collection of such tales.

All three of the forms discussed above ask to be taken at face value as history. Many examples of each, however, clearly belong to the realm of fiction, and so are comparable in one important respect to short examples of the romance (*[tsukuri] monogatari*), the only undisputedly fictional form of the classical age.

The titles of approximately 200 romances are known, all dating from the ninth century to around the early fourteenth, and there were probably many others. The forty or so survivors range in length from a few pages to the majestic bulk of the fifty-four-chapter *Tale of Genji* by Murasaki Shikibu, which occupies five volumes in a modern Japanese printed edition. Three antedate the *Genji*, among them *The Tale of the Bamboo Cutter*, a Chinese-influenced amalgam of folktale motifs, which a character in Murasaki Shikibu's work calls "the ancestor of all romances." The post-*Genji* examples, most of which were written under *Genji* influence, included a number of short tales—ten of them in a single collection, *The Riverside Counselor's Stories* (Tsutsumi chūnagon monogatari)—and some relatively long ones. Whether early or late, the longer ones, in particular, have in common a tendency to focus on romantic love and to combine more or less realistic depictions of aristocratic life with elements of fantasy—improbable adventures in China; Cinderella situations; plot developments hinging on miraculous events, dreams, or reincarnation; and, in one case, a brother and sister who switch sexes.

The Tale of Genji transcends both its genre and its age. Its basic subject matter and setting—love at the Heian court—are those of the romance, and its cultural assumptions are those of the mid-Heian period, but Murasaki Shikibu's unique genius has made the work for many a powerful statement of the fragility of human relationships, the impossibility of permanent happiness in love, the ineluctability of karmic retribution, and the vital importance, in a world of sorrows, of sensitivity to the feelings of others.[4] The book is not carefully plotted in the manner of a nineteenth-century English novel. Many of its chapters could be deleted with no damage to the story line; there is an abrupt break between the first two parts, in which the protagonist is Genji, the Shining Prince, and the late chapters, which deal with the next genera-

4. A number of writers have pointed out the correspondences between the *Genji* and the "novel of sensibility" pioneered by Virginia Woolf and others. See, for example, Haruo Shirane, *The Bridge of Dreams: A Poetics of 'The Tale of Genji'* (Stanford, Calif., 1987), p. 32.

tion; and the ending trails off inconclusively. This structural looseness is related to the manner in which the author is presumed to have written, turning out chapters in piecemeal, open-ended fashion to satisfy the demands of her mistress's salon, but it is also a trait shared by many important works in other classical forms. The readers of Japan's classical age were more concerned with feeling than with action, more attracted to the vignette than to the broad picture. And in the *Genji*, where feeling is very nearly all, Murasaki Shikibu probes her characters' psyches and records their musings, reminiscences, and internal conflicts in minute detail, making skillful use of poetry, of shifting points of view and voices, and of richly evocative metaphors and imagery drawn from the poetic canon. She also pauses, sometimes at great length, over such matters as gardens, costumes, concerts, dance rehearsals, incense blending, Buddhist services, and discussions of the art of fiction. These authorial techniques invest her work with some of the static quality of scenes in a picture scroll: the *Genji* becomes not an organic whole but the sum of many quasi-autonomous parts. Yet we cannot appreciate the book until we see it as a whole—until the finely wrought scenes have combined to draw us deeper and deeper into Murasaki Shikibu's world, to make the joys and sorrows of the characters our own, and to contribute, each in its way, to an ineffable emotional appeal that has been identified as the hallmark of an authentic literary masterpiece.

The main character in *The Tale of Genji* is a man who holds the highest bureaucratic offices and plays an important role in court politics, including decisions affecting the imperial succession. To contemporary readers, Murasaki Shikibu's story of his life and times, with its lengthy discussions of consorts in rivalry, family quarrels, marriages, birth celebrations, illnesses, funerals, and elegant entertainments, must have seemed not only vastly more amusing but also truer to life than the histories they knew, which were mere laconic chronological notations in Chinese, marking the prominent external events of successive reigns— enthronement ceremonies, formal receptions of foreign envoys, changes in bureaucratic assignments, and the like. And in an era when the distinction between fiction and history was of no great concern, it was perhaps inevitable that Murasaki Shikibu's dazzling achievement should have suggested the possibility of a vernacular history centering on a similarly memorable figure and using the same narrative techniques.

The subject chosen was Fujiwara no Michinaga, Chancellor, Regent, father-in-law of three Emperors, of one Retired Emperor, and of one Crown Prince, grandfather of two Emperors, and father of two Regents. *A Tale of Flowering Fortunes* (Eiga monogatari, ca. 1030's–40's?), the naïvely adulatory work that resulted, took the form of a long chronological narrative, two volumes in a modern printed edition. Told from a woman's viewpoint, it has been attributed tentatively to Akazome Emon, a lady-in-waiting who served Michinaga's principal consort, Rinshi. It was probably written shortly after Michinaga's death, when Emon, a poet of minor reputation, would have been around seventy.[5]

Lovingly detailed descriptions of everyday aristocratic life at the highest level make *Flowering Fortunes* an invaluable resource for the social historian, but its aging author lacked Murasaki Shikibu's gift for dialogue and the delineation of feelings and moods, her poetic descriptive powers, and her impeccable sense of form. For the student of literature, the book is noteworthy primarily as the first of six classical works, known as historical tales (*rekishi monogatari*), relating the history of Japan from 660 B.C. to 1333. One of the six, which dealt with the decade from 1170 to 1180, has failed to survive; the remaining four follow *Flowering Fortunes* in using vernacular narrative techniques to celebrate courtly life and aristocratic ideals. The most interesting as literature is the second, *The Great Mirror* (Ōkagami), which was probably written in the second half of the eleventh century or the first half of the twelfth. Like *Flowering Fortunes*, *The Great Mirror* takes as its topic Fujiwara no Michinaga and his times, but the author's style is dramatic and anecdotal, with emphasis on public events in the great man's career—for example, his display of courage on a certain rainy night at court, his magnificent appearance during an imperial progress to a shrine, and his defeat of a political rival in an archery match. Such occasions, symbolic of Michinaga's superiority to the ordinary run of mortals, are observed through the eyes of a former court servant, an old raconteur possessed of a seemingly inexhaustible store of setsuwa, who entertains a crowd with reminiscences while awaiting the arrival of a preacher at a Buddhist temple.

With the exception of *Flowering Fortunes*, all the extant historical tales appear to have been written by anonymous male authors who were

---

5. Michinaga died in the Twelfth Month of the year corresponding mostly to 1027, a date that fell in January 1028. An anonymous addition, probably written by another lady-in-waiting, carries the history of his descendants to 1092.

minor aristocrats or Buddhist monks. Unlike Akazome Emon's work and the feminine tradition from which it stemmed, they depict aristocratic life as it would have appeared to a bureaucrat serving at court. Their focus is not on the boudoir and the larger private residence but on formal and informal public events—annual ceremonies, Buddhist services, poetry contests, imperial excursions, and the like. They also take some cognizance of significant political developments, a subject almost never broached by women writers. In particular, the last of the six, *The Clear Mirror* (Masukagami, 14th c.), records both the revolutionary events of the late twelfth century and the efforts of Retired Emperor Go-Toba and Emperor Go-Daigo to regain power. But the historical tale, committed as it had become to the monotonous round of court events, proved too inflexible to accommodate itself to a growing demand for literary works reflective of the profound social changes that had transformed capital and countryside alike, and, especially, for information about the lifestyle, code of behavior, and exploits of the newly prominent warrior class. Instead, it gave birth to an offshoot, the so-called military tale (*gunki* [*monogatari*]), the last major tale type.

Two of the four main military tales, *A Tale of Hōgen* (Hōgen monogatari, 13th c.) and *A Tale of Heiji* (Heiji monogatari, 13th c.), are short accounts of brief armed clashes in 1156 and 1160, foreshadowings of the great war between the Taira and the Minamoto in the 1180's. A third and much longer one, *The Tale of the Heike* (Heike monogatari, 13th–14th c.), is concerned with the Taira-Minamoto struggle itself; and the last and longest, *The Great Peace* (Taiheiki, 14th c.), deals with the increasingly chaotic military conflicts of the fourteenth century. All four were recited or read before audiences, and much of their content is gossipy, anecdotal, and suited to oral presentation. *The Tale of the Heike* and *The Great Peace*, in particular, bear a superficial resemblance to multifaceted collections of setsuwa. They include not only tales from military camps, battlefields, and besieged strongholds, as the name "military tale" would suggest, but also short stories about love, poetry, and music, told in the courtly style; legends and snatches of history borrowed from Chinese and native sources; and Buddhist accounts of miracles and religious conversions. Their language, although more polished than that of a setsuwa collection, preserves many traces of oral presentation, especially in the battle accounts, where the reader finds conventionalized "dressing the hero" and "self-naming" motifs of a kind familiar from the Western epic, as well as stereotyped descriptions of combat, rhythmic poetic passages, and the like. There is also repeated treatment of plot motifs that seem to have been audience favorites, such as the loyalty or disloyalty of the hero's friend, the competition to lead the attack, and the identification of the anonymous head taken in battle.

Regardless of their degree of indebtedness to oral sources, these works have undergone an extensive process of shaping, pruning, amplifying, and refinement that places them closer in several respects to the historical tale than to any setsuwa collection. The best of them, *The Tale of the Heike*, stands as a landmark of Japanese literature, a favorite with generations of audiences and readers and a source of inspiration for writers working in many narrative and dramatic genres.

As noted, that work deals with the protracted struggle in the late twelfth century between the Taira (Heike) and Minamoto (Genji) clans. In romanticized but essentially truthful fashion, it chronicles the main events leading up to the war, the war itself, and the aftermath of the Minamoto victory. The *Heike* is not, however, an account of all the relevant happenings, much less an analysis of the political, economic, and social factors involved. Like the *Genji*, which focuses on the figure of the Shining Prince, and like *Flowering Fortunes*, with its single-minded attention to Michinaga, it is centrally concerned with the human drama represented by the catastrophic decline and annihilation of a seemingly invincible power, the great house of Taira. It invites the reader to consider the question of how such a thing could have happened.

In a sense, the answer is a simple one, supplied in the work's famous opening lines:

> The sound of the Gion Shōja bells echoes the impermanence of all things;
> The color of the *śāla* flowers reveals the truth that the prosperous must decline.
> The proud do not endure, they are like a dream on a spring night;
> The mighty fall at last, they are as dust before the wind.

Members of the aristocracy had always regarded "awareness of mutability" (*mujōkan*) as a mark of cultivation, even in their palmiest days; and by the end of the twelfth century, when the precarious position of the sovereign and his court was all too evident, and when even the least reflective warrior could not fail to recognize that death might be the price of glory on the battlefield, mujōkan had become far more than a fashionable upper-class air. *The Tale of the Heike,* a quintessentially medieval work, contains many explicit echoes of the Gion Shōja passage—as when, for example, the author says of the fleeing Taira, "Yesterday, they were 100,000 riders aligning their bridles at the foot of the Eastern Barrier; today, they were but 7,000 men untying their mooring lines on the waves of the western sea."[6] But it would not have captivated generations of readers if it had merely repeated platitudinous observations from time to time. It appeals not because it tells but because it shows. Just as each of the seemingly miscellaneous anecdotes in *The Great Mirror* plays its part in the creation of a total picture of Michinaga that is sharper and more realistic than Akazome Emon's, so their counterparts in the *Heike,* when viewed as a whole, can be read as a dramatic, precise demonstration of the manner in which the law of change worked against the Taira.

With the focus always on human acts and their karmic implications, the reader is introduced to a host of memorable characters, including Kiyomori, the arrogant, intemperate Taira chieftain; Kiyomori's sons, among them the model Confucian minister Shigemori and the craven Munemori; the crafty Retired Emperor Go-Shirakawa; the brilliant young Minamoto general Yoshitsune and his cousin and rival Yoshinaka; and innumerable other aristocrats, warriors great and small, monks, distressed ladies, pathetic children, and loyal servants, who exhibit all kinds of human behavior—ambition, treachery, cowardice, gullibility, shrewdness, bravery, fidelity, piety, aestheticism, rusticity—and who are all involved, through their deeds and fates, in the ultimate outcome of one of the crucial events in Japanese history. This work, infinite in variety and heroic in scope, creates a world strikingly different from Murasaki Shikibu's cloistered domain, but one no less remarkable.

Some modern Japanese writers, observing that *The Tale of the Heike* can be said to focus successively on Kiyomori, Yoshinaka, and Yoshitsune, have called the work a biography. We might make the same claim for many others in our Tales category, because the distinction between history and biography is often obscure, as is also the distinction between fiction and nonfiction. "Of History . . . is not the whole purport Bio-

6. "Author" is a term used for convenience. Many different hands contributed to the *Heike* we know today, which can be said to have come into being gradually between the early thirteenth century and 1371, when the best of many extant versions was completed.

graphic?" asked Thomas Carlyle. "Again, consider the whole class of Fictitious Narratives; from the highest category of epic or dramatic Poetry . . . down to the lowest of froth Prose. . . . What are all these but so many mimic Biographies?"[7] It is particularly difficult to establish a borderline between biography and fiction in the case of works drawing extensively on the poems of a single historical figure, such as the court noble who appears in episode after episode of *Tales of Ise*—a man unmistakably identifiable as the great poet Ariwara no Narihira (825–80). Nevertheless, substantial differences in emphasis, in narrative techniques, and in perceived truthfulness make it useful to distinguish the tales considered above from the types of personal history that constitute our second general category, Memoirs.

"Memoir" corresponds roughly to the Japanese term *nikki bungaku*, which is usually translated literally as "diary literature" or more freely as "literary diaries." The Japanese have long been conscientious diarists. One of the best extant descriptions of the state of Buddhism in Tang China is to be found in a lengthy journal written by a Japanese pilgrim-monk of the ninth century, and the voluminous diaries of Heian and medieval court nobles, often maintained for decades, are important primary sources for the historian. But the authors of such works typically wrote in corrupt, lifeless Chinese, confined themselves largely to statements of fact, and, like most of their latter-day successors, made little or no use of those resources of language that are commonly thought to mark a work as literature. Their writings are not *nikki bungaku*.

The classical nikki, a consciously crafted, frequently introspective literary artifact, differs in at least four respects from the layman's notion (and the dictionary definition) of a diary. First, it is not invariably narrated in the first person or written by the main character. *The Gossamer Journal* (Kagerō nikki, 10th c.), for instance, vacillates between the third person and the first, and *The Diary of Izumi Shikibu* (Izumi shikibu nikki, 11th c.) is written in the third person and may or may not have been composed by its protagonist. Second, some examples contain daily or near-daily entries, but many others arrest time or telescope it in a manner reminiscent of fiction, history, autobiography, or biography. Third, the content tends to be somewhat more diverse, and also somewhat more selective, than that of an ordinary nonliterary diary. *The*

7. *Critical and Miscellaneous Essays: Collected and Republished* (Boston, 1860), pp. 54, 56.

Diary of Murasaki Shikibu (Murasaki shikibu nikki, 11th c.) contains not only autobiographical passages but also extensive comments on the characters of the author's fellow ladies-in-waiting (set down in what appears to be a letter) and detailed descriptions, occupying some 65 percent of the whole, of ceremonial and other events centering on the birth of Empress Shōshi's first son. Conversely, the first book of *The Gossamer Journal* excludes almost every aspect of the author's life not related directly to her marital situation. And finally, most of them make use of poetic conventions and contain significant numbers of *waka*—sometimes, indeed, so many that the works resemble collections of poems, supplied with prefatory remarks in which the authors explain the circumstances and describe the emotions expressed or evoked by the act of composition. Such works are not so much diaries as autobiographical or possibly biographical notes, in part confessional and in part conservatorial, which record experiences and transmit information on subjects of interest to the authors and others. We shall call them either nikki or memoirs, rather than diaries.[8]

The oldest known literary memoir of importance is *A Tosa Journal* (Tosa nikki), by Ki no Tsurayuki, who was the principal compiler of *Collection of Early and Modern [Japanese] Poetry* (Kokin [waka]shū, ca. 905), the first and most influential of twenty-one imperially commissioned poetic anthologies dating from the tenth to the fifteenth century. Probably written in 935 or 936, shortly after the end of the author's tour of duty as Governor of Tosa Province, it is a short, day-by-day account of the return by boat from Tosa to the capital, ostensibly set down by a woman in the Governor's party. Most of its content is devoted to the introduction and recording of poems, close to sixty in all, which were inspired, Tsurayuki tells the reader, by the emotions of the travelers—notably, boredom and depression caused by weather delays, fear of pirates, longing for the capital, and grief for a dead child—and which echo the themes in the Travel section of *Collection of Early and Modern Japanese Poetry*.

In his reliance on the poetic tradition for the expression of personal feeling, Tsurayuki pioneered a method that later memoirists were to follow and, in a few cases, to exploit brilliantly. The nikki proper, as opposed to the travel account, became almost exclusively the domain of

8. The conventional translations "diary" and "journal" have been retained in the English titles.

women after *A Tosa Journal*. We know of approximately a dozen female writers whose works survive. The first, and one of the best, was the author of *The Gossamer Journal*, a provincial Governor's daughter called Michitsuna's Mother, whose treatment of her subject matter—a reflective examination of an unhappy marriage, with many poems and an exhaustive analysis of the nuances of the wife's feelings over the years—not only paved the way for Murasaki Shikibu's psychological probings in *The Tale of Genji* a generation later, but also produced a narrative of remarkably convincing honesty and grace.

Murasaki Shikibu may have had access to *The Gossamer Journal* through her association with Michinaga (whose father, Fujiwara no Kaneie, had been its author's husband) or through a marital connection. The father of Sei Shōnagon's mistress, Empress Teishi, was Michinaga's older brother Michitaka. But if Sei Shōnagon knew the work, she was little influenced by it. Her *Pillow Book*, the most famous of all Heian memoirs, is a high-spirited evocation of court life at its sunniest, conveying almost no hint of the sorrows that befell her cherished mistress after Michitaka's death in 995 enabled Michinaga to gain control of the government, install his own daughter as a rival Empress, and persecute his niece in many subtle and overt ways. It has been suggested that the author wrote it as a spokeswoman for the salon, or that she intended it as a pleasant memento for the small daughter Teishi left behind when she died in the Twelfth Month of 1000, at the age of around twenty-four.

At any rate, the *Pillow Book* is an occasionally autobiographical memoir containing reminiscences of the Empress, her family, and her ladies, of the Emperor and his attendants as viewed from within Teishi's salon, and of great and small events in the imperial palace and elsewhere, all narrated with wit, elegance, and a keen eye. Interspersed with such passages are miniature essays and casual comments inspired by aspects of nature, observed human behavior, and the author's own lively imagination—a household's putative reaction to an unwelcome visitor, events likely to follow a light snowfall, two handsome men playing backgammon, a scene after an autumn typhoon, and so forth. And there are also innumerable lists—trees, musical instruments, deities, stars, boring things, things that are hard to say, insignificant things that sometimes become important—either unembroidered or with added observations shading into short sketches.

This hodgepodge of disparate elements is unified by a distinctive authorial voice. Regardless of the extent to which she may or may not resemble the real Sei Shōnagon (she seems, for example, to be less willing than Michitsuna's Mother to appear in an unflattering light), the narrator of the *Pillow Book* could not be mistaken for any other in the classical canon. Her individuality is partly a matter of technique: she includes very few poems, showing herself instead to be a first-rate story-teller with a rare gift for poetic prose. More important, it resides in the personal qualities of the character we are invited to identify with the author, a woman respectful, admiring, and affectionate in her attitude toward her young mistress; fastidiously repelled by vulgarity, stupidity, and ugliness; clever, amusing, unorthodox; and possessed of an exuber-ant vitality that stands in sharp contrast to the pensive melancholy of other classical women writers.

Murasaki Shikibu wrote her own memoir in Michinaga's day, and an anonymous hand produced *The Diary of Izumi Shikibu*, a tale of courtly love centering on poetic exchanges between the protagonist, who was a leading poet of the age, and an imperial Prince. *The Sarashina Diary*, by a woman known only as Takasue's Daughter, displays the selectivity and introspection typical of the form, saying relatively little about the mi-nutiae of the author's life during the twenty-five years the work covers, but dwelling instead on religious retreats, pilgrimages, and other travel; dreams, omens, and their significance; poetic composition; and the narrator's youthful love of romances and passionate longing to meet a man exactly like Genji or his supposed son Kaoru.

Such Heian women established a tradition of feminine memoir writing that endured until almost the middle of the fourteenth century. Some of their medieval successors were pedestrian chroniclers—ladies-in-waiting who recorded poems and external events of significance pri-marily to themselves, their masters and mistresses, and their compan-ions—but one, the author of *The Confessions of Lady Nijō* (Towazugatari, ca. 1310?), ranks as the last of the major classical women writers. In the first part of her work, which all together reviews thirty-six years of her life, she discusses her sexual encounters, involvements in love triangles, infidelities, and pregnancies, and resultant pain and suffering with a frankness unprecedented in Japanese literature; in the last part, she appears as a traveling nun, who attempts without much success to for-get her troubles and to progress toward salvation. No other medieval work illustrates so vividly the contrast between the decadence of the thirteenth-century court and the appeal of the religious life.

The two principal male memoirists after Tsurayuki, Kamo no Chōmei (1155?–1216) and Yoshida Kenkō (1283?–ca. 1352), wrote in the thirteenth and fourteenth centuries, respectively. Chōmei's *An Account of My Hermitage* (Hōjōki, 1212) is a short essay in which man's experiences with his dwellings serve as illustrations of the Buddhist teachings that all things are impermanent, and that attachment to the impermanent is futile and a hindrance to enlightenment. After graphic descriptions of the widespread destruction of houses by fire, wind, earthquakes, and other such disasters, the author proceeds to a discussion of the personal misfortunes that have caused him to move into successively smaller houses, and finally, in a decisive act of renunciation, to retire as a monk to a tiny hermitage south of the capital. The description of his simple, self-sufficient life there, with its poetry, music, rambles in the hills, and Buddhist devotions, leads both reader and narrator to the realization that he has formed a new attachment, and that the ten-foot-square hut itself, the symbol of his rejection of worldly things, has become a hindrance to enlightenment. What is he to do? As with *The Tale of Genji* and other classical works of poetry and prose, the reader is left to ponder the implications of an ambiguous ending.

Although Chōmei retained a gentleman's interest in poetry and music, his basic response to the contemporary state of aristocratic life was to reject society and seek Buddhist enlightenment. Kenkō also became a monk, but he remained sentimentally attached to the court and its culture. His *Essays in Idleness* (Tsurezuregusa, ca. 1330?) is couched in the classical Japanese of the high Heian period, without the Chinese loanwords and grammatical changes characteristic of the less flowing and elegant, if richer, more vigorous, and clearer medieval language; and the work's form, 243 largely unstructured sections, shows the influence of Sei Shōnagon's *Pillow Book*. Despite a rather large number of setsuwa, the content—miscellaneous jottings about what the author has seen, done, heard, and thought—also bears a certain resemblance to the *Pillow Book*. The tone, however, is often nostalgic and antiquarian. For Kenkō, what was old was praiseworthy. Again and again, he criticizes the pursuit of novelty, sets the record straight in matters of usage, and laments the disappearance of ancient customs. "In general," he remarks, "oddities and rarities are valued by persons of inferior breeding." Or, "The Emperor faces southeast, not south, when he worships the Grand Shrine of Ise from afar." Or, "Nobody nowadays knows the proper way to hang up a quiver at a place where someone is under imperial censure."

In many other passages, he discusses the qualities of a cultivated man. Such a person, he says, prizes the suggestiveness of faded elegance above the surface attraction of shiny newness, regards the anticipation or recollection of a lovers' tryst as more pleasurable than the meeting itself, and finds true natural beauty not in the lifeless perfection of a meticulously groomed garden, or in the harvest moon on a cloudless night, or in the cherry tree in full bloom, but in plants left to grow as they will, in the moon glimpsed through cryptomeria trees deep in the woods, and in the fallen petals that invite the imagination to recreate the blossoming boughs.

Those opinions can be traced to a literary aesthetic developed around the end of the twelfth century and validated in the eighth imperial anthology, *New Collection of Early and Modern Poetry* (Shinkokinshū, 1206)—an ideal exemplified in the so-called "style of mystery and depth" (*yūgentai*), which was explained as follows by Kamo no Chōmei's poetic mentor, the monk Shun'e (b. 1113):

When one gazes upon the autumn hills half-concealed by a curtain of mist, what one sees is veiled yet profoundly beautiful; such a shadowy scene, which permits free exercise of the imagination in picturing how lovely the whole panoply of scarlet leaves must be, is far better than to see them spread with dazzling clarity before our eyes. What is difficult about expressing one's personal feelings in so many words—in saying the moon is bright, or in praising the cherry blossoms simply by declaring that they are beautiful? What superiority do such poems have over mere ordinary prose? It is only when many meanings are compressed into a single word, when the depths of feeling are exhausted yet not expressed, when an unseen world hovers in the atmosphere of the poem, when the mean and common are used to express the elegant, when a poetic conception of rare beauty is developed to the fullest extent in a style of surface simplicity—only then . . . will the poem [be true poetry].[9]

During the medieval period, suggestion, restraint, and understatement became criteria of excellence not only in literature but also in the

---

9. Quoted by Chōmei in his *Untitled Jottings* (Mumyōshō). Translation from Robert H. Brower and Earl Miner, *Japanese Court Poetry* (Stanford, Calif., 1961), p. 269.

noh drama, painting, the tea ceremony, and landscape gardening; and the ability to appreciate incompleteness, asymmetry, and surface plainness was recognized as one mark of a superior person. *Essays in Idleness* contains many amusing anecdotes, a great deal of esoteric lore, and much practical advice on how to behave—so much that it was studied in the Edo period (1603–1868) as a guide to deportment—but its deepest interest resides in the author's discussions of beauty and the nature of sensibility. Although Kenkō may sometimes seem eccentric, snobbish, or precious, the views he expounds have helped to shape what is for many the best and truest in modern Japanese taste.

Chōmei and Kenkō are the most prominent of numerous late Heian and medieval male authors who wrote belletristic prose after becoming Buddhist monks. The preferred vehicle of expression for many of the others, and the last major classical form remaining for consideration here, was the travel account, a type of memoir.

"Travel account" is a fairly literal translation of *kikō*, the Japanese term for such works. Almost all the well-known examples were written after the fact, even though they usually contain day-by-day entries; and all employ the devices of fiction to shape, dramatize, and distill the essence of the travel experience.

The Heian period produced a small amount of travel writing— notably, Ki no Tsurayuki's *Tosa Journal*, the recognized ancestor of the form, and a description in *The Sarashina Diary* of the author's girlhood trip from eastern Japan to the capital with her father, a returning provincial official—but the almost total lack of food and lodgings along the road precluded journeys of any length for all but the hardiest non-official travelers. As the medieval period progressed, accommodations gradually came into being, especially at post stations along the Eastern Sea Road, the main link between the capital and the military headquarters at Kamakura. Many people traveled, and many recorded their journeys in Chinese or Japanese, with particular attention to poems composed along the way.

Scholars have perceived some degree of literary interest in approximately seventy of the extant accounts in Japanese. Of that number, about one-half are official or quasi-official in nature, consisting primarily of poems produced during journeys undertaken by Retired Emperors, high military commanders, and other personages. Some of the remainder were written by members of court society and warriors; many others by men who led reclusive or semireclusive lives, often as Buddhist monks. Our concern is almost exclusively with the recluses, as we shall call them, even though most were probably less eremitic than is implied either by the English word or by its Japanese equivalents.[10]

Like Chōmei, the typical medieval recluse signified his understanding of impermanence and his emancipation from worldly ties by dwelling in an unsubstantial temporary abode. To reaffirm his lack of attachment, he also engaged in travel, which he regarded as another way of divorcing himself from everyday life. The physical hardships and hazards of a journey served as a form of religious discipline, leading to spiritual purification by bringing home the meaning of life's uncertainty, and the wild surroundings offered a unique opportunity to achieve a mystic union with nature. It was meritorious to worship at provincial shrines and temples and instructive to visit the sites of historic events, such as the execution of a once-powerful figure or the destruction of an army. For the dedicated recluse-poet, spiritual progress deepened sensibility, and intimate contact with nature renewed the creative impulse. It was exhilarating to behold for the first time places celebrated by generations of earlier writers, and to feel that one's conduct emulated that of the famous Saigyō (1118–90) and other wandering monk-poets of old. And for all but the most saintly and detached, the simple prospect of exchanging the monotony of a settled existence for the novelty and adventure of the road was an incentive to periodic rambles. It is not surprising, then, that the journeying recluse was a familiar figure from the thirteenth century on.

Of the many prose writings generated by medieval travel, only three are even moderately well known today to any but specialists. Two, *A Sea Road Journal* (Kaidōki, ca. 1223?) and *An Account of a Journey to the East* (Tōkan kikō, 1242?), are the products of anonymous recluses, erroneously attributed to Kamo no Chōmei in the medieval and Edo periods; the third, *The Journal of the Sixteenth-Night Moon* (Izayoi nikki, 1279–80), was written by the widowed nun Abutsu (ca. 1220–83), whose husband, Fujiwara no Tameie (1198–1275), had been the son and literary heir of the great poet Teika (1162–1241). Although not major works themselves, all are worth notice because they seem to have influenced the undisputed master of the travel account, Matsuo Ba-

---

10. Japanese literary historians refer to such writers as *inja* or *tonseisha*, both translatable as "recluse."

shō (1644–94), who wrote in his *Backpack Notes* (Oi no kobumi, 1690–91?), "The excellent travel accounts of Tsurayuki, Chōmei, and Abutsu give full expression to the feelings we experience on a journey. Later writers have been unable to progress beyond feeble imitations of their art."[11]

Poetic convention, the foundation on which the travel writer constructed his memoir, dictated that the narrator's predominant feelings should be sadness, loneliness, homesickness, fatigue, discomfort, and uneasiness. *A Tosa Journal* obeys the rules, as we have seen, and so do the other works Bashō praises. Abutsu goes so far as to maintain a resolutely gloomy tone throughout, but Tsurayuki ventures an occasional humorous remark or appreciative comment, and the other two authors sometimes indulge in enthusiastic praise of scenic wonders, exhibit curiosity about local places and their histories, and compose poems more appropriate for the Miscellaneous category of an anthology than for Travel. Bashō goes a long step further in his own *Narrow Road of the Interior* (Oku no hosomichi, 1694). The awareness of impermanence and related travel feelings receive expression, but there is also attention to all the other emotions that might conceivably be experienced by his narrator—a man of taste and education, dedicated to the art of poetry, who regards Saigyō as a mentor and the medieval poet-recluses as spiritual brothers, but who also breathes the air of the seventeenth century, a period when many ancient literary assumptions were being questioned.

The dedication of Bashō's narrator to his art is adumbrated in *A Tosa Journal* and *The Journal of the Sixteenth-Night Moon*; and his piety, his interest in local legend and folklore, and his tendency to philosophize at historical sites are foreshadowed in *A Sea Road Journal* and *An Account of a Journey to the East*. We can also trace an affinity between some of Bashō's narrative techniques and those of his predecessors, and can hazard the guess that he found the author of *An Account of a Journey to the East* the most congenial of the four. All three of the male writers make use of allusions to Chinese and Japanese literature and history—Tsurayuki sparingly, the author of *A Sea Road Journal* so insistently that his work sometimes verges on the unreadable, and the author of *An Account of a Journey to the East* frequently but aptly and unobtrusively, as Bashō himself does. Tsurayuki and Abutsu tend to emphasize poetry over

11. Sugiura Shōichirō et al., eds. *Bashō bunshū*, vol. 46 of *Nihon koten bungaku taikei* (1959), p. 53.

prose, the author of *A Sea Road Journal* veers in the opposite direction, and the author of *An Account of a Journey to the East* strikes a happy medium, as Bashō does. Tsurayuki and Abutsu write in classical Japanese, the author of *A Sea Road Journal* adopts an overblown Chinesey style, crammed with parallel constructions, and the author of *An Account of a Journey to the East* combines Japanese grace with Chinese vigor in a smooth, unaffected manner close to Bashō's practice, even though he fails to match Bashō's crispness, wit, and elegant simplicity. The author of *An Account of a Journey to the East*, feeling himself incompetent to produce a good enough poem at the famous Fuwa Barrier, flouts convention by passing the spot in silence; Bashō does the same at Matsushima.

Each of the four works alluded to in *Backpack Notes* has its merits, and each doubtless contributed something to *The Narrow Road of the Interior*. In all distinguished literary achievements, however, the sources of the author's inspiration are less important than the uses to which they are put. The *Narrow Road* stands alone among classical travel accounts in the variety and interest of its subject matter, the quality of its poetry and prose, and the complexity of its structure. Bashō makes extensive use of symbolism, allusion, metaphor, and wordplay, taking it for granted that his readers will possess a cultural background similar to his own, and that they will expect to find more in his work than appears on the surface. The opening lines of *The Narrow Road of the Interior*, for example, read as follows:

The sun and the moon are eternal voyagers; the years that come and go are travelers too. For those whose lives float away on boats, for those who greet old age with hands clasping the lead ropes of horses, travel is life, travel is home. And many are the men of old who have perished as they journeyed.

I myself fell prey to wanderlust some years ago, desiring nothing better than to be a vagrant cloud scudding before the wind. Only last autumn, after having drifted along the seashore for a time, had I swept away the old cobwebs from my dilapidated riverside hermitage. But the year ended before I knew it, and I found myself looking at hazy spring skies and thinking of crossing Shirakawa Barrier.

Even in translation, we can appreciate the subtlety with which Bashō moves back and forth between celestial, marine, and human imagery as he narrows his focus. But a reader in the classical age would have noticed a number of other things, too. The passage as a whole constitutes an affirmation of the interrelationship between Buddhist doctrine, travel, and the art of poetry. In the initial phrase, Bashō makes a veiled reference to impermanence by quoting the Tang poet Li Bo (701–62), who wrote, "Heaven and earth are universal innkeepers; the sun and the moon are eternal voyagers. But man's fleeting life is like a dream. How long does happiness last?"[12] Bashō elaborates the point and brings it closer to home with his reference to "men of old" (*kojin*). That term, which may also mean "great men of old," can be taken here to refer to four celebrated wandering poets who died in the course of their travels—Li Bo, Du Fu (712–70), Saigyō, and the medieval linked-verse master Sōgi (1421–1502).

The remainder of the passage (part of one long sentence in the original) asserts that the narrator is a man like Li Bo and the others, someone who no sooner returns from "drifting along the seashore" on one trip than he is moved by the advent of spring to set out again, this time toward a place particularly identified with a composition by the monk-poet Nōin (b. 988). Although the word "spring" does not appear in Nōin's poem (GSIS 518), the season is indicated by "haze" (*kasumi*), a spring image.

miyako o ba	Though I left the city
kasumi to tomo ni	with the hovering haze
tachishikado	as companion,
akikaze zo fuku	an autumn wind is blowing
shirakawa no seki	at Shirakawa Barrier.

That Bashō has Nōin's poem in mind is further suggested by his repetition of one of Nōin's rhetorical devices, a pun on the verb *tatsu*.[13] Elsewhere in the passage as well, nuances of language invite attention. The verb *sasoware* ("enticed [by the wind]," translated as "scudding [before the wind]") foreshadows the similar-sounding *sasurae* ("drifted"). To create a link with "boat," *ukabu* ("float") replaces the standard *okuru* ("spend") in the phrase *shōgai o okuru* ("spend one's life"). Some of the Sino-Japanese compounds are words charged with Chinese literary associations—for example, *haoku* ("dilapidated cottage") and *hyōhaku* ("roaming," which occurs in a phrase translated as "wanderlust"). The purely classical *izure no toshi yori ka* ("since what year might it

12. Wang Zaian, ed., *Li taibo quanji* (Taibei, 1975), p. 629.
13. Nōin's *tachishikado* means both "although [I] left" and "although [haze] was hovering." Bashō, exploiting a third possible meaning of *tatsu*, "arrive," writes *haru tateru kasumi no sora*, "hovering haze sky now that spring has arrived" (translated as "hazy spring skies").

have been," translated as "some years ago") quietly borrows the romantic atmosphere of *The Tale of Genji* by paraphrasing Murasaki Shikibu's well-known opening words, *izure no ontoki ni ka* ("in what reign might it have been").

The dense texture of *The Narrow Road of the Interior* derives not only from Bashō's genius but also from an 800-year-old tradition of emphasis on allusion, implication, overtones, compression, and wordplay. That tradition, founded and nurtured by poets, has exerted a far-reaching effect on the tales and memoirs in this anthology. Not every author represented here exploits its resources with Bashō's skill, but we would need to subject the work of each to minute scrutiny in order to do him or her full justice, a procedure that would result in a different kind of book. That we can nevertheless find such writers entertaining, stimulating, and moving is a testament to their literary ability and, especially, to the timeless relevance of their topics and themes, without which their works could claim little more than curiosity value. In the final analysis, we listen to these voices from the distant past because they speak with conviction on matters of universal concern—man's relationship to his fellow man and to nature, the ephemerality of worldly things, the quest for self-knowledge and spiritual growth, and the meaning of human existence.

The Ancestor of All Romances

The anonymous *Tale of the Bamboo Cutter* (Taketori monogatari) probably dates from the late ninth or early tenth century. Its story begins with the first of the three excerpted sections below, in which an old bamboo cutter finds a tiny girl three inches tall, seated inside a stalk of bamboo. He takes her home and gives her to his wife to rear. When she grows up in less than three months, her beauty fills the surroundings with light. She is given the name Nayotake no Kaguyahime, Radiant Maiden of the Pliant Bamboo, and the feasting for her naming ceremony lasts three days.

Many suitors are attracted by reports of Kaguyahime's charms. She rebuffs them all because she is actually a moon maiden, forbidden to wed a mortal. Nevertheless, five refuse to be discouraged, and the old man, anxious to see her settled before his death, urges her to choose one of them. In order not to seem disobedient, she agrees to accept the one who can prove his devotion by performing an impossible task. The first, Prince Ishitsukuri, is to bring her the stone begging bowl used in India by the historical Buddha; the second, Prince Kuramochi, a branch of a tree with silver roots, a golden trunk, and jeweled fruit from Penglai, the legendary Isle of the Immortals; the third, Minister of the Right Abe no Mimuraji, a robe made of the fireproof fur of the mythical Chinese fire-rat; the fourth, Major Counselor Ōtomo no Miyuki, a five-colored jewel from a dragon's head; and the fifth, Middle Counselor Isonokami no Marotari, one of the easy-birth shells supposedly possessed by swallows.

About half of the story is devoted to descriptions of how the suitors fail in their missions. The first three men try to palm off counterfeit objects—a begging bowl that fails to shine like a true holy relic, a fire-rat robe that burns when thrown into the flames, and the jeweled branch described in the second section below. The other two make fools of themselves by trying unsuccessfully to obtain the genuine articles.

Next, the Emperor woos Kaguyahime, only to see her turn temporarily into a shadow when he tries to take her to his palace. The two correspond for three years, and then the time comes for Kaguyahime to return to the moon. The bamboo cutter and the Emperor's soldiers try to resist the moon beings who come to fetch her, but their efforts are futile (third section below).

The tale is based on versions of two universal folkloristic themes: the supernatural wife—the maiden who comes to earth, is discovered and captured by a mortal man, marries the man, and eventually returns home—and the suitors who are set impossible tasks. It also shows other evidences of oral influence, such as the repetition of the number three, the folk etymologies accompanying several of the sections, and the conventional storyteller's phrase with which it ends, "Such is the story that has been handed down" (*to zo iitsutaetaru*). At the same time, it exhibits, if in embryonic form, two basic traits of the romance ([*tsukuri*] *monogatari*): detailed, realistic description, particularly of the suitors' quests; and a concern with the thoughts and emotions of the principal characters, particularly Kaguyahime and the Emperor, who are exemplars of courtly sensibility. It is this last quality that probably inspired Murasaki Shikibu to call *The Tale of the Bamboo Cutter* the "ancestor of all romances."

The Tale of the Bamboo Cutter

[1]

Once upon a time, there was an old bamboo cutter who went into the mountains and fields, cut bamboo, and put the stalks to all kinds of uses. His name was Sakaki no Miyakko[maro]. Now it happened that one stalk of bamboo shone at the base. Puzzled, the old man went up to it and found that the light was coming from its interior. When he examined it, he saw a dainty little girl, just three inches tall, sitting inside.

"Because she is here in this bamboo I cut every morning and evening, I can tell that she is destined to be my child," the old man said. He put her in his hand, took her home, and gave her to his wife to rear. She was the cutest thing in the world. The wife kept her in a basket because she was so tiny.

When the old man went to cut bamboo after having discovered that child, he kept finding stalks with gold between the joints, and he gradually grew wealthy.

The child shot up swiftly while they cared for her. By the time she was three months old, she was as big as an adult, so they put up her hair and dressed her in a train. They looked after her with great solicitude, making sure that she never emerged from behind her curtains. The incomparable beauty of her face and figure filled the house with radiance. Even if the old man felt ill or upset, a single look at her was enough to end his distress or soothe his anger.

After having cut bamboo for a long time, the old man became a person of consequence. He summoned a diviner, Inbe no Akita of Mimurodo, to confer a name on his daughter, who was quite grown up by then, and Akita named her Nayotake no Kaguyahime, Radiant Maiden of the Pliant Bamboo. The occasion was marked by a three-day celebration, with music and all kinds of other pastimes. Men of every status were invited, and the entertainment was very splendid.

[2]

Prince Kuramochi was an artful man. To the court, he submitted a request for a leave of absence so that he might visit the curative baths of Tsukushi; to Kaguyahime's house, he sent word that he was going to fetch the jeweled branch. Then he departed from the capital. All of his usual attendants accompanied him as far as Naniwa, but there he announced that he intended to set out with only a handful of people. It was to be a very private journey, he said. He embarked with just a few close attendants, and everyone else returned to the capital after seeing him off.

Three days after his pretended departure, the Prince came back again in the boat. He had already called in the six best metalsmiths of the day, and had built a house in an inaccessible spot and set up furnaces inside three sets of walls. Now he brought the smiths to stay in the house, joined them there, and supervised the fabrication of a jeweled branch, using all the resources of his storehouses and sixteen estates. He had them make the branch exactly according to Kaguyahime's specifications. Then, having managed the whole affair with the utmost resourcefulness, he sneaked into Naniwa.

The Prince sent word of his return to his mansion and sat around looking exhausted. A throng of people came to greet him. They put the jeweled branch in a chest, covered it, and bore it toward the capital. It is impossible to tell how the word spread, but everyone began to say, "Prince Kuramochi has come to the capital with a spray of *udonge* blossoms!"[1]

Kaguyahime was dismayed when she heard the news. "I'm going to be defeated by that Prince," she thought.

Presently, there came a knocking at the gate. "Prince Kuramochi has arrived," a voice announced. "He's still wearing his traveling clothes."

The old man received the Prince. "Please show this to Kaguyahime," the Prince said. "Tell her I've brought the jeweled branch for which I risked my life." The old man took the branch inside. There was a message attached:

itazura ni	Never would I
mi wa nashitsu tomo	have returned empty-handed
tama no eda o	without plucking
taorade tada ni	the branch adorned with jewels—
kaerazaramashi	not though it cost me my life.

Kaguyahime did not seem impressed.

The old man dashed inside the curtains. "The Prince has brought a jeweled branch from Penglai, exactly like the one you asked for. What reason can we give for putting him off? He's come in his travel robes without even stopping by his own house. You'll have to meet him right away," he said. Kaguyahime rested her cheek on her hand in silence, looking very sad and gloomy.

"Now that it's come to this, there's nothing left to discuss," said the Prince. He scrambled onto the veranda.

The old man considered his behavior reasonable. "There's no branch

1. The *udonge* was a legendary Indian tree that blossomed once in 3,000 years.

like that anywhere else in the country," he said as he sat in front of Kaguyahime. "How can we refuse this time? Besides, he's a good-looking man."

Kaguyahime was astonished and upset by the Prince's arrival with
the branch. "I asked for something hard to get because I didn't want to
be stubborn about refusing you," she said to the bamboo cutter. But the
old man arranged for the bedroom to be decked out.

"What kind of place was that tree growing in? What a rare, beautiful object!" the old man said to the Prince.

"It was around the Tenth of the Second Month, two years before last,
that I set out to sea from Naniwa," the Prince answered. "I realized that I
didn't even know which way to head, but I felt that there would be no
point in living if I failed in my quest, so I simply went with the uncertain winds. 'If I die, I die,' I thought. 'I'll go on like this as long as I
live, and perhaps I'll stumble across Mount Penglai.' At times, I almost
sank beneath stormy seas as I drifted on the waves far from Japan. At
times, I was driven by the wind to strange shores, where demonic
apparitions tried to kill me. At times, I was completely lost at sea,
unable to tell where I had been or where I was going. At times, my
provisions exhausted, I consumed the roots of island plants. At times,
indescribably horrible creatures appeared and tried to eat me. At times,
I clung to life by gathering shellfish. I contracted all sorts of ailments in
those places where there was nobody to help a traveler, and I had no idea
where to go.

"I drifted over the waves, content to let the boat take me wherever it
pleased. And then, just at the Hour of the Dragon [7:00 A.M.–9:00
A.M.] on the five hundredth day, I saw the faint outline of a mountain in
the middle of the ocean. Everyone in the boat was transfixed. It floated
on the water, a great peak, high and beautiful. I thought it must be the
one I was looking for, but somehow I couldn't help feeling afraid. I gave
orders for the boat to circle it.

"I kept the mountain under observation for two or three days. Then
a woman dressed like a heavenly being emerged from its depths and
began to dip water with a silver bowl. I disembarked and asked the
mountain's name.

"'This is Mount Penglai,' she said. At the same instant, she disappeared into the interior.

"There seemed to be no way of climbing the mountain. While I was circling it, I saw flowering trees of a kind unknown in this world. A stream with waters of gold, silver, and blue flowed from the mountain. It was spanned by a bridge of many-colored jewels, and there were shining, glittering trees growing nearby. The tree from which I broke this flowering branch was a sadly inferior one, but I chose it because I thought there might be trouble if I didn't follow the lady's instructions to the letter.

"The delights of the mountain were inexhaustible. Nothing in the world could compare with it. But I couldn't wait to leave after I picked the branch. I got back on board the boat and returned in a little more than four hundred days, assisted by favorable winds. Yesterday, I reached the capital from Naniwa, thanks, it may be, to Amida's vow to help sentient beings. And now I've come here, without even changing my brine-soaked robes."

With a sigh, the old man recited a poem:

kuretake no	Not in fields or in hills
yoyo no taketori	has he experienced hardships
noyama ni mo	to compare with yours—
sa ya wa wabishiki	this old bamboo cutter
fushi o nomi mishi	who has lived so many years.

"Today marks the final end of the suffering I have endured so long," the Prince said. This was his reply to the poem:

wa ga tamoto	Now that my sleeves
kyō kawakereba	are dry again today,
wabishisa no	all of my trials
chigusa no kazu mo	will surely be forgotten,
wasurarenubeshi	innumerable though they were.

Just then, six men filed into the courtyard. One of them held a letter on a stick. "I am Ayabe no Uchimaro, a smith from the Office of Palace Works," he said. "I fasted and labored with all my might for more than a thousand days in order to make the jeweled branch, but I still haven't received any recompense. Reward me so I can reward my helpers." He held up the letter.

The bamboo cutter cocked his head in bewilderment. "What can that smith be talking about?" he said. The Prince was dumbfounded, flabbergasted.

"Take the man's letter," said Kaguyahime, who had heard everything. The letter read, "His Highness the Prince hid with us humble artisans for a thousand days while we made him a fine jeweled branch. He promised us official posts. After thinking the matter over, we have decided to ask for our reward here, because we have heard people say, 'The branch must be something needed by Kaguyahime, the lady the Prince is to wed.'"

Kaguyahime had been growing more and more distraught as night-time approached, but the smith's demands for payment made her laugh with joy. She called the old man inside. "I thought it must be a genuine jeweled branch. Now that we know it's only a shabby counterfeit, please return it at once," she said. The old man nodded in agreement. "We have learned that it was undoubtedly made by human hands, so it will be very easy to return it," he answered.

In high spirits, Kaguyahime composed a reply to the Prince's original poem:

makoto ka to	I thought it genuine,
kikite mitsureba	as I thought your words sincere,
koto no ha o	but the jeweled branch,
kazareru tama no	like the leaves of your words,
eda ni zo arikeru	stems from a tree of deceit.

The jeweled branch was returned with the poem.

Now that he knew the Prince's story was nothing but a lie, the old bamboo cutter pretended to doze off. The Prince sat there until darkness fell, embarrassed to go and embarrassed to stay. Then he slipped away.

Kaguyahime called in the petitioners, seated them, and gave them many presents. "You are delightful men!" she said.

The smiths were overjoyed. "Things turned out just as we hoped," they said. But Prince Kuramochi waylaid them on their return, beat them until the blood ran, and scattered their presents to the winds. They ran away, none the better for Kaguyahime's generosity.

"This has been the humiliation of a lifetime," the Prince said. "Not only did I fail to win the girl, but everybody in the country will be thinking embarrassing things about me." He went far into the mountains, all by himself. His stewards and attendants divided into search parties to look for him, but he was nowhere to be found. They wondered if he might be dead.

The Prince was not seen for many years after he had apparently tried to hide from his attendants. That is how people began to use the expression *tamasaka naru* to mean "infrequent."[2]

[3]

[*Kaguyahime has told the old couple that messengers from the moon will come for her on the Fifteenth of the Eighth Month. The bamboo cutter has asked the Emperor for help.*]

On the Fifteenth, the court dispatched 2,000 men from the six guards headquarters to the bamboo cutter's house, with Lesser Captain Takano no Ōkuni as their commander. When the 2,000 arrived, they mounted guard over every inch of the premises. There were 1,000 of them on top of the earthen wall and another 1,000 on the building, in addition to all the people from the bamboo cutter's household. The guards were armed with bows and arrows. Inside the main apartment, the women took turns standing watch. The old woman sat inside the strongroom with Kaguyahime in her arms, and the old man posted himself at the entrance to the locked strongroom door.[3]

"Not even heavenly beings can win out against a place guarded like this," the old man said. To the men on top of the building, he said, "If you see anything at all flying in the sky, shoot to kill immediately."

The answer was reassuring. "With this kind of a guard, we'll certainly shoot down or drive away anything at all, even a mosquito."

Kaguyahime heard them. "Even though you may lock me up and prepare a defense, you can't fight the people from the moon. You can't shoot them with bows and arrows. Even though I'm locked inside like this, everything will fly open when the people from the moon arrive; even though you try to fight, no man will be brave when the people from the moon arrive."

"I'll gouge out their leader's eyeballs with my long fingernails and smash them. I'll grab his hair and pull it down. I'll expose his butt and humiliate him in front of all those court officials," the old man stormed.

"Please don't talk in such a loud voice," Kaguyahime said. "They'll hear you on top of the roof. It's not the right way to act. I hate to go away

2. A conjectural translation of a possibly corrupt passage. The phrase may be a pun meaning also "infamous conduct with respect to jewels" or "taking leave of one's jewels / soul / senses."

3. The strongroom was partitioned off from the main apartment.

as though I didn't appreciate all your kindness. Ah! It must be because our karma-affinity was short that I have to leave so soon. It won't be easy to go without doing anything for my parents. These days, I have kept going out to the veranda to beg for permission to stay just this year, but my appeals have been rejected. That's why I've been so sad. I can't bear to go away knowing I've been nothing but a bother to you. People who live in the moon palace are blessed with beauty, eternal youth, and freedom from care, but it doesn't make me happy to be going there. I want to be here when you get old and feeble."

"Don't say such terrible things. I won't be defeated by any messengers from the moon; I don't care how beautiful they are," the old man said in a defiant voice.

Meanwhile, the night wore on. Just at the Hour of the Rat [11:00 P.M. – 1:00 A.M.], the air around the house began to shine with a light brighter than midday, a radiance like ten full moons combined. Even the pores on people's skins were visible. A group of men came down from the sky, riding on a cloud, and aligned themselves about five feet off the ground. For those inside and outside the house, it was exactly like seeing ghosts. They lost the will to fight. If they did pluck up the courage to grasp their bows and arrows, the strength drained from their arms, and they collapsed against whatever supports they could find. A few bold fellows brought themselves to shoot, but their arrows went astray, and they were left staring in stupefaction, unable to fight a real battle.

The people from the moon wore costumes of incomparable beauty. They had brought along a flying carriage topped by a silk parasol. One of them, who looked like a King, spoke with his face toward the house. "Miyakkomaro! Come out!" The formerly brave Miyakkomaro fell flat on his face, feeling just as he did when he drank too much wine.

"As a reward for a trifling meritorious deed on your part, we sent down a young person to help you," the King continued. "We meant to have her stay only a short time, but you have received much gold over many years and have come to be quite a different person. Kaguyahime had to spend some time in your humble dwelling because she committed a sin. Now that the sin has been expiated, we've come to fetch her. You can't stop us by weeping and wailing. Send her out right now."

"We have taken care of Kaguyahime for more than twenty years," the old man answered. "It's odd that you should talk about a short time. There must be somebody else called Kaguyahime in some other place."

He continued, "The Kaguyahime who lives here is desperately ill. She can't come out."

The King brought the carriage to the roof without bothering to answer. "Kaguyahime! Why do you linger in that unclean place?" he said. The locked strongroom door flew open in a twinkling; the wooden shutters opened of their own accord. Kaguyahime left the old woman's arms and went outside. Unable to detain her, the old woman wept with upturned face.

Kaguyahime went to the place where the distraught bamboo cutter lay weeping. "I'm unhappy, too, because I have to go. Won't you at least watch me leave?" she said.

"Why should I watch when I'm so miserable? What am I supposed to do when you desert me and fly off into the sky? Take me with you!" he said.

It distressed Kaguyahime to see him lying there in tears. "I'll leave a letter for you. Take it out to read whenever you miss me," she said. This is what she wrote, weeping: "If only I had been born on this earth, I would have stayed with you until no act of mine could have caused you grief. To leave before that hour is the last thing I would ever have wanted to do. Consider the robe I remove a keepsake, and look up on nights when the moon shines. I will be longing to come down from the skies for which I leave you now."

The heavenly beings had brought along a box, which one of them carried. It contained a heavenly feathered robe. There was also another box containing an elixir of immortality. One of the heavenly beings brought the elixir to Kaguyahime. "Drink the elixir in this jar. You must be feeling sick after having eaten food in an unclean place," he said. Kaguyahime took a tiny sip. She started to wrap the jar in the robe she had removed, with the thought of leaving it as a small keepsake, but the heavenly being stopped her. Someone took out the feathered robe and started to dress her in it.

"Wait a minute," Kaguyahime said then. "I've heard that once a person is dressed in a robe like that, she no longer possesses a human heart. There's something I need to say." She began to write on a piece of paper.

"It's getting late," one of the heavenly beings complained.

"Please don't talk as though you lacked sensitivity," Kaguyahime said. Very calmly, she wrote a letter for the Emperor. She did not seem to be in any hurry. "Although you were so kind as to send all those people to keep me here, the messengers who have come for me won't let me stay. Much as I regret it, they are going to take me away. It was because I was not an ordinary mortal that I couldn't serve you. You must have found my behavior hard to understand, and it grieves me to realize that my stubbornness must have seemed very rude." [Her poem:]

ima wa tote	With sad emotion,
ama no hagoromo	I think of His Majesty
kiru ori zo	as now I put on
kimi o aware to	the heavenly feathered robe,
omoiidekeru	saying, "The time has come."

She attached the jar of elixir to the paper, summoned the Head Chamberlain–Middle Captain, and gave instructions for the poem to be transmitted. It was a heavenly being who transmitted it. The moment the Middle Captain received it, someone dressed Kaguyahime in the heavenly feathered robe. No longer did the maiden consider the old man pitiful or pathetic, for one who dons such a robe is emancipated from sorrow. She entered the carriage and soared into the heavens, escorted by 100 heavenly beings.

A Ninth-Century Nobleman
and the Courtly Ideal

Tales of Ise (Ise monogatari) is a collection of short tales and anecdotes, each centering on one or more poems, that seems to have come into existence over a period extending from the late ninth or early tenth century to around 950. A passage in *The Tale of Genji* shows that it was already considered a classic at the beginning of the eleventh century. The description below applies to the textual line considered most reliable, which contains 209 poems in 125 sections.

During the Heian and medieval periods, *Tales of Ise* was attributed to Ariwara no Narihira (825–80), a middle-ranking bureaucrat of imperial descent who is known to history as a major poet and a legendary lover. Edo-period scholars pointed out that Narihira could not have included either his own death poem, which appears in Section 125, or a composition by the mid-tenth-century poet Tachibana no Tadamoto, which is to be found in Section 11, and it is now generally agreed that the work in its present form represents the accumulated labors of several authors, possibly including Narihira, who probably drew for their materials on existing poetry collections and orally circulating tales. A collection of Narihira's verse seems to have been the source of some of the 209 poems, because at least thirty are from his hand and most of the other identifiable authors were his associates. But 75–80 percent of the 209 are of unknown provenance.

Tales of Ise begins with an anecdote about a young nobleman recently come of age, continues with numerous episodes in which a male protagonist composes a poem known to be by Narihira or is described as holding one of Narihira's known offices, and ends with Narihira's death poem. The picture that emerges from these sections, taken in conjunction with many others where the principal character is simply "a man," is that of a single recognizable individual who consistently demonstrates the sensitivity of the ideal aristocrat, especially in his relationships with women. In Section 63, the only one that mentions Narihira by name, this attribute is made quite clear: "Most men show consideration for the women they love and ignore the feelings of the ones who fail to interest them. Narihira made no such distinctions."

The reader is thus invited to recognize Narihira as a real-life precursor of Prince Genji, to accept *Tales of Ise* as his biography, and to recognize sensitivity in courtly love as the work's main theme. There is doubtless some validity to these implicit claims, especially the last. At the same time, it must be noted that almost nothing is known about the character or personal life of the historical Narihira, that some of the episodes in which the Narihira-character figures are demonstrably fictitious, and that many other episodes have nothing to do with him.

The translation below contains thirty-nine of the 125 sections.

Tales of Ise

I

Once a man who had lately come of age went hunting on his estate at Kasuga Village, near the Nara capital. In the village there lived two beautiful young sisters. The man stole a look at the sisters and quite lost his head, so startling and incongruous did it seem for such women to be dwelling at the ruined capital. He tore a strip from the skirt of his hunting robe, dashed off a poem, and sent it in. The fabric of the robe was imprinted with a moss-fern design.

kasugano no	Like the random patterns
wakamurasaki no	on this robe dyed with young purple
surigoromo	from Kasuga Plain,
shinobu no midare	utterly confused is the heart
kagiri shirarezu	of one secretly in love.

It must have occurred to him that this was an interesting opportunity for an adaptation of the poem that runs:

Above: Two children play beside a well (Sec. 23). Below: A young noble steals a look at two women (Sec. 1). Only the skirts of the second are visible.

michinoku no	It is you alone
shinobumojizuri	who have set my heart astir
tare yue ni	with emotions
midaresomenishi	as confused as moss-fern patterns
ware naranaku ni	on cloth from Michinoku.

People were remarkably elegant in those times.

2

Once in the days after the move from Nara, when people were still not settled in the new capital, a certain man discovered a woman living in the western part of the city. She was charming to look at, and her disposition was even more delightful than her appearance. It seemed that she was not single, but the man made love to her anyway, even though he was an honorable fellow. His conscience must have bothered him after he got home, because he sent her this poem. It was early in the Third Month and a drizzling rain was falling.

oki mo sezu	Having passed the night
ne mo sede yoru o	neither waking nor sleeping,
akashite wa	I have spent the day
haru no mono tote	brooding and watching the rain—
nagamekurashitsu	the unending rain of spring.

4

Once when a Grand Empress was living on Gojō Avenue in the eastern sector of the capital, a certain woman occupied the western wing of her house. Quite without premeditation, a man fell in love with the woman and began to visit her. Around the Tenth of the First Month, the woman moved away without a word. The man learned where she had gone, but it was not a place for ordinary people to frequent, and he could do nothing but lament the wretchedness of life. In the First Month of the following year, when the plum trees were in full bloom, poignant memories drew him back to her old apartments. He sat and looked, he stood and looked, but it was hopeless to try to recapture the past. He burst into tears, flung himself onto the floor of the bare room, and lay prostrate until the moon sank low in the sky. He composed this poem with the preceding year in his thoughts:

tsuki ya aranu	Is this not the moon?
haru ya mukashi no	And is this not the springtime,
haru naranu	the springtime of old?
wa ga mi hitotsu wa	Only this body of mine,
moto no mi ni shite	the same body as before . . .

He went home at dawn, still shedding tears.

9

Once a certain man decided that it was useless for him to stay in the capital. Accompanied by one or two old friends, he set out toward the east in search of a province where he could settle down. Since none of the party knew the way, they simply blundered along as best they could. In time, they arrived at a place in Mikawa Province called Yatsuhashi. It was where the waters of a stream branched into eight channels, each with its own bridge, which was why it had come to be called Yatsuhashi [Eight Bridges]. They dismounted under a tree near this marshy area and sat down to a meal of parched rice. One of them noticed some irises blooming in the swamp. "Compose a poem on the subject, 'A Traveler's Sentiments,' beginning each line with a syllable from the word 'iris' [*kakitsubata*]," he said. The man recited:

karagoromo	I have a dear wife,
kitsutsu narenishi	familiar to me as skirts
tsuma shi areba	of a well-worn robe,
harubaru kinuru	and thus these distant travels
tabi o shi zo omou	darken my heart with sorrow.

They all wept onto their rice until it swelled with the moisture.

On they journeyed to the province of Suruga. At Mount Utsu, the road ahead was dark, narrow, and overgrown with ivy and maples. They were eyeing it, filled with dismal forebodings, when a wandering ascetic came into view. "What are you doing on a road like this?" he asked. Recognizing him as someone he had known in the old days, the man gave him a message for a woman in the capital:

suruga naru	Beside Mount Utsu
utsu no yamabe no	in Suruga Province,
utsutsu ni mo	I can see you
yume ni mo hito ni	neither when I am awake
awanu narikeri	nor, alas, even in my dreams.

A pure white snow had fallen on Mount Fuji, even though it was the end of the Fifth Month.

toki shiranu	Fuji is a peak
yama wa fuji no ne	indifferent to season.
itsu tote ka	What month does it think this,

| ka no ko madara ni | that snowflakes should be falling |
| yuki no fururan | to spot its slopes like deerskin? |

To speak in terms of the mountains around here, Mount Fuji is as tall as twenty Mount Hiei's piled on top of one another. It resembles a salt cone in shape.

As the travelers continued on their way, they came to a mighty river flowing between the provinces of Musashi and Shimōsa. It was called the Sumidagawa. They huddled together on the shore, saddened by involuntary thoughts of home. "We've come such a long distance," they said.

The ferryman interrupted their lamentations. "Hurry up and get in. It's late."

They embarked in wretched spirits, for not a soul among them but had left someone dear to him in the capital.

A white bird about as big as a snipe, with a red bill and red legs, was idling on the water, eating a fish. Its like was not to be seen in the capital, and nobody could say what it was. When they consulted the ferryman, he answered, "Why, that's a capital-bird, of course." Someone composed this poem:

na ni shi owaba	If you are in truth
iza koto towamu	what your name would tell us,
miyakodori	let me ask you,
wa ga omou hito wa	capital-bird, about the health
ari ya nashi ya to	of the one for whom I yearn.

Everyone in the boat shed tears.

10

A certain man, having reached the province of Musashi in his wanderings, began to court a Musashi girl. Her father told him that she was intended for someone else, but her mother was delighted by the prospect of such an elegant son-in-law. (Although the father came of ordinary stock, the mother was a Fujiwara, and she considered a match with a nobleman entirely suitable and most desirable.) She sent the suitor this poem. The family lived in Miyoshino Village in the Iruma District.

| miyoshino no | The wild goose tarrying |
| tanomu no kari mo | on the surface of the field |

A party of travelers sees capital-birds at the Sumida River (Sec. 9)

hitaburu ni	at Miyoshino
kimi ga kata ni zo	cries that it looks toward you
yoru to naku naru	and toward no other man.

His reply:

wa ga kata ni	When might I forget
yoru to naku naru	the wild goose that tarries

miyoshino no	on the surface
tanomu no kari o	of the field at Miyoshino,
itsu ka wasuren	crying that it looks toward me?

Even in the provinces, this man did not depart from his customary behavior.

12

Once there was a man who abducted someone's daughter. He was on his way to Musashi Plain with her when some provincial officials arrested him for theft. He had left the girl in a clump of bushes and run off, but the pursuers felt certain that he was on the plain, and they prepared to set fire to it. The girl recited this poem in great agitation:

musashino wa	Light no fires today
kyō wa na yaki so	on the plain of Musashi,
wakakusa no	for my young spouse,
tsuma mo komoreri	sweet as new grass, is hidden here,
ware mo komoreri	and I am hidden here too.

They heard her, seized her, and marched the two off together.

14

Once a man found himself in Michinoku in the course of his wanderings. A girl of the province, who was probably unaccustomed to meeting people from the capital, fell head over heels in love with him and sent him a poem as countrified as she was:

nakanaka ni	Far better it were
koi ni shinazu wa	to turn into a silkworm,
kuwako ni zo	even for a while,
narubekarikeru	than to be tortured to death
tama no o bakari	by a foolish passion.

He must have pitied her in spite of her crudity, because he went to her house and slept with her. He left in the middle of the night, whereupon she sent him this:

| yo mo akeba | When daybreak arrives, |
| kitsu ni hamenade | I'll toss him into the cistern— |

kutakake no   that pesky rooster
madaki ni nakite   who raises his voice too soon
sena o yaritsuru   and drives my lover away.

Presently, the man sent word that he was returning to the capital.
His poem:

kurihara no   Were it but human—
aneha no matsu no   the pine tree of Aneha
  hito naraba   at Kurihara—
miyako no tsuto ni   I would tell it, "Come and be
iza to iwamashi o   my keepsake in the city." [1]

The girl was overjoyed. "I'm sure he's in love with me," she said.

16

Once there was a man named Ki no Aritsune who served three
Emperors. He prospered for a time, but changes took place, and he
found himself even less well off than an average courtier. He was a person
of exceptional sensibility and refinement. Despite his poverty, he retained the tastes and attitudes of his more affluent past, untroubled by
the problems of everyday life. He and his wife of many years gradually
drew apart, and at length the wife made up her mind to take Buddhist
vows and go to live with an older sister, who had already become a nun.
Even though the couple had not been intimate for a long time, Aritsune
was deeply moved by the prospect of her departure, but he was too poor
to give her a farewell present. In great distress, he wrote of her decision
to an old friend. "She is leaving forever, and I must send her off without
so much as a trifling gift." He ended with this poem:

te o orite   When, telling by tens,
aimishi koto o   I count on bent fingers
  kazoureba   each of the years
tō to iitsutsu   we have lived as man and wife,
yotsu wa henikeri   the total amounts to four.

His friend found it most touching. He sent him both a robe and a
quilt, with this poem:

1. The man implies that he would like to take the girl home with him. (But the poem
can also be interpreted to mean, "I consider you scarcely human. Naturally, I won't take you
with me.")

toshi dani mo	In that marriage
tō tote yotsu wa	enduring over a span
henikeru o	of four decades,
ikutabi kimi o	many must have been the times
tanomikinuran	when she came to you for help.

Aritsune replied:

kore ya kono	Might this be the famed
ama no hagoromo	feather robe from the heavens?[2]
mube shi koso	Indeed, my lord,
kimi ga mikeshi to	you yourself must have deigned
tatematsurikere	to wear it as your own.

So great was his joy that he sent another poem:

aki ya kuru	That my sleeves seem as wet
tsuyu ya magau to	as though autumn had arrived
omou made	with its drenching dews—
aru wa namida no	the explanation is here
furu ni zo arikeru	in the joyous tears I shed.

17

After staying away for months, a man once visited a certain house to see the cherry trees in bloom. The woman who lived there composed this poem:

ada nari to	They are called fickle,
na ni koso tatere	these blossoms of the cherry,
sakurabana	yet they have waited
toshi ni mare naru	for someone whose visits
hito mo machikeri	come but seldom in the year.

His reply:

kyō kozu wa	Had I not come today,
asu wa yuki to zo	they would have fallen tomorrow
furinamashi	like drifting snowflakes.
kiezu wa ari tomo	Though they have not yet melted,
hana to mimashi ya	they are scarcely true flowers.

2. According to legend, the inhabitants of earth were visited occasionally by heavenly maidens who wore crowns of flowers and many-hued skirts and danced with marvelous

18

Once there was a rather shallow woman who wished to be thought elegant. A certain man lived nearby. Because the woman was fond of versifying, she decided to test the man's feelings with this poem, which she attached to a faded chrysanthemum:

kurenai ni	Where might it be—
niou wa izura	that beautiful crimson glow?
shirayuki no	We can see only
eda mo tōo ni	a whiteness as of snowflakes
furu ka to mo miyu	fallen thick on bending boughs.[3]

The man pretended not to understand. He answered:

kurenai ni	A white chrysanthemum
niou ga ue no	with petals snowy above
shiragiku wa	a crimson glow—
orikeru hito no	might it not bloom in the sleeve
sode ka to mo miyu	of the one who picked the flower?

19

Once a man in the service of an imperial consort began to make love to one of the consort's attendants. Presently, the affair came to an end. When the two met in the course of their duties at the house, the man behaved as if the woman were invisible, even though she saw him plainly enough. She sent him this poem:

amagumo no	Although you remain
yoso ni mo hito no	visible to the eye,
nariyuku ka	we are quite estranged:
sasuga ni me ni wa	you have become as distant
miyuru mono kara	as a cloud in the heavens.

His reply:

| amagumo no | That I spend my days |
| yoso ni nomi shite | ever as distant from you |

---

grace. Diaphanous robes made of birds' feathers enabled the maidens to fly between heaven and earth.

3. The gift of a fading white chrysanthemum, its petals tinged with red, showed that the woman appreciated the poignancy of the changes wrought by time. Her professed

furu koto wa	as a cloud in the sky
wa ga iru yama no	is the fault of the harsh wind
kaze hayami nari	on the hill where I would rest.

He meant that another man had been visiting her.

20

Once a man met, courted, and won a woman who lived in Yamato. After a time, he had to return to the capital, where he served an imperial personage. On the way, he was intrigued by the sight of a maple tree whose leaves were red, even though it was the Third Month. He broke off a branch and sent it to the woman with this poem:

kimi ga tame	As you may see,
taoreru eda wa	this bough I have broken off
haru nagara	just because of you
kaku koso aki no	is dyed with the red color
momiji shinikere	of autumnal foliage.[4]

Her answer came after he had reached the capital:

itsu no ma ni	How very swiftly
utsurou iro no	the color seems to have changed!
tsukinuran	I can only think
kimi ga sato ni wa	there is no springtime at all
haru nakarurashi	in the city where you live.

21

Once a man and a woman loved one another dearly. I am not sure what happened—nothing of any importance—but the woman grew unhappy with the relationship and decided to go away. She left behind this poem, scribbled on something in the house:

---

inability to see the reddened petals was a fashionable pose. "Reddish tinge" suggests passion; thus, the real message of the poem is, "I've heard you are something of a gallant, but I see no sign of it." In his response, which is a graceful evasion, the man surmises that the woman is wearing a robe in the "white chrysanthemum" color combination (white with a reddish lining).

4. "I send you this branch not only so that you may admire its beauty but also as a reminder of the flaming passion in my heart." In her reply, the woman pretends to misunderstand the man's feelings. She accuses him of losing interest, making an implicit pun on *aki* ("autumn"; "weary of"). "How quickly your sentiments have changed! For you, it seems, there is no spring—only *aki*."

idete inaba	If I go away,
kokoro karushi to	others will doubtless conclude
ii ya sen	that I am fickle.
yo no arisama o	They have no way of knowing
hito wa shiraneba	what has passed between us.

The man was astonished and bewildered that she should have written in that vein, because he could think of nothing at which she might have taken offense. He went outside the gate, weeping bitterly and wondering where to search first, but though he looked this way and that, he had no notion of where to start, and he finally went back inside. He recited this poem:

omou kai	In our marriage
naki yo narikeri	my love counted for nothing—
toshitsuki o	yet for all those years
ada ni chigirite	was I ever once untrue
ware ya sumaishi	to my pledge of constancy?

Then he sat staring gloomily into space. He also composed this:

hito wa isa	I wonder if she
omoi ya suran	might still be thinking of me.
tamakazura	Fair as a gemmed fillet,
omokage ni nomi	time after time her image
itodo mietsutsu	rises before my mind's eye.

After a long time, the woman sent him this, possibly because she could no longer control her feelings:

ima wa tote	Perhaps you believe
wasururu kusa no	it is time to forget me—
tane o dani	yet I would like
hito no kokoro ni	to stop the "forgetting-grass" seed
makasezu mo ga na	from being planted in your heart.

His reply:

wasuregusa	Had I so much as heard
uu to dani kiku	that you were planting the grass
mono naraba	of forgetfulness,
omoikeri to wa	I would have understood:
shiri mo shinamashi	"Ah, she still remembers me!"

With that, there began a new intimacy even closer than the old. One day the man composed this poem:

wasururan to	Because of these doubts—
omou kokoro no	these fears that even now
utagai ni	you are forgetting—
arishi yori ke ni	my misery is greater
mono zo kanashiki	than when we were estranged.

She replied:

nakazora ni	Because of your doubts,
tachiiru kumo no	I feel on the point of death,
ato mo naku	ready to vanish
mi no hakanaku mo	like a cloud in the heavens
narinikeru ka na	dissolving without a trace.

But in the end they found new partners and separated.

23

A boy and a girl, the children of two men who traveled over the countryside, used to play together beside a well. As they grew up, they both felt rather self-conscious about continuing the old relationship, but the boy had set his heart on marrying the girl, and she was determined that she would be his wife, and refused to agree when her father tried to betroth her to someone else. The boy sent the girl this poem:

tsutsui tsu no	Since last I saw you,
izutsu ni kakeshi	it seems to have grown until
maro ga take	I am the taller—
suginikerashi na	my height that we two measured
imo mizaru ma ni	against the curb of the well.

She replied:

kurabekoshi	The mid-parted hair
furiwakegami mo	I once measured against yours
kata suginu	hangs toward my waist.
kimi narazu shite	For whom should it be put up,
tare ka agubeki	unless it be for you?

After many such poems had passed between them, their wishes were realized and they became man and wife.

Some years later the wife's father died, leaving her without support, and the husband, tired of living with her in poverty, took to visiting a woman in the Takayasu District of Kawachi Province. The wife always saw him off with so little apparent resentment that he began to suspect her of having a lover. One day, after pretending to set out for Kawachi, he hid in the shrubbery and watched her. She made up her face with meticulous care and recited this poem, gazing into space:

kaze fukeba	Is he journeying
okitsu shiranami	alone in the dead of night
tatsutayama	across that mountain
yowa ni ya kimi ga	whose name recalls waves at sea
hitori koyuran	rising when the tempest blows?

His heart swelled with love for her, and his visits to Kawachi ceased.

On the rare occasions when the man did go to Takayasu, he observed that the woman there had abandoned all decorum, despite the great pains she had taken with her appearance at first. Watching her seize the rice ladle and heap her bowl to overflowing, he felt so disenchanted that he finally severed the connection altogether.

One day the woman in Kawachi composed this poem as she looked toward Yamato:

kimi ga atari	Though rain may fall,
mitsutsu o oran	I beg you, clouds, do not hide
ikomayama	Ikoma Mountain,
kumo na kakushi so	for I think only of seeing
ame wa furu tomo	the place where my beloved dwells.

With some reluctance, the man sent word that he would come. She waited in joyous anticipation, but he failed to appear. After the same thing had happened several times, she sent him this poem:

kimi komu to	Night after night,
iishi yogoto ni	I have awaited the visits
suginureba	you promised to make.
tanomanu mono no	Though I no longer trust you,
koitsutsu zo furu	I spend my days in longing.

But he never came again.

24

There was once a man who lived in a remote country district. One day he bade his wife an affectionate farewell and set off for the capital to seek employment in an aristocratic house. When three years had passed with no sign of him, his wife, tired of waiting, promised to marry someone who had been wooing her with great persistence. But on the very night she had selected for the first meeting, her husband appeared and knocked on the door to be let in. Instead of opening, she wrote this poem and passed it out:

aratama no	After three long years
toshi no mitose o	of wearisome waiting
machiwabite	for your return,
tada koyoi koso	on this very evening
niimakura sure	I am to wed another.

He replied:

azusayumi	Love your new husband
mayumi tsukiyumi	as I have loved you for years
toshi o hete	as numerous as bows
wa ga seshi ga goto	made of birch and spindlewood,
uruwashimi se yo	made from the zelkova tree.

Then he started to leave. His wife recited this poem:

azusayumi	It does not matter
hikedo hikanedo	whether others seek my love.
mukashi yori	From the beginning,
kokoro wa kimi ni	you were always the one
yorinishi mono o	for whom I truly cared.

All the same, he set out. His anguished wife went after him but could not overtake him, and at length she fell down beside a clear spring. She wrote this poem on a rock with blood from her finger.

aiomowade	I could not detain
karenuru hito o	the one who went away,
todomekane	rejecting my love,
wa ga mi wa ima zo	and now, it seems, the time has come
kiehatenumeru	to bid farewell to life.

She died on that very spot.

40

Once a young man took a fancy to a girl who was really acceptable enough, but his parents, a conceited couple, decided to send the girl away before the attachment became serious—or so they said, for at first they did nothing but talk. The boy was unable to oppose them, because he was dependent on them and had no strong will of his own yet; and the girl, being of low birth, was equally powerless. The two merely fell deeper and deeper in love. Then, quite abruptly, the parents resolved to get rid of the girl. The boy had no way of stopping them, bitterly though he wept, and she was carried off. Sobbing, the boy composed this poem:

idete inaba	It would not be hard
tare ka wakare no	to lose someone who had gone
katakaran	of her own free will,
arishi ni masaru	but the grief I feel today
kyō wa kanashi mo	strikes far deeper than before.

Then he lost consciousness. His parents were terribly upset. After all, they had spoken only out of concern for his welfare, never dreaming that the affair was so serious—yet there he lay in a faint. They offered agitated prayers to the gods and Buddhas.

Although the boy had lost consciousness at sunset, it was the Hour of the Dog [7:00 P.M.–9:00 P.M.] on the next day before he came around. Such were the depths of feeling that the young used to display. Sensibility of that order is not to be found nowadays, even among older people.

49

Once a man who was stirred by the beauty of his younger sister composed this poem:

ura wakami	It pains me to think
neyoge ni miyuru	that another hand will bind
wakakusa o	the young grasses—
hito no musubamu	the herbs so fresh and tender,
koto o shi zo omou	so ideal for sleeping.

She replied:

hatsukusa no	Why do you speak of me
nado mezurashiki	in words as unfamiliar
koto no ha zo	as the sight of young grass
ura naku mono o	when springtime comes? Have I not
omoikeru ka na	loved you in all innocence?

50

Once a man who was nettled by a woman's reproaches composed this poem:

tori no ko o	How can I love one
tō zutsu tō wa	who would care nothing for me
kasanu tomo	even were I able
omowanu hito o	to make layers of hens' eggs
omou mono ka wa	ten eggs high and ten eggs wide?

She answered:

asatsuyu wa	Of the morning dew
kienokorite mo	an occasional drop
arinubeshi	may perhaps remain,
tare ka kono yo o	but a relationship with you
tanomihatsubeki	is ephemeral indeed.

Then he wrote:

fuku kaze ni	It is less likely
kozo no sakura wa	that you should prove trustworthy
chirazu tomo	than that the breezes
ana tanomigata	should have failed to scatter
hito no kokoro wa	last year's cherry blossoms.

The woman's rejoinder:

yuku mizu ni	Less profitable
kaze kaku yori mo	than writing on the water
hakanaki wa	of a flowing stream—
omowanu hito o	such is the futility
omou narikeri	of unrequited passion.

The man:

yuku mizu to	Flowing waters,
suguru yowai to	the years gliding by,
chiru hana to	scattering blossoms—
izure mate chō	which of them will listen
koto o kikuran	if someone asks them to wait?

In spite of their mutual accusations of infidelity, both of them were probably involved in secret affairs with other people.

60

Once there as a man whose duties at a palace kept him so busy that his wife, tired of being neglected, ran off to another province with someone who promised to treat her better. Some time later, the first man was named imperial messenger to Usa. As he was journeying toward the shrine, he learned that his former wife was now married to one of the local officials responsible for providing him with accommodations on the way. He gave orders that she was to serve his wine. "Otherwise, I won't drink it," he said. When she presented the cup, he took an orange from a dish of relishes and recited this poem:

satsuki matsu	Scenting the fragrance
hanatachibana no	of orange blossoms that await
ka o kageba	the Fifth Month's coming,
mukashi no hito no	I recall a perfumed sleeve
sode no ka zo suru	worn by someone long ago.

The woman, overcome with shame, became a nun and entered a mountain retreat.

62

Once there was a woman whose husband had neglected her for years. Perhaps because she was not clever, she took the advice of an unreliable person and became a domestic in a provincial household. It happened one day that she served food to her former husband. That night, the husband told the master of the house to send her to him. "Don't you know me?" he asked. Then he recited:

inishie no	Where is the beauty
nioi wa izura	you flaunted in days of old?
sakurabana	Ah! You have become
kokeru kara to mo	merely a cherry tree
narinikeru ka na	despoiled of its blossoms.

The woman was too embarrassed to reply. "Why don't you answer me?" he asked. "I am blind and speechless with tears," she said. He recited:

kore ya kono	Here is a person
ware ni au mi o	who has wished to be rid

nogaretsutsu   of her ties to me.
toshitsuki furedo   Although much time has elapsed,
masarigao naki   her lot seems little improved.

He removed his cloak and gave it to her, but she left it and ran off—
nobody knows where.

69

Once a man went to Ise Province as an imperial huntsman. Because
the Ise Virgin's mother had sent word that he was to be treated better
than the ordinary run of imperial representatives, the Virgin looked after
his needs with great solicitude, seeing him off to hunt in the morning and admitting him to her own residence when he returned in the
evening.[5]

On the night of the second day of this hospitable treatment, the man
suggested that they get better acquainted. The Virgin was not unwilling, but it was impossible to arrange a private meeting with so many
people around. However, the man, as leader of the hunting party, had
been given accommodations rather close to the Virgin's own bedchamber
instead of in some distant quarter, and she went to his rooms around
eleven o'clock that night, after the household had quieted down. He was
lying there wide awake, gazing out into the night, when he saw her by
the faint light of the moon, standing behind a little page girl. Overjoyed, he led her into the bedchamber. But she left without pledging her
love, even though she stayed from eleven o'clock until two-thirty.

The disappointed man spent a sleepless night. Despite his impatience, he could not very well send a message on the following morning;
he could only wait anxiously for word from the Virgin. Soon after dawn,
she sent this poem without an accompanying letter:

kimi ya koshi   Might you have come here,
ware ya yukikemu   or did I perhaps go there?
omōezu   I cannot recall . . .
yume ka utsutsu ka   Was it dream or reality?
nete ka samete ka   Was I sleeping or waking?

5. The Ise Virgin was the chief priestess of the Inner Shrine at Ise, dedicated to Amaterasu, the ancestor of the imperial clan. At the beginning of each reign, a new incumbent
was chosen from among the unmarried daughters of Emperors and Princes.

With tears streaming from his eyes, he composed this and sent it to her:

kakikurasu	I wandered confused
kokoro no yami ni	in the darkness of a mind
madoiniki	bereft of reason.
yume utsutsu to wa	You must pronounce it tonight
koyoi sadame yo	either dream or reality.

Then he went out to hunt.

As the man galloped over the plain, his thoughts strayed to the coming night. Might he not hope to meet the Virgin as soon as the others had gone to bed? But word of his presence had reached the Governor of the province, who was also in charge of the Virgin's affairs, and the Governor proceeded to entertain him with wine all night long. It was impossible to see the Virgin. He was to leave at dawn for Owari Province, so there could be no further opportunity, even though he was quite frantic with longing—as was the Virgin herself.

Toward dawn, the Virgin sent a farewell cup of wine with a poem written on the saucer. The man picked up the saucer and examined it.

kachibito no	Our relationship
wataredo nurenu	was but a creek too shallow
e ni shi areba	to wet a walker's skirts . . .

The last two lines were missing.

The man completed the poem with a bit of charcoal:

| mata ōsaka no | I shall surely cross again |
| seki wa koenan | the Barrier to Meeting. |

The Virgin was the one who served during Emperor Seiwa's reign, the daughter of Emperor Montoku and the sister of Prince Koretaka.

81

A certain Minister of the Left once lived in a very interesting house on the bank of the Kamo River near Rokujō Avenue. Late in the Tenth Month one year, when the white chrysanthemums had taken on a reddish tinge and all the trees and bushes blazed in autumn hues, the Minister invited some imperial Princes to visit him for a night of wine and music. As dawn approached, the guests fell to composing poems in praise of the mansion's elegance. A humble old fellow, who had been creeping about below the veranda, recited this after the others had finished:

shiogama ni	When might I have come
itsu ka kinikemu	to Shiogama shore?
asanagi ni	How nice it would be
tsuri suru fune wa	were a boat trolling for fish
koko ni yoranan	to approach in the morning calm!

A traveler to Michinoku Province sees countless unusual and intriguing places. In all the sixty and more provinces of our country, there is nothing quite like Shiogama; thus, the old man heaped praise on the host's garden in saying, "When might I have come to Shiogama?"

82

There was once an imperial Prince named Koretaka. He owned a house at Minase, beyond Yamazaki, which he visited every year when the cherry trees were in full bloom, always taking with him a man who served as Director of the Imperial Stables of the Right. (It was so long ago that I have forgotten the man's name.) The Prince would go out hawking during such visits, but the hunts did not greatly interest him; they were, indeed, little more than pretexts for sipping wine and composing verses. On one occasion, he noticed some exceptionally lovely blossoms at the Nagisa House in Katano. He and some of the others dismounted to sit under the trees, decorated their caps with flowers, and began to compose poems. The Director of the Stables of the Right:

yo no naka ni	If ours were a world
taete sakura no	where blossoming cherry trees
nakariseba	were not to be found,
haru no kokoro wa	what tranquility would bless
nodokekaramashi	the human heart in springtime!

Someone retorted:

chireba koso	It is just because
itodo sakura wa	the cherry blossoms scatter
medetakere	that they win our praise.
ukiyo ni nani ka	Does anything last for long
hisashikarubeki	in this insubstantial world?

At dusk, shortly after they had left the trees to ride in the direction of Minase, the rest of the Prince's people came over the fields toward them with servants bearing wine, and the party continued together, looking for an attractive spot in which to drink. Presently, they arrived at a place called Amanogawa [River of Heaven], and there the Director of the Stables of the Right started to offer the Prince a cup.

"When you present the wine," the Prince said, "recite a poem on the subject 'Coming to Amanogawa After a Hunt at Katano.'" The Director recited:

> karikurashi   Having hunted all day,
> tanabatatsume ni   let us borrow a lodging
> yado karamu   from the Weaver Maid,
> ama no kawara ni   for we have come to the shore
> ware wa kinikeri   of the River of Heaven.

After the Prince had chanted the poem several times without hitting on a reply, Ki no Aritsune, who was one of the party, responded thus:

> hitotose ni   Since the Weaver Maid
> hitotabi kimasu   awaits her beloved spouse
> kimi mateba   who comes once a year,
> yado kasu hito mo   she is not at all likely
> araji to zo omou   to take us in for the night.

Back at the mansion, they drank and told tales far into the night. When the Prince prepared to retire, somewhat befuddled, the eleven-day-old moon was just ready to disappear behind the hills. The Director of the Stables of the Right recited:

> akanaku ni   Must the moon vanish
> madaki mo tsuki no   in such great haste, leaving us
> kakururu ka   still unsatisfied?
> yama no ha nigete   Retreat, O rim of the hills,
> irezu mo aranamu   and refuse to let it set.

Ki no Aritsune answered for the Prince:

> oshinabete   Would that every peak,
> mine mo taira ni   every summit far and near,
> narinanamu   might turn to flatlands,
> yama no ha naku wa   for without a mountain rim
> tsuki mo iraji o   the moon could not disappear.

83

Once an elderly Director of the Imperial Stables of the Right went along on one of Prince Koretaka's frequent hunting excursions to Minase. The Prince returned to his palace in the capital a few days later. But instead of dismissing the Director (who had intended to escort him home and then go to his own house), he detained him, saying that he wanted to drink with him and give him a present. The Director, impatient to be off, recited:

makura tote	I shall pull up
kusa hikimusubu	no grasses to be fashioned
koto mo seji	into a pillow:
aki no yo to dani	tonight will not last as long
tanomarenaku ni	as though the season were autumn.

(It was late in the Third Month.) Nevertheless, the Prince stayed up all night.

Such was the manner in which this Director made himself useful to the Prince; but one day, while he was still in constant attendance at the palace, he was astonished to learn that his patron had become a monk. When the First Month came around, he resolved to go and pay his respects to him at Ono, a place blanketed with snow at the foot of Mount Hiei. With much difficulty, he made his way to the hermitage, where he found the Prince looking bored and forlorn. The Director lingered on and on, reminiscing about the past, but his official responsibilities obliged him to start back at nightfall, even though he would have liked to remain longer. As he set out, he recited:

wasurete wa	When for an instant
yume ka to zo omou	I forget, it seems a dream.
omoiki ya	Did I imagine
yuki fumiwakete	that I might behold my lord
kimi o mimu to wa	only by tramping through snow?

He went back to the capital in tears.

84

Once there was a man of rather low rank whose mother was an imperial Princess. The mother lived at Nagaoka, and the son, who was in imperial service at the capital, found it hard to visit her as often as he would have liked. He was her dearly beloved only child. In the Twelfth Month of a certain year, a letter came from her. It was a matter of the utmost urgency, the messenger said. In great alarm, the man opened it and read this poem:

oinureba	Now more than ever
saranu wakare no	I long to look on my son,
ari to ieba	for when we grow old
iyoiyo mimaku	there is a kind of parting
hoshiki kimi ka na	none of us can evade.

Weeping bitterly, her son wrote:

yo no naka ni	For the sake of sons
saranu wakare no	who pray that their parents
naku mo ga na	may live a thousand years,
chiyo mo to inoru	how I wish that in this world
hito no ko no tame	there were no final partings!

85

Once there was a man who visited his former patron, a Buddhist monk, during the First Month of every year. He had attended this personage since his childhood, and he made his annual pilgrimage with undiminished loyalty, even though his duties at court prevented him from calling very often. One year, the hermitage was crowded with gentlemen and monks, all former attendants of the master. Wine was served in honor of the season. It snowed hard all day long, and the tipsy company began to compose on the theme "Snowbound." The man of whom I speak recited these lines:

omoedomo	Though I think of you,
mi o shi wakeneba	I am powerless to split
mekare senu	myself asunder:
yuki no tsumoru zo	thus I rejoice to see the snow
wa ga kokoro naru	fall and fall and pile in drifts.

The Prince took off a robe and gave it to him, deeply moved.

87

Once a man went to stay on some property he owned in Ashiya Village, Mubara District, Settsu—the very place mentioned in the old poem that runs:

ashinoya no	The salt-fire tenders
nada no shioyaki	by the Bay of Reed-Thatched Huts
itoma nami	have too little time
tsuge no ogushi mo	even to dress their hair
sasazu kinikeri	with simple wooden combs.

(From this, the place came to be called Ashiya-no-nada, Bay of Reed-Thatched Huts.)

The man held a minor official post that involved no very onerous duties, and certain Assistant Guards Commanders used the connection as an excuse for joining him. His older brother was a Guards Commander. One day, as the gentlemen were idling along the beach in front of the host's house, with no particular destination in mind, someone proposed going up into the mountains for a view of Nunobiki Falls. After making the ascent, they saw a spectacular cascade stretching like white silk across a rock face 200 feet high and 50 feet across. At the very top, the water rushed over a rock lip the size of a straw cushion, spraying globules as big as tangerines and chestnuts. The host called for waterfall poems, and the Guards Commander recited:

wa ga yo o ba	Which might be the higher—
kyō ka asu ka to	these falls or the cascade
matsu kai no	of the tears I shed
namida no taki to	in vain hope of prospering
izure takaken	today or tomorrow?

Next, the host composed this:

nukimidaru	There must be a man
hito koso arurashi	unstringing them at the top—
shiratama no	those transparent beads
ma naku mo chiru ka	scattering incessantly.
sode no sebaki ni	Alas for my narrow sleeves!

The others seem to have been much amused. They all praised the poem and refused to go on with their versifying.

The return journey was long, and twilight was falling as they passed
the dwelling that had belonged to Mochiyoshi, the late Minister of the
Imperial Household. Gazing ahead toward the Ashiya house, they saw
the fires of many fishing boats. The host recited:

haruru yo no	Might they be stars
hoshi ka kawabe no	twinkling in cloudless skies,
hotaru ka mo	or fireflies near the stream,
wa ga sumu kata no	or are they fish lures kindled
ama no taku hi ka	by the shore folk where I dwell?

So they returned.

The waves reared and tossed during the night, whipped by a south
wind, and maidservants went out early in the morning to gather the
seaweed that had been washed ashore. The lady of the house heaped the
seaweed on a pedestal tray and presented it to the guests, covered with an
oak leaf on which she had scribbled this poem:

watatsumi no	For these gentlemen,
kazashi ni sasu to	gladly the god of the sea
iwau mo mo	relinquishes
kimi ga tame ni wa	the seaweed he treasures
oshimazarikeri	to decorate his head.

How are we to judge this country person's poem? Was it good or bad?

88

Once a group of friends, no longer very young, were admiring the
moon together. One of them recited:

ōkata wa	As a general thing,
tsuki o mo medeji	I take but little pleasure
kore zo kono	in praising the moon.
tsumoreba hito no	Does not its every circuit
oi to naru mono	make us a little older?

90

Once there was a man who had been striving to win an unresponsive
woman for some time. Moved, perhaps, by pity, she finally agreed to
receive him on the following night with only a flimsy barrier between
them. The man was overjoyed, but could not help fearing that she might

change her mind. He sent her a poem attached to a beautiful spray of cherry blossoms:

sakurabana	Today, as we see,
kyō koso kaku mo	the cherry blossoms glow
niou tomo	with radiant beauty,
ana tanomigata	but none can be sure, alas,
asu no yo no koto	of what the morrow may bring.

His misgivings were probably justified.

91

Once there was a man who had been much depressed by certain troubles and, indeed, even by the passing of time. He composed this poem toward the end of the Third Month:

oshimedomo	With all my heart,
haru no kagiri no	I willed it to be otherwise,
kyō no hi no	and yet on this,
yūgure ni sae	the final day of springtime,
narinikeru ka na	the shades of evening fall.

92

Once a man, deeply in love, journeyed time and again to the neighborhood where a certain woman lived, but was always obliged to go home without seeing her. He could not even send her a letter. At length, he wrote this poem:

ashibe kogu	For how many times—
tananashiobune	how many dozens of trips—
ikusotabi	might the tiny boat
yukikaeruran	go and return among the reeds
shiru hito mo nami	with none to know of it?

93

Once a man of humble status fell in love with a woman who moved in the very highest circles. Can it be supposed that he had cause for optimism? He thought of her waking and sleeping, and one day, in miserable spirits, he composed this poem:

ōnaōna	We should fall in love
omoi wa subeshi	as befits our station in life,
nazoe naku	for it is bitter
takaki iyashiki	to feel the disparity
kurushikarikeri	between exalted and base.

Even in earlier times, may it not have been common wisdom that such attachments lead to unhappiness?

94

Once there was a man who stopped living with a woman for some reason. She formed another liaison, but she had borne him a child and he continued to send her an occasional letter, though with no great display of ardor. It happened that he asked her to paint a picture for him—she was something of an artist—but she replied that her new husband was with her just then. After first one day and then another had passed with no sign of the painting, he wrote in considerable irritation, "I suppose it's natural enough that you still haven't bothered to do as I asked, but you will understand that I find it annoying." He sent along a sarcastic poem (the season was autumn):

aki no yo wa	Autumn nights, it seems,
haruhi wasururu	have caused you to forget
mono nare ya	the days of springtime—
kasumi ni kiri ya	else why should mist be adjudged
chie masaruran	so vastly superior to haze?

The woman's reply:

chiji no aki	Not a thousand autumns
hitotsu no haru ni	can equal a single spring—
mukawame ya	yet in scattering
momiji mo hana mo	there is little difference
tomo ni koso chire	between foliage and blossoms.

95

Once there was a man who served the Nijō Empress. For some time, he had been in love with a lady-in-waiting whom he encountered constantly, and he finally begged to be allowed to visit her, keeping curtains between them if necessary, "for I should like to try to clear up a matter that has been very much on my mind." The lady received him, taking great pains not to be observed. He chatted awhile and then recited this poem:

hikoboshi ni	My longing for you
koi wa masarinu	makes the Ox-Driver's passion pale.
ama no kawa	Please put aside
hedatsuru seki o	the River of Heaven,
ima wa yamete yo	that barrier between us.

Struck with admiration, she accepted him as her lover.

96

Once there was a man who wooed a woman with such persistence that she gradually began to return his affection. (Not being made of stone or wood, she could scarcely have helped feeling sorry for him.) Unfortunately, it was the middle of the Sixth Month by then, and a boil or two had erupted on her skin. "Although I think of nobody but you, I am suffering from a boil or two just now—and besides, it's so frightfully hot. I promise to meet you as soon as the autumn winds begin to blow," she sent him word.

While the woman was waiting for autumn to arrive, some of the people around her started to complain that she meant to go off with the man, and her older brother came suddenly to take her away. She told a servant to gather some maple leaves that had just turned red. Then she composed a poem, attached it to the leaves, and left it to be sent to the man:

aki kakete	"In autumn," I pledged—
iishi nagara mo	but it was not to happen.
aranaku ni	Our relationship
ko no ha furishiku	proved to be as shallow
e ni koso arikere	as an inlet choked with leaves.

"If anyone comes from there, give him those leaves," she said.

To this very day, no one knows what became of her—whether she was happy or miserable, or even where she went to live. People say the man clapped his hands and uttered blood-curdling imprecations against her. "We shall soon learn whether one human being has the power to injure another through curses," he is supposed to have said.

97

There was once a personage known as the Horikawa Minister of State. On the day of a banquet in celebration of that Minister's fortieth year, which was held at the Kujō Mansion, an elderly Middle Captain composed this poem:

sakurabana	Scatter at random,
chirikaikumore	O blossoms of the cherry,
oiraku no	and cloud the heavens,
komu to iu naru	that you may conceal the path
michi magau ga ni	old age is said to follow.

105

Once a man sent word to a woman, "I'll die if things go on like this." She answered:

shiratsuyu wa	If the white dew
kenaba kenanan	must vanish, let it vanish.
kiezu tote	Even if it stayed,
tama ni nukubeki	I doubt that anyone
hito mo araji o	would string the drops like jewels.

The man considered the reply most discourteous, but his love for her increased.

107

Once a Private Secretary named Fujiwara no Toshiyuki began to court a girl who served a certain nobleman. The girl was still too young to write a decent letter or express herself properly—much less compose a poem—so her master wrote something for her to copy and send. Quite dazzled, Toshiyuki responded with this poem:

tsurezure no	Unable to meet you,
nagame ni masaru	I am lost in lonely thought,
namidagawa	my sleeves drenched with tears

| sode nomi hijite | as abundant as the waters |
| au yoshi mo nashi | of a rain-swollen river. |

The girl's master composed her reply:

asami koso	Because it lacks depth,
sode wa hizurame	it merely drenches your sleeve—
namidagawa	yon river of tears.
mi sae nagaru to	Were your body to float off,
kikaba tanomamu	I might have faith in your words.

People say Toshiyuki was so impressed that he rolled up the poem and put it in his letter box, where it remains to this day.

Somewhat later, after Toshiyuki had succeeded in winning the girl, he sent her a letter: "I am upset to see that it looks like it's going to rain. If I'm lucky it won't." The girl's master wrote this poem for her to send him:

kazukazu ni	Since I cannot ask,
omoi omowazu	point by point, whether your love
toigatami	is love or no love,
mi o shiru ame wa	the rain that knows of my plight
furi zo masareru	falls ever harder, harder.

Toshiyuki went rushing off to see her without even stopping to put on rain gear or a hat, and arrived sopping wet.

125

Once a man was taken ill. Sensing the approach of death, he composed this poem:

tsui ni yuku	Upon this pathway,
michi to wa kanete	I have long heard it said,
kikishikado	man sets forth at last—
kinō kyō to wa	yet I had not thought to go
omowazarishi o	so very soon as today.

Pioneering Memoirists
of the Tenth Century

Two long-lived prose forms, the travel account and the confessional memoir, were inaugurated in the tenth century by two consciously innovative writers, Ki no Tsurayuki (ca. 872–945) and the woman known as Michitsuna's Mother (937?–95). Tsurayuki's work, *A Tosa Journal* (Tosa nikki), was completed around 935; that of Michitsuna's Mother, *The Gossamer Journal* (Kagerō nikki), probably in the 970's.

Tsurayuki was an obscure young bureaucrat around 902, when he was named one of four compilers of the future *Collection of Early and Modern Poetry*. He emerged as the collection's principal compiler and the author of its influential kana preface, and subsequently became recognized as the leading professional poet of the age, although his official career never prospered. In addition to producing many screen poems and other verses on commission for the higher nobility, he compiled another anthology, *New Selection of Japanese Poetry* (Shinsen waka, ca. 935), which missed the honor of imperial sponsorship only because the sovereign who had commissioned it died before it could be presented. Aside from the kana preface, *A Tosa Journal* is his only important prose work.

Tsurayuki was appointed to a five-year term as Governor of Tosa, a province on the island of Shikoku, in 930. *A Tosa Journal*, which describes an anonymous Governor's return from Tosa to the capital, is believed to have been written shortly after the end of his tour of duty. The prose portion of the work is essentially a framing device for almost sixty poems, most of which were presumably composed by him during his own journey home, but which are attributed to a number of different members of the Governor's party by the narrator, who is proclaimed in the opening sentence to be a woman. Tsurayuki's assumption of a feminine persona pays lip service to the view that Chinese was the appropriate prose medium for a man. The device is, however, a transparent one—for example, the narrator tends to indulge in masculine locutions and crack masculine jokes—and the contemporary reader must have been intended to see through it. Tsurayuki's implicit suggestion is that the time has come to treat Japanese prose as the equal of Chinese, a point made for poetry thirty years earlier with the *Collection of Early and Modern Poetry*. The journal can also be regarded as a form of advocacy for the poetic style favored by Tsurayuki and embodied in the *Collection*, which emphasized elegance, witty conceits, wordplay, and mellifluous diction.

The translation below is complete.

Like many other aristocratic women, the author of *The Gossamer Journal* is known to history only by a name indicative of her relationship to a man, in this case a son. Nowadays, she is sometimes called the Gossamer Lady. Her father, Fujiwara no Tomoyasu, was a provincial Governor; her brother, Nagatō, was a poet of some repute. By the time she was around eighteen or nineteen, she was reported to be both an accomplished poet and one of the "three beauties of Japan," a reputation that attracted the attention of the twenty-five-year-old Fujiwara no Kaneie (929–90) and led him to take her as a second wife. It was a brilliant match for someone of her social status. The able son of the influential Minister of the Right Morosuke (908–60), Kaneie was destined to assume control of the government himself in the 980's. At the time of the marriage in 954, he held the kind of junior appointment considered suitable for a rising young man of high birth, and by 974, the last year covered in *The Gossamer Journal*, he was a Major Counselor.

Anecdotes in *The Great Mirror* and elsewhere depict Kaneie as a forceful, arrogant man, insensitive to the feelings of others. The Gossamer Lady's relationship with him was further complicated by his romantic adventures, but her failure to match the fecundity of his first wife, Tokihime, was probably the factor that imposed the greatest strain on the marriage. She produced only one child, Michitsuna (955–1020), whereas Tokihime gave birth to five, all of whom became important political assets for their ambitious father. Kaneie never broke with the Gossamer Lady completely, and he saw to it that Michitsuna pros-

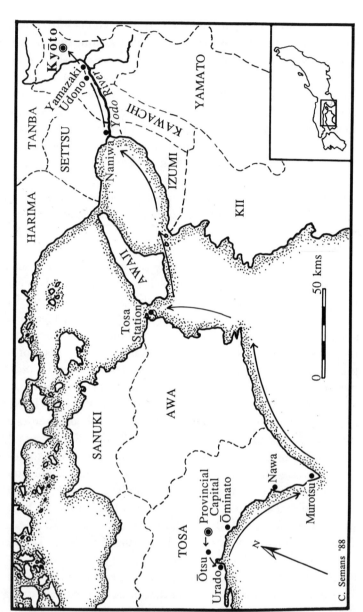

The *Tosa Journal* voyage

C. Semans '88

pered at court, but he communicated with her less and less often as time went on. Although her memoir is silent on the subject, she turned increasingly to literature for consolation, becoming a poet of professional stature who participated in contests and composed screen poems on commission. The poet-critic Teika (1162–1241) included her in his celebrated *One Hundred Poems by One Hundred Poets* (Hyakunin isshu); thirty-six of her compositions found their way into imperial anthologies; and she is represented in various unofficial anthologies as well. Takasue's Daughter, the author of *The Sarashina Diary*, was her niece; Murasaki Shikibu, a relative by marriage. She is thought to have become a nun toward the end of her life.

The Gossamer Lady tells the reader at the outset that her work is not a romance, a "conventional tissue of fabrications," but something new—an unvarnished account of what happens when a girl without powerful family backing embarks on a marriage with a man who can divorce her simply by ceasing to visit or communicate with her. Her memoir is divided into three books, covering, respectively, the years 954–68, 969–71, and 972–74. The first book, a self-contained entity with a definite beginning and ending, is a poem-studded retrospective account of the first fifteen years of the marriage, a period during which the narrator's primary emotions are anxiety, jealousy, resentment, and sadness. The second is a more detailed description of a three-year period during which she begins the painful process of reconciliation to increasing neglect; and the third, similarly detailed, presents her as a woman in her thirties who has learned to view Kaneie objectively, her old anger and misery gone, and to think of him as someone who is no longer a significant part of her life.

The first book is translated below.

A Tosa Journal

I intend to see whether a woman can produce one of those diaries men are said to write.

The departure took place during the Hour of the Dog [7:00 P.M.– 9:00 P.M.] on the Twenty-first of the Twelfth Month in a certain year. I will set down a few notes about the journey.

Having come to the end of a four- or five-year tour of provincial duty, a man finished the usual tasks, got a clearance, and set out from his official residence toward the port of embarkation. A throng of acquaintances and strangers saw him off. People who had been close to him during the past years were especially reluctant to say good-bye. The whole day was hectic, and there was still much commotion when it began to get late.

On the Twenty-second, prayers were offered for a safe voyage as far as Izumi Province. Even though the journey was to be made by boat, Fujiwara no Tokizane "pointed the horse's nose." People of all classes imbibed generously and made spectacles of themselves—stinking drunk, oddly enough, beside the salty sea.[1]

[Twelfth Month,] T W E N T Y - T H I R D   D A Y

A man by the name of Yagi no Yasunori, who apparently had had no connection with the provincial government, nevertheless made a splendid presentation of gifts. Possibly because of some shortcomings on the Governor's part, most of the local residents had dropped out of sight as soon as his term ended, but this admirable man risked embarrassment to come. I praise him not merely because he brought presents.

[xii] T W E N T Y - F O U R T H   D A Y

The head monk of the province came to present gifts. Everyone got staggering drunk—the high, the low, and the very children. People who did not even know the character "one" wrote "ten" with their feet.[2]

[xii] T W E N T Y - F I F T H   D A Y

Someone brought a letter of invitation from the Governor's residence. The former Governor went and was entertained for a day and a night.

1. "Pointing the horse's nose" was a term for a farewell present given to a traveler. Here the expression is intended as a jest, turning on the fact that the party is to travel by sea, not by land. "Stinking drunk" is an approximation of a wordplay on *azaru* ("rot"; "frolic"). Tsurayuki implies that nothing should rot in a place where salt is available as a preservative.
2. The character for one (*ichi*) consists of a single horizontal line; that for ten (*jū*) resembles a cross.

[xii] TWENTY-SIXTH DAY

There was another grand banquet at the Governor's residence, with presents for everyone, servants and all. People chanted Chinese poems, and the host, the guest of honor, and others exchanged Japanese poems. I cannot record the Chinese ones, but the host composed this in Japanese:

miyako idete	I left the city
kimi ni awamu to	and found my way to this place,
koshi mono o	longing to meet you—
koshi kai mo naku	yet my journey was in vain,
wakarenuru ka na	for now we must say farewell.

The departing ex-Governor recited:

shirotae no	Will you not one day
namiji o tōku	do as I am doing now,
yukikaite	you who have come here
ware ni nibeki wa	far along the white wave paths
tare naranaku ni	as another ventures forth?

There were also poems by others, but I doubt that they amounted to much. After talking awhile, the two Governors descended the steps, clasped hands, and wished one another well in hearty voices somewhat the worse for drink. Then the one started off and the other went back inside.

[xii] TWENTY-SEVENTH DAY

The boat rowed out from Ōtsu toward Urado.

During the bustle of departure and the other events of those days, one member of the party had looked on in silence, thinking of a little girl, born in the capital, who had died suddenly in the province. It ought to have been a cause of joy to be setting out toward the city, but the parent was lost in grief for the absent child. The others were deeply sympathetic. A certain person wrote a poem and brought it out:

miyako e to	"At long last," I think,
omou o mono no	"we head toward the capital"—
kanashiki wa	and yet this sadness

kaeranu hito no	because of one among us
areba narikeri	who will not be going home.

Again, another time:

aru mono to	Sharper still the grief
wasuretsutsu nao	when the forgetful parent,
naki hito o	thinking her alive,
izura to tou zo	asks where she can have gone—
kanashikarikeru	the child whose days have ended.

Meanwhile, at a place called Kako-no-saki, the boat was overtaken by the new Governor's brother and some other men, who came bringing wine and such. The former Governor went ashore and sat with them on the beach, where they all lamented the necessity of parting. One felt inclined to agree with those who called them the friendliest people at the Governor's house.

After the usual exchange of civilities, the party from the residence composed a poem on the beach, helping one another along like fishermen dragging a net:

oshi to omou	Hoping against hope
hito ya tomaru to	that the one we grieve to lose
ashigamo no	might resolve to stay,
uchimurete koso	we have come flocking here
ware wa kinikere	like wild ducks among the reeds.

They all stayed where they were, and everyone praised them to the skies. A departing traveler composed this:

sao sasedo	As when a boatman
sokoi mo shiranu	seeks in vain to plumb the sea,
watatsuumi no	thrusting with his oar,
fukaki kokoro o	even so do we behold
kimi ni miru ka na	the boundless depths of your hearts.

The boat captain, an insensitive fellow, had had as much as he wanted to drink and was anxious to leave. "The tide is full! The wind's coming up!" he shouted.

As the travelers prepared to board the vessel, the well-wishers recited Chinese poems suitable to the season and occasion. Even though Tosa is a western province, someone also sang a song from Kai Province.

"Magnificent singing!" people said. "The cabin dust has scattered and the clouds are standing still."[3]

That night we stayed at Urado, where Fujiwara no Tokizane, Tachibana no Suehira, and some others overtook us.

[xii] TWENTY-EIGHTH DAY

The boat rowed out from Urado, bound for Ōminato. Meanwhile, Yamaguchi no Chimine, the son of one of the Governor's predecessors in office, had arrived with wine and delicacies and sent them on board, so we went on our way drinking and eating.

[xii] TWENTY-NINTH DAY

The night was spent at Ōminato. The provincial medical officer came all the way to bring *tōso, byakusan,* and even wine.[4] It would seem that he was a very kind man.

[First Month,] FIRST DAY

Still in the same harbor. Someone had put the *byakusan* up against the boat cabin, thinking it would be safe overnight, but the wind gradually shifted it overboard, so nobody was able to have any. There were no dried taro stems, *arame* seaweed, or New Year health dishes, either. Such things are not ordinarily provided aboard boats, and the Governor had not asked for them. People simply kissed the lips of pressed salted trout.[5] Do you suppose the trout found it romantic?

"I can't help thinking about the capital today," everybody kept saying. "I wonder how it all looks—the straw festoons, with their mullet heads and holly, at the gates of the little houses."

3. A legendary Chinese singer, Yu Gung, is said to have made dust rise from the rafters, a story adapted here to a nautical setting. Another, Qin Qing, sang a lament so moving that it swayed trees and made clouds stand still.

4. *Tōso* and *byakusan,* two Chinese drinks consumed at the beginning of a new year to ward off illness, were compounds of medicinal substances steeped in rice wine. The medical officer had supplied the wine to make sure that the party would be able to prepare the potions.

5. I.e., nibbled at their heads. Salted trout were a Tosa specialty.

[i] SECOND DAY

Still at Ōminato. The head monk sent food and wine.

[i] THIRD DAY

Same place. The wind and waves seemed tiresomely reluctant to let us go.

[i] FOURTH DAY

Winds prevented our departure. Masatsura presented wine and delicacies. Unwilling to accept gifts with no return, the Governor did what little he could by way of recompense. There was nothing to serve as a proper acknowledgment. The presents created a prosperous atmosphere, but they were really a source of embarrassment.

[i] FIFTH DAY

The winds and waves refused to abate, so we remained in the same place. There was a steady stream of callers.

[i] SIXTH DAY

Same as the day before.

[i] SEVENTH DAY

The Seventh Day came, with the boat still in the same harbor. People thought in vain about the White Horse Banquet being held that day; for us, waves were the only white things in sight.[6] Meanwhile, someone who lived at a house called "The Pond" sent over a procession of servants shouldering long chests crammed with food. In addition to other things, the chests held *funa* and other river and sea fish—but no carp. There were young greens to serve as a reminder of the date, and also a very clever poem:

6. On the White Horse Banquet, one of the annual court New Year festivals, see William H. McCullough and Helen Craig McCullough, trs., *A Tale of Flowering Fortunes* (Stanford, Calif., 1980), 1: 382–83.

asajiu no	We dwell on a plain
nobe ni shi areba	where sparse cogon grasses grow,
mizu mo naki	and thus these young greens
ike ni tsumitsuru	have been gathered for your sake
wakana narikeri	from a pond without water.

"Pond" was a reference to the name of the place. Someone said a well-bred woman from the capital had come there with her husband to live.

The food from the chests was distributed to everyone on board, including the children, and they all ate as much as they could hold. The sounds made by the sailors drumming on their bursting bellies were enough to wake the sea god and raise the waves.

A number of things happened during that period. A man appeared on the same day with some servants carrying partitioned lunch boxes. (His name escapes me; I will remember it presently.) This person had come because he wanted to recite a poem. After a little preliminary talk, he spoke up in a doleful voice. "The waves are shockingly high, aren't they?" he said. Then he produced his composition:

yukusaki ni	Exceeding the sound
tatsu shiranami no	of the white billows rising
koe yori mo	where you are to go—
okurete nakamu	even so will be my wails
ware ya masaramu	when you have left me behind.

He must have had a loud voice! How well did his poem compare with the gifts he had brought? People said polite things, but nobody composed a reply. Although there were some who were capable of doing so, they merely uttered words of praise and kept right on eating. After nightfall, the poet withdrew, announcing that he would return soon. Then, to everyone's surprise, a little girl, the child of one of the passengers, said softly, "I'd like to answer the poem."

"That would be lovely. Can you really think of something? If so, let us hear it."

"I'll wait for the gentleman who went away. He said he wasn't leaving."

Someone went in search of the man, but he had gone straight home after all, possibly because of the lateness of the hour.

"Well, now, what was your poem going to be?" an inquisitive

person asked. At first, the bashful child was too embarrassed to answer, but after much urging she brought out these lines:

yuku hito mo	The rivers of tears
tomaru mo sode no	on the sleeves of one who goes
namidagawa	and one who remains
migiwa nomi koso	rise until they overflow
nuremasarikere	and make the beaches wetter.

Imagine the child's composing such an excellent poem! We might have been less surprised if we had not been thinking of her as a mere sweet infant.

"We can't present it as a child's composition; it must seem to come from an older person," someone said. "Right or wrong, it shall be sent at the first opportunity." The speaker apparently copied it down and saved it.

[i] EIGHTH DAY

The boat remained in the same place because of an obstacle to our departure. As the moon sank into the sea that night, someone recalled Narihira's poem:

> Retreat, O rim of the hills,
> and refuse to let it set.

If Narihira had been composing by the seashore, I wonder if he might have said:

> Rear up, O waves of the sea,
> and refuse to let it set.

With Narihira's poem in mind, a certain person composed some such lines as these:

teru tsuki no	Gazing at the course
nagaruru mireba	of the shining moon on high,
ama no kawa	we find that the mouth
izuru minato wa	of the River of Heaven
umi ni zarikeru	is none other than the sea.

[i] NINTH DAY

The boat rowed out from Ōminato shortly before dawn on the Ninth, bound for Nawa Harbor. Of the many people who had come separately to say good-bye, eager to see the Governor as long as he was still in the district, the most faithful had been Fujiwara no Tokizane, Tachibana no Suehira, and Hasebe no Yukimasa, who had followed him from place to place ever since his departure from the official residence. Those three had hearts as deep as the ocean. Knowing that the boat was to set out across open water from Ōminato, they had come for a final farewell. As the boat moved away, the figures on the seashore shrank, and the passengers became invisible from the land. Those on the shore must have had things they wished to say, and those in the boat felt the same way, but nothing could be done about it. Someone murmured this poem to himself before turning his mind to other things:

omoiyaru	Are they unaware
kokoro wa umi o	of how I send my spirit
wataredomo	across the water—
fumi shi nakereba	I who can neither walk there
shirazu ya aruramu	nor dispatch a letter?

Presently, the boat passed the pine woods of Uda. It was impossible to imagine how many trees might be standing there, or how many thousands of years they might have lived. The waves came up to their roots, and cranes flew back and forth among the branches. Too deeply moved to admire the spectacle in silence, one of the passengers composed a poem that went something like this:

miwataseba	They must think of them
matsu no ure goto ni	as friends for eternity—
sumu tsuru wa	those cranes far away
chiyo no dochi to zo	dwelling wherever a pine tree
omoubera naru	offers a bough for a home.

The poem was not the equal of the scene.

The boat moved on, with the passengers gazing at similar sights, until shadows gathered over mountains and sea. As the night deepened, one direction seemed the same as another, and everything concerning the weather conditions had to be left to the captain's discretion. It was a depressing experience for any man unaccustomed to such journeys—and as for the women, they simply pressed their heads against the floorboards and wailed. But the sailors and captain roared out boat songs without a care in the world. For example:

> Here I sob in the fields of spring.
> Is an old man wolfing them now?
> Is an old mother-in-law eating them now?—
> Those tender greens I picked
> While the young miscanthus
> Cut, cut my hands.
>
> KAERAYA[7]
> Just let me meet last night's girl again!
> I'll ask her for the money.
> She told a lie, she bought on credit,
> And now she doesn't bring the money,
> She doesn't even show her face.

There were many others that I will not record. The sound of the laughter they elicited was a relief; the seas were rough but our nerves were somewhat calmed.

We reached the harbor after traveling all day long. An old man and an old woman, who had suffered more than the rest of us, took to their beds without eating.

[i] TENTH DAY

This night was spent at Nawa Harbor.

[i] ELEVENTH DAY

The boat left for Murotsu before daybreak. Since everyone was still in bed, it was impossible to see the ocean; the best we could do was judge directions by the moon. Presently, the new day dawned. It was around noon by the time people had washed their hands and performed the usual offices. Just then the boat reached a place called Hane.

"Does Hane look like a bird's wing [hane]?" asked a child who had heard someone mention the name. Everyone laughed at the naïve question, and a little girl—the same one as before—composed a poem:

7. Interpreted as a word used to mark time (hayashikotoba). Its meaning, if any, is obscure.

makoto nite	If, true to its name,
na ni kiku tokoro	this place consisted of wings,
hane naraba	how nice it would be
tobu ga gotoku ni	to return to the city
miyako e mo ga na	like a flock of flying birds.

"Exactly so," the others thought. Even though her composition was not very good, it was remembered by men and women alike, for everyone longed to reach the capital as soon as possible.

With her question about Hane, the child had stirred thoughts of another, no longer among the living, who was never forgotten. The mother seemed especially sad that day. Prompted by the reflection that those who had traveled to the province were not all returning, someone recalled the old poem, "Not the full number, it seems, is making the journey home." He composed these lines:

yo no naka ni	Ponder as we may
omoiyaredomo	the sorrows of this bleak world,
ko o kouru	we find none more sharp
omoi ni masaru	than the grief a parent feels
omoi naki ka na	mourning the loss of a child.

And even as he spoke . . .

[i] TWELFTH DAY

No rain. The boat carrying Funtoki and Koremichi, which had been delayed, reached Murotsu by way of Narashi Harbor.

[i] THIRTEENTH DAY

A little rain fell before dawn on the Thirteenth. It stopped after a while. The women went ashore to bathe at a suitable place in the vicinity. Gazing out across the sea, someone composed a poem:

kumo mo mina	Each fleecy white cloud
nami to zo miyuru	assumes the guise of a wave.
ama mo ga na	O for a fisher
izure ka umi to	to answer when we inquire,
toite shirubeku	"Which of them might be the sea?"

The gibbous moon was delightful. Out of fear of the sea god, none of the women had worn handsome deep-red robes since boarding the vessel on the first day, but now, convinced that there was nothing to worry about, they found shelter of sorts behind a sparse stand of reeds, tucked up their skirts to their shins, and calmly displayed mussels and abalones.[8]

[i] FOURTEENTH DAY

Rainfall, which began before daybreak, kept the boats in the same harbor. The chief passenger abstained from eating flesh. In the absence of vegetarian foods, he broke his fast at noon with a sea bream caught on the previous day by the captain, to whom he gave some rice for lack of money. The same thing was done on later occasions: the captain brought sea bream again, and received rice or wine several times, which he seemed to find agreeable.

[i] FIFTEENTH DAY

To the disappointment of all, no bean-gruel was made on this day. Furthermore, the boat had now been inching along for more than twenty days because of bad weather. Finding no better way of passing the time, people stared absently at the sea. A little girl recited a poem:

tateba tatsu	When it rises,
ireba mata iru	they rise along with it;
fuku kaze to	when it rests, they rest.
nami to wa omou	Might the two of them be friends—
dochi ni ya aruramu	the blowing wind and the waves?

It was a suitable composition for a child.

[i] SIXTEENTH DAY

We stayed in the same place, detained by continuing high wind and waves. Everyone kept wishing for calm seas and a quick passage around the cape. Someone composed a poem as he watched the surging waves:

shimo dani mo	In these parts, they say,
okanu kata zo to	the nights are not cold enough

8. It was believed that the sea god might claim a woman who excited his interest. In the ill-understood last part of this sentence, of which the translation is a loose paraphrase, Tsurayuki plays on the names of mollusks that were probably thought to resemble a woman's genitals.

iu naredo	even to set frost—
nami no naka ni wa	and yet we see fallen snow
yuki zo furikeru	white among the ocean waves.

Twenty-five days had passed since we boarded the boat.

[i] SEVENTEENTH DAY

The dark clouds cleared to reveal a delightful late-night moon, and the crew took the boat out and began to row. Sea and sky seemed to merge. It was not without reason that the man of old said, I believe, something like this:

> The oar strikes through the moon on the waves;
> The boat presses against the sky in the sea.

But I know little about such things.
Someone composed this poem:

minasoko no	A cinnamon tree!
tsuki no ue yori	Surely it is no other
kogu fune no	catching the oar
sao ni sawaru wa	of the boat rowing over
katsura narurashi	the moon in the watery depths.

Someone who had been listening recited this:

kage mireba	With a forlorn heart
nami no soko naru	I gaze into the moonlight
hisakata no	where beneath the waves
sora kogiwataru	stretches a limitless sea
ware zo wabishiki	to be traversed by this boat.

Day finally dawned while such poems were being recited.
"Some black clouds have come up out of nowhere," the captain announced. "The wind is going to blow. I'm taking the boat back." A depressing rain fell as the boat returned to the harbor.

[i] EIGHTEENTH DAY

Still in the same place. The boat could not be taken out while the waves were so rough. The scenery at the harbor was very nice, both in the distance and closer at hand, but everyone was too miserable to appreciate it. I got the impression that some of the men were reciting Chinese poems, possibly in order to cheer themselves up. Someone composed this as a way of killing time:

isofuri no	Snow falls constantly
yosuru iso ni wa	with no regard for season
toshitsuki o	on the wild seashore
itsu to mo wakanu	where great breakers thunder in
yuki nomi zo furu	to shatter against the rocks.

It was the poem of a person unaccustomed to composition. Someone also composed this:

kaze ni yoru	Forever blooming
nami no iso ni wa	on rocky strands where the wind
uguisu mo	drives the wild waves home:
haru mo eshiranu	flowers unfamiliar
hana nomi zo saku	to the warbler and to spring.

The elderly chief passenger, intrigued by the efforts of the others, tried some lines of his own, which he hoped might relieve the gloomy atmosphere of the past weeks:

tatsu nami o	It seems to intend
yuki ka hana ka to	to deceive our human eyes—
fuku kaze zo	the wind blowing waves
yosetsutsu hito o	forever toward the seashore
hakarubera naru	to break like snow, like blossoms.

After listening intently to the comments on the poems, a certain person produced one that proved to contain thirty-seven syllables. To his indignation, everyone burst out laughing. One would try in vain to recite such a poem. Even if it were written down, it would be impossible to read. If it was so difficult on the very day of its composition, imagine what it would be like later!

[i] NINETEENTH DAY

The weather was too bad for the boat to leave.

[i] TWENTIETH DAY

Same as the preceding day; the boat failed to leave. Everyone was worried and gloomy. The passengers' nervousness and depression made them count the days until their fingers almost cramped. "How many has it been today?" "Twenty. . . ." "Thirty. . . ." They were too miserable to sleep at night.

The Twentieth-night moon appeared. With no mountain rim from which to emerge, it seemed to rise out of the sea. Just such a sight must have greeted the eyes of Abe no Nakamaro when he prepared to return home from China long ago. At the place where Nakamaro was to board ship, the Chinese gave him a farewell party, lamenting the separation and composing poems in their language. The moon rose from the sea as they lingered there, seemingly reluctant to let him go. Nakamaro recited a composition in Japanese, remarking, "Such poems have been composed by the gods in our country ever since the divine age. Nowadays people of all classes compose them when they regret the necessity of parting, as we are doing, or when they feel joy or sorrow":

aounabara	When I gaze far out
furisakemireba	across the blue-green sea plain,
kasuga naru	I see the same moon
mikasa no yama ni	that appeared above the hills
ideshi tsuki ka mo	of Mikasa at Kasuga.

Nakamaro had feared that the poem would be unintelligible to the Chinese, but he wrote down its gist in characters and explained it to someone who understood our language, and then it received unexpectedly warm praise. They may have been able to appreciate his emotion, after all. Although China and this country use different languages, moonlight must look the same in both places, and thus it must evoke the same human feelings.

With those days in mind, someone composed:

miyako nite	It is the same moon
yama no ha ni mishi	I saw at the mountain rim
tsuki naredo	in the capital,
nami yori idete	yet now it comes from the waves
nami ni koso ire	and into the waves retreats.

[i] TWENTY-FIRST DAY

Our boat set out around the Hour of the Hare [5:00 A.M. – 7:00 A.M.]. All the others left, too, giving the appearance of scattered autumn leaves on the springtime sea. Thanks, it may be, to the fervent prayers we had offered, it proved to be a beautiful, calm day as we rowed along. A child who had come with the party, asking to be used as a servant, sang a touching boat song:

> And still, and still,
> I can't help looking far into the distance
> Toward my homeland
> When I think that there my father lives,
> There my mother lives.
>
> KAERAYA

The boat moved on, with the passengers listening to such songs, and presently we reached a rock where a flock of black water birds had gathered. White waves broke at its base.

"White waves approach black birds," the captain said. It was not a particularly felicitous phrase, but it had a literary ring. One was struck by it because it did not seem to fit the man's station in life.

The boat continued its progress while similar remarks were being exchanged. Gazing at the waves, the chief passenger said, "Ever since our departure from the province, I have been worrying about rumors that the pirates plan to seek revenge. And then the sea has been terrifying! My hair has gone completely white. I see now that the ocean can make a man turn seventy or eighty years old:

wa ga kami no	Tell me, guardian
yuki to isobe no	of yon island in the sea,
shiranami to	which is the whiter:
izure masareri	the snow covering my head
okitsushimamori	or waves on a rocky shore?

"Captain, I rely on you to transmit my message."

[i] TWENTY-SECOND DAY

We headed from the previous night's harbor toward another stopping place. Mountains were visible far in the distance. A boy of about nine, young for his age, noticed that the hills seemed to be moving with the boat. To everyone's surprise, he composed a poem:

kogite yuku	Gazing from the boat
fune nite mireba	as it goes rowing along,

ashihiki no	we see that the hills,
yama sae yuku o	the very hills, are moving.
matsu wa shirazu ya	Don't the pine trees know it?

It was a suitable poem for a child.

The sea was choppy that day; snow fell on rocky shores and wave flowers bloomed. Someone composed this:

nami to nomi	Our ears tell us waves—
hitotsu ni kikedo	waves alone—yet our eyes,
iro mireba	observing their hue,
yuki to hana to ni	lead us into confusion
magaikeru ka na	with snowflakes and blossoms.

[i] TWENTY-THIRD DAY

Sunshine followed by clouds. Prayers were offered to the gods and Buddhas because there was said to be danger from pirates in the area.

[i] TWENTY-FOURTH DAY

Same place as on the preceding day.

[i] TWENTY-FIFTH DAY

The captains having pronounced the north wind unfavorable, the boats were not taken out. People kept saying the pirates were pursuing us.

[i] TWENTY-SIXTH DAY

Whether it was true or not I can't say, but there were rumors that pirates were on our trail. This caused us to delay our departure until around midnight. As the boat proceeded, we came to a place where travelers make offerings to the gods for a safe journey. The captain was commissioned to present strips of sacred cloth. The offerings went flying off toward the east, and he prayed, "Grant that the boat may travel swiftly in the direction taken by the sacred strips." A little girl who was listening composed a poem:

watatsuumi no	O wind scattering
chifuri no kami ni	the sacred strips we present

tamuke suru	to gods who protect
nusa no oikaze	travelers on the broad sea:
yamazu fukanamu	may your blowing never cease!

Meanwhile, elated by the fair wind, the captain gave orders to hoist the sail. The flapping noise delighted the children and old women, possibly because of their eagerness to reach the capital. One of the group, the Awaji Grandmother, composed a poem:

oikaze no	Now that fair winds blow,
fukinuru toki wa	we clap our hands joyously,
yuku fune no	echoing the sound
hote uchite koso	of the halyards clattering
ureshikarikere	as the vessel speeds along.

The captain offered prayers for fine weather.

[i] TWENTY-SEVENTH DAY

The wind and waves were high, so the boat was not taken out. There were despairing sighs in all quarters.

The men attempted to amuse themselves with Chinese poetry. A woman composed this waka, after having caught the gist of a verse that said something like "When I look at the sun, the capital seems far away":

hi o dani mo	Even the far sun
amakumo chikaku	rides close to the heavenly clouds,
miru mono o	and yet how distant
miyako e to omou	is the end of this journey
michi no harukesa	toward the longed-for capital!

Someone else recited:

fuku kaze no	Because the white waves
taenu kagiri shi	will certainly raise their heads
tachikureba	whenever the wind blows,
namiji wa itodo	long indeed must be our trip
harukekarikeri	across the billowing sea.

The wind blew all day long, and the passengers went to bed snapping their fingers in vexation.

[i] TWENTY-EIGHTH DAY

It rained all night and into the morning.

[i] TWENTY-NINTH DAY

The boat was taken out. We were rowed along in bright sunlight. Noticing that my nails had grown excessively long, I reckoned up the days and found that it was a Day of the Rat; thus I refrained from cutting them. Since it was the First Month, people began to talk of the Day of the Rat in the capital. "Wouldn't it be nice to have a little pine tree?" someone said.[9] But that was scarcely possible on the open sea. One of the women jotted down a poem, which she showed around:

obotsukana	How unreal it seems!
kyō wa ne no hi ka	Is this the Day of the Rat?
ama naraba	Were I a fisher
umimatsu o dani	then I might at least uproot
hikamashi mono o	pine of the sea, but alas . . .

What shall we say of that as a Day of the Rat poem composed at sea? Someone also composed this:

kyō naredo	Though it is today,
wakana mo tsumazu	I cannot even pick greens,
kasugano no	for on the beaches
wa ga kogiwataru	I pass in this rowing craft
ura ni nakereba	there is no Kasuga Plain.

The boat proceeded on its way amid such talk. Presently, we approached a beautiful spot.

"Where are we?" someone asked.

"Tosa Harbor."

Among the passengers there was a woman who had once lived in a place called Tosa. "Ah," she sighed. "It has the same name as the Tosa where I lived long ago." She recited this poem:

toshigoro o	It bears the same name
sumishi tokoro no	as the place in which I lived
na ni shi oeba	while the years went by,

9. A Day of the Rat in the First Month was the proper time for picking healthful young greens in the fields. People on such outings also pulled up tiny pine trees, which were valued

| kiyoru nami o mo | and thus I feel affection |
| aware to zo miru | even for its approaching waves. |

[i] THIRTIETH DAY

No rain or wind. We left around midnight, having heard that the pirates were inactive at night, and began to negotiate the Awa Strait whirlpool. It was too dark to tell one direction from another, but we managed to get through, with both sexes praying frantically to the gods and Buddhas. We passed Nushima Island at around the Hour of the Tiger [3:00 A.M. – 5:00 A.M.] or the Hour of the Hare [5:00 A.M. – 7:00 A.M.], and then Tanakawa; and by traveling at full speed we reached a place called Izumi-no-nada.

The gods and Buddhas must have been blessing us, for the sea was almost perfectly calm that day. It was our thirty-ninth on board the boat.

Now that we had reached Izumi Province, pirates were no longer a threat.

[Second Month,] FIRST DAY

Rain fell in the morning. When it stopped, around the Hour of the Horse [11:00 A.M. – 1:00 P.M.], we set out from Izumi-no-nada. As on the preceding day, the surface of the sea was calm and windless. We traveled past the Kurosaki [Black Cape] pine woods. With the name of the place black, the color of the pines green, the waves on the rocky beach snow-white, and the shells red, we lacked only one of the five colors [yellow].

Meanwhile, at a place called Hako-no-ura [Bay of Boxes], the sailors began to pull us with a towrope. As we were progressing in that manner, someone recited a poem:

tamakushige	When waves are thus calm
hako no uranami	in this bay that calls to mind
tatanu hi wa	gemmed comb boxes,
umi o kagami to	who could fail to find the sea
tare ka mizaramu	exactly like a mirror?

---

as symbols of longevity. "Pine of the sea," mentioned in the poem below, was a type of seaweed.

"To think a new month has begun . . . ," the chief passenger sighed. Miserably depressed, he decided to cheer himself up with a poem, since someone else had already recited one:

hiku fune no	Forty or fifty
tsunade no nagaki	are the days I have endured,
haru no hi o	spring days stretching out
yosoka ika made	as long as the long towrope
ware wa henikeri	with which sailors pull our boat.

It would seem that those who heard his composition began to make private remarks about its lack of ingenuity, but there were only a few whispers after someone warned, "He went to a lot of trouble over that poem, and he's probably proud of it. He'll be annoyed if he hears you."

The wind and waves suddenly rose, forcing the boat to stop.

[ii] SECOND DAY

The wind and high seas continued. People prayed to the gods and Buddhas all through the day and night.

[ii] THIRD DAY

The sea remained the same as on the day before, preventing the sailors from taking the boat out. The ceaseless wind seemed to roll back the waves as they approached the shore. Someone was moved to compose a poem:

o o yorite	What good might it do
kai naki mono wa	to make thread of twisted hemp?
ochitsumoru	We cannot use it
namida no tama o	to string the jewel-like tears
nukanu narikeri	we shed in such abundance.

So the day ended.

[ii] FOURTH DAY

The captain refused to take the boat out, pronouncing the wind and clouds too threatening, but the elements remained calm all day long. The stupid fellow couldn't even predict the weather.

There were many beautiful shells and rocks of all kinds on the shores of that harbor. Someone on board, lonely as always for an absent child, recited:

yosuru nami	You incoming waves,
uchi mo yosenamu	wash ashore the forgetting-shells
wa ga kouru	that may bring surcease
hito wasuregai	from longing for my dear love:
orite hirowamu	I will go and gather them.

Too deeply affected to remain silent, and hopeful also of relieving the gloom on board, a certain person composed this:

wasuregai	I shall not gather
hiroi shi mo seji	seashells for forgetfulness,
shiratama o	but make a keepsake
kouru o dani mo	of this longing for a child
katami to omowamu	as fair as a precious white pearl.

Grief for a daughter seems to damage a parent's powers of judgment. Some may object that the girl could not have been as pretty as a pearl. But there is also an old saying, "The dead child had a beautiful face."

One of the women composed this poem, unhappy because day after day was being spent in the same place:

te o hidete	The days have gone by
samusa mo shiranu	in this Izumi—a spring
izumi ni zo	where sleeves can be soaked
kumu to wa nashi ni	with no feeling of coldness,
higoro henikeru	where no water can be drawn.[10]

[ii] FIFTH DAY

On this day, the boat finally left Izumi-no-nada for Ozu Harbor. Pine woods stretched before us as far as the eye could see. The whole party got heartily sick of them, and someone composed a poem:

yukedo nao	On and on we press,
yukiyararenu wa	yet we cannot journey past
imo ga umu	pine trees on the shore

10. The poem puns on the name of the province and a homophone meaning "spring."

| ozu no ura naru | fringing the Bay of Ozu, |
| kishi no matsubara | known for fair spinners of hemp. |

Such was the talk as we moved along.

"Take advantage of the good weather. Row as fast as you can," the Governor urged.

"Orders from His Excellency!" the captain said to the crew. "Hurry up and get the towrope going before the morning northerly begins." His speech sounded like a poem but was quite spontaneous and uncalculated.

"That's odd. He seems to have recited a poem," said someone who had been listening. The speaker wrote down the words; there were indeed thirty-one syllables.

The wind and waves remained tranquil in response to the pleas of the passengers, who prayed throughout the day for calm seas.

The boat came to a place where a flock of seagulls was at play, and one of the children recited this poem, happy at being so close to the capital:

inorikuru	The wind has died down
kazama to mou o	in divine recognition
aya naku mo	of our many petitions—
kamome sae dani	but why should we seem to see
nami to miyuramu	white waves where the seagulls flock?

As we journeyed on, we saw delightful pine-covered shores, stretching far into the distance, at a place called Ishizu. Then the boat passed Sumiyoshi, and someone recited:

ima mite zo	What I now behold
mi o ba shirinuru	informs me of my true plight:
suminoe no	I am older still
matsu yori saki ni	than the venerable pines
ware wa henikeri	on Suminoe's beaches.

The dead child's mother, who never forgot her for a day or an hour, composed this:

suminoe ni	Please take the boat in
fune sashiyose yo	to the Suminoe shore.
wasuregusa	Before we journey on,

> shirushi ari ya to   I will pluck forgetting-grass
> tsumite yukubeku   to test the truth of its name.

It is unlikely that she wanted to forget completely. She was probably seeking temporary relief from her longing, hoping to regain the strength to bear it.

We were proceeding in that way, composing poems and admiring the scenery, when a sudden wind blew up. Although the sailors rowed with all their might, the boat was forced steadily backwards, and we were soon in imminent danger of sinking.

"This Bright Divinity of Sumiyoshi is like all the gods. He must want something," the captain said. How modern of a god to be so covetous!

"Please make an offering of sacred strips," the captain said. We did as he asked, but the storm showed no sign of abating, and the wind and waves reached ominous heights.

The captain spoke up again. "He isn't satisfied with the strips; that's why he won't let His Excellency's boat proceed. Please give him something nice enough to make him happy."

The Governor felt compelled to obey. "Precious though my eyes are, I have two of them. I'll give the god my one mirror," he said. With a heavy heart, he threw the mirror into the sea, and the surface itself instantly became like a mirror. Someone composed a poem:

> chihayaburu   I cast a mirror
> kami no kokoro o   into the turbulent waves
> aruru umi ni   of the raging sea,
> kagami o irete   and the thing it reflected
> katsu mitsuru ka na   was the heart of the mighty god.

That was certainly not the same god people praise with talk of Suminoe [Limpid Inlet], forgetting-grass, and young shore pines. I saw his heart clearly in the mirror: it was the same as the captain's.

[ii] SIXTH DAY

After setting out from the channel marker, we arrived at Naniwa and entered the [Yodo] river. All the passengers, and especially the elderly men and women, raised their hands to their foreheads in an access of joy. In her delight at hearing that it was no longer far to the capital, the seasick old Awaji Grandmother lifted her head from the bilge and recited a poem:

itsu shi ka to	Now the august boat
ibusekaritsuru	comes at last to the inlet,
naniwagata	to long-awaited
ashi kogisokete	Naniwa, and with its oars
mifune kinikeri	pushes its way through the reeds.

Everyone was amazed to hear a poem from so unexpected a source. The ailing chief passenger was particularly impressed. "A fine composition," he said. "Quite a contrast with the seasick face we saw earlier!"

[ii] SEVENTH DAY

On this day we got well up the river, but were dismayed to find the water level falling as we rowed farther from the sea. It is no easy task for a boat to ascend a river.

The chief passenger was still feeling ill. Furthermore, he was an unrefined man, ignorant of the art of composition. But he decided to try a poem—possibly from a combination of admiration for the old lady's feat and relief at being near the capital. This was the rather eccentric result of his labors:

ki to kite wa	Despite our great haste,
kawanoboriji no	the water is but shallow
mizu o asami	in this river course,
fune mo wa ga mi mo	and thus the boat, like myself,
nazumu kyō ka na	goes indifferently today.

He must have been thinking of his indisposition when he composed it. Since a single poem was not enough to express all his sentiments, he produced another:

toku to omou	That it labors so—
fune nayamasu wa	the boat I would see speed on—
wa ga tame ni	is surely because
mizu no kokoro no	the river's feeling for me
asaki narikeri	is as shallow as its waters.

The poem was probably inspired by a desire to show his joy at the proximity of the capital. Recognizing that it was inferior to the Awaji woman's, he was impatient with himself for composing it. Meanwhile, night settled down and everyone went to bed.

[ii] EIGHTH DAY

Struggling onward up the river, we spent the night near Torikai Pasture. The chief passenger's illness flared up after dark, causing him acute distress. Someone brought fresh fish, for which rice was given in return. The men apparently whispered among themselves that it was a case of catching a bluefish with a grain of rice. It was not the first time such an exchange had taken place. But the fish went to waste because it was a day of abstinence.

[ii] NINTH DAY

With the sailors manning the towrope, we started upriver again before dawn, full of eager anticipation, but the extreme dearth of water forced us to crawl along. At a place called Wada Port Junction, some people asked for rice and fish, which we gave them.

Later, as the sailors continued to pull the boat upstream, we were able to see Nagisa House. It was a delightful sight for nostalgic eyes. Pine groves stood on the hill to the rear, and plum trees bloomed in the inner garden. People remarked that it was a famous old spot, and someone said it was the place where Ariwara no Narihira, the Middle Captain, composed this poem when he visited it with Prince Koretaka:

yo no naka ni	If ours were a world
taete sakura no	in which flowering cherry trees
sakazaraba	were never in bloom,
haru no kokoro wa	what tranquility would bless
nodokekaramashi	the human heart in springtime!

A member of our party recited some lines appropriate to the setting:

chiyo hetaru	Although the pine trees
matsu ni wa aredo	have endured a thousand years,
inishie no	there has been no change
koe no samusa wa	in the cold voice of the wind
kawarazarikeri	blowing as in bygone days.

Someone also composed this:

kimi koite	Blossoms of the plum,
yo o furu yado no	nostalgic for their master
ume no hana	at the old dwelling,
mukashi no ka ni zo	bloom with the same sweet fragrance
nao nioikeru	as in times now long past.

We continued upstream, rejoicing in the thought that the capital was drawing ever nearer.

There had been only one child in the Governor's party on the journey from the capital to Tosa, but a number of women had given birth in the province. After watching the parents as they carried their youngsters off the boat and back on again at the various stops, the dead child's grieving mother recited a poem:

nakarishi mo	Even those others
aritsutsu kaeru	who went out with no children
hito no ko o	return as parents.
arishi mo nakute	How bitter that a mother
kuru ga kanashisa	should come home with empty arms!

She began to weep. How must the father have felt as he listened? Such poems are not composed for pleasure. Both in China and in our land, they spring from emotion too strong to be borne.

We stopped at Udono that night.

[ii] TENTH DAY

Something prevented us from continuing up the river.

[ii] ELEVENTH DAY

A light rain stopped after a time. Traveling upstream, we saw a mountain just ahead to the east, which proved upon inquiry to be the site of Yawata Shrine. Everyone offered joyful prayers. Then the Yamazaki Bridge came into view, and our happiness knew no bounds. The boat was halted briefly in the vicinity of Sōōji Temple so that some decisions could be made. A great many willows bordered the river near the temple, and their reflections in the water suggested a poem:

| sazarenami | One might imagine |
| yosuru aya o ba | reflected young willow threads |

aoyagi no	weaving the pattern
kage no ito shite	traced by incoming ripples
oru ka to zo miru	on the surface of the stream.

[ii] TWELFTH DAY

We spent the night at Yamazaki.

[ii] THIRTEENTH DAY

Still at Yamazaki.

[ii] FOURTEENTH DAY

Rain fell. On this day, someone was sent to the capital to fetch carriages.

[ii] FIFTEENTH DAY

People came bringing carriages. Depressed by shipboard life, the Governor moved to a private residence, where he was entertained with every appearance of delight. The owner's hospitality was indeed so marked as to seem almost excessive. Various kinds of return gifts were presented. The members of the household were most well bred and proper.

[ii] SIXTEENTH DAY

Setting out for the capital toward evening on this day, we noticed that there had been no changes in the pictures of small boxes at Yamazaki or in the shapes of the big fishhooks at Magari. But as they say, "Who knows what's in a shopkeeper's heart?"

As we continued toward the capital, someone entertained us at Shimasaka. There was no particular reason for him to do so. People were more hospitable during the return journey than when we traveled to Tosa. We gave return gifts to this host as well.

Wishing to enter the city after nightfall, we went along at a leisurely pace. Presently, the moon rose, and we crossed the Katsura River by its light. "Since this is not the Asuka, its pools and rapids haven't changed at all," people said. Someone composed a poem:

hisakata no	There has been no change,
tsuki ni oitaru	not even in the moonlight
katsuragawa	on the Katsura,
soko naru kage mo	the river whose name recalls
kawarazarikeri	the celestial cinnamon tree.

Someone also composed this:

amakumo no	Now I have crossed it,
haruka naritsuru	drenching my sleeve as I passed—
katsuragawa	Katsuragawa,
sode o hidete mo	the stream that once seemed as distant
watarinuru ka na	as clouds in the firmament.

This was also composed:

katsuragawa	No affinity
wa ga kokoro ni mo	guides the Katsura River
kayowanedo	through my heart's channels—
onaji fukasa ni	yet in depth it seems the same
nagarubera nari	as this flood of happiness.

Too much elation at returning to the capital had resulted in too much poetry.

Because we were arriving late at night, the familiar places were not visible, but it was a joy merely to make our way deeper into the city. When we reached the house and entered the gate, the surroundings stood out clearly in the bright moonlight. The disrepair was terrible— far worse than we had been told. The consciences of the people to whom the Governor had entrusted the house were obviously in as bad shape as the buildings themselves. There was a boundary fence between the house and the one next door, but the two were like a single establishment, so the neighbors had volunteered to look after things. It was not an onerous responsibility, but still the Governor had sent them presents at every opportunity . . . Nevertheless, he refused to let his people utter noisy complaints that night. Heartless as the neighbors had shown themselves, he made up his mind to thank them.

There had been a stand of pine trees beside a pond of sorts, but half of them had died and new ones had crowded in. One wondered if their thousand-year lifespans had somehow been exhausted in five or six years. The sheer desolation of the scene evoked exclamations of grief and despair.

Memories came flooding back. Among many sad, nostalgic thoughts, the most poignant were of the little girl, born in that house, who had not returned with the party. The children of others from the boat, chattering and shouting in noisy groups, made the grief of a certain person more unbearable than ever. He murmured a poem to someone who understood his feelings:

umareshi mo	What sadness to see
kaeranu mono o	how young pine trees have sprung up
wa ga yado ni	inside the garden
komatsu no aru o	of one who is bereft
miru ga kanashisa	even of a child once born.

He also composed this, possibly because his feelings still demanded expression:

mishi hito no	If the child's lifespan
matsu no chitose ni	had been a pine's thousand years,
mimashikaba	that distant parting,
tōku kanashiki	that sad, eternal farewell,
wakare semashi ya	would never have happened.

It is hopeless to try to record all the unforgettable and painful things that come to mind. After all, I suppose the best thing to do is to tear up these sheets at once.

The Gossamer Journal

There was once a woman who led a forlorn, uncertain life, the old days gone forever and her present status neither one thing nor the other. Telling herself that it was natural for a man to attach no value to someone who was less attractive than others and not very bright, she merely went to bed and got up day after day. But then it occurred to her, as she leafed through the many current tales of the past, that such stories were only conventional tissues of fabrications, and that people might welcome the novelty of a journal written by an ordinary woman. If there were those who wondered what it was like to be married to a man who moved in the very highest circles, she might invite them to find an answer here. Her memory was not good, either for the distant past or for more recent events, and she realized in the end that she had written many things it might have been better to omit.

Eighth Year of Tenryaku [954]

After I had received overtures from various quarters, none of them serious enough to record, there was an offer of marriage from Assistant Guards Commander Kaneie, the son of an exalted house. Instead of employing a male intermediary, a young maidservant, or the like, as most men would have done, he chose to drop hints to my father in person, sometimes as though in jest and again with a serious air. We let him know that we considered the match unsuitable, but he sent a mounted Escort to pound on the gate in blithe disregard of our message. The Escort and his companions created such a commotion that our people could scarcely make themselves heard to ask where they had come from. The visit caught us unprepared, so I simply accepted the message—and then there was more commotion.

Upon inspection, the paper proved to be different from the kind usually chosen for love letters, and the gentleman's handwriting was unbelievably bad, even though I had heard it praised to the skies. It was all very strange. This was the sum total of the message:

oto ni nomi	I long in my heart
kikeba kanashi na	to converse with the cuckoo:
hototogisu	these rumors, alas,
koto katarawamu to	have of themselves rendered me
omou kokoro ari	a prey to melancholy.

While my ladies and I were trying to decide whether I needed to answer it, my old-fashioned mother intervened. We could not ignore the attention; I must write something, she said. This was my poem:

katawaramu	Please do not persist,
hito naki sato ni	O cuckoo, in fruitless song
hototogisu	outside a house
kai nakarubeki	where there dwells no person
koe na furushi so	with whom you might care to speak.

With that as a beginning, he sent repeated messages, to none of which I replied. Then this poem arrived:

obotsukana	Utterly distraught,
oto naki taki no	I can but liken you
mizu nare ya	to the Mute Cascade.
yukue mo shiranu	It is as hard to meet you
se o zo tazunuru	as to find where the shallows flow.

I said I would answer later—whereupon, quite irrationally, he sent this:

hito shirezu	How sharp is the pain
ima ya ima ya to	when an answer fails to come
matsu hodo ni	while I wait and wait
kaerikonu koso	in breathless expectancy,
wabishikarikere	hiding my feelings from others!

"It won't do to snub a man like him," my mother said. "You'll have to send a reply." So I had a suitable message composed by a waiting-woman skilled in such matters, and we sent it off. Absolutely delighted to receive even a communication of that nature, he besieged us with missives. This poem was added to something he sent:

hamachidori	No visible sign
ato mo nagisa ni	of tracks left on the strand
fumiminu wa	by the beach plover:
ware o kosu nami	might it be because a wave
uchi ya ketsuramu	has surged in to wipe them out?

On that occasion, too, I avoided a direct reply by having someone else write for me.

Another message came, its tone earnest. "I was pleased to receive such a serious response, but it grieves me that you should still refuse to write in your own hand." There was a poem at the end:

izure to mo	Happy though I am
wakanu kokoro wa	to hear from either person,
soitaredo	this time I address
kotabi wa saki ni	the lady whose handwriting
minu hito no gari	I have not been privileged to see.

Nevertheless, I used a surrogate again.

So the days and months passed while we kept up a sedate correspondence.

Autumn approached. In a postscript to one of his letters, Kaneie wrote, "It distresses me that you should seem so firmly on your guard. I try to put up with it, but what can be the reason for my plight?" [His poem:]

shika no ne mo	I live among men
kikoenu sato ni	where the cry of the stag
suminagara	does not reach one's ears.
ayashiku awanu	Is it not strange that my eyes
me o mo miru ka na	refuse to close in sleep?

My reply was simply this poem, with the comment, "Strange, indeed!"

takasago no	I had never heard
onoe watari ni	that you would be likely to lie
sumau tomo	thus sleepless alone,
shika samenubeki	even if you were dwelling
me to wa kikanu o	near the peak at Takasago

Again, after a while, this came:

ōsaka no	For all its closeness,
seki ya nakanaka	it cannot be swiftly crossed.
chikakeredo	I live in misery,
koewabinureba	unable to pass beyond
nagekite zo furu	the Meeting Hill Barrier.

My reply:

koewaburu	Please understand this:
ōsaka yori mo	the famed Nakoso, "Don't Come,"
oto ni kiku	is a stronger barrier
nakoso o kataki	than the one at Meeting Hill
seki to shiranamu	you say you cannot cross.

Many serious messages went back and forth, and then one morning there was this: [11]

yūgure no	The flow of my tears
nagarekuru ma o	resembles the Ōi,
matsu hodo ni	"Stream of Abundance,"
namida ōi no	as I await the hour
kawa to koso nare	when evening shadows fall.

11. A "morning-after" poem, ending the courtship stage of the relationship, which has followed the approved pattern of masculine ardor and feminine coyness.

My reply:

omou koto	My heart in turmoil,
ōi no kawa no	I can but weep to contemplate
yūgure wa	nightfall, the time
kokoro ni mo arazu	when sad thoughts are as abundant
nagare koso sure	as the Ōi River's flow.

This arrived on the morning after our third night together:

shinonome ni	Why might it have been?
okikeru sora wa	Most oddly, when I arose
omōede	just before daybreak,
ayashiku tsuyu to	my spirit fainted away
kiekaeritsuru	as though it were a dewdrop.

My reply:

sadame naku	And what might I be?
kiekaeritsuru	Forced to rely on someone
tsuyu yori mo	as fickle as the dew,
soradanome suru	am I not even worse off
ware wa nani nari	than those evanescent drops?

He came to see me while I was making a brief stay away from home for some reason. This note arrived the next morning: "I had hoped that I might spend a leisurely day with you today, at least, but I gathered that it would be inconvenient. How is everything? I can't help thinking you hid yourself in the hills to get away from me." This was my only reply:

omōenu	Planted near a fence
kakio ni oreba	where it had not thought to be,
nadeshiko no	the blossoming pink
hana ni zo tsuyu wa	spills dewdrops from its petals
tamarazarikeru	when someone comes to pluck it.

The Ninth Month arrived. Toward the end of the month, there was a letter after he had stayed away two nights in a row. My reply:

kiekaeri	Even from the sky,
tsuyu mo mada hinu	affliction too cruel to bear:
sode no ue ni	showers fall this morning
kesa wa shigururu	on sleeves still drenched with moisture
sora mo wari nashi	from dewdrops of bitter grief.

He answered at once:

omoiyaru	That raindrops should seem
kokoro no sora ni	to fall in showers this morning
narinureba	can only be because
kesa wa shiguru to	my passionate heart has merged
miyuru naruramu	with the sky above your house.

He arrived in person before I could respond.

If I remember correctly, I composed this poem on a rainy day after another brief absence, when he had sent word to expect him that evening:

kashiwagi no	Does the oak each evening
mori no shitakusa	still tell the grass it shelters,
kuregoto ni	"Depend on me,"
nao tanome to ya	although it knows full well
moru o mirumiru	that the rain is leaking through?

He smoothed the matter over by coming instead of sending a reply.

The Tenth Month began. A number of impatient letters came while our household was observing a period of ritual seclusion. This poem also arrived:

nagekitsutsu	Why must showers fall,
kaesu koromo no	adding their moisture to a robe
tsuyukeki ni	turned inside out
itodo sora sae	and drenched with the tears of one
shiguresouramu	whose heart is heavy with grief? [12]

My reply was far from original:

omoi araba	If the fire of love burns,
hinamashi mono o	it can surely keep things dry.
ika de ka wa	How might it happen
kaesu koromo no	that the garments you reverse
tare mo nururamu	should be as wet as mine?

Meanwhile, it was decided that my father, the person on whom I relied, was to take up a position in Michinoku. It was a melancholy season of the year, and my marriage was still so new that I did not feel on

12. According to a popular belief, turning one's sleeping-robe inside out would bring dreams of one's beloved.

intimate terms with Kaneie. Whenever he came, I sat with tear-filled eyes, unutterably gloomy and miserable. My sympathetic attendants seemed to be saying among themselves that his behavior showed he would never desert me, but I could not share their faith in outward appearances, and dismal forebodings crowded into my mind.

The day came when my father and his party had to go. Father could not restrain his tears. Needless to say, my own grief was sharper still—quite beyond words. Even when the others warned that it was getting late, Father could scarcely bring himself to leave. He rolled up a piece of paper, put it in a nearby writing box, and went away with tears streaming down his face.

It took a while to summon the spirit to see what he had written. After the party had disappeared, I composed myself, went to the box, and found a poem:

kimi o nomi	This thought fills the mind
tanomu tabi naru	of the traveler who trusts
kokoro ni wa	in Your Lordship alone:
yukusue tōku	may the marriage go on as long
omōyuru ka na	as the road that lies ahead.

In a fresh access of grief, I realized that Father must have left it as a message for the husband who was henceforth to assume responsibility for me. I put the poem back, and Kaneie arrived soon afterward. I was too miserable to meet his eye.

He tried to coax me into a good humor. "Why are you so sad?" he asked. "There's nothing unusual about going to serve in the provinces. You must be acting this way because you don't trust me." The poem in the writing box caught his attention. Moved, he sent an answer to the place from which Father was to start:

ware o nomi	You say you rely
tanomu to ieba	on me alone: when you return,
yukusue no	you will see that my pledge
matsu no chigiri mo	is as enduring as the pines
kite koso wa mime	at Sue-no-matsuyama.

The days went by. It saddened me to think of how Father must be feeling out there in the provinces—and what was even worse, Kaneie's affections seemed far from reliable.

The Twelfth Month began. A messenger came from Kaneie, who

had ascended Mount Hiei to do something at Yokawa: "I am snowbound here. I miss you terribly and think of you all the time." I sent this poem back by the same man:

kōruramu	Forlorn though it be,
yokawa no mizu ni	the snowflake on the frozen stream
furu yuki mo	at Yokawa
wa ga goto kiete	is less likely to vanish
mono wa omowaji	than this spirit faint with love.

Soon the year drew to a close.

Ninth Year of Tenryaku [955]

Around the First Month, at a time when Kaneie had not visited me for two or three days, I went to stay somewhere, leaving instructions with a servant to give him this poem if he came:

shirareneba	Its heart unfathomed,
mi o uguisu no	the disconsolate warbler
furiidetsutsu	ventures forth crying
nakite koso yuke	toward whatever field or hill,
no ni mo yama ni mo	leaving the city behind.

He replied:

uguisu no	Even though its flight
ada ni mo yukamu	may lead the capricious warbler
yamabe ni mo	into the mountains,
naku koe kikaba	I will not fail to seek it
tazunu bakari zo	as soon as I hear its cry.

It was at about that time that I became pregnant. A difficult spring and summer followed, and then, around the end of the Eighth Month, I gave birth. Kaneie was most thoughtful and solicitous, both before and after the delivery.

One day around the Ninth Month, after he had left, I idly opened a letter box and discovered a message intended for another woman. Dumbfounded, I scribbled a poem on the edge so that he would at least know I had seen it:

utagawashi	At sight of a note
hoka ni wataseru	intended for someone else,

fumi mireba	I can but wonder:
koko ya todae ni	might this perhaps spell the end
naramu to suramu	of your visits to my house?

Toward the end of the Tenth Month, he absented himself for three nights running, just as I had anticipated.[13] He was quite offhand about it. "I thought I would stay away for a little while to test your feelings, and the days slipped by before I knew it," he said. He left in the evening, with the excuse that a directional taboo would make it awkward to go from my house to the imperial palace in the morning. I told someone to follow him, my suspicions aroused, and was informed that he had stopped at a house on Machijiri Street. It was no more than I had expected, I thought. But for all my distress, I did not know how to bring the subject up.

Two or three days later, there was a rapping on my gate toward dawn. I thought it must be he, but was too miserable to have my people open the gate, and he went off in what seemed to be the direction of the house on Machijiri Street. The next morning, unwilling to let the incident pass, I composed a poem, wrote it out with special care, and attached it to a faded chrysanthemum:

nagekitsutsu	You cannot know
hitori nuru yo no	how long it seems until dawn
akuru ma wa	for someone who lies
ika ni hisashiki	on a solitary bed,
mono to ka wa shiru	lost in melancholy thought.

He wrote in reply, "I had intended to keep knocking until your people opened the gate, even if it meant staying there until dawn, but a messenger found me—someone sent from the court on urgent business—and I had to leave. I can see why you were angry." His poem:

ge ni ya ge ni	It is true what you say
fuyu no yo naranu	of winter nights. Yet I have learned
maki no to mo	that a pinewood door
osoku akuru wa	may cause painful waiting, too,
wabishikarikeri	when it is slow to open.

He was bafflingly matter-of-fact about the whole affair. I might not

---

13. Spending three consecutive nights with a woman usually indicated a serious commitment.

have minded so much if he had tried to be secretive for a time—
pretending to have to go to the palace or something like that—but his
disregard of my feelings was too much to bear.

Tenth Year of Tenryaku [956]

The Third Month of a new year arrived. I think we probably decorated the house with peach blossoms.[14] I waited for Kaneie on the Third,
but he failed to come. That was also the one day on which there was no
visit from the gentleman who ordinarily liked nothing better than to be
with my sister. Both men showed up early on the morning of the Fourth.
Our ladies had been expecting them since the night before. They produced the festival things from our respective apartments, saying that it
would be a shame to let them go to waste, and I scribbled off an idle
verse, vexed by the sight of blossoms broken from boughs meant for the
Third:

matsu hodo no	What good does it do
kinō sukinishi	to break off those flowers today?
hana no e wa	Yesterday you drank
kyō oru koto zo	blossom wine with another
kai nakarikeru	while I sat waiting for you.

I was determined not to show the poem to Kaneie, whose behavior I had
found altogether too provoking, but he noticed my efforts at concealment, captured the paper, and composed a reply:

michitose o	Please be sure of this:
mitsubeki mi ni wa	the one whose love is plighted
toshigoto ni	for three thousand years
suku ni mo aranu	will not drink blossom wine
hana to shirasemu	year after year with another.

My sister's husband heard about the exchange and composed this:

hana ni yori	We stayed away,
suku chō koto no	lest by seeking the blossoms
yuyushiki ni	and drinking the wine
yoso nagara nite	we might be considered
kurashiteshi nari	mere frivolous ladies' men.

14. The Third of the Third Month was the date of the Peach Festival, an occasion for
drinking peach wine, eating special cakes, and composing poetry.

Kaneie had now become open about his involvement at Machijiri Street. There were many times when he actually seemed to regard even his first wife, Lady Tokihime, as an impediment. My own situation was indescribably distressing, but I could do nothing about it.

It was embarrassing for everyone that I should be a witness to my brother-in-law's constant comings and goings, so that gentleman decided to move his wife to a place where they could feel more comfortable. The prospect of being left alone added to my gloom. Miserably aware that I would hardly ever be able to see my sister, I sent out this poem when the men brought the carriage up:

> nado kakaru
> nageki wa shigesa
> . masaritsutsu
> hito nomi karuru
> yado to naruramu

> How might it happen
> that my dwelling becomes a place
> where the tree of grief
> puts forth luxuriant leaves
> while the people fade away?

The gentleman answered:

> omou chō
> wa ga koto no ha o
> adabito no
> shigeki nageki ni
> soete uramu na

> Please do not equate
> this expression of regard
> with the leaves of words
> put forth by one whose faithlessness
> makes the tree of sorrow grow.

And with that the party left.

Just as I had expected, I spent the days and nights alone from then on. My marriage was satisfactory enough in material respects; it was just that Kaneie's feeling for me was not what I had thought it would be. But according to the gossips, I was not the only sufferer; he had also stopped visiting his wife of many years. Lady Tokihime was a person with whom I sometimes exchanged messages, so I sent her this on the Third or Fourth of the Fifth Month:

> soko ni sae
> karu to iu naru
> makomogusa
> ika naru sawa ni
> ne o todomuramu

> Where might be the swamp
> in which they can put down roots—
> those water oats
> the reapers have harvested,
> cutting to the very bottom?

Her reply:

> makomogusa
> karu to wa yodo no

> The marsh from which
> the water oats have vanished

sawa nare ya	is this one at Yodo:
ne o todomu chō	people said they had struck root
sawa wa soko to ka	in the bottom where you dwell.

The Sixth Month arrived. On the First, it was still pouring rain. Looking out toward the garden, I murmured to myself:

wa ga yado no	On the tree of grief
nageki no shitaba	growing at my dwelling,
iro fukaku	the lower leaves have turned
utsuroinikeri	while the long rains have fallen
nagamefuru ma ni	and I have lived in misery.

The Seventh Month arrived.

One day Kaneie came, just when I had persuaded myself that it was better to have the relationship end than to be visited merely for the sake of appearances. I received him in silence, which did not seem to please him. Then one of my attendants mentioned the poem about the lower leaves, and he composed this reply:

ori narade	The colored foliage
irozukinikeru	that assumed autumnal hues
momijiba wa	ere its season came
toki ni aite zo	has taken on new beauty
iro masarikeru	now that its proper time is here.

I pulled over the inkstone and wrote this:

aki ni au	Though I grieved to see
iro koso mashite	even the lower leaves turn,
wabishikere	I am far more wretched
shitaba o dani mo	now that all the foliage
nagekishi mono o	has encountered autumn's touch.

So the days went by. Kaneie's visits did not cease entirely, but it was impossible for me to feel at ease with him, and our relations grew more and more strained. There was even a time when he turned around and left at once, declaring himself vanquished by my sulkiness, a veritable "traveler falling down on Standing Mountain." [15] A close neighbor, who knew how things were going, sent over this poem after his departure:

15. Kaneie utters a brief phrase, *taoruru ni tachiyama,* that can be interpreted either as a quotation of a proverb, "[Travelers] fall down but Tachiyama [Standing Mountain] keeps on standing," or as a complaint against the author, "Talked down, I retreat." Tachiyama (2,992 m; now called Tateyama) is in Toyama Prefecture.

moshio yaku	That the salt-fire smoke
keburi no sora ni	should have drifted away
tachinuru wa	toward unknown skies—
fusube ya shitsuru	might it be because the flame
kuyuru omoi ni	of jealousy burns too hot?

Our mutual stubbornness had thus reached the point of provoking unwelcome comment from the neighbors. Around that time, there was an especially long period when I saw nothing of him.

Now that his affections had strayed, he removed his belongings from my house, something he had never done in the days when things were going well. I told myself that the end had apparently come; I was to be left without even a memento. But a letter arrived ten days later. He wrote this and that and added at the end, "Please send me the small-bow arrow I left tied to one of the pillars on the curtain-dais." I had forgotten that one thing, at least, had remained. I unfastened the arrow, took it down, and sent it off with a poem:

omoiizuru	I thought there would be
toki mo araji to	no time when a memento
omoedomo	might make me think of you,
ya to iu ni koso	but now this commission
odorokarenure	has called the arrow to mind.[16]

During this period when his visits had ceased, I tried in vain to keep from listening to his men clear the way with discreet coughs as he traveled at night past my house, which lay on his route home from the imperial palace. But I was not sleeping well—as the poem says, "the nights were long; sleep would not come"—and I was always aware, with feelings quite beyond description, whenever he went by. There were times when I longed above all never to hear of him again, but then I would learn to my annoyance that another man was trying to persuade one of my attendants to act as a go-between, because "people say she no longer receives visits from the gentleman who used to come so often," and I would spend every evening in misery.

According to the gossips, Kaneie was also staying away altogether from Lady Tokihime, the consort who had borne him so many children. I

16. Line 4, loosely translated as "but now this commission," contains a pun that yields two meanings: "Now that you say, '[Send] the arrow [ya]'" and "Now that you say, 'Hey [ya]!'"

sent her a solicitous message, in the thought that her position was even worse than mine. Because it happened to be around the Ninth Month, I added this poem to my expressions of sympathy:

fuku kaze ni	Even though the web
tsukete mo towamu	long trodden by the spider
sasagani no	may vanish in the sky,
kayoishi michi wa	I trust the wind if need be
sora ni tayu tomo	to tell you of my concern.

Her reply was cordial:

iro kawaru	When I consider
kokoro to mireba	how it causes things to change,
tsukete tou	I find it odious—
kaze yuyushiku mo	that wind you have enlisted
omōyuru ka na	to tell me of your concern. [17]

Unable to maintain my pose of aloofness forever, I did see him occasionally. And so the winter arrived. Living with the baby as my sole companion, I found myself murmuring the old poem, "What is the reason? I long to question the whitefish gathered at the weir." [18]

First Year of Tentoku [957]

The new year began, bringing with it the springtime. Kaneie sent a messenger to fetch a book he had left by mistake—one he had been carrying around to read. I wrote this on the paper in which I wrapped it:

fumi okishi	Because the wild waves
ura mo kokoro mo	have rolled in to ravage
aretareba	the beach it once trod,
ato o todomenu	no longer does the plover
chidori narikeri	leave its tracks in the sand.

Although he would have done better to remain silent, he sent back a glib answer:

17. Tokihime views the wind as responsible for the changing color of the autumn leaves. A pun on *iro* ("color"; "feelings") yields a second meaning: "I'll dislike the wind if it deprives me of your friendship by causing your feelings to change."

18. A slight misquotation of a poem in *Tales of Yamato,* Sec. 89: ika de nao / ajiro no hio ni / koto towan / nani ni yorite ka / ware o towanu ("Somehow, I would like to ask a question of whitefish gathered at the weir: tell me where he goes and why he fails to come to

kokoro aru to	You may return the book,
fumi kaesu tomo	thinking my affections have strayed,
hamachidori	but the beach plover
ura ni nomi koso	wishes to leave its tracks
ato wa todomeme	on no other shore than yours.

The messenger was still there, so I replied:

hamachidori	Were I to seek
ato no tomari o	the place where the beach plover
tazunu tote	leaves its tracks these days,
yukue mo shiranu	I would doubtless see many shores
urami o ya semu	as I sought to find the way.

With such exchanges, the summer passed.

His favorite's confinement approached. He selected an auspicious direction, got into the carriage with her, and rode past my very gate, preceded by disagreeably loud shouts, and followed by a procession so long that the whole city must have buzzed with gossip. My maids and the others raised a great fuss when they saw me faint and speechless. "What a cruel thing to do! There were plenty of alternative routes." I wanted to die as I listened to them, but we cannot control the length of our life. I hoped that I might at least never have to see him again.

A letter arrived two or three days later, while I was still seething with resentment. Astonished by his insensitivity, I opened it to read, "I have been unable to call lately because someone here has been ill, but the affair ended safely yesterday. I fear I would be unwelcome if I were to visit you in a state of defilement." Could anything have been more shocking or bizarre? I replied only that I had received the message. Someone asked the messenger about the birth, and he announced that the child was a boy, tidings that deepened my distress.

Three or four days later, Kaneie himself put in a nonchalant appearance. I made it clear that I could see no reason for the visit, and he left in embarrassment before long. The same kind of thing happened several times afterward.

The Seventh Month arrived. Around the time of the wrestling matches, he had the effrontery to send me an old set of robes and the material for a new set, the former to be repaired, he said, and the latter to

---

me"). The speaker, a woman, assumes that because the fish approach (*yoru*) the weir, they must know whom the man visits (*yoru*) and why (*nani ni yorite*) he fails to come to her.

be freshly tailored. I was so angry I could hardly see straight when I looked at them.[19] "Poor fellow!" my old-fashioned mother said. "Apparently they can't sew very well at his house." But the maids crowded around and agreed that the request was unreasonable: I ought to say my women were too clumsy to do a proper job. After I had sent the things back, I learned that he had had to farm them out in one place and another, just as I had foreseen. No doubt he found my refusal annoying; I heard nothing for more than twenty days.

A letter arrived one day—I have forgotten just when. "I would like to visit you but feel unsure of my welcome. If you will extend a definite invitation, I will try to summon the courage to come." I wanted to ignore it, but several people said, "That would seem dreadfully rude. It would be going too far." So I sent this:

ho ni idete	I have no intention
iwaji ya sara ni	of begging you to come.
ōyoso no	I shall simply wait
nabiku obana ni	for the pliant miscanthus
makasete mo mimu	to bend wherever it pleases.

He replied:

ho ni ideteba	Once the plumes appear,
mazu nabikinamu	the feathery miscanthus,
hanasusuki	eager to yield,
kochi chō kaze no	will follow whenever
fukamu manimani	the east wind bids it come.

The messenger was still there. With an effort, I composed a conciliatory response:

arashi nomi	Were it to beckon,
fukumeru yado ni	I fear it would do no good—
hanasusuki	the plumed miscanthus
ho ni idetari to	growing at the dwelling
kai ya nakaramu	where the harsh gale ever blows.

Then we saw him again.

This exchange took place as we lay gazing at the riot of color in the garden. (Both of us must have been annoyed about something.) Kaneie:

19. They appear to have been intended for the woman in Machijiri Street.

momokusa ni	That all kinds of flowers
midarete miyuru	should offer this spectacle
hana no iro wa	of different hues—
tada shiratsuyu no	might it simply be because
oku ni ya aruramu	white dewdrops tinge their petals?[20]

My reply:

mi no aki o	To ask is to know
omoimidaruru	the function of those dewdrops
hana no ue no	on the flowers
tsuyu no kokoro wa	blooming in many colors
ieba sara nari	now that autumn is here.

Thus another coolness developed between us.

On the night of the Nineteenth, he began to show signs of leaving around the time when the moon rose above the rim of the hills. I must have looked as though I were thinking that he might at least spend that night with me, for he said, "If there is any reason why I should stay . . ." But I had no wish to seem insistent. I composed this poem:

ikaga semu	If the restless moon
yama no ha ni dani	chooses to course through the sky
todomarade	rather than to stay
kokoro mo sora ni	at the rim of the hills,
idemu tsuki o ba	what can I do to stop it?

He stayed after making this reply:

hisakata no	Whenever the moon
sora ni kokoro no	sets forth on its journey
izu to ieba	across the heavens,
kage wa soko ni mo	its reflection must appear
tomarubeki ka na	in the depths of the water.[21]

Then again, he came two days after an autumn gale of nearly typhoon force. "Most people would have sent to see if we were all right after a storm like the one the other day," I said. He may have taken my point, for he answered with a nonchalant verse:

20. Dew was thought to produce autumn colors. Puns give the poem another meaning: "I can see that you're fretting about something. Obviously, you don't trust me enough to speak out." Lady Gossamer's reply can be taken to mean, "If I fret, it's because I fear you have tired of me. Look into your heart for an explanation of my behavior."

21. "Because you accuse me of restlessness, I'll stay with you tonight."

koto no ha wa	I kept my letter,
chiri mo ya suru to	fearing that the leaves of words
tomeokite	might be blown astray,
kyō wa mi kara mo	but today, as you can see,
tou ni ya wa aranu	I have come to ask in person.

I replied:

chirikite mo	Though it might have strayed,
toi zo shitemashi	an inquiry would surely
koto no ha o	have arrived at last,
kochi wa sa bakari	its leaves of words delivered
fukishi tayori ni	by an east wind such as that.

He countered with this:

kochi to ieba	You can hardly say
ōzō narishi	the east wind blew toward you alone.
kaze ni ikaga	Think of the gossip
tsukete wa towamu	if I had relied on it
atara nadate ni	to convey my inquiry!

Determined not to be put down, I retorted:

chirasaji to	Had you been concerned
oshimiokikeru	to prevent those leaves of words
koto no ha o	from being scattered,
kinagara dani zo	you would have made inquiry
kesa wa towamashi	when you arrived this morning.

He seemed to concede that I was right.

Again, around the Tenth Month, he started to take his leave, explaining that he had something important to attend to at home. The heavy rain, a downpour rather than a seasonal shower, did not seem to deter him. Taken aback, I could not help murmuring this poem:

kotowari no	I can understand
ori to wa miredo	the importance of the affair,
sayo fukete	but need you rush off
kaku ya shigure no	so late at night, regardless
furi wa izubeki	of these torrential showers?

He left anyway. Was ever a man so headstrong?

Second Year of Tentoku—Second Year of Ōwa [958–62]

Kaneie seemed to have lost interest in his former favorite after the birth of her child. It had been my spiteful wish that the woman might live to know my agony, and that very thing was happening now. What was more, she had even lost the son whose arrival had created such a commotion. The unrecognized daughter of an eccentric Prince, she had lived in abject poverty, managing to survive only through the recent help of those who were attracted by her lineage and knew nothing of her true situation. I could imagine how she must be reacting to this latest abrupt turn of events; it was a satisfaction to reflect that her suffering was worse than mine.

I heard that Kaneie was now paying regular visits to his first wife. Unhappily, I myself saw him as seldom as ever.

It was around this time that my son began to talk. "I'll come again soon," he kept saying, imitating the parting words with which his father invariably took his leave.

With things as they were, I could not help feeling uneasy and depressed. Well-meaning people urged me to cheer up and stop acting childish, but it was not easy to follow their advice. Kaneie ignored my unhappiness. He defended his behavior as perfectly acceptable, made no attempt at concealment, and acted as though he could not possibly be considered blameworthy. I longed desperately to let him know exactly how I felt, but whenever I tried to broach the matter my resolution faltered, my heart began a disagreeable pounding, and I found myself struck dumb. So I decided to set down my thoughts in writing for him to see. I composed this poem, which I left on the lower shelf of a two-tiered cabinet:

omoe tada	Please feel for me!
mukashi mo ima mo	Does it not seem fated
wa ga kokoro	that the uncertainty
nodokekarade ya	I suffer now as in the past
hatenubeki	must last all my days?
misomeshi aki wa	In the autumn when we met,
koto no ha no	I could not restrain
usuki iro ni ya	the fears I knew in secret
utsurou to	that the vows you swore
nageki no shita ni	might fade into somber hues
nagekareki	like leaves on a tree.

fuyu wa kumoi ni	In the winter, I was sad,
wakareyuku	my sleeves drenched by tears
hito o oshimu to	as by seasonal showers,
hatsushigure	my spirits as gloomy
kumori mo aezu	as skies overcast with clouds,
furisobochi	grieving to have lost
kokorobosoku wa	the father who went away
arishikado	toward a distant land,
kimi ni wa shimo no	but I assured myself,
wasuru na to	"There is nothing to fear"—
iiokitsu to ka	for had I not been informed
kikishikaba	of his words to you,
sari tomo to omou	his plea not to forget me?
hodo mo naku	And yet all too soon—
tomi ni harukeki	in the twinkling of an eye—
watari nite	you grew indifferent,
shirakumo bakari	as remote as a white cloud
arishikaba	high in the heavens,
kokoro sora nite	and I went on in a daze,
heshi hodo ni	uncomprehending,
kiri mo tanabiki	until a mist came hovering
taenikeri	to make the break complete.
mata furusato ni	To no avail did I wait,
karigane no	thinking constantly,
kaeru tsura ni ya to	"Surely the time must come
omoitsutsu	when he will return
furedo kai nashi	like a homing wild goose."
kaku shitsutsu	Thus have I lived on,
wa ga mi munashiki	comparing my existence
semi no ha no	to your affection,
ima shi mo hito no	for both have proved as hollow
usukarazu	as a cicada husk.
namida no kawa no	Nor is it merely of late
hayaku yori	that your cruelty
kaku asamashiki	has made my tears fall without cease,
soko yue ni	flow in swift streams:
nagaruru koto mo	long indeed have I suffered
taenedomo	from your shallowness.
ika naru tsumi ka	Heavy must be the burden
omokaramu	of sin I shoulder—
yuki mo hanarezu	the karma-tie denying me

kakute nomi
hito no ukise ni
    tadayoite
tsuraki kokoro wa
    mizu no awa no
kieba kienamu to
    omoedomo
kanashiki koto wa
    michinoku no
tsutsuji no oka no
    kumatsuzura
kuru hodo o dani
    matade ya wa
sukuse tayubeki
    abukuma no
aimite dani to
    omoitsutsu
nageku namida no
    koromode ni
kakaranu yo ni mo
    fubeki mi o
nazo ya to omoedo
    au bakari
kakehanarete wa
    shikasuga ni
koishikarubeki
    karagoromo
uchikite hito no
    ura mo naku
nareshi kokoro o
    omoite wa
ukiyo o sareru
    kai mo naku
omoidenaki
    ware ya semu
to omoi kaku omoi
    omou ma ni
yama to tsumoreru
    shikitae no
makura no chiri mo
    hitorine no

freedom from you,
condemning me to exist
    in uncertainty,
the hostage of a fickle heart.
    I long to perish,
to vanish like a bubble
    on the water,
yet it saddens me to think
    of my father.
Ought I to sever our ties
    by not even waiting
until he comes from the north,
    that land where vines curl
on the Hill of Azaleas?
    I must bide my time
until we can meet again—
    so I think as I grieve.
"Why not pronounce Buddhist vows,"
    I have asked myself—
"why not embark on that life
    in which tears of grief
never dampen one's sleeves?"
    But though I were a nun,
what longing I would feel,
    knowing I had lost
all hope of being with you!
    Whenever I recalled
how once you came visiting
    and there was nothing
to mar our intimacy,
    I fear I could not
but shed nostalgic tears:
    to no avail
would I have turned my back
    on this cruel world.
While I have agonized thus,
    my thoughts in turmoil,
the total of all the nights
    I have spent alone
must have exceeded by now
    the number of motes

kazu ni shi toraba	in the mountain of dust
tsukinubeshi	on the pillow.
nani ka taenuru	In vain do I tell myself,
tabi nari to	"This absence won't last."
omou mono kara	When you appeared the other day
kaze fukite	in the wake of the storm,
hitohi mo mieshi	it was only to go off
amagumo wa	like a cloud in the sky.
kaerishi toki no	"I'll come again soon," you said,
nagusame ni	and the child, trusting
ima komu to iishi	those soothing words, waited
koto no ha o	expectantly,
sa mo ya to matsu no	repeating, "I'll come again,"
midorigo no	over and over.
taezu manebu mo	Each time I had to listen
kiku goto ni	to his mimicry,
hitowarae naru	I wept in embarrassment;
namida nomi	tormented by grief,
wa ga mi o umi to	I shed tears that gushed forth
tataedomo	like a lake in flood.
mirume mo yosenu	Though I fear it be vain—
mitsu no ura wa	for you come no more
kai mo araji to	than seaweed to the lakeshore
shirinagara	at Mitsu-no-ura—
inochi araba to	I would like to ask of you,
tanomekoshi	if by chance you approach
koto bakari koso	as a white wave nears the beach,
shiranami no	whether you meant it
tachi mo yorikoba	when you won my trust with the words,
towamahoshikere	"Never as long as I live."

He appeared after the usual interval, but I did not go out to join him, and he left discomfited, taking along my poem. Presently, this came from him:

orisomeshi	Do not think me like
toki no momiji no	the ordinary man whose love
sadame naku	wanes with the years,
utsurou iro wa	fading as each autumn
sa nomi koso	the leaves on the trees
au aki goto ni	lose the color they flaunted
tsune narame	when first we picked them.

nageki no shita no
   ko no ha ni wa
itodo iioku
   hatsushimo ni
fukaki iro ni ya
   narinikemu
omou omoi no
   tae mo sezu
itsu shika matsu no
   midorigo o
yukite wa mimu to
   suruga naru
tago no uranami
   tachiyoredo
fuji no yamabe no
   keburi ni wa
fusuburu koto no
   tae mo sezu
amagumo to nomi
   tanabikeba
taenu wa ga mi wa
   shiraito no
maikuru hodo o
   omowaji to
amata no hito ni
   sekasureba
mi wa hashitaka no
   suzuro nite
natsukuru yado no
   nakereba zo
furusu ni kaeru
   manimani wa
toikuru koto no
   arishikaba
hitori fusuma no
   toko ni shite
nezame no tsuki no
   maki no to ni
hikari nokosazu
   morite kuru
kage dani miezu

Indeed, your father's message
   seemed to deepen
my feeling for you in your grief,
   just as frostfall,
the first of the year, tinges
   the leaves on the trees.
The fire of my passion
   burning as ever,
I longed ardently to see
   the child who waited—
yet when I sought to approach
   as waves to the shore
at Tago-no-ura Beach
   in Suruga,
I was received by billows
   of jealous smoke,
rising as from Mount Fuji,
   unremitting,
and you kept your distance
   like a cloud in the sky.
Although I came as ceaselessly
   as thread spins on a reel,
you thought my visits too few:
   "He does not love me."
You encouraged your people
   to be unfriendly,
to make me feel embarrassed
   and ill at ease.
But there was no other place
   where I felt at home,
and thus there were occasions
   when I came to you
from the palace, like a hawk
   flying to its nest.
And I lay perforce alone
   with a single quilt:
wakeful in the night, I saw
   not a trace of you.
There was naught but the moonlight,
   streaming in through crevices
in the door made of pinewood.

arishi yori	It was from then on
utomu kokoro zo	that I began to feel
tsukisomeshi	distant from you;
tare ka yozuma to	it was not through dalliance
akashikemu	with casual amours.
ika naru tsumi no	You say you wonder what sin
omoki zo to	you have committed.
iu wa kore koso	Is there no transgression
tsumi narashi	in that very speech?
ima wa abukuma no	Why wait until your father
ai o mide	returns from the east?
kakaranu hito ni	Entrust your fortunes at once
kakare ka shi	to a better man.
nani no iwaki no	I am not as insensible
mi naraneba	as stone or wood:
omou kokoro mo	I will do nothing to stop you
isamenu ni	if you wish to be free.
ura no hamayū	And if by any chance
ikukasane	a river of tears
hedatehatesuru	should drench the sleeve of your robe
karagoromo	after barriers
namida no kawa ni	manifold as crinum leaves
sobotsu tomo	have set us apart,
omoi shi ideba	then if you but call to mind
takimono no	the trials you endured,
kono me bakari wa	the memory will suffice
kawakinamu	to dry your eyes, at least.
kai naki koto wa	Although I know it is vain
kai no kuni	to try to hold you—
hemi no mimaki ni	as vain as for a warden to seek
aruru muma o	to impose restraints
ika de ka hito wa	on a horse that has run wild
kaketomemu to	at Hemi Pasture
omou mono kara	in the province of Kai—
tarachine no	yet it is saddening
oya to shiruramu	to wonder if the young colt
katagai no	doomed to live half-trained—
koma ya koitsutsu	the child who seems to know
inakasemu to	his father's face—
omou bakari zo	must neigh disconsolately,
aware narubeki	longing for someone who is gone.

The messenger was still there, so I sent this:

natsukubeki	This must be the last
hito mo hanateba	of the horse from the pasture
michinoku no	in Michinoku,
mumaya kagiri ni	left to its own devices
naramu to suramu	by the one who should tend it.

I am not sure what moved him, but he sent a prompt reply:

ware ga na o	If I resembled
obuchi no koma no	the wild horse of Obuchi—
areba koso	the one that ran away—
natsuku ni tsukanu	then you might think of me
mi to mo shirareme	as impossible to tame.

I answered:

komauge ni	Because the keeper
narimasaritsutsu	dislikes the horse more and more,
natsukenu o	he does not tame it:
konawa taezu zo	it has had to pin its hopes
tanomikinikeru	on the small rope of a colt.

And he replied in turn:

shirakawa no	The barrier
seki no sekeba ya	of Shirakawa holds
komaukute	the horse in check:
amata no hi o ba	that is why its coming
hikiwataritsuru	has been so long delayed.

"But I shall come to see you the day after tomorrow," he said. It was the Fifth of the Seventh Month. He was observing a fairly long period of ritual seclusion, which was why he wrote as he did. I answered:

amanogawa	By promising
nanuka o chigiru	a visit on the Seventh,
kokoro araba	are you telling me,
hoshiai bakari no	"Be content to meet as often
kage o mi yo to ya	as the Tanabata stars"?

Perhaps he saw my point, for he seemed a little more considerate during the next several months.

I learned with satisfaction that the unspeakable woman in Machijiri

Street was now frantically engaged in futile efforts to recapture his affections.

I was far from easy about my own marriage, but I kept telling myself that matters were out of my hands: unbearable as life sometimes seemed, it was probably my karma to be unhappy. Meanwhile, Kaneie received Fourth Rank after having been a Lesser Counselor for a number of years, and he ceased both to serve in his old office and to attend His Majesty in the Courtiers' Hall. Then, much to his annoyance, the new appointments list named him Senior Assistant Minister of a ministry that dealt with a very undesirable class of people.[22] He stopped going anywhere except to his wives' houses, and there were times when he spent a leisurely two or three days with me.

This message came from the Prince who headed the distasteful ministry:

midareito no	Now that our duties
tsukasa hitotsu ni	join us like random threads
narite shi mo	ordered in a skein,
kuru koto no nado	why should it be, I wonder,
taenitaruramu	that the spinning has ceased?[23]

Kaneie replied:

tayu to ieba	It is very sad
ito zo kanashiki	to hear talk of breaking off.
kimi ni yori	I shall have gained nothing
onaji tsukasa ni	by changing to the office
kuru kai mo naku	where I hoped to be with you.

The Prince sent a prompt rejoinder:

natsuhiki no	It is as natural
ito kotowari ya	as to spin thread in summer:
futame mime	time is bound to pass
yoriariku ma ni	while one goes around calling
hodo no furu ka mo	on two or three different wives.

22. The appointment was to the War Ministry, where Kaneie's duties would have brought him into contact with the military, a class held in contempt by the nobility. The head of the ministry, mentioned below, was probably Prince Noriakira (924–90), a son of Emperor Daigo.

23. A pun on *kuru* ("spin"; a form of *ku,* "come") yields another meaning: "Why have you ceased to come?" Kaneie, in his reply below, pretends to think that it is the Prince who will not be appearing at the ministry.

Kaneie replied:

nanahakari	The number, I fear,
ari mo koso sure	may total seven or more.
natsuhiki no	I would not lack time
itoma ya wa naki	were it merely a question
hitome futame ni	of one or two *me* of thread.[24]

And from the Prince:

kimi to ware	Let the two of us
nao shiraito no	agree to go separate ways
ika ni shite	with feelings intact:
ukifushi nakute	let our relations be as smooth
taemu to zo omou	as cleanly twisted white thread.

"'Two or three wives' was a grave understatement! I am observing ritual seclusion now, so this must be the end," the Prince said. Kaneie replied:

yo o fu tomo	A man and his wife
chigiri okiteshi	may go their separate ways
naka yori wa	after many years,
itodo yuyushiki	but no such painful breach need part
koto mo miyuramu	one comrade from another.

Shortly after the Twentieth of the Fifth Month, I avoided a forty-five-day directional taboo by moving into a house belonging to my father, which was just across a hedge from the place where the Prince was staying. The seasonal rains, which persisted into the Sixth Month, were so heavy as to keep both the Prince and Kaneie indoors.[25] My father's house was a leaky, ramshackle affair. The interior got soaked, and the resultant commotion elicited an embarrassing poem from the Prince:

tsurezure no	Bored and disheartened
nagame no uchi ni	by these interminable rains,
sosoguramu	I have found amusement
koto no suji koso	in observing the furor
okashikarikere	where there seems to be a leak.

Kaneie replied:

izuko ni mo	Since this is a time
nagame no sosogu	of general commotion

24. *Me* (a unit of weight) puns on a homophonous word for wife.
25. Kaneie is staying with the author when this exchange occurs.

koro nareba	as the long rains cause leaks,
yo ni furu hito wa	the exceptional man alone
nodokekaraji o	may boast of a tranquil heart.

Again, from the Prince, "So you say you are upset":

ame no shita	Since this is a time
sawagu koro shi mo	when continual rains cause
ōmizu ni	general commotion,
tare mo koiji ni	everyone's robes must be drenched
nurezarame ya wa	by mud from the flooding waters. [26]

Kaneie:

yo to tomo ni	There must be no time
katsu miru hito no	for his muddy robes to dry—
koiji o mo	that gentleman
hosu ma araji to	who never ceases to roam
omoi koso yare	from one brief love to another.

Again, the Prince:

shika mo inu	You are the one
kimi zo nururamu	whose robes are drenched by your failure
tsune ni sumu	to stay as I stay.
tokoro ni wa mada	Mud has yet to stain a man
koiji dani nashi	who keeps always to the same place.

I read it with Kaneie. "Really, how he talks!"

Another message came from the Prince on a day when Kaneie had taken advantage of a clear spell to visit his first wife. "I told the man His Lordship was not here, but he insisted on leaving this anyway," the maid said when she brought it in. The poem:

tokonatsu ni	Are you not aware
koishiki koto ya	of how I have lingered
nagusamu to	beside your hedge,
kimi ga kakio ni	hoping to comfort a heart
oru to shirazu ya	ever longing to see you?

"But I have given it up as a bad job and left."

I showed Kaneie the poem when he arrived two days later. "It's no

26. Puns give the last two lines a second meaning: "All the men (including you) must be drenching their sleeves with tears because the rain prevents them from pursuing their amours."

use answering now; too much time has elapsed," he said. He merely sent a note: "I am sorry not to have heard from you recently." The Prince replied:

mizu masari	It is the season
ura mo nagisa no	when ever-rising waters
koro nareba	make the shore disappear:
chidori no ato o	that must be why the plover
fumi wa madou ka	finds no place to leave its track.[27]

"This is what I thought when I saw your letter," he wrote in the cursive script used by women. "Your complaint was quite unreasonable. But I am delighted to hear that you plan to call on me." Kaneie responded in masculine script, which made me feel sorry for the Prince:

uragakure	If the plover's tracks
miru koto kataki	be hidden on the shore,
ato naraba	impossible to see,
shiohi o matamu	I must suffer the suspense
karaki waza ka na	of waiting for the ebbtide.

Again, the Prince:

ura mo naku	It would be pointless
fumi yaru ato o	to wait for the ebbtide
watatsuumi no	on the boundless sea,
shio no hiru ma mo	merely to search for tracks
nani ni ka wa semu	where there is no shore to be found.[28]

"That is how I feel. Why do you persist in these odd misinterpretations?"

Meanwhile, people elsewhere had presumably performed the purification ceremonies, for it was now the day before Tanabata, the fortieth of my directional retreat. I had been suffering from a racking cough and other painful symptoms, so I decided to go up to the usual mountain temple, both to commission prayers against a possible spirit possession

27. The main message, conveyed by puns: "I wrote to you; the letter must have gone astray." The Prince continues with a reference to a portion of Kaneie's letter not mentioned by the author.

28. Puns yield another meaning: "The letter was sent with no ulterior motive; why wait for one to appear?" The Prince's comment below conveys a similar message: "My original letter was of no importance. I have a feeling that you have read it and interpreted it as a love letter to your wife."

and to escape the heat, which was still unbearable in my cramped quarters.

On the Fifteenth and Sixteenth, throngs of people came to the temple for the Festival of the Dead, carrying their offerings in all sorts of strange ways—on shoulder poles, on their heads, and the like. I watched the spectacle with Kaneie, touched and amused.

When I left with my health restored, it was to go to the city, my directional retreat at an end.

The autumn and winter passed uneventfully.

Third Year of Ōwa [963]

Nothing of importance happened after the start of the new year. With Kaneie so uncharacteristically attentive, I felt completely happy. He had received Courtiers' Hall privileges early in the First Month.

On the day of the Kamo Virgin's purification, a message arrived for Kaneie from the same Prince (the head of the ministry): "I would like to join you in your carriage if you plan to view the procession." There was a poem near the edge of the paper.[29] Having learned that the Prince was not at his usual residence, we tried his house on Machijiri Street but were told, "Only Her Ladyship is here." I composed a poem to send in, using a borrowed inkstone, and the Prince's consort joined us for the outing.

Some time afterward, I called on the consort while she was staying at the Prince's house of which I have spoken, the one across the hedge from us. The miscanthus there, which I recalled as having put forth delightful plumes the year before, was now forming healthy, slender-leaved clumps. "If you intend to divide them, I wonder if I might have one or two," I said. Then a little later, when I happened to be on my way to the riverbed, I pointed out the house to an attendant and sent a message to the staff. "I would like to visit Her Ladyship, but there is someone with me just now. Please ask her not to forget the miscanthus I mentioned the other day." With that, I went on.

The purification did not take long, and I was soon home. "The miscanthus has arrived from the Prince's house," someone said. The plants had been set elegantly erect in a long box, with an amusing poem on green paper attached to one of the stalks:

29. Missing except for an initial line. The author's poem referred to immediately below, apparently a polite greeting from one lady to another, is too garbled to be intelligible.

ho ni ideba	With deepest regret,
michi yuku hito mo	I dig up the miscanthus
manekubeki	that would beckon
yado no susuki o	even the casual wayfarer
horu ga wari nasa	when it put forth its plumes.

I wonder how I responded. Since I have forgotten my poem, it could not have been a creditable performance. It is just as well not to try to recall it. (To be sure, I have already recorded others that should doubtless have been consigned to oblivion.)

First Year of Kōhō [964]

Another spring passed. As the summer wore on, I began to feel that Kaneie was spending a great many nights on duty at the imperial palace. In what struck me as a rather suspicious pattern of behavior, he would come to my house early in the morning, spend the day, and set out for the palace at nightfall. One day, startled and moved by the first cicada song of the year, I composed a poem that seemed to make it hard for him to leave:

ayashiku mo	All day long today,
yoru no yukue o	I hear the cicada's voice,
shiranu ka na	but how distressing
kyō higurashi no	not to know where it goes
koe wa kikedomo	when it takes its leave at night!

Things went along in much the usual way after that, but I remained uneasy.

One moonlit night, I could not help feeling sad as I mentally contrasted our perfunctory conversation with the old intimate talk. I found myself murmuring this poem:

kumoriyo no	Which is the dimmer:
tsuki to wa ga mi no	the course followed by the moon
yukusue no	on a cloudy night,
obotsukanasa wa	or the future awaiting
izure masareri	one who has nowhere to turn?

He replied in a jesting tone:

| oshihakaru | In my judgment, |
| tsuki wa nishi e zo | the course followed by the moon |

yukusaki wa　　　　　　　leads toward the west.
ware nomi koso wa　　　　It is enough that I alone
shirubekarikere　　　　　should know its destination.

His manner seemed reassuring, but our relationship could not be satisfactory to me as long as he appeared to consider someone else his principal wife. A woman's lot cannot be happy unless she produces a large family of children. I had failed to do so despite the length of my marriage, and I was tormented by thoughts of my own inconsequentiality.

Troubled though my life was, I managed to cope as long as my mother was alive, but she died in the early autumn after a long illness, leaving me with nowhere to turn, more miserable by far than if I had been someone in ordinary circumstances. I was the most painfully affected of all her children. In a frenzy of grief, I begged to die with her—and somehow, as though in answer to my pleas, my limbs stiffened and I wavered on the brink of death. It was in the mountain temple that I fell into this extremity. My last words ought to have been addressed to Kaneie, but he was in the capital, so I called the young Michitsuna to my side and gasped out a few phrases. "I feel utterly drained—on the point of death. Please repeat this to your father: 'Don't bother about me, but please commission pious works on Mother's behalf after the family has taken care of the funeral and so forth.'" I tried to continue, but could utter only a broken expression of despair.

The family and others had become more or less reconciled to the loss of the one who had been ill for so long, but they all clustered around me in the utmost agitation, shedding floods of tears and exclaiming, "What shall we do? What can be the matter?" Although I could not speak, I was still alive and able to see.

My father came to my side. "You have more than one parent, haven't you? Why are you in such a state?" He forced medicine into my mouth, and I gradually recovered the use of my arms and legs after I drank it.

I still felt that I did not have long to live. At the root of my misery was the memory of how my mother, too ill to carry on a conversation, but seeing me grieve night and day over the precarious state of my marriage, had merely murmured again and again in a faint voice, "Ah, what are you going to do?"

Kaneie came to the temple when he learned of my illness. I was still in a daze, only half-conscious. One of my attendants met him with a description of my suffering. He burst into tears, made as if to go to me, heedless of the danger of defilement, and stood weeping when she barred the way. It did seem then that he truly loved me.

Many people helped with the funeral arrangements, and presently all was accomplished. Then everyone assembled for the tedious mourning period at the temple with its sad memories. Lying sleepless and miserable throughout the night, I saw how the morning mist indeed "enveloped the base of the hills." The thought of having nobody to return to in the city made me want to perish on the spot, but there was someone to keep me alive, alas.[30]

The Tenth passed. I heard two monks gossiping during a pause in the Buddha-invocations. "A place exists where this dead woman would be clearly visible. People say that the apparitions disappear when someone approaches, but that they can be seen from a distance," one said.

"Where is it?" the other asked.

"I have heard its name given as Mimiraku [Ear-Pleasing] Island."

As I listened, I felt a sharp longing to see the island, coupled with a fresh access of grief. A poem sprang to my lips:

ari to dani	If you are in truth
yoso nite mo mimu	what your name seems to make you,
na ni shi owaba	Ear-Pleasing Isle,
ware ni kikase yo	tell me, that I may see her,
mimiraku no yama	though it be from afar.

My brother heard me and composed this in tears:

izuko to ka	Where might it be?
oto ni nomi kiku	I long to find the person
mimiraku no	hidden on the isle
shimagakurenishi	called Mimiraku, a place
hito o tazunemu	known to me only by name.

Meanwhile, Kaneie came and stood outside or sent messages of inquiry every day. I lacked the spirit to respond, but he kept writing with quite tiresome diligence about how impatient he was for the defilement to end and how lonesome he felt. I cannot remember any of the letters now, possibly because I was so dazed at the time.

30. Her son. "Enveloped the base of the hills" refers to a poem by Kiyowara no Fukayabu (SIS 202): kawagiri no / fumoto o komete / tachinureba / sora ni zo aki no / yama

Although I was in no hurry to go home, the decision was not mine to make. The day came when we were all scheduled to leave the mountains. On the journey to the temple, I had exhausted myself in frantic endeavors to ease the ordeal for the mother who lay with her head in my lap, but I had never quite abandoned hope that everything would come out right in the end. This time, the very comfort of the carriage and its astonishing spaciousness made the trip unbearably sad.

Once home, I felt overwhelmed with grief. After the onset of Mother's illness, no attention had been paid to the plants whose pruning the two of us had supervised as we sat on the veranda together, and they had grown into unruly masses of riotous color. While the other mourners busied themselves with observances of their own, I simply sat idle, gazing dispiritedly at the garden and murmuring, "The miscanthus plant . . . insect voices."[31] A poem occurred to me:

te furenedo	Left untended,
hana wa sakari ni	they have yet put forth blossoms
narinikeri	in profusion—
todomeokikeru	those plants nourished by the dew
tsuyu ni kakarite	of past solicitude.

I was vaguely aware that my male relatives, none of whom served at the Courtiers' Hall, seemed to be arranging makeshift individual rooms with a view to spending the period of defilement together, but I kept to myself in utter dejection, bursting into tears with the night's first Buddha-invocations and weeping until dawn.

Everyone assembled at my house for the forty-ninth-day services. It was because Kaneie seemed to have assumed responsibility for the affair that so many people came. I commissioned a Buddhist painting as an offering. The others all went off to their own houses at the end of the day, leaving me more depressed and forlorn than ever. Kaneie sought to comfort me by increasing the frequency of his visits.

With nothing better to occupy my time, I began to restore order to the things that had been jumbled together when we went to the temple.

---

wa miekeru ("When from the river the rising mist envelops the base of the hills, autumn foliage appears on mountains in the sky").

31. Miharu no Arisuke, composed after the death of Fujiwara no Toshimoto (KKS 853): kimi ga ueshi / hitomurasusuki / mushi no ne no / shigeki nobe to mo / narinikeru ka na ("The miscanthus clump once planted by our master has spread far and wide, making the garden a field alive with insect voices").

It was almost more than I could bear to see the letters Mother had written and the personal belongings she had used every morning and evening. I discovered a surplice, the property of one of the monks, among her effects. It had been draped over her weakened body when she had received the commandments and had been left unclaimed because of the defilement. Seized with a desire to return it, I rose before daylight to start a letter. "This surplice . . ." Tears blinded my eyes. I sent the garment off with a poem, prefaced by the notation, "Thanks to this":

hachisuba no	She has doubtless become
tama to naruramu	a gem on a lotus leaf.
musubu ni mo	Ah, this morning dew:
sode nuremasaru	its moisture drenches my sleeve
kesa no tsuyu ka na	when I tie the surplice cords.

The same monk's older brother was also a monk, a holy man I had commissioned to recite prayers and otherwise relied on. I now learned that he had died too—very suddenly, in his case. It was most disturbing, both because I could imagine his brother's feelings and because I seemed to be losing everyone I had depended on. I sent the brother consolatory gifts on several occasions. The dead monk had lived at the Urin'in [Cloud Forest Cloister], so I sent this after the forty-ninth-day services:

omoiki ya	Did I ever dream
kumo no hayashi o	that he would abandon
uchisutete	the forest of clouds
sora no keburi ni	for another realm, rising
tatamu mono to wa	as a smoke plume in the sky?

My own loneliness was so acute that I could think of nothing but retiring as a nun to some moor or mountain. A gloomy autumn and winter went by.

My brother and aunt were living with me. I looked on my aunt as a parent, but that did not keep me from missing Mother dreadfully, and I wept the days away.

Second Year of Kōhō [965]

The spring and summer of another year passed, and then it was time for the rituals marking the first anniversary, the only observances for which we returned to the temple. The memories evoked by the surroundings made the occasion even more painful than it would have been otherwise. I grew faint at the sound of the chief officiant's first words, "Those present have not come here merely to enjoy the scenery in the autumn hills. It is their desire to have the scriptures expounded in the place where the deceased closed her eyes." I was unaware of what happened afterward.

We changed out of mourning as soon as we returned home from the services. A poem came to my mind while we were sending all our dark gray things downstream, even the fans, but I was crying too hard to recite it to anyone:

fujigoromo	More copious still
nagasu namida no	than when I donned these mourning
kawamizu wa	robes,
kishi ni mo masaru	my tears form a river
mono ni zo arikeru	overflowing its banks
	as I send them downstream.

With time hanging heavy on my hands again after the anniversary, I dusted off the zither and struck a few desultory notes, nothing that could really be called playing. Ah, I thought, the time has already come when there is no prohibition against music. How pitiful to think of that transitory existence! A poem arrived from my aunt's apartments:

ima wa tote	The past returns
hikiizuru koto no	and I am desolate again:
ne o kikeba	the sound of a zither
uchikaeshite mo	taken out to be played,
nao zo kanashiki	"now that the mourning is over."

It was not a remarkable composition, but the thought of what she must be feeling elicited a new storm of tears. [My reply:]

naki hito wa	She who is no more
otozure mo sede	does not come back again:
koto no o o	nothing returns
tachishi tsukihi zo	save the sorrow of those days
kaerikinikeru	when the zither's strings were stilled.

My older sister, the one among my numerous brothers and sisters on whom I relied the most, was preparing to leave for a distant province, a journey originally scheduled for the summer but postponed until the end of the mourning period. The prospect of losing her was indescribably painful. I went to see her on the day of her departure, taking as gifts a set of robes and some odds and ends in an inkstone box. The house was full of people bustling noisily about, but the two of us simply sat face to face, unable to look each other in the eye or restrain our tears. The maids all remonstrated with us. "There is no need to be so upset," they said. "Please try to be brave. This is a very unlucky way to act."

Just as I was thinking that it would be too much to watch her get into the carriage, a message came from Kaneie at my house. "Come home at once; I have arrived." I ordered my carriage, and the two of us removed and exchanged outer garments before we parted. Hers was a short blue mantle, mine a russet gossamer robe. It was a few days past the Tenth of the Ninth Month. Back home, I could not help weeping so violently that Kaneie chided me for my inauspicious behavior.

Later, I sat gazing at the lonely moon, thinking that my sister would be traversing the barrier mountain today if she had not already done so yesterday. The sound of a zither revealed that my aunt was up too. A poem arrived from her apartments:

hikitomuru	Powerless to detain
mono to wa nashi ni	the one who approaches,
ōsaka no	Ōsaka Barrier,
seki no kuchime no	I can but shed bitter tears
ne ni zo sobotsuru	at the sound of the zither.

She wrote in that vein because she was also a close relative. [My reply:]

omoiyaru	Merely through listening,
ōsakayama no	I have wept until my sleeve
seki no ne wa	seems doomed to decay—
kiku ni mo sode zo	that zither played by one whose thoughts
kuchime tsukinuru	linger at Ōsaka Mountain.

The longing for my sister stayed uppermost in my mind as the year drew to a close.

Third Year of Kōhō [966]

Around the Third Month, Kaneie fell ill just after he had arrived at my house. Racked with pain, he was quite at a loss to know what to do, and I was frantic with anxiety as I tried to help him.

"I wish I could stay," he said, "but it would be a great inconvenience for you if I commissioned treatment here, so I'd better go home. Please don't think I am callous. I suddenly have a terrible feeling that I may not live much longer. How sad that there is really nothing to make you remember me if I die!" He wept as he spoke, and I burst into tears, numb with grief.

"Don't cry. You make me feel even worse. This abrupt parting is the hardest thing of all. What will you do? I'm sure you won't stay single. But please wait until after the first anniversary of my death to remarry. Even if I do pull through, this will probably be my last visit here. I doubt that I'll be well enough to come anymore. I hope you can manage somehow to be with me as long as I survive. But if I die now, I'll never see you again." So he ran on, lying there with tears streaming from his eyes. He called my attendants to his side. "Do you realize how kindly I have felt toward you? It saddens me to think that I won't see you again if I die," he said. They all shed tears. I wept on, speechless with grief.

In worse and worse agony, he called for his carriage and told his attendants to lift him to his feet. He turned around and looked at me with a steadfast, sorrowful gaze. I need say nothing of my own feelings.

"These tears are most inauspicious," my brother said. "His Lordship is going to be perfectly all right. Please hurry up and get into the carriage." He entered the carriage himself and drove off with Kaneie in his arms. My anxiety was beyond description.

I sent two or three messages every day. It might not be appreciated in certain quarters, I knew, but I could not help it. Kaneie had one of his senior ladies-in-waiting reply. "His Lordship keeps saying, 'If only I could write in person!'" The news that he was much worse reduced me to hopeless misery. As he had predicted, there was no way for me to be with him and nurse him.

More than ten days went by. Then, thanks to sutra recitations and esoteric rituals, he improved enough to send an answer himself, just as I had hoped. He had seized a private moment to write in detail. Among other things, he said, "Oddly enough, time passes and I don't seem to recover. It worries me, but perhaps it's just that I have never had the experience of being so ill before." He added, "My mind is clear now. I know you would not want to come here in the daytime, but please come at night. It's been so long."

For all my worry about what people might think, I was desperate to see how he was—and then, too, he kept repeating the same thing. There seemed no alternative to asking him to send a carriage. He lay waiting for me near the threshold of a nicely prepared and furnished room in a distant gallery.

I had had the lights extinguished before leaving the carriage and could not find my way in the dark.

"Oh, really! I'm right here." Amused, he grasped my hand to guide me. "Why did it take you so long to come?" He went on to describe in rather disjointed fashion all that had been happening of late. Then he said, "Light a lamp; it's pitch black in here." To me, he added, "There's no need at all to feel uneasy; don't worry about it." Someone lit a faint lamp behind a folding screen.

"I haven't eaten any fish yet. I was thinking we might dine together if you came tonight. What do you say?" He gave orders for trays to be brought. It was already late by the time we had eaten a light meal, and the resident monks were arriving to begin their protective rites. "You might as well rest now; I'm feeling a little better than usual," Kaneie told them.

"Your Lordship does seem improved." They withdrew.

Toward dawn, I asked for an attendant to be called.[32] "Must we?" Kaneie said. "It's still dark; wait awhile."

When the sky lightened, he summoned men to raise the shutters so that we could see out. "Look at the garden," he said. "What do you think of its design?" I was alarmed when I looked outside. "It's much too light already."

"There's nothing to worry about," he said as I began hasty preparations for my departure. "Eat a little rice before you go."

It was soon broad daylight. "Let's go back to your house together. I know it would be unpleasant for you to come here again," he said.

"I worried enough about how it would look if I visited you like this; it would truly distress me if people thought I had come to fetch you."

"All right, then." He told his men to bring up the carriage.

When the carriage arrived, he went out on unsteady feet to the entrance. It touched me to watch him. "When will it be . . . your next visit?" Tears filled my eyes as I spoke.

He seemed to find it very hard to say good-bye. "I won't be easy in my mind," he said. "I'll do my best to come tomorrow or the next day."

---

32. Probably a maid to help her get ready to leave.

The attendants pulled the carriage a short distance away and yoked the ox. I saw him watching with a steady gaze from the room to which he had returned, and I found myself looking back again and again as we drove off.

A long letter arrived before nightfall. This poem was included:

kagiri ka to	Still sharper than the grief
omoitsutsu koshi	when I returned home, thinking,
hodo yori mo	"Was it the last time?"—
nakanaka naru wa	this loneliness following
wabishikarikeri	a fleeting interlude.

"You still seemed to be so ill that I can't stop worrying," I answered. "As regards the 'fleeting interlude'":

ware mo sa zo	I have felt the same.
nodokeki toko no	My heart was in strange turmoil
ura narade	as I returned home
kaeru namiji wa	from that bed where we two
ayashikarikeri	could not lie together at ease.

He still seemed unwell, but he came two or three days later in spite of his discomfort. Then he gradually recovered, and his visits resumed their old pattern.

In the Fourth Month, I went to watch the festival procession. Lady Tokihime had also come out, and I told my men to stop across the avenue from the carriage I took to be hers. Presently, bored with the wait, I attached some heartvine to an orange on a branch and sent it over with these lines:

aoi to ka	Although I had heard
kikedomo yoso ni	that this is a day for meeting,
tachibana no	you remain aloof.

A reply arrived after a longish interval:

kimi ga tsurasa o	It is rather you who today
kyō koso wa mire	show yourself to be unfeeling.

"She has probably resented you for years. Why does she limit herself to today?" said one of my attendants.

I told Kaneie about the incident after I went home. To my vast amusement, he said, "I wonder if she didn't mean something like this":

| kuitsubushitsubeki | Were I to do as I wished, |
| kokochi koso sure | I would chew the orange to bits. |

There was a great stir in anticipation of the Sweet Flag Festival, which was to be held again that year.[33] I longed desperately to witness the events but had no seat. When Kaneie hinted that he might be able to arrange something, I countered with a challenge to a game of backgammon. "All right," he said, "the festival shall be the stakes." I won and began my preparations in high spirits. Meanwhile, the first part of the night wore on and the household settled down to sleep. I drew over an inkstone, dashed off an idle verse, and gave it to him:

ayamegusa	Eagerly I await
oinishi kazu o	the Fifth Month Festival,
kazoetsutsu	the time when people
hiku ya satsuki no	pull up the sweet flags, counting
sechi ni mataruru	the sum of their well-grown roots.

Smiling, he replied:

kakurenu ni	Is there anyone
ouru kazu o ba	who can tally the number
tare ka shiru	of the sweet flags
ayame shirazu mo	growing in a hidden marsh?
mataru naru ka na	Why, then, this frenzied waiting?[34]

But he had intended all along that I should witness the spectacle. He arranged for the partition of a two-bay structure next to the Prince's viewing stand, ordered one side to be fitted out in handsome style, and put it at my disposal.

Although this apparently secure marriage had lasted eleven or twelve years, I had lived in constant misery, tormented day and night by the inferiority of my position. My feelings were natural enough. It was lonely with so few waiting-women on the nights when he failed to come. Also, my father, the only person on whom I could rely, had spent most of the last ten or more years in the provinces, and during his occasional sojourns in the city, had stayed in the Shijō-Gojō area, far from the place where I lived, which was next to the riding grounds of the Bodyguards of the Left. With no one to order repairs and look after things, my house

---

33. It had been canceled in the two previous years because of the death of Kaneie's sister, Empress Anshi (927–64).

34. He suggests teasingly that he may not be able to find her a seat.

and its environs had become more and more dilapidated, and it upset me that Kaneie should come and go blithely in such a place, without seeming to care whether its condition bothered me or not. When he spoke of having many affairs to see to, I reflected gloomily that his tasks were apparently more numerous than the clumps of mugwort in my garden. So the Eighth Month arrived.

One day, when he and I were taking our ease together, a trivial exchange led to harsh words on both sides, and he left the room with a final cutting remark. He went to the veranda and summoned Michitsuna. "I won't be coming again," he told him. Then he departed. The boy rushed inside to me and began to wail. When he refused to explain himself, I guessed that his father must have said something to him, but his grief was so wild that I stopped asking questions and did my best to soothe him, mindful of listening ears.

Five or six days passed without a word, an abnormally long interval. "Really, this is too unreasonable. I never dreamed he was serious. It has always been a shaky relationship; something like this could end it," I thought.

In wretched spirits, I noticed the bowl of water he had used while dressing his hair on the day of his departure. It was as he had left it, except that now it was filmed with dust. Startled, I realized how long his absence had lasted. A poem came to my mind:

taenuru ka	Has it all ended?
kage dani araba	If there were a reflection,
toubeki o	I might question it,
katami no mizu wa	but mossy growth has appeared
mikusa inikeri	on this water, my keepsake.

He came that same day. Everything was as before, and the quarrel receded into the past.

It was miserable to be constantly frightened and upset by such incidents.

When the Ninth Month arrived, I consulted my women about visiting a holy place. The scenery would be delightful, and I could also pray for a happier future. The decision reached, I went very quietly to a certain shrine. These were the poems I attached to my offerings. First, at the lower shrine:

ichijiruki	If your powers
yamaguchi naraba	be miraculous, O god

koko nagara	at the foot of the hill,
kami no keshiki o	vouchsafe to tell me here
mise yo to zo omou	the will of the god above.

At the middle shrine:

inariyama	Long have I worshipped
ōku no toshi zo	the deities who preside
koenikeru	at Inariyama:
inoru shirushi no	I pin my hopes on the cedar
sugi o tanomite	where lies the answer to my prayers.

At the last shrine:

kamigami to	Painfully have I toiled
noborikudari wa	uphill and down to offer prayers
waburedomo	at every shrine,
mada sakayukanu	yet I cannot but fear
kokochi koso sure	it has been of small avail.

I made a similar pilgrimage late in the same month. At each shrine, I presented two offerings, along with petitions in verse that were none the less earnest for its being a season when the gods were unlikely to answer prayers.[35] At the lower shrine:

kami ya seku	Is it blocked above,
shimo ni ya mikuzu	or has litter massed below?
tsumoruramu	Something obstructs
omou kokoro no	the flow of the pure waters
yukanu mitarashi	before the sacred shrine.

Also:

sakakiba no	With offering strips
tokiwa kakiwa ni	tied to green *sakaki* leaves,
yūshide ya	I pray you, O gods:
katagurushi naru	do not make me bear the pain
me na mise so kami	of unrequited love.

And at the upper:

| itsu shi ka mo | I wait and wait, |
| itsu shi ka mo to zo | burning with impatience: |

35. Presumably because the gods were preparing for the Tenth Month, the period during which they left their shrines to assemble at Izumo. The first poem below is a veiled inquiry about the deities' failure to answer earlier prayers.

machiwataru	when shall I behold
mori no koma yori	the light of divine favor
hikari mimu ma o	penetrating the forest?

Also:

yūdasuki	If I find surcease
musubōretsutsu	from this pent-up misery,
nageku koto	this constant sorrow,
taenaba kami no	I shall believe that the gods
shirushi to omowamu	have responded to my prayers.

Once the autumn had ended, people of all degrees became preoccupied with the various winter events, and I had to spend many nights alone.

Fourth Year of Kōhō [967]

Toward the end of the Third Month, I got some waterfowl eggs and, just as way of killing time, decided to try constructing a layer of ten. I made a long thread of raw silk by tying together shorter lengths, encircled first one egg and then another, fastening each in turn, and dangled the finished product triumphantly in the air. It seemed a shame to leave it at that, so I sent it to Lord Morosuke's daughter, the Junior Consort, attached to a spray of *unohana* blossoms. I wrote nothing special, merely my usual sort of letter with a note at the end. "Though I have made this layer of eggs, I must still feel the same way." [36] She replied:

kazu shirazu	A layer of ten
omou kokoro ni	will not bear consideration
kurabureba	when it is compared
tō kasanuru mo	with the countless numbers
mono to ya wa miru	of my loving thoughts of you.

My rejoinder:

omou hodo	No worth attaches
shirade wa kai ya	to regard of which the extent
arazaran	remains unknown:

36. A jest. "I cannot love you, because, like the person in the old poem [*Tales of Ise*, Sec. 50], you care nothing for me." The Junior Consort was Kaneie's sister Fushi, who did not actually receive that title until 968.

kaesugaesu mo   by all means, let me see
kazu o koso mime   the numbers you have in mind.

I heard that she later gave the eggs to the Fifth Prince.[37]

The Fifth Month arrived. Shortly after the Tenth, news of Emperor Murakami's illness threw the capital into an uproar, and then, very soon, His Majesty succumbed. (It was just a few days past the Twentieth.) The Crown Prince succeeded to the throne at once. Kaneie, who had previously been Assistant Master of the Crown Prince's Household, was now to serve as a Head Chamberlain, a promotion that caused a great stir. Although everyone was supposed to be upset about the Emperor's death, we were deluged with congratulations. I felt a bit more confident of my status as I replied to the good wishes; my innermost sentiments remained the same, but the burst of activity made it seem as though my life had changed.

Listening to talk of the tomb and such things, I was saddened by thoughts of what the imperial favorites must be feeling. After a little time had elapsed, I sent a solicitous note to Lady Jōganden.[38] My poem:

yo no naka o   How sad you must feel
hakanaki mono to   as you think of the mountain
misasagi no   where he lies buried—
umoruru yama ni   how ephemeral must seem
nagekuramu ya zo   all that happens in this world!

The tone of her reply was melancholy indeed:

okureji to   Might it have set forth
uki misasagi ni   across the Shide Mountains—
omoiiru   the heart of one who yearns
kokoro wa shide no   not to be left behind,
yama ni ya aruramu   but to join him in the grave?

After the end of the forty-ninth-day services (it was the Seventh Month by then), one of the late Emperor's courtiers, the Assistant Commander of the Military Guards, abandoned his mother and wife, ascended Mount Hiei, and became a monk, even though he was still a young man with no apparent worries. While everyone was uttering

37. Morihira, Emperor Murakami's fifth son and his third by Kaneie's sister Anshi; the future Emperor En'yū (959–91; r. 969–84).
38. Kaneie's sister Tōshi (d. 978), a Junior Consort of Emperor Murakami.

exclamations of shock and pity, we heard that his wife had taken religious vows too. All the more grieved and astonished because she and I had been correspondents, I sent her some words of sympathy:

okuyama no	It was sad enough
omoiyari dani	even to imagine him
kanashiki ni	deep in the mountains,
mata amagumo no	but what sorrow that you too
kakaru nani nari	should have renounced the world!

She sent a moving answer in the old familiar hand:

yama fukaku	I longed to seek out
irinishi hito mo	the person who made his way
tazunuredo	deep into the hills,
nao amagumo no	but he is as remote from me
yoso ni koso nare	as a cloud in the heavens.

While others were undergoing such painful experiences, Kaneie enjoyed one promotion after another, first to Middle Captain and then to Third Rank. He moved me into a different house, explaining, "With all the work I have to do now, it's inconvenient for us to live so far apart. I've got hold of a suitable house close to mine." He seemed pleased that he could reach the new place in a short time, even without a carriage. This happened around the middle of the Eleventh Month.

Toward the end of the Twelfth Month, Lady Jōganden came to stay in the apartments west of mine.

The last day of the year arrived. I decided to give the exorcism rites a try, and my attendants set up a fearful racket while it was still broad daylight. I sat alone, unable to keep a straight face.

First Year of Anna [968]

The next day our guest's quarters were quiet, there being no gentleman callers to offer New Year greetings. My part of the house was equally peaceful. Listening to the commotion at Kaneie's mansion next door, I smiled and murmured, "The sound for which I yearn."[39]

39. Monk Sosei (SIS 9): aratama no / toshi tachikaeru / ashita yori / mataruru mono wa / uguisu no koe ("Ever since that dawn when the departing year gave way to the new, the voice of the warbler has been the sound for which I yearn"). It is Kaneie's voice announcing his arrival that the author wants to hear.

Meanwhile, one of my attendants amused herself by plaiting a net to hold a gift of shells and chestnuts, which she placed on the shoulder of a wooden doll depicting a working-class man with a tumor on his leg. When she brought out her creation, I took it, pasted a piece of paper to the afflicted limb, and sent it to Lady Jōganden with a poem:

katakoi ya	It must be painful
kurushikaruramu	to suffer a swollen leg,
yamagatsu no	but one would suppose
ōko nashi to wa	a woodsman might at least
mienu mono kara	lay claim to a carrying pole.[40]

Lady Jōganden returned it with the shells and chestnuts replaced by dried seaweed, which was cut into short lengths and suspended in two bundles from the ends of a carrying pole. A second tumor, bigger than the first, had been glued to the formerly normal leg. This was her poem:

yamagatsu no	When we compare them,
ōko machiidete	now that the woodsman has acquired
kurabureba	a carrying pole,
koi masarikeru	we find one tumor to be
kata mo arikeri	far larger than the other.

Lady Jōganden seemed to be dining on festival dishes as the day advanced. I did the same. I followed the usual forms on the Fifteenth too.

The Third Month arrived. A letter from Kaneie, intended for our guest, was delivered to me by mistake. "I do not mean to be inattentive: I would like to call soon. I wonder, though, if there is not someone with you who thinks, '. . . for anyone but me.'"[41] He had probably permitted himself the jest because the two had always been close, but I felt that I could not let it pass in silence, so I added a poem in very small writing. Then I returned the letter to the messenger with instructions to take it to Lady Jōganden. [My poem:]

| matsuyama no | The pine-clad mountain |
| sashikoete shi mo | will never be inconstant: |

40. Puns yield another meaning: "When I consider that an opportunity to meet is not lacking, this one-sided longing to see you is hard to bear." Lady Jōganden's response can mean, "Now that there is an opportunity for us to see one another, comparison shows that I have been the more anxious for the meeting."

41. *Tales of Ise,* Sec. 37: ware narade / shitahimo toku na / asagao no / yūkage matanu / hana ni wa ari tomo ("Though your love may resemble a morning-glory blossom, gone before nightfall, do not loosen your undersash for anyone but me").

araji yo o	the waves make a fuss
ware ni yosoete	merely because they think it
sawagu nami ka na	as frivolous as themselves.[42]

The lady replied at once:

matsushima no	He is like the waves
kaze ni shitagau	following the course of the wind
nami nareba	at Matsushima:
yoru kata ni koso	we may know the wind blows strongest
tachimasarikere	toward the beach where the surf is high.

Because Lady Jōganden was acting as surrogate mother to the Crown Prince, the time came when she had to return to the palace. She hated to leave without seeing me again, she said; could I visit her even briefly? After several such messages, I went to her part of the house in the early hours of the night. Most inopportunely, Kaneie arrived while I was away. Her Ladyship called my attention to his voice, which was clearly audible, and when I showed a disposition to ignore it, she said, "The little one sounds as though he is ready for bed. He's going to be peevish. Wouldn't it be best to go?"

"He can get along without a nurse," I said. I was reluctant to leave, but a messenger came to ask her to excuse me, and I had to cut my visit short. She left for the palace at sundown on the following day.

In the Fifth Month, Lady Jōganden retired from the palace as a preliminary to changing out of mourning for the late Emperor. Kaneie invited her back to share my house, but she chose his mansion instead because she had had an inauspicious dream. More warning dreams kept coming, and she racked her brains for a way to counter their effect. On a bright, moonlit night during the Seventh Month, she sent me this poem:

mishi yume o	I have come to know
chigaewabinuru	how hard it is to sleep
aki no yo zo	on an autumn night
negataki mono to	when one has struggled in vain
omoishirinuru	to escape a warning dream.

42. "Pine-clad mountain" (*matsuyama*) and "waves" (*nami*) are metaphors for Lady Jōganden and Kaneie. The author refers to an old song (KKS 1093): kimi o okite / adashigokoro o / wa ga motaba / sue no matsuyama / nami mo koenamu ("Would I be the sort to cast you aside and turn to someone new? Sooner would the waves traverse Sue-no-matsu Mountain"). Lady Jōganden's reply means, "The letter was misdelivered because you are the one my brother loves best."

I replied:

sa mo koso wa	I fear it is true:
chigauru yume wa	to escape a warning dream
katakarame	must be difficult.
awade hodo furu	But need I suffer too
mi sae uki ka na	from lack of your presence here?

She answered promptly:

au to mishi	I have spent the days
yume ni nakanaka	utterly bemused by a dream
kurasarete	in which you and I met.
nagori koishiku	The memory is too precious:
samenu narikeri	I have no wish to awaken.

I sent this:

koto tayuru	What is the reason
utsutsu ya nani zo	that we are no longer friends
nakanaka ni	in the waking world?
yume wa kayoiji	You speak of the path of dreams,
ari to iu mono o	but I do not see you there.

"Do you really mean that we are no longer friends? What an unlucky thing to say!" she answered. Her poem:

kawa to mite	When I gaze, grieving,
yukanu kokoro o	toward one as inaccessible
nagamureba	as a stream's far shore,
itodo yuyushiku	ought I to be addressed
ii ya hatsubeki	in such inauspicious terms?

My reply:

wataraneba	Since you will not come,
ochikatabito ni	my corporeal being
nareru mi o	must remain distant,
kokoro bakari wa	but my heart crosses the stream,
fuchise ya wa waku	heedless of depths and shallows.

These exchanges occupied an entire night.

I wanted to make the arduous pilgrimage to Hasedera, the temple whose deity I had worshipped for so many years. I thought about going in the Eighth Month, but I was not free to do as I pleased, and it was only in the Ninth Month that I reached a definite decision.

"The Acting Consort will set out from here when they hold the Great Thanksgiving Purification in the Tenth Month. I could go along if you waited until after the ceremonies," Kaneie said.[43]

But the Purification was no concern of mine. I made up my mind to leave without further talk. On the day before my departure, I went from my house to Hosshōji to avoid an inauspicious direction. Then, by starting before dawn, I reached the villa at Uji during the Hour of the Horse [11:00 A.M. – 1:00 P.M.].

It was a sad, lonely feeling to glimpse the shining expanse of the Uji River through the trees. In an effort to avoid notice, I had left with only a few attendants, so it was my own fault, but I could not help thinking of the stir my entourage would have created if I had been a different kind of wife.

I gave orders for the carriage to be turned around and for curtains to be erected so the passengers in the rear could get out.[44] Then I sat facing the river with the blinds raised. Weirs stretched across the water, and more boats than I had ever seen were plying back and forth—all in all, a most diverting spectacle. When I glanced to the rear, it was moving to see the menservants gulping miserable-looking citrons and pears, exhausted by their long walk.

After lunch, the men loaded the carriage onto a boat, and I was soon traveling beyond the river, with my attendants pointing out Nieno Pond, the Izumi River, and other sights. There was something touching about the waterfowl; I found it fascinating to watch them. It was because I was traveling in such quiet style that everything moved me to tears.

We stopped for the night at Hashidera, still on the same side of the Izumi River. It was around the Hour of the Cock [5:00 P.M. – 7:00 P.M.] when I left the carriage and settled down to rest. Before my women served the main meal, they produced some minced daikon radish, dressed with citron juice, from their makeshift kitchen.[45] Their creation, so appropriate to the place, left an amusing, strangely memorable impression.

The next morning, we crossed the river and journeyed on. Moved by the sight of dwellings inside brushwood fences, I wondered where the

43. The Acting Consort was to be Chōshi, one of Kaneie's daughters by Tokihime.
44. The curtains made a circular, roofless enclosure for privacy.
45. The radish and citron were local products. Travelers carried the bulk of their provisions with them.

house in *The Tale of Kamo* might have been situated. That night, we also stayed at a place resembling a temple.

We stopped at Tsubaichi on the following night. The next morning, people wearing cloth leggings bustled along the frost-whitened road in both directions—pilgrims going to and from Hasedera, by the look of them. The hostelry shutters were up, and I watched as I waited for the water to be heated, reflecting that each of those different passersby must be burdened with his own special care.[46]

Presently, a man appeared with a letter. He stopped outside and announced, "A message from His Lordship."

Kaneie had written, "I have been worrying about you for the last two days. Are you all right? Isn't it inconvenient with so few attendants? Do you still plan to spend three days at Hasedera as you said you wanted to? I can at least come to meet you if you'll let me know when you will be coming back."

"I have reached Tsubaichi without any problems. I am thinking of going deeper into the mountains; it's impossible to say when I might get back," I wrote. But my attendants disliked the idea of spending three days in retreat, and the messenger heard them say so before he left.

There were no famous spots along the way as we journeyed onward from Tsubaichi, but the feeling of being in remote mountains gave the surroundings a special charm. The sound of the river was extraordinary, the stands of cryptomeria soared toward the heavens, and the autumn leaves displayed an infinite variety of color. In the last rays of the setting sun, the water flowed with tumultuous force in its rock-strewn bed, a scene that brought tears to my eyes. The earlier part of the trip had not been particularly interesting. Too early for autumn leaves and too late for blossoms, the season had offered nothing except some withered miscanthus. But all was different here. I rolled up the blinds, tucked away the inner curtains, and observed that even the colors of my robes seemed unbelievably fresh and bright. When I put on a train of pale purple gossamer, it was pleasant to realize how well the crossed ribbons suited my outer robe, which was dyed in the reddish fallen-leaf color.

The beggars sitting behind their bowls were pitiful. One felt drawn into the world of the lower orders rather than cleansed by entering a holy spot.

Unable to sleep, and with little in the way of devotions to fill the

46. The water was for the author's purificatory ablutions before her arrival at Hasedera.

time, I listened idly to the sounds of the temple.[47] An apparently young-
ish blind man was unburdening himself in a loud voice, not caring
whether people heard him or not—a pathetic recital that moved me to
tears.

I would have liked to stay awhile longer, but my attendants hurried
me off at daybreak. For all my desire to remain incognito, people along
the way kept offering hospitality, and the return became a lively affair.
We had planned to reach the capital on the third day, but darkness
overtook us, and my women prevailed on me to stop at Kuze-no-miyako
in Yamato Province. Sordid place though it was, we had no alternative
but to wait there until morning.

We set out while it was still dark. As we journeyed, a shadowy figure
wearing something on his back came galloping toward us. He dismounted and knelt at some distance, and I recognized him as one of
Kaneie's Escorts. When my people questioned him, he replied, "His
Lordship arrived at the Uji villa yesterday during the Hour of the Cock.
He ordered me to go and see if Her Ladyship had returned yet." My
outriders told the men in front to hurry the ox along.

Near the Uji River, we encountered an unsettling fog, so dense that
we could see nothing behind us. My attendants unyoked the ox and
began bustling noisily about. Meanwhile, we heard shouts from a large
party of Kaneie's men: "Unyoke the carriage and set it down beside the
river."

The weirs I had noticed before were visible below the fog, an indescribably charming sight. I dashed off a poem to send to Kaneie, who
seemed to be still on the other side of the river.

hitogokoro	Though you asked to know
uji no ajiro ni	the day of my return,
tamasaka ni	mere chance brings you here
yoru hio dani mo	to watch the whitefish gather
tazunekeru ka na	at the Uji River weirs.

A reply arrived while the arrangements for my crossing were being made
in proper form:

kaeru hi o	Only for your sake
kokoro no uchi ni	have I come visiting weirs
kazoetsutsu	after inwardly

47. She is now staying in one of the Hasedera halls.

| tare ni yorite ka | counting and counting again |
| ajiro o mo tou | the days until your return. |

As I was reading the poem, the men loaded the carriage onto a boat and began to pole us across with lusty shouts. Sons of quite good family (though not of the best) and officials of secretarial status had placed themselves between the shafts at the front and rear. On the far side, where the sun was breaking through the fog here and there, the Assistant Commander of the Guards and other gentlemen stood looking in our direction. Kaneie waited among them, dressed like the others in a hunting robe. My party guided the boat to a towering bank, laboriously hoisted the carriage, and set it down with the shafts resting on a veranda.

Food had been prepared to allow me to break my vegetarian fast. While we were eating, someone reported that the Inspector–Major Counselor Morouji, who owned a property across the river, had come down to view the weirs in autumn.[48]

"He's probably heard that we're here; I'd better pay my respects," Kaneie decided. But then a message arrived, accompanied by a pheasant and a whitefish attached to an attractive branch of colored leaves. "I hear that both of you are there. I wish I could join you, but I am not free at the moment. Unfortunately, this is the one day when I have nothing nice to send you."

"Please forgive my remissness; I have only just learned of your presence," Kaneie replied. "I would like to call at once to pay my respects." He took off a singlet to reward the messenger, who seems to have gone back across the river with the garment still draped over his shoulder. Carp, sea bass, and a succession of other gifts arrived from the Major Counselor.[49]

A tipsy crowd of pleasure-loving gentlemen assembled. "What a splendid night—the rays of the sun shining on the moon-wheels of Her Ladyship's carriage!" someone said. They stuffed flowers and autumn leaves behind the carriage body, and one young gentleman remarked, "The time is at hand when flowers will bloom and fruit will ripen for this lady." My attendants in the rear made appropriate responses.

Meanwhile, the gentlemen were about to board boats for the crossing to the other side of the river. Everyone said the Major Counselor

48. Morouji (913?–70) was Kaneie's uncle.
49. The author now re-enters her carriage as Kaneie and his retinue prepare to visit Morouji.

would make the visitors drink until they were besotted, so Kaneie set out with a select group of tipplers. I had my carriage drawn up facing the river, its shafts on a stand, and watched as they crossed in two boats.

They all came back singing drunken songs. "Hitch up Her Ladyship's ox! Get it hitched up!" they began to shout at once. I found it very trying and depressing in my fatigued state, but such was the return home—a most unpleasant experience.

The next morning, Kaneie told me that there was still much to do before the Purification. Would I see to certain things? I said, "Of course," and rushed about until the tasks were accomplished.

When the day arrived, the procession of formally decked carriages stretched on and on. I almost felt myself part of a court ceremony as I watched the brilliant display—the marching maidservants and menservants and the like.

From the start of the next month on, Kaneie was busy supervising the Thanksgiving preparations, and my own time was occupied with getting ready to view the festivities. Then toward the end of the month, Kaneie seemed to have his hands full with other duties.

So time passes, but the advent of a new year brings no joy to one who is sunk in grief, her life far from what she would have desired. When I reflect on the perpetual uncertainty in which I exist, it seems to me that this has been the journal of a woman whose fortunes are as evanescent as the gossamer shimmer of a heat wave in the sky.

A Court Lady's Musings

Sei Shōnagon's personal name is unknown. Sei, the first element in her court name, is the Sino-Japanese reading for the first character used in writing Kiyowara, her surname; Shōnagon (Lesser Counselor), the second, may have been an office held by a male relative. Her clan, the Kiyowara, was not politically influential but included a number of scholars and minor poets and traced its lineage to a seventh-century Emperor. Her father, Motosuke (908–90), a scholar and minor bureaucrat, was one of the compilers of the second imperial poetic anthology, *Later Collection* (Gosenshū, ca. 951).

There is little definite information about Shōnagon's life. Some scholars hold that she was married to a certain Tachibana no Morimitsu, and that the failure of the match led her to enter court service. She is conjectured to have been a lady-in-waiting to Empress Teishi from around 993 until the end of 1000, when the Empress died, and to have written her *Pillow Book* (Makura no sōshi) around the first decade of the eleventh century.[1] Nothing reliable can be said of her later years. There is a theory that she married again, to a man who predeceased her, and a persistent legend holds that she died as a poverty-stricken nun, presumably in karmic retribution for her sharp tongue.

At court, she was prominent among the thirty or forty women who attended Teishi, the consort of Emperor Ichijō. Teishi had been pre-

---

1. There is no consensus concerning the meaning of the *Pillow Book*'s title, which seems to date from the medieval period. A *sōshi* was a sewn book or booklet, as opposed to a scroll; *makura* means "pillow." It has been variously suggested that a pillow book may have

sented as an imperial bride early in 990, when she was around thirteen or fourteen and the Emperor was ten, and had received the title of Empress in the Tenth Month of the same year, subsequent to the appointment of her father, Fujiwara no Michitaka, as the imperial Regent. The *Pillow Book* depicts her as presiding with gentle grace and humor over a light-hearted, fashionable salon in which Shōnagon, a mistress of urbane badinage, played a highly visible role. Her palace apartments appear to have been irresistibly attractive to the youthful Emperor and his gentlemen, and to have retained their gaiety and literary tone even after 995, the year in which Michitaka's death shattered his children's prospects.

The *Pillow Book* is divided into approximately 320 sections, the exact number varying from one textual line to another. About eighty-five, including many of the longest, consist of random reminiscences; about sixty others record opinions, comments, and imaginative sketches; and the remainder are devoted to lists. The twenty-one sections presented here are weighted in favor of the first two categories but include a few representative examples of the third.

PRINCIPAL CHARACTERS

Emperor. Emperor Ichijō (980–1011; r. 986–1011)

Empress. Fujiwara no Teishi (976?–1000). Oldest daughter of Michitaka by his principal wife; consort of Emperor Ichijō; mistress of Shōnagon

Imperial Lady. Fujiwara no Senshi (962–1001). Mother of Emperor Ichijō; sister of Michitaka

Kamo Virgin. Princess Senshi (964–1035). Daughter of Emperor Murakami by Empress Teishi's paternal grand-aunt, Fujiwara no Anshi

Korechika (973–1010). Oldest son of Michitaka by his principal wife

Matsugimi. Childhood name of Korechika's son Michimasa (993–1054)

Michitaka (953–95). Son of Fujiwara no Kaneie; Imperial Regent; father of Empress Teishi

Michiyori (971–95). Son of Michitaka by a secondary wife

Mikushigedono (ca. 983–1002). Fourth daughter of Michitaka by his principal wife

Naka-no-kimi (981?–1002). Genshi, second daughter of Michitaka by his principal wife; became consort of the Crown Prince in 995, after the

---

been a memorandum book, a collection of secret jottings, a notebook kept under a pillow or otherwise close at hand, etc.

events described in Section 256 (called Lady Shigeisha from the palace building where she lived after her marriage, thus the use of the name is anachronistic here)

Regent, *see* Michitaka

Ryūen (980?–1015). Third son of Michitaka by his principal wife; became a monk

San-no-kimi (?–?). Third daughter of Michitaka by his principal wife; married a Prince

Shigeisha, *see* Naka-no-kimi

Tadataka (Minamoto; ?–?). Court official; Chamberlain, Secretary of Ceremonial later

Takaie (979–1044). Second son of Michitaka by his principal wife

Ukon-no-naishi. Lady-in-waiting to Emperor Ichijō

Chūnagon, Kohyōe, Kowakagimi, Saikyō-no-shōni, Saishō, Uemon, Ukon. Ladies-in-waiting to Empress Teishi

The Pillow Book of Sei Shōnagon

I

In spring, the dawn. As the light gradually increases, the rim of the hills reddens just a bit, and we see slender purplish-red clouds trailing in the sky.

In summer, the night. I need not mention the times when the moon is visible, but it is pleasant also to watch fireflies flitting to and fro in the darkness. Even the falling rain has its charm.

In autumn, the evening. When the bright setting sun has sunk very close to the mountaintops, it is moving even to see crows flying toward their roosts in groups of three or four or two. Still more delightful is a file of wild geese looking very tiny. Then, too, the wail of the wind and the plaints of insects when the sun has quite disappeared.

In winter, the early morning. The morning after a snowfall needs no comment. When the frost is very white, or even when the air is bitter with frost, the sight of servants hastily kindling fires and carrying glowing charcoal here and there seems peculiarly appropriate to the season. Toward midday, when the temperature rises a little and the cold gradually abates, the fires in the braziers turn into disagreeable white ash.

5

It is sad when parents make a beloved son into a monk. The decision has its reassuring aspects, to be sure, but it is pathetic that people should think of the young man as no more human than wood or stone. A monk eats coarse vegetarian fare and cannot even fall asleep without incurring criticism. If he is young, he will probably have his full share of curiosity. Why should we expect him to avert his eyes from women, all hypocritical abhorrence? Yet some people will be ready to blame him for a single glance. And an exorcist's lot is even worse. He goes around to Kinbusen, Kumano, and all the other mountains, exposing himself to ghastly hardships, and finally succeeds in acquiring wonder-working powers. Then word of his prowess spreads, people summon him to all kinds of places, and he becomes a harried victim of his own popularity. It is no simple matter to subdue a malignant spirit when the patient is desperately ill. The exorcist may easily nod off, exhausted by the strain. And then it is awkward, indeed, to hear someone say in a censorious voice, "That exorcist spends all his time sleeping." We can imagine how he must feel.

But I am talking about the past. Monks nowadays seem to lead a comfortable life.

7

The Emperor's cat, Lady Myōbu of Fifth Rank, was a sweet little creature, and His Majesty took a lively interest in her welfare. One day, her attendant, Uma-no-myōbu, noticed that she had ventured out to the edge of the veranda. "You naughty thing! Come back inside," she said.

The cat went on dozing in the sun. Uma-no-myōbu called one of the palace dogs to give her a scare. "Where are you, Okinamaro? Come and bite Lady Myōbu!"

The foolish Okinamaro bounded up, thinking she was serious, and the cat ran behind the blinds in a panic.

The incident was a great shock to the Emperor, who had witnessed it from the Imperial Dining Room. He tucked the cat into his bosom, summoned his attendants, and issued a command to Chamberlain Tadataka when that gentleman reported. "Punish Okinamaro and exile him. Do it right now!" A group of men set out in noisy pursuit of the dog.

The Emperor scolded Uma-no-myōbu. "I'll have to find someone else to take care of Lady Myōbu. Her present attendant is unreliable," he said.

Uma-no-myōbu stayed away from the imperial presence to show her remorse. Meanwhile, the men found the dog and told the Palace Guards to chase him away.

We all felt sorry for Okinamaro. "Poor fellow! He used to have such a self-satisfied air! On the Third of the Third Month, the Controller–Head Chamberlain took him around with a willow wreath and peach blossoms on his head and cherry blossoms girdling his middle. He could never have dreamed that this would happen to him," we said.

Three or four days went by. Then around noon one day, we heard a dog uttering piteous yelps. We pricked up our ears as the howls continued, and all the other dogs rushed yapping to investigate. A cleaning woman hurried in. "Two Chamberlains have been ordered to beat the dog. He's going to die! They're punishing him because he came back after His Majesty sentenced him to exile," she said.

Alas! It could only be Okinamaro. The howling finally ceased, just as we were about to send to make the Chamberlains desist. (They were Tadataka and Sanefusa, it seemed.) "The dog was dead, so they dragged him outside the gate and left him," someone said.

That evening, while we were all feeling depressed about Okinamaro's sad end, a hideously swollen, repulsive dog came into view, trembling miserably. "Could he be Okinamaro? There certainly hasn't been any dog like that around here lately," I said. One of the other ladies called him by name, but he paid no attention. Some said he was Okinamaro; others disagreed.

"Ukon would recognize him," Her Majesty said. "Somebody call her."

Ukon was in her room. A messenger went to tell her that she was needed on urgent business, and she presented herself. Her Majesty pointed to the dog. "Is that Okinamaro?"

"There is a resemblance, but this is a frightful-looking animal. And

Okinamaro always dashed up happily when I called him, but this dog won't come at all. It must be a different one. People say they flogged Okinamaro to death and threw his corpse away. He couldn't have survived a beating by those two men," Ukon said. Her Majesty looked grieved.

We offered the dog some food at nightfall, but he rejected it, and we decided that he was definitely not Okinamaro.

The next morning, I went to do Her Majesty's hair. She performed her ablutions and inspected her coiffure while I held the mirror. As I waited on her, I noticed the same dog crouched beside a post. "Ah," I murmured to myself, "they gave Okinamaro a merciless beating yesterday. How sad to think that he must have perished! I wonder what kind of body he has been reborn into. It must have been a dreadful experience for him." To my astonishment, the dog, which had seemed sound asleep, began to shudder and weep.

"Then it is Okinamaro, after all! He tried to keep from being recognized last night!" I was both touched and diverted. Letting the mirror fall, I said, "Well, so you're Okinamaro!" He barked frantically, flat on his belly.

Her Majesty laughed in surprise. The ladies-in-waiting gathered around, and the Empress summoned Ukon-no-naishi to tell her what had happened. The Emperor appeared, attracted by the sound of laughter and voices. "It's astonishing! Who would have expected such sensibility from a dog?" he laughed.

His Majesty's ladies-in-waiting also heard the news and assembled, and this time Okinamaro stood up and moved when he was called. But his face still looked swollen. "I wish we could get somebody to treat him," I said. "Now the truth comes out," Her Majesty smiled. "You've been on his side all along."

Tadataka sent a message from the Table Room when he got wind of the affair. "Is it really true? Let me see him."

"The very idea! The dog isn't here," we answered.

"Very well; I'll find him eventually. You won't be able to hide him forever."

Later, Okinamaro was pardoned and restored to his old status. But I still felt mixed emotions when I thought of how he had come forward, trembling and barking, after my words of commiseration. It had been a novel and interesting spectacle, but also a most pathetic one. Tears came to my eyes whenever I heard people mention it.

22. Things That Violate Our Expectations

A dog barking in the daytime.[2]
A weir in springtime.[3]
A red-plum robe in the Third or Fourth Month.[4]
A birth chamber when the baby has died.
A brazier or hearth with no fire in it.
An ox-driver when the ox has died.
A learned doctor who sires a succession of girls.

Going to a house to avoid a directional taboo and being offered no entertainment. This seems especially inappropriate and disappointing if it happens at the change of seasons.

A letter from the provinces with no accompanying souvenir. Some might say the same of a letter from the capital, but it is quite enough that such a communication should describe recent events and tell the recipient other things he or she would like to hear about.

After having taken great pains to prepare and send off an attractive letter, one waits in breathless anticipation to see what response it will elicit, but the reply is astonishingly slow to arrive. Then, while one is still agog, the original letter comes back. Whether rolled or formally twisted, it is now so dirty and crumpled that even the superscript has disappeared. "The person was not at home," the messenger reports. Or: "They could not accept it because they were observing ritual seclusion." This is exceedingly depressing and disconcerting.

Again, one is waiting after having dispatched a carriage to fetch a guest whom one confidently expects to come for a visit. At the sound of returning wheels, people go out to meet her, only to see the carriage attendants enter the carriage shelter and thump down the shafts. When asked for an explanation, the attendants say, "She has gone out today. She won't be coming." Then they depart with the ox in tow.

2. Dogs were expected to bark at night as watchdogs.
3. Weirs were used as fish traps in the autumn and winter.
4. Red-plum robes (red with purple linings) were supposed to be worn only from the Eleventh Month to the Second.

It is also disconcerting when a man's visits cease after the whole household has made a great point of welcoming him as a son-in-law. And when his heart has been captured by some high-born lady in court service, how miserable the deserted wife feels as she yearns wistfully for his return!

A baby's nurse leaves the house with a promise to return shortly. When the child misses her, others try to distract him, meanwhile sending to her to come at once. "I am afraid I won't be able to get back tonight," she replies. This is more than disconcerting; it is downright hateful.

We can imagine the feelings of a man who expects a woman in vain. And when a woman expects a man, the sound of a discreet knock on the gate in late evening makes her heart beat a little faster. She sends to see who it is, but it proves to be someone else, a person of no possible interest. What could be more disconcerting?

An exorcist trying to expel malignant spirits puts on a confident expression, instructs the medium to hold a vajra and a string of prayer beads, and sits chanting a sutra in a strident voice, but the spirits show not the slightest inclination to retreat, nor does the spirit protector of the Law enter the medium. This is most disconcerting for the assembled men and women of the household, who are also offering prayers. After two hours of chanting, the exorcist tires. "The guardian spirit refuses to enter your body. Be off with you," he tells the medium. "Well, that did no good at all," he remarks as he takes back the beads. He rubs his forehead, yawns, leans against something, and falls asleep.

Expectations are cruelly dashed at the house of a man who fails to get a post when official appointments are conferred. It has been rumored that the master is sure to receive something this year, and his dispersed former attendants—people from the countryside and others—have congregated in such numbers that there seems barely room to put down the shafts of all the carriages that arrive and depart. These people are eager to accompany the candidate when he goes to offer prayers; they eat and drink and generally raise a commotion. But the appointments ceremonies draw to a close. By dawn on the following morning, there has still been no knock at the gate. Voices are heard clearing the way as the senior nobles leave the imperial palace. And then a group of servants come trudging in with crestfallen faces—men who have waited for news outside the office since evening, shivering with cold. Nobody has the heart to question them. When outsiders ask, "What is His Lordship's present title?" the reply is always the same: "He is the Former Governor of Such-and-such Province." Those who have pinned their hopes on the gentleman are devastated. During the course of the morning, the once-dense throng gradually melts as people steal away by ones and twos. Longtime household members, who cannot very well leave, count over next year's likely provincial vacancies on their fingers and walk around looking pathetically glum. We can imagine how disconcerting it has been for them all.

When somebody sends off what seems a fairly good poem, it is disconcerting to receive no answer. If the missive is a love letter, the author must simply accept the situation, but it is disappointing that there should not be any acknowledgment when one has devised a clever treatment of a subject. Again, expectations must inevitably be dashed when an old-fashioned person with an abundance of leisure sends a mediocre poem about the past to someone who is busy and popular.

Eager to provide herself with precisely the right fan for an important occasion, a woman asks to have one designed by a person whose taste she trusts. The fan arrives on the day of the event, decorated with a picture that is not at all what she had in mind.

When a messenger comes with a farewell present, a gift for a birth celebration, or the like, it is disconcerting to receive no reward. People should always give him something, even if he brings no more than a medicinal ball or a hare stick. He will be delighted to receive an unexpected gratuity. On the other hand, he is bound to feel disappointment if he goes away empty-handed after having arrived in high hopes, confident that so important an errand as today's must merit some recompense.

It is disconcerting when there is no commotion about getting a birth chamber ready, even though the daughter of the house has already been married four or five years.

Also disconcerting are parents who nap together in the daytime when they have grown children—or worse, grandchildren crawling about. Even a child of ten or so will probably be quite taken aback by the sight of his mother and father napping together. And if they bathe in hot water after awakening, they actually arouse feelings of anger.

Constant rain late in the Twelfth Month. Shall we compare it to the feeling we have when we slip up during a 100-day regimen of vegetarian fare?[5]

Layered white robes in the Eighth Month.[6]

A wet nurse who has run out of milk.

24. Things People Look Down On

The north side of a house.

A person with a reputation for excessive good nature.

A very old man.

A loose woman.

A crumbling earthen wall around an establishment.

39

A preacher ought to be handsome. It is only when we keep our gaze fixed firmly on a good-looking monk's face that we feel the holiness of the text he expounds. If the man is ill-favored, our gaze wanders and we lose track of what he is saying. For this reason, it seems to me that listening to an ugly monk's sermon may actually lead us into sin. But I must not write these things. Although it might have been all right when I was a little younger, the thought of sin terrifies me now.

When I contemplate my own sinful heart, I wonder about the honesty of those who make a point of being the first to arrive wherever there is to be a sermon, informing us that sutra expositions are holy occasions and that they themselves are bursting with piety.

40

In earlier times, men who had stepped down from the office of Chamberlain would not even serve as imperial outriders, much less show their faces at the palace during the first year after their departure. Things seem very different nowadays; they bear the title of Former Fifth-Rank Chamberlain and receive many commissions to discharge. Still, they are

5. The rain is inopportune because it interferes with the preparations for New Year events. Scholars are at a loss to explain the reference to vegetarian fare.

6. Their season was summer.

less busy than before, and it must seem to them that they have a great deal of time on their hands. Thus they find themselves bustling off to hear a sermon, and after the first two or three times it becomes a habit. Even in the torrid heat of summer, we see them sitting in vivid red underrobes with their feet tucked into pale blue or dark gray trousers. Sometimes they wear ritual seclusion tags on their hats, as though to tell us, "Even though today is a day of seclusion for me, there can be no harm in going out to perform a pious act." Or they may hurry in, chat with the preacher, take it on themselves to find places for ladies' carriages, and otherwise show themselves at home.

To his profound amazement, one such gentleman spots a friend whom he has not seen for a long time. He sits down next to him, talks, nods, tells an amusing story, spreads his fan wide, presses it to his lips and laughs, idly fingers his ornate prayer beads and flicks the tassels toward his companion to emphasize everything he says, pronounces on the merits of the carriages, and compares the sutra services and Eight Expositions sponsored by this person and that. Meanwhile, he ignores the preacher's remarks. But his inattention does not matter. He hears similar sermons all the time. They are an old story to him, and he certainly does not see anything novel about this one.

People of quite a different type may arrive shortly after the lecturer has taken his seat. A carriage draws up, preceded by unobtrusive shouts from its outriders, and three or four slim young gentlemen emerge, some clad in hunting robes and others wearing cloaks lighter than cicada wings, with baggy trousers and thin silk singlets. When they enter, accompanied by an equal number of attendants, those present move over and make room for them to sit at the foot of a pillar near the dais. They give the impression of having stopped in on the spur of the moment, but they rub their beads, prostrate themselves, and listen closely. The lecturer, who must consider the visit a signal honor, begins to preach with all the eloquence at his command, determined to give a performance so impressive that everyone will be talking about it. The gentlemen choose an opportune moment to withdraw, before the final pious exclamations and prostrations. On their way out, they glance toward the carriages, exchanging comments. The ladies inside the carriages wonder what they are saying. If we recognize them, the incident has a special charm; if not, it is amusing to speculate about their identities as we watch them leave.

When someone announces, "There was a sutra exposition at such-

and-such a place," or "At such-and-such a place, they held an Eight Expositions service," and we reply, "Was So-and-so there?" it is really too much to have the other person say, as though the answer were obvious, "Why, my dear, of course." To be sure, there is no reason to avoid such events altogether. Even lower-class women seem to attend them with great frequency. But in the old days, a gentlewoman did not go out on foot. Under exceptional circumstances, she might venture forth in an elegant travel costume, but not to any destination other than a shrine or temple. And so far as I have heard, not many such people went to hear sermons. If one of them were alive to see what goes on today, how critical and censorious her eye would be!

49. Elegant Things

A young girl's trailing white summer robe, worn over a lavender chemise.

Shaved ice, mixed with vine syrup and put into a new metal bowl.

Fallen snow on plum blossoms.

A sweet infant eating a strawberry.

A duck egg, broken.

Crystal prayer beads.

65. Bridges

The bridges of Asamutsu, Nagara, Amahiko, Hamana, and Hitotsu. The Sano Boat Bridge. The bridges of Utashime, Todoroki, and Ogawa. Anything spanning a ravine or providing passage across the face of a cliff. Seta Bridge. The bridge on the Kiso Road. Horikawa Bridge. The Raven Bridge. The Lovers' Meeting Bridge. The floating bridge at Ono. Yamasuge Bridge (an interesting name). Utatane Bridge.

74

Secret trysts are especially enjoyable in the summertime. The short night slips by before the lovers can get a wink of sleep. The latticed shutters have all been left up, and the garden looks delightfully cool. As the couple exchange a few essential last words, a crow flies directly in front of them, cawing in a loud voice. Most amusingly, they suddenly feel very much exposed.

75

It is also pleasant to hear a temple bell, its sound seeming to emanate from some remote fastness, when one is buried under the bedclothes with a lover on a bitter night. I find it intriguing that the initial cockcrow should sound infinitely far away (the bird's beak still being tucked under his wing), and that the second and third should seem closer and closer to the garden.

78

Of the cubicles assigned to the ladies-in-waiting at the imperial palace, those in the corridor are especially interesting.[7] The wind comes sweeping through when the upper shutters are raised. In summer it is delightfully cool, and in winter I enjoy the occasional flurry of snow or hail that finds its way inside. Because the rooms are considered too cramped to accommodate children, young visitors are told to sit hidden behind the folding screens, and to refrain from laughing and making noise as they do in apartments elsewhere—which is all to the good.

During the daytime, the occupants can never relax their vigilance, and at night, amusingly enough, they must be even more careful. Footsteps echo all night long. I like it when the sound of shoes breaks off, someone raps with a single finger, and the person inside recognizes the knock instantly. The tapping goes on without eliciting a response. The woman, not wishing to be thought asleep, makes a little movement or rustles her clothing, and the man realizes that she is still up. The sound of a fan being wielded is another sign that she has not retired. If the season is winter, the man may hear the faint noise of fire tongs being thrust into a brazier, even though someone is trying to be quiet. This inspires him to knock with renewed vigor and to call out. Sometimes the woman slips close and listens behind the locked door.

Perhaps a group of courtiers may come along chanting poems. Nobody has knocked, but a woman has opened her door, and they all come to a halt, whether they had intended to visit her or not. There are too many to fit inside, so some of them stand outside chatting for the rest

7. Probably the corridor on the west side of the Tōkaden, a building assigned to Empress Teishi. The corridor led directly to the Seiryōden, where the Emperor lived, and was used by courtiers and others going back and forth between the Seiryōden and the Genkimon Gate, the main northern entrance to the imperial residential compound.

of the night—an entertaining spectacle. The blinds are delightfully green, the stand-curtains bright and fresh. The callers catch the merest glimpse of the woman's skirts. It is interesting to see well-born gentlemen, their informal cloaks open at the back, and olive-clad, self-satisfied Chamberlains of Sixth Rank standing before the earthen wall with their sleeves aligned primly, unable to find a place by the door.

I enjoy watching from elsewhere while a man pushes against the blinds of a room and seats himself halfway inside, dressed in deep purple trousers and a resplendent informal cloak, with the tips of a brilliantly colored inner robe peeping out at the bottom. It is also pleasant if the visitor pulls over a tidy inkstone and scribbles off a note, or if he borrows a mirror to comb a few errant locks on the side of his head.

A woman sits behind a portable curtain-stand three feet high but, most interestingly, there is a little space between the top of the stand and the decorative cloth edging the beam from which the blinds hang—a gap just big enough for a man standing outside and a woman seated inside to look each other in the face. There may be a difficulty if one person is very tall and the other short, but this is the way it works for people of ordinary height.

79

The dance rehearsal before the Kamo Special Festival is uncommonly diverting.[8] People from the Bureau of Grounds hold long torches aloft, their necks buried in their collars against the cold, and the tips seem in constant danger of hitting something. There is a delightful sound of music, the flutes begin to play, and we sense the uniqueness of the occasion. If some gentlemen in formal court attire drop by to chat, the warnings of the courtiers' Escorts are subdued and quiet: they are clearing their masters' way, to be sure, but their voices harmonize with the music in a manner pleasantly different from the usual shouts. Toward dawn, as we await the performers' departure, we hear a group of nobles singing, "The Ears of Rice Growing in Untilled Paddies," their voices a little more interesting than earlier. An earnest fellow, striding homeward at a brisk pace, evokes a burst of laughter. "Wait awhile," somebody says. "I believe one of the ladies wonders why you're wasting a

8. The rehearsal, which took place in the courtyard east of the Seiryōden, was not visible from the cubicles on the west side of the Tōkaden, but the music was audible, and some of the participants used the corridor.

Sei Shōnagon converses with one of the Emperor's gentlemen (Sec. 79)

night like this by hurrying off." But perhaps he is in a bad humor, for he dashes ahead, all but falling in his haste, as though he were in danger of being pursued and arrested.

91

Once while Her Majesty was staying in the Empress's Office, she decided to hold continuous sutra recitations in the western eave-chamber. Sacred images were hung, and monks came to officiate as usual. On about the second day, we heard an ill-bred female voice at the outer edge of the veranda.

"You must have some leftovers from the offerings by now, haven't you?"

"How could we have? The services are just starting," a monk answered.

I got up to investigate. The speaker was an old, monkey-like nun. She wore a pair of filthy men's trousers, as short and narrow as two bamboo pipes, and an equally disreputable garment that ended five inches below the belt. (It could hardly have been called a robe.)

"What's this all about?" I asked.

She put on a bright, refined voice. "I am a disciple of the Buddha. I asked for some leftover offerings, but these monks don't want to give me anything."

"People like her aren't pathetic unless they act dejected. She's absurdly lively," I thought. "Don't you eat anything except the Buddha's leftovers. You *are* holy," I said.

"Is it likely that I would refuse anything else? It's because I don't have any other food that I'm asking for leftovers," she replied, taking her cue from my attitude.

I got her some fruit and flat rice-cakes, which moved her to become excessively friendly and talkative.

The younger ladies-in-waiting came out to ask questions. "Do you have a husband?" "Where do you live?" She replied with amusing remarks and sly jokes. Someone asked, "Do you sing? Are you a dancer?"[9] Without further invitation, she burst into song: "Who shall I sleep with at night? I'll sleep with Hitachi-no-suke. That sleeping man's skin feels good!" After favoring us with a number of other verses, she started to roll and shake her head in a repulsive manner, chanting:

> Ah, the colored leaves on Otokoyama's peak—
> Ah, yes, they have a reputation!
> Ah, yes, they have a reputation![10]

The ladies shooed her away with disgusted laughs.

"Let's give her something," I said, amused.

9. Itinerant female entertainers often dressed as nuns.

10. Ambiguities and wordplays produce a second meaning: "I have a reputation for promiscuity."

Her Majesty overheard it all. "That was horrid! Why did you encourage her in such distasteful behavior? I couldn't bear to listen; I had to stop up my ears. Give her one of those robes and send her away," she said.

I tossed the nun a robe. "Her Majesty condescends to give you this. Your robe is dirty. Wear this clean one," I said. She made a bow, which she supplemented with an imitation of a courtier's formal dance of gratitude, with the robe draped over her shoulder. Everyone went inside, feeling utterly revolted.

Possibly emboldened by her initial success, the woman proceeded to haunt our neighborhood, trying her best to be noticed. We dubbed her Hitachi-no-suke. She was still wearing the same dirty clothes, and we wondered contemptuously what she had done with the new robe.

Once when Ukon-no-naishi stopped by, Her Majesty said, "My ladies seem to have made a friend of a beggar woman. She keeps coming here." She told Kohyōe to show Ukon how Hitachi-no-suke had acted that first time.

"I'd love to get a look at her. Do let me! She seems to be a favorite with you. I promise faithfully not to try to wean her away," Ukon laughed.

Later, another beggar nun appeared, this one well bred. We summoned and questioned her as we had done with Hitachi-no-suke. Her air of embarrassment aroused our compassion, and Her Majesty gave her a robe. Beggar or not, she went away with a genteel bow, shedding tears of joy. Hitachi-no-suke happened to see her go. She dropped out of sight for a long time afterward, but nobody missed her.

There was a big snowstorm shortly after the Tenth of the Twelfth Month. When it ended, the ladies-in-waiting set to work making piles of snow in lids and other receptacles.

"As long as we're doing this, why not get people to make us a real mountain in the courtyard?" somebody said.

We summoned samurai in Her Majesty's name, and a group of men gathered to make the mountain.[11] All the courtyard cleaners and sweepers came over too, and together they built it very high. Officials from the

11. Shōnagon says *saburai* ("one who serves"), which is an earlier form of samurai. In the classical age, some saburai were armed retainers; others served in a general capacity.

Empress's Household arrived to offer advice as the edifice grew. Three or four men appeared from the Chamberlains' Office, and the Bureau of Grounds contingent swelled to around twenty.

Messengers were even sent to summon off-duty samurai from their homes. "Those who help build the mountain today will get three days of leave," we said. "Those who fail to report will lose the same number of days." There were some who dropped everything and rushed to the palace in a flurry of excitement the minute they were notified. (It was impossible to get word to those who lived far away.)

When the mountain was finished, we summoned the household officials and gave them double rolls of silk to toss onto the veranda. Each of the workers came up, took one, and tucked it into his waist with a bow. Then they all left. Some of the household officials were dressed in formal robes; others wore hunting robes.

"How long do you think the snow mountain will last?" the Empress asked. Almost everybody suggested a date in the near future. For instance, somebody said, "Probably a little more than ten days." Then she asked me for my opinion. "Until the Fifteenth of the First Month," I said. She looked skeptical, and the other women all insisted that it could not possibly survive until the end of the year, much less any longer. I had to agree inside. "What possessed me to choose a date so far in the future? They're right. It can't last that long. I ought to have said something like the First," I thought. But I had committed myself, whether it lasted or not, and I put up a stubborn argument for my prediction.

Some rain fell on the Twentieth, but the snow mountain showed no sign of melting. It merely got a little lower as time went on. I offered frantic prayers: "O Kannon of Shirayama, don't let that mountain melt!"

On the day when the snow mountain was built, Secretary of Ceremonial Tadataka came over with a message from His Majesty. I put out a cushion and chatted with him. "People are building mountains everywhere after this snowfall today," he said. "His Majesty is having one made in the front courtyard, and there are others at the Crown Prince's residence and the Kokiden. I hear they have one at the Kyōgoku Mansion too." I replied:

koko ni nomi	The snow mountain
mezurashi to miru	we had considered unique
yuki no yama	proves to be commonplace:

tokorodokoro ni	we ought to have realized
furinikeru ka na	that snowflakes fell everywhere. [12]

"I can't bring myself to spoil a witty composition with a feeble answer. I'm going to tell His Majesty's ladies-in-waiting about it," he said. He rose to his feet and left. It seemed odd behavior on the part of a man who was supposed to be an enthusiastic versifier.

"He must have been thinking that he'd have to come up with something really outstanding," said Her Majesty, who had heard the exchange.

Toward the end of the month, the mountain looked as though it had shrunk a bit, but it was still fairly tall. Hitachi-no-suke appeared around noon on a day when some of us had gone out to sit on the veranda.

"Why did you stay away so long?" we asked her.

"It's not worth mentioning. There was something that upset me," she said.

"What was it?"

"This is how I felt." She recited a poem in an affected voice:

urayamashi	Consumed with envy,
ashi mo hikarezu	I lacked the will to visit you.
watatsumi no	Is she so special—
ika naru ama ni	the one in holy orders
mono tamauramu	whom you favor with your bounty?

We all laughed in disgust and paid her no further attention. Finding herself ignored, she climbed onto the snow mountain, scrabbled around aimlessly, and left. After she had gone, we sent to tell Ukon-no-naishi what had happened.

"Why didn't you get someone to bring her over here? Poor thing! She felt so cheap that she had to ramble around on the snow mountain," she answered. We laughed again.

The snow mountain remained unchanged as the new year began. On the First, there was another heavy snowfall. I was delighted when I saw how much had accumulated, but Her Majesty said, "This won't do. Clear away everything above the old level."

As I was going toward my room early one morning after a night on duty, I met a Head Samurai who was shivering with cold. The sleeve of

12. The poem puns on *furu* ("fall"; "grow old," "become commonplace").

his citron-green night-duty robe held a letter, written on green paper and attached to a sprig of pine needles.

"Where is the letter from?" I asked.

"From the Kamo Virgin."

Knowing at once that it would be something out of the ordinary, I went back to the Empress, who was still in bed. By pulling the *go* table over to stand on, I managed to raise the heavy shutter opposite the curtain-dais—a hard task for one person. But with nobody helping from the other side, there was such a loud squeak that Her Majesty woke up.

"Why are you doing that?" she asked.

"A letter has come from the Kamo Virgin. Could it be that I wouldn't hurry to give it to you?" I said.

"It has arrived very early." She got up. The letter contained two hare sticks, each about five inches long, which were wrapped at the top like hare wands and decorated daintily with spearflower berries, club moss, and wild sedge. There was no message.

"There must be something else." Looking again, she discovered a poem, which was inscribed on the small piece of paper wrapped around the head of one of the sticks:

yama toyomu	The echo of axes
ono no hibiki o	reverberating in the hills
tazunureba	proves to be none other
iwai no tsue no	than the sound of men felling trees
oto ni zo arikeru	to make the festive wands.

The manner in which the Empress wrote her reply was splendid. Whenever she sent a letter to the Virgin or answered one from her, she took great pains and rewrote often. She gave the messenger a white unlined robe with a woven design; also a brown one. I believe the brown one must have been a plum-blossom robe. The man made an interesting picture as he trudged off through the snow with the garments draped over his shoulder. To my disappointment, I did not learn what Her Majesty wrote that time.

The snow mountain showed no more sign of melting than if it had been a real peak in the north. It had turned black and was no longer worth looking at. Sensing the possibility of victory, I longed desperately for it to last until the Fifteenth, but the other women insisted that it could not survive beyond the Seventh at most.

While we were all waiting to find out what would happen, it was suddenly decided that Her Majesty would move to the Emperor's residential compound on the Third. "This is dreadful! Now I won't see what becomes of the mountain," I thought in despair. The other women also lamented that they had been counting on watching the outcome, and the Empress herself expressed disappointment.

Now that there was no hope of showing Her Majesty the mountain as proof that I had been right, I hit on another plan. I waited until everybody else was engrossed in the business of transferring the Empress's belongings. Then I summoned a garden watchman, a fellow who stayed in a kind of lean-to built against the earthen wall. I called him close to the veranda. "I want you to guard this snow mountain very carefully. Don't let children trample on the snow or scatter it or break it up; see that it lasts until the Fifteenth. I know Her Majesty will reward you with a handsome present if you take good care of it until then. I will also express my deep personal gratitude," I said. I gave him a generous portion of the fruits and other delicacies that were kept in the Table Room as gratuities for the lower orders.

"There won't be any problem at all," he said, his face wreathed in smiles. "You can count on me. But I'm afraid the children will want to climb on it."

"Don't let them. Tell me if anybody disobeys you," I instructed him.

Once Her Majesty had moved into the residential compound, I remained on duty until the Seventh. Then I went home. All during the time before I left, I fretted about the snow mountain, dispatching a stream of maids, bath attendants, and elderly cleaning women to keep my agent on his toes. I also sent the watchman some leftovers from the Seventh Day Festival, and we all laughed when the messenger came back with a description of his obeisances.

After my return home, the mountain was always on my mind. I sent someone to check it every day at dawn. On the Tenth, I was delighted to learn that it was still five or six feet high. But on the night of the Thirteenth, there was a rainstorm that seemed certain to melt whatever remained of it. In wretched spirits, I stayed up until all hours. To think that it was going to disappear just a day before the Fifteenth! The people who heard my lamentations laughed and said I was crazy.

On the morning of the Fourteenth, I arose at the first sound of activity. My efforts to arouse a servant produced nothing but a fit of temper, and I ended by sending the person who had got up in the first place.

"A pile the size of a cushion is left," the woman reported. "The watchman is being very conscientious about keeping children away. He says, 'It's sure to last until tomorrow or the next day. I'll get my reward.'"

I could hardly wait. "The minute tomorrow comes, I'll compose a poem and send it to Her Majesty with some of the snow in a container," I exulted.

Before daylight on the morning of the Fifteenth, I gave a servant a large cypress-wood box and sent her off with meticulous instructions. "Put the whitest snow in the box and bring it back. Scrape the dirty part away," I said.

To my amazement, she came back in no time, carrying the box dangling in her hand. "The snow was all gone," she announced.

So much for the poem over which I had groaned and labored, hoping to produce something that would set people talking!

"What happened? How could it have melted overnight when there was so much left yesterday?" I asked, crestfallen.

"The watchman was wringing his hands and saying, 'I'm not going to get the reward,'" she said in great agitation.

Just then, a message arrived from the Empress at the palace. "Tell me, did the snow last until today?"

I tried to swallow my mortification. "Everyone else said, 'It will melt before the end of the year; it won't even last until the First,' but it was still there until dusk yesterday, which I consider most creditable. For it to have lasted until today would have been too much. I think somebody who was jealous must have got rid of it during the night. Tell that to Her Majesty," I said.

After I resumed my duties on the Twentieth, the snow mountain was the first thing I mentioned in the Empress's presence. I told Her Majesty of my disappointment when the servant returned—exactly like the monk who brought back only a dangling lid, saying, "Everything else disappeared"—and of how I had intended to make a little mountain on a lid and present it with a poem nicely written on white paper.[13] She went off into peals of laughter, and the other ladies laughed too.

"I am afraid I committed a sin by frustrating the scheme that meant

13. The reference to the monk is no longer understood.

so much to you. You were right; I did send samurai to dispose of the snow on the evening of the Fourteenth. How amusing that you hit on the truth in your reply! The old man came out wringing his hands and protesting, but the samurai said, 'We're acting on Her Majesty's orders. You're not to tell anyone from that house. If you do, we'll tear down your shack.' They threw all the snow onto the other side of the south wall at the Office of the Bodyguards of the Left. I understand that they said the mountain was still quite big and tall, so it might have lasted until the Twentieth. And a new snowfall might have made it even bigger. His Majesty heard about it and told the courtiers nobody else would have thought of arguing the way you did. Come on, recite your poem. Now that I've confessed, it's just the same as though you had won. Give us the poem," Her Majesty said.

The others also asked to hear my composition, but I was miserable. "What would be the point of reciting it after what I've just heard?" I said.

The Emperor came in. "You've always seemed to be one of Her Majesty's favorites. I wonder what possessed her to do such a thing," he said.

I was so upset that I felt like crying. "Ah, what a cruel world this is! Just when I was so happy about the new snowfall, Her Majesty said, 'This won't do,' and ordered people to scrape it away."

His Majesty laughed. "She certainly seems to have been determined to keep you from winning."

101. Things That Make One Uncomfortable

While conversing with a guest whom one has received, one hears people inside the house saying all sorts of indiscreet things. It is irritating to have no way of shutting them up.

A man of whom one is fond gets frightfully drunk and keeps repeating the same thing with a sagacious air.

Someone relays a bit of gossip without knowing that the subject is listening. Even if the person is only a servant, this makes one feel uncomfortable.

A group of lower-class people disport themselves near the place where one is staying during a sojourn away from home.

The doting parents of an unattractive young child pet him, play with him, and repeat his sayings, imitating his voice.

With a knowing air, an ignoramus drops the names of historical figures in front of a learned person.

Someone makes another person listen to a mediocre poem of his own and announces that So-and-so has praised it. This also causes one to feel uncomfortable.

When someone is wide awake, chattering away, it is disconcerting if a companion simply lies there half-asleep.

Someone performs complacently on an out-of-tune zither in front of an expert musician.

A conspicuously neglectful son-in-law encounters his father-in-law at a public function.

124

It is interesting if the weather is very cold, with ice and the prospect of snow, when one stays in retreat at a temple during the First Month. The possibility of rain is most distasteful.

When I visit Hatsuse and wait for a room to be prepared, my attendants halt the carriage at the foot of the gallery and I watch as the young monks, wearing sashes but no outer robes, dash blithely up and down the steps in their high clogs, reciting miscellaneous snatches of sutras and intoning bits of songs from the *Abhidharmakośa-śāstra*—a scene delightfully appropriate to the place. The ascent strikes me as so perilous that I always go to the side and grasp the handrail, but the monks treat the gallery stairs like flat wooden floors, which I also find interesting. When my room is ready, someone brings shoes and helps me out of the carriage.

One sees women who have tucked up their skirts and others who are ostentatiously attired in trains and formal jackets. The sound of leather boots and half-boots shuffling along the gallery is amusingly reminiscent of the imperial palace. A woman pilgrim is escorted by a group of kinsmen and trusted household youths, who tell her, "There is a low place there," "That place is high," and the like. Who might she be? They warn off anybody who walks too close or who tries to pass, saying, "Just a minute! This is a person of importance. Kindly keep your distance." Some people defer and drop back a little; others ignore the party and press on, determined to be the first to enter the sacred presence.

I find it unpleasant to have to pass before rows of seated worshippers on the way to my room, but a feeling of great holiness steals over me when I gaze beyond the latticed barrier, and a sudden rush of piety causes me to marvel that I have stayed away for so many months. The central image, very holy in appearance, glitters in the almost frighteningly brilliant light of all the worshippers' votive lamps (to say nothing of the perpetual lamps). The monks face the platform and pray, each holding a petition aloft. It seems impossible to hear any particular one of them in the din, which fills the hall and sets it atremble, but a voice manages to emerge, faintly audible, from the clamor of supplicants who shout with all their might. "A pledge of a thousand lights for So-and-so," the speaker declaims. I put on a sash and pray, and a monk appears with a branch of star anise, declaring himself at my service. Such things deepen one's feeling of sanctity and have an interest of their own.

The monk approaches from the direction of the latticed barrier. "I have presented your petition in complete detail," he says. He asks how long I intend to remain in retreat, tells me that So-and-so is also staying there, and sends in a brazier and some fruit as soon as he takes his leave. The temple folk also supply a jug of wash water and a handleless basin. "That cell over there is at the disposal of your attendants," they say. In response to their repeated invitations, my attendants go off by turns to rest.

When a bell announces the start of a sutra recitation, I am comforted by the thought that it may be ringing for me. I hear a man of some substance performing unobtrusive obeisances in the next room. Although he takes care to be quiet in his movements, he seems deeply distressed; his devotions continue throughout the night with touching persistence. Whenever he stops for a moment's rest, he recites a sutra in a barely audible voice, a most holy sound. Just as I think that I would like to hear him better, he blows his nose—not in a disagreeably loud manner but very softly. What can be worrying him? I wish that it were within my power to grant his petition.

In the past, nothing much has happened during the daytime when I have spent several days at a temple. My menservants and pages usually go off to monks' cells, and I sit with time on my hands until the sudden shock of the conch shell, blaring nearby, announces the coming of noon. Perhaps the bearer of a spotless twisted letter puts down his offerings for sutra recitations and summons a temple page, his voice resounding impressively through the hall. The handbells begin to ring more briskly, and I wonder about the petitioner's identity. Then the name of an exalted personage is pronounced, followed by prayers for a safe delivery. Anxious and uneasy, I feel a desire to intercede for the woman too.

Such is the ordinary tenor of daytime events. The First Month, by contrast, is a hectic time. Pilgrims arrive in an endless stream, each seeking fulfillment of some aspiration, and the sight distracts me so that I find it impossible to settle down to my own devotions.

A party arrives at dusk with the apparent intention of staying. I watch as some young monks dextrously move tall screens, which seem almost too heavy to carry, and lay thin, bordered matting with a smart slap. After the newcomers make their appearance in the room, they proceed to hang blinds against the latticed barrier with practiced skill, producing most comfortable accommodations. Next, a large group of people emerge from their quarters with a rustle of silk robes. It seems that they are leaving the temple, for I hear one of them, who sounds like an elderly woman, issue an order in a refined, subdued voice: "Be careful with the fire in that room; it isn't safe."

A boy of seven or eight summons an attendant in a winsome, imperious voice and chatters away to him, which I also find entertaining. Again, a half-asleep three-year-old utters an adorable cough. When he calls his nurse by name or demands his mother, I feel that I would like very much to know who the mother might be.

The monks perform noisy rituals all night long, putting sleep out of the question. Once the late devotions are finished, I drowse off, and then, half-asleep, I hear a rough voice declaiming the sutra associated with the temple's principal deity. The sound inspires no particular reverence, but I start awake and listen with a full heart, aware that the recitant is probably a wandering ascetic.

Again, I observe the devotions of a respectable-looking man who does not stay for a retreat. He wears a great many padded white robes over a pair of dark gray trousers and brings with him a modishly dressed young boy, who appears to be his son, as well as a number of other young people. I watch with interest as a throng of attendants bow and seat themselves in prayer. Their master has temporary folding screens installed, and I infer that he is performing brief prostrations.

When I fail to recognize someone, I am consumed with curiosity; if I do know the person, I have a pleasant sense of satisfaction. Sometimes young men will tend to loiter near the rooms of the women in retreat. With never a glance toward the sacred image, they summon a temple official, talk to him in low voices, and leave. Still, they seem to belong to good families.

It is also agreeable to be in retreat at a temple around the last day of the Second Month or the First Day of the Third Month, when the cherry trees are in full bloom. It seems exactly right to see two or three dapper gentlemen clad in attractive cherry-blossom or willow hunting robes, their trousers elegantly tied and bloused. They have brought along a servant to carry a handsome provision bag, and their page boys are dressed in pink or yellowish-green hunting robes, worn over divided skirts stenciled with variegated patches of color. It is diverting to watch them strike the gong, escorted by a group of slender men laden with sprays of blossoms—samurai, by the look of them.

I am sure I recognize someone who, of course, has no way of knowing that I am inside. Even though I feel no special desire to meet the person, it is disappointing to see him go past my room. To my own amusement, I say, "I wish I could tell him I am here."

When I go to stay in a temple, or indeed in any unfamiliar place, I feel that the trip has been scarcely worthwhile if I am accompanied only by attendants. I would always wish to invite one or two or a group of others belonging to my own class—congenial friends with whom to discuss amusing things or to talk about whatever may come up. Some of my women are good enough conversationalists; I suppose it is over-familiarity that causes me to look elsewhere. Judging from the efforts that men make to find agreeable traveling companions, they must feel the same way.

155. Adorable Things

A child's face drawn on a melon.

A baby sparrow that comes hopping over when we imitate a squeaking mouse. It is also a pretty sight when the parent bird comes to feed the chick an insect after we have tied a string to its leg.

When a child of two is crawling briskly along, it is adorable to see it alertly spot a tiny curl of dust, pick it up with its dainty fingers, and show it to an adult.

A child's shoulder-length hair gets in her eyes, but she merely tilts her head to look at things instead of brushing the hair back. This is adorable—as is the fresh whiteness of the skirt cord tied above the waist to hold back her sleeves.

The tiny pages at the Courtiers' Hall are adorable as they walk about in their splendid costumes.

A sweet child falls asleep, clinging to someone who has picked him up to pet him for a moment. This is also a pretty sight.

Doll things. A very small lotus leaf plucked from a pond. A small heartvine leaf. Anything small is adorable.

A roly-poly two-year-old with a delightfully fair complexion crawls into view, dressed in a long, purplish-blue gossamer robe with the sleeves tied back.

It is adorable to hear a boy of eight, nine, or ten chant a Chinese text in his childish voice.

A long-legged baby chick, its white body amusingly suggestive of a short skirt, walks cheeping in someone's wake or follows the mother hen.

Duck eggs. Wild pinks.

165

While we were in mourning for the Empress's father, Lord Michitaka, Her Majesty had to leave the imperial residential compound to get ready for the purification on the last day of the Sixth Month. The direction of the apartments belonging to the Empress's Household Office was pronounced inauspicious, so she moved into the Aitandokoro Hall in the Council of State compound. As was to have been expected of the season and the end of the month, the night was hot and pitch black.

The confined quarters and tiled roof were not the kind of thing we were accustomed to. Also, the usual shutters were absent and the rooms were merely enclosed by blinds—an arrangement that nevertheless seemed a diverting novelty.

The ladies-in-waiting amused themselves by visiting the garden, where masses of brilliant day lilies beside a rough-woven fence seemed perfectly suited to the formal surroundings.

With the Timekeepers' Office immediately adjacent, the sound of the gong was not as we had usually heard it. Intrigued, some two dozen of the younger women went over to the staircase next door and climbed into the tower. In their gray trains and formal jackets, gray double unlined underrobes, and red divided skirts, they looked from our vantage point as though they might have descended from the sky—though, to be sure, one would not see heavenly beings dressed in mourning. I was amused by the sight of some other women, equally young but too senior in status to join the party, who gazed upward with envious faces.

After nightfall, the older women joined the younger in venturing out under cover of darkness to see the Guards Office. Some of the people there objected to their larking, chatter, and laughter. "Please don't act that way. You ladies ought not to sit in the senior nobles' chairs. And you are knocking over the Council officials' benches and damaging them," they said. But nobody paid any attention to their remonstrances.

We slept outside the blinds at night to escape the stifling heat in the ancient structure, which may have been caused by the tiled roof. Because of the building's age, centipedes dropped down on us all day long, and stinging insects swarmed over a huge nest in a terrifying manner.

His Majesty's courtiers paid daily visits, sometimes talking until dawn. Most amusingly, one of them intoned, as though reciting a poem: "Never would I have believed it! A lair of fox beauties in the Council of State grounds!"[14]

Autumn began, but our domicile seemed a place where the breeze was not cool "on a single side."[15] We did hear the sound of insects.

Her Majesty returned to the imperial residential compound on the Eighth. Probably because of the confined quarters, the stars had seemed closer than usual when we celebrated the Tanabata Festival.

204

Around the Fifth Month, it is pleasant to travel by carriage to a destination in the mountains. When one goes straight ahead for a long distance across a marshy green expanse, its surface covered with flourishing growth, the abundant water underneath splashes up amusingly as the men trudge through it, even though it is not deep.

---

14. Foxes were said to possess the ability to turn into bewitching women.

15. Ōshikōchi no Mitsune, composed on the last day of the Sixth Month (KKS 168): natsu to aki to / yukiau sora no / kayoiji wa / katae suzushiki / kaze ya fukuramu ("Are there cold breezes blowing on a single side of the celestial path where summer and autumn meet, going their opposite ways?").

A branch tip enters the passenger compartment from a hedge on the left or right. One makes a hasty effort to snap it off, but it whips out and the carriage rolls on—most disappointing.

It is delightful to savor the pungent scent of crushed mugwort, caught underneath and brought close as the wheels turn.

256

It had been decided that the Imperial Lady and the Empress would both go to witness the dedication of the sacred canon at Hokoin Saku-zenji on the Tenth of the Second Month, a ceremony that was being sponsored by His Lordship the Regent. By way of preparation, Her Majesty moved to the Nijō Palace around the First.[16] It was late at night when we arrived, and I was too sleepy to notice the appearance of the palace.

A bright sun shone in the sky when I arose next morning. The palace was beautifully clean and new; everything seemed to have been put into place the day before, even the blinds. I wondered when there had been time to install the imperial lion and Korean dog.[17]

A cherry tree about ten feet high stood at the foot of the stairs, apparently in full bloom. Our first reaction was astonishment that it should have flowered so early, just in the season for plum blossoms. Then we saw that the flowers were artificial, but they were quite as gorgeous as the real thing. What a tedious task it must have been to make them! It was sad to think that they would perish in the first rain.

A great number of small dwellings had been demolished to make way for the new residence, so there were no groves or other points of interest yet. One could say only that the building itself was inviting and tasteful.

His Lordship the Regent came calling, dressed in dark greenish-

16. S(h)akuzenji was a subsidiary temple founded by Michitaka within the precincts of Hokoin (Hōkōin), the former residence of Michitaka's father, Kaneie, which Kaneie had converted to religious purposes some time earlier. The Nijō Palace was a new residence built by Michitaka for Teishi's use when she was away from the imperial palace. It was close to both Hōkōin and Michitaka's own house.

17. Appurtenances of royalty. These sizable beasts sat facing one another on opposite sides of the entrance to the curtain-dais. Their ostensible functions were to keep the curtains from blowing in the wind and to ward off evil spirits, but they were essentially status symbols.

It had been decided that the Imperial Lady and the Empress would both go to witness the dedication of the sacred canon at the Hokoin Sakuzenji on the Tenth of the Second Month, a ceremony that was being sponsored by His Lordship the Regent. By way of preparation, Her Majesty moved to the Nijō Palace around the First (Sec. 256).

gray bound-patterned trousers and a cherry-blossom informal cloak over three red robes. The Empress and all her ladies wore bound-patterned and unfigured bombycines in deep and pale red-plum colors—a brilliant spectacle. Some of the jackets were yellowish-green, pale green, and pink.

His Lordship seated himself in front of the Empress and began to converse with her. As I looked on, I wished that people away from court might be privileged to catch a glimpse of the flawless manner in which she replied.

"I wonder how Her Majesty feels when she sees so many splendid attendants lined up together," His Lordship said, his gaze wandering to the ladies-in-waiting. "It's an enviable sight. I don't detect a single ugly face. It must be because they are all daughters of good families. Most impressive! You must take great care of them while they're in your service. But you ladies—what decision about Her Majesty's character prompted you to flock to her side? Even though she shows a tendency to be shockingly stingy, I have done my very best for her ever since she was born—and yet she has never given me so much as a cast-off robe. I say this to her face, not behind her back." We all burst out laughing, amused by his raillery. "It's the truth! You mustn't laugh at me for a fool. I'll be embarrassed," he said.

Meanwhile, a messenger arrived from the Emperor, a Secretary attached to the Ministry of Ceremonial. Major Counselor Korechika took the letter and gave it to His Lordship, who removed the outer wrapping.

"What do you suppose is in this letter? If Her Majesty doesn't mind, I'd like to open it and read it," His Lordship said. "But I see that she looks nervous. Also, I wouldn't want to be guilty of lese majesty." He gave the Empress the message. Most admirably, she refused to commit the discourtesy of opening it in her father's presence. The ladies-in-waiting had brought the messenger a cushion from a corner room, and three or four of them had seated themselves near the curtain-stand. "I'll go over to the other place to see about a reward." His Lordship said. He took his leave, and then Her Majesty read the message. She wrote her reply on red-plum paper, a perfect match for the color of her robe. I thought it a great pity that nobody was likely to guess what she had done.

His Lordship sent over the reward, together with a message proclaiming this to be a special occasion. It was a woman's costume with a red-plum semiformal jacket.

We had produced refreshments with a view to making the messenger tipsy, but he went off. "I am responsible for an urgent matter today. I must ask you to excuse me," he said to the Major Counselor.

His Lordship's other daughters had performed elaborate toilets and put on red-plum robes designed to hold their own in any company. The third daughter, San-no-kimi, was larger and plumper than the other two, Mikushigedono and Naka-no-kimi. She seemed well suited to the role of wife.

The Empress's mother, Lord Michitaka's consort, had also come to visit. Her curtain-stand was drawn close to shield her from the gaze of Her Majesty's newer attendants, which made us feel uncomfortable.

The assembled ladies-in-waiting consulted one another about their costumes and fans for the dedication day, and a certain spirit of rivalry crept into the discussion. "Oh, I'm not planning anything special. I'll just make do with whatever I have," someone shrugged. "That's what you always say," someone else retorted in a resentful voice. Many of them left in the evening. Since they were going home to prepare for the great event, Her Majesty could not very well detain them.

We saw His Lordship's wife every day and also at night, and the Empress's sisters came too, their visits keeping Her Majesty nicely provided with company. There were daily messages from the Emperor.

The passing of time did nothing for the blossoms on the cherry tree in the garden. They faded and deteriorated when the sunlight struck them and then, as a crowning blow, a night of rain left them in ruins the next morning. "One feels that those are not quite the kind of faces from which one would part in tears," I said, after having arisen very early.[18] Her Majesty overheard me. "I thought I heard rain falling. How did the cherry blossoms fare?" she asked as she awakened. Just then, some samurai and menservants arrived from His Lordship's mansion. Congregating in a large group under the blossoms, they began to pull down the branches and take away the flowers. "His Lordship said, 'Go over there quietly and take away the flowers while it's still dark.' It's already light. We shouldn't have been so slow. Hurry up! Hurry up!" the samurai told the servants. "If one of them were a man of quality, I'd like to ask if he remembers Kanezumi's poem, 'Let him censure me as he sees fit,'" I thought, vastly amused.[19] But I merely said, "Who are these

18. Anonymous (SIS 302): sakurabana / tsuyu ni nuretaru / kao mireba / nakite wakareshi / hito zo koishiki ("When I see the faces of cherry blossoms moistened by dew-drops, how I long for the person from whom I parted in tears!").

19. Unidentified. Possibly a mistaken reference to a poem by Sosei (GSS 50): yama-mori wa / iwaba iwanamu / takasago no / onoe no sakura / orite kazasamu ("Let the watch-

people stealing our blossoms? Shame on you!" They laughed and ran away, dragging their spoils. His Lordship had shown admirable judgment. I went back inside, reflecting that sodden blossoms on the boughs would not have been worth looking at.

Her Majesty arose after the women from the Housekeeping Office and the Bureau of Grounds had opened the shutters and done the cleaning. Upon seeing that the blossoms had vanished, she exclaimed, "Whatever can have become of them?" She continued, "I thought I heard a voice say something about thieves just as it was beginning to get light, but I assumed that it was only somebody breaking off a few branches. Who can have done it? Did you see them?"

"No," I said. "It was still too dark to see much. I made out some white figures and called to them because I was afraid they intended to help themselves to the blossoms."

"But why would they take everything? They must have had secret orders from my father," she laughed.

"Oh, I don't think it was that at all. It was probably a spring breeze," I said.

"You're just saying that to hide the truth. They weren't stolen; the rain spoiled them." Accustomed though I was to her quick mind, this seemed to me an impressive display of wit.

Since His Lordship was expected, I withdrew to the background lest he think my sleepy morning face inappropriate to the time.[20] The moment he arrived, he said in an astonished voice, "What's happened? The cherry blossoms have disappeared. How could you have let them be stolen? To think your ladies didn't notice anything! They must be late risers."

"And yet," I said, "I did believe 'I was not the first.'"[21]

---

man censure me as he sees fit: I shall deck my head with blossoms from the cherry trees on Takasago's high hill").

20. This presumably means that Shōnagon, preoccupied with the cherry blossoms, has not made her morning toilette despite the relative lateness of the hour. She puns on *asagao,* "morning glory" (literally, "morning face"), a summer-blooming flower "inappropriate to the time," which was the Second Month.

21. Probably an allusion to a poem in the collected works of Mibu no Tadami: sakurami ni / ariake no tsuki ni / idetareba / ware yori saki ni / tsuyu zo okikeru ("When I went out to view the cherry blossoms as the dawn moon shone, I was not, it seemed, the first: the dew had risen before me"). Shōnagon obliquely defends herself against the charge of oversleeping, at the same time suggesting that the dew may have been the thief.

"I thought so!" he shot back with a hearty laugh. "Nobody else would have gone to investigate. I guessed that if anybody caught me, it would be you or Saishō."

Her Majesty responded with a smile and an apt allusion. "But Shōnagon 'made the wind bear responsibility.'"[22]

"Really," His Lordship continued, "it was aggravating to have my men discovered after I had taken such pains to warn them. Your ladies are too vigilant." He proceeded to chant the poem about the mountain paddies, after first remarking, "'Spring breeze' was a clever way of pretending ignorance."

Her Majesty laughed. "Considered as a bald statement, it was rather extravagant. I wonder how the cherry blossoms looked this morning."

"Shōnagon saw them very early. According to her, the rain had ruined them; they were sopping wet," Kowakagimi said. There was an amusing expression of chagrin on His Lordship's face.

I was planning to make a trip home around the Eighth or Ninth. Her Majesty suggested that I wait until closer to the dedication, but I decided to go anyway. She sent me this message on an unusually sunny day: "Have the flowers opened their hearts? What do you say?"[23] I replied, "Although autumn has yet to arrive, I feel my spirit wander nine times in one night."

To go back a bit. On the night of Her Majesty's departure from the imperial palace, no arrangements had been made concerning the order in which the attendants' carriages were to depart, and there was a brisk struggle to be first. I stood aside with three companions who also found the scene distasteful.

"All this commotion about getting into carriages is most unseemly; they're falling all over themselves like people trying to see the Kamo Return. Oh, well, Her Majesty will be bound to hear of it and send for us if we can't get a carriage now," we laughed.

22. *Collected Works of Tsurayuki*: yamada sae / ima wa tsukuru o / chiru hana no / kagoto wa kaze ni / ōsezaranamu ("Already men till the paddies in the mountains. Do not make the wind bear responsibility for the scattering blossoms").

23. "Do you miss me? Why not come back?" The Empress alludes to a poem by Bo Juyi, as does Shōnagon in her reply, "It is too early for me to return, but yes, I do miss you": "In the Ninth Month, the west wind rises: / The moonlight is cold; dew-flowers form. / When I think of you, the autumn night seems long; / My spirit wanders nine times in one night. / In the Second Month, the east wind comes: / The grasses put forth buds; the flowers open their hearts. / When I think of you, the spring day seems slow to pass; / My heart contracts nine times in one day."

We stood in the background until all the others had filled the carriages to overflowing. Then an official asked if everybody was accounted for. "We're still here," we replied. Someone from the Empress's Household Office came over to us. "Which ladies are you?" he asked. "This is very odd," he went on. "I thought everyone had found a place. How is it that you were so slow? I was just about to put the maids from the Kitchen Office into their carriage. Most peculiar!" He ordered a carriage to be drawn up.

"Use that for the maids, since you seem bent on taking care of them. We'll wait our turn," I said.

He overheard me. "What spiteful tongues you ladies have!" he said.

We got in. Since the next vehicle did indeed carry the maids, we proceeded with little in the way of torchlight, which we found amusing. Thus we arrived at the Nijō Palace.

Her Majesty had entered the gate in her palanquin long ago. After settling into her splendid apartments, she had commanded that I should present myself as soon as I arrived. Two of her younger attendants, Saikyō-no-shōni and Ukon, were checking each new contingent, but I was nowhere to be seen as the other women left their carriages and reported in groups of four.

"How very strange! What can have become of Shōnagon?" Her Majesty said.

The two emissaries finally spied me coming along in the wake of all the others, quite unaware that I was wanted. "Her Majesty keeps asking for you. What took you so long?" they said. They seized me and led me inside. Most interestingly, the Empress looked as much at home as though she had lived there for years.

"Why were you so late that people had to go and look for you?" the Empress asked.

When I did not volunteer an explanation, one of my three companions stepped into the breach with a merry laugh. "Your Majesty has expected too much," she said. "Someone who rode in the last carriage could scarcely have arrived any earlier. We almost lost our chance at that carriage too, but the kitchen maids took pity on us and relinquished their claim to it. It was a dark, dreary trip."

"What were the officials thinking of? Why didn't you say anything? I can see that a new lady-in-waiting might hesitate, but Uemon could have spoken up," said Her Majesty.

"We didn't like to thrust ourselves forward at the expense of others."
Uemon's reply probably did not sit well with some of those present.

Her Majesty was displeased. "It was not admirable to crowd into the
carriages any which way. Surely it would be better to observe the rules in
a dignified manner," she said.

I tried to smooth things over. "Perhaps people simply couldn't face
the long wait while the front carriages discharged their passengers."

I returned to duty on the evening before the Empress was to attend
the dedication. Upon joining my fellow attendants in the northern eavechamber of the south enceinte, I found a number of low lamps burning
on inverted pedestal trays.[24] Some of the women were seated with a
friend or two behind folding screens, some behind curtain-stands, others
in large groups. Needless to say, they were busily assembling layered
skirts, attaching train streamers, and applying makeup. Some fussed
with their hair as though the next day would mark the high point of their
lives.

"Her Majesty will set out during the Hour of the Tiger [3:00
A.M. – 5:00 A.M.]. Why are you just now getting here? A person with a
servant carrying a fan was asking for you," someone said to me.

I dressed, wondering if the Empress might really leave during the
Hour of the Tiger. Then I waited while the sky brightened and the
sun rose.

Informed that we were to meet the carriages under the Chinese eaves
in the west wing, we all set out along the gallery, a trying journey for
those of us who were inexperienced newcomers. The west wing contained His Lordship's living quarters. The Empress was there too, and a
group of august spectators stood in a row inside the blinds to watch us
enter the carriages: the Empress herself, Lady Shigeisha, His Lordship's
third and fourth daughters, His Lordship's consort, and the consort's
three sisters.

The Empress's brothers, Lord Korechika and Lord Takaie, stood to
the left and right of the carriages, raising the blinds and parting the
inner curtains to help the women in.

We might have been able to hide our faces if we had all been crushed
together, but each name was called in order from a list so that we might
enter in groups of four. It was miserably uncomfortable to step forward.

24. The Empress and her entourage have moved to Michitaka's mansion.

To say that we were fully exposed would be putting it mildly. I could not bear the thought that the Empress might disapprove of my appearance as she watched with the others behind the blinds. Perspiration started from my body, and I felt that my meticulously coiffed hair must be standing on end. Once I had managed to pass Her Majesty, it was like being in a dream to find myself undergoing an inspection by the two smiling gentlemen, who were dressed with intimidating splendor. I could not decide whether to be proud or ashamed of reaching the carriage without fainting.

After all the women had been accommodated, the carriages were taken through the gate and their shaft stands were put down on Nijō Avenue. It was pleasant to see them lined up like sightseeing carriages. My heart beat faster at the realization that passersby must be thinking the same thing. A large group of men of Fourth, Fifth, and Sixth Rank came out from the mansion to posture and chat beside the carriages.

First of all, His Lordship the Regent, the courtiers, and the gentlemen of lesser status went off to the Imperial Lady Senshi's palace to escort her to Sakuzenji. Since Empress Teishi was not to leave until after the Imperial Lady had passed, we awaited the party's return with great impatience.

The Imperial Lady came into view when the sun was well up in the sky. There were fifteen carriages, including her own—four of them occupied by nuns. Her Chinese carriage led the procession. Then came the nuns' carriages, with impressive displays of crystal rosaries, gray surplices, and gray robes at the rear entrances. The blinds were down; the inner curtains were of lavender shading to a deeper purple at the bottom. The ten carriages containing ordinary ladies-in-waiting followed, resplendent with cherry-blossom formal jackets, lavender trains, red robes, and taffeta mantles. The day was balmy and fair, but a pale green haze hovered in the air, setting off the costumes to perfection and making them more beautiful and interesting than the most elaborate bombycines or colored jackets.

It was splendid to witness the solicitude with which Lord Michitaka and both of his younger brothers attended the Imperial Lady. We were overcome with admiration as we watched the spectacle. Those in the procession must have been equally impressed by our row of twenty carriages.

We awaited Her Majesty's appearance with eager anticipation, unable to imagine what could be taking so long. At last, attendants led out eight mounted Provincial Maids, all dressed in shaded green trains, with formal streamers and scarves fluttering prettily in the wind. The girl called Buzen, who was on intimate terms with the physician Shigemasa, wore grape-colored bombycine trousers, which was most unusual. "I wonder if Shigemasa has received permission to wear the forbidden colors," Lord Michiyori laughed.[25]

Her Majesty's palanquin appeared when all the members of the escort had ridden out and taken their places. It was a scene incomparably more magnificent than the one we had just witnessed. The palanquin's onion-flower finial glittered in the brilliant rays of the ascendant sun, and the very curtains shone with lustrous color.

The palanquin set forth, its guide ropes taut. When the curtains swayed, we women demonstrated the truth of the old saying about people's emotions making their hair stand on end. It would certainly be a convenient excuse for anyone who found her coiffure in disarray later. I basked in reflected glory, stunned by the grandeur of the occasion and the marvel of having become the close attendant of such a personage.

While the palanquin was passing us, the men swiftly yoked all the oxen to the shafts again, and our carriages fell into line behind the Empress. No words could describe my admiration and excitement as we followed her.

When Her Majesty reached the temple, Chinese music played near the main gate, and lion and Korean-dog performers leaped and danced. Dizzied by the blare of the *shō* mouth organs and the beating of the drums, I felt as though I had been swept aloft into some unknown Buddha-land. Inside the gate, there were brocade tents of many colors, all equipped with fresh green blinds and interior hangings—a scene of unearthly beauty.

Lord Korechika and Lord Takaie were waiting when we drew up near Her Majesty's viewing-stand. "Get out quickly," they said.

The experience of entering the carriages had been bad enough, but now we were even more devastatingly exposed. Dignified and handsome

---

25. Special authorization was required to wear the forbidden colors (*kinjiki*), one of which was purple (*murasaki*). Michiyori suggests playfully that grape (*ebizome,* light purple) might fall within the ban. Shigemasa seems to have lent Buzen a pair of trousers (*sashinuki*), a garment not ordinarily worn by women, for her excursion on horseback. A Provincial Maid (*uneme*) was a girl sent to the capital by a provincial official for service in the women's quarters of the imperial palace.

in an underjacket with a voluminous long train, Lord Korechika raised our blind and urged us to hurry. I thought that my hair, with its carefully inserted switch, had probably made an ugly bulge inside my jacket; also, the light was bright enough to show the difference in color between the black hair and the reddish switch. Feeling acutely self-conscious, I cringed at the thought of getting out.

"Let the people in the rear go first," I said.

One of the women in the rear may have shared my feelings. "Please withdraw. You do us too great an honor," she said to the gentlemen.

"Someone seems to be embarrassed." They moved away, laughing, but returned when I finally steeled myself to leave the carriage. "We are under instructions from Her Majesty to spirit you out without letting Munetaka see you.[26] It would be inconsiderate of us to leave," they said. They helped me down and took me to the Empress. It made me feel unworthy to think that she might truly have issued such a command.

When I reached the imperial presence, I saw that the women who had been the first to leave the carriages, some eight in all, were seated toward the front where they could view the proceedings. Her Majesty sat on a threshold beam about two feet high.

"Here she is. I screened her with my body," Major Counselor Korechika announced.

The Empress moved toward me from behind her curtain-stand. "Well, Shōnagon." She was still resplendent in a formal jacket. Her costume consisted of a magnificent red robe over a Chinese damask robe in the willow combination; a fivefold grape-colored robe; a red jacket; and a train of stenciled Chinese gossamer with a design edged in gold leaf. The colors were incomparable. "How do I look?" she asked.

"Marvelous!" I said. It was a sadly inadequate response.

"You must have had a long wait. The Master of the Household Office decided that people might criticize him if he escorted me in the same underjacket everyone had seen him wear when he accompanied the Imperial Lady, so we were delayed while the women sewed another. He's very particular about his dress," she laughed. In those bright, festive surroundings, she looked more striking and splendid than ever. It was wonderful even to see the distinct slight slant of her parted hair, caused by the ornamental pin in the upswept front tresses.

26. Munetaka is unidentified.

Lady Chūnagon and Lady Saishō were seated on a crosswise strip of matting on the threshold beam, separated from the rest of us by a pair of three-foot curtain-stands arranged back to back. Chūnagon was a daughter of Lord Michitaka's uncle Tadakimi, the Commander of the Military Guards of the Right; Saishō was a granddaughter of the Tomi-no-kōji Minister of the Left Akitada. The Empress looked at them. "Sit over there, Saishō, and watch with everyone else," she said.

Saishō understood what she had in mind. "Three can see very well from here," she said.

"Well, then." Her Majesty told me to sit on the beam.

"It seems that a Palace Attendant has won permission to ascend to the Courtiers' Hall," a woman on the lower level smirked.

"Do you mean that a Palace Attendant has become a Courtiers' Hall page?" I asked.

"Let us say, rather, a page holding a horse's bridle." [27]

Despite such remarks, I entered the inner area and sat down to watch. It was a signal honor.

I know that it sounds boastful to tell a story like this about myself, and also that it may seem to reveal a lack of consideration for Her Majesty. It would be dreadful if so august a personage were troubled by people who put on sage airs and criticized her for partiality to someone so insignificant. But ought I to leave out things that actually happened? I do realize that I was probably favored above my station on more than one occasion.

It was splendid to look across at the viewing-stands occupied by the Imperial Lady and other important guests. His Lordship the Regent first called at the Imperial Lady's stand and then, after a short time, came over to us. Major Counselors Korechika and Michiyori accompanied him. Middle Captain Takaie remained near the guard station, a fine military figure with a quiver on his back.

27. A conjectural reading of a corrupt passage, based on emendations. If the interpretation is correct, the other women object to Shōnagon's receiving preferential treatment, which they regard as inappropriate to her status as a newcomer and a person of modest lineage. In an earlier era, the minor functionaries called Palace Attendants (*udoneri*) had been chosen from among the sons of relatively important men, holders of Fourth and Fifth Rank, a fact to which Shōnagon probably alludes in her reply. A Courtiers' Hall page (*warawa tenjō*) was a child of good family placed in court service to learn palace etiquette. "A page holding a horse's bridle" is a reference to Shōnagon's social inferiority to Saishō, whose father was Director of the Stables of the Right. Contemporary writings show that such spitefulness was not uncommon at the Heian court.

The Regent was also accompanied by all the courtiers and other men of Fourth and Fifth Rank, who seated themselves in rows.

His Lordship entered Her Majesty's viewing-stand and surveyed the group inside. Everyone was wearing a train and formal jacket, even Mikushigedono. The only exception was His Lordship's wife, who had put on a semiformal coat over a train. "You all look beautiful—just like a picture. But one person's costume seems a little pedestrian today," he said. To his third and fourth daughters he added, "Remove Her Majesty's train. The Empress is supreme here. How many people can boast of having Imperial Bodyguards stationed in front of their viewing-stands?" He wept as he spoke. His natural joy and pride brought tears to everyone's eyes.

His Lordship looked at the red jacket I was wearing over my fivefold cherry-blossom robe. "There was a last-minute commotion because I lacked one set of having enough formal vestments to give the monks. I ought to have borrowed your jacket. You didn't by any chance shorten some holy man's vestment to make it, did you?" he said.[28] We laughed.

Lord Korechika overheard the question from his seat a little to the rear. "It probably belonged to Bishop Sei," he said. For a comeback, it was rather amusing.

It was interesting to watch Bishop Ryūen circulate among the ladies-in-waiting, a veritable bodhisattva in his red gossamer robe, purple surplice, pale purple underrobes, and bloused trousers. "How shocking for a senior cleric to cast dignity aside and mingle with women!" we laughed.

Little Matsugimi was brought over from the viewing-stand of his father, Lord Korechika. He wore an informal cloak of grape-colored bombycine, a deep red robe of glossy damask, and a deep pink bombycine inner robe. As usual, numerous men of Fourth and Fifth Rank attended him. Once inside the stand, he joined the ladies-in-waiting. When, presently, some mishap reduced him to tears, his wails seemed to add an extra liveliness to the occasion.

The dedication ceremonies began. The scrolls of the canon, each borne on a red lotus, were carried in procession by monks, senior nobles, courtiers, non-courtiers of Fourth and Fifth Rank, men of Sixth Rank, and lesser figures, a most holy sight. The lecturer came for the sermon,

28. Monks' formal vestments were red.

and then the sacred dances were presented. My eyes were drooping with fatigue by the end of the day.

Most splendidly, a Chamberlain of Fifth Rank attended the ceremonies as an imperial messenger. He stayed on afterward, announcing that His Majesty had commanded him to accompany the Empress to the imperial palace. The Empress indicated a desire to return to the Nijō Palace first, but the Chamberlain-Controller arrived, and His Lordship the Regent also received an imperial letter.[29] Her Majesty then decided to do as the Emperor wished.

Someone came from the Imperial Lady's viewing-stand with an attractive gift and a message: "Salt kilns at Chika!"[30] The gesture added to the splendor of the occasion.

The Imperial Lady departed after the end of the ceremonies. This time half of the senior nobles escorted her.

All our personal servants had gathered expectantly at the Nijō Palace, where they awaited us in vain until late at night, unaware that the Empress was going to the imperial palace. We for our part waited at the palace for them to bring our night things, but saw neither hide nor hair of them. There was nothing to do but keep wearing our stiff new finery, our irritation increasing as the night grew colder. We upbraided the servants for their stupidity when they appeared on the following morning, but they countered with perfectly reasonable excuses.

It rained on the day after the dedication. "This shows what a good karma I have," Lord Michitaka told the Empress. "Don't you think so?" His relief seemed quite natural.

320. Disagreeable Sights

Someone wearing a robe with a crooked back seam.

Someone wearing a collar pulled back.

A senior noble's carriage with dirty inner curtains.

A child brought into the presence of a person the parent rarely sees.

A child wearing high clogs with a divided skirt. (I realize that the practice is currently popular.)

29. The Chamberlain-Controller was probably Takashina no Sanenobu, the Empress's maternal uncle. He was sent as a second imperial messenger.

30. Chika, the name of a place in northeastern Japan known for its salt kilns, suggests *chikashi*, "close"; salt suggests *karashi*, an adjective that can mean both "salty" and "hard to endure." The message means: "It is hard to be so close without meeting you."

A woman in travel costume walking fast.

A monk wearing a yin-yang master's paper headdress while he performs a purification ritual.

A thin, dark, plain woman with a switch in her hair sleeps with an emaciated, heavily bearded man in the daytime. Who could possibly enjoy looking at the two of them lying there? At night nobody can see them, and besides, everyone else is asleep, so there is no need for them to stay up in order to spare their companions an ugly sight. They will be sufficiently considerate if they rise and go away early in the morning.

A very superior person may appear moderately attractive after awakening from a summer nap, but an ordinary face will be glistening, puffy, and perhaps even distorted. When a couple see each other under such circumstances, they must wonder if life is worth living.

It is most disagreeable to see a swarthy person wearing a singlet made of thin unglossed silk. Glossed-silk singlets are transparent too, but they do not look indecorous.[31]

31. In the remainder of the sentence, which is too corrupt to be fully intelligible, Shōnagon speculates about the reason for the difference.

A Historian-Biographer of the Eleventh Century

The selection below is taken from the earliest Japanese vernacular history, *A Tale of Flowering Fortunes* (Eiga monogatari). The work consists of two parts: a thirty-chapter "main portion" (*seihen*), conjectured to have been written between 1030 and 1045 by Akazome Emon (ca. 960?– 1040's?), and an anonymous ten-chapter "continuation" (*zokuhen*), thought to date from around the start of the twelfth century. The main portion, which begins with the accession of Emperor Murakami in 946 and ends with the death of Fujiwara no Michinaga in 1027, takes as its principal subject the fortunes of the Fujiwara clan, following them from the generation of Morosuke (a leading figure in Murakami's reign) through that of Kaneie (Morosuke's son and Michinaga's father) to that of Michinaga, and devoting seventeen chapters—50 percent of its total length—to an admiring account of the last eleven years of Michinaga's life. The continuation, which carries the history of Michinaga's descendants from around 1030 to 1092, consists largely of descriptions of court events.

Akazome Emon, the minor poet who probably wrote the original thirty chapters, was the stepdaughter of Akazome no Tokimochi, an obscure officer in the Gate Guards (*emon*). She married the scholar Ōe no Masahira (952–1012), probably in the 970's, and seems to have become a lady-in-waiting to Rinshi, Michinaga's principal consort, before Rinshi's marriage in 987. At some point after Masahira's death in 1012, she apparently left Rinshi's service and became a nun, but her involve-

Translation by William H. and Helen Craig McCullough.

ment in court life continued. She is last heard of as a participant in a poetry contest held in 1041, when she would have been around eighty. She and Masahira had two children: a son, Takachika (d. 1046), who followed in the Ōe clan's scholarly tradition; and a daughter, Gō Jijū, a poet of modest renown, who appears to have served Rinshi's daughter Kenshi.

Kenshi, the second of Michinaga's four daughters by Rinshi, is the subject of the excerpts below, which together trace her life from childhood to death. Her older sister, Murasaki Shikibu's mistress Shōshi, was married in 999 to Emperor Ichijō (980–1011; r. 986–1011); received the successive titles of Empress, Grand Empress, and Senior Grand Empress; became a nun with the honorary title Jōtōmon'in in 1026; and lived to the age of eighty-six. Kenshi began her own court career in 1004 at the age of ten, when she was named Principal Handmaid to Emperor Ichijō. In 1010, at sixteen, she married the thirty-four-year-old Crown Prince, the future Emperor Sanjō, who had been happily married for years to another woman, Fujiwara no Seishi. In 1012, the year after Sanjō's accession, she received the title of Empress; and in 1018 she was named Grand Empress. Meanwhile, in 1016, Emperor Sanjō was forced off the throne by Michinaga to make room for the older of Shōshi's two sons. He died the following year, leaving Kenshi a widow at twenty-three. Shōshi was also a widow by that time, but she remained a power at court as the mother of the child sovereign, Go-Ichijō, and of the future Emperor Go-Suzaku (1009–45; r. 1036–45). Kenshi, by contrast, lacked influence because her only child was a girl, Princess Teishi.

If friction existed between Kenshi and her more fortunate sister, we have no knowledge of it today. There is evidence, however, both in poems and in *A Tale of Flowering Fortunes*, that Akazome Emon was devoted to Shōshi and regarded Kenshi with some coolness. This putative authorial bias does not prevent her from giving Kenshi the praise due to a child of Rinshi and Michinaga, but an occasional note of criticism creeps in, with the result that Kenshi becomes one of the more credible and interesting of the characters who receive extended treatment in the book. Emon's painstaking account of Kenshi's activities also brings home, through sheer accumulation of detail, the contrast between the glittering career of a young woman who enjoyed powerful family backing and the quiet life of an unimportant official's daughter like Michitsuna's Mother, who appears in *The Gossamer Journal* as a virtual recluse despite her beauty, literary gifts, and status as a recognized wife of Kaneie.

The excerpts below are identified by the chapter numbers in William H. and Helen Craig McCullough, *A Tale of Flowering Fortunes*, 2 vols. (Stanford, Calif., 1980).

PRINCIPAL CHARACTERS

Atsunori (997–1054), Atsuhira (999?–1050). Sons of Emperor Sanjō by Seishi

Go-Ichijō, Emperor (1008–36; r. 1016–36). Son of Emperor Ichijō by Shōshi

Ishi (999–1036). Third daughter of Michinaga by Rinshi. Married Emperor Go-Ichijō in 1018

Kenshi (994–1027). Second daughter of Michinaga by Rinshi. Married future Emperor Sanjō; named Empress in 1012 and Grand Empress in 1018

Kintō (996–1041). Son of former Regent Yoritada; second cousin of Michinaga; father-in-law of Norimichi

Kishi (1007–25). Fourth daughter of Michinaga by Rinshi. Became consort of future Emperor Go-Suzaku in 1021; died shortly after giving birth to a son

Koichijōin (994–1051). Son of Emperor Sanjō by Seishi. Was Crown Prince until forced by Michinaga to resign in 1017

Michinaga (966–1027). Most influential figure at court. Held top posts; took Buddhist vows in 1019

Norimichi (996–1075). Second son of Michinaga by Rinshi. Became Palace Minister in 1021; later held top positions

Okisada, Prince. The future Emperor Sanjō (976–1017; r. 1011–16)

Rinshi (964–1053). Principal wife of Michinaga

Sanesuke (957–1046). Grandson and adopted son of former Regent Saneyori; second cousin of Michinaga. Called the Ono-no-miya Minister of the Right

Sanjō, Emperor, *see* Okisada

Seishi (972–1025). Daughter of Michinaga's second cousin Naritoki; original consort of Emperor Sanjō

Shōshi (988–1074). Oldest daughter of Michinaga by Rinshi. Married Emperor Ichijō; named Empress in 1000, Grand Empress in 1012, and Senior Grand Empress in 1018. Mother of Emperor Go-Ichijō

Tadanobu (967–1035). Son of former Chancellor Tamemitsu; prominent court figure

Teishi, Princess (1013–94). Daughter of Kenshi and Emperor Sanjō. Married future Emperor Go-Suzaku in 1027. Called Princess of First Rank

Yorimichi (992–1074). Oldest son of Michinaga by Rinshi. Held top posts; Regent from 1017 to 1067

Yorimune (993–1065), Yoshinobu (995–1065), Nagaie (1005–64). Sons of Michinaga by his second consort, Meishi (b. ca. 965?)

A Tale of Flowering Fortunes

8

So began the fifth year of the Kankō era [1008]. The mists on the peaks were transformed overnight, and the skies stretched calm and hazy to the horizon. The Kyōgoku Mansion was gay with the seasonal finery of the ladies in attendance on Michinaga's second daughter, Kenshi (known to everyone by her official title of Principal Handmaid), and on her younger sister Ishi.[1] When Michinaga went to visit Kenshi, who was then fourteen or fifteen years old, he found her seated in a chamber decorated with a charmingly youthful touch. She wore a number of lined robes in different hues, and her lustrous hair, of which every strand seemed polished, brushed the hem of her red-plum bombycine mantle, longer than her height by seven or eight inches. The aristocratic refinement of her features was softened by a radiant charm that made her, Michinaga thought, almost too beautiful for her parents' peace of mind. There were seven or eight young ladies in attendance, all looking happy and proud to be serving such a mistress.

. . .

With the coming of the Twelfth Month [of 1009], it was time for Kenshi's marriage to Crown Prince Okisada. The presentation that had been so long in the planning was carried out with spectacular magnificence. Indeed, it made people realize what an extravagant place the

1. The Kyōgoku Mansion, also called the Tsuchimikado Mansion, was Michinaga's principal residence.

world had become. The wives and daughters of the senior gentlemen in Michinaga's service all assembled at the mansion to accompany the bride, whose retinue included forty ladies, six girl attendants, and four maids.

I fear that a long description of Kenshi's appearance would impress the reader as tiresomely familiar and repetitious, but it seems a pity to write nothing at all. She was sixteen, and her hair shone with an almost theatrical beauty, even richer and more abundant than the elegant tresses of her sisters. The delighted Crown Prince treated her with the utmost consideration.

Life at the Crown Prince's palace must have been gayer and more fashionable after Kenshi's arrival. People had talked about "radiant Fujitsubo" when Empress Shōshi had first entered the imperial palace, but I could not possibly describe the splendor of even the most trifling of Kenshi's belongings. When one considers that ten years had elapsed since Shōshi's marriage, each bringing its own changes, it is not difficult to imagine the degree of luxury that had been attained.

The Crown Prince treated Kenshi with a gracious consideration that she found rather embarrassing, coming as it did from someone so much older. Confronted with this slip of a girl after his many years of devotion to Seishi, the Prince had felt at first as though one of his own daughters had been installed at his side, but he was wholly enchanted as the days passed and he came to know her. By night he called her to his bedchamber, and in the daytime he visited her apartments, where he set out her belongings, inspected them one by one, and marveled at their beauty. Needless to say, he was particularly fascinated by the articles from the trays and the tiny containers inside the comb boxes, which had been supplied by her mother and brothers in a spirit of keen rivalry. . . .

Prince Okisada's other wife, Seishi, had inherited a pair of gold-lacquered comb boxes, made for an earlier Sen'yōden Consort by order of that lady's husband, Emperor Murakami. The Prince had always liked nothing better than to examine their contents, but now they struck him as distinctly old-fashioned in comparison with Kenshi's. Emperor Murakami, who had had better taste than any other sovereign, had personally supervised the creation of the articles in question, instructing the Office of Palace Works by word and by brush, and sending back whatever failed to meet his standards. Yet to Prince Okisada, Kenshi's boxes appeared incomparable. He knew that his preference might simply reflect the changed tastes of his time, but he remained convinced of their superiority, which seemed to him still another illustration of Michinaga's astonishing faculty for doing things well.

Seishi's folding screens were splendid works of art from the brushes of Tameuji and Tsunenori, with calligraphy by Michikaze himself on the colored-paper sections; and they were as clean and bright as new ones, despite their age. Kenshi's were the work of Hirotaka, with calligraphy in what appeared to be Yukinari's hand. Confessing himself unable to choose between them, the Prince appealed to Michinaga and Yorimichi, who felt embarrassed and very much on their mettle in dealing with so mature, discriminating, and sophisticated a critic.

Magnificently attired in bombycine jackets and trains decorated with dramatic marine designs, Kenshi's bevies of ladies sat in groups, hiding their faces behind fans, whispering, and uttering mysterious laughs. They seemed a bit overwhelming to the Crown Prince, who was never quite at ease during his visits.

Seishi took care of the Prince's wardrobe, contriving elegant color effects and scents for even the least of his garments. There is a special air about any Emperor or Crown Prince, however young and childish, but Prince Okisada's maturity, dignity, and refinement inspired a profound sense of awe in those who saw him. Kenshi put the other consorts in the shade with the exquisite sleeves and skirts that lent distinction to her most casual costume. It was clear that Michinaga was keeping her provided with ample supplies of beautiful robes.

"How do you feel about it all? Is your sleep troubled?" Seishi's attendants and others asked her.

"The marriage ought to have taken place years ago," she answered. "I grieved for the Crown Prince because of the delay, and now that it has finally happened I am much relieved." She worked early and late on the Prince's elegant costumes, and saw to it that he received incense balls whenever she made new ones. It seems natural that he should have thought of her as a mother.

[*Crown Prince Okisada becomes Emperor Sanjō in 1011.*]

10

On several occasions, Emperor Sanjō remarked to Michinaga that he considered it proper to raise Kenshi to imperial status. Michinaga always protested. "Seishi has been with Your Majesty for years," he would say, "and she also has a large family of children. It would be only right to promote her first. Kenshi's future will take care of itself; there's no need for haste."

"Your attitude is not as I would have it," the Emperor finally told him in an aggrieved voice. "Do you object to the connection with me?"

"If such is Your Majesty's pleasure, by all means issue the decree as soon as an auspicious date can be chosen," Michinaga answered. He left the palace and set swiftly about the necessary preparations. Since there were no obstacles or other reasons for postponement, it was decided to make Kenshi an Empress, with the title Chūgū, on the Fourteenth of the Second Month [of 1012]. Michinaga worked frantically to get things ready on time.

Though the ritual on the day of the investiture was merely the usual one, it seemed exceptionally dignified and impressive. In the past, it had been almost impossible to distinguish the various ranks of Kenshi's attendants, who had all dressed as they pleased. Some of them had disapproved of such laxity, but many of those very ladies found their prescribed costumes a source of embarrassment on the day of their mistress's elevation. The timid and conservative were obliged by the regulations to put on bombycine jackets, whereas others who had prided themselves on their elegance were suddenly confronted by the devastating necessity of appearing in plain silk. The affair had its amusing side, but everything was different now that Kenshi was an Empress. It was only natural that distinctions should be enforced, and thus that everyone should envy certain ladies who had formerly seemed undistinguished— like Ōsaishō-no-kimi, whom people had derisively nicknamed Granny, but who now waited on Kenshi in a stunning bombycine jacket in grape colors—and that no attention should be paid to others who had thought rather well of themselves. All the ladies were secretly upset, but they concealed their distress as best they could, unable to complain to Kenshi. One could not help feeling sorry for them. Some very pretty daughters of gentlemen of Fifth Rank had been told to act as Lady Chamberlains, and they too were most pathetic as they stoically carried trays, ran errands, and performed similar duties, all of which seemed to them dreadfully humiliating.

Wearing a white costume and a formal coiffure, Kenshi took her place on the dining bench, with a fierce-looking lion and a Korean dog mounting guard beside her curtain-dais. The coiffure suited her admirably, lending an impressive air of dignity to her plump, girlish face, and everyone agreed that she made a perfect Empress. She was just nineteen. "It can't be more than three or four years since her presentation, and here she is already an Empress," people calculated. Grand Empress Shōshi had entered the palace at twelve and received imperial status at thirteen, but Kenshi was much more grown up. The fire posts in the courtyard and the new guard station were staffed by low-ranking guards officers, who performed their duties with a great air of importance; and freshly appointed Head Samurai and others bustled officiously about. The great banquet was to take place directly. Michinaga's oldest brother, Major Counselor Michitsuna, had been selected to serve as Master of the Empress's Household, and almost all the other offices had been filled. It was rare indeed, people said, for two sisters to have the good fortune to become Empresses in succession.

Although the Emperor was anxious to promote Seishi, he could not bring himself to speak to Michinaga about it. Seishi herself did not mind, but various people who claimed connections with her ladies made a point of passing along the views of those outside the court. "Her Ladyship must be miserable. It's a disgrace! I've never heard of anything so unfair," the visitors said, putting on knowing airs. Some of the ladies showed Seishi letters from such people. "See what So-and-so has to say about it," they urged her.

"Why must they repeat those disagreeable things?" Seishi said in a serious voice. "If people choose to gossip, I don't want to know about it. I've given up any idea of becoming an Empress; nowadays I think of nothing but my lot in the next world." Her protests merely provoked sage comments from the ladies. "Yes, but Her Ladyship is looking at things from a very special point of view—one that isolates her from human emotions and worldly concerns."

11

Empress Kenshi had taken up residence at Major Counselor Tadanobu's Ōimikado house after her withdrawal from the imperial palace early in her pregnancy. Now, several months later, she decided to move to Tsuchimikado, just as everyone was expecting the baby to be born at Tadanobu's. Her host racked his brains for a suitable gift. She had moved to Ōimikado after a fire at the Higashisanjōin Mansion, where she had stayed first, and he was determined to find exactly the right farewell present to mark her departure. It would be best not to attempt anything elaborate, he concluded. Expensive trifles were unlikely to intrigue a lady accustomed to every luxury. So he prepared a diary-like tale of life at Emperor Murakami's court, made up of four large picture scrolls, with calligraphy by Sukemasa's daughter and Enkan, and presented it to her in an elegant set of boxes, together with appropriate copybooks. She was delighted. To the ladies-in-waiting, he presented big partitioned cypress-wood boxes, filled with cosmetic powder and incense balls.

At the Tsuchimikado Mansion, all the prayers that had been offered for Shōshi were recited again. With the weather so unbearably hot, Michinaga could not help worrying.

I should mention, perhaps, that a number of Tadanobu's Chief Stewards were honored by promotions in rank.

Kenshi's labor began on the evening of the Sixth of the Seventh Month in the second year of Chōwa [1013], while Michinaga was still fretting and offering prayers. The prayer-monks raised a deafening chorus of mystic incantations and scattered rice furiously. A succession of imperial messengers arrived, a cacophony of calamity-averting chants rang out, and the child was safely delivered during the Hour of the Dog [7:00–9:00 P.M.]—an answer, perhaps, to all the months of supplication. There was a brief interval of noisy prayer, and then the afterbirth appeared. The monks were still quite fresh.

It was splendid that everything had gone so well, but Michinaga realized that the child must be a girl when those in attendance avoided mentioning its sex. Although he was disappointed, he told himself that it was not so bad; this was not his first grandchild, and besides, Kenshi would produce a son in time. He set about making the preparations for a bathing ceremony to be held that very night.

No formal announcement was made to the Emperor, but he naturally learned of the birth, and a messenger came from the palace with a sword. It was not usual to send a sword to a newborn Princess, but there was no need to be constrained by the usages of the past in so flourishing an era, especially since the baby was Michinaga's grandchild; and thus a precedent was set. The messenger's reward was a magnificent robe, as white as crane plumage, which shines even in the dark.

One of the Crown Prince's nurses, Ōmi-no-naishi, was summoned for the rite of the first suckling. Numerous others were available, but Naishi was the daughter of one of Rinshi's own nurses, and she had also served Shōshi as a Handmaid.

The reader will be able to imagine the splendor of the bathing ceremonies performed during the next several days. Twenty men of Fifth and Sixth Rank were commanded to serve as bow-twangers. (Those of Fifth Rank were Chamberlains.) Since the baby was a girl, the Emperor was at pains to select handsome men.

Everyone would probably have preferred a boy, but if people had spoken of the birth of Michinaga's first grandchild, the Crown Prince, as "the first blossom in the flowering of Michinaga's fortunes," then might not one say that the birth of this little Princess was a bud? For although the present might be a time of uncertainty and impatient waiting, the petals of a brilliant destiny would one day unfold.

The white furnishings and all the other arrangements were just as they had been for Shōshi's confinements.

There seemed to be innumerable applicants for the office of nurse. Certain ladies in the Empress's entourage, the mothers of children fathered by men of some consequence, had apparently convinced themselves that their past services made them the only suitable candidates, but Kenshi had made up her mind to ignore their pleas and bring in new people from outside.

Despite the oppressive heat, each of the ladies took infinite pains to make her white costume appear unusual and interesting, with most pleasing results.

Just as had happened after the births of Shōshi's sons, senior nobles of the first three ranks and ordinary courtiers of every rank down to the Sixth presented themselves for the birth ceremonies, which were sponsored by Michinaga on the Third Night, by the Empress's Household on the Fifth, by the court on the Seventh, and by Grand Empress Shōshi on the Ninth.

The Crown Prince was not yet weaned, so the new baby's attendants were soon deluged with messages demanding Ōmi-no-naishi's return. There was no lack of volunteers to take her place. Kenshi was not entirely satisfied with any of them, but at length the honor fell to a daughter of the Governor of Ise, a lady who was married to the late Regent Michitaka's son Chikayori, the Senior Assistant Minister of Central Affairs. She put the Princess to the breast on the night of her arrival, freeing Naishi to go back to the Crown Prince. Lavish presents were bestowed on Naishi, and it was announced that her service would not be confined to the first suckling; she was to be counted among the Princess's regular nurses.

The infant Princess's hair was so long that it parted, and they decided to let it hang naturally. How splendid it all was! Emperor Sanjō waited impatiently to see her, charmed by glowing reports of her beauty.

Things happened to be fairly quiet elsewhere, and Michinaga took to appearing at odd hours of the night on errands connected with the baby. His visits upset the ladies, who were too oppressed by the intolerable heat to worry about appearances when they went to bed. The new nurse found the intrusions particularly embarrassing.

Aware that the Emperor was anxious to see the baby, Michinaga decided to arrange an imperial visit to Tsuchimikado during the Ninth Month. (Empress Kenshi had been in poor health since the birth, and it seemed unlikely that she would be returning to the palace very soon.) A great deal of preparatory polishing and repairing went on at the mansion.

The Emperor had hoped to hold the Fiftieth Day ceremonies at the palace, but now they were to take place at the Tsuchimikado Mansion because of Kenshi's inability to travel.[2] Michinaga assumed responsibility for all the preparations. Supplies poured in from the Courtiers' Hall, from the Office of the Ladies-in-Waiting, and even from Grand Empress Shōshi's Household. It would have been impossible to count all the different varieties of boxed dainties and fruit baskets. The Emperor showed a gratifying interest in every detail of the proceedings, adding many admirable touches of his own. With the ceremonies scheduled for a date shortly after the Twentieth of the Eighth Month, the ladies worked early and late on their costumes, at the same time hurriedly preparing as best they could for the imperial visit in the following month.

All of Emperor Sanjō's principal ladies-in-waiting went to the Tsuchimikado Mansion for the baby's birth, and also for the Fiftieth Day celebration. The daughter of Tachibana Naishi-no-suke (the Emperor's nurse), Minamoto Naishi-no-suke, and other prominent gentlewomen,

2. A child was fed from an assortment of 50 special rice cakes on or around the 50th day after his birth, probably as a formal indication that his future diet would include solid food. An elaborate banquet accompanied the event.

such as Sakari Shōshō, were registered on Kenshi's duty-board, and they seem to have been very faithful about visiting the mansion.

Once the Ninth Month had begun, everyone sensed that the imperial visit was imminent, and there was much rushing about. Aware that Kenshi's ladies would be magnificently attired, the attendants of her sister and mother, Ishi and Rinshi, had determined not to be outshone. Great pains were also taken with the boat music. The visit itself I shall not describe in detail, since it followed the usual pattern. It was exactly like the one after the birth of Grand Empress Shōshi's son, the Crown Prince.

The mansion and grounds were a marvelous sight. To the delight of the spectators, the ivy on the island pines flamed with far greater brilliance than in ordinary years, as though caught up in the spirit of the occasion. The Emperor felt he had never beheld such dazzling splendor. And when the boats glided into sight as the dancing began, it seemed to him that such beauty must come from another world. The sound of the wind, sighing through the pines like the strains of a zither, blended harmoniously with the music, and the ladies' dresses, billowing out at the edges of the blinds, were magnificent beyond description.

As soon as the Emperor went inside, he asked to see his daughter. Michinaga carried her in, and the Emperor took her in his arms to look at her. She was a plump, sweet infant, whose hair, he noted with some surprise, was parted in the middle. When he spoke to her, she babbled enthusiastically, giving him a bright smile.

"Isn't she cunning? She seems to know me. I've never seen such an appealing baby. And what a head of hair! It will be down to her hips by next year," he said, already very much the adoring father.

He observed that Kenshi was wearing a set of Chinese damask robes in white chrysanthemum colors—an auspicious reminder, he thought, of those other garments of white. "How did you manage in all that heat?" he asked. "It must have been terribly hard on your hair." But her hair lay coiled on her skirts in thick, luxuriant masses. "Really! What kind of hair is that for a mother?" he said. "Women who are old hands at child-bearing have pitiful, skimpy locks and sallow faces. You must be some sort of a freak. And the baby takes after you, I can see."

"Where is the nurse?" the Emperor asked presently. Michinaga himself took custody of the baby and carried her away. "The nurse is rather countrified in her ways," he said. "She's too shy to show herself."

Stepping inside Kenshi's curtain-dais, the Emperor began to chat about the events of the past months, very much at his ease. "Just think," he mused, "this has been my first glimpse of that beautiful baby. She will have a splendid future. But life is hard for a man in my position. When I am worried about someone dear to me, it's sad not to be able to see the person at once." Then he said, "What do you say to having the baby brought here to lie between us? She's such a little doll. When Seishi's daughters were babies I thought them pretty, but they were ordinary by comparison. It's the long hair, I suppose, that makes this child so remarkably attractive. Come back to the palace as soon as you can. You won't need any nurses there; I'll take care of her myself." Kenshi gave him a small, indulgent smile.

Soon twilight fell, and there began a nostalgic, moving musical performance, presented by the senior nobles. The faint sound of other instruments, drifting shoreward from an island in the lake, mingled with the lapping of the waves and the murmur of the wind in the pines.

Since the Emperor seemed in no hurry to emerge, Michinaga went to fetch him. "It's getting late, and the music is quite nice. Perhaps Your Majesty should watch," he suggested.

"I like listening from here. It's more interesting to hear a performance than to watch it. As for the dances, I've seen them all," the Emperor answered in an indifferent voice. Michinaga withdrew in something of a huff.

When darkness had settled over the scene, Michinaga came back again with his request, and the reluctant Emperor emerged from behind the curtains, repeating to Kenshi, "Don't forget, you must come very soon—within the next day or two if you can." Then His Majesty summoned the Major Captain of the Left to write out a list of honors—sons of the house and stewards were to have promotions, and the baby's nurse was to be granted Fifth Rank. The Major Captain read off the names to the Empress, after which Michinaga performed the obeisance of gratitude. So the young Princess's nurse acquired court rank. Ōmi-no-naishi also received a promotion. Michinaga gave the usual presents to the Emperor, senior nobles, and others—all very handsome, as may be imagined.

The Tsuchimikado Mansion was amazingly favored by fortune. It is indeed cause for envy when a single private residence is honored by repeated imperial visits, and when it sees its daughters depart for the palace, one after another, to become Empresses. Even the humblest of the humble thought, with smiles of satisfaction, "This is what people mean when they talk about 'celebrated places'; this is what is called 'flowering fortunes.'" Human beings derive pleasure from the good fortune of others, just as they feel involuntary compassion in the face of suffering, and all the common people greeted the successes of Michinaga's sons and daughters with admiration and joy.

After the Emperor's return, he thought of little but the baby. He sent off many messengers begging Empress Kenshi not to linger in the city. Kenshi, who had not fully recovered her strength, seemed content to stay at home, but he made such a nuisance of himself that she agreed to go to the palace around the Tenth of the Eleventh Month. Since the Gosechi dances and the Kamo Special Festival were to follow almost at once, it may be imagined that her ladies had their hands full with the quantities of robes required for their costumes. The younger ones seemed especially eager to make a gay and fashionable appearance after their long absence from court.

Two more nurses for the baby had arrived. One was Ben-no-menoto, a daughter of Masatoki, the Governor of Awa, and the other was Nakatsukasa, a daughter of Takakata, a former official in Ise Province. There also seemed to have been a considerable increase in the number of Kenshi's attendants during those months. One who came was Go-no-onkata, the fifth daughter of the Hōjūji Minister of State Tamemitsu. Another was a lady who had been Mistress of the Crown Prince's Wardrobe while Emperor Sanjō was the heir apparent. (Her parents were the late Regent Michitaka and the Lady in the Wing Chamber; the Reikeiden Principal Handmaid Suishi had presumably been her sister.) A third was a daughter of Treasury Minister Masamitsu by Minamoto no Takaakira's second daughter—a lady who also bore the title Mistress of the Wardrobe. And there were a great many other daughters of important men. Those were times in which the wives and daughters of all the great nobles entered imperial service. If anyone stayed at home, the gossips interpreted it as a sure sign that she suffered from some dreadful defect. She might even be a cripple, they said. What a queer world it had become, with Chancellors' daughters leaving home to serve as ladies-in-waiting! The daughters of former sovereigns would be doing the same thing before long, people predicted.

There was little work for the nurses after Kenshi's arrival at the palace. In a somewhat excessive display of parental love, Emperor Sanjō carried the tiny Princess about and dandled her in his arms all day long. He had resolved to make himself responsible for even the most trifling of her furnishings.

Soon the year ended and the third year of Chōwa began [1014]. From the First of the First Month on, there was a fresh new feeling in the air. With the passing of the old year, the dwellers in the realm above the clouds raised bright faces skyward, and the spring haze appeared overnight, trailing its banners of purple and lavender, as though to share in man's welcome to the new season. The sun shone mild and clear, a myriad birds chirped in swelling choruses, the buds on bare limbs suddenly burst into bloom, and new green clothed the hedge grasses. Searchers pushed through the reeds on the burnt fields at Ashita-no-hara, and at Kasuga, too, the Tobuhi watchman gathered the first tender sprouts of a "myriad generations" spring. The breezes that melted the ice blew in gentle silence through the boughs, and the voices of warblers from the valleys lingered in the ear, singing, it seemed, of a long, happy reign. On the Day of the Rat, the pines at Funaoka impressed everyone with their eternal green, as though they were destined to live forever, transformed by the imperial example. Even the bamboo leaves at the lip of the wine-crock seemed to presage a long and prosperous reign, and the rose bushes at the foot of the stairs to await summer with impatience. It was all very pleasant and auspicious.[3]

The Congratulations and other ceremonies went off in splendid style. The gorgeous, richly scented costumes of Kenshi's attendants occasioned no particular surprise, since her ladies invariably appeared to great advantage, even on occasions of much less importance. Certain of the gentlemen assigned to drink the leftover spiced wines seem to have disrupted the ceremonies in an unforgivable manner, a result of their having got disgustingly drunk and noisy.

In spite of the pressure of official functions, the Emperor found time to visit Kenshi's apartments. Dressed in a splendid informal cloak and several dazzling inner robes, he seemed to the intimidated ladies a model of masculine beauty and breeding. Kenshi was half hidden behind green curtains. She wore eight or nine red-plum robes under a float-patterned

---

3. Many of the images in this paragraph are drawn from *Collection of Early and Modern Poetry* and other anthologies.

mantle of deep purple, and she too was an awesomely aristocratic and elegant sight as she languidly concealed her face behind a purple fan, which was decorated on one side with a huge painted mountain. The Emperor gazed in fresh astonishment at her long, abundant hair. The hair that inspired the saying "tangled locks on bombycine" must, after all, have been thin and scanty. Kenshi's beautiful tresses covered her whole skirt.

When the Emperor asked about Princess Teishi, the nurse Myōbu brought the baby in. Ben-no-menoto carried the sword. Observing that the Princess's hair had been trimmed at the ends, her father said in an affectionate voice, "Ah! Now she looks like a baby again." He carried her in his arms to show her the mirror cakes, all the while reciting the auspicious phrases in a long-winded manner that the onlookers found hilarious. "He sounds like someone offering hare-wand congratulations," one of the ladies whispered. He noticed the surreptitious titters and asked pleasantly, "What are you laughing at?"

The nurses had all done their best to make a splendid appearance, with brilliant results.

The Emperor chatted with Kenshi, laughing from time to time. How nice it would have been to paint the scene as the younger ladies sat in a group beside the curtains! Major Counselor Yorimichi put in an appearance, and he and the Emperor went off together after a little more talk. . . .

At last the ceremonies ended and everyone was able to relax. Emperor Sanjō sent Kenshi a poem suggested by some pine boughs covered with frozen snow: [4]

haru kuredo	Though springtime has come,
suginishi kata no	the ice of the departed year
kōri koso	refuses to melt:
matsu ni hisashiku	long indeed has it lingered
todokōrikere	on the branches of the pine.

Her reply:

chiyo fubeki	Though springtime has come,
matsu no kōri wa	something has made the ice

4. The Emperor's poem appears to be a complaint about Kenshi's prolonged absence from the imperial palace. Her answer implies that she is annoyed with him for some reason.

haru kuredo   reluctant to melt
uchitokegataki   on the branches of the pines
mono ni zo arikeru   that will live a thousand years.

[*Emperor Sanjō abdicates in 1016 and dies in mid-1017. The year 1017 is now ending.*]

13

At the Ichijō Palace, Empress Kenshi occupied the quiet days with religious rites. Startled awake one night by the sound of a bell announcing the predawn services, she raised a lattice shutter and looked out, murmuring a poem:

minahito no   With cold wintry blasts,
akazu nomi miru   the wind sweeps them all away—
momijiba o   those autumn leaves
sasoi ni sasou   of whose red and yellow hues
kogarashi no kaze   no eye can ever tire.

Presently, there was the usual excitement about the Gosechi dancing. In Kenshi's apartments, the commotion served only to call forth poignant memories of bygone days. Whenever a prominent courtier came to pay his respects, the younger ladies would emerge to seek consolation in a chat, and no doubt the Empress's brothers, in particular, made a special effort to be kind.

The Emperor, who had not yet visited Kamo, was to go there on the Twenty-fifth. The prospect was arousing great interest. Since the procession was to pass the north gate of the Ichijō Mansion, Empress Kenshi's ladies thought they might permit themselves the pleasure of watching, but the Empress was afraid of what people might think if there was any sort of public display at her residence. "How much can Her Majesty see by simply peeking out through a gate?" protested the disgruntled ladies. They had been going on in the same vein for several days when Michinaga called. "Do you intend to watch the imperial procession?" he asked the Empress. "It will pass your north gate."

"No," she said. "My ladies seem to be talking about it, but how could I?"

"What odd things you say! People might be critical if you were to build a viewing-stand and make a spectacle of the affair, but nobody would expect you to close your eyes to a procession passing right in front of you," he answered. Her best course, he advised in parting, would be to contrive a vantage point by breaking down part of the north embankment in such a way as to create a natural effect. The younger ladies were delighted.

The procession was a brilliant one. To the imperial spectator at the Ichijō Palace, everything was indescribably beautiful—Emperor Go-Ichijō's litter, shared by Grand Empress Shōshi, the elegant carriages of the ladies-in-waiting, and all the rest. The last to pass was Michinaga, a magnificent figure.

[*In 1018, Kenshi is named Grand Empress; in 1019, her father, Michinaga, takes Buddhist vows.*]

16

In the Eighth and Ninth Months [of 1021], the weakening leaves could no longer cling to the branches. Insects shrilled as though aware of the pathos of life, a cold wind sighed through the reeds, and the plaintive calls of migrant geese lingered in the ear. On a melancholy, depressing evening, when it seemed that even the belling of the deer in their mountain recesses must sound sadder than ever, Grand Empress Kenshi's ladies sat gazing into space and making conversation.

"With everything so uncertain, it's a serious business to simply go through life accumulating karma burdens," someone said. "Why don't we get the gentlemen to help us make a copy of the *Lotus Sutra* to dedicate? We can do a chapter apiece." "That would be splendid," the others agreed. They went to Kenshi with their plan and asked for her opinion. "An excellent idea," she said, "but if you start you must be conscientious about finishing."

"We ought to be able to manage with thirty capable people. First of all, for the Preface, Go-no-onkata," they decided. "For the 'Tactfulness' chapter, the Tsuchimikado Mistress of the Wardrobe . . ."

With the main decisions made, they all began to wonder aloud about the best way to proceed, making such a commotion that it was impossible to understand them. The married ones were afraid that their husbands' modest resources might prove unequal to the occasion, and the others felt even more uneasy, since they were going to have to rely on nobles and other men with whom they were friendly. The enterprise seemed indeed to have become less a pious work than a contest, which might, one feared, have the contrary effect of creating a karma burden.

More than ten days of hectic activity followed. (The time was around the Twentieth of the Ninth Month.) The sutra boxes commissioned by Kenshi were ready, the copying had been completed in spite of sundry misgivings, and the ladies were occupying themselves with preparations for the dedication, which they hoped to hold before the end of the month. They had settled on Master of Discipline Yōshō as lecturer, and had assembled a set of damask and gossamer night-duty robes and 100 rolls of silk as his recompense. Michinaga happened to drop by while they were trying to select a site for the ceremony. Kenshi mentioned the matter to him in the course of conversation. "My ladies have copied a sutra and are wondering where to hold the dedication."

"Of course they mustn't think of having it anywhere except at my Buddha Hall," he said.

"Very well, we shall plan on it."

"Who is to be the lecturer? What are you going to give him?"

"We intend to have Yōshō."

"Excellent. What do you have for him?"

"A damask and gossamer night-duty costume and one hundred rolls of silk," said Naishi-no-suke, one of the ladies in attendance.

"Much too extravagant," Michinaga replied. "I suggest that you give fifty rolls to the lecturer and the rest to the title-chanters. But when is the dedication to take place?"

"We were thinking of today or tomorrow."

"Two days from now would be an auspicious date. I'll have my people clean the Buddha Hall. And they'd better straighten up this old monk's living quarters too. It would be embarrassing if the young ladies-in-waiting laughed at me." He hurried off home.

Back at the Buddha Hall, Michinaga began hasty preparations. "There is to be a sutra dedication. Decorate the Amitābha Hall with rich furnishings, and arrange seating in the south corridor for the ladies-in-waiting. Our friends and relatives among the senior nobles will be coming, so the Kitchen Office will have to get ready for them—and there must be fruits and other dainties for the ladies."

It was easy to see that Kenshi's attendants were abashed and agitated by such attentions. The Amitābha Hall was being fitted out with the utmost magnificence.

Each of the ladies produced her work when Michinaga called at Kenshi's apartments early on the morning of the dedication. The sutra was indescribably magnificent. Some chapters were true chrysographed texts, inscribed in gold on lustrous cobalt-blue paper. Others were written over pictures superimposed on damask, or contained pictures above and below the text, or provided textual illustrations—the "Gushing Forth" chapter, for instance, depicted the emergence of multitudes of bodhisattvas from the earth, and the "Eternal Life" chapter showed the Buddha's eternal abode on Vulture Peak. It was all quite beyond words. The "Devadatta" chapter was illustrated with a drawing of the dragon king's abode; others were attached to branches of silver or gold . . . But it would be impossible to describe them all. Their splendor and sumptuousness made them resemble collections of elegant verses rather than sutras. Jeweled rollers had been used, and almost every scroll was embellished with the seven treasures. Nobody had ever seen anything so gorgeous. Kenshi's sandalwood sutra boxes bore gold-edged figured designs into which multicolored gems had been worked, and she had had the corner decorations made of dark blue Chinese brocade with a tiny figure. Ah, the splendor of it! One would have liked to make just such a sutra to keep always at one's side.

"I'll put it in the sutra treasury," said Michinaga, overcome with admiration. He went off with it, leaving word for the ladies to follow at once.

Four or five household carriages were summoned, and Go-no-onkata and the rest of the thirty ladies crowded inside for the journey to the Buddha Hall. They had kept on their usual dress with much reluctance—it would have been only proper, they thought, to make suitable preparations for so grand an event—but to the onlookers, watching them cram themselves helter-skelter into the carriages and start off, it seemed that even the most elaborate special costumes would have served no better, so brilliantly did their attire capture the hues of the season's chrysanthemums. They alighted at the gallery south of the Amitābha Hall, where the senior nobles were seated in a row against the balustrade of the eastern veranda.

"I didn't expect the project to amount to much," said Michinaga, "but I was absolutely astounded and dazzled when I saw the results." The gentlemen were impressed by the warmth of his praise.

Attractive dishes of fruit were brought to the ladies' seats, and the gentlemen also partook of refreshments. Yoritō, Koreyori, Tamemasa, and other officials from Kenshi's household looked after the ladies. Tokinobu, acting on Kenshi's behalf, took charge of the offerings for the lecturer and title-chanters.

When all was in readiness, the lecturer made his appearance, clad in gorgeous red vestments, and the anticipation of the congregation mounted as he raised his censer in an impressive gesture of homage to the Buddha. He ascended to the high seat, spoke of the nature of the occasion and its significance, read a small portion of the supplication, described what had been done, and explained the general meaning, titles, and text of the sutra, proceeding with such clarity and skill that Michinaga and the others showered him with praise. During the exposition, which began with the *Sutra of Innumerable Meanings* and continued through the *Sutra of Meditation on the Bodhisattva Fugen*, the ladies basked in reflected glory, and Kenshi's situation was admirable indeed.

Ten million people aspired to enlightenment while the Buddha lived on earth [Yōshō said], but never before, perhaps, have ladies entered into a compact, held consultations, and, like these, conceived a desire for enlightenment so fervent as to have written out, richly adorned, and presented a copy of the *Lotus Sutra*, "impossible to comprehend, impossible to penetrate." This is a rarity of rarities. Those who copy and dedicate the *Lotus Sutra* are assured of birth in the Heaven of the Thirty-three Divinities. What is more, it is unthinkable that any of these ladies-in-waiting should have failed to read the *Lotus*, and thus they will undoubtedly be born in the Tuṣita Heaven, there to lead a life of bliss. Consider, too, that they have made use of gold, silver, beryl, and pearls in copying their dedicatory text. What a noble enterprise! Their resolve is loftier than Mount Sumeru and deeper than the four great seas. Today their flowery sleeves are dyed in exquisite hues and shades, and the scents of Indian sandalwood and aloeswood permeate their robes. They paint their faces with cosmetics of many colors, and like the woman of Śrāvastī, they find themselves most comely when they see their reflections in the mirror. Their amusements within the Ninefold Palace are like those of damsels in the Heaven of the Thirty-three Divinities; they are not inferior to those of the Garden of Joy; they are superior to those of the Joyful-to-see Palace. Yet what thoughts can have entered the minds of these ladies, who, like fair maidens in the Heaven of the Thirty-three Divinities, sit on the soft, pearly stone beneath the kalpa trees, bathe in the marvelous Mandākinī Pond, savor the four kinds of nectar, and listen to the music of the five tones? Beholding the scattering of springtime blossoms, they have understood ephemerality; beholding the falling of autumn leaves, they have felt sadness. The cock's crow at dawn has brought tears to their eyes. The morning frost vanishing before the ascendant sun, the evanescence of the evening dew, the sound of the vesper bell marking the end of yet another day—those things have moved them to pronounce their great vow. They pray for the safety of their mistress, the Grand Empress, in whom they place their trust, and for that of the Princess of First Rank; likewise, they hope that their private petitions, encompassing this life and the next, may be granted, and that through their intercession every sentient being may also achieve peace in the present life and rebirth in paradise. There can be no lack of efficacy in a single character of this scripture elucidating the marvelous truth of the One Vehicle. The Jewel of the One Vehicle has been fastened inside garments adorned with damask, gauze, brocade, embroidery, gold, and gems. Can anyone doubt that so great a petition, encompassing this life and the next, will be granted?

There were many other moving and splendid things, but I cannot describe them all. Yōshō looked especially impressive as he took his leave at the end of the ceremony, after having received some silk and the package containing his reward. The Buddha Hall officers and title-chanters also went off with presents of silk, and the gentlemen, much impressed, felt that Kenshi had handled matters admirably. The sutra was stored in the treasury.

19

At the Biwa Mansion [Kenshi's residence], elaborate preparations had been under way since spring for Princess Teishi's Assumption of the Train, which was to take place in the Fourth Month [of 1023]. Michinaga was providing indescribably splendid articles for the Princess's use, and every effort was being made to lend distinction to the attendant events. Shōshi was to attach the train, and her ladies, faced with the need for costumes to see them through three days of festivities, found themselves almost as busy as the ones at Kenshi's house.

The Princess was to proceed to the Tsuchimikado Mansion[5] early in the morning on the First of the Fourth Month, the day on which she was to assume the train. It was clear that her nurses had devoted much anxious thought to their attire. Although such women are expected to appear as quiet, conservative figures, they had decorated their jackets and sashes with gorgeous mountain and river designs, gold and silver

5. Where Shōshi was living.

edging, mother-of-pearl appliqué, gold and silver lacquer, gold and silver damascene work, and bits of glass. And of course the young attendants had indulged their fancies with an extravagance verging on lunacy.

Shōshi had assembled presents of many kinds for the Princess.

All the ladies-in-waiting with any claim to superiority had placed themselves at the Princess's disposal, including elderly women who had previously retired to their homes, feeling unequal to the rigors of court service, but who were now coming in to sew and perform other tasks. The whole group assembled at the Biwa Mansion during the night of the Thirtieth, some of them just before dawn on the First.

At the Tsuchimikado Mansion, the west wing had been decorated for the occasion. Its appearance was impressive enough under ordinary circumstances, but now each of the furnishings had been specially brought in, and they gleamed with indescribable brightness and purity. Throngs of people from the staffs of the two mansions streamed in to look, expressing a noisy admiration that was in itself a diverting spectacle.

Their other preparations complete, Kenshi's ladies-in-waiting were making up their faces in a state of great agitation. Meanwhile, people sent by Ishi, Kishi, Yorimichi, and others kept bringing in different kinds of elegant clothing boxes containing sets of robes and tasteful accessories, such as fans and incense. So much was going on that the messengers received no replies. Koichijōin also sent splendid gifts. There seem to have been innumerable poems, too, but it must have been hard for Kenshi to tell one from another, what with the bustle and confusion of the ladies' carriages being brought up and the gentlemen assembling. A variety of handsome fans arrived from Princes Atsunori and Atsuhira, who had assembled exactly the right numbers and kinds to provide every lady-in-waiting with one appropriate to her age. Some of the recipients seem to have preferred creations of their own design, and it was those they chose to carry.

Michinaga was deeply concerned about the preparations. Since he felt he should not appear in public to keep an eye on things (to do so, he thought, would be inauspicious), he besieged Yorimichi with urgent instructions about tasks that needed to be performed. Early in the morning, the Regent betook himself to the Biwa Mansion, and there, in his eagerness to hurry matters along, he went so far as to urge the ladies-in-waiting to greater speed. Then he rushed off again. "It's time to begin," he said. "I'll see that everything is in order at the Tsuchimikado Mansion and then come back."

The gentlemen had assembled.[6] "Here's Yorimichi already," someone said. "Princess Teishi will be leaving at the Hour of the Hare [5:00–7:00 A.M.]." But it was not until the Hour of the Dragon [7:00–9:00 A.M.] that the party from the Biwa Mansion set out. Because it would have been undesirable for the Princess to travel separately, Kenshi used a Chinese carriage instead of the customary palanquin, and the two rode together, accompanied by Go-no-onkata. Fifteen carriages followed in an indescribably splendid and glittering procession, escorted by the Regent, the Palace Minister, and a host of other notables. Needless to say, the courtiers were also present. There were no ordinary men among the samurai attached to the imperial carriage; they were all Kenshi's own people. The other samurai and Head Samurai in the service of the two personages accompanied the party on foot. Even for the short distance between the Tsuchimikado and Biwa Mansions, they all wore elaborate court costumes, including boots. Their faces were flushed with embarrassment, for despite their low status they were the sons of men of Fourth and Fifth Rank, and they found it trying to endure the stares of the crowds in sight-seeing carriages and elsewhere along the way—to say nothing of having to suffer the inspection of the illustrious ladies they were escorting.

In deference to Shōshi's presence, Kenshi's men unyoked the ox at the Tsuchimikado Guards Office and drew the carriage in by hand. The Regent and the Palace Minister stood waiting at the point of descent to help the Grand Empress.

That day, the ladies-in-waiting from the Biwa Mansion wore robes of different colors under trains stenciled with designs of their own choosing. Shōshi's ladies sat from the south to the west side of the main hall, their skirts and sleeves billowing from behind the blinds. Ten were attired in wisteria colors, ten in deutzia, ten in azalea, and ten in kerria—a magnificent spectacle. Kenshi's ladies were seated along the eastern side of the west wing, their robes visible all the way to the south corner. Rinshi sat in privacy in a two-bay room with a southern exposure, somewhat to the west of the eastern side of the main hall. (It was

6. At the Tsuchimikado Mansion.

the chamber in which continuous sutra-recitations were performed for Shōshi.)

The day drew to a close amid ceremonies of many kinds, and then Michinaga sent a number of messages pointing out that it was time for Shōshi to join Kenshi. In the ordinary course of events, the guest would have gone to the hostess in the main hall, but Michinaga had probably decided to arrange things otherwise so that Shōshi could see the jewel-like perfection of the west wing's furnishings. Kenshi proceeded along the middle corridor to the hall in order to welcome her sister to the wing. What a splendid sight the two Empresses presented as they crossed in turn! Both were wearing semiformal coats, trains, and formal coiffures, and the spectacle was so magnificent that one longed to capture it in a painting.

Thus Shōshi arrived at the west wing to view the furnishings. The bombycine lavender curtains, shading to purple toward the bottom, were embroidered with branch designs, and their streamers, braided in the Chinese style, were cluster-dyed in purple. The curtain-dais was decorated in the same manner. The folding screens and other accessories were also very splendid, and Shōshi gazed at them with astonished eyes, accustomed as she was to considering her own apartments the last word in luxury. The curtain-stands and the frames of the screens were inlaid with mother-of-pearl and gold lacquer. On the five-foot screens, there were quotations from Chinese works, inscribed in elegant Chinese script on colored-paper sections by Major Counselor Yukinari; and on the four-foot Chinese damask screens, their colored-paper sections lightly tinted with purple, there were texts in Yukinari's cursive script, the calligraphy and underlying designs combining to produce an effect of indescribable brilliance and taste. The edgings were of Chinese brocade. The articles for the Princess's use were decorated with gold lacquer and mother-of-pearl, with gems inlaid wherever space permitted. But I could not possibly describe everything. The blinds were edged in green bombycine with a large figure.

Princess Teishi was looking very drowsy in the dim glow of the lamps. There were repeated messages from Michinaga; he was sure it must be past time for the ceremony to begin. Finally, Naishi-no-suke, one of the imperial nurses, brought up a lamp and stood next to the Princess. Shōshi looked at her niece. She was an exquisite child, with hair that seemed to fall in an extraordinarily splendid manner. A doll may be all very interesting, but its stiffness is disappointing; and a picture may be painted with admirable skill, but it can neither move nor speak. Princess Teishi, though she might have been mistaken for either, was so sweet, dainty, elegant, and radiant that Shōshi found it impossible to turn her eyes elsewhere.

The nurses waited behind curtains and screens, barred from closer approach.

The Princess changed into a white costume, and Assistant Handmaid Ben-no-saishō came forward to put up her hair. It would have been appropriate for Ōmi-no-sanmi to perform the ritual, but Kenshi had felt that she would not be a particularly novel choice, considering that she had been one of the Princess's nurses ever since she had been called on for the first suckling. Ben gazed in delighted admiration at the sweet little figure. Shōshi had always thought of the Crown Prince as having a special radiance, but her small niece's refined, winsome air made her long to keep the child where she might see her day and night.

"If she was beside His Majesty looking like that, wouldn't they be as cute as two dolls?" said Ben. The Empresses laughed.

The Princess looked incomparably pretty and lovable in the lamplight as her hair was being dressed. She seemed half asleep while Shōshi was tying the sash. Since the train had now been attached and the hour was late, Shōshi took her leave. "We'll meet tomorrow," she said. As before, Kenshi escorted her.

The magnificent costumes presented as gifts[7] included robes made of bombycine, damask, gossamer, and other fabrics in various colors, rolled together in sets of five and three. They were packed in beautifully decorated chests, which had been built to match their length, and which far excelled the ordinary sort of box trimmed with gold edging and lacquer. Since there were ten chests, they must have contained about 100 rolls. Modern colored paper always seems to be assembled in copybook form, but the sheets of paper presented by Kenshi followed the old style, and their different colors and shapes were more interesting than I can say. And then there were the dinner things—silver dishes on standing trays made of aloeswood, sapanwood, and sandalwood. Instead of following the usual design, the tray tops imitated the appearance of the sea, with mountainous islands and indented shorelines on which

7. From Kenshi to Shōshi.

many kinds of objects were arranged. Silver and gold were the only materials used. Shōshi put the trays and their contents on top of a cabinet, where, she said, they were to remain as ornaments, which no one must touch.

That evening, a splendid room was set aside for Ben-no-saishō, the Assistant Handmaid who had put up the Princess's hair; and all of its luxurious furnishings were given to her to keep. Her presents included two clothing boxes containing costumes in sets of two, with appropriate accessories. She also received the things that had been presented before the Princess that night.[8] And everything in her room went to her—the screens and curtain-stands, the double-tiered cabinet, the inkstone box, the comb box, the incense burner, the water jug and basin, and even the mats. Such largesse was not without precedent, but it was unlikely, people agreed, that any other Assistant Handmaid had been so lavishly rewarded for putting up a young lady's hair. For Shōshi's ladies-in-waiting, her household staff, and even her lesser servants, there were garments or rolls of silk appropriate to their status, and also, of course, presents of food. Every gentleman was given similar cause for rejoicing.

Emperor Go-Ichijō sent Shōshi a letter announcing promotions for three nurses in the service of the Princess of First Rank. Shōshi rewarded the messenger, and Kenshi also gave him an indescribably splendid present. The nurses were Ben, Tayū, and Chūjō. When Michinaga heard what had happened, his awe and gratification moved him to tears, inauspicious though they were on such an occasion. "His Majesty's act was everything that one might have wished for," he thought.

On the following day, Shōshi's ladies made a splendid appearance in China-pink robes, their colors paling toward the bottom, and Kenshi's wore layers of yellow kerria, which were a delightful complement to the red.

Kenshi would ordinarily have stayed until the Third, but the day was unlucky for her, so it was decided that she would go home on the night of the Second. Shōshi gave Princess Teishi an incomparable present—a set of gold and silver boxes containing all twenty scrolls of *Collection of Early and Modern Poetry* in Tsurayuki's own hand, Prince Kaneakira's transcription of *Later Collection*, and a copy of *Collection for a Myriad Ages* made by Michikaze. All of the manuscripts had probably

8. The dinner tables and trays.

been inherited from Emperor En'yū by Emperor Ichijō, and all were quite unique.

After amusing themselves until nightfall, the senior nobles and courtiers escorted Kenshi home. There had naturally been rewards for everyone on the preceding day, and all the members of Kenshi's party now received additional presents from Shōshi. Princess Teishi's three nurses, Kenshi's nurses, and the ladies-in-waiting were given robes, and there were other gifts for the senior nobles and courtiers, the Master of the Household Office, and the lesser household officials. High and low joined in singing the praises of the two sisters, whose warm regard for one another made it worthwhile indeed, people said, to be in their service.

When the company reached the Biwa Mansion, they found a sumptuous feast in readiness. The senior nobles in the escort stayed for a while, and on their departure they received fine quilts and oversized lined robes of the kind usually presented on official occasions. The courtiers were remembered in the customary fashion. Preparations were also made to receive visitors on the following day, which, as the last of the three, called for the same kind of entertainment.

24

[In 1025, Kenshi holds a New Year Banquet.]

Those of Grand Empress Kenshi's ladies who had been staying at home returned to the Biwa Mansion during the evening of the Twenty-second and the early morning hours of the Twenty-third. The wing to the east of the main hall and the other areas required for the banquet had been decorated on the Twenty-second. Although everything was more or less the same as at the Regent's banquet, there were differences in the presents for the guests, and also, presumably, in the disposition of the senior nobles, who were to go first to the east wing and then to Kenshi's south veranda.

After such a long period of impatient waiting, the younger ladies must have been consumed with excitement when the great day arrived. At last they were to match colors and combinations with their rivals! Regular ladies-in-waiting with assigned quarters dressed in their rooms, but the ones who came from outside were jammed together in the Table Room inside flimsy enclosures of screens and curtain-stands, where they

were joined by their male friends. In some of the cubicles, a last-minute frenzy of sewing went on, while the occupants moaned, "Oh, dear! My hair hasn't even been done yet!" In others, ladies who had finished most of their preparations calmly blackened their teeth and added other touches to their toilettes. Some members of the group, skeptical about the quality of the folding fans Kenshi might dole out, had asked that theirs be provided by friends or personal painters, and now they either waited nervously for the fans to come or discussed their merits. "How did you manage to get such a good one? Mine isn't at all what I wanted." Others passed judgment on the luster of their glossed silks or fussed

Grand Empress Kenshi's ladies prepare for a banquet (Chap. 24)

about the patterns in their bombycines. The ones who were authorized to wear forbidden colors sat with smug faces, aloof from the hubbub. The others, provoked by the superior airs of their companions, were filled with a burning desire not to be outshone. But the situation was hopeless for women who were condemned to appear in unfigured jackets, and even those who planned to wear bound-patterned fabrics complained because the figures were indistinct.

At dawn, the lattice shutters were raised, the doors and half-shutters were thrown open, and there was a flurry of hair-tidying and face-freshening. In some places, people tramped in with enormous bags and bundles; in others, pairs of bearers carried stacks of trunk and chest lids, packed with unbelievable quantities of clothing. The amazed onlookers asked themselves how many robes one woman could wear.

As the sun rose, some of the ladies breakfasted in a pleasantly un-affected manner on food brought from home. For others, busily thread-ing fans or burning incense balls, breakfast was the least of their con-cerns. "This is ridiculous!" their people said. "You shouldn't get so excited. You've been in such a state that you haven't eaten a bite for days. This morning, at least, please have a little watered rice or something. If you don't, how can you stand the weight of all those robes? Didn't you see what happened yesterday? Her Majesty had Saemon put on several layers so she could look at them, and Saemon couldn't budge—she simply stood there all hunched up." Absorbed in their tasks, their mistresses paid no attention.

When the sun had reached the Hour of the Dragon [7:00–9:00 A.M.], Kenshi sent attendants, housekeepers, bath maids, and other messengers to tell all the ladies not to dawdle. They went on with their primping—ceremonies were always late in starting, they said—and only moved to assemble after repeated warnings that the sun had risen much too high. Accompanied by court officials holding curtain-stands, and preceded by others clearing the way, they walked toward the Grand Empress with attendants carrying their skirts. They were graceless fig-ures, their robes too numerous and thick to let them raise their fans to their faces. It looked as though the seams of their jackets had split open because of their bulky garments and had had to be held together with cluster-dyed yarn. As they filed in, one imagined how elegant Kenshi herself must look.

After all of the ladies-in-waiting had made their entrances, hand-some curtain-stands were set up in the bay above the central stairway of the main hall, and the ladies took their seats, two in each bay west of the stairs and across the gallery to the southeast side of the west wing. East of the stairs, their ranks extended to the section of the gallery above the garden stream. I cannot tell you how many there were, but it must have been a huge number. The blinds were braided with cluster-dyed string and fitted with striking borders of an unusual kind. The long lines were grand beyond words.

The senior nobles assembled at about the Hour of the Sheep [1:00–3:00 P.M.].

Although the weather was mostly fair, a sudden flurry of snow added a delightful touch to the scene, enhancing the brilliance of the sand in the garden and bringing fresh charm to the murmur of the brook. It was just at that time that the gentlemen arrived. Their Escorts, dressed in exceedingly handsome costumes, resembled figures in a painting as they stood leaning on their bows near the inner gate. As I was admiring the grand entry of the Regent with his imposing company of Escorts, I noticed the Ono-no-miya Minister Sanesuke coming in. Young for his years, he still had a fine, attractive face, and I found him more appealing than any of the others. Because he held the title of Major Captain, he was accompanied by an impressive group of Escorts. All the senior nobles seated themselves in the inner chamber of the east wing, facing west. The courtiers took seats in the southern eavechamber. In the inner chamber, the seat of honor was on the south; in the eavechamber, it was on the west.

With all in readiness, the ceremonies proceeded as usual. Glancing toward the west wing, Kenshi could see a magnificent display of layered skirt edges, spilling out at the foot of the blinds like rows of pillow books made of differently colored brocades. The layers seemed to be more than a foot thick. And the sleeve openings were amazing, as large and round as small braziers. It was so astonishing and embarrassing an exhibition that she must have blushed with discomfort at the thought of the guests' reactions.

After the ceremonial obeisances, Yorimichi, as Minister of the Left, led a stately procession up the east steps of the main hall. He occupied the seat of honor east of the south steps. The Ono-no-miya Minister of the Right was next to him, and then came Tadanobu and all the others. They sat on square cushions facing north, with the tails of their underjackets draped over the balustrade behind them. The color combinations of the jackets were glossed silk, willow, cherry, grape, and, in the case of the younger men, red plum—a delightful, glittering array.[9]

Once seated, the gentlemen inspected the edges of the row of blinds in front of them. By mutual consent, each of the ladies on the other side was wearing three of the same five color combinations—willow, cherry,

9. The glossed silk colors (*kainerigasane*) were red for both the front and the lining.

kerria, red plum, and yellowish-green. Some wore five robes in each of their three combinations, a total of fifteen; others, six or seven, amounting to eighteen or twenty-one in all. Some were wearing Chinese damasks; others seemed to have on bombycines that were either bound- or float-patterned, the difference being determined by the color combination. Some of the mantles were five-layered; others seemed to be glossed unlined garments dyed in pale green and other such colors. The jacket colors were chosen from among the same five combinations, and the trains were decorated with seashore patterns. The stand curtains were in red plum, yellowish-green, and cherry colors, deepening toward the bottom, and were decorated with paintings and brilliant green streamers. The unlined ones were all leaf green. The gentlemen exchanged amazed glances, dazzled by the display.

Kintō and Norimichi were not among the guests at the event, which took place in the month that marked the death anniversary of Norimichi's wife. But Norimichi was uneasy about absenting himself altogether from such an occasion. He also felt curious about what was going on, so he appeared at the mansion in an informal cloak and went behind the blinds, where he wandered among the ladies-in-waiting, arranging their sleeve openings and smoothing their hair. The ladies, distressed by his attentions, thought it the kind of situation for which the phrase "dripping with sweat" must have been invented. They felt their faces redden at the same time that their bodies chilled with perspiration. What would Kenshi think? Each was painfully aware that her mistress was scrutinizing every detail of her personal appearance and behavior, as well as the style and coloring of her costume. The row of gentlemen did not much concern the ladies. Knowing they could not be recognized, they felt like the "thin men" at the Sacred Spirit Service, who mask their faces with hand towels. But the intrusion of the smiling Palace Minister was very upsetting.

A marvelous assortment of scents and perfumes, borne on the breeze from the gentlemen's seats, mingled with the fragrance of a superb plum-blossom incense burning inside. On that occasion, the ladies felt, the "gentleman-in-waiting" was superior even to the Ministers of the Left and the Right.[10]

In the garden, where musicians waited to the west of the east

10. "Gentleman-in-waiting" was the name of an incense.

corridor, the splendid fragrance of a plum tree near a fire-post was diffused by the movements of the crowd. The musicians emerged by fours in the usual fashion to present exhilarating performances of the dances "Ten Thousand Years" and "Universal Peace." (It may have been because of the season that the music sounded especially fine.) The performers kept their eyes raised to the edge of the Grand Empress's blinds, a delightful touch that seemed to enhance the beauty of their playing.

Sanesuke went up to Yorimichi. "A man of my age has been present at a good many brilliant and showy events, but I have never seen anything like the costumes the ladies-in-waiting have on today. Their ostentation appalls me!" he said. Yorimichi's smile must have made the ladies behind the blinds speculate uneasily about the subject of the conversation. "At Your Lordship's banquet the other day," Sanesuke continued, "I thought all the arrangements indescribably magnificent—the appearance of the mansion itself and every other detail—but that was 'brocade on a dark night' compared to this. Today I keep feeling as though I were facing a bright mirror—I am so ashamed of my appearance that that's exactly how it seems. At a man's place, the ladies-in-waiting are far away, and things are more relaxed, aren't they? Here everything has been done in such lavish style that it becomes trying." His remarks were most interesting. . . .

The winebowls were filled again and again, and the guests seemed to find it increasingly hard to preserve their dignity. When the sun went down, post torches were lit here and there in the garden, and portable lights made the surroundings as bright as day. The oil lamps inside were being lit by smug-looking female servants in unconventional attire, whose lofty indifference to possible criticism struck the onlookers as most intriguing. One realized that such servants were not to be found in humble places. Guards in unfamiliar costumes resembling hunting robes had come into the garden and were cheerfully tending the fires. What could possibly go wrong, they seemed to be thinking. Kenshi's eyes lingered on the scene, which she found very noble.

The gentlemen ushered in the darkness with a delightful concert, the tones of the instruments most impressive. Something that might have been either a plum blossom or a snowflake drifted into a winebowl, and Tadanobu began to sing:

> Plum blossoms swathed in snow fly above the zither;
> Willow-color merging into mist enters the wine.

The abundant flow of wine suggested another song:

The cold light of a single lamp—night beyond the clouds;
Many cups of warm cordial—spring amid the snow.

Although the voices were beautiful, some people said "Ten Thousand Years, a Thousand Autumns" would have been a more appropriate choice.

The guests cast away their inhibitions and made merry in a number of diverting ways. When it became apparent that some of them were getting drunk, Kenshi took pity on them and brought out the gifts. It was too dark for me to see, but I heard that they were magnificent. The departure was rather noisy.

Yorimichi went behind the blinds to speak to Kenshi. "Things went too far today," he said. "Everybody has been indulging in excessive display during the last few years. All you ladies let your attendants wear lavish costumes when the Buddha Hall was dedicated, but there was a limit to what they could do in the summertime. There is no excuse for anyone's wearing twenty robes, I don't care who she is. Your ladies are outlandish! Those excellent nobles Sanesuke and Tadanobu both protested to me that they had never seen or heard of such ostentation, and who could blame them? I was also amazed by the gaudiness of the makeup." He continued in the same vein, his manner so affable and charming that one could not believe he was the forbidding First Noble who had taken part in the day's ceremonies. "If Father asks for an account of today's events," he said, "I hate to think of the scolding I'll get about the robes. He's all smiles when the Empresses behave well, but he pounces on every irregularity. You've been very foolish. He always praises Shōshi and Ishi for not letting their ladies wear more than six robes. You're the one who's a problem, he says." He took his leave.

The ladies-in-waiting, stiff from so much sitting, could barely struggle to their feet. There was great bustling back and forth as carriages were drawn up at the Guards Office for the ones who were leaving the mansion. The others returned to their rooms, where they propped themselves up or stretched out, faint with fatigue.

The banquet had lasted far into the night. On the following day, Michinaga sent word for Yorimichi to call at once. The Regent hastened to obey, curious about the summons, and found that his father merely wanted to chat. The conversation probably touched on the appointments list that was to be announced soon.

"Now tell me," Michinaga said, "how did Kenshi's banquet turn out yesterday?"

As Yorimichi described the event, Michinaga deluged him with questions, smiling in great good humor. But he was infuriated by the answer to his inquiry about the ladies' costumes. "Such extravagance is simply appalling! In my opinion, it's too much for them to wear even seven or eight, and I've told them all—Ishi, Shōshi, and the rest—to limit their ladies to six, even on the grandest occasions. The others have never failed to observe the limitation, but this Imperial Lady flouts my wishes! I won't put up with that kind of behavior!" Yorimichi could not help being amused by his indignation over something that was already past and done with.

Michinaga proceeded to dress Yorimichi down. "Let's forget about Kenshi for the moment," he said. "I'd like to know how you, a Minister of State, found it possible to tolerate such conduct. Who do you think is supposed to be the court's guardian? What kind of man would ignore that sort of thing?" Yorimichi admitted to being at fault.

Yorimune, Yoshinobu, and others also visited Michinaga and exclaimed about the lavishness of the banquet.

28

Although the gossips were always speculating about whether Princess Teishi was destined for the Emperor or for the Crown Prince, no word of any match had reached the Biwa Mansion. Finally, in the Third Month [of 1027], hints of marriage to the Crown Prince were received, and the ladies-in-waiting huddled together in discussions of what the future might hold.

Messengers kept arriving from Michinaga. Yorimichi paid a visit, and there were long talks with Yoshinobu, the Master of the Empress's Household. The ladies promptly assumed that all the comings and goings had to do with the marriage and were impatient for matters to be decided as soon as possible. On the Sixth of the Third Month, it was decided that Yorimichi should come to settle things that very day, which had been found to be auspicious. The Grand Empress's household officials assembled, and the Chancellor appeared at about the Hour of the Sheep [1:00–3:00 P.M.]. He called for an inkstone, jotted down a few notations "as a formality," and went off again.

Michinaga took advantage of the auspicious day to send over quantities of silk and damask, which arrived at about the Hour of the Cock [5:00–7:00 P.M.]. "Distribute them to your ladies today," he said. "I'm afraid you'll have to work day and night if you're going to be ready. The presentation is to be on the Twenty-third, which leaves practically no time. I've already told the weavers to make bombycines for the jackets and mantles; you'll have to get the rest of the costumes together as soon as you can." Kenshi distributed the fabrics to the ladies who were to take part in the ceremonies, and they set feverishly to work. "How can we ever get glossy robes ready in time?" they complained. "And we can't just wear bombycine the way it's given to us. What's to be done? The time is so short!"

Kenshi called in several of the ladies who had been begging for positions at the mansion. She also sent for one of the numerous daughters of the late Governor-General–Middle Counselor Minamoto no Tsune-fusa, but Middle Captain Sanemoto responded that the family could not consider the arrangement.[11] When Michinaga heard of Sanemoto's refusal, he told him to send his sister to Kenshi, but Sanemoto declared to the Grand Empress that he really could not consent. Then Michinaga instructed Kenshi not to let the Middle Captain or his relatives visit her mansion, and vowed that he would not have anything to do with them, either. Sanemoto offered his apologies.

Michinaga sent Kenshi more supplies than her staff could cope with. "Don't neglect anything," his letter said. "With my health so much worse than it was last year, I simply can't visit you, much as I want to. This marriage is the only thing that keeps me alive; I don't intend to go until it takes place. Please, my dear, be sure that the arrangements are perfect." There were many other messages in the same ominous tone, which the Grand Empress found deeply distressing. Since it was a time of happy beginnings, she tried to keep her worries to herself, but tears often filled her eyes. Her ladies also looked as if they found it difficult to control their emotions.

Meanwhile, Kenshi was in and out of bed, plagued by a mysterious indisposition. Miserable and feverish, she would have her legs massaged and then be up and down again. She couldn't imagine what was wrong, she said, but somehow she managed to carry on with the wedding arrangements. In the thought that it might be a disorder of the nervous system, her ladies dosed her in vain with magnolia-bark tea.

11. Sanemoto was Tsunefusa's son.

After four or five days, Yorimichi came to call. What was making Her Majesty look so peaked, he asked. "She's been that way for several days," Naishi-no-suke answered. "It seemed to be a nervous disorder, so she drank magnolia-bark tea, but that didn't help."

"How very awkward." He had a samurai send for Morimichi, and the diviner proceeded to perform purification rituals in the Grand Empress's presence, giving it as his opinion that the cause of the illness was probably either a curse by the clan deity or a transgression against the Earth God.

"She isn't eating anything," one of the ladies told Yorimichi. "What a time for her to fall ill!"

Yorimichi set out toward the Hōjōji, leaving orders for the purification rituals to be repeated two or three times a day.

"This is most unfortunate," Michinaga said when he heard the news. "Do whatever else seems necessary." He told the Ninnaji Master of Discipline Jōten, who had recently been performing esoteric rites for Princess Teishi, to begin prayers and rites on Kenshi's behalf. The Grand Empress was determined to carry on, as appalled as everyone else by the untimeliness of her affliction. It was almost more than she could bear, but the marriage could not be halted. To Michinaga's distress, his own infirmity, from which he had been suffering since the previous year, forced him to remain a distant witness to these events.

Jōten became a Bishop. During his expressions of gratitude, he spoke of the promotion as a sure sign that his prayers would succeed.

Great preparations were afoot at the Biwa Mansion. All marriages tend to be lavish affairs, but Kenshi and Teishi's nurses had talked about the Princess's ever since her infancy, and the ladies must have been determined to spare no effort. Their instructions were to avoid outlandish extravagance and concentrate on making the conventional attire as fine as possible. Each was putting together three sets of costumes. There were to be the same numbers of ladies, girl attendants, and maids as for the earlier imperial marriages.

The mansion buzzed with activity as the wedding day drew ever closer.

After learning that the Crown Prince's messenger would come on the Seventeenth, which was auspicious, Kenshi's people made elaborate arrangements for his reception.[12] Everything was quite perfect, even to

12. The messenger brought the letter and poem with which the betrothal was sealed.

the pleasantly cool effect of the garden stream. Yorimichi, Norimichi, and the others were all waiting to greet the messenger when he arrived at the Hour of the Monkey [3:00–5:00 P.M.]. He was Lesser Captain Yukitsune, Yukinari's son, and his impressive bearing, as he proceeded through the east corridor to the main hall, bore witness to the excellence of his father's instruction. The Crown Prince's letter, written on willow-combination paper and attached to a willow branch, seemed extraordinarily elegant and splendid, but perhaps I only thought so because I barely caught a glimpse of it. I have no idea what it said. . . .

The usual ceremonies were observed, and the messenger left after dark with Teishi's reply. After that, there were daily messages from the Prince.

Rinshi was at the Biwa Mansion, working with the same anxious concern as the Princess's mother. The quiet spring rains, an added complication, caused exasperating delays. Since Michinaga was taking care of everything else, the sole task at the mansion was the preparation of the ladies' costumes, but Rinshi feared that even that might prove too much, in spite of the many hands at work. And then there was the added worry about Kenshi. Now that the wedding date was upon them, the Grand Empress was determined to bear up, but she was so miserable that it was hard for her to think of anything else.

It must have been unsettling for Michinaga to have to rely on others for news about the progress of things at the mansion and the state of Kenshi's health.

Yorimichi had been counting all along on having Kenshi join the Princess at the palace, but he now learned, to his distress, that there was no precedent to sanction the residence of an imperial lady who was neither the mother nor the wife of the reigning sovereign.

Early on the morning of the Twenty-third, the appropriate people went to the palace to decorate Teishi's apartments. Others were dazzled by the splendor when they peered into the Kokiden through the new blinds.

At the Biwa Mansion, the ladies-in-waiting slaved over their toilettes, and the Princess's nurses seemed equally convinced that their preparations were matters of crucial importance. Yorimichi appeared at midday to issue the necessary orders. The other brothers rushed around, eager to do their part, and there was a parade of messengers from Michinaga.

Messengers arrived from Shōshi and Ishi at the height of the confusion, but everyone was too excited to pay any attention to them. Kenshi must have been upset when she discovered what had happened. Shōshi's costume was an indescribably beautiful set of robes in shaded cherry-blossom layers, accompanied by a folding fan, incense balls, and other accessories, all showing meticulous attention to detail. Apt classical texts had been inscribed on the clothing box. Ishi had sent robes with wisteria designs woven in shades of purple.

Vast quantities of folding fans came from Koichijōin, Prince Atsunori, and Prince Atsuhira. From Yorimichi there were splendid costumes for the Princess's girl attendants—inner robes of red, others of yellowish-green bombycine, trailing robes in the globeflower and cherry-blossom combinations, and triple-layered trousers—every article a masterpiece, down to the last folding fan. Norimichi was responsible for the four maids, who were to wear robes of different colors, surmounted by green mantles and willow-combination jackets. The train patterns were far more elegant than the random stencil-designs one usually sees on maids' trains.

Toward sunset, there was much noise and confusion as the ladies' carriages were brought in from the establishments of various gentlemen. Princess Teishi, who looked uncommonly lovely that evening, had been led to believe that the purpose of the outing was to avoid a directional taboo. On learning that her mother would not be going, she refused to budge, but Kenshi managed to allay her fears. The Grand Empress watched with loving eyes as she entered the carriage, which had been drawn up to the bay at the head of the south stairs; and Rinshi was also deeply moved. Anxious messages streamed in from Michinaga.

The appearance of the ladies' carriages may be imagined.

The Princess's arrival at the palace and her descent were accompanied by singularly impressive ceremonies. The hand-drawn carriage and things of that sort took time, and it was rather late at night when the ladies-in-waiting alighted from the carriages in their beautiful costumes.

Numerous messengers came from the Crown Prince, all imploring Teishi to come at once. Meanwhile, the hour grew very late. Yorimichi was doing his best to persuade the Princess to go, talking to her like an affectionate father. All the other uncles were showering her with attention, mindful of the instructions they had received from Michinaga, who desired, he said tearfully, that everyone who loved him should act as Teishi's faithful servant in his place. At length, Yorimichi took the girl by the hand and led her to the Prince's apartments, where she remained motionless until the Prince came out to carry her behind the curtains. She looked so sweet and charming that His Highness must have been well pleased with the match.

Teishi's retinue withdrew, except for her chief ladies, who remained on duty in the Courtiers' Hall.

After the cocks had crowed a number of times, ladies and gentlemen began to arrive to escort Teishi back, but it was almost light by the time she left.

Kenshi's motherly anxieties and physical ailments kept her from sleeping that night, and she stayed up until dawn talking to Rinshi. There had been an extraordinary hush over the mansion since the Princess's departure.

At the palace, the Crown Prince's messenger came around sunrise.[13] He was Yoshiyori, the Provisional Assistant Master of the Crown Prince's Household. Teishi's stand curtains were of triple-layered bombycine in the wisteria combination, and her dais curtains repeated the colors. Everything was done in the usual splendid style, but this time the atmosphere seemed more dignified. Perhaps it was the fatefulness of the occasion that made it so very impressive. The Princess was using the eastern eavechamber of the Kokiden, and the edges of her ladies' robes, billowing out from behind the blinds, made an indescribably beautiful spectacle during the messenger's reception. The nurses and senior ladies-in-waiting all wore splendid double-patterned mantles in different colors.

Another Emperor's daughter who had made a similar marriage was Princess Shōshi, Emperor Suzaku's daughter, who had become Emperor Reizei's consort. But that happened long ago, and apparently the marriage was not all that might have been desired, because Emperor Reizei was an invalid. Everything was perfect in Teishi's case.

Yorimichi and the other brothers were all present, and they set out to get the messenger drunk. Since Yoshiyori was partial to wine, their relentless hospitality soon had him befuddled. He was an interesting sight as he took his leave and staggered, red-faced, back to the Crown Prince.

13. The messenger brought the expected "morning-after" letter and poem from the Crown Prince to Teishi.

The gentlemen thought it a great pity that Kenshi had been unable to witness the marriage proceedings or see the room furnishings.

Princess Teishi paid many visits to the Crown Prince, who was besieging her with messengers. There was a certain arranged look to the whole affair, but the Prince's affection seemed genuine, which must have pleased and reassured Michinaga and Kenshi. Both of them sent costumes to the palace.

Four or five nights after the presentation, Teishi was seized by a sudden severe pain as she was about to leave for the Prince's apartments. Yorimichi tried in alarm to make it go away by applying firm hand pressure, while messengers streamed in from the Prince. What was the matter? What had happened? When the pain subsided a bit, they persuaded the Princess to go ahead, and the perturbed bridegroom greeted her with a burst of anxious questions. She had seemed better, but another attack came on, and Yorimichi had to lead her away. Michinaga offered prayers for her as soon as he heard the news. It seemed that the attacks might well be the work of malignant spirits. The Crown Prince's nurses gathered solicitously at the Kokiden.

Teishi began to feel better toward dawn. Word of her improvement caused great joy at the Biwa Mansion, where Kenshi's concern had made her forget her own sufferings.

The Crown Prince thought it a pity that Teishi should have to journey to and from his apartments every night. In the future, he decided, he would sleep in her quarters. The Shōkyōden was prepared for his use.

There were preparations at the Hōjōji and the Biwa Mansion for the coming Change of Dress. The people at the mansion were also assembling a costume to be presented by Princess Teishi to the Crown Prince's son, Prince Chikahito, whose Assumption of the Trousers, they had been informed, was being arranged by Shōshi for the Second of the Fourth Month. [14]

The Crown Prince was to begin his visits from the Shōkyōden on the Ninth of the Fourth Month. All the stand curtains installed for the Change of Dress were made of triple-layered bombycine in the deutzia combination. The ladies' rooms in the corridors and elsewhere were decorated to reflect the individual tastes of the occupants, and the

14. The Change of Dress took place annually on the First of the Fourth Month. Prince Chikahito, the future Emperor Go-Reizei (1025–68; r. 1045–68), was the Crown Prince's son by Michinaga's daughter Kishi. Shōshi was his grandmother.

ladies themselves were wearing layered bombycines in the wild-pink combination.

That day, the Princess bestowed suitable gifts on the Crown Prince's nurses, supplementing the usual items with quantities of plain silk, damask, and the like. The gifts for the Prince's ladies-in-waiting, lower female servants, and maids probably followed the precedents set on earlier occasions.

29

Kenshi was much worse. A twenty-one-day series of esoteric rites, undertaken by Bishop Meison, had produced no improvement. The Bishop's efforts were reinforced by those of other notable monks, who were directed to perform two- and three-altar rites, but the disease proved impervious to their outpourings of mystic invocations; the Grand Empress did not so much as yawn. Every conceivable purification and oblation ritual was tried.

In the quiet aftermath of the Kamo Festival, Kenshi had ample time to fret about her daughter in the palace, and she deluged the Princess and her ladies with costumes. The ailing Michinaga must have felt similarly harried by responsibilities—the Buddha Hall, the Buddhas and bodhisattvas of the Ten Days of Fasting, and so forth. . . .

Kenshi's worries were assuaged by news of Teishi gleaned from the Emperor's ladies-in-waiting, who were frequent callers at the Biwa Mansion, and she found some consolation for her physical suffering in the constant visits of her anxious mother, Rinshi. But her condition was very frightening; the illness hung on with no hint of change. Casting about for something else to do, Rinshi summoned another group of eminent monks and told them to begin the customary sutra-reading rites. All the efficacious holy texts were recited—the *Life Sutra*, the *Kannon Sutra*, the *Healing Buddha Sutra*, and others. The Crown Prince sent a stream of official inquiries, and Princess Teishi's grief knew no bounds. It was too much, the Princess felt, that something should happen to her mother just when she herself was trying to contend with the uncertainty inspired by every aspect of her new situation. No success whatever was resulting from the current series of rites at the mansion, performed by Bishop Shin'yo of Miidera, Bishop Meison, and Jakushō. Rinshi was disheartened and gloomy. . . .

Michinaga had been intending every day to visit Kenshi, whose state caused him keen concern, but he had been unable to go. It was a dreadful disease, so unresponsive to treatment that even the ministrations of the Zenrin Archbishop Jinkaku were of no avail. Prayers of every conceivable kind had been offered at the mansion and at mountains and temples everywhere, but all had proved distressingly ineffective.

Michinaga's visit took place in bright moonlight on the evening of the Sixteenth of the Sixth Month [of 1027]. The spirits were driven into mediums, and he himself performed some mystic invocations, expressing great confidence in their efficacy. "How could the Buddhas and sutras fail to respond after I have prayed to them for so many years?" he said. He and Kenshi must have felt very sorry for each other, but they were both too ill to keep up a conversation. Excusing himself for leaving early and promising to come again soon, he went back home. . . .

Rinshi was spending all her time at the Biwa Mansion. Gloomy and pessimistic, she struggled in vain to adopt a cheerful attitude.

It was now the Eighth Month. The sad days slipped by, with Kenshi no longer aware of their passing. Feeling that something had to be done, Michinaga decided that the Grand Empress should go into retreat at the Hōjōji Hall of the Five Great Mystic Kings, where he proposed to arrange esoteric rites on her behalf. In a touching display of concern, he undertook a major reconstruction of the north side of the hall to accommodate her.

Daily messengers arrived from the Crown Prince, and Ishi and Shōshi were frantic with apprehension.

It was the sixth month of the illness, which had begun in the Third Month. Kenshi had stopped eating and was as thin as a shadow. Sometimes she would ask for a bath during a lull in her suffering, and the boiler-house servants would be pathetically happy as they went about their chores. The ladies-in-waiting and samurai competed with one another to be of service to their mistress, never allowing themselves a sound night's sleep, but they worried in private conversation about what such a long illness must lead to, and walked around brushing tears from their eyes. Since the lattice shutters were not being lowered at night, the gentlemen slept where they were, seated on the veranda with their backs propped against the balustrade. One's heart went out to them. . . .

Kenshi directed her ladies to prepare costumes for the Hōjōji retreat, which she had decided to begin on the Thirteenth of the Eighth

Month. If she recovered, she vowed, she would make a pilgrimage of gratitude to the temple in the Tenth Month. Furniture was transported on the appointed day, and rooms were suitably decorated. That evening, the ladies-in-waiting assembled before her in all their finery. Princess Teishi wore a coat in fallen-leaf colors over aster robes. Kenshi was a white figure, her two or three robes matched by her complexion. Her hair was disheveled at the knot where it had been tied in back, but not a strand was out of place below. One marveled at its length, which appeared to have increased during her illness.

On arriving at the temple, Kenshi took up residence on the north side of the eastern eavechamber in the Hall of the Five Great Mystic Kings. Michinaga occupied a room at the northwest corner of the building. A curtained chamber had been prepared for the Grand Empress's people in the northern eavechamber of the Golden Hall.

Five-altar esoteric rites were begun, sponsored by Michinaga with the aid of Yorimichi, Norimichi, Rinshi, and the Master of the Grand Empress's Household, Michikata, but two or three days passed without a sound from the possessing spirits. Michinaga and the monks were dismayed. Because Kenshi often sank into a comatose state at night, the monks would assemble to perform mystic invocations during the hours of darkness, but not even a yawn rewarded their efforts. Except that her condition remained unchanged, one might have believed that all the spirits had departed. Kyōmei and the others worried and lamented, humiliated by the futility of their ministrations, which they compared to scooping up water to throw at a rock.

Michinaga had assembled a large number of clerical vestments for the dedication of his 100 Śākyamuni images, planned for the Twenty-third, as well as other robes for an Eight Expositions Service, to be held immediately afterward. To his disappointment, it now appeared that he would have to cancel the ceremonies because of Kenshi's illness.

"There's no need to give up your plans," Kenshi protested. "I'm used to being sick by now, and I'll be able to hold out."

"How happy you make me!" he exclaimed. He rubbed his beads. "O Buddhas! For that noble speech, grant that she may be restored to instant health!" He went ahead with his preparations. Worshippers were to forgo the usual ostentation in making their offering-branches, he said; they must strive for decorous beauty instead.

On the dedication day, Shōshi arrived before dawn and went to the northern eavechamber of the Healing Buddha Hall. As Princess Teishi and Rinshi were proceeding toward the southeast, a dozen or so yards from Kenshi's quarters, they were astonished to see the Grand Empress slip smoothly out on her knees to greet them. Overcome with joy, they interpreted the encounter at a miraculous boon from a Buddha.

The ceremonies began—first the dedication of the images at the Śākyamuni Hall and then the Eight Expositions. From the outset, the lecturers spoke of nothing but Kenshi's illness, which became the subject of endlessly repeated prayers. Michinaga distributed clerical robes to the participating monks, who numbered 100 as usual.

"If she directs a single thought to the hundred Śākyamuni images, it will mean another hundred years of life," one monk declared. The holy words of hope stirred the listeners to the bottoms of their hearts.

There were illustrations from the *Lotus Sutra* on the pillars, but most of the monks seemed too preoccupied with Kenshi to appreciate them.

The days of the Expositions passed swiftly. Michinaga distributed magnificent gifts to the monks at their conclusion. Shōshi regretted not having seen Kenshi when she was so close, but exalted personages are governed by inflexible restrictions on their conduct.

So the month ended. The nights lengthened with the coming of the Ninth Month. Kenshi was much worse. She seldom slept through until morning, and the strain of her nurses' labors left them nodding with fatigue, sturdy as they were. Asleep on her feet, Naishi-no-suke took to napping in the daytime.[15]

The distracted Michinaga recalled how Minister Kamatari, suffering long ago from an intractable malady, had recovered after a nun from China had made an offering of the *Vimalakīrti-nirdeśa-sūtra*. He summoned Ryūsei, Iseki, Keinyū, and other worthy Nara monks to do the same, but there was no response. It seemed to him that Kenshi was simply waiting to go. Unable to look at her without bursting into tears, he felt as though years were being taken from his own life.

"Nothing can do any good now," Kenshi said. "Whether I live or die, I want to be at Biwa."

"It would never do to go back to the place where you fell ill," Michinaga answered. "The spirits must have put the idea into your head."

Shortly before dawn on the Seventh of the Ninth Month, Kenshi

15. Naishi-no-suke was Kenshi's childhood nurse.

moved to the New Southern Hall. Her failure to recover was a bitter blow to Michinaga, who had been confident of the curative powers of a retreat at his temple. The east side of the main hall was decorated for her.

Early on the morning of the Ninth, several kinds of fish arrived from Yorimichi. . . . It had been some time since Kenshi had tasted any, but she pulled a robe over her head in utter indifference. Despite all that had been done, the end seemed at hand, and bitter grief filled every heart.

The Tenth of the Ninth Month passed. Esoteric rites were performed at the New Southern Hall, with the Rain Bishop Ninkai and Bishop Shin'yo as officiants. Many of the ladies who had worked so hard at the Hall of the Five Great Mystic Kings went off home, promising to return on the following evening. The yin-yang masters all agreed that the patient would improve on the Fourteenth, and on the preceding night she did indeed rally enough to exchange a few words with her people.

Early on the morning of the Fourteenth, Kenshi expressed a desire for a bath. Orders were issued to the samurai, and the delighted boiler-house servants set about preparing water, but then she said that she was in a hurry: a small amount would do. Her ladies instructed Kaneyasu in the Serving Office to boil water and bring it as soon as possible. Kaneyasu hastened to obey, and when it arrived Kenshi slipped down to the bathing chamber on her knees to take her bath. The robes and mats she had been using for the past several days were all removed. After the bath she put on bright, fresh clothing, lay down, and sent someone to fetch Michinaga. He was in the bath himself, her father answered, but he would come at once. He rushed off to her apartments in his bath attire, afraid that she might be dying. There was no doubt that she was worse. He spoke to let her know he was there, and she gestured as though to cut her hair.

"Do you mean that you want to become a nun?" he asked.

She nodded, and he performed the necessary acts with tears streaming down his face. Her voice was very firm as she pledged to keep the commandments. Rinshi, who had arrived in the meantime, was too distraught to realize what was happening. Bishop Shin'yo, Past Lecturer Kyōen, and other holy monks assembled to perform mystic invocations, but the Grand Empress was sinking steadily. At the urging of Nagaie, Yorimune, and Yoshinobu, who were also present, she recited the name of Amitābha Buddha in a strong, clear voice. It was heartrending to hear her chant mingling with the monks' frantic invocations. There was pandemonium everywhere inside and outside the hall. In the midst of it all, Kenshi's brothers and others came crowding noisily in the room.

As Kenshi's life ebbed, Michinaga cried out in anguish, "How can you leave your old father and mother? Take us with you!" The ladies who had gone home had suddenly reappeared, and their wails reverberated through the hall at the sound of his sobbing.

Death came to Kenshi at the Hour of the Monkey [3:00–5:00 P.M.] on the Fourteenth Day of the Ninth Month in the fourth year of Manju [1027]. She had been ill since the Eighth of the Third Month. She lay covered by a robe and surplice belonging to Michinaga, placed over her by Rinshi, with her own brilliant robes pulled over her head. Her hair, which looked as if it had been cut to hip length, had been clipped just above the tie. The shorn locks had appeared to be about six feet long when Michinaga held them up for the Mii Bishop to look at. "See what long hair she had!" he said. Dazed by emotion, the Bishop had burst into tears. It was he who administered the commandments immediately afterward. When Her Majesty was pledging so firmly to uphold them, who could have thought that the end would come so soon?

The hall echoed with wails. As the ladies talked on about their terrible loss, even their mistress's age became a subject of mournful complaint. Dismal and inauspicious though the tearful voices sounded, one could not help recognizing the special sadness of their plight.

Michinaga pulled the robes away from Kenshi's face. "I can't believe it's true," he cried. "Please wake up!" Rubbing his prayer beads, he rambled on in tears. "How cruel the Buddha is! To think that he would let me survive to know such sorrow!" No words could do justice to his misery. Rinshi had sunk to the floor in a faint.

Yorimichi looked after his mother with medicinal decoctions. Her sobbing, ever more violent, continued even after the lamps had been lit. The faint sound of Princess Teishi's frenzied weeping came from the room to which her uncles had taken her. Her grief was most natural, infinitely pathetic.

Yorimichi took Rinshi by the hand and led her away. "You must go too," the brothers told Michinaga. "You aren't looking at all well." Their father scraped his feet against the floor, bursting into tears, but they drew him from the room, unwilling to let him stay. His chronic ailment seemed to be bothering him more than ever, and they led him off with touching solicitude. Yorimune, Yoshinobu, and Nagaie remained near Kenshi with the ladies-in-waiting. Naishi-no-suke was in a dreadful state, lying unconscious in her room with no notion that people were trying to get her to drink medicine.

At Michinaga's request, Bishop Shin'yo had stayed on after completing the esoteric rites that morning. His presence could no longer make a difference, but they left his altar intact, a mark of the special regard in which he was held.

Long though autumn nights may be, there was no peaceful sleep for anyone that night. Michinaga was stupefied with grief.

Aware that he could not abandon himself to sorrow, Michinaga summoned Morimichi to inquire about funeral arrangements. "I never dreamed it would come to this when I performed the purification rituals after Her Majesty first fell ill," Morimichi said. "The results of the divination were unfavorable, but I thought they would be changed by all the things you were doing. What a terrible tragedy!" Tears started from his eyes. "Well now, as to the day for the funeral, it seems that tomorrow would be best. It is a day of ritual seclusion for the Regent, but you need not avoid it for that reason. It is only days of seclusion for the Imperial Lady Shōshi that must be shunned, and tomorrow does not happen to be one. If the present opportunity is missed, it will be some time before there is another."

"Then tomorrow it seems fated to be," Michinaga answered, weeping. "I could see that theirs was an extraordinarily close relationship."

"There is a broad flatland called Ōtani east of Gion," Morimichi said. "That is the place for the funeral."

"Then go and make the necessary arrangements tomorrow," Michinaga directed. Morimichi withdrew.

Since Kenshi had given up her imperial status, it would have been improper to use a palanquin. Michinaga decided on a string-decorated carriage instead, in accordance with precedents established after the deaths of Empresses Senshi and Junshi.

On the following day, Michinaga supervised the activities of Kenshi's household officials and others close to her, who had begun to crowd into the hall early in the morning. Crews set to work on the roads along the funeral route. Michinaga admitted tearfully that he felt too drained to manage the walk. The sobbing household officials went about their business with frantic haste as the day drew to a close. Moved by the contrast with the happy splendor that had always characterized their mistress's outings, the ladies-in-waiting shed floods of tears.

Soon it was time to put the body in the coffin. Because the task was beyond the ladies' strength, it was performed by Yorimune, Yoshinobu, Nagaie, Koretsune, and Korenori. Appropriate objects were added. Yorimichi was in ritual seclusion and could not be present. Four or five carriages were provided for the ladies. Weeping without restraint, they all begged to be allowed to go, but of course there was room only for the ones who had been closest to the Grand Empress.

The reader may imagine the wailing when the hearse set out. The departure was especially poignant because it coincided with the removal of the flooring [16] in the eastern corridor where Princess Teishi was to stay. Kenshi's nurses were too upset to see the body off, and Teishi's lamentations were more than the family could bear. How inadequate it seems to call such things pathetic or sad! It was chilling to see the ladies wearing mourning robes over the chrysanthemum and autumn-leaf costumes that had been their habitual attire in recent days. The funeral procession was a melancholy spectacle, utterly different in costumes and general appearance from the imperial lady's usual progresses, but it was also very grand as it moved along beneath the fine cloudless sky, which seemed a reminder of autumn's end.

A brilliant moon shone throughout the night, illuminating the mourners, the surroundings, and even the colors of the ladies' robes. Someone with a natural understanding of things gazed reflectively at the ladies' carriages, her thoughts moving from the unendurable sadness of the occasion to musings on the impermanence of worldly things. To console her aching heart, she recited these poems to herself:

fujigoromo	Like layered mourning robes,
kaesugaesu mo	our sorrows accumulate,
kanashiki wa	grief added to grief,
namida no kakaru	on this tear-bedewed journey
miyuki narikeri	our imperial lady makes.

16. To create an earthen-floored mourning chamber.

hanamomiji	An end now to sleeves
orishi tamoto mo	woven of springtime blossoms
ima wa tote	and autumn leaves.
fuji no koromo o	How grievous it is to wear
kiru zo kanashiki	wisteria mourning robes!

Because Michinaga was in no condition to walk, his sons and some of the others carried him on their shoulders. It must have been hard for them.

The mourners found a spacious building awaiting them at Ōtani.[17] Everything was clearly visible in the moonlight, which was brighter than day. The rites were slow to start, and it was late at night before the Buddha-invocations began. The chants of the monks, their voices broken by sobs, were so moving that it was difficult to restrain tears, even for people with no understanding of the fundamental causes and meanings of things. With the Hiei Abbot Ingen and the Provisional Archbishop Kyōmei serving as Leader and Invoker, Kenshi's remains vanished without a trace into smoke—a dreadful sight.

Naishi-no-suke acted as waitress that night, and of course the other ladies who had been close to the Grand Empress all descended from their carriages to help.[18] I must leave the scene to the reader's imagination. Remembering the First Month, when she had also served her mistress's repast, Naishi-no-suke shed floods of tears.

The rites were completed near dawn, and then the Kohata Bishop Jōki and Assistant Household Master Yoritō took the remains to Kohata.

So Kenshi went alone to mingle with the clouds and mist, leaving the others to turn homeward without her. What their number was I do not know, but their plight was deeply moving.

17. Erected for the cremation.
18. It seems to have been customary to serve a final meal to the deceased.

Short Tales of Aristocratic Life

"The Lesser Captain Plucks a Sprig of Flowering Cherry," "The Lady Who Admired Vermin," and "Lampblack" are three of a group of ten short tales preserved in a collection called *The Riverside [Middle] Counselor's Stories* (Tsutsumi chūnagon monogatari). One of the ten, "The Provisional Middle Counselor Who Failed to Cross the Divide," was written by an identifiable lady-in-waiting for a short story contest held in 1055 by her mistress, an imperial Princess; most of the others, all of which are anonymous, probably date from the late eleventh and early twelfth centuries. If the title is to be trusted, the compiler was a court noble who held the relatively high office of Middle Counselor, but nothing more is known of him. The style of most of the tales is amply descriptive; the subject of all is the private life of the aristocracy, with emphasis in most cases on the vicissitudes of courtly love; and the authors devote less attention to plot than to atmosphere, mood, state of mind, and the everyday occupations and interests of a gossipy leisured society.

The three tales presented here are among the longest and liveliest in the collection. "The Lady Who Admired Vermin," well known in the West from Arthur Waley's early translation, is a humorous but surprisingly sympathetic portrayal of an unconventional girl with intellectual aspirations, a type for whom polite Heian society had little tolerance; "The Lesser Captain Plucks a Sprig of Flowering Cherry" develops as a

Translation by Robert L. Backus.

typical tale of romantic adventure but takes a bizarre turn at the end; and "Lampblack," in somewhat similar fashion, shifts abruptly from the celebration of courtly sensibility to slapstick comedy.

The Lesser Captain Plucks a Sprig of Flowering Cherry

Deceived by the moon into thinking it was dawn, he had risen in the depths of night from the bed where she must still be lying, wondering why he had gone, alas; but now that he had come too far to retrace his steps, he must press on: past cottages where none of the usual daylight noises could be heard, while in the streaming moonlight clusters of blossoming cherry rose dimly to shade off into the haze. One of these, a little more attractive than the others he had seen, made him reluctant to pass it by, and he was moved to think aloud:

sonata e to	I cannot bring myself
yuki mo yararezu	to take another step beyond this spot,
hanazakura	when I am being drawn
niou kokage ni	so urgently beneath the shade
tachiyoraretsutsu	of a tree where flowering cherry glows.

When suddenly the memory of one whom he had courted here before made him pause, and at that moment from a break in the earthen wall he thought he saw a white figure emerge, coughing loudly.

The place was sadly in ruin with no sign of being inhabited, so that however much he peered in one direction or another, no one was there to challenge him.

The person he had noticed was just going back, when he called to her, "I knew the lady who used to live here. Is she still in residence? Tell her that someone has come who would have a word with the mistress of these wilds."

"The lady does not reside here. She is pleased to live in some other place."

"How sad!" he thought uneasily when she told him this. "Can she have become a nun or some such thing?"

Then with a smile he said to her, "I wouldn't be surprised if you were going to meet that fellow—you know—Mitsutō." And as he bantered with her he heard the soft sound of a side door opening.

He sent his men a little farther down the road and concealed himself in a clump of miscanthus that grew thickly by an openwork fence, to watch.

"Lady Shōnagon! Is it dawn already? Go out and see."

She was a likely little girl, of charming appearance and dressed for night duty, her garments much wilted from sitting in, who was lovely to look at with her glossy chemise showing—ruby colored it may have been—and the fringe of her neatly combed hair set off against the back of her robe. Shielding her eyes with a fan against the brightness of the moon, she murmured, "'The moon and the blossoms . . . ,'" and as she stepped toward the blossoms closer to him, he wanted to give her a start, but kept still and watched for a while longer.[1]

Then an elderly lady spoke up: "Why isn't that fellow Suemitsu out of bed yet? Lady Ben! Oh, here you are. You should be on your way to prayers." This meant that they must be going to visit a holy place.

The girl he had seen would no doubt stay behind. "I am so disappointed!" she said. "Anyhow, I can just accompany you and stay somewhere nearby. I won't go to the shrine."[2]

To which the other replied, "You foolish child!"

Five or six people appeared, all dressed to go out. Apparently much distressed as she descended the stairs was the one who must have been the mistress, or so it appeared to him; and as he regarded her carefully, the tiny figure with her mantelet thrown back struck him as ever so child-like. And while her speech was pretty too, it also impressed him with its elegance.

"How lucky I am to have seen her!" he thought, and as day was beginning to dawn he took himself home.

He awoke to a sun shining high in the sky and wrote a letter to the

1. Minamoto no Saneakira (GSS 103): atarayo no / tsuki to hana to o / onajiku wa / kokoro shiramu / hito ni misebaya ("The moon and the blossoms on such a night too good to miss—if I could have my way, how I would like to have one see them who was a friend and shared my thoughts!").

2. The girl was apparently ritually defiled, perhaps by a recent death in her family or by menstruation.

lady with whom he had stayed the night before. "To have left you, my dear, so soon in the night, when your whole demeanor suggested how perfectly natural you thought it was for me to go—can you imagine how painful that was!" This and similar sentiments he put down on a sheet of soft paper, a dark green, which he attached to a sprig of willow and sent to her with the poem:

sarazarishi	To think that my feelings
inishie yori mo	are running like green willow threads
aoyagi no	so much more tangled
itodo zo kesa wa	on the morning of this day
omoimidaruru	than ever before we came to this!

Her answer was quite acceptable to the eye:

kakezarishi	Those threads of yours
kata ni zo haishi	some time past did creep in my direction,
ito nareba	where you had never meant to go;
toku to mishi ma ni	and hardly did they seem to straighten out
mata midaretsutsu	before they kept on getting tangled up again.

While he was reading this, the Minamoto Middle Captain and an Assistant Commander of the Military Guards came with attendants carrying their target bows for them.

"Where were you keeping yourself last night? You were invited to a party at the palace, but we had to go without you."

"Why, I was here all the time. How strange that you didn't find me!"

The sight of blossoms falling so plentifully from the cherry trees, which were blooming in profusion, called forth the first half of a verse:

akade chiru	When I see blossoms
hana miru ori wa	falling to the ground too soon,
hitamichi ni	I feel with all my heart . . .

To which the Assistant Commander added:

wa ga mi ni kaeba	that if I could but take their place myself,
yowarinishi ga na	gladly would I fall and waste away.

"I'm afraid that wouldn't do much good," said Milord the Lesser Captain. He recited:

chiru hana o	Even if, sorry to see them go,
oshimi tomete mo	I kept the falling blossoms in their place,
kimi naku wa	were you not here to look at them,
tare ni ka misemu	with whom else could I wish to share the
yado no sakura o	pleasure
	of the cherries that are blooming in my
	yard?

And so in a playful mood they set off together. The Lesser Captain was thinking how much he would like to visit the place where he had seen the lady.

That evening he went to pay his respects to the family; and his features, when he raised the blinds and gazed out at the sunset in a darkening sky thick with haze, with blossoms falling in splendid profusion, were so ineffably ashine that even the glow of the blossoms, one felt, was quite overshadowed beside him. He tuned a lute to the *ōshiki* mode, and the play of his hands so serene and melodious over the strings seemed hardly within the powers of the most superb of women. He summoned others to him of similar talents, and they amused themselves in ensembles of varied composition.

"How could any woman fail to admire him? And indeed, near Guardsmen's Gate there is one who plays admirably. She appears to be most remarkable in everything she does."

Overhearing these remarks, which a certain Mitsusue let drop to his companions, he said, "Where do you mean? The run-down house with all the cherry trees? How did you see it, young man? Tell me what you know."

"Why, sir, it so happens that I have had occasion to go there."

"I saw such a place! Tell me everything you know about it."

It turned out that the young man was courting the girl whom he had seen among the lady's attendants.

"The mistress is the daughter of the late Minamoto Middle Counselor. She is really a beautiful lady, I hear. They tell me that her grandfather, the Major Captain, intends to take her in hand and present her to the palace."

"Still, you must work out something for me before that happens."

"I would like to, but I wonder how," said the youth and took his leave.

One evening the girl, who was very good at putting things into words, explained to her lover exactly how matters stood: "What would you have me do when Milord the Major Captain is forever making himself so difficult that Mistress's grandmother is terribly strict with us even about passing letters to her!"

Later, when this same house was filled with talk of the happy event soon to come, his appeal took on a special urgency; so that she, perhaps because she was a young person wanting in discretion, told him, "I'll do it if I get the chance." But she made it a point not to transmit a letter, so as to give no inkling of what was afoot.

Mitsusue presented himself and reported: "I have talked her around. Tonight should be a good time."

Overjoyed, the Lesser Captain started off rather late in the night. It was in Mitsusue's carriage that he went. The girl, after going about to see that all was quiet, let him in. In the dim surroundings—for she had taken the lamp away and put it behind something—lay a very small figure asleep in the main chamber, whom he swept up in his arms, lifted into the carriage, and then drove hastily away, as the figure cried out in uncomprehending amazement, "What are you doing! What are you doing!"

Now, as it happened, the lady's nurse, Chūjō, had overheard something, and her grandmother had felt apprehensive, so that she had made her bed there. She was a small woman to begin with; while at the same time, since she had also become a nun in her old age, her tonsured head was cold, and she had been lying there with her garments pulled over it. No wonder he mistook her for the other.

As the carriage drew up at its destination, she said in a voice cracked with age, "Good gracious, young man, who are you!"

As to what happened after that, who knows? It must have been the height of folly. Though she did have the looks of a peerless beauty.

The Lady Who Admired Vermin

Next to the place where lived the lady who admired butterflies was the daughter of the Inspector–Major Counselor, whose parents tended her with such infinite care that she grew up to be a creature of intriguing and exceptional beauty.

This lady collected great numbers of frightful-looking vermin. "The way people lose themselves in admiration of blossoms and butterflies is positively silly and incomprehensible," she would say. "It is the person who wants the truth and inquires into the essence of things who has an interesting mind."

And she put them into different kinds of screened boxes to see how they would develop. "What intrigues me the most is the caterpillars, which have a certain appeal," she would say, and she would lay them out on the palm of her hand and watch them from morning till evening with her hair drawn back behind her ears.

Since her young ladies were dismayed at this behavior, she gathered around her a band of fearless and disreputable boys, and amused herself by giving them the vermin in the boxes to hold, asking their names and assigning names to the unfamiliar ones.

"As a rule it is wrong for people to make themselves up," she would say, and never plucked her eyebrows, and never applied tooth blackening because she thought it was bothersome and dirty. And she doted on the vermin from morning till night, all the while showing the gleaming white of her teeth in a smile.

Whenever people fled from her in consternation, this "lady" would shout at them in a very peculiar manner. The people thus frightened she would transfix with a stare from under heavy black eyebrows, calling them "Disgraceful!" "Vulgar!" so that they were bewildered all the more.

"That she should be so peculiar and behave so differently!" her parents thought. But at the same time they wondered, "Can there be some meaning in this that she has comprehended? Whenever we think that something she does is odd and tell her about it, she contradicts us no end. It makes one feel so intimidated!" And they were very embarrassed by this behavior too. "That may be," they told her. "But you are getting a strange reputation. What people like is good looks. If society were to hear that you enjoy playing with weird-looking caterpillars, it would put you in a very peculiar light."

"I don't care. Only when one examines all things and looks at their outcome do things have significance. That's being very childish, because caterpillars turn into butterflies." She took out some in which that phase was emerging, and as she showed them, said, "The clothes that people wear by the name of 'silk' are produced by worms before they grow wings, and when they become butterflies, why then they are completely ignored and are worthless!" Against this they could find no argument and were confounded.

Nevertheless, she was lady enough not to display herself even to her parents, and she held the opinion that "Devils and women are better invisible to the eyes of mankind." Thus would she deliver herself so cleverly from behind a curtain stand set out by a slightly raised blind in the main chamber of the house.

Her young ladies would listen to all of this. "She puts on quite a show, but leaves you positively bewildered. These playthings of hers! I wonder what kind of people serve the lady who admires butterflies," said one of them who was called Hyōe, and recited:

ikade ware	What means have I
tokamu kata naku	to make her understand?
ide shi ga na	Oh, to go away!
kawamushi nagara	I would never look upon those things
miru waza wa seji	in their caterpillar stage again.

Another, who was called Little Tayū, recited laughing:

urayamashi	I do envy them.
hana ya chō ya to	"Ah, the blossoms! Ah, the butterflies!"
iumeredo	they will be exclaiming;
kawamushi kusaki	while what have we to look upon
yo o mo miru ka na	but a world that reeks of caterpillars!

"Too harsh, really," said one who was called Sakon. "Her eyebrows look like furry caterpillars all right, but her bare teeth you would think have been skinned.

fuyu kureba	In wintertime
koromo tanomoshi	we can depend on having coats
samuku tomo	however cold it is,
kawamushi ōku	in a place like this where one can see
miyuru atari wa	so many worms with furry skins.

We could easily get along without clothes, you know."

They were overheard telling each other such things by a faultfinding

woman, who said, "Whatever are you young people saying! I find nothing at all admirable about a person who is supposed to admire butterflies. You are quite inexcusable! And besides, would anyone line up
caterpillars and call them butterflies? It's just that they molt, you know.
She examines that stage. That is good sense. When you catch a butterfly,
its dust sticks to your hand and makes it very unpleasant, you know.
Also, they say that if you catch a butterfly, it gives you the ague. Horrid
things!"

But this only made them even more malicious in their remarks to
one another.

To the boys who caught the vermin the lady gave interesting things,
things they desired; and so they collected various kinds of frightful-
looking creatures and presented them to her. Although the caterpillars
had fine-looking fur and all, they did not suggest anything to her
imagination, and for that reason she found them lacking. So they would
collect such things as mantises and snails, and she had them sing loud
songs about them for her to hear, and raised her voice herself to chant the
ditty:

katatsuburi no tsuno no	Why do the horns of the snail
arasou ya nazo	battle each other to no avail?

She was disappointed to find that the boys' names were so ordinary,
and so she named them after insects and other low creatures. She em-
ployed them under such names as Mole Cricket, Toady, Dragonfly,
Grasshopper, and Millipede.

Such things became known in public, and there were people who
said very disagreeable things, among them a certain young man well
connected by marriage, who was high-spirited, fearless, and personable.
Hearing about the lady, he said, "Well, I bet she will be afraid of this."
And he fashioned the end of a sash—very beautiful to look at—into the
close likeness of a snake, fixed it so that it could move and all, put it into
a bag that had a scaly pattern and a string to draw it closed, and tied a
note to it which read:

hau hau mo	Ever so slowly
kimi ga atari ni	creeping, creeping would I follow
shitagawamu	by my lady's side,
nagaki kokoro no	I who am long in faithfulness
kagiri naki mi wa	that stretches on without an end.

When they saw what was written, they brought it into her presence in all innocence. "These bags are always so strangely heavy just to lift!" they remarked as they drew it open. And there was the snake with its head raised up. Her people cried out in bewilderment, but the lady was very calm. "Praised be Amida Buddha! Praised be Amida Buddha!" she intoned.

"It must be an ancestor reborn in this present form. Don't carry on so!" she quavered; and averting her face, she muttered as she drew it close to her, "Right now, while it is still so young and lovely, I want to have a feeling of kinship for it. How low-minded all of you are!"

But even a woman of her temperament felt so afraid that she fidgeted up and down like a butterfly, and the strained voice in which she spoke made a terribly funny sound, so that her people broke into laughter as they fled noisily away. Whereupon the news spread.

"What an appalling, unearthly thing is this I am hearing!" exclaimed His Lordship. "How unnatural that all of them should have left her with such a creature right there in front of their eyes!" And he rushed to her, sword in hand. When he looked at the thing closely, he saw that the gentleman had fashioned it into a very good likeness; and so, taking it into his hands, he said, "How very good this person is at making things! Apparently he has done this because he heard about the wise airs you put on and the kind of things you appreciate. Write an answer and send it to him at once." And with that he took his leave.

When her people heard that it was artificial they said angrily, "What an outrageous thing to do!"

"He will be left in suspense if you don't answer him," everyone told her, and so she wrote an answer on a very stiff and coarse piece of paper. Since she had never written in a cursive hand, it was done in the angular script.

chigiri araba	If we are bound by fate,
yoki gokuraku ni	one day I shall encounter you
yukiawamu	in that good paradise.
matsuwarenikushi	No easy thing to get involved with
mushi no sugata wa	is the shape of a lowly creature.

"In the garden of bliss."

When the young man, who was the Assistant Director of the Stables of the Right, saw it, he thought, "What a curious and different sort of letter this is!" And hoping to find some way to have a look at her, he made an arrangement with a certain Middle Captain whereby they disguised themselves as common women, proceeded to the home of the Inspector–Major Counselor at a time when he was out, and watched from a position by a latticework on the north side of the quarters where the lady resided. They noticed some boys who were doing nothing unusual, loitering about and walking among the grasses and trees, when one of them said, "Look! Here's a whole bunch of them crawling all over this tree! These are very fine ones!"

"Would you look at these?" they said, raising one of the blinds. "We've got some wonderful caterpillars for you!"

"Oh what fun!" said the lady in a brisk voice. "Bring them here!"

"I don't think we can sort them out. Would you just come and look at them here?"

At that she trod brusquely into the open.

As the men watched her push the blind outward and stare wide-eyed at the branches, they saw that she wore a mantelet over her head; and her hair, though the sidelocks made a pretty curve downward, had a prickly look about it, perhaps because she did not groom it, while her eyebrows stood out very dark in gaudy relief and looked crisp. Her mouth was attractively formed and pretty, but since she did not apply tooth blackening, it was most unconventional. One felt that had she used cosmetics she would certainly be good-looking. How depressing! What a pity it was to see that she had let herself go so badly, yet was not unattractive, but looked quite different from the ordinary, was remarkably genteel, and had an air of brightness about her. She wore robes of figured silk in pale yellow under the outer robe with a katydid design, and preferred her trousers white.[3]

She went out because she wanted to examine the worms as closely as possible. "What a splendid sight!" she said. "They are coming this way because it hurts them to be burned in the sun. Round them up, boys, and don't miss a single one!"

As the boys knocked them off they fluttered to the ground. She held out a white fan with calligraphy on it that she had practiced in black strokes of India ink. "Pick them up and put them on this," she commanded, and the boys got them out.

3. The pale colors were appropriate for a middle-aged or older woman.

The two gentlemen were appalled. "How extraordinary in a place that has misfortune enough!" they thought; and in their opinion of her, as far as the gentlemen were concerned, she was incredible.

One of the boys, who was standing there, looked at them suspiciously and said, "Over there alongside that latticework some good-looking but strangely dressed men are standing and peeking at us!"

"How awful! I fear Milady is exposed to view because of her interest in playing with vermin the way she does. I shall go and inform her," said Lady Tayū; and when she came into her mistress's presence she found her outside the blind as usual, shouting and having the caterpillars brushed off so that they fell to the ground. Since they frightened her very much, she announced without coming too close, "Come inside, Madam! The veranda is exposed to view."

Believing that she spoke only to restrain her from what she was doing, the lady replied, "Well, what of it! I am not ashamed."

"Oh, what a sorry business! Do you think I am lying? Why do you act this way when they say that some very magnificent-looking persons are over by the latticework! Come inside and look!"

"Mole Cricket, go over there and take a look!" said the lady.

He ran over and then reported, "They are really there!"

At this the lady jumped to her feet, and the caterpillars she gathered up and put into her sleeve before she ran inside. Her figure was nicely proportioned, and her hair fell very abundantly the full length of her robes. Since it was untrimmed at the edges, it did not form a cluster, yet it flowed evenly and looked only the more beautiful.

"Most people are not this well favored. Is it so regrettable that they try to improve their personal appearance and manner? One ought really to be repelled by her appearance, yet she is very nice looking and genteel, and it is surely only her troublesome qualities that make her different. Oh, how regrettable! Why does she have such a weird mind, and when she looks so nice too!"

So the gentlemen thought. The Assistant Director was highly dissatisfied with the prospect of just going away. He would at least let her know that he had seen her. Therefore he used the juice of a plant to write on a sheet of folded paper:

kawamushi no	Now that I have seen
kebukaki sama o	significant depths in caterpillar fur,
mitsuru yori	I have every hope

| torimochite nomi | that I may keep yours in hand for good |
| mamorubeki ka na | to watch and guard with tender care! |

He tapped with his fan, whereupon a boy appeared. "Present this to the lady," he said, giving it to him.

The lady called Tayū accepted it from the boy as he told her, "The person standing over there says to present this to Her Ladyship."

"Oh, how awful!" she said. "This does indeed seem to be the work of the Assistant Director of the Stables of the Right. He must have seen your face, Madam, while you were amusing yourself with those wretched bugs!" And she told her mistress a thing or two.

To which the lady replied, "When one thinks things through, one realizes that nothing is shameful. Who among men can stay long enough in this dreamlike and illusory world to look at bad things or look at the good and wonder about them?"

There was no point in saying anything to that, and her young people turned to each other in despair. The men stood by for a while on the off chance that there might be a reply, but the ladies called all the boys inside. "A sorry business!" they said to one another.

There must have been some among those present who understood what was required, for one of them did rise to the occasion and out of sympathy wrote:

hito ni ninu	The depths of a heart
kokoro no uchi wa	so unlike the hearts of other human
kawamushi no	beings
na o toite koso	I certainly wish to reveal;
iwamahoshikere	but only when I have asked the person's
	name
	as I do with caterpillars whom I do not
	know.

The Assistant Director recited:

kawamushi ni	No one at all
magiruru mayu no	could equal the tip of a single hair
ke no sue ni	growing on those eyebrows,
ataru bakari no	which are all but indistinguishable
hito wa naki ka na	from furry caterpillar forms!

Then, laughing, he apparently went home.

What happened next you shall read in Scroll Two.

Lampblack

In the lower part of the city, a man of no mean quality, whose affairs were not prospering as well as they might, had for years been living happily enough with a certain woman, when he took a fancy to the daughter of a friend of his while frequenting their house, and was visiting her in private. Perhaps because of the novelty of the experience, he felt a deeper regard for the girl than for the wife he already had, and took so little care to keep from being seen when he visited her that her parents got wind of it. "Even though he has a wife of long standing, how can we stop him?" they said and left him alone with her.

His regular wife heard about it and kept wondering what to do. "This looks like the end," she thought. "They will hardly be satisfied just to have him visit her. I wish there were somewhere I could go. I must leave him before he makes my life totally unbearable." But she had nowhere to go.

The new woman's parents put their views forcefully: "Here we had a young man with no wife or anybody, who was eager to have her, and we should have married her to him. But then you started coming like this much against our will! It is really too bad, but since it would do no good to say anything, we have been letting it go on. But it makes us uneasy the way society is talking about it. 'A man who already keeps a wife!' they say. 'Even if he says he loves her, he will certainly set greater store by the one he keeps at home.' That's what they say, and they're right too!"

"I don't count for as much as most people, I admit," said the man. "But at least in my regard for your daughter, I doubt that you will find anyone who loves her more than I. If you feel slighted because I haven't moved her to my place, I'll move her right now. You really surprise me!"

"Do that much for her at least," they urged; and in the face of such insistence he could only wonder, "Alas, where am I to send the other one?"

Even though he was sad at heart, the new woman was more important to him; therefore, he decided to tell the old one what was happening and see how she would take it, and with that he went home to her.

The sight of her, refined and angelic, if slightly haggard from days of worrying, moved him to pity. It pained him to see her so subdued, too embarrassed to speak to him as she usually did; but since he had made that promise, he said, "As far as my regard for you is concerned, that has not changed; but I started seeing her like this without letting her parents know, so I keep on going because I feel sorry for her. When I think how unbearable it must be for you, now I reproach myself. Why did I ever do it, I wonder. But I really can't see any way for a clean break now. They keep telling me to move her here because they will have to violate the soil over there.[4] What do you think? Are you wondering whether to go away? How can it hurt for you to stay here? You can stay on the same as you are, in a side room, you know. Where would you go if you sneaked away all of a sudden?"

"I guess he is telling me this because he means to bring her here," the woman thought. "She has parents and family, so she doesn't need to live here! What a thing to have him talk like this when it is perfectly plain that I have had nowhere to go for years!"

Although she despaired to think what he was doing, she answered unconcernedly, "Of course, you should. Move her as soon as possible. I will go away somewhere or other. Certainly it will be enough for me to have lived all these years without concern and free of the cares of the world."

The man felt so sorry for her that he added for her sake, "Why do you talk like this? It's not for good but only for a while. When she goes home I will bring you back." And after he had left, the woman spent the rest of the day weeping alone with her maid.

"The ways of the world are misery! What should I do? If that woman forces her way in here, I will look positively cheap in front of her. That would be too degrading. It may be a terrible-looking, low place to live in, I know, but I will go to Imako's house in Ōhara. I don't know anyone else." (The Imako she mentions must be a woman whom she used to employ.)

"That hardly seemed to me the sort of place you could stay in for a moment, Madam. Even so, you might go there for the time being until something better comes along."

So they discussed it together, and the sorrow she felt as she had the maid sweep the house and clean up was so intense that she wept and wept as she gave her personal letters and things to burn.

Since the man was busy getting ready to move the new woman in on

4. "Violating the soil" might offend the Earth God, who inhabited the kitchen fire-place in spring, the gate in summer, the well in autumn, and the yard in winter. If it was necessary to build or make repairs in the quarter the god happened to be occupying, the

the very next day, she could not easily make known to him what she needed. "Whom shall I borrow a carriage from?" she wondered. "Certainly I ought to ask him to escort me." It was absurd to ask for help now, but she sent word to him anyway: "I would like to go somewhere tonight, so if I could have the carriage for a while . . ."

When the man received the message he thought, "Alas, where does she plan to go? I must at least see her as she leaves." And he came promptly to her unobserved.

She was sitting near the veranda waiting for the carriage. In the bright moonlight she wept incessantly.

wa ga mi kaku	Could I have thought
kakehanaremu to	that I would be torn away
omoiki ya	from home like this,
tsuki dani yado o	when even the moon is settled here
sumihatsuru yo ni	forever serene in the house?

She was weeping as she spoke; and when at that moment he arrived, she acted as if nothing were the matter and remained seated with her face turned away.

"You wanted the carriage," he said. "But there is a problem with the ox. I can give you a horse."

"It's only a short distance, so it would be overdoing it to take a carriage. Well, the horse will do. But I must be going before it gets late."

At the urgency in her voice he felt how very sad it all was, but since everybody seemed to expect him the next morning at the other place, he could hardly get out of it; and so, regretting every moment, he had the horse led out, and it was brought up to the veranda. When she stepped forward to mount, he noticed how tiny she appeared in the brightly shining moonlight, how glossy and very pretty her hair looked as it fell the length of her figure. As the man helped her to mount with his own hands and went around arranging her clothing, she felt terribly unhappy, but controlled herself and said nothing. The way she looked as she sat on the horse, the tilt of her head, was so very beautiful that he was moved to say, "I will come along too, and escort you."

"I can manage," she said. "It is quite close. I will send the horse back

---

family moved elsewhere to avoid the consequences of disturbing him and stayed away until the work was completed.

soon. You wait here until then. It is such a shabby place that I could not have you see it."

"I suppose so," he thought, and stayed behind, seated on the edge of the veranda.

She did not have a lot of people accompanying her; she left with one page boy whose company she had been long accustomed to. As long as the man watched her, of course, she hid her feelings bravely, but as soon as the horse was led out the gate she wept bitterly on the road; until the boy was much affected, and as they proceeded farther, with the maid showing the way, he said, "You said it was quite close, Madam. How come you are going so far without anyone to accompany you?"

As it was a mountainous area and no one was abroad, she rode on weeping, feeling quite forsaken; while back home the man, too, sat deep in thought, all alone in the run-down house, and felt such a fondness for the memory of that most beautiful woman who used to live there that he found himself wondering of his own accord what she must be thinking on her journey, until, with the gradual lengthening of time, he had lain back on the veranda with his legs hanging down.

The woman arrived before midnight. She found the house to be very small.

"How can you mean to stay in such a place, Madam?" said the boy, looking at it with very evident regret.

"Hurry and take the horse back," she told him. "Your master must be waiting."

"If he asks me where you have put up, Madam, how shall I answer?"

"Tell him this," she said weeping.

izuko ni ka	If anyone asks
okuri wa seshi to	whither you attended her,
hito towaba	you have come as far
kokoro wa yukanu	as the disheartening river of tears,
namidagawa made	where the heart, withal, does not
	consent to go.

The boy was weeping too when he heard this, and mounting the horse, he arrived back home in a short while.

The man started from his sleep and saw that the moon had at length come close to the rim of the mountains. "Strange how late he is coming back! They must have gone a long way all right!" The thought affected him so much that he said aloud:

> suminareshi   Oh, this longing
> yado o misutete   aroused by the light of the setting moon
> yuku tsuki no   as it goes away,
> kage ni ōsete   abandoning to solitude a house
> kouru waza ka na   where once it was wont to dwell serene!

And just then he noticed that the boy had returned. "This is very strange. Why have you come back so late? Where were you?" he asked; and when the boy told him her poem, the man was so stricken that he broke into tears.

"Her not crying when she was here, why that was only pretending she didn't care!" The realization moved him so deeply that he decided to go after her and bring her back; and he said to the boy, "I never thought she was going to such a horrible place! Why, in a place like that she'll just waste away and die! Now I'm sure that I must go after her and bring her back."

"Oh, she kept weeping without letup, did Milady, all the way there!" said the boy. "What a shame when she deserves better!"

"We must get there before daylight," the man said, and, with the boy accompanying him, reached the place very quickly.

The house was indeed very small and run-down. The sight of it saddened him; and when he knocked, the woman, who had lain weeping new tears ever since her arrival, sent someone to ask who it was.

> namidagawa   That river of tears,
> soko to mo shirazu   not knowing where to find it,
> tsuraki se o   I kept crossing
> yukikaeritsutsu   and recrossing pitiless shallows,
> nagarekinikeri   until at last I have drifted here!

When she heard this spoken in the man's voice, the woman was caught completely unawares, and was amazed not least to recognize the voice.

"Open up!" he said; and although they had no idea what he was doing there, they opened the door and let him in. He came over to where she lay and confessed his fault in tears, but she kept weeping throughout without so much as answering him.

"I can scarcely tell you everything I want to say now. Certainly I never thought you would come to a place like this when I sent you away. If anything, it is rather you who have been a great trial and embarrassment to me. I will tell you everything later when we have time. Let's get back before daylight," he said, and gathering her in his arms, he put her on the horse and departed.

The woman was taken totally by surprise and went home all confused, wondering what had gotten into him. He helped her dismount, and they went to bed together. He comforted her on every score. "I will never go there again," he said. "To think that you feel this way!"

He loved her more than anyone in the world, and sent word to the person whom he had intended to move into the house: "I fear this is a bad time to have you over right now, because someone here is sick. It would be improper. I will come for you when this is over." And since he stayed home all the time, her father and mother were left to wonder in sorrow. His wife, on the other hand, thought herself as happy as if she were living in a dream.

This man was very impulsive by nature. "I won't be long," he said, and went off to his new woman's house in daylight. When they saw him come in, a sudden cry went up: "The Master is here!" The woman, who at the time was taking her ease, started up excitedly. "My box! Which one is it? Where is it?" she said; and, drawing her comb box to her, she meant to powder her face, but took out a packet of lampblack by mistake and was dressing herself up without even looking in the mirror.

"Tell him to wait a moment where he is. Not to come in," the woman said, and as she coated her face heedless of what she was doing, the man lifted the blind.

"My, you are quick to turn a fellow away, aren't you!" he said, and came in. She hid the packet and, with the makeup spread hit or miss, concealed her mouth behind her sleeve, and in the gathering dusk sat blinking about goggle-eyed, with fingerprints of the stuff splotched on her face, believing that she had made herself presentable. The man looked at her in amazement and wonder. She was such a fright that he could not think what to do; and so, without going near her, he said, "All right, I'll come back later on." For even a brief look was so scary that he quit the house.

The woman's father and mother had come to her room on hearing that he had arrived, but were told he had already left. "What a lack of sensibility!" they said in blank surprise; and when they looked at the young lady's face, they were startled to see it so scary. It was so bad that even her father and mother collapsed with fright.

"Why are you carrying on like this?" the daughter asked.

"Your face," they stammered, but could not find the words to ask what had happened to it.

"Strange. Why are they carrying on like this?" she wondered, and looked in the mirror. The reflection she saw there frightened her too, and she threw the mirror away, crying in tears, "What has happened to me? What has happened to me?"

The whole house was thrown into an uproar. "They're supposed to be doing everything they can over at his place to put him off from this girl. So see what has happened to her face because he was here!" And so they called in a diviner and were making a great fuss over her, when, noticing that her skin was normal where the tears had run down, her nurse crumpled up a piece of paper and wiped her face; and with that the skin was back to normal again.

It is certainly most amusing, the commotion they made because they thought she had been ruined over a thing like that.

Heian and Medieval Setsuwa

The eight tales below are drawn from two setsuwa collections, *Tales of Times Now Past* (Konjaku monogatari, ca. 1120?) and *A Collection of Tales from Uji* (Uji shūi monogatari, ca. 1210–20?). The first is a huge compendium containing more than 1,000 tales in thirty-one numbered books, three of which (8, 18, and 21) are missing. Books 1–5 consist of tales from India, almost all of them related to Buddhism; Books 6–7 and 9–10, of Buddhist and secular tales from China; Books 11–17 and 19–20, of Japanese Buddhist tales; and Books 22–31 of Japanese secular tales, concerning, respectively, the Fujiwara clan, feats of strength, masters of the arts and crafts, warriors, the workings of karma, the supernatural, humorous incidents, criminals and animals, love, and strange happenings. The collection is thought to have been put together by one or more monks for use as a preachers' handbook.

A Collection of Tales from Uji contains 197 stories, many of them humorous or concerned with the supernatural. About 40 percent of the total are related to Buddhism in one way or another, but the collection as a whole is less didactic in tone than *Tales of Times Now Past*. Nothing is known of the compiler.

The first four tales are from *Tales of Times Now Past* (16: 28, 25: 12, 27: 2, and 30: 5); the last four, from *A Collection of Tales from Uji* (78, 79, 125, and 166).

Tales of Times Now Past

How a Pilgrim to Hatsuse Acquired Riches Through Kannon's Aid

Once in the past, there was a young samurai in the capital who had no father, mother, wife, children, or friends. He went to Hatsuse and addressed the statue of Kannon. "I am a poor man with no resources at all. If my whole future is going to be like this, I'll starve myself to death in front of you. If there is any chance that you might help me a little, tell me so in a dream. I'll never leave here unless you answer me." He prostrated himself and lay face down.

"Who are you, talking this way?" the monks at the temple demanded. "We don't see that you have anything to eat. You would defile the temple if you died here. Who is your master?"

"I'm a poor man; how could I have a master? Kannon is the only one I can rely on. I don't have anything at all to eat," he said.

The monks assembled in conference. "This man is trying to intimidate Kannon by refusing to go away. It could be a serious matter for the temple; we'd better all see that he gets fed," they decided. They took turns feeding him. Thus sustained, he never left his place in front of the image, but stayed there resolutely, day and night, for thrice seven days.

Toward dawn on the twenty-first night, the man had a dream in which a monk emerged from inside the curtains to speak to him. "It is exceedingly improper of you to pester Kannon like this, just as if you didn't know that your poverty is the result of sins in a former life. But the bodhisattva will give you a little help for compassionate reasons. When you leave the temple, keep whatever touches your hand; be aware that it is a gift you are receiving," he said. After that, the man awoke.

Next, the man went to ask for food at the cell of a monk who had befriended him. He ate and started off. At the main gate, he tripped and fell on his face. When he rose, supporting himself with his hands, he clutched something that proved to be a piece of straw. "How could this be the bodhisattva's gift?" he thought. But he started home with it because of the dream. Meanwhile, a new day dawned.

As the man went on his way, a bothersome horsefly began to circle around his face. He broke off a branch from a tree and chased it away, but it came back again. He caught it by the leg, tied it in the middle with his piece of straw, and carried it along. Bound at the waist, the insect made frantic efforts to fly.

Presently, an aristocratic lady from the capital came riding toward the man in a carriage. She was accompanied by a pretty young child who was sitting with the blind rolled up. "What's that man carrying? Ask him to give it to me," the child said.

A samurai on horseback came over to the man. "You, there! The young master wants the thing you're carrying. Give it to me."

"This was a present from Kannon, but since it's called for in this way, I'll give it to you." The man handed it over.

"He was very nice about giving it up," said the people inside the carriage. They offered him three big tangerines wrapped in fragrant, thick, white crepe paper. "You're probably thirsty. Eat these," they told him.

"A single piece of straw has turned into three big tangerines," the man thought. He tied the fruit to a branch, shouldered it, and went on.

After a time, the man saw an important-looking gentleman who was traveling incognito, making a pilgrimage on foot to Hatsuse with a group of samurai. The gentleman was stumbling with fatigue. "My throat is parched. Get me some water to drink. I feel faint," he said.

In great agitation, the members of the party rushed around looking for water nearby, but there was none to be had. Just as they were at their wits' end, the man with the tangerines strolled up.

"Do you know a place near here where there's clean water?" they asked.

"There's no water nearby. What's the matter?" the man said.

"Someone on his way to Hatsuse is tired from walking and his throat is dry. We're looking for water."

"I have three tangerines. I'll give them to you," he said.

They awakened the master, who had fallen into an exhausted sleep, and gave him the tangerines. "A fellow here is giving you his tangerines."

"I was dying of thirst," the master said. He ate the tangerines. "I would probably have fallen by the roadside if it hadn't been for these. What splendid luck! Where is the fellow?" he said.

"He's here."

"What can I do to make him happy? Have our people brought up the food? Send him on his way with a meal."

No sooner had the master's instructions been conveyed to the man than some people came into sight leading pack animals. They proceeded to erect curtains and lay mats in preparation for the noonday meal. They also fed the man.

The master gave the man three bolts of spotless cloth. "Words cannot express my appreciation for those tangerines. It's impossible to repay you adequately while I am traveling; this is a mere token of what I intend to do for you. I live at Such-and-such place in the capital. Be sure to call on me there," he said.

The man took the cloth, put it under his arm, and went on in high spirits. "The one piece of straw has turned into three bolts of cloth. Kannon must be helping me," he thought. At nightfall, he sought shelter in a small dwelling near the road. When dawn came, he jumped up and continued on his journey. During the Hour of the Dragon [7:00 A.M.—9:00 A.M.], he met a man on a fine horse who was loitering along the way, putting the beast lovingly through its paces. As he watched in admiration, the horse suddenly collapsed and expired. The dismayed owner dismounted, tore off the saddle, and tried to think of something to do, but it was all in vain. The horse was dead. The owner transferred the saddle to a nag from his entourage and rode off, vexed enough to clap his hands and weep.

One of the owner's servants had been left behind with orders to drag the body away and hide it. The man with the cloth walked up to where he was standing guard over the dead animal. "What kind of horse could it be that would die so suddenly?" he asked.

"The master thought he had a real treasure when he brought it to the capital from Mutsu Province. Lots of people offered to pay anything he asked for it, but he wouldn't give it up, and now he hasn't even got two bolts of cloth out of it. I'd like to skin off the hide, at least, but I don't know what I could do with it while we're on this trip, so I'm just standing here guarding the carcass."

"I was thinking what a wonderful horse it was when it dropped dead. Living things are strange! I don't suppose you could dry the hide right away, even if you did take it off. I live around here; I can take it off and put it to some use. Give the horse to me and go on home," the man said. He offered him a bolt of cloth.

"This is a gain I didn't expect," the servant thought. He seized the cloth and took to his heels like a fugitive, afraid the man might reconsider.

The man must have bought the dead horse because he thought, "Thanks to Kannon's oracle, I got a piece of straw that changed into three tangerines. Then the tangerines became three bolts of cloth. Maybe this dead horse will come back to life and the three bolts of cloth will turn into a horse." He washed his hands, rinsed his mouth, and bowed toward Hatsuse. "If this has happened through your aid, restore the horse to life at once," he prayed.

The horse opened its eyes, raised its head, and tried to get up. The man went over, took hold of it, and helped it to its feet. In great glee, he led it to a secluded spot in case anyone happened along, and there he let it rest until the end of the hour. When it had returned to its old self, he led it to a local house, exchanged a bolt of cloth for a cheap saddle, mounted, and started off toward the capital.

The sun set while he was in the vicinity of Uji, so he stopped at a house and converted his last bolt of cloth into food and horse fodder. When morning came, he went on to the capital.

In the neighborhood of Kujō Avenue, he noticed a house where people were hurrying around as though someone were setting out on business. "If I take this horse farther into the city, someone may recognize it and accuse me of stealing it. That would be awkward; I think I'll sell it here. A horse is a necessity at a place where a person is setting out on a trip," he thought. He dismounted and went over to the house. "Would you like to buy a horse?" he asked.

The master had just been looking for a mount. He was delighted to see such a splendid beast. "I don't happen to have any silk cloth on hand at the moment," he said. "Would you be willing to exchange it for some fields in a paddy area south of here, plus a little rice?"

"I need silk cloth, but I'll do as you ask because you need a horse," the man said. The master mounted, tried the horse out, and found it ideal. He bought it for two and a half acres of fields in his Kujō paddy area, plus a little rice.

After arranging about the bill of sale, the man went to stay in the house of an acquaintance in the capital, where he used the rice to feed himself. Two months later, when the rice was gone, he agreed to let a local farmer cultivate his fields in exchange for half the crop, which became his source of sustenance.

The man went on to establish a household and lead a happy life, blessed by one piece of good luck after another. Well aware that he owed everything to the Hatsuse Kannon, he made constant pilgrimages to the temple.

This shows that Kannon's miracles have few parallels. So the tale has been told, and so it has been handed down.

How Minamoto no Yorinobu's Son Yoriyoshi Shot Down a Horse Thief

Once in the past, there was a warrior named Minamoto no Yorinobu. This Yorinobu learned that a certain man in the east possessed a superb mount. He dispatched someone to ask for the horse, and the owner had no choice but to send it off toward the capital. A horse thief saw the animal on the way, coveted it, and slunk along behind in the hope of stealing it. But the members of the warrior escort never relaxed their vigilance, and the thief had to follow the party all the way to the capital without accomplishing his purpose on the road. The warriors left the horse in Yorinobu's stable.

With matters in this state, someone told Yorinobu's son Yoriyoshi, "They've brought our lord a superb mount from the east today."

"Some fellow who doesn't deserve that horse may get my father to give it to him. I'd better look at it first. If it's really a superb mount, I'll ask for it myself," Yoriyoshi thought. He went to his father's house that very evening, braving a torrential downpour in his eagerness to inspect the horse.

"Why haven't I seen you for so long?" Yorinobu said. Then it occurred to him that Yoriyoshi had probably heard about the horse and come to ask for it. He continued before Yoriyoshi could answer. "They tell me a horse has arrived from the east, but I haven't seen it yet. The man who sent it said it was a superb mount. It's too dark to see anything tonight. Look at it tomorrow and take it away if you like it."

Yoriyoshi was delighted that Yorinobu had anticipated his request. "All right, I'll stand duty here tonight and look at it in the morning," he said.

In the early part of the night, the two talked; later, Yorinobu went into his bedroom and slept while Yoriyoshi rested nearby.

Around midnight, the horse thief entered the grounds under cover of the noise made by the rain, which was still falling. He got the horse, led it out, and left.

Minamoto no Yorinobu's son Yoriyoshi shoots down a horse thief
(*Tales of Times Now Past*, 25.12)

There were shouts from the direction of the stables. "A horse thief has gone off with the horse they brought this evening!"

When Yorinobu heard the faint cries, he did not say to Yoriyoshi, "Did you hear that?" He sprang to his feet, pulled on a robe, tucked up his skirts, donned a quiver, and ran to the stables. Then he personally led out a horse, saddled it with a cheap saddle that happened to be handy, mounted, and set out in pursuit, heading toward the Ōsaka Barrier mountain. He probably chose that direction because he thought, "The thief must have been an easterner who coveted that superb mount and followed it to the capital, unable to steal it on the way. He has taken advantage of the rain to make off with it."

Yoriyoshi, who also heard the shouts, thought as his father thought and followed the same course of action. Without a word to Yorinobu, he sprang to his feet, donned his quiver (he had slept in his clothes), and set out in pursuit alone, heading from the stables toward the barrier mountain. The father thought, "My son will undoubtedly come in pursuit." The son thought, "My father has undoubtedly gone ahead in pursuit."

Yoriyoshi galloped his horse, eager to catch up. Once he had passed the Kamo riverbed, the rain stopped and the sky cleared. He galloped even faster, and presently he arrived at the barrier mountain.

The thief was riding the stolen horse through some water near the mountain. No longer worried about pursuit, he was splashing along at a walk instead of galloping hard. Yorinobu hear the noise. Although it was too dark to see whether Yoriyoshi was there or not, he spoke up, just as though the two had arranged from the start to act at that spot. "Shoot! There he is!" A bow twanged before the last word left his mouth, and there was the sound of a hit, together with the clatter of stirrups on a horse running riderless.

Yorinobu uttered a few brief words. "You've shot the thief. Hurry up! Gallop after the horse and bring it back." Then he went home without waiting for Yoriyoshi to come back with the horse.

Yoriyoshi galloped after the animal, overtook it, caught it, and started back. Retainers who had got wind of the affair came to join him as he returned, one or two at a time. There were twenty or thirty of them when he arrived at the house in the city.

It was still dark when Yorinobu reached home, so he went back to bed without knowing how things had turned out. Yoriyoshi entrusted the repossessed horse to the retainers and went to bed too.

The next morning, Yorinobu emerged from his quarters and called Yoriyoshi in. He did not say, "Congratulations! You kept the horse from being stolen. That was a fine shot," or anything of the sort. He merely told his men to lead the horse out. They did so, and Yoriyoshi saw that it was indeed a superb mount. "Thank you. I'd like to have it," he said.

Although the subject had not been mentioned on the previous evening, the horse carried a splendid saddle. I wonder if Yorinobu meant it as a reward for shooting the thief in the night.

Those are hard people to understand, but such is the warrior mentality. So the tale has been told, and so it has been handed down.

How Retired Emperor Uda Confronted
the Spirit of the Kawara-no-in
Minister of the Left Tōru

Once in the past, there was a house called the Kawara-no-in, the residence of Minister of the Left Tōru. The Minister had laid out his garden to resemble Shiogama in Mutsu Province, filled its lake to the brim with sea water, and otherwise arranged things in the most splendid and tasteful manner imaginable. After his death, his descendants gave the property to Retired Emperor Uda. The Retired Emperor went there to live, and Emperor Daigo, his son, honored the mansion with occasional visits.

One night around midnight during the Retired Emperor's term of residence, there came a sound as of someone opening the storeroom in the western wing chamber, followed by the swish of approaching skirts. The Retired Emperor looked in that direction and saw that a man in formal daytime attire, with a sword at his waist and a baton in his hand, had seated himself respectfully two bays away.

"Who are you?" the Retired Emperor asked.

"I am the elderly master of this house."

"Lord Tōru?"

"Yes."

"Why are you here?"

"This is my house; I live in it. With all respect, your presence is inconvenient. I don't quite know what to do."

"This is very strange. I certainly wouldn't seize possession of somebody else's house; I am here because your descendants gave it to me. Whether you're a spirit or not, what you say is unreasonable!" the Retired Emperor shouted.

The spirit disappeared in an instant and was never seen again.

When the facts became known, the people of the day talked about the Retired Emperor in awed voices. "He is no ordinary mortal. Nobody else could have stood up to Lord Tōru's spirit like that," they said. So the tale has been told, and so it has been handed down.

How an Impoverished Man's Deserted Wife
Became the Spouse of the Governor of Settsu

Once in the past, there lived in the capital a poverty-stricken man of inferior status. Because he possessed no friends, parents, kinsmen, or dwelling, he took service in someone else's household. Then, having failed to find favor there, he moved from place to place in search of a better situation. But it was the same everywhere, and he was left with no recourse whatever, unable even to obtain employment in a noble household. In despair, he spoke to his wife, a young, pretty woman of gentle disposition who had followed him faithfully.

"I had always hoped that we would be together like this for as long as we lived in the world, but we get poorer every day. Maybe we're poor because it's a mistake to stay together. It's my feeling that we ought to separate and try our luck apart. What do you say?" he asked.

"I don't agree at all. I've been resigned to starving with you because I thought our plight was karmic retribution from a previous existence. But please go ahead and leave me. Then you can see whether all this ill fortune has been caused by our staying together," she said.

"That's the thing to do," the man thought. With a promise to meet again, the two went their separate ways in tears.

After that, the wife, who was young and pretty, entered the service of a person called ———. Her master liked her because of her gentle disposition. After his wife's death, he made her his personal attendant and mistress and loved her dearly; and in time, he recognized her as his wife and placed all the household affairs in her charge.

Meanwhile, the master became the Governor of Settsu. The woman lived a splendid life. But her first husband had fallen on worse and worse times after deserting her to seek his fortune alone. At last, unable to remain in the capital, he wandered off to Settsu Province and became a humble farm worker. He did not know how to till paddies, cultivate dry fields, cut wood, or perform other menial agricultural tasks, so his master sent him to Naniwa Bay to cut reeds. While he was at work there, the Governor of Settsu went to the province with his wife. The Governor halted his carriage near Naniwa, strolled around, ate and drank, and otherwise amused himself, attended by a throng of retainers and kinsmen. His wife remained in the carriage to enjoy the interesting scenery at Naniwa Bay with her ladies-in-waiting.

Among the many laborers cutting reeds along the shore, there was one fellow who appeared to have seen better days. The Governor's wife stared at him, struck by his resemblance to her former husband. She looked hard again, wondering if she might be mistaken, and decided that it was undoubtedly he. "Alas!" she thought as she watched the shabby figure cutting reeds. "He's as feckless as ever. What karma from a previous life has brought him to this?" Tears filled her eyes to overflowing, but she summoned an attendant in an unconcerned manner.

"Call over one of those reed-cutters, that one there," she said.

The messenger ran to the man. "You're wanted by someone in the carriage." The man straightened up in amazement.

"Get a move on!" the messenger shouted in a threatening voice. The man dropped his reeds, tucked his sickle into his waist, and presented himself in front of the carriage. When the Governor's wife observed him at close hand, there was no question about his identity. He wore a dirt-blackened sleeveless hemp singlet, cut off at the knees, and a semiformal cap like a commoner's hat. His dirt-encrusted face, hands, and feet were indescribably filthy, and his shanks and the backs of his knees were spattered with blood where leeches had sucked them. Upset by the sight, the lady told someone to give him food and drink, which he gobbled down in a repulsive manner as he faced the carriage. Then she sent him out a robe, explaining to the ladies-in-waiting in the carriage that she had felt sorry for him when she saw him among the reed-cutters; he looked as though he had seen better days. She wrote this poem on the edge of a piece of paper:

ashikaraji	You went away from me,
to omoite koso wa	thinking you would not fare so ill
wakareshika	if we were apart.
nado ka naniwa no	Why, then, are you dwelling here
ura ni shi mo sumu	by the Bay of Naniwa?

The man was astonished by the gift of the robe. Inspecting it in amazement, he saw something written on the edge of a piece of paper. He picked up the paper and read the poem. "Ah! That lady is my former wife. What a miserable, humiliating turn of fate!" he thought. After requesting the loan of an inkstone, he presented this reply:

kimi nakute	Harder than ever,
ashikarikeri to	this existence by the Bay
omou ni wa	of Naniwa,
itodo naniwa no	when I think how ill I have fared
ura zo sumiuki	since we two have been apart.

The Governor's wife felt sadder than ever. The man abandoned his reed-cutting and ran away into hiding. Thereafter, the Governor's wife did not mention the subject to anyone.

People utter foolish complaints about their lot through ignorance of the fact that everything is determined by karma from a previous existence.

Might the Governor's wife have related the story in her old age? At any rate, people learned of it and repeated it. So in these later generations the tale has been told, and so it has been handed down.

A Collection of Tales from Uji

The Mimuro Archbishop and the Ichijōji Archbishop

Also in the past, there were two esteemed prelates of the Miidera school, the Ichijōji Archbishop and the Mimurodo Archbishop. The Mimurodo Archbishop was the fourth son of Governor-General Takaie; the Ichijōji Archbishop was the fifth son of Major Counselor Tsunesuke. The Mimurodo Archbishop was called Ryūmyō, the Ichijōji Archbishop Zōyo. Both were holy living Buddhas.

The Mimuro Archbishop was a man of portly figure. Unable to fare forth and practice austerities, he remained steadfastly in front of his temple's principal image, his bell ringing day and night as he performed the rituals. The occasional visitor always found the gates closed. By knocking on the gate, a caller could sometimes scare up an attendant, who would ask, "Who is it?" Upon being told, "So-and-so has come," or "It is a messenger from the Retired Emperor," the attendant would say, "I shall inform His Reverence," and go inside.

The bell would keep on ringing for a long time. When it stopped, a functionary would unbolt the gate and open one half just wide enough to admit a single person. Inside, the visitor would behold a pathless court-yard overgrown with vegetation. Then, making his way through the dew to the hall, he would reach a small outer eavechamber, only one bay wide, with sliding screens at the corner doorway, their paper sooty and ancient-looking. Presently, a black-robed monk would appear on noise-less feet. "Please wait a little while. His Reverence is performing rituals just now." After a short delay, a voice would speak from the interior. "Please enter." Incense smoke would drift out as the visitor opened the sooty sliding door. The Archbishop, clad in a wrinkled robe and a torn surplice, would remain silent, and the visitor would sit opposite him without quite knowing what was happening. Then the Archbishop would fold his arms and lower his eyes. When a short time had elapsed, the visitor would be told, "The prayers you wanted have been said. Please go home right away." He would leave, his message unspoken, and the gate would be locked again. Archbishop Ryūmyō was a man whose religious observances all took place inside his temple.

The Ichijōji Archbishop had twice traversed the Great Peaks. He performed a ritual that made a snake appear, and he could conjure up visions of dragons with horses' legs and other improbable things. The congestion outside his dwelling extended for one or two blocks, *dengaku* and *sarugaku* players assembled in great numbers, and Escorts and Impe-rial Guardsmen came and went all the time. When someone came to sell a saddle, sword, or other piece of property, the Archbishop always paid whatever price was asked. His grounds turned into a veritable market-place, and he accumulated all kinds of treasures.

This reverend monk was very fond of a certain young acrobat at the temple, a boy whom he had first seen helping with the field planting at Toba. (At the Archbishop's suggestion, one of the other planters, a man who had performed on stilts earlier, had astonished the spectators by coming out from behind a tent with the boy standing on his shoulders in the modern fashion.)

In an excess of affection, the Archbishop said to the boy, "It's no good this way. Become a monk and stay with me day and night."

"Well, I don't know," said the boy. "I think I'd like to go on as I am for a while." But the infatuated Archbishop insisted, and the boy yielded against his will.

Time passed, and the spring rains began to fall. Bored by the constant drizzle, the Archbishop called in one of his people. "Do we have the costume the boy used to wear?" he asked.

"Yes, it's still in the storeroom."

"Get it out and bring it here," he said.

When the costume was produced, the Archbishop told the boy to put it on.

The boy demurred. "It wouldn't look right."

"Just put it on," the Archbishop insisted.

The boy retired to a corner, put on the robes and the dance helmet, and came out, looking exactly as he had in the old days. The Archbishop's face puckered up at the sight, and the boy's own face looked different.

"Do you recall the steps?" the Archbishop asked.

"No, I don't—but I remember a little of the 'Katasarawa' because I performed it so often." The boy danced and leaped his way through one of the patterns. Then, helmet in hand, he crossed the room in one-beat time.

The Archbishop sobbed. "Come here," he said, and began to fondle him. "Why did I force you to become a monk?" He wept as he spoke.

"That was why I wanted to wait a while," the boy said.

The Archbishop had the boy remove the costume and took him into an inner room. I can't say what happened after that.

How a Monk Stole and Ate Whitefish in Someone's House

Also in the past, a certain monk went to someone's house. The host offered wine and brought out some whitefish, which had just come into season, as a special treat. Something came up that required the host's presence inside for a while. When he returned, he saw to his surprise that an amazing number of the whitefish had disappeared, but it was awkward to bring the matter up. Then, as the two sat talking, a whitefish suddenly emerged from one of the monk's nostrils.

"What's this?" the astonished host said. "A whitefish has come out of your nose."

"These whitefish nowadays keep falling out of people's eyes and noses all the time," the monk shot back in an instant.

Everyone burst out laughing.

A monk eats whitefish (*A Collection of Tales from Uji,* Sec. 79)

How Yasusuke Robbed People

Also in the past, there was a younger brother of the Tango Governor Yasumasa, Yasusuke by name, who was a Military Guards Lieutenant of Fifth Rank. This Yasusuke was the captain of a band of robbers. Far back in the grounds of his house, which was situated south of Ane-ga-kōji and east of Takakura, he had built a storehouse over a pit as deep as a well. He would call in all kinds of people with things to sell—swords, saddles, armor, helmets, silk, and ordinary cloth—and would agree to buy their wares at the asking price. Then he would say to his men, "Pay this fellow; take him back to the storehouse." When the seller went, expecting to receive payment, the gang would call him inside the storehouse, push him into the pit, and keep the goods he had brought. Nobody who took things to Yasusuke's house ever returned. Other sellers thought it was odd, but nobody revealed the truth because everyone who knew about it died in the pit.

Furthermore, this Yasusuke went boldly out into the city streets to commit robberies. There were vague rumors about his activities, but somehow he was never caught and arrested.

The Prodigious Strength of Ōi no Mitsutō's Younger Sister

Also in the past, there was a wrestler called Ōi no Mitsutō of Kai Province, a man outstanding in appearance, character, and every other respect—short but solid, tenacious, strong, and fast on his feet. He had a younger sister who was a slender, pretty woman of twenty-six or twenty-seven, with a pleasant disposition and gentle manners. She lived in a house separate from his.

One day, a fellow who was trying to evade pursuers dashed inside the sister's gate, took her hostage at swordpoint, and pressed his weapon against her belly. A member of the household went running to tell the master, Mitsutō, "Someone has taken Her Ladyship hostage."

Mitsutō was not in the least perturbed. "A man would have to be as strong as Ujinaga of Satsuma if he wanted to make her a hostage," he said.

Puzzled, the other went back and peered out from behind something that offered concealment. As befit the time of year, which was the Ninth Month, the sister was wearing a set of lavender robes and an autumn-leaf divided skirt. She had raised her sleeve to hide her face. Her captor, a huge, fearsome fellow, had clamped his legs around her from the rear and was holding a long sword against her belly with a backward grip.

The sister wept with her face hidden by her left hand. But with her right hand, she toyed with a pile of twenty or thirty unfinished bamboo arrow shafts that happened to be lying in front of her. Using a finger to grind the joints against the wooden floor, she pulverized them as easily as a person might crush soft, rotten wood.

The robber panicked at the sight. "Her brother, the famous strong man, couldn't even do that with a hammer. There's something weird about strength like hers. The next thing I know, she'll be mashing *me* flat. This is terrible; I've got to get away from here," he thought. He waited until the others had relaxed their vigilance for a moment; then he leaped out and fled. People pursued him, seized him, and took him to Mitsutō.

"Why did you run away?" Mitsutō asked.

"I was amazed when Her Ladyship crushed the big joints on those arrow shafts like rotten wood; I got scared and ran away," he said.

Mitsutō burst out laughing. "You'd never have been able to run her through, no matter what you did. If you had tried it, she'd have grabbed your arm and twisted it until the shoulderbone popped out of the socket. Your arm would probably have been torn right off. It must have been karma from a previous existence that saved you. I could kill you with my bare hands myself. Would you still be alive after I twisted off your arm and stamped on your belly and chest? But my sister is as strong as two of me. If I lay a hand on her in fun, she grabs my arm so hard that I lose my grip and she gets away, even though she looks so slim and ladylike. If she were a man, nobody could stand up to her. What a pity she's a woman!"

The robber felt faint. He had taken the sister for an ordinary woman, an ideal hostage, but his plan had been a disastrous failure.

"I ought to kill you, but I'll let you go because my sister was in no real danger," Mitsutō said. "You saved your life when you ran off. She can put a big deer antler across her knee and snap it like a twig from a dead sapling—that's how strong she is!" He let the man go.

Women Memoirists of the
Medieval Period

The first of the two selections below is taken from *The Confessions of Lady Nijō* (Towazugatari, ca. 1310?), a memoir covering the period from 1271, when the author was thirteen, to 1306, when she was forty-eight. During thirteen of those years, described in the first three of the work's five books, Lady Nijō acted as a lady-in-waiting and concubine to Retired Emperor Go-Fukakusa (1243–1304; r. 1246–59). In 1283, she was dismissed from the Retired Emperor's palace, and by 1289, the first year recorded in the fourth book, she had become a Buddhist nun. Her life thereafter alternated between travel in the provinces and residence in the capital area, where she met the Retired Emperor on three occasions, and where, in 1306, she attended Buddhist services marking the second anniversary of his death, the last event she discusses.

Unlike most of the authors represented in this volume, Nijō belonged to the highest stratum of the aristocracy. Her paternal grandfather was a Chancellor; her father, Major Counselor Masatada (1228–72), was the head of the Minamoto clan, on the verge of becoming a Minister of State at the time of his death; and her mother was the daughter of a Major Counselor and the niece of both a Chancellor and an Honorary Empress. But she was orphaned at the age of fourteen, and the loss of paternal support, together with the hostility of Go-Fukakusa's principal consort and her own indiscreet conduct, finally made her position at the Retired Emperor's palace untenable.

One of the causes of Nijō's downfall may have been her involvement with Go-Fukakusa's brother, Emperor Kameyama (1249–1305; r.

1259–74). Although the *Confessions* usually depicts the two men as friendly, their relationship was actually far from cordial, as Nijō occasionally hints. In 1259, after having abdicated thirteen years earlier in favor of the three-year-old Go-Fukakusa, their father, Go-Saga (1220–72; r. 1242–46), had forced Go-Fukakusa to cede the throne to Kameyama, who was then ten. Nine years later, in 1268, Go-Saga arranged for Kameyama's son, rather than Go-Fukakusa's, to be named Crown Prince; and in 1272, after Go-Saga's death, the Kamakura shogunate recognized Kameyama, rather than Go-Fukakusa, as the head of the court. In 1274, Kameyama abdicated in favor of his son, Go-Uda (1267–1324; r. 1274–87), and began to reign through a new Retired Emperor's Office. To placate the incensed Go-Fukakusa, the shogunate agreed to make his son Crown Prince. The son, Fushimi (1265–1317; r. 1287–98), acceded in 1287, whereupon Go-Fukakusa angered Kameyama by establishing his own Retired Emperor's Office. Two years later, Fushimi's son, the future Go-Fushimi (1288–1336; r. 1298–1301), became Crown Prince, an event that drove Kameyama to take Buddhist vows. By the last date in the *Confessions*, a son of Go-Uda, Go-Nijō (1285–1308; r. 1301–8), was on the throne and the succession was alternating between Go-Fukakusa's descendants, the so-called Jimyōin line, and Kameyama's, the Daikakuji line.

The first book, translated below, describes Lady Nijō's life at court from the beginning of 1271 to the end of 1274, the year in which the future Emperor Fushimi became the Crown Prince.

The second selection is a complete translation of *The Journal of the Sixteenth-Night Moon* (Izayoi nikki, 1279–80), by the nun Abutsu (ca. 1220–83). Almost nothing is known of Abutsu's early childhood other than that she was the adopted daughter of Taira no Norishige, a provincial Governor. As a young girl, she served in the palace of Princess Ankamon'in (1209–83), a granddaughter of Emperor Takakura (1161–81; r. 1168–80), where she bore the name [Ankamon'in no] Shijō. When she was around eighteen, an unhappy love affair led her to retire from society, but by the middle of the thirteenth century she had met and married the much older Fujiwara no Tameie (1198–1275), after having given birth to two sons and a daughter of unknown paternity. She took the name Abutsu when she became a nun after Tameie's death.

Tameie sired two sons by Abutsu, Tamesuke (1263–1328) and Tamemori (1265–1328), in addition to four by an earlier marriage— Tameuji (1222–86), Tamenori (1227–79), and two who became monks. Himself a man of mediocre literary talent, he had inherited the headship of the Mikohidari, a poetic school made famous by his distinguished grandfather and father, Shunzei (1114–1204) and Teika (1162–1241), to whom Abutsu alludes with pride in her memoir. The school had lost much of its luster in his day and was soon to split into the three lines that dominated the later history of the waka—the Nijō, Kyōgoku, and Reizei, descended, respectively, from Tameuji, Tamenori, and Tamesuke.

As the strong-willed favorite of her husband's old age, Abutsu was able to secure many of the Mikohidari archives for her sons. She also persuaded Tameie to bequeath rights in his Hosokawa estate (a property in Harima Province) to Tamesuke, rather than to Tameuji, to whom the estate had been promised, but a dispute over the property developed after his death, with Tameuji refusing to cede it and Abutsu pressing her son's claim. In the Tenth Month of 1279, Abutsu went to argue the case in Kamakura, where she seems to have died, her mission unaccomplished.

Abutsu is best known for *The Journal of the Sixteenth-Night Moon*, which begins with an account of her fourteen-day trip along the Eastern Sea Road to Kamakura, records poems exchanged with correspondents during her stay there, and ends with a long poem (*chōka*) reiterating the importance of the Mikohidari heritage and the righteousness of her suit, two of the work's recurrent themes. She was also the author of many poems, including forty-eight in imperial anthologies, and of *Dozing* (Utatane, ca. 1240?), a short confessional memoir describing her youthful disappointment in love.

The Confessions of Lady Nijō

[*Eighth Year of Bun'ei: 1271*]

Spring with its seasonal haze arrived overnight, and the ladies-in-waiting sat in rows on the long-awaited morning, each wearing a magnificent costume designed to eclipse all the others. I joined them, attired, if I remember rightly, in seven budding-plum inner robes, a red outer robe, a green mantle, and a red formal jacket. My two short-sleeved underrobes were woven in a plum-blossom and vine pattern and were embroidered with plum blossoms and Chinese fences.

My father, Major Counselor Masatada, served the imperial medicinal draughts to Retired Emperor Go-Fukakusa. After the end of the formal ceremonies, the Retired Emperor had the participants come inside and summoned ladies-in-waiting from the Table Room for an informal party. The men had already drunk nine rounds during the ceremonies—three from each of three bowls. Father proposed the same number again, but His Majesty said, "This time, it shall be nine threes!"

After everyone was befuddled, the Retired Emperor gave Father the imperial bowl. "Let this spring be the time when the wild goose sheltering on your field comes to me," he told him.[1] Father made a deep bow. Again, His Majesty made a confidential remark as Father was about to withdraw after accepting the final round. I saw it all but had no way of knowing what was going on.

When I returned to my room after the Felicitations, I found a note. "From this day forth, I hope to tread where the snow lay yesterday." It was accompanied by a cloth-wrapped package containing eight lined robes in colors shading from red to white—also a red singlet, a green mantle, a jacket, a divided skirt, a set of three inner robes, and another set of two robes. Startled and disconcerted, I was preparing to return everything when I noticed a poem on a thin piece of paper attached to one of the sleeves:

tsubasa koso	Although we may fail
kasanuru koto no	to emulate birds with wings paired
kanawazu to	in conjugal bliss,
kite dani nare yo	accustom yourself, at least,
tsuru no hagoromo	to wearing these crane-feathered robes.

It seemed unfeeling to reject a gift offered in such a spirit, but I sent it back with a poem and a note:

yoso nagara	Would I do well
narete wa yoshi ya	to wear these robes at night
sayogoromo	all by myself?

---

1. An allusion to *Tales of Ise*, Sec. 10.

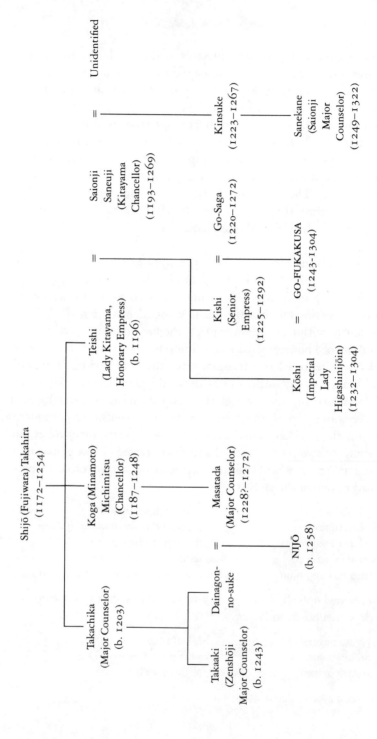

Principal characters

itodo tamoto no	Surely the time would come
kuchi mo koso sure	when tears would rot the sleeves.

"Perhaps if your affection were really to endure . . ."

Someone rapped softly on the rear door toward midnight, while I was away on night duty. The unsuspecting little maid opened it, and an unseen hand thrust something inside. It was the same package with another poem:

chigiriokishi	If in the future
kokoro no sue no	you will be true to the pledge
kawarazuba	spoken in the past,
hitori katashike	please lie abed at night
yowa no sagoromo	with these garments spread alone.

It would have been awkward to send it away again, so I kept the things.

I wore the new robes on the Third, when Priestly Retired Emperor Go-Saga came to visit His Majesty. "The colors and luster of your robes are remarkably beautiful," Father said. "Were they a gift from His Majesty?" It was upsetting, but I managed a show of indifference. "No, they came from Lady Tokiwai," I said.[2]

On the evening of the Fifteenth, someone came from Kawasaki with word that he had been instructed to escort me there.[3] It was inconveniently short notice, but I could not very well demur. To my surprise, everything looked much grander than usual when I reached the mansion. The folding screens, the matting, and even the curtain-stands and room hangings seemed to have been chosen with special care. I supposed that it must have something to do with New Year. So the day ended.

The next morning, people rushed around with talk of a repast of some kind, and there were consultations concerning courtiers' horses and senior nobles' carriages. My step-grandmother, the nun, arrived and engaged in whispered conversations.

"What's going on?" I asked.

Father smiled. "His Majesty has declared that he will come here tonight to avoid a directional taboo, and we're taking special pains because it's the New Year season. I've brought you home to serve his meal."

2. Lady Tokiwai was Nijō's great-aunt.
3. Kawasaki, an area east of Ichijō and Kyōgoku avenues near the west bank of the Kamo River, was the site of one of Masatada's houses.

"This isn't the date of the seasonal change. What kind of taboo is it?" I asked.

Everyone laughed. "Listen to the child!" they said.

For a reason I could not have been expected to divine, some especially splendid folding screens and curtain-stands had been brought to the room where I always stayed. "Why are these decorations so elaborate? Is His Majesty going to see this room too?" I said. People laughed, but nobody gave me a clear answer.

At dusk, someone delivered three white singlets and a deep red divided skirt, which I was instructed to wear. The room was perfumed to an extraordinary degree. After the lamps had been lit, my stepmother brought in a beautiful short-sleeved robe for me to put on.

Father appeared a little later. He fiddled with the robes on display. "Hold yourself in readiness until His Majesty comes; don't go to bed. A lady-in-waiting should never act willful; she must be perfectly obedient," he said. I had no way of understanding what prompted the admonition. Vaguely annoyed, I leaned against a brazier and dozed off.

Just what happened next I cannot say. His Majesty arrived without my knowing it. Father busily supervised the placement of the carriage and the like. When the food came, he said in a flurry, "That worthless girl has gone to sleep. Wake her up."

His Majesty overheard. "It's all right. Let her sleep," he said. So nobody disturbed me.

After having leaned for a while against the brazier just inside the sliding door, I had fallen into a sound sleep with a robe over my head. Some time later, I started awake to find the lamps dim, the curtains apparently drawn, and a man lying near me at his ease, just inside the doorway. In a panic, I tried to rise and flee, but he held me down. "You've haunted my thoughts ever since you were a little girl. I've been waiting for you to turn fourteen." He said other things—so many that I have no words to record them all—but I merely wept without listening. My tears drenched his sleeves, to say nothing of my own. Unable to soothe me, he did not resort to force but said, "I've felt frustrated for so long that I decided to seize this opportunity. Other people must have made assumptions about us by now. Do you think a display of coldness is likely to end the relationship?"

I realized that he was right. It was not a secret tryst but a matter of public knowledge. And would not tonight's brief dream prove a source of misery tomorrow? Looking back now, I am astonished that I should have been so prescient.

Why couldn't the Retired Emperor have explained what he was going to do? Why didn't he talk it over with Father, I asked myself. "I'll never be able to show my face again," I wailed. His Majesty laughed, amused by my naïveté, and I felt worse than ever. I did not even answer any of his remarks for the rest of the night.

A stir outside indicated that dawn had come. "Isn't His Majesty supposed to go home this morning?" someone said.

"I'll be leaving just as though this had been a real tryst," His Majesty remarked half to himself. As he prepared to rise, he addressed me with mingled annoyance and compassion. "This quite unexpected behavior has made me feel that it was a waste of time to pledge my devotion back in those days when you wore your hair parted in the middle. I advise you to avoid a manner others might consider strange. People are bound to wonder if you shut yourself off from everybody." I made no answer.

"It's hopeless." He got up and put on his informal cloak. His attendants called for the carriage, and I heard Father ask, "Will you have some rice gruel?" It was as though Father were another person; I could not endure the thought of seeing him again. If only I might have recaptured yesterday's innocence!

Even after I heard people saying His Majesty had left, I stayed there with the robe over my head. A letter arrived with disconcerting speed. My step-grandmother and stepmother came in to ask why I was still in bed. Distressed by their questions, I said, "I haven't been feeling well since last night." They seemed to take it for granted that I was merely suffering from bridal nerves, which made me feel still more forlorn. The letter was produced with much fuss, but I was in no mood to read it.

"You're keeping His Majesty's messenger from going back. What about your reply?" people said in consternation.

"We'd better tell the Major Counselor," someone suggested. I found it all unbearable.

Father came in. "They say you're ill."

The others pressed the letter on him. "What kind of nonsense is this? Do you intend to let it go unanswered?" I could hear him opening it as he spoke. It was a poem inscribed on thin purple paper:

amatatoshi   For many long years,
sasuga ni nareshi   you have been as dear to me
sayogoromo   as a well-worn robe:
kasanenu sode ni   I prize the lingering scent
nokoru utsuriga   on the sleeve I spread alone.

When the others saw the poem they all said, "She isn't a modern girl." It was too depressing; I could not bring myself to get up. Father apparently decided in some agitation that a reply by proxy would seem ruder than no answer at all. I gathered that he merely gave the messenger a present and said, "My childish daughter is still asleep; she hasn't read His Majesty's kind letter yet."

A letter from an unexpected quarter arrived around noon:

ima yori ya   If the smoke plume's tip
omoikienan   ends by trailing away
hitokata ni   in one direction,
keburi no sue no   the fire of hopeless longing
nabikihatenaba   must surely snuff out this life.

"Unhappy though my existence has been, I've managed to go on in the hope that we might exchange vows some day, but what am I to do now?" The thin, dark blue paper was decorated with a colored design in which I could make out the words of an old poem, ". . . that I may no longer feel the anguish of love."[4] I tore off the bit where "Mount Concealment" appeared and sent it back with this:

shirareji na   You cannot know
omoimidarete   the innermost feelings
yūkeburi   of the evening smoke,
nabiki mo yaranu   its heart too uncertain
shita no kokoro wa   to drift in one direction.

I could not help realizing that I was being indiscreet.

The day drew to a close. I refused to swallow anything, even hot water, and my attendants told one another that I must truly be ill. At twilight, I heard people announcing His Majesty's arrival. No sooner had I begun to wonder what would happen this time than the door opened and he entered with a nonchalant air. "They say you aren't feel-

---

4. Fujiwara no Masatsune (SKKS 1094): kiene tada / shinobu no yama no / mine no kumo / kakaru kokoro no / ato no naki made ("Let me simply die, that I may no longer feel the anguish of love as secret as the name of cloud-veiled Mount Concealment").

ing well. What's the matter?" he asked. I merely lay there, unwilling to answer. He stretched out beside me and murmured all kinds of endearments. There seemed little alternative to saying, "If this were a world . . ."[5] But I also felt that it would be too heartless to disregard the emotions with which someone else would learn that the evening smoke had suddenly trailed off in one direction. At my wits' end, I made no reply at all.

His Majesty's behavior that night was callous. I think my thin robes must have ripped rather badly, but he did as he pleased with me. I hated being alive, hated even the dawn moon. The words of a poem kept running through my mind:

kokoro yori	When, in days to come,
hoka ni tokenuru	might gossip sully the name
shitahibo no	of someone whose robes
ika naru fushi ni	have had their strings unfastened
ukina nagasan	though her heart did not consent?

How strange that I should have foreseen the future so clearly at such a time!

The Retired Emperor showered me with reassurances. "The marital bond transcends rebirth. I may not be with you every night, but you will always be in my heart," he said. Meanwhile, the sound of the dawn bells announced the close of the spring night, too short even for dreams. He got up, telling me he did not want to inconvenience the household by lingering in bed.

"Even though you may not be sorry to see me go, won't you at least come out to say good-bye?" he urged. My sleeves were drenched with the tears I had shed all through the night, but I shrugged on a thin singlet and went outside, unable to refuse so small a favor. It was the hour when the Seventeenth-night moon sinks toward the west while horizontal clouds trail in the east. What tutelage might have been responsible for the sudden attraction I felt as I looked at him standing there in a red-lined green-banded hunting robe, a lavender inner robe, and a pair of bound-patterned baggy trousers? I marvel at the complexity of a woman's heart.

My uncle, Major Counselor Takaaki, brought up the carriage. He

5. Anonymous (KKS 712): itsuwari no / naki yo nariseba / ika bakari / hito no koto no ha / ureshikaramashi ("If this were a world in which there were no such things as false promises, how great would be my delight as I listened to your words!").

was wearing a blue hunting robe. The single courtier in attendance was Lord Tamekata, who was an Assistant Chief in the Auditors' Office at the time. There were also two or three junior North Guards and some minor palace functionaries. A rooster heralded the dawn with knowing crows as the carriage arrived, and the sound of the bell from the Kannon Hall seemed to echo in my sleeves. I wondered if Prince Genji might have felt the same way when he composed the poem, ". . . my left sleeve and my right."[6]

His Majesty lingered. "I'm going back all alone; please keep me company awhile," he pleaded. Even though it seemed presumptuous to fret over my inability to probe his mind, I stood there in confusion while the bright late moon gradually lost its color.[7]

"Ah, it worries me to see you looking like that," he said. He swept me into the carriage, and we started away before I could so much as leave word of my departure. It was like an old romance. But what would the future bring? I composed this poem:

> kane no oto ni   Dawn moon in the sky:
> odoroku to shi mo   how grievous the memory
> naki yume no   of the dreamlike night
> nagori mo kanashi   when no temple bell was needed
> ariake no sora   to arouse one who had not slept!

On the way to the palace, he promised to love me always, quite as though he were a man who had just abducted a woman. A dispassionate observer would probably have found the situation delightfully intriguing, but I felt more and more miserable as the journey progressed. There was nobody to tell me what the future held—not unless it might have been the tears I shed.

We arrived at the palace. The men took the carriage to the middle gate of the Corner Palace,[8] and His Majesty alighted. "She is such a helpless child that I couldn't bring myself to leave her alone; that's why

6. Ushi to nomi / hitoe ni mono wa / omōede / hidari migi ni mo / nururu sode ka na ("It is not as though sadness alone fills my heart: my left sleeve and my right have been dampened by tears of two different kinds"). Genji, living in Suma, is moved both by the unhappiness of exile and by fond memories of imperial kindnesses.

7. "Probe his mind" is an allusion to a poem addressed to Genji by Yūgao in *The Tale of Genji*: yama no ha no / kokoro mo shirade / yuku tsuki wa / uwa no sora nite / kage ya taenamu ("May its light perhaps vanish in mid-heaven—the journeying moon, unable to probe the mind of the rim of the hills?"). "How do I know you won't desert me?"

8. A building in the southeast corner of the compound at Go-Fukakusa's palace, the Tomi-no-kōji Mansion.

I've brought her with me," he said to Takaaki. "I don't want anyone to know about it for the time being. Look after her." He entered his private apartments.

I felt threatened and ill at ease in the palace, which did not seem at all like the familiar place where I had served since my childhood. If only I had refused to come! I broke down in tears, unable to stop worrying about the future. As I wept, I heard Father's voice and wondered, with a twinge of pity, if he might be feeling anxious about me. Takaaki told him what the Retired Emperor had said. "She's been put in an ambiguous position," Father answered. "It would have been better to let her go on serving him as usual. There will be unpleasant gossip when the truth comes out." I felt trapped and miserable as I listened to him leave. What indeed lay ahead for me? Then His Majesty entered the room and swore over and over that he would never stop loving me. In spite of my misgivings, my spirits gradually rose. Perhaps our relationship was the predestined result of a karmic bond.

His Majesty visited me for ten nights running. Foolishly enough, I could not help worrying about how the author of the smoke-plume poem must be feeling. Meanwhile, Father kept telling His Majesty that I ought not to stay in the palace under such circumstances, and so I went home. Unbearably sensitive to the eyes of others, I kept myself apart on the pretext of a lingering indisposition.

An affectionate letter arrived from His Majesty. "I miss you dreadfully after having seen you so often. Come soon." His poem:

kaku made wa	You cannot love me
omoiokoseji	as much as I love you.
hito shirezu	I yearn to show to you,
misebaya sode ni	unknown to others, these sleeves
kakaru namida o	drenched with the tears I shed in secret.

Although I had found his letters distasteful in the past, I greeted this one eagerly and happily. I am afraid my answering poem may have sounded a bit artificial:

ware yue no	I cannot think myself
omoi naranedo	the one for whom you yearn,
sayogoromo	but my sleeves, too, are wet
namida no kikeba	when I hear of the tears
nururu sode ka na	moistening your robe at night.

Before long, I went to the palace to resume my regular duties.

Already beset by vague misgivings, I soon found myself the object of malicious gossip. "The Major Counselor thinks nothing is too good for her," people said. "He presented her to the Retired Emperor with as much ceremony as if she had been a Junior Consort." And life began to seem bleak indeed when the Imperial Lady Higashinijōin showed herself increasingly displeased. I simply got through the days as best I could.

I was in no position to complain about the Retired Emperor's failure to visit me at night, but it was disappointing to wait in vain time after time. Nor could I very well grumble like my companions about the women who visited him from outside the palace, but I rebelled inwardly against the conventions whenever I had to escort one of them. Was the time likely to come when I would recall this period in my life with nostalgia?[9] The days went by and autumn arrived.

The approach of Higashinijōin's confinement, which was to take place in the Corner Palace, was causing concern because of the Imperial Lady's relatively advanced age and history of difficult births. I believe the time was around the Eighth Month. Every conceivable large ritual and secret ritual had been commissioned—prayers to the Seven Healing Buddhas and the Five Mystic Kings, prayers to Fugen for the prolongation of life, prayers to Kongō Dōji and the Mystic King Aizen, and so on. At Father's special request, he assumed responsibility for the prayers to Kongō Dōji this time, in addition to the ones to Kuṇḍalī, which had always been supported by Owari Province in the past.[10] The exorcist was the Jōjūin Bishop.

Shortly after the Twentieth, there were agitated reports that the birth was impending. There ensued two or three days of breathless waiting, which reduced everyone to a state of frantic anxiety, and then word was sent to the Retired Emperor that there seemed to have been a change for the worse. His Majesty went inside and saw that the Imperial Lady looked alarmingly weak. He told the exorcist to pray just outside the curtain-stand. He also called in His Reverence of Omuro, who had been serving as chief officiant at the Aizen altar. "She doesn't look as though she can survive. What shall we do?" he asked.

"The Buddhas and bodhisattvas have vowed that bad karma-results

9. Fujiwara no Kiyosuke (SKKS 1843): nagaraeba / mata kono goro ya / shinobaremu / ushi to mishi yo zo / ima wa koishiki ("If I live long enough, will I recall these days, too, with nostalgia? I cherish the memory of a time that once seemed hard").

10. Masatada had been granted the revenues from Owari Province.

can be changed into good ones. I'm sure she won't die." The monk began to pray.

The exorcist hung a picture of Fudō in front of the Imperial Lady—possibly the very one that had saved Shōkū's life.[11] Rubbing his beads, he intoned, "An ascetic who serves Fudō is the same as a Buddha; a monk who achieves command of the mantra enjoys Fudō's eternal protection." In a mighty effort to subdue the possessing spirits, he rubbed his beads again. "Long ago, when I was a boy, I devoted my nights to prayer in the hall; now that I am a man, I spend my days in difficult, painful austerities. Can there be no divine response, no divine protection in return?" he said.

There were signs that the Imperial Lady was about to give birth. Encouraged, the monk redoubled his exertions, praying hard enough to raise smoke. All the ladies-in-waiting passed out singlet sets and raw silk robes under the blinds to the presiding official, who handed them over to courtiers. Members of the North Guards presented them to the recitants.

The senior nobles sat below the stairs, looking as though they were hoping for a boy. The yin-yang masters put an eight-legged table in the courtyard and performed the thousandfold purification. Courtiers picked up the ritual articles, and ladies-in-waiting thrust out their sleeves to receive and transmit them. Escorts and junior members of the North Guards led in sacred horses, which His Majesty inspected and dispatched to the Twenty-one Shrines as offerings. How fortunate the Imperial Lady seemed! We felt that anyone born into this world as a human being and a woman would want to be exactly like her.

His Majesty summoned the chief officiant from the Seven Healing Buddhas altar and ordered him to have the *Healing Buddha Sutra* chanted by three junior officiants with especially fine voices. The birth took place just as the three intoned, "The beholders rejoice."

Amid all the congratulations inside and outside the hall, the rice steamer rolled toward the north.[12] It was a disappointment for the Retired Emperor, but the exorcist received the usual series of rewards.

11. Fudō, one of the Five Great Mystic Kings of esoteric Buddhism, was said to have saved Shōkū, a prelate favored by Go-Saga, when the monk offered his own life in exchange for that of his dying teacher.

12. A sign that the baby was a girl. *The Tale of the Heike*: "When an Empress gives birth, it is customary to roll a rice steamer down from the ridgepole of the building she occupies, directing it to the south for a Prince and to the north for a Princess."

Although the baby was a girl, Priestly Retired Emperor Go-Saga made a great fuss over her. The fifth and seventh nights after the birth were observed with particular splendor. On the seventh night, the two former sovereigns chatted in Retired Emperor Go-Fukakusa's apartments after the celebratory banquet. Around the Hour of the Ox [1:00 A.M.– 3:00 A.M.], there was a tremendous noise in the Orange Tree Courtyard—a sound like storm-driven waves crashing onto a rocky shore.

"What's happening? Go and look," His Majesty said to me. When I went out, I saw ten ladle-shaped, bluish-white objects streaking through the air, their heads ranging in size from plates to earthen vessels, and their long, slender tails shining with dazzling brilliance. I fled inside, aghast.

"Why are you so upset?" asked the senior nobles in the eavechamber. "They were only meteors."

But then a voice shouted, "Something that looks like seaweed starch is scattered under the big willow tree."

The diviners were put to work at once. They reported that Priestly Retired Emperor Go-Saga's spirit had been wandering, and spirit-summoning rituals were begun that very night, along with prayers to the Taishan deity.

Around the Ninth Month, we heard that the Priestly Retired Emperor had fallen ill. His body swelled and he seemed to fail daily, despite constant frantic applications of moxa. Thus the year ended.

[Ninth Year of Bun'ei: 1272]

The New Year season brought no improvement in the patient's condition. It was a far from festive time.

Late in the First Month, when the end seemed near, the Priestly Retired Emperor journeyed to the Saga Detached Palace by palanquin.[13] Retired Emperor Go-Fukakusa also went, and I sat in the rear of his carriage to attend him. The two Imperial Ladies shared a carriage, with Mikushigedono to see to their needs.[14] Medicinal decoctions, meant to be drunk on the way, had been prepared and put into two water flasks in

13. The Saga Detached Palace was Go-Saga's residence west of the capital.

14. The Imperial Ladies were the Senior Empress (Go-Saga's consort) and Higashinijōin (Go-Saga's adopted daughter and Go-Fukakusa's consort). Mikushigedono was one of Go-Fukakusa's mistresses.

the imperial presence by the physicians Tanenari and Moronari; and Nobutomo, a junior member of the North Guards, had been detailed by Tsunetō to carry them.[15] But both flasks turned out to be dry when the imperial attendants sought to administer their contents at Uchino. It was very strange. We heard that the former sovereign seemed worse after the incident, which must have made him feel more despondent than ever.

Retired Emperor Go-Fukakusa took up residence in the Ōidono Palace,[16] whence he dispatched men and women of all degrees by day and by night with anxious inquiries about his father's condition. Cold shivers ran down my spine when I heard the waters of the Ōi River as I traversed the long galleries on such errands.

By the beginning of the Second Month, the end seemed to be merely a matter of time. The two Rokuhara deputies paid a call around the Ninth, with the Saionji Major Counselor Sanekane transmitting their expressions of concern. The reigning sovereign, Emperor Kameyama, came on the Eleventh and stayed through the Twelfth. There was a stir in preparation for his departure on the Thirteenth, but no ceremonial music sounded in the hushed palace. The Emperor and Retired Emperor Go-Fukakusa both shed floods of tears when they met—a sight to make even a casual observer weep.

Around the Hour of the Cock [5:00 P.M.–7:00 P.M.] on the Fifteenth, a huge cloud of smoke rose in the direction of the capital. While we were all wondering whose house was on fire, someone said, "The South Rokuhara Lord Tokisuke has been attacked and killed. The smoke is from the fires that were set."[17] It was beyond words! The man who had paid the sick call on the Ninth had gone before the one whose every day seemed likely to be his last. We know well enough that some people die early in this world and some late, but I was deeply moved nevertheless. This latest manifestation of the law of impermanence remained unknown to the Priestly Retired Emperor, who had scarcely uttered a word since the night of the Thirteenth.

On the morning of the Seventeenth, we heard that the former sovereign's condition was critical. The news caused a great commotion.

15. Tsunetō, a Middle Counselor, was one of Go-Saga's close attendants (*kinshin*).

16. Part of the Saga Detached Palace complex.

17. The Hōjō Regent in Kamakura, Tokimune, had suspected his deputy Hōjō Tokisuke of conspiring against him.

Two spiritual guides, Archbishop Keikai and the Ōjōin Abbot, urged the dying man to call on the name of Amida Buddha. "As one who has occupied the throne and commanded the allegiance of all officialdom in his life on earth, you can feel confident about facing the future on the path of the dead. Go quickly now to your lotus pedestal on the highest level of the Pure Land; then look back and help those who remain behind in this world where you have dwelt," they said, alternating words of comfort with exhortations. But he seemed powerless to rid himself of worldly attachments or confess his sins. He breathed his last at the age of fifty-three, during the Hour of the Cock on the Seventeenth Day of the Second Month in the ninth year of Bun'ei, with no indication that he had heeded the advice of the holy men. The heavens darkened, the nation sorrowed, and flowery sleeves gave way to black garb.

The body was taken to the Yakusōin Hall[18] for cremation on the Eighteenth. A Head Chamberlain–Middle Captain came from the reigning sovereign's palace as an imperial messenger, and all of the dead man's priestly sons accompanied the cortege—the Omuro, Enman'in, Shōgoin, Bodaiin, and Shōren'in Princes. No brush could do justice to the sadness of that night. The Priestly Retired Emperor's special favorite, Tsunetō, had been expected to take religious vows and forsake the world, but he surprised everyone by wearing a soft crepe hunting robe as he carried away the cinerary urn.

Retired Emperor Go-Fukakusa's grief in those days was quite extraordinary. He wept day and night, and the spectacle of his misery moved his attendants to tears of sympathy, mere onlookers though they were. Because the country was in mourning for an imperial parent, we heard no timekeepers announcing the hour, no voices clearing the way for important personages. I wondered if the cherry trees at Kameyama might put forth charcoal-colored blossoms.[19]

Father had received permission to wear especially black robes.[20] He suggested to Retired Emperor Go-Fukakusa that it would be appropri-

18. A cloister in the Saga Detached Palace complex.
19. Kamusuke no Mineo, composed after the burial of the Horikawa Chancellor at Fukakusa (KKS 832): fukakusa no / nobe no sakura shi / kokoro araba / kotoshi bakari wa / sumizome ni sake ("If you have feelings, flowering cherries in the fields at Fukakusa, will you not just this one year put forth charcoal-colored blooms?"). Kameyama was a mountain near the Saga Detached Palace.
20. A mark of closeness to the deceased.

ate for me to go into deep mourning too, but His Majesty said, "She's very young. Let her dress like everyone else; there's no need for anything special."

Father made repeated applications to the Senior Empress and Retired Emperor Go-Fukakusa for permission to take Buddhist vows, but the two replied that they had their reasons for not consenting. He visited the grave daily, perhaps because he felt the loss more than others did. He also renewed his request to the Retired Emperor through an intermediary, Major Counselor Sadazane. "I enjoyed His Majesty's favor on every possible occasion, from the time when I first came to his notice and entered court service at the age of nine. I was especially grateful for his kindness when my stepmother charged me with unfilial conduct after my father's death, and I did my best to repay him with loyal service. Blessed with offices and ranks beyond my deserts, I smiled when I opened official communications on the mornings after appointments ceremonies; I performed my duties with a light heart, free of resentment and envy. I gazed with pleasure at the moon from the palace. Night after night, I joined the Toyo-no-akari drinking and dancing; for many years, I wore purification tunics at Special Festival rehearsals and saw my image reflected in the sacred stream. Now I hold Senior Second Rank, serve as the senior Major Counselor, and head my clan. When His Majesty died, I was just refusing his offer of a ministerial post, giving as my reason a document in which my older brother, Major Captain Michitada, had recommended prior service as a Major Captain in the Bodyguards. But now my patron has gone and I have nobody on whom to rely; I would gain nothing by remaining at court, no matter what office I might occupy. How many years are left to me at fifty? 'It is by severing the bonds of kindness and entering the realm of the eternal that we truly repay kindness.'[21] With your permission, I will become a monk and pray for His Majesty's welfare in the next life."

The Retired Emperor responded to this fervent plea with another refusal. He also discussed the matter with Father directly. So things went along, a day at a time. It was not that anyone ceased to miss the dead, but time slipped by while people worked day and night to arrange for the religious services and so forth. The forty-ninth day came, and everyone returned to the capital after the final rites.

21. From a verse chanted by those taking Buddhist vows.

Thenceforth, it was necessary to send messengers to Kamakura and otherwise deal with increasingly vexatious political problems. Soon the Fifth Month arrived.

Perhaps because the Fifth Month is always a time when dew besprinkles our sleeves, Father seemed more prone to tears than if the season had been autumn. He had never wanted to spend a night without a woman, but now he invariably slept alone. He also gave up drinking parties altogether. People wondered if it was his new way of life that was making him so thin. On the night of the Fourteenth of the Fifth Month, as he was returning in his carriage from listening to Buddha-invocations at Ōtani, one of his attendants said, "Your Lordship's face has turned quite yellow. I wonder why." This impelled him to consult a physician. The problem was diagnosed as jaundice (a disease that afflicted those who tend to brood, he was told), and a series of moxa treatments was begun. I could not help worrying about what might happen.

To my infinite distress, Father's health deteriorated steadily. Then, on top of everything else, I discovered around the Sixth Month that I was pregnant. Miserably ill though I felt, I could not very well say anything to Father in his condition.

Father refused to order prayers for himself. "I feel that I can't recover," he said. "I want to join His Majesty as soon as possible." On the night of the Fourteenth of the Seventh Month, after a brief sojourn in his Rokkaku Kushige house, he left the young children behind and moved to Kawasaki to prepare quietly for the end. I went to Kawasaki alone, considering myself a grown child. When he saw that I looked peaked, he began to comfort me because he thought I had been too worried to eat, but then he seemed to notice something.

"You must be pregnant!" he said. He resolved immediately to try to survive until the baby was born. For the first time, he commissioned all sorts of pious exercises—seven days of formal prayer to the Taishan deity at the Enryakuji Central Hall, seven field-music performances on the grass at the seven Hiyoshi shrines, a one-day summary reading of the *Great Wisdom Sutra* at Yawata, the construction of a stone pagoda on the Kamo riverbed, and so forth. I felt a deep sense of guilt as I witnessed all this activity, for it was motivated not by love of life but by a desire to see what the future held for me.

Since Father appeared to be in no imminent danger, I returned to the palace around the Twentieth. His Majesty was especially attentive after he learned of my pregnancy. If only there were reason to believe it would always be that way, I kept thinking. Too, it was frightening to remember Mikushigedono's death in childbed in the Sixth Month, a fate I might easily share. Nor did it seem likely that Father would pull through in the end—and what would become of me then? Gloomy thoughts filled my mind as the last days of the Seventh Month approached.

One night, around the Twenty-seventh or thereabouts, there happened to be fewer people in the palace than usual. His Majesty told me to accompany him to the deserted main hall, where he began to chat quietly about the past and the present. After a melancholy comment on the ephemerality of worldly things, he continued with tear-filled eyes. "I don't think there is any hope for the Major Counselor. You will have nowhere to turn if he dies; there will be nobody but me to care about you." His solicitude merely deepened my depression. There was no evening moon at that time of month, only the dim light from the lamps outside. Late at night, as the two of us talked alone in the dark room, we heard an agitated voice asking for me.

"Who is it?" I said.

"I've come from Kawasaki. It looks as though His Lordship may be dying."

I left at once, just as I was, and traveled with desperate speed, afraid that the end might already have come. The distance seemed as long as the road to the eastern provinces. To my great joy, Father was still alive when I reached the mansion. "The dew awaiting the wind has yet to vanish. I don't like to linger this way. But it worries me to leave with you pregnant." He spoke in a faint voice, weeping.

Just as the late night bells began to sound, we heard voices announcing the Retired Emperor. Even Father was excited by the news of the visit, which was completely unexpected. I hurried out when I heard the carriage being drawn up. His Majesty had come incognito, accompanied only by two junior North Guards and a single courtier. The bleak light of the late moon, which had just cleared the rim of the hills, sufficed to show that he had departed on the spur of the moment, clad in a lavender-banded hunting robe with a woven burnet design. It was a great honor.

Father sent out a messenger. "I lack even the strength to pull on a hunting robe, so I can't hope to receive Your Majesty. The news of your visit will be my most precious memory of this world." The Retired Emperor promptly opened the door and went inside. Father made a futile effort to rise.

"Stay where you are." His Majesty sat down on a cushion near the pillow and burst into tears. "You have been close to me ever since I was a child. When I heard that you were dying, I felt so miserable that I had to see you one last time."

"The happiness of your visit is far more than I deserve. But my heart aches with pity for this child. She lost her mother at the age of two, and I reared her in the knowledge that I was all she had. It's leaving her that upsets me more than all my other worries, especially now that she is pregnant. I can't express my grief and pity." Father wept bitterly as he spoke.

"The parting can't be prevented, but I'll take your place. Don't let anxiety bar you from the true Way." To these kind words, His Majesty added, "You must rest now." Then he left the room.

A little after daybreak, His Majesty said, "I can't let myself be seen looking this way." As he was making hurried preparations to depart, Father sent people out to the carriage with two gifts—an heirloom lute that had belonged to my grandfather, the Koga Chancellor, and a sword that had belonged to Retired Emperor Go-Toba, which I think the former sovereign had given to my grandfather around the time he went into exile. A piece of thin blue paper was attached to the sword cord:

wakarete mo	Although I must go,
miyo no chigiri no	I look to what lies ahead:
ari to kikeba	we are told that the bond
nao yukusue o	between lord and man endures
tanomu bakari zo	through past, present, and future.

"Ah, how sad! Don't worry about anything at all." His Majesty repeated the words over and over as he set out. An answer to the poem arrived very soon, written in his own hand:

kono tabi wa	When we meet again,
ukiyo no hoka ni	it will be far away
meguriawan	from this cruel world,
matsu akatsuki no	in that long-awaited dawn
ariake no sora	when the pale moon hangs in the sky.

It was somehow pitiful and moving to observe the joy with which Father concluded that he had liked the gifts.

Takaaki brought the sash of maternity very early—it was only the Second of the Eighth Month.[22] "When His Majesty gave it to me, he instructed me not to dress in mourning," he said. He wore an informal cloak, and his outriders and attendants were splendidly attired. I guessed that His Majesty had wanted to hasten the presentation so that Father could see it. Delighted, Father gave orders for Takaaki to be offered wine. It was sad to think that this might be his last memorable moment. His present to the envoy was a prized ox, Shiogama, which had been given to him by the Omuro Prince.

Father seemed a little better around that time. I wondered, as I sat with him one night, whether he might recover after all. The hour grew late. I stretched out beside him, intending to rest a minute, and began to doze. Then I started awake, and he said, "What an innocent girl you are! I am too worried about you even to grieve that I must tread an unknown path today or tomorrow, and now you make me feel worse by drifting off to sleep like a child."

He went on to speak at greater length than usual. "After you lost your mother at the age of two, I was the only one who worried about you. I have sired many other children, but I feel that you have received all the love 'due to three thousand.'[23] When I watch you smile, you seem to me to possess 'a hundred charms'; when you look unhappy, I share your sorrow. It's been this way for the springs and autumns of fifteen years, but now we're going to part.

"If His Majesty continues to favor you, take care to serve him faithfully. If his affection wanes and life in society becomes difficult, as may happen in this uncertain world, you must hasten to enter the true Way so that you may improve your lot in the next life, repay the kindnesses of your parents, and pray for our rebirth on the same lotus pedestal. If you should choose to remain in society by serving another master or by seeking protection in somebody's household, no matter

22. The presentation of the sash constituted the Retired Emperor's formal recognition of paternity.

23. An allusion to Bo Juyi's "Song of Everlasting Sorrow": "There were three thousand beauties in the Rear Palace, / But one woman received the imperial affection due to three thousand." "A hundred charms" in the next sentence echoes Bo's description of the same favorite, Yang Guifei.

whose, simply because you feel rejected and helpless, you must consider yourself disinherited, dead though I shall be.

"There's no denying that the conjugal bond outlasts a single life-time. But nothing could be more humiliating than for you to sully the honored name of our house by taking up with a man instead of becoming a nun.[24] Once you have left society, it will make no difference what you do." I thought miserably that these were the last admonitions I would ever receive from him.

When the dawn bell sounded, Nakamitsu came in with the usual steamed plantain leaves to be spread under the patient. "Let me replace the old ones for you," he said.

"It's almost over. There's no use doing anything. Just see that this child gets something to eat—it doesn't matter what," Father said. I wondered how I could force anything down at such a time, but he insisted, "Hurry, while I can still watch her." Ah, I thought, he may be here to see me this one time, but what of the future?

An attendant brought some chopped sweet potato balls in an un-glazed pottery dish. "Those are supposed to be bad for pregnant women," Father said, looking annoyed. I picked at the food and got rid of it to avoid trouble.

As dawn was breaking, Father told us to send for a holy man. Earlier, around the Seventh Month, he had summoned the Yasakadera Abbot, who had shaved his head, administered the Five Command-ments, and given him the Buddhist name Renshō, and since then he had planned to make that Abbot his spiritual guide on his deathbed, but now, for some reason, my grandmother insisted that we call Shōkōbō, the Kawara-no-in Abbot. We dispatched a messenger with word that Father was in critical condition, but Shōkōbō was slow to appear.

Meanwhile, Father said, "I'm dying. Lift me up." He summoned Nakamitsu to support him from the rear. (Nakamitsu was Nakatsuna's oldest son, a boy Father had reared and kept as a personal attendant.[25]) A lone lady-in-waiting sat to the front, and I sat to one side. "Take hold of my wrist," Father told me. I obeyed. He called for the surplice the holy man had given him, and we draped it over the upper half of a glossed silk *hitatare*, the only garment he wore. "I'm going to invoke the sacred

24. Presumably, such a relationship might stem from a similar one in an earlier life.
25. We learn later that Nakatsuna was the husband of Nijō's nurse.

name. You, too, Nakamitsu," he said. The two chanted for half an hour.

Just as the sunlight began to enter the room, Father dozed off, leaning a little to the left. I jogged his knee, intending to rouse him so that he could go on with the chant. He started awake, his eyes wide open, and the two of us exchanged a long look. "Ah, what will happen?" he said. He died as he spoke, early in the Hour of the Dragon [7:00 A.M.–9:00 A.M.] on the Third Day of the Eighth Month in the ninth year of Bun'ei. His age was fifty.[26]

Alas! There could have been no doubt about his future if he had died intoning Amida's name, but he had gone with other words on his lips because I had been foolish enough to rouse him. My brain felt paralyzed. When I looked up, the sky seemed as dark as if the sun and moon had fallen to earth; when I lay on the ground and wept, it seemed that my tears must bring forth a flowing river.

Although I had lost my mother at the age of two, her death had never preyed on my mind; it was merely something that had happened in the past, before I reached the age of understanding. But Father and I had spent fifteen years together, beginning with the forty-first day of my life, when I had nestled in his lap for the first time. When I consulted my mirror in the morning, it pleased me to see that I looked like him; when I dressed in the evening, I felt gratitude for his generosity. Greater than the height of Mount Sumeru was my obligation for the gift of life; deeper than the four seas was my debt for the care with which he had reared me in a mother's stead! How could I ever repay him? What could I do that would be enough? As I recalled the unforgettable words he had uttered on more than one occasion, it seemed to me that nothing could end the agony of this final parting.

I longed for a way to keep his body and witness its changes, but there is a limit to everything. We took the remains to Kaguraoka on the night of the Fourth. I would not have minded turning into smoke too, if only I might have set forth as his companion on the way. But such thoughts were of no avail, and I went home with the tears on my sleeve as my sole keepsakes. Gazing at the empty apartments, I remembered Father's appearance the day before. Ah, if I were ever to see him again, it would

26. If the text is correct here, Masatada was five years older than he is shown in two generally reliable early sources, *Kugyō bunin* and *Sonpi bunmyaku*, which both indicate 1228 as the probable year of his birth.

have to be in a dream. Even his last worries about my diet came to my mind again and again, evoking feelings that were quite beyond description.

wa ga sode no	O sea of tears
namida no umi yo	on my sleeve, please join your flow
mitsusegawa ni	to the Three Crossings stream:
nagarete kayoe	let me at least behold
kage o dani min	his reflection in the water.

On the evening of the Fifth, Nakatsuna came in wearing a monk's somber robes. I knew he must have counted on becoming a steward of Fourth Rank if Father were made a Minister of State—but now he suddenly appeared in this unexpected garb. "I'm going to visit His Lordship's grave. Do you have any message?" he said. The sight of his drenched black sleeve moved everyone to tears.

On the Ninth, the seventh day after Father's death, my stepmother, two of the ladies-in-waiting, and two samurai took Buddhist vows. The holy man from Yasaka had been summoned to officiate. I watched with inexpressible sorrow, tinged with envy, as the monk intoned, "Trans-migrating through the three worlds," and administered the tonsure. The thought of following their example never left my mind, but it was out of the question for someone in my condition. I merely lay prostrate, shedding futile tears.

The rituals marking the twenty-first day were celebrated with special magnificence. We received generous expressions of sympathy from Retired Emperor Go-Fukakusa. I wished sadly that Father might have been there to witness the arrival of His Majesty's messengers, who never missed a day.

The Kyōgoku Imperial Lady was Minister of State Saneo's daughter, Emperor Kameyama's Empress, and the Crown Prince's mother. Neither in status nor in age was she a person whose loss could be viewed with equanimity, but she had fallen ill—apparently, everyone surmised, through a return of the possessing spirits that had plagued her for so long—and now we heard agitated reports of her death. It was all too easy to understand her father's misery and the Emperor's anguish. My heart ached for them both.

When the thirty-fifth day arrived, Retired Emperor Go-Fukakusa sent a crystal rosary attached to a gold-and-silver maidenflower, with word that it was to serve as a prayer offering. Also attached was a slip of paper bearing a poem:

sarade dani	Tears of longing
aki wa tsuyukeki	for one who lives no more
sode no ue ni	must be drenching the sleeves
mukashi o kouru	these autumn dews would dampen
namida souran	even were it otherwise.

Knowing how much Father would have treasured such a message, I wrote, "I am sure he is overwhelmed with gratitude and happiness under the moss." My poem:

omoe tada	Please imagine
sarade mo nururu	how the white dew of autumn,
sode no ue ni	season of parting,
kakaru wakare no	drenches sleeves that would be damp,
aki no shiratsuyu	even were it otherwise.

Everything seemed a source of grief as I lay sleepless during the long autumn nights. The sleeves spread on my lonely bed were drenched with tears called forth by "a thousand blows, ten thousand blows" on the fulling blocks;[27] the image of the dead never left my mind's eye.

On the morning of Father's death, there were condolatory messages from the reigning and retired sovereigns and other members of the imperial family. The senior nobles and courtiers also called and sent messages. Major Counselor Mototomo was the only one who failed to observe the usual courtesies.[28]

On a moonlit night shortly after the Tenth of the Ninth Month, I received a visit from a person who had sent daily messages of inquiry, the first a solicitous note before dawn on that fateful Third. In mourning like everyone else, he wore a plain black informal robe, which made me feel as though he were expressing sympathy with my own dark attire. It seemed inappropriate to resort to an intermediary; I met him in the south apartment of the main hall.

"What with one thing and another, this has been a sadder year than most. One's sleeves never have a chance to dry," he said. "During a

27. From a poem by Bo Juyi: "Long, indeed, are the nights in the Eighth and Ninth Months; / A thousand blows, ten thousand blows, the fulling hammers never fall silent."

28. Mototomo, who appears to have been a political rival, succeeded Masatada as head of the Minamoto clan.

drinking party on a snowy night last year, your father asked me to look after you always. I could tell from that how much he loved you."

We spent the whole night in such talk, weeping and laughing. When the temple bell announced the dawn, I felt just as the poem says: "The length of an autumn night depends on one's companion." [29] The cocks crowed while there were still many things left unsaid.

"People will call this a most unusual morning farewell," he remarked as he took his leave. [30] Reluctant to see him go, I sent a maid to the carriage with a poem:

wakareshi mo	To that other grief
kesa no nagori o	is added the sorrow
torisoete	of this morning's parting:
okikasanenuru	once again, the falling dew
sode no tsuyu ka na	drenches sleeves already wet.

His reply:

nagori to wa	I cannot believe
ikaga omowan	you sorrow to see me go.
wakarenishi	Your sleeves are wet, I think,
sode no tsuyu koso	only from the ceaseless dew
hima nakarurame	evoked by that final parting.

Memories of our nightlong conversation lingered the next day, somewhat to my surprise. (It was not as though it had been a lovers' tryst.) While the night was still on my mind, a samurai in a dark russet hunting robe appeared near the middle gate with a letter box. He was a messenger from my caller. The letter was a long one, with this poem at the end:

shinobu amari	Overcome with grief,
tada utatane no	I merely dozed awhile,
tamakura ni	head pillowed on arm,
tsuyu kakariki to	but will the faultfinders say
hito ya togamuru	your tears fell on my sleeve?

In my grief and loneliness, I found even such trifles affecting. My reply, which was lengthy, ended with this poem:

29. Ōshikōchi no Mitsune (KKS 636): nagashi to mo / omoi zo hatenu / mukashi yori / au hito kara no / aki no yo nareba ("That they all drag on is not the right view to take. As the ancients knew, the length of an autumn night depends on one's companion").

30. Because it was not a romantic tryst and because both were wearing mourning.

aki no tsuyu wa	The dews of autumn
nabete kusaki ni	fall on every grass and shrub
oku mono o	and on every tree:
sode ni nomi to wa	could it be that faultfinders
tare ka togamen	would single out your sleeve as wet?

Lesser Captain Masaaki took charge of the rituals on the forty-ninth day.[31] After the Kawara-no-in holy man had finished chanting a petition full of phrases that even we lay people had used until they were threadbare—"the 'single-wing' pledge exchanged under the mandarin-duck quilt" and so forth—Dharma Seal Kenjichi officiated at the dedication of some passages from the *Lotus Sutra*, which Father himself had copied onto the backs of old letters. Major Counselor Michiyori, Middle Counselor Morochika, and Major Counselor Takaaki came to attend the services and left with words of sympathy.[32] It was a wrench to see them go. Since the day was the one on which the mourners were to disperse, I decided to move to my nurse's house at Shijō Ōmiya. I could not help weeping as I left. Nor could I possibly describe the feelings with which I settled down alone, separated from those with whom I had at least been able to exchange expressions of grief while we were all together in Father's house.

His Majesty had visited me in private even during those first grim days. "With everyone in mourning, it will be quite all right for you to wear black at the palace. Come as soon as the forty-nine days are up," he said. But I was too wretched to do anything but immure myself in the Shijō-Ōmiya house. The forty-ninth day had fallen on the Twenty-third of the Ninth Month, almost at the end of autumn, and it was saddening to hear the weakened voices of the insects, which sounded as though they were commiserating with me in my grief. His Majesty sent to ask why I was staying away so long, but I lacked the spirit even to choose a date for my return.

The Tenth Month arrived. Some time after the Tenth Day, there was a message from another quarter. "Although I have wanted to write every day, I feared that His Majesty might think, 'I did not know it was time,' if his messenger encountered mine, so I've had to let the days accumulate."[33]

31. Masatada's son; Nijō's younger half brother.
32. Nijō's second cousins and her uncle.
33. The thought attributed to the Retired Emperor quotes a poem from *The Tale of Genji*, in which Kaoru accuses Ukifune of infidelity: nami koyuru / koro to mo shirazu / sue

My nurse's house stood at the intersection of Shijō and Ōmiya avenues. The tile-capped earthen wall was in an advanced stage of dilapidation on the Shijō side nearest Ōmiya, and the grounds were separated from the street only by two large greenbrier vines, which had climbed onto what was left of the wall. "I suppose you post a night watchman there," the messenger remarked to someone. "No, we don't," the other answered. Then, so I was told, the messenger cut down the stalks with his dagger before he took himself off. "This would make an ideal passageway," he said. I wondered at the deed, but it never occurred to me to anticipate what actually happened.

Later, while the moon was shining (I think it must have been during the Hour of the Rat [11:00 P.M. – 1:00 A.M.]), there came a soft tapping on the outer door. I heard a young girl called Chūjō open the door. "What's that noise? Is it a clapper rail?" she said. A moment later, she reported back in consternation, "A gentleman outside wants to know if you will go and speak to him." I was too surprised to frame a reply. The caller came in before I could collect my wits—guided, I suppose, by the sound of the girl's voice. As I remember, he wore a hunting robe with an embossed maple-leaf design and a pair of bloused trousers in the aster combination, both garments showing by their lack of starch that the visit was a secret one.[34]

In view of my condition, I felt that I must do my best to evade him that evening. "If you care for me, let it be 'like Later Rapids Mountain,'" I begged.[35]

He answered with honorable promises. "I wouldn't dream of doing anything wrong while you're pregnant; I merely want to say a few quiet words about the love I have cherished so long. The Mimosuso River goddess herself will surely let me lie down alone for a while."

Weak-willed as always, I could not bring myself to utter a flat refusal, and he came all the way in to the place where I slept.

---

no matsu / matsuramu to nomi / omoikeru ka na ("With confident heart, I thought you waited for me. I did not know it was time for the waves to cross Sue-no-matsu Mountain"). Kaoru's poem in turn alludes to an anonymous song in *Collection of Early and Modern Poetry* (KKS 1093): kimi o okite / adashigokoro o / wa ga motaba / sue no matsuyama / nami mo koenamu ("Would I be the sort to cast you aside and turn to someone new? Sooner would the waves traverse Sue-no-matsu Mountain").

34. Starched garments would have rustled. The aster combination was probably lavender with a green lining.

35. Lady Sakanoue's Elder Daughter (MYS 737): ka ni kaku ni / hito wa iu tomo / wakasaji no / nochise no yama no / nochi mo awamu kimi ("Though others may talk, let us meet again later—later, like the name of Later Rapids Mountain in the land of Wakasa").

He rambled on during the long night in a manner pitiful enough to draw tears from the eyes of the proverbial Chinese tiger. Even though I had no desire to risk everything for his sake, I was not made of rock or wood, and I ended by sharing a pillow against my will. It was terrifying to think that His Majesty might be watching in a dream.

We were awakened by a cock's crow. His departure before dawn left me with a forlorn feeling. I did not reach the point of hoping to doze off into dreams of him, but I did linger in bed. His letter arrived before daybreak:

kaerusa wa	As I returned home,
namida ni kurete	my eyes were blinded by tears.
ariake no	It was painful
tsuki sae tsuraki	even to see the late moon
shinonome no sora	in the brightening heavens.

"How could my love have had time to swell to such enormous proportions? I don't see how I can survive until tonight. You must imagine how upset I am by the need for all this secrecy."

My reply:

kaerusa no	I can know nothing
sode wa shirazu	of your sleeves as you returned,
omokage wa	but your face wavered
sode no namida ni	in the tears on my sleeves
ariake no sora	when the late moon shone in the sky.

Now that matters had reached this stage, my previous strong resistance had become meaningless. I knew it was my own fault, but it was easy to imagine the difficulties the future held in store. Around noon, a letter from His Majesty arrived as I sobbed in private, its tone more intimate than usual. "What is the attraction that makes you stay away so long? Don't you know how boring it is in the palace nowadays with almost nobody here?" I felt horribly guilty.

That night, to my alarm, the gentleman did not even wait until the hour grew late. I kept silent, feeling as though we were meeting for the first time. To make matters worse, that was the very night on which my nurse's husband, Nakatsuna, chose to put in an appearance. Nakatsuna had gone to live with the Senbon holy man after taking religious vows, leaving the Shijō-Ōmiya house with no male resident, but now he had come "for a rare visit," as he said. The children of the family were also assembling with much distasteful commotion. One would never have guessed from Nurse's ill-bred agitation that she had been reared in the famous old household of an imperial Princess. I could not imagine what had come over her; she was disgustingly like Lady Imahime's foster mother.[36] But it was hard to object on the grounds that I was entertaining that particular guest. I put out the lights and pretended to be watching the moon, leaning against a brazier near a sliding door, with my caller hidden in the bedroom. Sure enough, Nurse appeared. It was most annoying.

"Father says, 'Autumn nights are interminable. I'll play Her Ladyship a game of marbles to amuse her.' Come and join us," she said, her manner disagreeably insistent. "What would be fun to do? So-and-so has come, also Thus-and-so." She ran on at depressing length, reeling off the names of sons and stepsons, proposing a party, and the like. One might have thought she was counting the hot-spring boards in Iyo.

My reply was evasive. "I don't feel very well."

"It's always like this. You never pay any attention to me." She flounced off.

It was Nurse's opinion, expressed frequently with an air of wisdom, that girls should be kept under close surveillance; thus, my room adjoined the same garden as her living quarters. I thought in embarrassment that the noise was worse than the booming of the foot pestle at Yūgao's dwelling.[37] With matters in such a state, I felt too ill at ease to tell my caller all the things I had planned to say, yet I hated to leave the words unspoken. I could only lie there, longing for the household to quiet down.

Someone who turned out to be Nakayori pounded on the gate. "I'm late because I had to serve the Emperor's meal," he said. "A handsome wickerwork carriage with an eight-petaled lotus design is standing at the Ōmiya corner. When I got close, I saw that it was full of drowsy attendants, with the ox tethered some distance away. I wonder where the owner has gone." I listened in consternation.

As usual, Nurse spoke up. "Send someone to find out who it is."

Nakatsuna's voice answered. "What for? It's none of our business. If anyone is taking advantage of Her Ladyship's retirement to pay her a private visit, he could come in through the gap in the wall, just like the

36. A character in a romance, *The Tale of Sagoromo* (Sagoromo monogatari).

37. Yūgao, one of the ladies wooed by Genji in *The Tale of Genji*, lived in humble surroundings.

man who said, 'I wish he might fall asleep every evening.'[38] You can't trust a woman, whether she's pregnant or not. High-born or low, they're all the same."

Nurse's reply was distinctly audible. "No good can come of this. Who do you suppose the man is? There would be no need for secrecy if it were the Retired Emperor." To my distress, she added, "His Majesty will probably scold me for letting her get involved with some low-ranking fellow."

Now that still another son had joined the group, the noise put sleep out of the question. Presently there was a stir, apparently in response to the arrival of the refreshments they had ordered. "Tell Her Ladyship to come," voices clamored. I heard someone approach and speak. "She is unwell," answered the maid who was waiting on us. Then a peremptory tattoo on the sliding door announced Nurse's arrival. Upset and frightened, I felt as though she were a stranger.

"What's wrong? Come and see what we have," she said, rapping on the panel next to my pillow.

I could not very well remain silent, so I said, "I'm too sick."

"I wouldn't urge you except that we have your favorite white thing. If that isn't typical! When we don't have it, you ask for it; when we offer it, you refuse it. Well, suit yourself." She went off, grumbling. Under ordinary circumstances, I would have essayed a witty response, but now I was ready to faint with embarrassment.

"What is the white thing you like?" my caller wanted to know.

Doubtful that he would believe me if I named something elegant like frost, snow, or hail, I told the truth. "Sometimes I enjoy a special, white kind of *sake*. My nurse has blown it all out of proportion."

I shall never forget his smiling reply. "It's a good thing I came tonight. If you'll come to my house, I'll get you something white even if I have to go to China." On many painful occasions, it has seemed to me the most precious memory I am likely to have.

As the nights accumulated, I grew fonder of my lover and less inclined to return to the palace.

38. *Tales of Ise*, Sec. 5. A man who is visiting a woman in secret finds a watchman posted at the gap in the wall through which he had been entering. His poem: hito shirenu / wa ga kayoiji no / sekimori wa / yoiyoigoto ni / uchi mo nenanan ("I wish he might fall asleep every evening—this watchman who guards the secret passageway where I go back and forth").

My maternal grandmother, Gondainagon, had fallen ill around the Twentieth of the Tenth Month. Because she had seemed in no immediate danger, I had felt no particular alarm, but now, only a few days later, word came that she had breathed her last. She had lived for many years at Ayato, near Zenrinji Temple in the eastern hills. The news of her death was a grievous blow. Dreamlike and evanescent though worldly ties may be, it was bitter to realize that all of mine were now severed. First it had been Father, then this.

aki no tsuyu	The sleeves of my robe
fuyu no shigure ni	I wring and wring again.
uchisoete	To autumn dew
shiborikasanuru	has been added moisture
wa ga tamoto ka na	from showering winter rains.

Having heard nothing from His Majesty of late, I feared that news of my indiscreet behavior might have leaked out, but an unusually warm letter arrived. He asked how I had been getting along during our separation and announced that he was sending a carriage to fetch me that night.

"My aged grandmother died a couple of days ago," I responded. "I will come after the mourning period." I added a poem:

omoiyare	Please imagine it:
suginishi aki no	my sleeves, dampened earlier
tsuyu ni mata	by last autumn's dews,
namida shigurete	are saturated again
nururu sode o	by showers of wintry tears.

His reply was prompt:

kasanekeru	I had not yet known
tsuyu no aware mo	that yours was the sadness of one
mada shirade	doubly bereaved:
ima koso yoso no	now my own sleeves are wet through
sode mo shiorure	with tears of sympathy.

When I reported for duty early in the Eleventh Month, it seemed as though things had suddenly changed at the palace. I could not forget seeing Father in so many different places, nor could I help feeling awkward and ill at ease. Then, too, the Imperial Lady Higashinijōin seemed to resent my presence. It was all very disheartening. His Majesty issued kind orders on my behalf to my grandfather and uncle, Takachika and Takaaki. "See that she is as well cared for as when her father, the Major Counselor, was alive. Use some of my tribute goods to provide her with robes," he told them. But my only remaining desire was to get through with the birth and lead a quiet life, praying for my parents and for my own release from worldly things. I left the palace again toward the end of the month.

I went to stay with a connection, Abbess Shingan, at Daigo Shō-tokuteiin, where I thought I might listen to some recitations of scriptures. The Abbess's cloister reminded me of the old poem, "Of smoke, at least . . ."[39] Wood fires were burning, and the water had ceased to flow through the frozen conduits. The year-end preparations also had a makeshift air, quite different from the usual arrangements.

One night, a little past the Twentieth, Retired Emperor Go-Fukakusa came to pay me a secret visit. The late moon was just rising. Even though it was an incognito journey in a plain wickerwork carriage, Major Counselor Takaaki rode with him. "His Majesty has been staying at the Fushimi Palace," Takaaki said. "Something happened to make him think of you." I wondered uneasily how he had known where I was, but he treated me with special affection that night, lingering until the dawn bells rang.

The moon was still visible in the western skies, and a bank of horizontal clouds at the rim of the eastern hills sent white flakes fluttering like blossoms onto old patches of snow, as though to add an elegant touch to the occasion. It was affecting to see His Majesty's unfigured hunting robe and matching black trousers—attire that echoed my own dark gray. Unaware of the imperial presence, the nuns were emerging for the dawn offices, dressed in scruffy robes and carelessly draped, shabby surplices. "I've finished my sunrise recitations. What's become of Sister So-and-so and Sister Thus-and-so? Sister Something Amidabutsu!" I watched with a pang of envy. I think some of them took to their heels and hid, tardily aware of what was going on, when they saw the carriage being brought up by the junior North Guards in their black hunting robes.

"I'll see you again soon," the Retired Emperor said as he left. The

39. Izumi Shikibu (GSIS 390): sabishisa ni / keburi o dani mo / tataji to ya / shiba orikuburu / fuyu no yamazato ("Someone burns firewood in the winter-bound mountains. Does he think, 'Of smoke, at least, there shall be no end in this lonely dwelling'?").

sadness of the parting lingered in the tears on my sleeves; the scent transferred during our exchange of vows seemed to have permeated my robes. I listened attentively to the nuns' voices as they performed their devotions. Even the words of the hymn, "Exalted is the status of a chakravartin, yet he follows the Three Paths in the end," seemed to merit special reflection; even the dedicatory prayer evoked regret that the service had ended.

A letter from His Majesty arrived after daybreak. "Never have I known such emotion as when the pale moon shone on our parting this morning," it said. I replied:

kimi dani mo	Would that I might show
narawazarikeru	the reflection on my sleeve
ariake no	left from that dawn parting
omokage nokoru	when my lord himself felt grief
sode o misebaya	such as he had not known.

Toward evening about three days before the end of the year, I was sitting in front of the Abbess in an especially melancholy mood. "We probably won't have another quiet time like this," she remarked. Then, as though trying to cheer me up, she chatted away and called in the older nuns to tell stories about the past. The water in the conduit leading to the cistern had frozen depressingly hard, and the sound of an ax, chopping firewood in the mountains across the way, seemed strangely moving, quite like an old romance. Lights from altar lamps became visible here and there as darkness closed in.

The evening offices were performed, and the nuns began to talk about making an early night of it. Just then, to my surprise, someone tapped softly on the corner door near my room. I could not imagine who was there, but it proved to be he.

My welcome was cold. "This is awkward. It would be terribly embarrassing if I were found indulging in loose conduct at this temple. Besides, now that I have begun a retreat, I have to remain pure if my prayers are to be heard. His Majesty's visit was special; I couldn't do anything about that. But I can't engage in licentious, unchaste behavior. Please go away," I said.

A heavy snow chanced to be falling, accompanied by violent winds— a veritable blizzard. "It's unbearable out here," he protested. "At least let me come inside until this snowstorm ends."

Some of the nuns with the Abbess must have overheard. "That's dreadful! How cold-hearted! It doesn't matter who he is. He must have had his heart set on visiting our temple or he wouldn't have made such an effort to get here. The wind from the mountain is freezing." They unlocked the door and built up a fire, and he took advantage of the opportunity to slip inside.

As though to rebuke my lack of hospitality, the snow accumulated until it had buried peaks and eaves alike. Even after day began to break, my visitor stayed in bed, dismayingly at home. "The blizzard raged all night," he said. "It sounded frightful." There was nothing I could do; I simply worried.

After the sun had risen high in the sky, two of the gentleman's attendants appeared with articles of various kinds, and I watched nervously as their master meted out things for the Abbess to distribute. "Now we can ignore those cold year-end winds," the nuns said. He also provided invocation-recitants' surplices and robes for offerings, and the nuns all chorused, "At last, a light has shone on these humble rustic surroundings!"

I found their enthusiasm unbecoming. They ought to have regarded an imperial visit as second in importance only to the advent of the heavenly host, but His Majesty had been seen off by a scant handful of people, and I had heard nobody use words like "awe-inspiring" or "a great honor." Someone among them might have been expected to point out the shocking irregularity of the present situation, but they were all transfixed with joy by the visitor's bounty. Although such behavior is common enough, it was distasteful all the same. There was a New Year costume for me (nothing showy, but with many layers, which were blue, I believe)—also a set of three white narrow-sleeved inner robes. I could not help worrying lest someone learn all there was to know about our relationship, but we spent the whole day drinking.

He left the next morning, after explaining that it was impossible for him to stay longer. "Please come to the veranda to see me off, at least," he urged.

When I got up and went outside, the white snow on the peaks was glittering in the faintly brightening dawn sky—a chill, lonely sight. Two or three attendants appeared in colorless hunting robes. The anguish with which I watched the departure seemed shameful even to me.

People came from Nurse's house to fetch me on the last day of the

Twelfth Month. They insisted that it would not do for me to stay far back in the mountains in my condition, so I had to greet the new year in the capital, little as I wanted to.

[*Tenth Year of Bun'ei: 1273*]

No brilliant events ushered in the year. Retired Emperor Go-Fukakusa's palace was dull on the first three days, my own grief welled up anew, and altogether it was a wretched holiday season. Prevented by defilement from paying my usual New Year visit to the family shrine, I traveled as far as the gate and offered prayers there.[40] (I have written elsewhere of my petition and of the dream in which Father appeared; thus, I shall say nothing more here.)

On the evening of the Tenth of the Second Month, it became evident that I was about to give birth. What with His Majesty's difficulties and my own sorrow, it was not a cheerful time, but my uncle, Major Counselor Takaaki, took charge and rushed around issuing orders. His Majesty asked the Priestly Imperial Prince at Omuro to offer prayers to the Mystic King Aizen in the main cloister. He also commissioned offerings at Narutaki to Fugen, the Prolongation of Life Bodhisattva, and instructed the Bishamondō Archbishop to offer prayers to the Seven Healing Buddhas. (The rituals at Narutaki and the Bishamondō took place in the main cloisters too.) My relatives arranged the usual sort of thing— for example, prayers to Kannon, offered by Dharma Seal Shingen. The Shichijō Archbishop Dōchō, who had just returned from practicing austerities at Kinbusen, came to be with me. "I can't forget how your late father worried about you, and how he asked me to do whatever I could," he said.

I began to suffer excruciating pains around midnight. There was a minor stir when my aunt, Lady Kyōgoku, arrived as a messenger from the Retired Emperor.[41] My grandfather, Takachika, also put in an appearance. Ah, I thought, the tears starting to my eyes, if Father were still alive . . . As I sat leaning against an attendant, I dozed off and saw Father come up behind me with an anxious expression, looking just the same as ever. The delivery took place at the same instant. Would it be proper to say that a Prince had entered the world? Although I was happy

---

40. The Minamoto tutelary shrine was at Iwashimizu. Nijō's mourning robes and her pregnancy were both sources of defilement.

41. Kyōgoku was one of Go-Fukakusa's ladies-in-waiting.

to have got through the ordeal safely, the possible consequences of my misconduct came home to me for the first time.

A sword was forwarded discreetly from His Majesty, and Takaaki provided conservative gifts for the exorcists. I could not help letting my mind dwell on the thought that the birth would probably have taken place at the Kawasaki house if Father had been alive.[42] But Takaaki had made all the arrangements for the nurses' costumes and the like, and the bow-twanging and many other ceremonies were all performed. The year slipped by as though in a dream. It depressed me to remember the birth—the dream of Father, the bow-twanging, the embarrassment of exposing myself before so many people. Nor was I comforted by the divine gift of a son, for it seemed unlikely to lead to anything good.

In the Twelfth Month, all of His Majesty's people were fully occupied with the annual prayers to the gods and other activities. I retired from the palace with the intention of performing some private Buddhist austerities, but my visitor came again, guided by the light of the proverbially bleak Twelfth Month moon, and we talked all night long. "I had planned to leave when the widow crows cawed, but here it is dawn already. I can't very well go now," he said. To my great alarm, he stayed on. A letter came from His Majesty while we sat together, its expressions of tenderness more numerous than usual.

mubatama no	What did I behold
yume ni zo mitsuru	in a dream dreamt on a night
sayogoromo	black as leopard-flower seeds!
aranu tamoto o	The sleeve of another man
kasanekeri to wa	was spread on top of your robe.

"I wish I could have seen him more distinctly."

Horrified, I wondered what he could possibly have seen, but I could not admit that there was any basis for his suspicions. I replied:

hitori nomi	The light of the moon
katashikikanuru	lodges night after night
tamoto ni wa	in the sleeve of one
tsuki no hikari zo	who grieves to spread her robe
yadorikasanuru	on a bed where she sleeps alone.

Aware that my behavior was brazen, I prevaricated all the same.

The two of us spent a quiet day together. All the women in my part

42. Nijō was probably staying in a house provided by her uncle, Takaaki.

of the house knew what was going on, but I could offer no explanation; I simply bore my uneasiness as best I could. That night, I dreamed that my lover gave me a silver oil flask, proffering it on a fan with black-lacquered ribs and a gold-lacquered design of pine trees, and that I hid it in my bosom. I awoke to the sound of the dawn bell. Then, while I was musing about the strangeness of it all, he revealed that he had dreamed exactly the same thing! I wondered what it meant.

[*Eleventh Year of Bun'ei: 1274*]

No sooner had the new year begun than Retired Emperor Go-Fukakusa, the dream of the past year very much on his mind, commanded twelve monk-scribes to copy sacred texts according to form at the Rokujō Palace temple. He used articles from his storerooms to defray the expenses so that he would not have to inconvenience others. It was his intention to begin copying the *Lotus Sutra* himself in the First Month, using blood from his fingers to write on the backs of sheets bearing his father's calligraphy, and thus he avoided all his ladies and otherwise observed ritual purity from the First Month to the Seventeenth of the Second Month.

Late in the Second Month, I fell ill and lost my appetite. At first, I thought it was a cold, but gradually I came to suspect the dream about the oil flask. There was no way of concealing the truth; I was going to pay for my sin. The realization plunged me into the depths of despair, but I could not tell anyone my troubles.

I stayed away from the palace as much as possible, using as my excuse the services in honor of the gods.[43] My lover, who visited me constantly, guessed somehow that I was with child and became even more affectionate than before. "If only there were a way of concealing the truth from His Majesty!" he said. He offered a succession of fervent prayers. I wondered which of us was at fault.

I began to visit the palace again after the end of the Second Month. Around the Fifth Month, His Majesty assumed that I was in the fourth month of my pregnancy, although it was actually the sixth. I could not imagine what I would do when the discrepancy came to light.

On the Seventh of the Sixth Month, my lover insisted that I leave the palace. When I did so, my curiosity piqued, I found that he had person-

43. Ladies-in-waiting usually stayed away from Shinto events.

ally prepared a maternity sash for me. "I wanted you to have this. Even though the fourth month was the proper time, I delayed because I was afraid of gossip, but I heard that His Majesty intended to send you one on the Twelfth, and I was determined to get mine to you first," he said. Despite this evidence of his devotion, I could not help agonizing over what lay ahead.

He visited me in secret for three days running. I had meant to return to the palace on the Tenth, but that night I fell ill suddenly and was unable to go. On the evening of the Twelfth, Takaaki brought a sash. "Here I am, just as before," he announced. "'Dewdrops do not form in autumn alone,'" I thought.[44] My tears flowed unchecked as I remembered how Father had fussed over Takaaki's entertainment on that other night.

No matter how hard I tried, I could not think how to account for a pregnancy that was more than a month further along than it ought to have been. On the other hand, I could not make up my mind to jump into the river. Time passed uneventfully, and the Ninth Month arrived while I was still searching frantically for a way out of my predicament.

Nervous about gossip, I found an excuse to hurry away from the palace around the Second Day. My lover appeared promptly on the same night, and we put our heads together. "First of all, you'll have to report that you're desperately ill. Then make it known that the yin-yang masters have pronounced the disease one to be avoided by His Majesty," he said, sitting at my side. I did as he advised. I stayed in bed all day long, denied myself to intimates and outsiders, and dispensed with all my attendants except two maids with whom I was on close terms. We put it about that I was too sick even to sip hot water, but it turned out that there were no callers anyway. In miserable spirits, I thought of how different things would be if Father were still alive.

I sent word to the Retired Emperor that I did not want to be a nuisance; he was pleased not to have people inquire about me. He let a little time elapse and then sent a letter. It was terrifying to contemplate the all-too-probable future in which my sham would be exposed, but everyone seemed deceived for the moment.

44. Retired Emperor Go-Toba (SKKS 470): tsuyu wa sode ni / monoomou koro wa / sazo na oku / kanarazu aki no / narai naranedo ("Whenever we grieve, the tears descend like dew onto our sleeves. Those dewdrops do not form in autumn alone—and yet . . .").

Takaaki called often. "You can't go on like this. What do the doctors say?" he would ask.

I always declined to receive him. "They tell me it's a highly contagious disease. It will be better if we don't meet."

One time, he insisted that he was too worried to leave without seeing me. I darkened the room and lay silent under a robe, and he went away convinced. It was a frightening experience. Since nobody else ever came, my lover stayed with me. He had let it be known that he was to spend a period of retreat at Kasuga Shrine, but had sent a surrogate instead. To my alarm, he whispered, "I've told him to reply as best he can if anyone writes to me there."

Shortly after dawn on a day toward the end of the month, I began to feel that the baby was on its way. I said nothing except to my one or two intimate attendants, who set about hasty, sketchy preparations. It was painful to think of what would happen to my reputation if I died in childbirth, and sad also to witness the depth of my lover's emotion.

The day passed uneventfully. Signs that the birth was imminent appeared around lamp-lighting time, but I did not arrange for people to twang bows; I merely lay in lonely misery under a robe. Around the hour of the midnight bell, I sat up, unable to endure the pain. "They say someone is supposed to hold the mother around the waist. Maybe the birth is slow because nobody's doing that. Be brave!" My lover supported me. I clung to his sleeve, and the baby arrived safely. "Hurry up with the gruel!" he ordered, vastly relieved. The maids marveled at his knowledgeability.

He lit a lamp to look at the child. It had a beautiful head of black hair and its eyes were wide open. A single glance was enough to tug at a parent's heart, but he wrapped it in a nearby white inner robe, took the knife from the scabbard of his sword, which was lying close to the pillow, cut the umbilical cord, picked the baby up, and carried it outside in silence. I did not see it again. Much as I wanted to beg for one more glimpse, I kept quiet, aware that it would merely make the parting harder. The tears I wept into my sleeve must have shown how I felt, for he did his best to comfort me. "Now, now. This doesn't mean you'll never see it again. There are sure to be other opportunities as long as you both stay alive." Still, I could not forget how the baby had looked when we gazed into each other's eyes that one time. It was a girl, which made it especially hard not even to know where she had been taken. But it was useless to ask to have her back; I merely sobbed quietly into my sleeve.

At daybreak, we sent a message to the Retired Emperor. "The severity of Her Ladyship's illness caused her to miscarry shortly before dawn today. It was possible to tell that the child was a girl."

He sent back quantities of medicines. "The doctors say such things are bound to happen when a woman runs a high fever. Take good care of yourself during your convalescence." It was frightening to contemplate the enormity of my sin.

Time passed with no particular postpartum complications, and my lover went home. His Majesty had sent word that I was to return after 100 days. Meanwhile, I remained in melancholy seclusion. My lover came every night without fail, but neither of us could keep from fretting about the danger of discovery.

The son I had borne in a previous year was being reared privately by Takaaki. Around that time, I heard that he had fallen ill. Then I was told that he had vanished with the dew, disappeared like a raindrop after an early winter shower. I believe it was the Eighth of the Tenth Month, just when I was thinking that the future could hold little promise for a sinner like me. Even though I was prepared for the news, my feelings of emptiness and shock were beyond description. It seemed that I alone must suffer the dual sorrows of outliving one child and being separated in life from another. As though it were not bad enough to have lost my mother in infancy and my father during my best years, now there were these new griefs to be wept over by one who had nowhere to turn.

Nor was that all. The morning partings from my lover became harder to bear as our intimacy increased, and I used to lie in bed alone weeping. On evenings when I waited for him, my sobs mingled with the sound of the bells marking the hours, but once he had arrived, I worried about gossip. When I was away from the palace, I missed His Majesty; when I was there, I resented the many nights he spent with other women and mourned the waning of his affection.

Life in this world holds nothing but pain. It seemed that the scriptural "eight hundred million and four thousand sorrows in a day and a night" had all descended on me alone, and that I ought simply to leave the world of attachment for the life of a nun. At the age of nine, I had seen a picture scroll entitled, "A Record of Saigyō's Religious Travels."

In one section, the artist had depicted a scene deep in the mountains. A stream flowed in the foreground, and near it the poet sat under scattering blossoms, gazing at the water and reciting:

kaze fukeba	White waves of blossoms
hana no shiranami	cascade over the rocks
iwa koete	when the breezes blow.
watariwazurau	How difficult to ford
yamakawa no mizu	the waters of the mountain stream!

I had envied Saigyō ever since. Perhaps it would not do for a woman to become a journeying ascetic, but I wished that I might at least abandon the world and wander wherever I pleased, savoring the beauty of dew under blossoming trees, lamenting the scattering of autumn leaves, and setting down a similar record of religious endeavor—something to serve as a memento after my death. But I could not escape the miseries of the Three Subjugations.[45] Through no choice of my own, I had long been governed by my father's will, and now I still remained in this world of sorrows as His Majesty's attendant. The more I thought about it, the more distasteful secular life became.

I believe it was in the autumn of the same year that Retired Emperor Go-Fukakusa also became dissatisfied with his situation. He renounced his title of Retired Sovereign, declaring himself humiliated because Emperor Kameyama was staffing a Retired Emperor's Office. He also mustered, paid off, and dismissed his Escorts. "Hikinori alone will stay to help me with some last things," he said. Moreover, he announced his intention of taking religious vows. When he designated those whom he wished to have join him in holy orders, he said, "As ladies-in-waiting, Higashi-no-onkata and Nijō." Thus, it seemed that a sad event was to lead to happiness for me. But the authorities in Kamakura adopted a placatory stance. His Majesty's young son by Higashi-no-onkata was named Crown Prince, and life at the palace became brilliant and gay.

The portrait that had been kept in the Corner Palace was transferred to the Ōgimachi Mansion,[46] and the Corner Palace became the Crown Prince's residence.

One of the Retired Emperor's attendants was Lady Kyōgoku, the former Lady Shinsuke. I was not on close terms with her, but there was a

45. To father, husband, and son.
46. The portrait is conjectured to have been of Retired Emperor Go-Saga.

certain bond because of her connection with Father. Seeing her launch forth onto a new career as lady-in-waiting to the Crown Prince, with the name Dainagon-no-suke, I felt a surge of revulsion against the ways of the world. My thoughts dwelt on "the wilds beyond the hills," but I seemed powerless to make the final break.[47] Perhaps some karmic condition prevented it. The end of the year approached while I sighed over my lot. Then His Majesty sent me an insistent summons, which I obeyed, unable, after all, to sever worldly ties.

My grandfather took care of all my costumes and other needs at court, if in a somewhat perfunctory manner. I suppose I ought to have felt happy, but after the boy's death, I brooded incessantly over my lover's sin and my own wrongdoing. I recalled how His Majesty had paid a private visit to Takaaki's house and seen the innocent smile on the infant countenance, the very image of his own. "It's exactly like looking at my face in the mirror," he said. The memory evoked an endless succession of gloomy thoughts, and I spent the days in wretched spirits.

Meanwhile, for some unaccountable reason, the Imperial Lady Higashinijōin denied me further access to her apartments and expunged my name from her duty board, even though I had committed no particular offense to justify the action. Her displeasure increased my reluctance to continue in palace service. Although His Majesty assured me that he would not cast me out because of her attitude, everything seemed to be conspiring to make life disagreeable, and I began to withdraw more and more from the activities of the court. But then His Majesty showed that he felt sorry for me, and his sympathy gave me the courage to perform my duties in earnest.

The Ise Virgin, a daughter of Retired Emperor Go-Saga, had left her position to go into mourning, but had stayed on at Ise for three years while awaiting formal permission to retire. Around the autumn of this present year, she had come back to the capital to live in an area called Kinugasa at Ninnaji Temple. I remembered with nostalgia how Father had placed himself at her disposal because of family ties, especially at the time of her journey to the shrine. It was touching that she should have settled in so lonely a spot, and I visited her frequently in the hope of relieving the tedium of her days. Sometime after the Tenth of the

47. Anonymous (KKS 950): miyoshino no / yama no anata ni / yado mo ga na / yo no uki toki no / kakurega ni semu ("I long for a house in the wilds beyond the hills of fair Yoshino—a hidden dwelling to use when the world is hard to bear").

Eleventh Month or thereabouts, it was arranged that she should go to the Saga Mansion for a visit to the Senior Empress.

"It will seem inhospitable if I receive her alone," the Senior Empress sent word. "Please come."

The Senior Empress had not been on close terms with His Majesty during the dispute over affairs of state and the commotion attendant on the nomination of the Crown Prince, but more recently she had taken to sending him cordial messages. Reluctant to cause offense by refusing this invitation, he decided to accept. "You visit the Virgin often; you'd better come along," he said to me. I rode in the back of his carriage, attired in a thin red-plum robe over a set of three yellow robes lined in pale green.[48] We had all been decked out in formal jackets ever since the appointment of the new Crown Prince, so I wore a red one. I was the sole attendant; there was nobody from the Table Room.

His Majesty went to the Senior Empress's apartments and began to chat in a relaxed manner. After a time, he said, "I've reared this child since she was an infant, so she's pretty well accustomed to court service. That's why I like to keep her with me wherever I go. But others have misunderstood, and now she has been forbidden to serve Her Majesty. Still, I don't feel that I can reject her too. She is a memento from her mother and father, two loyal servants who entrusted her to my care."

"I quite agree that you can't abandon her. A person needs trained attendants; it's most inconvenient to have to make do with amateurs for even a short time," the Senior Empress said. To me, she added in a kind voice, "Please don't hesitate to consult me about any problem you may encounter." I could not help wondering how long my good fortune would last.

After an evening of leisurely conversation, the Retired Emperor dined in the Senior Empress's apartments. When the hour grew late, he announced his intention of retiring. He went to a room facing the kick-ball court. There was no lady-in-waiting to serve him, so I saw to his needs. The Saionji Major Counselor Sanekane, the Zenshōji Major Counselor Takaaki, Nagasuke, Tamekata, Kaneyuki, and Sukeyuki were in attendance.

The next morning, the Retired Emperor indicated that a party should be dispatched to escort the Virgin, and some minor functionaries

48. Neither part of Nijō's costume could have been worn without special permission.

and junior North Guards set out from the Senior Empress's palace. His Majesty took special pains with his appearance in anticipation of the meeting, donning a yellow-banded hunting robe with a woven burnet design and a pale green lining, a lavender robe with a woven gentian design, and a pair of aster-colored trousers, all meticulously perfumed.

At nightfall, we heard that the Virgin had arrived. The south side of the main hall was opened, dark gray curtain-stands were brought out, and low curtain-stands were also set up. We learned that the Senior Empress had received the guest. Then, very soon, a lady-in-waiting came with a message for His Majesty. "I am afraid our visitor finds the atmosphere lonely and inhospitable here. Please come and talk to her." He set out at once. I accompanied him as usual, carrying his sword.

The Senior Empress was wearing a dark gray robe over a pale black garment of fine silk gauze with a woven design. The draperies on her low curtain-stand were also dark gray. The Virgin wore three red-plum robes over a green singlet—a rather showy costume. The ladies-in-waiting on duty were attired in sets of five robes in colors shading from white to purple. They did not wear formal jackets or trains. The Virgin was a little past twenty, a woman in her prime. It was small wonder that the goddess should have wished to detain her. Anyone who compared her to a blossoming cherry tree would have been hard-pressed to choose the more beautiful; anyone who glimpsed the face hidden behind her raised sleeve would have lost his heart. Aware that she had probably already fascinated the susceptible Retired Emperor, I could not help pitying her, even though it was no concern of mine.

As the conversation proceeded, the Virgin spoke in a diffident manner of her life at Ise and other things, punctuating her remarks with frequent pauses.

"It's very late. Please get some rest now. We'd like to have you see the bare trees on Arashiyama Mountain before you leave tomorrow," the Retired Emperor told her.

His Majesty spoke to me as soon as he returned to his own apartments. "What would be the best thing to do?" Just as I predicted, I thought in amusement. "You've served me ever since your childhood. If you manage to bring this off, I'll take it as a mark of true loyalty," he went on.

I set out promptly as his envoy. The oral message was commonplace enough. "It was a pleasure to meet you. I hope you're not finding the night away from home too dull." There was also a private communication on thin white paper:

shirareji na	You cannot know
ima shi mo mitsuru	how my mind has become obsessed
omokage no	with visions of you—
yagate kokoro ni	with the face and figure
kakarikeri to wa	I have beheld for the first time.

It was so late that the Virgin's attendants were all lying down. She herself was asleep inside a circle of low curtain-stands. When I went up to her with my message, she turned scarlet and said nothing. She thrust the poem aside without reading it.

"What shall I say to His Majesty?" I asked.

"There is really no way for me to answer such an unexpected message." She composed herself to sleep without another word.

Unable in conscience to insist, I went back and reported. His Majesty's response left no room for argument. "Then you'll just have to take me to wherever she's sleeping. Come on," he said. The task was easy enough; I guided him there. He stole inside, wearing a wide-mouthed divided skirt instead of his banded hunting robe, which seemed too elaborate for the occasion.

When I slid the door open softly in front of him, I saw that the Virgin was sleeping as before. It seemed that all her attendants must also be asleep, for there was not a sound from anybody. I cannot say what happened after His Majesty made himself small and crept inside the curtain-stands. It would not have done to go off and leave him there, so I stretched out beside one of the women on night duty. She roused herself sufficiently to ask who I was.

"It seemed hard on you to be so short-handed; I've come to share the night duty," I answered.

With regrettable lack of caution, she accepted my story and began to chat.

"I'm sleepy; it's late." I pretended to go to sleep.

Lying not far from the Virgin's bed, I guessed that she must have yielded even before His Majesty had exhausted his powers of persuasion—a disappointingly prompt capitulation. It would have been more interesting if she had held out until morning.

His Majesty returned to his quarters before dawn. "Cherry trees are beautiful, but their branches are weak; it's easy to pick the blossoms," he remarked. Just as I thought, I said to myself.

The Retired Emperor slept until the sun was high; it was around noon when he awakened. He uttered a rueful exclamation. "What a morning to oversleep!" I believe the Virgin's reply to his hasty epistle was merely, "The face I saw in a dream refuses to leave my mind's eye."

"Have you thought of anything to do today that might amuse the lady who is paying us this rare visit?" the Retired Emperor asked the Senior Empress. When she answered that she had made no particular plans, he told Takaaki to arrange a banquet with wine. In the evening, Takaaki reported that everything was ready, and His Majesty invited the Senior Empress to his quarters. I was chosen to pour because it was possible for me to enter the presence of both guests.

I did not pour for the Virgin during the first three rounds. Then the Senior Empress asked the Virgin for her bowl and offered it to His Majesty, protesting that it must not remain empty. Sanekane and Takaaki sat in attendance below the threshold beam outside the curtain-stands. I received His Majesty's bowl and poured for Sanekane. Sanekane tried to yield place because Takaaki was the one who had arranged the evening's entertainment, but Takaaki refused. "Nijō wants you to drink. That settles it," he said. Thus, Sanekane drank first and Takaaki afterward.

"We have had no real drinking parties since your father's death. Please don't hesitate to have a good time this evening," the Senior Empress said to her son. She summoned a lady-in-waiting to play the zither and asked His Majesty to take the lute. Sanekane also played the lute, and Kaneyuki played the oboe. The hours advanced in an increasingly pleasant fashion. The two senior nobles sang sacred songs and, as usual, Takaaki performed "Serifu Village."[49]

I told His Majesty that I could not persuade the Virgin to drink, no matter what I said. "I'll pour for her myself," he announced. The Senior Empress intervened as he picked up the ladle. "If you're going to pour, it's up to you to produce a tidbit to go with the wine, even though this is not the beach at Koyurugi," she said.[50] He responded with a modern song:

49. Probably the name of a popular song.
50. She puns on *sakana* ("tidbit"; "supplementary entertainment"), alluding to a song in which seaweed from Koyurugi figures as food.

baiten no okina wa	Pathetic is the old man,
aware nari	the charcoal seller.
onore ga koromo wa	Although his robe is fashioned
usukeredo	of flimsy cloth,
takigi o torite	he waits for the winter,
fuyu o matsu	felling his firewood.
koso kanashikere	How piteous is his plight!

It was delightful to listen to him.

"I'll drink from that bowl," the Senior Empress said. After drinking three times, she offered the bowl to the Virgin. His Majesty took it again and placed himself in front of his mother.

"The adage says, 'The Son of Heaven has no father or mother,' but don't you think I deserve some of the credit for your having become Emperor, insignificant though I am?" she said in a plaintive voice. Then she asked him to do something to amuse her.

"I owe you everything—my life, my elevation to the throne, and my title of Retired Sovereign. How could I refuse your command?" he said. He sang another modern song three times:

omae no ike naru	The cranes have come flocking
kameoka ni	to disport themselves
tsuru koso mureite	where Turtle Island rises
asobu nare	from the garden lake.
yowai wa kimi ga	It is for Her Majesty
tame nareba	that they live so long:
ame no shita koso	all is tranquility
nodoka nare	under the heavens.

His Majesty offered the Senior Empress wine three times. Then he said, "I'll take the bowl now." He drank and gave the bowl to Takaaki. "Our lovely Nijō has shown that she's partial to Sanekane. Aren't you jealous?" he said. Wine was sent down to the courtiers and the affair ended.

I was positive that His Majesty would visit the Virgin that night, but he said, "I drank too much; I feel terrible. Massage my back." He went to bed and slept until morning.

The Virgin went home on the following day, and the Retired Emperor journeyed to the Imabayashi Mansion,[51] where he stayed overnight

---

51. The residence of his maternal grandmother.

because his grandmother, the Honorary Empress, had come down with a cold. He returned to his palace in the capital on the second day.

On the evening of our return, Lady Chūnagon arrived with a message from the Imperial Lady Higashinijōin.

"What is it?" we asked.

This was the message. "I removed Lady Nijō from my service because her behavior was quite consistently unacceptable, and then you went out of your way to favor her. I am told that she rides in your carriage wearing a set of three robes, and that everyone takes her for me—a most distressing state of affairs. Since I must suffer constant humiliation, I request permission to leave your court. I will retire as a nun to some place like Fushimi."

His Majesty replied as follows: "I have received your message. I don't wish to hear anything about Nijō now. I esteemed her mother, the late Dainagon-no-suke, above all my other ladies-in-waiting because she served me faithfully day and night; I was casting about for a way to repay her when she died a sadly premature death. She begged me at the last to look after Nijō—to regard the child as a memento from her—and I agreed to do so. Furthermore, Nijō's father, the late Major Counselor Masatada, also entrusted her to me when he was dying. A sovereign can be a sovereign only when he can rely on his subjects' loyalty; a subject can be a subject only when he can rely on his sovereign's benevolence. I freely granted Masatada's dying request, and thus he said, before breathing his last, 'Now there's nothing to hinder me in the life to come; my mind is at ease.' A ruler can't go back on his word. I am sure Masatada is watching from the grave. How could it be right to drive his guiltless daughter from the palace and send her off somewhere?

"There is nothing new about Nijō's wearing a set of three robes. When she made her initial appearance in the palace at the age of four, she was permitted to ride in a carriage with five streamers on the blinds, and also to wear double-patterned silk and numerous inner robes, because Masatada said, 'My status is low; she is being presented as the daughter of her grandfather, the Koga Chancellor.' Besides, Dainagon-no-suke served at court as the adopted daughter of the Kitayama Chancellor Saneuji, and Nijō entered service as the child of Saneuji's wife, the lady who personally tied the waist cord when the girl performed the Assumption of the Divided Skirt. As everyone knows, Nijō was given permission at that time to wear thin robes and white divided skirts because her family connections on both sides made her eligible to do so. She has also been authorized for years to use the carriage portals. I cannot understand why all these matters should be brought into question at this late date. Have insignificant junior members of the North Guards said that Nijō has been acting as though she were you? If she has, I will look into it and take appropriate action, but I can't go so far as to drive her from the palace and send her off to an unknown place. I will employ her as a female servant in some minor capacity.

"It is well known that Masatada declined the honor when the girl was given the name Nijō. In consequence, nobody called her that, nor did I insist on it. 'I have presented her as her grandfather's child because my status is low,' Masatada said, 'but it would be going too far to give her an avenue name. Please just let her serve for the time being as though she were your own daughter. She can receive a name when I become a Minister of State as I expect to do.'

"As a Chancellor's daughter, the girl is entitled to wear thin robes. Moreover, every family presses its own claims, but I need not point out that the Kazan and the Kan'in houses must go far back indeed before they get to Fujiwara no Fuhito. The Koga are a relatively new house; the descendants of Emperor Murakami's seventh son, Prince Tomohira, who was the younger brother of Emperors Reizei and En'yū, and their daughters do not ordinarily seek to serve at court. In Nijō's case, Masatada implored me to treat her as a memento from the mother who served me, which is why I have kept her here ever since her childhood. I am sure you know all these things, and I find it odd that you should talk this way now.

"As regards your becoming a nun: the religious impulse appears when the time is ripe, engendered by meritorious deeds in a previous existence. It would be wrong for you to defer to another's opinion." He said nothing else.

I became increasingly nervous about the precariousness of my position, but took comfort in the thought that there was one exalted personage, at least, who loved me.

I must not forget the former Virgin. Retired Emperor Go-Fukakusa had never seen her after the one dreamlike episode at Sagano. I pitied her when I imagined her emotions, and I also felt somewhat piqued that my good offices had borne so little fruit. "Do you think you ought to let the year end without meeting her again?" I asked. "I suppose you're right," he said. He sent a note: "Please think about coming whenever you happen to be free." The nun who acted as the Virgin's foster mother acknowledged the message, and I presented myself to her. She received me with a woebegone face, trying in vain to hold back tears with her sleeve.

"I thought my lady's only ties were with the goddess, but she's been more and more distraught ever since she wandered in confusion during that fleeting, dreamlike night." She grumbled on at tiresome length.

"I have simply been sent to ask if she happens to be at leisure," I replied.

"She is always at leisure," she said.

On my return, His Majesty remarked, "No doubt I would be bursting with ardor if it were a question of making one's way through 'foothills and wooded hills.'[52] As it is, I feel that I've already crossed to the other side." But he sent a senior noble's carriage to fetch the Virgin for a secret visit. I think it was around the time when the Twelfth Month moon shone in the sky. The journey was so long that it was late at night when she arrived. The private quarters fronting on Kyōgoku Avenue were in use by the Crown Prince, so the carriage was drawn up beside a gallery leading to the Great Willow Hall. The Virgin was taken to a four-bay room next to the Daytime Chamber. On duty as usual outside the folding screen, I found it only natural that she should be heard to complain about the time His Majesty had let elapse since their earlier meeting. It was enough to make anyone weep to see her set out in the morning, her sobs mingling with the sound of the dawn bell.

The arrival of the last day of the year deepened my gloom. I could not even leave the palace. There were indications that Higashi-no-onkata would be going to the imperial bedchamber, so I withdrew to my room after the evening repast, using a stomachache as a pretext. While I was there, my lover appeared at the doorway with a comment on the lateness of the hour. Terrified of gossip though I was, I let him steal inside, unable to deny the justice of his reproaches when he spoke of how long we had been separated. Our parting before dawn cost me a sharper pang than the farewell to the old year—an indication, I admitted to myself, that I was far too fond of him. Even now, tears dampen my sleeve as I recall our love.

52. Minamoto no Shigeyuki (SKKS 1013): tsukubayama / hayama shigeyama / shigekeredo / omoiiru ni wa / sawarazarikeri ("All those watchful eyes, many as foothills, as wooded hills at Tsukuba Mountain, will not deter one whose heart burns with passionate longing").

The Journal of the Sixteenth-Night Moon

Young people nowadays seem to be completely unaware of the connection between themselves and the name of a certain book that is reputed to have been taken from a wall in antiquity.[53] My late husband's written injunctions were as numerous as flutterings of kudzu leaves, and quite beyond dispute, but parental admonitions availed nothing. I came to realize, moreover, that I was the one person who had suffered exclusion from the all-embracing benevolence of the sovereign's rule, the only one who had failed to win the generous sympathy of His Majesty's loyal ministers. I could not reconcile myself to a situation that was a source of inconsolable grief and worry.

When I thought the matter over, it also seemed to me that there might be people who regarded the art of poetry as lacking in seriousness, as mere frivolous amusement. But our wise men have told us that this art has helped to regulate society, and to calm unrest in the Land of the Rising Sun, ever since the time when the heavenly rock-door opened and the assembled divinities accompanied the dance with song.[54] Furthermore, many individuals have compiled anthologies, but very few, I believe, have received a second imperial command and submitted selections to more than one sovereign.[55] I had formed a connection with remarkable men of the latter kind and, by karmic chance, had become the guardian of three sons and of countless old bits of paper having to do with poetry,[56] but other hands had gratuitously dammed the flow of "Narrow River," the Hosokawa estate bequeathed with the solemn understanding that its revenues should foster the art of poetry, provide care for the children, and support prayers for my husband in the afterlife. I marveled that I had managed to survive so long under those circumstances, sustaining a precarious, miserable existence month after month

53. A thrust at her stepson Tameuji. The Chinese *Classic of Filial Piety* (Xiao jing) was believed to have been hidden in the wall of Confucius's house.

54. According to Japanese myth, the Sun Goddess, Amaterasu, plunged the world into darkness by shutting herself inside the rock-cave of heaven. The other gods enticed her out with a bawdy dance.

55. Teika was one of the compilers of *New Collection of Early and Modern Poetry* (Shinkokinshū) and the sole compiler of the ninth imperial anthology, *New Imperial Collection* (Shinchokusenshū); Tameie was the sole compiler of the tenth, *Later Collection Continued* (Shokugosenshū) and one of the compilers of the eleventh, *Collection of Early and Modern Poetry Continued* (Shokukokinshū).

56. "Three sons" is probably a copyist's error for "two sons."

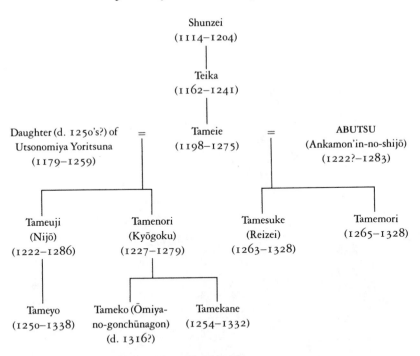

The Mikohidari house

and year after year, without knowing which would flicker out first, the flames in the memorial lamps or the lives of the parent and children who strove to guard the art and preserve the house. It was easy to think of bidding farewell to my own life, because I held it in no special affection, but I could not bear the darkness of heart that arises from worry about a child,[57] nor could I overcome my feelings of regret when I contemplated the present state of poetry. Obsessed by the thought that the merits of our case must appear as cloudless reflections in the tortoise mirror of the east,[58] I forgot every cause for hesitation, put aside every thought of self, and resolved to set off for Kamakura at once, following the beckoning of the Sixteenth-night moon.

My trip was not inspired by a Fun'ya no Yasuhide, nor was I seeking

57. An allusion to a poem by Fujiwara no Kanesuke (GSS 1103): hito no oya no / kokoro wa yami ni / aranedomo / ko o omou michi ni / madoinuru ka na ("The hearts of parents are not realms where darkness reigns—yet how easily we wander at a loss on the path of love for a child").

58. The tortoise's shell reveals the truth through divination, the mirror through reflection.

The nun Abutsu

a province in which to dwell. The season was early winter, the time of
unpredictable skies, and there seemed no end to the showers, "ever
falling, ever ceasing."[59] All nature conspired to depress my spirits; the
very leaves fell in concert with my tears, scattering before the gale as
though vying to go first. But "no one was forcing me to undertake the

59. Anonymous (GSS 445): kannazuki / furimi furazumi / sadame naki / shigure zo
fuyu no / hajime narikeru ("The start of winter: we know it by the showers in the Godless
Month, the unpredictable rains ever falling, ever ceasing"). Fun'ya no Yasuhide (9th c.)
invited a fellow poet, Ono no Komachi, to visit him in his province of Mikawa; Ariwara no
Narihira set out toward the east "in search of a province in which to settle" (*Tales of Ise*,
Sec. 9).

journey."[60] I could not linger just because it was hard to go, and I set about my preparations briskly.

When my eye fell on the gardens and rough-woven fences, which had shown increasing signs of neglect even while I was present to look after them, I realized that their appearance would soon be far worse. The people who loved me were inconsolable, their sleeves wet with tears. Tamesuke and Tamemori, in particular, seemed crushed with grief. I said what I could by way of comfort, my heart aching. My glance strayed to the bedchamber where all remained unchanged, even to Tameie's old pillow, and I jotted down these lines on something nearby, saddened anew:

todomeoku	If I go away,
furuki makura no	will there be any hand
chiri o dani	to so much as dust
wa ga tachisaraba	the old familiar pillow
tare ka harawan	I must now leave behind?

I wrote colophons for the booklets containing poems by successive generations of authors, selected and ordered the ones that were worth keeping, and added two compositions of my own, with a view to sending them to Tamesuke:

waka no ura ni	Make it a keepsake,
kakitodometaru	a memento of the past—
moshiogusa	this briny seaweed
kore o mukashi no	raked together on the beach
katami to mo mi yo	at Waka-no-ura.[61]

ana kashiko	If you feel yourself
yokonami kaku na	one of uncommon descent,
hamachidori	take care, beach plover,
hitokata naranu	that you do not dash crosswaves
ato o omowaba	onto those illustrious tracks.[62]

---

60. Minamoto no Sane (KKS 388): hitoyari no / michi naranaku ni / ōkata wa / ikiushi to iite / iza kaerinamu ("No one forces me to undertake this journey. I think on the whole I will call it too trying and turn around and go back").

61. The coastal area in Kii Province known as Waka-no-ura, a name translatable as Poetry Beach or Bay of Poetry, was a common metaphor for the art of poetry. Abutsu uses seaweed as a metaphor for poems.

62. "Don't stray from the Mikohidari teachings."

Tamesuke produced his answers at once:

tsui ni yomo	Quite impossible
ada ni wa naraji	that it should lead to nothing!
moshiogusa	This salty seaweed
katami o miyo no	has been left as a keepsake
ato ni nokoseba	from three generations.

mayowamashi	The beach plover
oshiezariseba	might have wandered from the path,
hamachidori	had it not been taught,
hitokata naranu	"These are the tracks left behind
ato o sore to mo	by illustrious forebears."

Reassured and moved by the maturity of his replies, I wished that I might recite them for Tameie, and my tears flowed again.

Tamemori, accustomed to being always at my side, was distraught when he learned that I was going off without him. I observed that he had written a poem as calligraphy practice:

harubaru to	With what emotions
yukusaki tōku	shall I gaze toward those skies,
shitawarete	yearning for the one
ika ni sonata no	who embarks on a journey
sora o nagamen	to a far-off destination?

Touched as by nothing else, I jotted down some words of consolation on the same piece of paper:

tsukuzuku to	Do not gaze sadly
sora na nagame so	at the heavens above.
koishikuba	If you should miss me,
michi tōku tomo	I will return in haste,
haya kaerikon	no matter how long the road.

Tamesuke's older brother, the Master of Discipline, came down from Mount Hiei to see me off.[63] He was also very sad, but he added these lines when he saw the two poems on the practice sheet:

ada ni nomi	Let us not be too swift
namida wa kakeji	to shed tears: the travel robe
tabigoromo	will be worn merely

63. This monk and the mountain ascetic who appears immediately below were Abutsu's sons by an earlier marriage.

kokoro no yukite	until she comes back again
tachikaeru hodo	with her mission accomplished.

His brusque words were only an attempt to distract our attention from his tears, which overflowed even while he tried to avoid inauspicious behavior. His bluffness and Tamemori's grief were both pathetic, each in its own way.

The Holy Teacher—the mountain ascetic who was the older brother of these other sons—stood ready to escort me on the journey. Declaring that he must not be unrepresented on Tamemori's sheet, he wrote this:

tachisou zo	How happy I am
ureshikarikeru	to serve as a guardian,
tabigoromo	accompanying
katami ni tanomu	the parent in whom we trust
oya no mamori wa	as she journeys on her way!

I did not have a whole bevy of daughters—only the one, an attendant of the Imperial Lady who lived near me. She had recently presented the Retired Emperor with a daughter. She was a person of firm, trustworthy character; thus, when writing to say how much I would miss seeing the Princess, I took the opportunity to speak in detail of my hope that she would look after Tamesuke and Tamemori. I added a poem at the end:

kimi o koso	I rely on you
asahi to tanome	as on the morning sun.
furusato ni	Let not the wild pinks,
nokoru nadeshiko	flowers left at the old home,
shimo ni karasu na	suffer from the blighting frost.

She wrote a moving, equally full response. This was her reply to my poem:

omoioku	If your loving heart
kokoro todomeba	remains behind with them,
furusato no	they will not wither
shimo ni mo kareji	even in the old home's frosts—
yamatonadeshiko	the wild pinks of Yamato.

In a sense, I suppose it has been foolish to record every poem composed by my five children, but I have assembled them here because all of them touched a mother's heart.

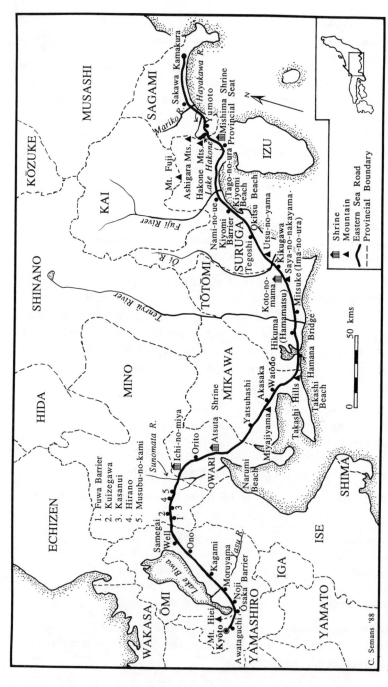

The Eastern Sea Road. Some of the place-names shown are mentioned in *An Account of a Journey to the East*, whose author had made his way along this route some 30 years earlier.

C. Semans '88

Aware that I would have to put weakness aside, I steeled myself to the parting and set out. I sent the carriage back at Awataguchi, and soon I was passing Ōsaka Barrier.

sadame naki	I make this journey
inochi wa shiranu	not knowing what lies ahead
tabi naredo	for my fleeting life,
mata ōsaka to	but I journey past Meeting Hill,
tanomete zo yuku	pledged to meet them again.

Not a soul was visible at Noji, either behind us on the road or ahead, and I could not repress a feeling of gloom as the sun declined toward the horizon. To make matters worse, a drizzling rain had begun to fall.

uchishigure	Far extends the way
furusato omou	from Noji-no-shinohara,
sode nurete	where a drizzling shower
yukusaki tōki	adds its moisture to sleeves
noji no shinohara	already drenched by thoughts of home.

We had planned to spend the night at Kagami, but darkness overtook us and we stayed at Moruyama instead, still pursued by showers.

itodo nao	Might it be to add
sode nurase to ya	new moisture to my drenched sleeves
yadoriken	that we stay the night
ma naku shigure no	at Moruyama, the hill
moruyama ni shi mo	where showers drip ceaselessly?

It was the night of the Sixteenth. I was exhausted when I lay down to sleep.

Toward dawn, we set out from Moruyama in the faint light of the lingering moon. The fog was thick when we crossed the Yasu River, and only the clop of horses' hoofs revealed the presence of travelers ahead.

tabibito wa	All together,
mina morotomo ni	the travelers take their leave
asa tachite	when morning arrives;
koma uchiwatasu	they ford the stream on horseback
yasu no kawagiri	through the Yasu River fog.

We spent the night of the Seventeenth at Ono Post Station. When the moon rose, it was delightful to be able to make out each tree in the row of pines on the mountaintop.

We left before daylight, groping through dense fog. At the Samegai

Well, I reflected that I would not be going on by if the season were summer. The foot travelers did seem to be stopping to drink. I thought:

musubu te ni	Samegai's waters:
nigoru kokoro o	were I to cup them in my hands
susuginaba	and cleanse my impure heart,
ukiyo no yume ya	might I awaken from the dream
samegai no mizu	of this transitory world?

Eighteenth Day. I put together these lines as we crossed the Fuji River near the barrier in Mino Province:

wa ga kodomo	If I did not wish
kimi ni tsukaen	my sons to be of service
tame narade	to their sovereign,
wataramashi ya wa	would I be likely to cross
seki no fujikawa	the Fuji River barrier?

The "eaves fashioned of wood at the Fuwa Barrier Post" were still unchanged.[64]

hima ōki	How they must filter through
fuwa no sekiya wa	at the Fuwa Barrier Post
kono hodo no	with its many gaps—
shigure mo tsuki mo	the season's drizzling showers
ika ni moruran	and the light of the moon!

From the barrier on, the rain became no longer a mere succession of showers but a steady downpour from black skies. The road was so bad that we had to stop at Kasanui Station, even though it was still daylight.

tabibito wa	At Kasanui,
mino uchiharau	I take lodgings to escape
yūgure no	the evening rain—
ame ni yado karu	this downpour in which travelers
kasanui no sato	must brush raincoats made of straw.

Nineteenth Day. We set out again. Near a place called Hirano or something of the sort, the road was in such a dreadful state from the

64. Fujiwara no Yoshitsune (SKKS 1599): hito sumanu / fuwa no sekiya no / itabisashi / arenishi nochi wa / tada aki no kaze ("Eaves fashioned of wood at the Fuwa Barrier Post where no human dwells: after the fall into decay, only the autumn wind"). The Fuwa Barrier, a government checkpoint near the Ōmi-Mino border, had been abandoned in the eighth century. The Fuji River was a small local stream, not to be confused with the Fuji River in Suruga Province.

previous night's rain that we struck out across the paddy fields, judging it impassable. The rain tapered off as dawn approached. Around noon, I noticed a prominent shrine near the road we were following. I asked about it, and someone said it was dedicated to Musubu-no-kami.[65] I composed this poem:

<table>
<tr><td>mamore tada</td><td>If you are indeed</td></tr>
<tr><td>chigiri musubu no</td><td>a god who vows to help men,</td></tr>
<tr><td>kami naraba</td><td>then please protect me:</td></tr>
<tr><td>tokenu urami ni</td><td>do not let me wander lost</td></tr>
<tr><td>ware mayowasade</td><td>in eternal resentment.</td></tr>
</table>

At a river called, I believe, the Sunomata, there was a floating bridge made of boats, which were aligned and fastened with what looked like ropes made of vines. Dangerous though it was, we crossed. Two poems came to my mind when I observed that the water was deep near the dike and shallow on the other side:

<table>
<tr><td>katafuchi no</td><td>My design is as deep</td></tr>
<tr><td>fukaki kokoro wa</td><td>as the pooling waters</td></tr>
<tr><td>arinagara</td><td>beside the dike,</td></tr>
<tr><td>hitomezutsumi ni</td><td>but may I not be held in check</td></tr>
<tr><td>sazo sekaruran</td><td>by interfering eyes?</td></tr>
</table>

<table>
<tr><td>kari no yo no</td><td>As ephemeral</td></tr>
<tr><td>yukiki to miru mo</td><td>as the goings and comings</td></tr>
<tr><td>hakanashi ya</td><td>in this transient world—</td></tr>
<tr><td>mi o ukifune o</td><td>the floating bridge made of boats</td></tr>
<tr><td>ukihashi ni shite</td><td>drifting like my wretched self.</td></tr>
</table>

Again, on passing Ichi-no-miya Shrine:

<table>
<tr><td>ichi no miya</td><td>I feel affection</td></tr>
<tr><td>na sae natsukashi</td><td>for the First Shrine's very name:</td></tr>
<tr><td>futatsu naku</td><td>it will surely guard</td></tr>
<tr><td>mitsu naki nori o</td><td>the dharma of which there exists</td></tr>
<tr><td>mamoru narubeshi</td><td>neither a second nor a third.</td></tr>
</table>

65. Musubu-no-kami is an abbreviation of Takamimusubi-no-kami, the name of a Shinto god who gives birth to all things. Abutsu chooses to interpret it in a Buddhist sense as part of the phrase *chigiri o musubu* ("pledge," "promise"; in this context, "help toward enlightenment"). Acknowledging that her attitude toward Tameuji is a hindrance to enlightenment, the poem calls on the god to help her win the lawsuit so that she can achieve a better state of mind.

Twentieth Day. We passed Orito Station in Owari Province. It was impossible not to visit Atsuta Shrine, which stood squarely on our route. I took out my inkstone, wrote some poems, and presented them as offerings:

inoru zo yo	I pray that my wish
wa ga omou koto	may come true: the divine gods
narumigata	bestow their favors
katahiku shio mo	as they ordain the ebb flow
kami no manimani	baring the beach at Narumi.

narumigata	If Narumi Beach
waka no urakaze	shuns not the sea breeze blowing
hedatezuba	from Waka-no-ura,
onaji kokoro o	the gods will accept my plea
kami mo ukuran	with sympathetic hearts.

mitsu shio no	Like the swelling tide,
sashite zo kitsuru	I have come toward this strand,
narumigata	hoping that the gods
kami ya aware to	of Narumigata Beach
mirume tazunete	will look on me with pity.

ame kaze mo	It seems that the gods
kami no kokoro ni	may direct as they desire
makasuran	even the rains and winds:
wa ga yukusaki no	let me suffer no hindrance
sawari arasu na	on the road that lies ahead.

The tide was out when we passed Narumi Beach; we followed the dry shoreline with no difficulty. Large flocks of beach plovers ran ahead as though to show us the way.

hamachidori	Though I had not thought
nakite zo sasou	to let my footsteps linger
yo no naka ni	in the world of men,
ato tomen to wa	crying plovers of the strand
omowazarishi o	entice me to journey on.

I had always heard that the Sumida River crossing was the place to see capital-birds, the waterfowl with the red bills and red legs, but there were some in this inlet too.[66]

66. Abutsu alludes to Narihira's poem on capital-birds in *Tales of Ise,* Sec. 9.

koto towan	I want to ask you:
hashi to ashi to wa	are you those capital-birds,
akazarishi	red of leg and beak,
wa ga sumu kata no	whose name recalls the city,
miyakodori ka to	the dear home where I dwell?

Night fell as we made our way beyond the Futamura Mountains on a long journey across hills and plains.

harubaru to	Traveling ever on,
futamurayama o	we have made our way across
yukisugite	the Futamura hills,
nao sue tadoru	yet still we must plod ahead:
nobe no yūyami	evening gloom on the plain.

I was told that we would spend the night at Yatsuhashi. The bridges were invisible in the darkness.

sasagani no	Ah! Night had fallen
kumode ayauki	before we made the crossing
yatsuhashi o	at Yatsuhashi,
yūgure kakete	the perilous Eight Bridges
watarinuru ka na	spanning the spider-leg stream.

Twenty-first Day. From Yatsuhashi, we traversed plains under a cloudless sky, with mountains in the distance. Around noon, we headed toward a hill splendid with colored leaves, some of which, clinging to the boughs despite the wind, were as brown as though they had already fallen. Evergreen trees also grew there; it was like looking at a brocade with a green ground. Upon making inquiries, I learned that the hill was called Miyajiyama.

shigurekeri	How it has showered!
somuru chishio no	A thousand dippings in dye,
hate wa mata	until at last
momiji no nishiki	the old colors disappear
iro kaeru made	from the autumn-leaf brocade.

It seemed to me that I had seen the hill before—and even the season was the same.[67] [I composed these lines:]

67. In the Tenth Month of an earlier year, Abutsu's adoptive father, Norishige, had taken her to Tōtōmi Province in an effort to make her forget her grief over the love affair mentioned earlier. Her childhood memoir, *Dozing*, describes the journey and her brief stay in the province.

machikeri na	Miyajiyama,
mukashi mo koeshi	the mountain I crossed of yore!
miyajiyama	It has awaited
onaji shigure no	the second meeting that comes
meguriau yo o	as showers fall again.

There was a thatched cottage in a bamboo grove at the foot of the hill. One wondered why the occupant had taken up his abode there and how he managed to live.

nushi ya tare	Who might dwell there?
yama no susono ni	Who has fixed his abode
yado shimete	at the foot of the hill,
atari sabishiki	with none for his neighbor
take no hitomura	save a lonely bamboo grove?

When the sun had set and it was too dark to tell one thing from another, we stopped for the night at a place called Watōdo or something of the sort.

On the Twenty-second, we set out before dawn by the light of the late moon, a departure that somehow seemed more depressing than usual. These lines came to my mind:

sumiwabite	I have taken leave
tsuki no miyako o	of the moon-palace city
ideshikado	where life was so hard—
ukimi hanarenu	yet the light of the dawn moon
ariake no kage	stays with me as I journey.[68]

Upon hearing a companion say, "Even the late moon wears a *kasa*":[69]

tabibito no	It wears a kasa,
onaji michi ni ya	the lingering moon at dawn.
idetsuran	Has it also,
kasa uchikitaru	like these human travelers,
ariake no tsuki	embarked upon a journey?

We crossed the Takashi Hills. The scenery was delightful where the ocean was visible. A strong shore wind wailed through the pine trees and whipped up the surf.

68. "Moon-palace city" (i.e., city as beautiful as the fabled palace in the moon) is an epithet for the capital. "Since I have left the palace in the moon behind, the moon itself ought to be far to the rear, but it accompanies me as a reminder of my troubles."

69. *Kasa* can mean both a traveler's rain hat and a ring around the moon.

wa ga tame ya	Might it be for me
nami mo takashi no	that the waves rise high
hama naran	at Takashi Beach?
sode no minato no	Never do the billows rest
nami wa yasumade	on sleeves recalling Sode Port.[70]

A flock of black birds on a snow-white sandspit proved to be cormorants:

shirahama ni	As black as ink sticks:
sumi no iro naru	cormorants, "birds of the isles,"
shimatsutori	on the white beach sands!
fude mo oyobaba	If my brush possessed the skill,
e ni kakitemashi	I would put them in a picture.

Looking out from Hamana Bridge, I saw flocks of gulls flying in every direction. Some were diving toward the depths; others were perched on rocks.

kamome iru	I feel a kinship
susaki no iwa mo	with the rocks on the sandspit
yoso narazu	where gulls go to perch,
nami no kakekosu	I who am well accustomed
sode ni minarete	to sleeves flooded by waves.

We spent the night at Hikuma Station. Hamamatsu (the name of the region thereabouts) had been the home of some people I had got to know fairly well. I saw in my mind's eye the faces of those who had dwelt there for years, and was deeply moved that I had lived to revisit the spot.

hamamatsu no	I hoped to find friends
kawaranu kage o	unchanged as the shore-pine shade,
tazunekite	yet they are no more:
mishi hito nami ni	I can but question the waves
mukashi o zo tou	for tidings of days gone by.

I invited the children and grandchildren of those past friends to my lodgings.

On the Twenty-third Day, Saigyō's experience came depressingly to mind as we boarded the boat at Tenryū Crossing.[71] There was only a

---

70. *Sode* means sleeve.

71. Saigyō is said to have been struck with a whip by a warrior who wanted his place in a crowded ferry boat at the crossing.

single bound-together craft, so besieged by travelers that the boatman
had no chance to rest.

mizu no awa no	Behold the state
ukiyo ni wataru	of each who goes through a life
hodo o mi yo	as brief as a bubble:
hayase no obune	a small craft in the rapids,
sao mo yasumezu	with its pole never at rest.

We spent the night at the Mitsuke provincial seat in Tōtōmi, a
ramshackle, rather frightening place. There was a spring nearby.

tare ka kite	More fearsome than ever
mitsuke no sato to	seems the journey when I hear,
kiku kara ni	"The name of this place
itodo tabine no	is Mitsuke, 'the village where
sora osoroshiki	someone comes to observe.'"

Twenty-fourth Day. We started across Saya-no-nakayama in the
middle of the day. The colored leaves were at their brilliant best near a
shrine called Koto-no-mama or something of the sort. I suppose the
sheltering hills had protected them from the storm winds. As we penetrated deeper, I found it lonely and disheartening to gaze at the ranges
near and far, which seemed quite unlike other mountains. We spent the
night at Kikugawa, a village at the foot of the hills.

koekurasu	Until dusk we crossed,
fumoto no sato no	and in the darkened village
yūyami ni	nestled at its base,
matsukaze okuru	it sends a wind through the pines:
saya no nakayama	Saya-no-nakayama.

Arising toward dawn, I saw the moon in the sky:

kumo kakaru	O moon of the dawn,
saya no nakayama	tell them in the capital
koenu to wa	that I have traversed
miyako ni tsuge yo	Saya-no-nakayama,
ariake no tsuki	those heights where the clouds come to rest.

The sound of the stream struck chill and lonely on the ear:

wataran to	Had I ever thought
omoi ya kakeshi	to be crossing these waters?

azumaji ni	Of the Chrysanthemum River
ari to bakari wa	I had merely heard men say,
kikugawa no mizu	"It is on the eastland road."[72]

On the Twenty-fifth, we left Kikugawa and crossed the Ōi River. In contrast to the stories we had heard, the water was very low and presented no difficulties. The other side of the riverbed seemed many leagues away; one could imagine the scene when it was full.

omoiizuru	Not even the sum
miyako no koto wa	of the rocks in the rapids
ōigawa	on the Ōi River
ikuse no ishi no	would equal the number
kazu mo oyobaji	of my thoughts of the city.

Just as we were crossing Utsu-no-yama, we met a mountain ascetic known to the Holy Teacher. I felt as though we were deliberately imitating that ancient time when someone recited, "even in my dreams."[73] It seemed a strange, amusing, touching, and elegant coincidence. The man said he was in a hurry, so I could not write a lot of letters; I merely sent a message to one important person:

wa ga kokoro	I am not at all
utsutsu to mo nashi	in command of my senses
utsu no yama	here at Mount Utsu:
yume ni mo tōki	I yearn for a capital
miyako kou tote	distant even in my dreams.

tsuta kaede	At Utsu Mountain,
shigurenu hima mo	tears turn my sleeves red-brown,
utsu no yama	even in intervals
namida ni sode no	when no wintry showers
iro zo kogaruru	fall on ivy and maples.

We spent the night at Tegoshi. It was very crowded, apparently because a certain Archbishop was passing through on his way to the capital. Despite some difficulty, we managed to find accommodations.

72. "Chrysanthemum River" is a literal translation of Kikugawa. Since the stream near the post station appears to have been very small, "creek" might be a better translation for *kawa* (*gawa*), which can mean a stream of any size.

73. A reference to the encounter with the ascetic in *Tales of Ise*, Sec. 9. Abutsu's first poem below puns on Utsu and *utsutsu* ("reality"; in the present context, with the negative *nashi*, "not in command of my senses").

Twenty-sixth Day. After crossing a river that was called, I think, the Warashina, we emerged onto Okitsu Beach, where I thought at once of the poem, "O moonlight shining where I left . . . crying."[74] I stretched out exhausted at our noonday stop, resting my head on a wretched little boxwood pillow. There was an inkstone, so I scribbled a poem on the sliding door as I lay:

naozari ni	The borrowed pillow
mirume bakari o	is just for a fleeting nap:
karimakura	do not tell others
musubiokitsu to	I have plighted a lasting troth
hito ni kataru na	with someone at Okitsu.

We passed Kiyomi Barrier in the gathering dusk. To my amusement, the breaking waves looked as though they were dressing the rocks in white silk:

kiyomigata	I would question you,
toshi furu iwa ni	O rocks borne down with years
koto towan	at Kiyomi Beach:
nami no nureginu	how many might you have worn
ikukasane kitsu	of "drenched robes" woven from waves?[75]

Night fell soon, and we took lodgings at a nearby hamlet close to the sea. The disagreeable odor of smoldering smoke from next door, which perhaps had something to do with fishermen's work, made me think of the poet's words, "Their night's lodging stank."[76] The wind raged all night long, and the waves seemed to be crashing next to my pillow.

narawazu yo	Never have I known
yoso ni kikikoshi	wakefulness like this:
kiyomigata	wild surf near my bed
araisonami no	at Kiyomi Beach, a strand
kakaru nezame wa	once only a name to me.

No smoke rose from Mount Fuji. I remembered distinctly that I had

74. Fujiwara no Teika (SKKS 934): koto toe yo / omoiokitsu no / hamachidori / nakunaku ideshi / ato no tsukikage ("O moonlight shining where I left with heavy heart, crying like these birds, beach plovers at Okitsu: please tell me how things are going").

75. *Nureginu* ("drenched robes") can mean "false accusations." Abutsu probably has the lawsuit in mind.

76. An inexact quotation of a passage from "The Bound Barbarians," a poem by Bo Juyi describing the suffering of wounded Tibetan captives marching to southeastern China: "At night, their stinking bodies soil the beds and matting."

seen the Fuji smoke plume morning and evening from Tōtōmi Province, which I had visited when I traveled eastward at my adoptive father's behest long ago (the time when I composed "Is it my uncertain fate" and other poems). I asked about the year in which the smoke had ceased to rise, but nobody could give me a clear answer.

ta ga kata ni	In whose direction
nabikihatete ka	might it have fluttered away?
fuji no ne no	No trace lingers now
keburi no sue no	of the smoke that once issued
miezu naruran	from Fuji's lofty peak.

The words of the preface to *Collection of Early and Modern Poetry* came to mind.[77] [I composed these poems:]

itsu no yo no	From what bygone age
fumoto no chiri ka	came the dust at the bottom
fuji no ne o	that made Fuji's peak
yuki sae takaki	grow into a high mountain,
yama to nashiken	home even to drifted snows?

kuchihateshi	If smoke no longer
nagara no hashi o	ascends from Mount Fuji,
tsukurabaya	I would like to rebuild
fuji no keburi mo	the bridge at Nagara,
tatazu narinaba	long fallen into ruin.

At Nami-no-ue that night, I was unable to sleep a wink because of the clamorous waves.

Twenty-seventh Day. We crossed the Fuji River after daybreak. The morning cold at the river was frightful. By my count, we crossed fifteen channels.

saewabinu	How bitter the cold!
yuki yori orosu	The sleeves of my winter robe
fujikawa no	freeze in the river wind
kawakaze kōru	whipping down from the snow
fuyu no koromode	at the Fuji River.

That day, we reached Tago-no-ura under balmy skies. On seeing fishermen plying their trade:

77. "As a high mountain grows from the dust and mud at its base to tower where heavenly clouds trail, so too must it have been with poetry. . . . When people today hear

kokoro kara	Of your own accord,
oritatsu tago no	you go down to the sea,
amagoromo	fishers of Tago.
hosanu urami to	Do not complain to others
hito ni kataru na	that you lack time to dry your clothes.

We spent the night at the Izu provincial seat. During a visit to Mishima Shrine, paid in the lingering rays of the setting sun, I composed and presented these poems:

aware to ya	Might they look on me
mishima no kami no	with pity—the Mishima gods,
miyabashira	deities of this shrine?
tada koko ni shi mo	Directing my steps hither,
megurikinikeri	I have journeyed long and far.

onozukara	The gods must know it:
tsutaeshi ato mo	there exists a successor
aru mono o	on whom the heritage,
kami wa shiruran	the way of Shikishima,
shikishima no michi	quite naturally has devolved.

tazunekite	I take it as a sign
wa ga koekakaru	of a successful outcome—
hakoneji o	this Hakone Road
yama no kai aru	with its mountain valleys
shirube to zo omou	that I have come to traverse.[78]

Twenty-eighth Day. We left the Izu provincial seat for the Hakone Road. It was still very dark.

tamakushige	Though we hurry across
hakone no yama o	the mountains at Hakone
isogedomo	of gemmed comb boxes,
nao akegataki	the dawn comes but slowly
yokogumo no sora	through cloud banks in the heavens.[79]

We had decided to go by way of Hakone because the route across the Ashigara Mountains was supposed to be longer.

---

that smoke no longer rises above Mount Fuji, or that Nagara Bridge has been rebuilt, the poetry [of the past] is their sole consolation." Nagara Bridge was a symbol of age.

78. *Kai* means both "valley" and "successful outcome" (of the lawsuit).

79. An implied second meaning: "There is a box (*hako*) here, but it is hard to open (*akegataki*, which can also mean 'dawn with difficulty')."

yukashisa yo	What might they look like—
sonata no kumo o	those Ashigara Mountains
sobadatete	holding themselves apart
yoso ni nashinuru	behind the towering clouds
ashigara no yama	they raise as barriers?

We descended a mountain so steep that people could hardly keep from slipping. It was called Yusaka. After just managing the descent, we came to a river at the bottom called the Hayakawa [Swift River]. It was swift enough! I inquired about all the wood floating in the stream and was told that fishermen were sending fuel for salt fires down to the coast.

azumaji no	When I survey the scene
yusaka o koete	after crossing Yusaka Hill
miwataseba	on the eastland road:
shioki nagaruru	the swift Hayakawa,
hayakawa no mizu	bearing saltwood in its flow.

From Yusaka we came out onto the coast. The evening shadows were beginning to gather, but our destination for the night lay far ahead. Nobody could tell me when I asked the name of the beach, which afforded a panoramic view all the way to the Great Island of Izu. There was no sign of human habitation except for some fishermen's dwellings.

ama no sumu	Let us find lodgings
sono sato no na mo	where white waves approach the beach
shiranami no	at this settlement,
yosuru nagisa ni	unknown to us even by name—
yado ya karamashi	this place where fisherfolk dwell.

We groped our way across the Mariko River in the pitch dark and spent the night at Sakawa, planning to enter Kamakura on the following day.

Twenty-ninth Day. We left Sakawa and traveled a great distance along the beach. A slender moon had risen above the brightening surface of the sea.

uraji yuku	With what poignance
kokorobososa o	it brings home the loneliness
namima yori	of travel on the strand—
idete shirasuru	the lingering morning moon
ariake no tsuki	rising from between the waves.

A mist spread over the waves as they advanced and retreated on the shore, and the many fishing boats disappeared from view.

amaobune	Coastal morning mist
kogiyuku kata o	hanging over cresting waves:
miseji to ya	is it reluctant
nami ni tachisou	to reveal the whereabouts
ura no asagiri	of the fishers' tiny craft?

It seemed a dream that I had journeyed so far from the capital.

tachihanare	Had my husband lived,
yomo ukinami wa	I would not have known this spray
kake mo seji	from cresting breakers,
mukashi no hito no	nor experienced these trials
onaji yo naraba	so far from the capital.

The place where I lived in the eastland was called Tsukikage Valley. It was close to the sea at the foot of a hill, a dreadfully windy spot. The Mountain Temple was nearby, so the environs were both peaceful and lonely. The murmur of the waves and the soughing of the wind in the pines never ceased.

Just as I was awaiting news from the capital with the greatest impatience and anxiety, a safe hand brought what appeared to be replies to the poems I had dispatched by the ascetic we had met at Mount Utsu.

tabigoromo	Even between showers
namida o soete	at Utsu-no-yama Mountain,
utsu no yama	showers must have fallen,
shigurenu hima mo	for tears added their moisture
sazo shigururan	to the traveler's garments.

yukuri naku	The hesitant moon
akugareideshi	that rose on the Sixteenth Night
izayoi no	shall be my memento
tsuki ya okurenu	of one who fared forth in distress
katami narubeki	on a journey unforeseen.

It seemed that my correspondent must have remembered the moon on the date of my departure—the Sixteenth of the Tenth Month. I replied only to the second poem (a most elegant and moving composition):

meguriau	I pin all my hopes
sue o zo tanomu	on the time of its return—

yukuri naku	the hesitant moon
sora ni ukareshi	that chanced by accident
izayoi no tsuki	to float in Sixteenth-night skies.

Tamenori's daughter, Ōmiya-no-gonchūnagon, was a poet with compositions in more than one imperial anthology, and I used to be in touch with her morning and evening on matters having to do with poetry. Perhaps for that reason, she sent a letter expressing concern about my journey. A poem was included:

harubaru to	From this far distance,
omoi koso yare	I wonder with anxious heart:
tabigoromo	what might be the state
namida shigururu	of travel robes when teardrops
hodo ya ika ni to	descend like wintry showers?

My reply:

omoiyare	Only think of it—
tsuyu mo shigure mo	moisture from sleeves where dewdrops
hitotsu nite	mingled with showers
yamaji wakekoshi	as I made my way hither
sode no shizuku o	along the mountain roads.

Her elder brother, Lord Tamekane, wrote in the same solicitous vein:

furusato wa	They must be growing
shigure ni tachishi	still colder from the snow—
tabigoromo	the travel garments
yuki ni ya itodo	in which you left the city
sae masaruran	as the rains of winter fell.

My reply:

tabigoromo	The shore wind strikes chill
urakaze saete	on travel robes: in this month
kaminazuki	when gods are absent,
shigururu kumo ni	snowflakes too fall from the clouds
yuki zo furisou	whence come the wintry showers.

The Koga Chancellor's daughter, Shikikenmon'in-no-mikushige-dono, was a well-known poet with compositions in two or three imperial anthologies, from *Later Collection Continued* on, and with many poems in unofficial anthologies as well. She was now serving in the Imperial Lady

Ankamon'in's entourage, where she was called Onkata. On the day before my departure for the east, I had gone to the Kitashirakawa Palace to say good-bye to her, but she had been out. Afterward, everything had had to be done on the one last evening, and I had been in too great a hurry even to send word of my plans before rushing off. The matter preyed on my mind, so I wrote her, telling of my depression as the year bid fair to end while I was still away, describing the incessant snows, and so forth. I included a poem:

kiekaeri	There is darkness, too,
nagamuru sora mo	in the sky at which I gaze,
kakikurete	lost in somber thought:
hodo wa kumoi zo	it will soon be snowing there
yuki ni nariyuku	in the distant capital.

Her answer was prompt. "I kept meaning to write as soon as an opportunity arose, and then today, on the Twenty-second of the Twelfth Month, your long-awaited letter arrived. It was a marvelous treat. I was so happy! I wanted to tell you all about everything, but things are in an uproar because Her Highness is moving tonight to avoid an inauspicious direction. It is very annoying, but I can't write as I wanted to.

"On the day when you came to say you were leaving the next day, I had taken some of the younger ladies-in-waiting to see the colored leaves at the Mine Mansion; it was only later that I learned of your plans. But why didn't you ask where I had gone?" [Her poem:]

hitokata ni	Had I regretted
sode ya nuremashi	nothing more than not knowing
tabigoromo	when you were to leave,
tatsu hi o kikanu	then perhaps these sleeves of mine
urami nariseba	might merely have been dampened.

She continued, "Here is my reply to 'it will soon be snowing there'":

kakikurashi	To gaze at the sky,
yuki furu sora no	somber with lowering clouds
nagame ni mo	where snowflakes fall,
hodo wa kumoi no	is to know the misery
aware o zo shiru	of one in a distant place.

I contented myself with a reply to "not knowing when you were to leave":

kokoro kara	Why express regret
nani uramuran	and plead ignorance of the day
tabigoromo	when I was to leave?
tatsu hi o dani mo	Was it not by your own choice
shirazugao nite	that you were absent when I called?

Having learned that someone who could carry messages was to leave before dawn, I stayed up all night writing letters for the capital. In the one to my older sister, with whom I was on close, loving terms, I spoke in detail of the little boys and then, with the winds and waves raging as usual, I added a description of my present circumstances:

yomosugara	Staying up alone
namida mo fumi mo	while the wind blows across the beach,
kakiaezu	I try in vain all night long
iso kosu kaze ni	to brush away the teardrops
hitori okiite	and put my brush to paper.

Again, I wrapped together a few bits and pieces from the beach to accompany a letter to my younger sister, the nun, with whom I was equally intimate, and who would be longing for me in the old home:

itazura ni	Though I seek solace
me kari shio yaku	in idly gathering seaweed
susabi ni mo	and kindling salt fires,
koishi ya nareshi	how I long to see the nun
sato no amabito	in the old familiar home!

Presently, I received touching replies from both sisters. The elder wrote:

tamazusa o	Reading your letter,
miru ni namida no	I bedewed it with teardrops.
kakaru ka na	It seemed that I, too,
iso kosu kaze wa	listened to the wind
kiku kokochi shite	blowing across the beach.

That sister was the wife of the Naka-no-in Middle Captain. Her husband was now called the Novice of Third Rank. He was still alive, but had taken up residence elsewhere and immersed himself in religious pursuits.

My younger sister responded with gentle delicacy to "gathering seaweed and kindling salt fires." Among other things, she said, "There is also a sea in the capital—a sea of tears under a pillow, shed by someone who yearns for you." This was her poem:

morotomo ni	Were it but a shore
me kari shio yaku	where you and I together
ura naraba	reaped seaweed and burned
nakanaka sode ni	salt fires—ah, then the waves
nami wa kakeji o	would not wash onto my sleeves.

She too had served Ankamon'in. In a manner both touching and amusing, her letter rambled on about things a person would not ordinarily disclose to others.

Soon the old year ended and spring arrived. Haze veiled the landscape. Although I lived near the mouth of a valley, I did not even hear a warbler's first song. I felt a sharp pang of nostalgia for the past, especially for the springtime skies I knew so well. Just then, someone told me of another opportunity to communicate with the capital, and I addressed letters to the usual places. To the author of the "hesitant moon" poem I sent these lines, as well as a number of other inconsequential musings:

oboro naru	The misty moon
tsuki wa miyako no	looks as it does in the skies
sora nagara	above the city,
mada kikazarishi	but how unfamiliar the sound
nami no yoruyoru	of breakers night after night!

I received an answer before long, transmitted through reliable hands:

nerareji na	With the sound of waves
miyako no tsuki o	breaking in strange surroundings
mi ni soete	night after night,
narenu makura no	sleep must be impossible,
nami no yoruyoru	though you see the city's moon.

Because Lady Gonchūnagon was a dedicated poet, I copied and sent her a group of compositions I had written lately for calligraphy practice. "Close to the sea as I am, I sometimes look for shells, but this beach is not Nagusa Strand: I have the feeling that it is quite barren."

ika ni shite	I cannot achieve
shibashi miyako o	even brief forgetfulness
wasuregai	of the capital:
nami no hima naku	like ever-breaking waves
ware zo kudakuru	is the turmoil in my heart.

shirazarishi	Even the hill breeze
urayamakaze mo	on an unfamiliar shore
ume ga ka wa	brings a scent of plum.
miyako ni nitaru	Ah, how this dawn in springtime
haru no akebono	recalls the royal city!
harekumori	Now clear, now clouded,
nagame zo waburu	it is hard to keep in view—
urakaze ni	the moon on a spring night
kasumi tadayou	with haze adrift in the breeze
haru no yo no tsuki	blowing shoreward from the sea.
azumaji no	Through rifts in the haze
isoyamakaze no	where the wind blows from the shore hills
taema yori	on the eastland road,
nami sae hana no	even the cresting breakers
omokage ni tatsu	resemble flowers in bloom.
miyakobito	Capital dweller,
omoi mo ideba	if you should remember me,
azumaji no	send a note to ask,
hana ya ika ni to	"What might be your opinion
otozuretemashi	of the blossoms in the east?"

Those and other things I jotted down just as they occurred to me, but the messenger was in a hurry and I had to bring my letter to an abrupt end.

Lady Gonchūnagon's answer was prompt. "I had been worrying about you for a long time, but your letter made me feel as though the skies had cleared on a hazy day." [Her poems:]

tanomu zo yo	I await the day
shiohi ni hirou	when, like an incoming wave
utsusegai	seeking the sea again,
kai aru nami no	you will return home to us,
tachikaeru yo o	your journey crowned with success.
kurabemi yo	They may look the same
kasumi no uchi no	to one with a clouded heart,
haru no tsuki	but please compare the scenes
harenu kokoro wa	when the springtime moon shines clear
onaji nagame o	and when it is veiled in haze.
shiranami no	The very idea
iro mo hitotsu ni	raises it before my eyes—

chiru hana o	that scene of blossoms
omoiyaru sae	scattering from cherry trees,
omokage ni tatsu	one in hue with the white waves.

azumaji no	Though you may be gazing
sakura o mite mo	at the eastland cherry trees,
wasurezuba	please ask a question
miyako no hana o	about the city's blossoms
hito ya towamashi	if you have not forgotten me.

On alternate days toward the end of the Third Month, I suffered two bouts of what seemed to be the kind of fever children have. It struck me as very odd. Dazed and exhausted, I arose before dawn when the next attack was due, settled myself in front of the sacred image, and recited the *Lotus Sutra* with all the energy I could muster. Perhaps for that reason, the fever disappeared without a trace. There was a chance to communicate with the capital just then, so I sent word of my illness to the people at home. I took the occasion to write this to Lady Gonchū-nagon: "I have fallen desperately ill on my journey, but have managed to survive thus far—thanks, perhaps, to the protection of the *Lotus Sutra*." [My poem:]

itazura ni	Were I to vanish,
ama no shio yaku	carried away on the wind,
keburi to mo	who would find the sight
tare ka wa mimashi	even as notable as smoke
kaze ni kienaba	from a fisherman's salt-fire?

Shocked, she sent a reply at once:

kie mo seji	Never will it die—
waka no uraji ni	the fisher's seaweed salt-fire,
toshi o hete	which for many years
hikari o souru	has burned with ever brighter light
ama no moshiobi	at Waka-no-ura Bay.

"I was awed by the efficacy of the sutra":

tanomoshi na	Trustworthy, indeed!
mi ni sou tomo to	The promise of the Flower
narinikeri	of the Wondrous Law
tae naru nori no	has become for you a friend
hana no chigiri wa	ever present at your side.

Around the beginning of the Fourth Month, I used an opportunity to write again to Lady Gonchūnagon, mentioning, among other things, my nostalgia for last year's spring and summer:

mishi yo koso	The world I used to see
kawarazarurame	probably remains the same—
kurehatete	even the branches,
haru yori natsu ni	changing as the season turns
utsuru kozue mo	and spring yields place to summer.

natsugoromo	Capital dwellers,
haya tachikaete	their costumes already changed
miyakobito	into summer styles,
ima ya matsuran	must be waiting eagerly
yamahototogisu	for the cuckoo from the hills.

I received an answer to that letter too:

kusa mo ki mo	The grasses and trees
kozo mishi mama ni	look precisely as they did
kawaranedo	when I saw them last year—
arishi ni mo ninu	and yet I have fallen prey
kokochi nomi shite	to quite different feelings.

"As regards your inquiry about the cuckoo":

hito yori mo	More than other folk,
kokoro tsukushite	I set myself to listen,
hototogisu	and thus this very day
tada hitokoe o	I heard the cuckoo utter
kyō zo kikitsuru	a solitary note.

"Your letter seemed especially elegant because it reminded me of the poem that Middle Captain Sanekata is supposed to have sent from Michinoku when the Fifth Month arrived without his having heard a cuckoo." [Sanekata's poem:]

miyako ni wa	The cuckoo's singing
kikifurusuran	must be a familiar sound
hototogisu	in the capital.
seki no konata no	How miserable to dwell
mi koso tsurakere	beyond the barrier post!

Meanwhile, the Fourth Month drew to a close and I abandoned hope of hearing even a faint echo of the cuckoo's song. I thought of this poem when someone said people had been hearing the birds often at a place called Hiki-no-yatsu [Low Valley]:

shinobine wa	The cuckoo who sings,
hiki no yatsu naru	low-voiced in the "Low Valley,"
hototogisu	Hiki-no-yatsu:
kumoi ni takaku	when will he announce his name
itsu ka nanoran	high in the realm of the clouds?

But nothing came of it. I suppose there have never been many cuckoos anywhere in the east as far as Michinoku. One could accept it if there were none at all, but it makes one fidgety and envious to learn that others hear them occasionally. It seems as though they are playing favorites.

After many years in the service of the Fukakusa Former Virgin (a position in which her father had placed her), Middle Counselor Teika's daughter, the lady known as Katokumon'in-no-shinchūnagon, had been transferred to the service of her present mistress, the Imperial Lady Katokumon'in, who was the Virgin's adopted daughter. She was the elder sister of Minbukyō-no-suke, the author of the poem, "the boat plying the waters . . . to harvest the seaweed."[80] Because she felt that anyone with a famous father like Teika ought not to produce inferior compositions for other people to hear, she was usually very secretive about her own poems, but she worried about my being far away under travel skies and wrote me all manner of touching things. She added this at the end, treating it as though it were not a poem but merely a part of the letter—something that seemed to me to show exceptional prudence:

ika bakari	How often its call
ko o omou tsuru no	must sound in the alien skies
tobiwakare	at its journey's end—
narawanu tabi no	the crane that has flown away
sora ni nakuran	from the young for whom it yearns!

My reply:

sore yue ni	Only for their sake
tobiwakarete mo	did it fly away from them—
ashitazu no	and yet the reed crane
ko o omou kata wa	can but droop in misery
nao zo kanashiki	when it remembers its children.

80. ShokuGSS 947: nigorie ni / ukimi kogaruru / mokaribune / hate wa yukiki no / kage dani mo mizu ("We no longer see even the reflection of the boat plying the waters of the turbid inlet to harvest the seaweed"). Wordplays yield a second meaning: "Despite my yearning, I no longer see even the shadow of the man who came and went here."

In the thought that she would be the one person to find it moving, I took occasion to tell her that Tameie had appeared to me in a dream, traveler though I was. I sent these poems:

miyako made
kataru mo tōshi
omoine ni
shinobu mukashi no
yume no nagori o

I long to describe
my dream of happier days,
dreamt when I fell asleep,
my mind filled with yearning thoughts—
yet how distant is the city!

hakanashi ya
tabine no yume ni
mayoikite
samureba mienu
hito no omokage

But a fleeting sight—
the figure of the person
who came from nowhere
into a traveler's dream
and vanished when she awoke.

She went out of her way to find a means of replying. Discreet though she was about revealing her compositions, she let herself be guided by circumstances. Her poems:

azumaji no
kusa no makura wa
tōkaredo
katareba chikaki
inishie no yume

However distant
the pillow fashioned of grass
on the eastland road,
close it seems when spoken of—
that dream of bygone days.

izuku yori
tabine no yuka ni
kayouran
omoiokitsuru
tsuyu o tazunete

Whence might he have come
visiting the bedchamber
where the traveler slept—
the one who sought the dewdrop
he sorrowed to leave behind?

To my great alarm, there was a strange dearth of news during the summer. I became even more uneasy on learning that there had been trouble in the vicinity of the capital: the Shiga waves had risen, it seemed, and Mount Hiei and Miidera were quarreling.[81] A messenger finally arrived on the Second of the Eighth Month, and I received an accumulation of delayed letters from different people. Tamesuke wrote that he had composed fifty poems, which he sent along without having had time to make fair copies. His compositions have become most inter-

81. The monks of Enryakuji on Mount Hiei and those of Onjōji (Miidera) near Lake Biwa often came to blows. "The Shiga waves had risen" means that there was discord in Shiga, an area bordering the lake.

esting. I marked eighteen of the fifty as meritorious, which did seem unusual, I admit. Perhaps it was simply maternal blindness. This was one of them:

kokoro nomi	Although in spirit
hedatezu tote mo	we are always together,
tabigoromo	the traveler, alas,
yamaji kasanaru	dwells afar under white clouds
ochi no shirakumo	beyond many a mountain road.

I was sure it had been inspired by thoughts of these travel skies of mine. Touched, I added a reply in small characters beside it:

koishinobu	Ah! My loving heart
kokoro ya taguu	accompanies the white clouds
asayū ni	of this distant land
yukite wa kaeru	as they journey ceaselessly
ochi no shirakumo	toward the city and back again.

I also added a reply to another poem with "Travel" as its topic. [Tamesuke's poem:]

karisome no	Dew dampens my sleeve
kusa no makura no	at the very thought of it—
yonayona o	the makeshift pillow
omoiyaru ni mo	on which the traveler's head
sode zo tsuyukeki	must repose night after night.

[The reply:]

aki fukaki	As autumn deepens,
kusa no makura ni	I weep into a pillow
ware zo naku	fashioned of grass,
furisutete koshi	crying like the bell insect
suzumushi no ne o	for the ones I have left behind.

I added something more at the end of the fifty poems—general comments on the art of composition, and a final poem written with Tameie in mind:

kore o miba	Were he to see them,
ika bakari ka to	what happiness he would feel!
omoiizuru	I can but shed tears
hito ni kawarite	in his place, weeping aloud
ne koso nakarure	as thoughts of him fill my mind.

Tamemori had also sent some poems, thirty of them, saying, "Please mark these and point out all the faults." He had turned sixteen that year. To me the verses seemed excellent—quite professional—but then I thought in embarrassment that I was probably just being a doting parent again. His travel poems, like Tamesuke's, seemed to have been written with me in mind. I had sent the boys a day-by-day account of the journey to Kamakura, which he had doubtless read before composing them.

[A travel poem by Tamemori:]

tachiwakare	How sorely the sight
fuji no keburi o	of smoke above Mount Fuji
mite mo nao	must have sharpened
kokorobososa no	the misery of the traveler
ika ni soiken	separated from her dear ones!

I added a reply to that one too:

karisome ni	Just for a while,
tachiwakarete mo	I have parted from my dear ones,
ko o omou	but to me Fuji's smoke
omoi o fuji no	suggested the fire of love
keburi to zo mishi	burning in a mother's heart.

Lady Gonchūnagon sent another detailed letter. "I have had no companion with whom to compose since you left, and now that autumn is here, I miss you more than ever. I look at the moon alone all night long." [Her poem:]

azumaji no	Tears of longing becloud
sora natsukashiki	even the moon, the reminder of one
katami dani	for whose sake I hold
shinobu namida ni	the skies of the eastland road
kumoru tsukikage	in nostalgic affection.

In my reply, I wrote of my longing for home and other such things. [My poem:]

kayourashi	Looking at the moon
miyako no hoka no	thus distant from the capital,
tsuki mite mo	I yearn for those skies.
sora natsukashiki	It seems that the two of us
onaji nagame wa	have gazed with similar thoughts.

Many poems from the capital have accumulated since then. I shall try to record them elsewhere.

* * *

shikishima ya	Ah, how awesome
yamato no kuni wa	the power first manifest
ametsuchi no	here in Yamato,
hirakehajimeshi	the land of Shikishima,
mukashi yori	in days long ago,
iwado o akete	after the separation
omoshiroki	of heaven and earth,
kagura no kotoba	when the rock-cave door opened
utaiteshi	and entertaining
sareba kashikoki	words set to divine music
tameshi tote	were intoned aloud,
hijiri no miyo no	thus making clear the Way
michi shiruku	of imperial rule!
hito no kokoro o	Poetry takes as its seed
tane to shite	the human heart,
yorozu no waza o	it expresses a myriad things
koto no ha ni	in the leaves of words,
oni kami made mo	it touches the emotions
aware tote	of spirits and gods.
yashima no hoka no	With calming touch, it quiets
yotsu no umi	the billows rising
nami mo shizuka ni	on the four seas that border
osamarite	our eight islands;
sora fuku kaze mo	likewise, it tempers the winds
yawaraka ni	blowing in the sky,
eda mo narasazu	that the branches may be still;
furu ame mo	and it determines
toki sadamareba	the season when rain may fall.
kimikimi no	And thus, many times,
mikoto no mama ni	in faithful obedience
shitagaite	to august edicts
waka no uraji no	from successive sovereigns,
moshiogusa	men have raked together
kakiatsumetaru	collections of salt seaweed
ato ōku	from Poetry Bay.
sore ga naka ni mo	And among that company
na o tomete	there have been, in truth,

miyo made tsugishi
　hito no ko no
oya no toriwaki
　yuzuriteshi
sono makoto sae
　ari nagara
omoeba iyashi
　shinano naru
sono hahakigi no
　sono hara ni
tane o makitaru
　toga tote ya
yo ni mo tsukae yo
　ikeru yo no
mi o tasuke yo to
　chigirioku
suma to akashi no
　tsuzuki naru
hosokawayama no
　yamagawa no
wazuka ni inochi
　kakei tote
tsutaishi mizu no
　minakami mo
sekitomerarete
　ima wa tada
kuga ni agareru
　io no goto
kajio taetaru
　fune no goto
yoru kata mo naku
　wabihatsuru
ko o omou tote
　yoru no tsuru
nakunaku miyako
　ideshikado
mi wa kazu narazu
　kamakura no
yo no matsurigoto
　shigekereba
kikoeageteshi

a father, son, and grandson
　successively famed.
Now, there is actual proof
　of a property
granted to that grandson's son
　by special bequest.
Might it be because the heir
　grew within a womb
of no account (suggesting
　hahakigi trees
on the Sonohara plain
　in Shinano)?
Might that be the reason why
　they dam the upper course
of the mountain stream whence flowed—
　as through a conduit
barely sustaining life—
　waters descending
from Hosokawayama,
　the domain beyond
Suma and Akashi,
　willed in covenant:
"Be of service to the state;
　let this property
ensure your livelihood"?
　For love of that son,
now driven to his wits' end,
　bereft of support,
as forlorn as a fish
　stranded on dry land,
or as a boat with its rope
　severed from the oar,
his mother, weeping aloud
　like a crane in the night,
has embarked on a journey
　from the capital,
but she is of small account,
　and affairs of state
proliferate like grasses
　at Kamakura.
The pleas she has presented—

koto no ha mo
eda ni komorite
    mume no hana
yotose no haru ni
    narinikeri
yukue mo shiranu
    nakazora no
kaze ni makasuru
    furusato wa
nokiba mo arete
    sasagani no
ikasama ni ka wa
    narinuran
yoyo no ato aru
    tamazusa mo
sate kuchihateba
    ashihara no
michi mo sutarete
    ika naran
kore o omoeba
    watakushi no
nageki nomi ka wa
    yo no tame mo
tsuraki tameshi to
    narinubeshi
yukusaki kakete
    samazama ni
kakinokosareshi
    fude no ato
kaesugaesu mo
    itsuwari to
omowamashikaba
    kotowari o
tadasu no mori no
    yūshide ni
yayoya isasaka
    kakete toe
midarigawashiki
    sue no yo ni
asa wa ato naku
    narinu to ka

the leaves of her words—
remain as buds on the branches,
    and now the plum trees
have blossomed in the springtime
    of a fourth year.
How piteous must be the state
    of her old dwelling,
abandoned to the onslaughts
    of the skyborne winds
blowing from every quarter,
    its eaves in ruins,
its chambers festooned with webs
    woven by spiders!
And what will be the outcome
    if they also rot—
those precious writings bequeathed
    by generations?
May not others then forsake
    the Way of poetry?
Upon reflection, our plight
    is not merely cause
for private lamentation:
    it is sure to prove
a most serious matter
    for society.
If there be those who think them
    nothing but falsehoods
pure and simple—those traces
    from the brush of one
who, in various manners,
    wrote down documents
providing for the future—
    pray make offerings
and briefly consult the god
    of Tadasu Woods,
the shrine whose name promises
    correction of wrongs.
With no concern for myself,
    I trust the government,
holding firm to the belief
    that if there be those

isameokishi o	who remember the warning
wasurezuba	left as legacy
yugameru koto o	in these degenerate
mata tare ka	late days of the Law—
hikinaosubeki	"hemp seems to have disappeared
to bakari ni	without a trace"—
mi o kaerimizu	someone will surely straighten
tanomu zo yo	that which has been bent.[82]
sono yo o kikeba	Upon hearing of the past,
sate mo sa wa	I feel a kinship
nokoru yomogi to	with the one who received grace
kakochiteshi	after complaining,
hito no nasake mo	"the surviving mugwort plants."[83]
kakarikeri	Her case, too, was thus.
onaji harima	Her land was in Harima,
sakai tote	the same province as ours,
hitotsunagare o	and she traced her descent
kumishikaba	from the same lineage.
nonaka no shimizu	If only the government
yodomu tomo	will reach a verdict
moto no kokoro ni	without delay—if only
makasetsutsu	it will emulate
todokōri naki	the meadow spring whose waters,
mizuguki no	though once they stagnate,
ato sae araba	flow again as in the past—
itodoshiku	eternal radiance
tsuru ga okabe no	will render ever brighter
asahikage	the morning sunlight
yachiyo no hikari	at Tsurugaoka Shrine,

82. According to contemporary opinion, the history of the Buddhist religion had entered its final stage, an era of degeneracy in which the doctrines barely survived. The quotation is from a poem by a Kamakura Regent, Hōjō Yasutoki (SCSS 1154): yo no naka ni / asa wa ato naku / narinikeri / kokoro no mama no / yomogi nomi shite ("In the present world, hemp has vanished without a trace; nothing remains but mugwort bushes growing exactly as they please"). In Yasutoki's poem, hemp, a straight plant, functions as a metaphor for uprightness and justice; mugwort, a sprawling plant, as a metaphor for disorder and unrighteousness.

83. The poet known as Shunzei's Daughter (actually his granddaughter) is said to have won a dispute over land rights by sending this composition to Yasutoki: kimi hitori / ato naki asa no / mi o shiraba / nokoru yomogi no / kazu o kotoware ("If you alone, my lord, know me to be someone as upright as vanished hemp, please judge the number of the surviving mugwort plants").

sashisoete	and ever greater
akirakeki yo no	will be the prosperity
nao mo sakaen	of this enlightened rule.

[*Envoy*:]

nagakare to	Today I express
asayū inoru	in the speech of Yamato
kimi ga yo o	the prayers I offer
yamatokotoba ni	both morning and evening
kyō zo nobetsuru	that our lord's rule may endure.

Medieval Recluse-Memoirists

The first of the three memoirs below, *An Account of My Hermitage* (Hō-jōki), was written in 1212 by Kamo no Chōmei (1155?–1216). The Kamo clan traced its ancestry to a god who had settled at Kamo (now a part of Kyōto) after having marched with Emperor Jinmu, the legendary founder of the Japanese state. In Chōmei's day, its leading members held low court ranks and prospered as priests at the influential Upper and Lower Kamo Shrines and their subsidiaries. Chōmei's father, Nagatsugu (d. ca. 1173), had become head priest of the Lower Kamo Shrine at around the time of his son's birth.

Chōmei seems to have been a pampered child, untouched by the political turbulence of the times, and to have looked forward to a career in the Shinto priesthood. When he was eighteen or twenty, however, the death of his father left him without backing, and he turned increasingly to music and literature. He participated in numerous important poetry contests from around 1191 on, and in 1201 was honored by appointment to the Poetry Office, an organ established by Retired Emperor Go-Toba in preparation for the compilation of *New Collection of Early and Modern Poetry*. Go-Toba also proposed to make him a priest at Tadasu, a Kamo subsidiary at which Nagatsugu had once served, but the Kamo Chief Priest insisted on the selection of his own son instead. The loss of the appointment was apparently a devastating blow to Chōmei. Although the Retired Emperor offered to create an opening for him at a less prestigious shrine, he severed his ties with the Poetry Office, took Buddhist vows, and went to live at Ōhara near Mount Hiei, an area favored by recluses. A few years later, probably around 1208, he built a hermitage in the remote mountains at Hino, his final home.

Chōmei's only lengthy absence from Hino was occasioned by a visit to Kamakura in the autumn of 1211. The journey had been arranged by Asukai Masatsune (1170–1221), a former member of the Poetry Office who had once been on close terms with Minamoto no Yoritomo (1147–99), the founder of the Kamakura shogunate. Masatsune may have wanted to help his old colleague by introducing him to Yoritomo's son, the shogun Sanetomo (1192–1219), an ardent versifier who was already in correspondence with the famous Teika. But nothing came of the visit, and Chōmei returned to the hermitage.

Soon after the trip to Kamakura, Chōmei put together *Untitled Jottings* (Mumyōshō, ca. 1211), a miscellaneous assortment of anecdotes and notes about poets, poems, and the art of composition, with many quotations from his teacher, Shun'e (fl. ca. 1160–80). Later, around 1214, he assembled a group of Buddhist anecdotes, *A Collection of Tales on the Awakening of Faith* (Hosshinshū). Both works are fairly well known today, as are several of his approximately 340 extant poems. But it is undoubtedly his short essay on the futility of attachment to worldly things, *An Account of My Hermitage*, that has caused him to rank with Yoshida Kenkō (Kaneyoshi) as one of the two main figures among identifiable male prose writers of the medieval period.

The translation of *An Account of My Hermitage* is complete.

Yoshida Kaneyoshi (1283?–ca. 1352), the author of *Essays in Idleness* (Tsurezuregusa, ca. 1330?), belonged to a branch of the Urabe clan whose members had been hereditary priests at Yoshida Shrine before they entered the secular bureaucracy. In his youth, he became a steward to the Horikawa, one of the main Fujiwara houses, thus establishing a connection to which he probably owed his court career and his ability to participate in the life of the upper aristocracy. He held the respectable posts of Chamberlain and Assistant Commander of the Military Guards of the Left, and was active as a poet in the conservative Nijō school, which compiled most of the medieval imperial anthologies.

Around 1313, for unknown reasons, he took Buddhist vows, changed the reading of the characters in his name from Kaneyoshi to the more religious-sounding Kenkō, and went to live at Ono-no-shō outside the capital. As was often true of lay monks, or novices (*nyūdō*), he retained many of his former interests, receiving visitors, making trips to the capital, participating in poetry contests, and otherwise keeping in touch with the world. In 1322, he sold the land that had been his chief source of income, and thereafter, if scholarly opinion is correct, supported himself by increased activity as a poet—perhaps teaching, and probably actively seeking patrons. It was probably in the 1320's that he made two trips to eastern Japan and lived in two other places close to the capital.

In 1336, Emperor Go-Daigo, the sovereign whose supporters had crushed the Kamakura shogunate three years earlier, was forced by the rebel warrior Ashikaga Takauji (1305–58) to flee to the Yoshino Mountains, where, during the next fifty-seven years, he and his successors presided over what came to be called the Southern Court, while a rival Northern Court in the capital conferred a species of legitimacy on Takauji's Muromachi shogunate. Casting his lot with the Northern Court, Kenkō took up residence in the capital. He won recognition as a major poet and an expert on ancient usages, became acquainted with powerful figures like Takauji's brother Tadayoshi (1306–52), and secured the patronage of an influential warrior, Kō no Moronao (d. 1351), whom he is said to have coached in the niceties of court etiquette. His last years are obscure.

Despite Kenkō's fleeting prominence as a poet, *Essays in Idleness* is regarded today as his only significant literary legacy. Sixty of the work's 243 sections are translated below.

Nothing is known about the author of *An Account of a Journey to the East* (Tōkan kikō, 1242?) except what can be inferred from the work itself—namely, that he was a well-educated man, presumably nearing fifty, who professed to be reclusive and weary of the world, but who was apparently not unwilling to contemplate the possibility of employment in Kamakura. The translation of his memoir is complete.

An Account of My Hermitage

I

The waters of a flowing stream are ever present but never the same; the bubbles in a quiet pool disappear and form but never endure for long. So it is with men and their dwellings in the world.

The houses of the high and the low seem to last for generation after generation, standing with ridgepoles aligned and roof-tiles jostling in the magnificent imperial capital, but investigation reveals that few of them existed in the past. In some cases, a building that burned last year has been replaced this year; in others, a great house has given way to a small one. And it is the same with the occupants. The places are unchanged, the population remains large, but barely one or two survive among every twenty or thirty of the people I used to know. Just as with the bubbles on the water, someone dies at night and someone else is born in the morning. Where do they come from and where do they go, all those who are born and die? And for whose benefit, for what reason, does a man take enormous pains to build a temporary shelter pleasing to the eye? The master in his dwelling is like the dewdrop vying in ephemerality with the morning glory where it forms. The flower may remain after the dew evaporates, but it withers in the morning sun; the flower may droop before the moisture vanishes, but the dew does not survive until nightfall.

2

I have witnessed a number of remarkable occurrences in the more than forty years since I began to understand the nature of things. Around the Hour of the Dog [7:00 P.M.–9:00 P.M.] on a very windy night—I believe it was the Twenty-eighth of the Fourth Month in the third year of Angen [1177]—a fire broke out in the southeastern part of the capital and burned toward the northwest. In the end, it spread to Suzaku Gate, the Great Hall of State, the Academy, and the Ministry of Popular Affairs, reducing them all to ashes overnight. Its source is said to have been a temporary structure housing some dancers, located near the Higuchi–Tomi-no-kōji intersection. Spread here and there by an erratic wind, it burned in a pattern resembling an open fan, narrow at the base and wide at the outer edge. Suffocating smoke engulfed distant houses; wind-whipped flames descended to earth everywhere near at hand. The sky was red to the horizon with ashes lit by the fiery glare, and winged flames leaped a block or two at a time in the lurid atmosphere, torn free by the irresistible force of the gale. Everything must have seemed as unreal as a dream to the people in the fire's path. Some of them fell victim to the smoke. Others died instantly in the embrace of the flames. Still others managed to escape with their lives but failed to rescue their

1. Chūwain
2. Imperial Palace (Dairi)
3. Court of Abundant Pleasures (Burakuin)
4. Court of Government (Chōdōin)

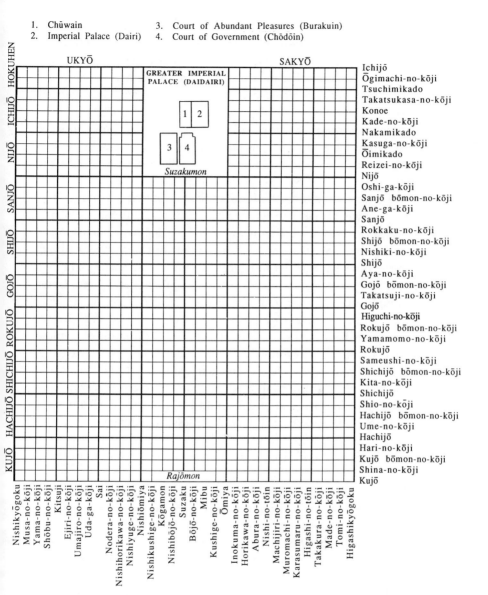

The Heian capital (Heian-kyō). Names in capital letters are districts; names in italics are gates.

belongings, and all their cherished treasures turned to ashes. The value of so much property may be imagined! The fire claimed the houses of sixteen senior nobles, to say nothing of countless others of less importance. It was reported that fully one-third of the capital had been destroyed. Dozens of men and women were killed; innumerable horses and oxen perished.

All human enterprises are pointless, but it must be counted an act of supreme folly for a man to consume his treasure and put himself to endless trouble merely to build a house in a place as dangerous as the capital.

Again, around the Fourth Month in the fourth year of Jishō [1180], a great whirlwind sprang up near the Nakamikado–[Higashi]Kyōgoku intersection and swept all the way to Rokujō Avenue. Not a house, large or small, escaped destruction within the area of three or four blocks where the blast wreaked its full fury. In some cases, entire buildings were flattened; in others, only crossbeams and pillars were spared. Gates were caught up and deposited four or five blocks distant; fences were blown away and neighboring properties merged. And I need hardly mention what happened to smaller objects. Everything inside a house mounted to the skies; cypress-bark thatch and shingles whirled like winter leaves in the wind. Dust ascended like smoke to blind the eye; the terrible howl of the storm swallowed the sound of voices. It seemed that even the dread karma-wind of hell could be no worse. Not only were houses damaged or destroyed, but countless men suffered injury or mutilation while the buildings were being reconstructed. The wind moved toward the south-southeast, visiting affliction on innumerable people.

Whirlwinds are common, but not ones such as that. Those who experienced it worried that it might be an extraordinary phenomenon, a warning from a supernatural being.

Again, around the Sixth Month in the fourth year of Jishō, the court moved suddenly to a new capital.[1] Nobody had dreamed of such a thing. When we consider that more than 400 years had elapsed since the establishment of the present imperial seat during Emperor Saga's reign, surely a new one ought not to have been chosen without exceptional

---

1. The move took place soon after the suppression of a preliminary attempt to overthrow the Taira. The new capital was at Fukuhara (now a part of Kōbe), where Taira no Kiyomori had established his principal residence some years earlier.

justification. It was more than reasonable that people should have felt disquiet and apprehension.

But complaints were useless. The Emperor, the Ministers of State, the senior nobles, and all the others moved. Nobody remained in the old capital who held even a minor court position. Those who aspired to office and rank, or who relied on the favor of patrons, strove to move with all possible dispatch; those who had lost the opportunity to succeed in life, or who had been rejected by society, stayed behind, sunk in gloom. The dwellings that had once stood eave to eave grew more dilapidated with every passing day. Houses were dismantled and sent floating down the Yodo River, and their former locations turned into fields before the onlookers' eyes.

In a complete reversal of values, everyone prized horses and saddles and stopped using oxen and carriages. Properties in the Western and Southern Sea circuits were sought; those in the Eastern Sea and Northern Land circuits were considered undesirable.

It happened that something took me to the new capital in Settsu Province. The cramped site, too small for proper subdivision, rose high on the north where it bordered the hills and sank low on the south beside the sea. The breaking waves never ceased to clamor; the wind from the sea blew with peculiar fury. The imperial palace struck me as unexpectedly novel and interesting, situated in the hills as it was, and I asked myself whether Empress Saimei's log house might not have been rather similar.[2]

I wondered where people were erecting the whole houses that were being sent downstream daily, their numbers great enough to clog the river. There were still many empty parcels of land and few houses. The old capital was already in ruins; the new one had yet to take form. Not a soul but felt as rootless as a drifting cloud. The original inhabitants grieved over the loss of their land; the new arrivals worried about plaster and lumber. On the streets, those who ought to have used carriages rode horseback; those who ought to have worn court dress or hunting robes appeared in *hitatare*. The customs of the capital had been revolutionized overnight, and people behaved like rustic warriors.

I have heard that such changes portend civil disturbance—and that was precisely what happened. With every passing day, the world grew

2. The log house was a temporary residence in Kyūshū used by Empress Saimei (594–661) when the Japanese were preparing to attack the Korean state of Silla in 661.

more unsettled, people lost more of their composure, and the common folk felt more apprehension. In the end, a crisis brought about a return to the old capital during the winter of the same year.[3] But who knows what became of the houses that had been torn down everywhere? They were not rebuilt in their former style.

We are told that the sage Emperors of old ruled with compassion. They roofed their palaces with thatch, neglecting even to trim the eaves; they remitted the already modest taxes when they saw the commoners' cooking-fires emit less smoke than before. The reason was simply that they cherished their subjects and wished to help them. To compare the present to the past is to see what kind of government we have today.

Again, there was a dreadful two-year famine. (I think it was around the Yōwa era {1181–82}, but it was too long ago to be sure.) The grain crops were ruined as one calamity followed another: drought in the spring and summer, typhoons and floods in the autumn. It was vain for the farmers to till the fields in the spring or set out plants in the summer; there was no reaping in the fall, no bustle of storage in the winter. Some rural folk abandoned their land and wandered off; others deserted their homes to live in the hills. Prayers were begun and extraordinary rituals were performed, but they accomplished nothing.

The capital had always depended on the countryside for every need. Now, with nothing coming in, people were beside themselves with anxiety. In desperation, they offered all their treasures at bargain rates, but nobody took any notice. The rare person who was willing to trade thought little of gold and much of grain. The streets were overrun with mendicants; lamentations filled the air.

The first of the two years dragged to a close. But just as everyone was anticipating a return to normal in the new year, a pestilence came along to make matters even worse. Like fish gasping in a puddle, the starving populace drew closer to the final extremity with every passing day, until at last people of quite respectable appearance, clad in hats and leggings, begged frantically from house to house. These wretched, dazed beings fell prostrate even as one marveled at their ability to walk.

Countless people perished of starvation by the wayside or died next to tile-capped walls. Since there was no way to dispose of the bodies, noisome stenches filled the air, and innumerable decomposing corpses

3. The rebellions of provincial Minamoto leaders had produced serious military disturbances.

shocked the eye. Needless to say, the dead lay so thick in the Kamo riverbed that there was not even room for horses and ox-carriages to pass.

With the woodsmen and other commoners too debilitated to perform their usual functions, a shortage of firewood developed, and people who possessed no other means of support broke up their own houses to sell in the market. The amount a man could carry brought less than enough to sustain him for a day. It was shocking to see pieces of wood covered with red lacquer or gold and silver leaf jumbled together with the rest. On inquiry, one learned that desperate people were going to old temples, stealing the sacred images, tearing away the fixtures from the halls, and breaking up everything for firewood. It is because I was born in a degenerate age that I have been forced to witness such disgraceful sights.

Some deeply moving things also happened. Whenever a couple were too devoted to part, the one whose love was greater was the first to die. This was because he or she put the spouse's welfare first and gave up whatever food came to hand. Similarly, a parent always predeceased a child. One sometimes saw a recumbent child sucking at his mother's breast, unaware that her life had ended. Grieved that countless people should be perishing in that manner, Dharma Seal Ryūgyō of Ninnaji Temple sought to help the dead toward enlightenment by writing the Sanskrit letter "A" on the forehead of every corpse he saw.[4]

The authorities kept track of the deaths in the Fourth and Fifth Months. During that period, there were more than 42,300 bodies on the streets in the area south of Ichijō, north of Kujō, west of Kyōgoku, and east of Suzaku. Of course, many others died before and afterward. And there would be no limit to the numbers if we were to count the Kamo riverbed, Shirakawa, the western sector, and the outlying districts, to say nothing of the provinces in the seven circuits.

People say there was something similar during the reign of Emperor Sutoku, around the Chōshō era [1132–35], but I know nothing about that. I witnessed this phenomenal famine with my own eyes.

If I remember correctly, it was at more or less the same time that a terrible seismic convulsion occurred. It was no ordinary earthquake. Mountains crumbled and buried streams; the sea tilted and immersed the land. Water gushed from fissures in the earth; huge rocks cracked

---

4. In esoteric Buddhism, of which Ninnaji was a center, "A," the first syllable in the Sanskrit syllabary, was regarded as symbolic of the unity of all things.

and rolled into valleys. Boats being rowed near the shoreline tossed on the waves; horses journeying on the roads lost their footing. Not a Buddhist hall or stupa remained intact anywhere in the vicinity of the capital. Some crumbled, others fell flat. Dust billowed like smoke; the shaking earth and collapsing houses rumbled like thunder. If people stayed indoors, they were crushed at once; if they ran outside, the ground split apart. If men had been dragons, they might have ridden the clouds, but they lacked the wings to soar into the heavens. It was then that I came to recognize an earthquake as the most terrible of all terrible things.

The violent shaking subsided fairly soon, but aftershocks followed for some time. No day passed without twenty or thirty earthquakes of an intensity that would ordinarily have caused consternation. The intervals lengthened after ten or twenty days, and then there were tremors four or five times a day, or two or three times a day, or once every other day, or once every two or three days. It must have been about three months before they ceased.

Of the four constituents of the universe, water, fire, and wind create constant havoc, but the earth does not usually give rise to any particular calamities. To be sure, there were some dreadful earthquakes in the past (for instance, the great shock that toppled the head of the Tōdaiji Buddha during the Saikō era [854–57]), but none of them could compare with this. Immediately after the event, people all talked about the meaninglessness of life and seemed somewhat more free from spiritual impurity than usual. But nobody even mentioned the subject after the days and months had accumulated and the years had slipped by.

Such, then, is the difficulty of life in this world, such the ephemerality of man and his dwellings. Needless to say, it would be utterly impossible to list every affliction that stems from individual circumstance or social position. If a man of negligible status lives beside a powerful family, he cannot make a great display of happiness when he has cause for heartfelt rejoicing, nor can he lift his voice in lamentation when he experiences devastating grief. In all that he does, he is ill at ease; like a sparrow near a hawk's nest, he pursues his daily activities in fear and trembling. If a poor man lives next door to a wealthy house, he abases himself before the neighbors and agonizes over his wretched appearance whenever he goes out in the morning or returns in the evening. Forced to witness the envy of his wife, children, and servants, and to hear the rich household dismiss him with contempt, he is forever agitated, constantly distraught.

He who lives in a crowded area cannot escape calamity when a fire breaks out nearby; he who settles in a remote spot suffers many hardships in his travels to and fro and puts himself at grave risk from robbers. The powerful man is consumed by greed; the man who refuses to seek a patron becomes an object of derision. The man who owns many possessions knows many worries; the impoverished man seethes with envy.

He who depends on another belongs to another; he who takes care of another is chained by human affection. When a man observes the conventions, he falls into economic difficulties; when he flouts them, people wonder if he is mad. Where can we live, what can we do, to find even the briefest of shelters, the most fleeting peace of mind?

3

For a long time, I lived in a house inherited from my paternal grandmother. Later, my fortunes declined through lack of connections, and I found myself unable to remain in society, despite many nostalgic associations. Shortly after I entered my thirties, I moved voluntarily into a simple new dwelling one-tenth the size of the old place. I built only a personal residence, with no fashionable auxiliary structures, and although I managed an encircling earthen wall, my means did not extend to a gate. The carriage-shelter was supported by bamboo pillars, and the house was unsafe in a snowfall or windstorm. The site was near the riverbed, which left it vulnerable to floods, and there was also danger from robbers.

For more than thirty miserable years, I endured an existence in which I could not maintain my position. Every setback during that time drove home the realization that I was not blessed by fortune. And thus, at fifty, I became a monk and turned my back on the world. Having never had a wife or children, I was not bound to others by ties difficult to break; lacking office and stipend, I possessed no attachments to which to cling.

During the next five springs and autumns, I sojourned among the clouds of the Ōhara hills, leading a life devoid of spiritual progress.

Now at sixty, with the dew nearing its vanishing point, I have built a new shelter for the tree's last leaves, just as a traveler might fashion a single night's resting place or an old silkworm spin a cocoon. It is not a hundredth the size of my second house. Indeed, while I have sat around uttering idle complaints, my age has increased with every year, and my house has shrunk with every move.

This house is unusual in appearance. It is barely ten feet square, and its height is less than seven feet. The location was a matter of indifference to me; I did not divine to select a site. I built a foundation and a simple roof, and attached hinges to all the joints so that I could move easily if cause for dissatisfaction arose. There would be no trouble about rebuilding. The house would barely fill two carts, and the carters' fees would be the only expense.

After settling on my present place of retirement in the Hino hills, I extended the eastern eaves about three feet to provide myself with a convenient spot in which to break up and burn firewood. On the south side of the building, I have an open bamboo veranda with a holy water shelf at the west end. Toward the north end of the west wall, beyond a freestanding screen, there is a picture of Amida Buddha, with an image of Fugen alongside and a copy of the *Lotus Sutra* in front. At the east end of the room, some dried bracken serves as a bed. South of the screen on the west side, a bamboo shelf suspended from the ceiling holds three leather-covered bamboo baskets, in which I keep excerpts from poetry collections and critical treatises, works on music, and religious tracts like *Collection of Essentials on Rebirth in the Pure Land*. A zither and a lute stand next to the shelf. The zither is of the folding variety; the handle of the lute is detachable. Such is the appearance of my rude temporary shelter.

To turn to the surroundings: I have made a rock basin in which to collect water from an elevated conduit south of the hermitage, and I gather ample supplies of firewood in a neighboring stand of trees. The locality is called Toyama, "the foothills." Vines cover the paths. The valley is thickly forested, but there is open land to the west.

Aids to contemplation abound. In the spring, lustrous cascades of wisteria burgeon in the west like purple clouds. In the summer, every song of the cuckoo conveys a promise of companionship in the Shide Mountains. In the autumn, the incessant cries of the cicadas seem to lament the transitoriness of worldly things. And in the winter, the accumulating and melting snows suggest poignant comparisons with sins and hindrances.[5]

When I tire of reciting the sacred name or find myself intoning a sutra in a perfunctory manner, I rest as I please, I fall idle as I see fit. There is nobody to interfere, nobody to shame me. Although I do not make a point of performing silent austerities, I can control speech-induced karma because I live alone; although I do not make a fuss about obeying the commandments, I have no occasion to break them because mine is not an environment conducive to transgression.

On mornings when I compare my existence to a white wake in the water, I borrow Mansei's style while watching boats come and go at Okanoya; on evenings when the wind rustles the maple leaves, I imitate Tsunenobu's practice while recalling the Xinyang River.[6] If my interest does not flag, I often perform "Song of the Autumn Wind" as an accompaniment to the murmur of the pines, or play "Melody of the Flowing Spring" to harmonize with the sound of the water. I am not an accomplished musician, but my playing is not designed for the pleasure of others. I merely pluck the strings alone and chant alone to comfort my own spirit.

At the foot of the hill, there is a brush-thatched cottage, the abode of the mountain warden. The small boy who lives there pays me an occasional visit, and if I chance to feel at loose ends, I set out for a ramble with him as my companion. He is ten, I am sixty. Our ages differ greatly, but we take pleasure in the same things. Sometimes we pull out reed-flower sprouts, pick *iwanashi* berries, heap up yam sprouts, or pluck herbs. Or we may go to the rice fields at the foot of the mountains, glean ears left by the reapers, and fashion sheafs. When the weather is balmy, we scramble up to a peak from which I can look toward the

5. Amida and his attendants were thought to descend, riding on a purple cloud, to escort the believer to the Western Paradise at the moment of death. Possibly because the cuckoo's cry included notes that sounded like *shide*, the bird was considered a messenger from the land of the dead, which lay beyond the Shide Mountains. Sins and hindrances to enlightenment piled up in the course of daily life and were discharged periodically by repentance rites and confessions before a Buddha.

6. Mansei (8th c.) was the author of a frequently quoted poem on ephemerality (SIS 1327): yo no naka o / nani ni tatoen / asaborake / kogiyuku fune no / ato no shiranami ("To what shall I compare life in this world—the white wake of a boat rowing off at break of day"). Tsunenobu (1016–97) was a major poet known also as an expert lute player. Chōmei alludes to the first two lines of Bo Juyi's "Lute Song": "As I see off a guest at night near the Xinyang River, / The autumn wind rustles through maple leaves and reed plumes."

distant skies over my old home and see Kohatayama, Fushimi-no-sato, Toba, and Hatsukashi. Nobody owns the view; there is nothing to keep me from enjoying it.

When the going is easy and I feel like taking a long walk, I follow the peaks past Sumiyama and Kasatori to worship at Iwama or Ishiyama. Or I may traverse Awazu Plain, visit the site of Semimaru's dwelling, cross the Tanakami River, and seek out Sarumaru's grave.[7] On the way home, I search for cherry blossoms, pick autumn leaves, gather bracken, or collect fruit and nuts, depending on the season. Some of my trophies I present to the Buddha; others I treat as useful souvenirs.

On peaceful nights, I long for old friends while gazing at the moon through the window, or weep into my sleeve at the cry of a monkey. Sometimes I mistake fireflies in the bushes for fish lures burning far away at Maki-no-shima Island, or think that a gale must be scattering the leaves when I hear rain just before dawn. The *horohoro* call of a pheasant makes me wonder if the bird might be a parent; the frequent visits of deer from the peaks attest to the remoteness of my abode.[8] Sometimes I stir up the banked fire and make it a companion for the wakefulness of old age. The mountains are so little intimidating that even the owl's hoot sounds moving rather than eerie. Indeed, there is no end to the delights of the changing seasons in these surroundings. A truly reflective man, blessed with superior powers of judgment, would undoubtedly find many more pleasures than the ones I have described.

4

When I first began to live here, I thought it would not be for long, but five years have already elapsed. My temporary hermitage has gradually become a home, its eaves covered with rotted leaves and its foundation mossy. Whenever I happen to hear news of the capital, I learn that many illustrious personages have breathed their last since my retreat to these mountains. And it would be quite impossible to keep track of all the unimportant people who have died. A great many houses have also

---

7. Semimaru and Sarumaru were semilegendary poets.

8. Gyōki (Gyōgi): yamadori no / horohoro to naku / koe kikeba / chichi ka to zo omou / haha ka to zo omou ("When I hear the voice of the pheasant, mountain bird, crying *horohoro*, I think, 'Might it be a father? Or might it be a mother?'"). Saigyō: yama fukami / naruru kasegi no / kejikasa ni / yo ni tōzakaru / hodo zo shiraruru ("To see at close hand deer grown accustomed to me deep in the mountains is to know my remoteness from the affairs of the world").

suffered destruction in recurrent conflagrations. Only in my temporary hermitage is life peaceful and safe. The quarters are cramped, but I have a place where I can lie at night and another where I can sit in the daytime. There is ample room for one person. The hermit crab likes a small shell because it knows its own size; the osprey lives on the rocky coast because it fears man. It is the same with me. Knowing myself and knowing the world, I harbor no ambitions and pursue no material objectives. Quietude is what I desire; the absence of worries is what makes me happy.

Men do not usually build houses for their own benefit. Some build for wives, children, relatives, and servants, some for friends and acquaintances, some for masters, for teachers, or even for household goods, treasures, oxen, and horses. But I have built for myself this time, not for anybody else. Because of present conditions and my own situation, I possess neither a family to share my dwelling nor servants to work for me. If I had built a great house, whom would I have lodged in it, whom would I have established there?

Friends esteem wealth and look for favors; they do not necessarily value sincere friendship or probity. I prefer to make friends of music and nature. Servants prize lavish rewards and unstinting generosity; they do not care about protection, affection, or a safe, tranquil existence. I prefer to make my own body my servant. How do I do it? If there is work to perform, I use my body. True, I may grow weary, but it is easier than employing and looking after someone else. If there is walking to do, I walk. It is burdensome, but less so than worrying over horses, saddles, oxen, and carriages. I divide my body and put it to two uses: it suits me very well to employ hands as servants and feet as conveyances. My mind understands my body's distress: I allow the body to rest when it is distressed and use it when it feels energetic. I use it but do not make a habit of pushing it to extremes. If it finds a task irksome, I am not perturbed. It is surely a healthful practice to walk constantly and work constantly. What would be the point of idling away the time? To make others work creates bad karma. Why should I borrow their strength?

It is the same with food and clothing. I hide my nakedness under a rough fiber robe, a hemp quilt, or whatever comes to hand; I survive by eating starwort from the fields and nuts from the peaks. Because I do not mingle with others, I need not chide myself for having felt ashamed of my appearance. Because I possess little food, I find coarse fare tasty.

I do not describe such pleasures as a means of criticizing the wealthy;

I merely compare my own former life with my present existence. "The triple world is but one mind."[9] If the mind is not at peace, elephants, horses, and the seven treasures are trash; palatial residences and stately mansions are worthless. I feel warm affection for my present lonely dwelling, my tiny cottage. My beggarly appearance is a source of embarrassment on the infrequent occasions when something takes me to the capital, but after my return I feel pity for those who pursue worldly things. If anyone doubts my sincerity, let him consider the fish and the birds. A fish never tires of water, but only another fish can understand why. A bird seeks trees, but only another bird can understand why. It is the same with the pleasures of retirement. Only a recluse can understand them.

5

The moon of my life is setting; my remaining years approach the rim of the hills. Very soon, I shall face the darkness of the Three Evil Paths. Which of my old disappointments is worth fretting over now? The Buddha teaches us to reject worldly things. Even my affection for this thatched hut is a sin; even my love of tranquility must be accounted an impediment to rebirth. Why do I waste time in descriptions of inconsequential pleasures?

As I reflect on these things in the quiet moments before dawn, I put a question to myself:

You retired to the seclusion of remote hills so that you might discipline your mind and practice the Way, but your impure spirit belies your monkish garb. Your dwelling presumes to imitate the abode of the honorable Yuima, but you are worse than Śuddhipanthaka when it comes to obeying the commandments. Is this because you let yourself be troubled by karma-ordained poverty, or has your deluded mind finally lost its sanity?

The question remains unanswered. I can do no other than use my impure tongue for three or four repetitions of Amida's sacred name. Then I fall silent.

Late in the Third Month of the second year of Kenryaku {1212}
Set down by the monk Ren'in in the hermitage at Toyama[10]

9. *Kegon Sutra*: "The triple world is but one mind. Outside mind there is nothing; mind, Buddha, and all the living, these three are no different."

10. Ren'in was Chōmei's Buddhist name.

Essays in Idleness

How foolish I feel when I realize that I have spent another day in front of my inkstone, jotting down aimless thoughts as they occurred to me, all because I was bored and had nothing better to do.

I

One may conclude that any man born into this world will find a multitude of things to desire.

The position of the Emperor is too awe-inspiring for words, and so too the Princes, down to the last branch and leaf of the Imperial Tree— all of these being of august status as men not born of human seed. Likewise, it goes without saying that the Regent, first of all nobles, is to be envied; indeed, all nobles of sufficient rank to be granted the privilege of acting as Escorts at court are truly impressive—so much so that their children and grandchildren retain some of their importance even if they have come down in the world. And on down through the lesser ranks there are also those who may meet with success according to their various stations and look very self-satisfied, even though in reality they may be of little consequence.

The least enviable of men is the monk. Sei Shōnagon spoke the truth when she said that people think of him as no more than wood or stone. Even when he is at the height of his influence, ordering people about and making a great display of his power, one cannot consider him that impressive. It is as Monk Sōga said: "Fame is a burden; and the monk who attains it may be transgressing the Teachings." The determined recluse is probably a better ideal.

One of course wants a man to be excellent in appearance and to bear himself well, but the man who is easy to listen to, speaks with charm, and never talks too much—that is the sort of person of whose company I never tire. For how lamentable it is when a man one had thought of as quite outstanding reveals himself to be inferior in character! A man's social status and looks are of course determined at birth; but if he resolves to progress in wisdom, what is there to stop him? To see a man of good looks and disposition but no education mixing with men of inferior status and disagreeable appearance, who quite outstrip him in

Translation by Steven D. Carter.

talent and treat him as of no account—that is indeed a regrettable sight.

It is most desirable for a man to be trained in orthodox learning, the composition of poetry in Chinese and Japanese, and music. Furthermore, it is splendid to observe a man whose knowledge of court custom and ceremony is a mirror for the conduct of others. Finally, the man of breeding is one who is able to write smoothly and in an acceptable hand, has a voice good enough to lead songs, and who, though reluctant to partake when drink is pressed upon him, does not abstain from drinking entirely.

3

Superior though he may be in every other way, a man who has no capacity for love seems to lack something, like a fine *sake* cup without a bottom.

For a man in love is a true delight: his sleeves heavy with dew or frost, he drifts along toward no certain goal, taking great pains not to earn the complaints of his parents or the censure of the world; but, for all his trouble, his advances lead only to heartache, and most of the time he sleeps alone—on nights when he sleeps at all.

And yet it is good for a man not to give himself entirely to such pleasures, or to be regarded by women as too easy a mark.

4

One is inspired by the sight of a man who never forgets the life to come and is never lax in his attentions to the Way of the Buddha.

5

It is best for a man who has suffered some setback not to be quick to shave his head and become a monk; rather, he should close his gate so that no one knows whether he's at home or not, and then pass the days quietly, with no particular expectations for the future.

Middle Counselor Akimoto once said that he wanted to "see the moon of exile—but without committing any crime." [11] One can understand how he must have felt.

11. The purpose would presumably have been to gain an understanding of an exile's feelings.

7

Life would lose much of its attraction if it went on forever—if man did not melt away like the dew on Adashi Moor or drift off like the smoke over Toribe Mountain. Its very uncertainty is the thing that gives it savor.

Look at other creatures and you will see that none lives as long as man. There are even those like the mayfly, which dies waiting for evening, and the summer cicada, which lives to know neither spring nor autumn. Just being able to live one year to the fullest should be a source of peace. The man who laments every passing day could go on for 1,000 years and still feel it was all the dream of a single night. Besides, since we cannot live forever, what is to be gained by stretching our years until we have become old and ugly? Long life means an abundance of shame. The best thing a man can do is to die before he reaches forty. Once he goes beyond that age, the desire to mingle in society blinds him to proper embarrassment about the figure he cuts; and the affection inspired by his grandchildren in his sunset years makes him want to be spared to see them achieve success. His attachment to worldly things grows stronger and stronger, until he finally loses all ability to appreciate the charm of ephemerality—a most shameful end.

8

Nothing exceeds lust in the power to deceive the human heart. And what a foolish thing that heart is!

Scents, for instance, are ephemeral, and we know that perfume burned into robes lasts only a moment; yet still our hearts thrill at a wonderful fragrance.

The wizard called Kume reportedly lost his power to work wonders after seeing the white legs of a girl washing clothes—something one can believe, since nothing is more beautiful than hands, legs, and skin that are fair, full-fleshed, and lustrous.[12]

10

One knows that it is only a temporary dwelling, but still it is a source of pleasure to have a house that suits one's needs, that is just what

12. The wizard fell to earth after seeing the girl's legs while he was flying.

one would want. At the house where a man of breeding lives in quietude, even the moonlight seems to shine down with greater effect. Though neither modern nor ornate in style, such a place will be surrounded by venerable trees, and in the garden the grass will appear to grow as it pleases, most naturally; the verandas and open-work fences will be joined with exquisite workmanship, and the furnishings, all placed artlessly around the room, will give off an aura of the past, making the place seem comfortable and refined.

On the other hand, a house that carpenters have labored over and polished, full of rare and imposing furnishings, both Chinese and Japanese; a house where everything down to the trees and grasses has been so trained that not a trace of natural beauty remains—now that is truly an ugly and cheerless sight. How could anyone hope to live long in such a place? Just one look is enough to picture it going up in a puff of smoke. One can indeed tell the personality of a person from the sort of place he lives in.

Once the poet Saigyō saw that the Go-Tokudaiji Minister had stretched a rope across the rooftop of his house to keep the kites from roosting there. "What would it hurt if kites *were* to perch there? So this is what the Minister is really like!" Saigyō said. It is reported that he never visited the house again.

I remembered this incident when I saw a rope pulled along the ridge of the roof of the Kosaka Palace of the Aya-no-kōji Prince. Upon hearing my story, a man of the Prince's household said, "The truth is that crows used to gather on the roof and catch frogs from the pond—something His Highness could not bear to watch." Why, of course, I thought, much impressed. I wonder if the Go-Tokudaiji Minister might also have had a good reason.

11

Once, during the Godless Month, I was passing through a place called Kurusu Moor on my way to visit a friend in the hills nearby. Making my way down a long, narrow path covered with moss, I came upon a hut where someone was living a forlorn existence. Save for water dripping from a bamboo pipe buried in fallen leaves, there was not a hint of sound; and chrysanthemum blossoms and autumn leaves scattered about on the altar inside were the only indication that someone was indeed living there.

"Ah, so a man can live even in such a lonely state," I reflected, much moved at the thought. But then, in the garden beyond, I saw a large tangerine tree firmly fenced about on all sides—a sight that quite destroyed the effect of the place and left me thinking, "If only that tree hadn't been there!"

13

To sit alone with a book spread out before you in the lamplight is one of life's greatest pleasures. Among my own favorite books are the more engaging chapters of *Wen xuan*, the collected poems of Bo Juyi, the sayings of Laozi, and Zhuangzi's writings. As for things written by scholars of our own country, I find many works of the past very captivating.

22

In all respects, I am drawn to things of ages past. Nowadays, standards of taste are growing more vulgar all the time. Even in the fine furnishings crafted by our woodworkers, I am most pleased by those done in old styles.

Even when it comes to letters, I prefer the language I find on old scraps left from long ago. And the same is true of spoken language, which is also getting worse all the time. In the past, people would say, "Bring the coach!" or "Light the lamps!"; now they say, "Bring it round!" and "Light 'em up!" When they ought to say, "Men of the Grounds Bureau—to your posts!" they say, "Torchers, let's have some light!"; and instead of referring to the place where the Emperor listens to lectures on the *Sutra of Golden Light* as the "Imperial Attendance Chamber," they call it the "Lecture Hall"—a sad state of affairs, an old gentleman once lamented to me.

23

One hears it said that ours is a degenerate time, the age of the End of the Law. Yet how far from that world, how rare a delight is the venerable air that dominates the ninefold imperial palace.

The Open Stage, the Dining Court, the This Chamber, the That Gate—such places sound splendid as a matter of course. But at the palace even the names of things that may likewise be found in the commonest dwellings—half shutters, small plank floors, high sliding doors, and the like—have a most delightful ring.

And how splendid it is to hear the command, "Prepare for night!" from the Guards Hall, or the call, "Bring the lamps—and be quick about it!" from the Imperial Bedchamber. At such times, the looks of self-satisfaction on the faces of senior nobles as they go about their duties in the Guards Hall are to be expected; but to find the same expressions among the minor men of the palace staff is amusing indeed. And what comical sights those same men make when you see them napping here and there on a chilly night!

Once the Tokudaiji Chancellor Kintaka declared of the chimes in the Repository of the Sacred Mirror that they made "a most delightful and elegant sound."

25

Our world is a place as changeable as the pools and shallows of the Asuka River: time moves along, things pass away, happiness is overtaken by sorrow; a splendid dwelling becomes a field without inhabitants, while another house stays the same on the outside but has new occupants—leaving us with no one who can share in our reminiscences, since the peach and plum blossoms are unable to speak.[13] And the ephemerality of things is all the more intense at the site where once stood the mansion of a great man of the remote past whose glory we never saw.

The grand designs of His Lordship Michinaga are still visible in the Kyōgoku Mansion and the Hōjōji Temple. But how heartstruck one is to see how they have been altered by time! When he labored over those buildings, and provided for their maintenance by grants from private estates, he was doubtless convinced that his house would flourish into the distant future as the abode of the Emperor's guardians, of the chief pillars of the state—never envisioning a time in which the place would fall so completely into ruin. The main gates and the Golden Hall lasted until quite recently; but during the Shōwa era [1312–17] the south gate burned, and since then the Golden Hall has fallen over and remains in a state of collapse, with no sign that it will be put right again. Only the

13. An allusion to a line of Chinese poetry by Sugawara no Fumitoki (WKRES 538): "O blossoms of the peach and plum, you will not say how many springs have passed."

Muryōjū-in survives as a reminder of the past, with its row of nine sixteen-foot Buddhas still inspiring awe. And still impressive are the plaque with calligraphy by Kōzei and the door inscribed by Kaneyuki, whose strokes remain vivid to this day. And the Lotus Hall is still standing as well. But how long will even these last? Here and there in the temple precincts are places that show no such hint of their past, except for an odd foundation stone; today no one knows anything about those places at all.

In all things it is vain to make plans for a future we will never see.

27

How terribly forlorn it is when, after the Abdication Banquet, the three regalia—the Sword, the Necklace, and the Mirror—are formally transferred to the new Emperor.

I understand that our recently retired sovereign wrote this poem in the spring of the year in which he stepped down from the throne:[14]

tonomori no	Even the groundsmen
tomonomiyatsuko	who served me at the palace
yoso ni shite	now neglect to come,
harawanu niwa ni	leaving my unswept courtyard
hana zo chirishiku	strewn with wind-blown flowers.

Preoccupied with all the official functions of the new reign, people don't visit the old sovereign, who seems a lonely figure. It is in such situations that people's true feelings become known.

28

There is no time more moving than a period of national mourning.[15] The very appearance of the temporary palace is a poignant sight, with its plank floors low to the ground, its blinds of rough reed stalks and valences of coarse cloth, its rustic furnishings. Even the attire of the attendants—down to their swords and decorative sword-belts—is different than usual and most affecting.

---

14. The reference is to Emperor Hanazono (1297–1348; r. 1308–18).

15. "National mourning" (*ryōan*) was a one-year period during which a reigning sovereign mourned the death of a parent.

29

In times of quiet thought, I realize that of all feelings the most difficult to suppress is longing for things past.

After all is quiet, with everyone in bed, I often while away the long night hours by putting the things around me in order; and as I throw out notes I would not want left behind, I come across a scrap of calligraphy or an idle drawing by one who is no longer with us and feel exactly as I did back then. Or then again I find a letter written by a friend still living but sent long ago, and am moved deeply as I wonder what the occasion might have been, or in what year it was written. It is somehow sad to think that the things that have become one's own over time will go on, oblivious and unchanging, long after one is gone.

31

On a morning made beautiful by snowfall from the night before, I sent off a letter to a person with whom I needed to correspond. In reply to my note, which had said nothing of the snow, she wrote back, "Am I expected to consent to the requests of a man so ill-natured that he fails even to ask me how I am liking the snow?" What an amusing thing to say!

Since the lady is no longer with us, I find even so minor an incident impossible to forget.

32

Once, around the Twentieth of the Ninth Month, I made good on an invitation to visit a certain gentleman and spent the night with him, walking about to enjoy the moon. Remembering an acquaintance along the way, the man showed me the woman's house and then went inside. Waiting in the run-down, dew-drenched garden, I caught a scent of a most discreet perfume that could not have been prepared for our visit. The snatches of conversation I overheard left me deeply moved.

In good time my friend emerged from the house. But I was still so taken with the elegance of the scene that I hid myself and watched to see the woman push open the double doors and gaze up at the moon. How disappointing it would have been had she just locked the door and withdrawn into her rooms immediately! Since she could not have known that anyone would be staying around to watch what she did, her behavior can only have been the result of a practiced sensibility.

I heard later that not long thereafter the lady died.

38

What utter foolishness it is to use oneself up in the search for fame and profit, with never a moment's peace, making life a constant toil.

Much wealth has a way of consuming life: it is an agent that invites danger, beckons trouble. And after your death, even if you have left a pile of riches high enough to make a pillar for the North Star, it will bring only grief to your heirs. The pleasures that delight the eye of a foolish man are simply not worth the trouble. For a man of sensibility will think of big carriages, fat horses, and ornaments of jewels and gold as entirely useless things. Better to abandon your gold to the mountains and throw your jewels into a deep pool. Only a complete fool troubles himself over a desire for profit.

Of course anyone would like to leave behind a name that will last far into the future. But do we only call superior those of high rank and exalted status? No: for we know of many foolish and quite stupid men born into fine houses who, blessed with opportunity, advanced to high rank and lived most glamorous lives; and there are also many sages and holy men who, not meeting with good fortune, resigned themselves to low status and ended in obscurity. Next to desire for profit, desire for a lasting name is most foolish.

Again, one wants to leave a reputation for excellence in learning and character. But consider the matter carefully and you will realize that to love praise really means only that you find joy in the commendation of others. And neither those who praise nor those who condemn last long in this world. Those who have heard what such men say also are quick to disappear. So whose low opinion should we fear? Whose recognition should we desire? Indeed, it is a high reputation that lays the foundation for slander. No good comes from leaving a high name after one is gone. After desire for fame and profit, this is next most foolish.

Speaking to those who seek knowledge out of a desire to become wise, I would say that with wisdom comes falsehood, and with great ability comes an increase in harmful passions. True wisdom is not something heard from another or learned through study. And what is true wisdom anyway? What one should do and what not are part of a continuum. And what are we to call "good"? A man of true excellence has no knowledge, no virtue, no accomplishments, no fame. Who can know of him? Who can make him known? And this is not because he hides his virtue or keeps his stupidity to himself, but because he is beyond the realm of wise or foolish, virtue or vice.

If a man is deluded enough to seek fame and profit, he will end as I have described. All desire must be denied. There is nothing worth talking about; there is nothing worth wanting.

43

Once, toward the end of spring, beneath mild, fair skies, I happened by a noble-looking mansion set well back in spacious grounds, with venerable trees all around and a garden strewn with fallen blossoms that I could not pass without venturing in for a better look. The southern exposure of the main building was entirely open, with the shutters all down, and there seemed to be no one about. But, going around to the eastern side, I caught sight, through a door left conveniently ajar and a tear in the reed blinds within, of a man of fine features who looked to be perhaps twenty years old. Although at his leisure, he was most dignified and elegant in manner, looking down at a book spread out before him on a desk.

Even now I would like to find out who he was.

52

At Ninnaji Temple there was a certain monk who, although already advanced in years, had never visited Iwashimizu Hachiman Shrine. Regretting that fact, he resolved to go, setting off on foot to make his pilgrimage. He did his obeisances at Gokurakuji and at Kora; then, thinking that was all there was to the place, he went back home.

Upon returning, he met one of his comrades. "Well," the monk said, "I've finally done what I've been thinking about all these years, and the shrine was more grand than I had heard it to be. But, tell me: why was it that all the other pilgrims there climbed on up the mountain? I wanted to see for myself, but my intent was only to worship the god, so I didn't go up."

It appears that even in the smallest things it is best to have a guide.

53

Here's another story about a monk at Ninnaji.

This happened at a farewell party for an acolyte who was about to go off and become a full-fledged monk. Caught up in the revelry and thoroughly drunk, one of the other monks got up to take his turn at entertaining the group and made to put a three-legged cauldron over his head. Since it would not go on smoothly, he flattened his nose and pushed the cauldron down over his face, and then began to dance around, much to the amusement of all assembled.

After dancing awhile, the monk tried to pull the cauldron off, but to no avail. At this everyone sobered up and began wondering what to do. First one way, then another, they tried pulling the pot off, scraping the monk's neck until the blood flowed; but his neck only swelled up, making it difficult for him to breathe. Then they tried to break the pot, but it would not be broken, and the reverberations were too much for him to bear. Now quite at a loss for what to do, they put a cloak over the three legs of the pot, gave the monk a stick for support, and took him by the hand off to a doctor in Kyōto. Along the way, everyone stared at the monk in wonderment.

What a strange sight the monk must have presented sitting there in front of the doctor! He spoke, but his voice was so muffled that his words could not be made out. "There's nothing in my books about a situation like this," the doctor said. "Nor is there anything about it in the oral teachings." So the monk went back to Ninnaji, where his aged mother and other close friends gathered around his pillow, crying and lamenting his fate—although one doubts that he could even hear them. With the situation getting no better, one man said, "Even if we take off his ears and nose doing it, we have to save his life. Let's just grab on and pull with all our might." So they took dry rice-stalks and pushed them up between his head and the metal and pulled as if to yank his head off, leaving only holes in place of his ears and nose but at last succeeding in freeing him. The story has it that the monk survived in the end, but was ill for a very long time.

55

A house should be designed for summer. In winter, you can stay anywhere; but it's hard living in a house that's no good in the heat.

Deep water doesn't seem to cool; it's shallow water flowing fast that is refreshing. When you're reading tiny writing, a room with sliding door panels provides more light than one with hinged shutters. A room with a high ceiling is cold in winter and dark when lit by lamplight.

I once heard a discussion in which it was concluded that a house containing some unused space is nice to look at and can be put to all sorts of uses.

58

Some people say, "If you are dedicated to the Way, where you live makes no difference. What difficulty can it present to your hopes for the next life if after taking vows you stay at home, still mixing with family and friends?" But those who say such things know nothing about how to prepare for the life to come. One who aspires to overcome the cycle of life and death can surely have no interest in serving his lord morn and eve, or in the day-to-day business of running a household. The mind is moved by its surroundings, after all: without quietude, the Way is hard to pursue.

People today cannot match the capacities of those of old. Even if they go off into the mountain groves, they must have some means of staving off hunger and protecting themselves from storms. How then can they not give the appearance of having worldly desires on occasion? Yet it is going too far to say that there is no use in leaving the world, that one may as well not abandon lay life. For even if a man who has entered the Way and turned his back on the world still has some desires, they will not resemble in number or intensity the desires of a man still embroiled in mundane affairs. With his paper bedclothes, his rough hempen robes, his one rice bowl, and his herb broth, will such a man be a drain on others? His demands are easily answered; his heart is quickly satisfied. And even if he does harbor some desires, he is somewhat shy because of his status, so he will usually retreat from evil and move toward good.

Certainly a man should try somehow to sever his worldly bonds while in this life, in token of his being born a man. The man who puts all his effort into worldly gain and makes no attempt to pursue higher understanding is really no different from the beasts.

72

Things that seem common: too many furnishings where one is sitting; too many brushes around an inkstone; too many sacred statues in a home chapel; too many stones and trees and bushes in a garden court; too many children and grandchildren in a house; too many words used when talking to people; too much praise for oneself in a written petition.

Things that don't offend good taste even if numerous: books on a bookcart; trash on a trash pile.

74

Like ants they crowd together, hurrying off to east and west, running along to north and south. Some are noble, others common; some are old, others young. All of them have places to go and homes to return to. At night, they go to bed; in the morning, they get up. But what do they hope to accomplish in their coming and going? Greed for long life, desire for greater wealth—these are things that never come to an end. And what do they think to gain by preserving their lives? All that awaits them is old age and death, which are quick to come and never rest for a minute, leaving them little to truly enjoy. Yet still there are those who wander in error, fearing nothing. Some stay infatuated with fame and profit because they have never given a thought to their final destination. And then there are the fools who lament their fate, pleading to live on forever because they are ignorant of the universal principle of change.

78

I simply cannot abide people who get hold of the latest fad and then spread its praises all about. More admirable by far is the kind of man who learns of such things only after they are old news.

When a new person arrives at a gathering, some man lacking in both understanding and breeding can be counted upon to bring up topics already familiar to him and his companions, exchanging cryptic phrases and clever glances, with much laughter—all in a way that makes the new person feel completely uninformed.

81

When the painting or calligraphy adorning a screen or sliding door is clumsily done, one is less critical of the work itself than of the master of the house.

For it is all too often the case that a man's accoutrements serve to show the inferiority of his sensibility. By this I don't mean that one must allow oneself only the finest of possessions. Rather, I speak of those who make things tasteless and ugly in an attempt to make them last well, or who out of a desire to be original end up filling their homes with useless things that reveal only the fussiness of the owner. The best furnishings are those that seem a little old, are not terribly pretentious, and stand up over time.

82

Once when someone remarked that silk was unsatisfactory as a backing for picture or book scrolls because it showed wear too readily, Ton'a replied, "To the contrary, I find that it's only after the silk has frayed at top and bottom and some of the mother-of-pearl has fallen from the roller that a scroll becomes truly attractive." This is an excellent sentiment. In the same way, while most people say that if a set of books is not uniform it is not pleasing to the eye, I am persuaded by Bishop Kōyū's comment on the subject: "To insist on complete sets of things is a mark of insensitivity. Incompleteness is far superior."

Another person has said this: "To want everything uniform and complete shows bad taste. Leaving things imperfect is more pleasing and gives one a future to look forward to. When a palace is built, something is always left unfinished." Indeed, even among the Confucian and Buddhist classics written by the ancient sages, there are many missing chapters.

97

How many are the things that work within other things to waste and spoil! The body has lice; a house has mice; a country has brigands; the common man has wealth; the man of high station has benevolence; and the monk has his Law. [16]

16. In his fourth and fifth examples, Kenkō echoes the Taoist work *Zhuangzi*, which argues that the petty man who seeks wealth and the gentleman who cultivates the Confucian

104

Once a man went to call on a woman who was living rather despon-
dently in a run-down out-of-the-way house to which she had withdrawn
during a time of personal trial. It was still early in the month, and as the
man searched quietly for the house in the dim moonlight, the dogs of the
place came toward him, barking so ferociously that they brought out a
kitchen maid. She asked him who he was, and he persuaded her to let
him into the house.

For a few minutes he stood on the crude wood floor in the hallway,
wondering how the woman could bear to stay in so wretched a place,
until a woman's voice, composed but youthful, said, "Come this way,
Sir." A sliding door then opened—not too smoothly—and he went
inside.

The interior was not in such a sorry state; indeed, it looked very
dignified in the glow from a lamp at the other end of the room, whose
light, albeit faint, made it possible to see the comeliness of the furnishings. And the scent of incense, which had obviously been burning since
well before his appearance, made the place seem a more comfortable one
in which to live.

"Shut the gate," someone said, adding, "and it may rain, so pull the
carriage in under the gate roof. Then find a place for his men to sleep."
This was followed by someone whispering, "Ah, maybe tonight at least
we'll get some rest." Despite the speaker's attempts to be discreet, the
quarters were so close that the visitor could not help overhearing.

The night went by, and as the man was relating what had gone on
in his life since their last meeting, the first cock crowed. He went
on, speaking with great earnestness of both the past and the future, until
the cock crows became more ardent, and more frequent, making him
wonder if perhaps the day had already dawned outside. But since the
lady's house was hardly the sort of place one needed to leave under
cover of night, he took his time. Only when he could see the white
of daylight through the crack in the door did he rise to go, choosing
final words of parting the lady would not be likely to forget. It was early
in the Fourth Month, and the faint dawn light made the treetops and
garden plants glow in lovely green hues that impressed the man with
their beauty and charm. Even today, he often remembers the scene,

---

virtue of benevolence are equally guilty of failure "to follow the true form of their inborn
nature." (Quote from Burton Watson, tr., *Chuang Tzu* [New York, 1968], p. 103.)

and takes care when he passes the house always to gaze at it until the great cinnamon tree above it disappears from sight.

105

It was a time when the unmelted snow in the shade of the north side of my house had turned to ice, and even the shafts of a carriage pulled up there were glistening with frost. The dawn moon shone brightly, although partially obscured. At a chapel in an unfrequented section of the city, a quite proper-looking man was sitting with a woman near the veranda, on the threshold of an inner room. The two were talking, and whatever it was they were talking about, they gave no sign of tiring of it. The woman's face and features were very fine; and her perfume, when a hint of it came to me on the wind, was most charming. What snatches of their conversation I caught left me wanting to hear more.

107

During the reign of Emperor Kameyama, there were some ladies in his service who, convinced that it was the rare man who could give a quick and estimable response to a woman's query, made it a point to test every young man coming to the palace. "Have you ever heard a cuckoo?" they would ask. One man, who I understand went on to become a Major Counselor, answered, "No. Men of my low station cannot hear such things." The Horikawa Minister, on the other hand, declared, "Yes. I seem to recall hearing one at Iwakura." When they discussed the matter, the ladies deemed the Minister's response satisfactory. Of the other man, however, they concluded, "But to say one is of too low status to hear such things—now that was a bit much."

A man should be taught from his youth how to avoid being laughed at by women. I believe I heard somewhere that it was thanks to the care Lady Ankimon'in took in preparing him as a boy that the former Jōdoji Regent was so adept in conversation. The Yamashina Minister of the Left once declared, "I'm so ill at ease around women that I have to be on my guard even with serving girls." If there were no women in the world, we could don our robes or wear our caps any way we wanted, and no man would take any care with his appearance at all.

From this one might conclude that women must be splendid beings indeed, to make men feel so at a loss. But the fact is that women are by nature perverse—self-centered in the extreme, intensely greedy, and with no concept of reason. Their fickle hearts are quick to follow delusion; and their words flow too easily one moment, only to cease the next, when one asks for a response to even the most innocent question. And don't think this silence shows reserve, either, for they may also come forth with the most astonishing things without even being asked. So well devised and highly polished are their statements that you may even think them superior to men in intellect. But when their deceptions come out later, will they ever admit them? No: dishonest and stupid, that is what a woman is. How disgusting it is to see any man following a woman around, trying to gain her favor! Why would anyone let himself be chagrined so? Even if there was such a thing as an intelligent woman, one can be sure that she would be aloof and without charm. Only when you let her wiles become your master does a woman seem attractive and worthy of attention.

117

There are seven kinds of people who make bad friends. First is the man of high and noble station; second is the man still young in years; third is the strong man who never falls ill; fourth is the man who likes rice wine; fifth is the strong-willed man of arms; sixth is the man who tells lies; seventh is the man who is exceedingly worldly.

There are three kinds of people who are good to have as friends. First is the friend who gives you things; second is the man of medicine; third is the friend who has wisdom.

122

The most essential accomplishments for a man are: first of all, to be well versed in the classics and knowledgeable in the writings of the sages. Next, a man should have a good hand: even if he does not make calligraphy his chief study, he should learn it for the great help it will be in all other forms of scholarship. Next, a man should study the medicinal arts: for without medicine one cannot provide for one's own health, be of help to others, or fulfill one's duties and filial obligations. Then come archery and horseback riding, two of the Six Arts, and both well worth looking into. Thus training in letters, arms, and medicine is indispensable. Those who gain these skills will never be called useless.

Next, since food is what sustains life, the man who can prepare tasty meals has a great advantage. And then comes skill with one's hands, which is useful in all sorts of ways.

When it comes to other matters, however, one must remember that to be skilled in many things is unseemly in a gentleman. Talent in poetry and excellence in music have always been considered elegant avocations that a gentleman should pursue with devotion. In our time, though, we seem no longer to rely on such means to govern the world—just as we recognize gold as the most excellent of metals, but deem it less versatile than iron.

127

When changing something would result in no benefit, it is best not to change it.

137

Should we look at the blossoms only in full bloom, or the moon only when it is unobscured by clouds? No: for to yearn for a moon hidden behind rain clouds or to ignore the progress of spring from inside drawn blinds is equally moving, and a source of great charm. Indeed, boughs on which flowers are about to bloom, a garden strewn with fallen blossoms—these are things that are truly worth seeing. After all, is a poem prefaced with "Going to see the blossoms and finding them already fallen" or "Unable to see the blossoms" inferior to one introduced with "Seeing the blossoms"? To sigh after fallen blossoms or the setting moon is only natural; but only a truly insensitive person would say, "These boughs are bare now—there's nothing left to see."

In everything, it is beginnings and ends that are of greatest interest. Does love between a man and a woman refer only to when they are together? To suffer misery when one must give up before ever meeting the object of one's affections; to lament a pledge that has come to nothing; to stay up through a long night alone, with one's thoughts as far away as the clouds; to sit in a reed-choked house thinking of the past—this is what love really means. More so than gazing out on a moon shining unimpeded over a thousand leagues, then, it is moving to wait for the waning moon near dawn, when it takes on a greenish hue. And certainly nothing could be more moving than to see moonlight shining through cryptomeria branches deep in a wood, or to look at the moon as it hides behind masses of clouds that have just brought rain showers. The way the moonlight on scrub oaks makes the leaves glisten as if wet is striking indeed, making one wish for a friend of fine sensibility to share it with, and for a quick return to the capital.

And do we really see the moon and blossoms only with our eyes? One is more certain to be captivated when staying inside the house in spring-time, or imagining the autumn moon from one's bedchamber. For the man of breeding never flaunts his tastes and is reserved even when deeply impressed. Only a rustic shows his admiration with no restraint. When he goes to see the cherry blossoms, he works his way forward through the throng, his eyes so fixed on the blossoms that he has not a glance for those he pushes aside; then he drinks his rice wine, composes some linked verse, and leaves, thoughtlessly breaking off a big branch to take home with him. At a spring, he has to soak his hands and feet; when there's snow, he gets down on it and leaves his footsteps behind. Never is he able to enjoy anything from a proper distance.

Such people have a curious way of watching the Kamo Festival. "The procession's slow in coming," they say. "There's no use sitting here on the stand waiting." So off they go to a shack at the rear to amuse themselves by drinking, eating, and playing *go* and backgammon. But they leave someone to keep a lookout for the procession, and when he calls out, "It's coming!" they all rush back, nearly knocking each other down in their resolve to get to their places and miss nothing. "Would you look at that! Look what's coming!" they say, remarking on everything that goes by. Then, after one group has passed in parade, they say, "Tell us when the next group's coming!" and get down from the stands again. Such people seem to come only to see the processions themselves. The high-born of the capital, in contrast, occasionally nap, showing no desire to see everything. Their servants are up and down, serving their masters, but even those in attendance on the high ones, seated behind their masters, never lean forward in an unseemly manner or make an effort to see everything that goes by.

140

A wise man will not leave any treasures behind after his death. If he has saved things of no worth he will seem ridiculous, and if he has stored things of value he will appear to have been vain and silly. And it is particularly regrettable if he has left a vast array of things behind, for there are sure to be those who will cry, "I'll have this!" and start bickering over his goods—a most undignified scene. Certainly it would be better to turn over whatever things he has decided should go to particular people while he is still alive.

There are of course some few things that one cannot do without in one's daily life; but otherwise one is better off owning nothing.

145

When the Escort Hada no Shigemi said of the North Guard Shingan of Shimotsuke, "His is the face of a man who will fall from his horse; he should take care," no one believed he could be right. But Shingan did indeed fall from his horse and die. Then people thought that the words of Shigemi, a man expert in reading faces, must be as sure as the words of the gods.

When someone asked him just what in a man's face boded such a fate, however, Shigemi replied, "I could see that the man's seat wasn't too firm in the saddle, and he liked unruly horses; that's why I made the pronouncement. Have I ever been wrong before?"

146

When Abbot Meiun asked a face-reader whether his countenance boded danger from weapons of war, the face-reader replied most respectfully, "Yes, I fear it does." The Abbot went on, "What sign is it that you see, then?" To this the man replied, "Why, a man of My Lord's status should have no fear of being killed in such a way; thus that you even asked me the question is itself a sign that there may be danger to come."

As it turned out, the man was right: it was an arrow that did the Abbot in. [17]

147

Recently some people have been saying that a man who has too many burns from moxa treatments is ritually unclean and should forbear participation in Shinto rites, but in the regulations I find no evidence of such a rule.

17. The Abbot was killed by a stray arrow in 1183, during a battle in which he had imprudently become involved.

149

One mustn't put the new antlers of a deer up to one's nose and smell them. There are little bugs inside them that crawl in through your nose and eat your brain.

150

People who aim to master an art seem to say to themselves, "While I'm still not too good at this, I'll keep it to myself and not let anyone know what I'm doing. People will be more impressed if I practice in private and show myself only after I've developed true skill." But anyone who says such things will never learn a single art well. For it is the man who mingles with the masters even as a beginner, uninhibited by ridicule or laughter, always pushing ahead coolly—it is that man, even if he has no special gift from birth, who will not stumble along the way or become too casual in his attitude. As the years pass, such a man will surpass one with natural gifts but no dedication, in the end arriving at a higher level of performance, expanding his talent constantly, and gaining the high opinion of the public as an artist of matchless reputation.

155

The man who would follow the ways of the world should first learn to sense the mood of the moment. A word spoken out of turn will grate on the ear of the listener, offend his sensibilities, and lead to no good end. Thus one would do well to recognize such exigencies. But falling ill, bearing children, and dying—these things alone follow no schedule; untimely or not, they cannot be put off. The truly crucial events—being born, taking on years, going through changes, and final dissolution—flow on like the waters of a raging river, stopping never for a moment, continuing always on course. And in the same way, when it comes to the truly important things—whether in lay life or after one has taken holy orders—one should not stop to consider the prevailing moods, but instead stride on without hesitation.

Summer doesn't begin only after spring has ended, nor does autumn come only with summer's demise. Rather, in time the spring itself begins to feel like summer; and in summer already autumn appears. Then autumn suddenly turns cold, and it is the Tenth Month, the first month of winter—but with weather again springlike as the grass turns green and buds swell on the flowering plum. And even with falling leaves, it isn't the case that the new growth comes out after the leaves have fallen, but rather that the leaves fall because of pressure from below. So great is the anticipation of life within that the opportunity comes and is taken with the greatest speed.

Even more rapid, however, are the changes of human life—birth, aging, illness, and death, compared to which the seasons follow a determined order. For death does not wait for a convenient time; it may not even attack from the front, but steal up from behind. We all know death must come; the problem is that it comes when we feel no urgency to prepare for it, when we are not expecting it, just as when a high tide surges in over a tideland that had seemed to keep the sea far away.

157

Pick up a brush, and you end up writing something; pick up an instrument, and you want to make music. Pick up a cup, and you think of *sake*; pick up dice, and you think of gambling. The mind always follows what the hand touches. It is for this reason that we should not engage in sinful pleasures for even a moment.

If by chance we glance at a line of holy writ, we somehow end up reading on, perhaps even correcting an erroneous notion of many years. And if we had not opened the book, would we have ever realized our mistake? This is the value of chance stimulation. For if you sit before the altar, beads in hand, sutra open, you may accumulate merit despite a general lack of devotion; and if you sit in meditation—even with distracted thoughts—you may find yourself moving toward a sense of concentration without knowing it.

Phenomenon and essence are not two things, but one. If we are true to the outward form, the inner reality cannot fail to mature. Thus it is wrong to declare such things empty formalities; they deserve praise and respect.

164

People meet, and there's never a moment of silence. Always there is talk. And if you listen to what is being said, it's all useless jabber: the rumors that are circulating, gossip about people, good and bad—all of which is harmful to both the people talking and those being discussed, and does no one any good.

When people talk like this, they don't realize that what they say profits no one.

166

Watching people strive to attain success reminds me of people making a snow-buddha on a spring day; they take pains to decorate it with precious metals and pearls, and then build a pavilion to display it. But will there be enough time to place their buddha on the altar? Too many men wait for success in the same way, supposing they have plenty of time, while beneath them life is melting away like snow.

172

When a man is young his body overflows with energy, his heart is easily moved by things, he is full of passion. He throws himself into danger as he might toss a jeweled ball to the ground, almost wanting it to shatter. So much does he love the beauty of women that he seems ready to waste his fortune in pursuit of it, only to relent and cast all that aside, debasing himself in the mossy robes of the priesthood. In an excess of bravado, he gets into a fight, then feels ashamed, and ends up envying the very man he has attacked. Thus his affections change from day to day, always unsettled. He loses himself in lust, is moved by the kindness of another, commits himself to good works; then he risks his future chasing after the example of those who have thrown their lives away—not thinking for even a moment that he might want to live safe and long. Pulled along by his whims, he makes a scandal of his life that may well be talked about for years to come. Yes, leave it to the young man to ruin his life.

When a man grows old, his spirit too loses vitality. He is impassive, easygoing, and never excited by things. Because his heart has arrived at a natural state of serenity, he engages in nothing unneedful; he cares for his body and thus does not suffer from ill health; and he is mindful not to cause anyone trouble. The old man excels the young man in wisdom, just as the young man excels the old in beauty of appearance.

189

Today you had planned to do one thing, but something else comes up and takes the whole day. The person you are waiting for is detained, but someone you hadn't expected shows up instead. Something you had confidence in goes awry, but something you had no hope for works out. The task you worried over comes off without trouble, but the task you thought would be easy proves to be difficult. As the days go by, what happens bears no resemblance to what you had anticipated. It's that way for any year; it's the same for a lifetime.

But just as you start to think that things *never* turn out as planned, something does and you feel more at a loss than ever. The only way we can be sure of things is to realize the truth: that all is uncertainty.

190

If there's one thing a man is better off without, it's a wife. I am impressed to hear of a man who has always lived alone, and if I learn later that he has gone to So-and-so's as a son-in-law or taken some woman in to live with him, he comes down in my estimation. People are bound to deride him, saying, "He's decided for himself that his woman is something fine, but she's really not so special!" or, if the woman is fine indeed, "Look at him carry on; why it's as if he's got his own little guardian Buddha, that's what!" And it's worse if the woman really runs the house. Soon they have children, whom she spoils and frets over disagreeably. Even after the man dies, she goes on, becoming a nun and mocking her man's memory with her wizened form.

No matter who the woman is, if a man spends dawn to dusk with her every day, he will grow tired of her and hate her in the end—in which case the woman too is left dangling in thin air. So to live separately, visiting the woman occasionally, makes for a more secure relationship, and one that will stand the test of time. To come unannounced and stay the night is sure to make one's visits seem something special.

191

Only a person of no feeling would say that things lose their beauty at night. On the contrary, it is at night that all rich fabrics, decorations, and colors are most delightful. In the daytime, one can appear in simple, subdued apparel; but at night, showy, bright clothing is best. And personal appearance is also shown to greatest effect in lamplight, just as voices speaking in the dark, taking care not to be heard, are most elegant. Scents and sounds too are especially delightful at night.

I find it particularly pleasing when on a night of no special significance a man comes to a mansion well into the evening dressed in the finest attire. And since those among the young who pay close attention to such things are always observant, young people—especially at times when they might be tempted to let their guard down—should take great care with their appearance, making no distinction between normal and special occasions. How charming it is when a gentleman stops to groom his hair after dark, or when a woman, late into the evening, slips out of sight, takes out a mirror, and touches up her face.

202

One hears it said that Shinto rites should not be performed during the Tenth Month—the Godless Month—but I can find no such stipulation anywhere. There's not a word about it in the classics. It may be that the name was given only because there are no Shinto festivals during that month.

There are those who say that during the Tenth Month all of the gods gather at Ise Shrine, but no source for that idea exists. If there were any foundation to it, certainly that month would be a festival time at the Grand Shrine; but there is no such tradition. Historically, there have been many imperial processions to shrines during the Tenth Month, although most of those turned out not to bode well for the future.

204

When a criminal is to be beaten with rods, he is tied to a "torture device." No one now knows what the device should look like, or how to tie the man to it.

207

When the ground was being prepared for the building of the Kameyama Palace, workers hit upon a grave mound that contained great numbers of serpents all coiled up together. "They must be the gods of the place," someone said. The whole matter was reported to the Emperor, who sent out an official query asking what should be done. Everyone said, "It would be a hard thing to dig them out if they've occupied the place for a long time." Only Minister Sanemoto disagreed: "The serpents live in the Emperor's realm; why would they want to put a curse on a place where an imperial palace is to be built? The gods and spirits do not engage in evil deeds. Stop your worrying. Just dig the snakes out and let them go." So the workers destroyed the tomb and let the snakes go into the Ōi River.

No curse ever ensued.

209

Once a man lost a suit over a rice field and, out of spite, dispatched men with the command to harvest all of the rice from the field in question. When the men stopped at the first field along the way and began reaping, someone said, "This isn't the right field. What do you think you're doing?" The men replied, "Well, we've really got no business taking the rice from the other field either. Since we've come to do something unreasonable anyway, why shouldn't we do our reaping anywhere we please!"

Their logic was most amusing.

211

We can rely on nothing. It is because the foolish man trusts in things that he so often ends up full of hatred or anger. If you have power—don't depend on it: the man of strength is first to fall. If you have great wealth—don't depend on it: riches can vanish in an instant. If you have learning—don't depend on it: even Confucius was rejected by his age. If you have virtue—don't depend on it: even Yen Hui met misfortune.[18] Nor can you rely on the affection of your lord, whose retribution may strike swiftly. And don't put faith in servants: they can betray and abandon you. Don't trust in anyone's goodwill: sometime it must change. Don't trust agreements either, for sincerity is rare.

If you depend neither on others nor on your own state of being, you can rejoice at good fortune and not be bitter at bad. With open space left and right, you will suffer no impediment; with distance behind and in

18. Yen Hui, Confucius's peerless disciple, died young.

front, your way will not be blocked. In a narrow passage things get crunched and broken. When a man has too little leeway for thought, he runs into other people, gets into fights, and loses; but when he has room and is at ease, not a hair of his head suffers.

Man is the most marvelous of all creatures in heaven and on earth. And if heaven and earth know no bounds, why should man's nature be any different? When we are open and unconstrained, joy and sorrow will not forestall us, and no one will cause us trouble.

212

The autumn moon is a thing splendid beyond compare. Any man who fails to recognize this, thinking the moon is the same in all seasons, must be lacking in sensitivity indeed.

218

Foxes bite people. Once an attendant at the Horikawa Mansion was bitten as he slept. And a low-ranking monk at Ninnaji, passing by the main hall at night, was attacked so ferociously by three foxes that he drew his sword and ran two of them through while trying to defend himself. One of them died on the spot; the other two got away. The monk had bites all over him, but he escaped serious injury.

240

Any man who persists in visiting a woman against all odds, despite the obstacles presented by "those observant fisherwomen of Shinobu Bay" and "the watchmen of Kurabu Mountain," must indeed have the most profound feelings for the woman, with whom he will share unforgettable memories.[19] On the other hand, it can only be embarrassing to a woman if she is sent off by her parents and siblings without the least complication.

And what a waste it seems when a woman suffering financial hardship announces that she will go "if a stream beckons," provided only that the man—be he an unseemly old monk or a vulgar easterner—has money, and then goes off to be greeted in a new house, unknowing and

19. Shinobu (translatable as "hide") and Kurabu (partially homophonous with *kurashi*, "dark") both suggest covert trysts. It is unclear whether Kenkō is alluding to specific poems.

unknown.[20] How will the two ever begin a conversation? By contrast, those who can reminisce about the pains of a long courtship, when they "met despite mountains between," will never run out of things to talk about.[21]

When people are brought together by an outsider, there is bound to be a great deal of unpleasantness. Even in the case of a woman of high birth, if she goes to a man of lower status who is ugly and advanced in years, the man may think to himself, "What reason could they have for throwing away such a fine woman on the likes of me?" and then conclude that she must be of inferior character. Then again, he may feel embarrassed by his own mean figure in his wife's presence—a most miserable situation.

The man who has never paused beneath a hazy moon on a night heavy with the scent of plum blossoms, or who has no fond memories of the sky near dawn when he went out into the dew near his lady's hedge—that man had best not fall in love at all.

242

Men find themselves caught up in cycles of prosperity and adversity for the sole reason that they are too concerned with pursuing pleasure and avoiding pain. Pleasure is liking something so much that we become infatuated with it. And we seek such things endlessly. Our foremost pleasure comes from fame, of which there are two kinds: praise for our deeds and praise for our artistic accomplishments. Our next chief pleasure comes from lust, and our third from appetite. No other desires exceed these three. They all result from a backward view of things and are the source of much trouble. To not pursue them at all is the best course.

243

When I turned eight years old, I confronted my father with this question: "What sort of being is a Buddha?" My father said, "Why, a

20. Ono no Komachi (KKS 938): wabinureba / mi o ukikusa no / ne o taete / sasou mizu araba / inamu to zo omou ("In this forlorn state, I find life dreary indeed: if a stream beckoned, I would gladly cut my roots and float away like duckweed").

21. The quotation is probably an allusion to a poem by Minamoto no Shigeyuki (SKKS 1013): tsukubayama / hayama shigeyama / shigekeredo / omoiiru ni wa / sawarazarikeri

Buddha is what a man has become." So I went on: "How does a man become a Buddha?" My father replied, "Through the teachings of a Buddha." Then I asked, "And the Buddha that taught the man—what sort of being was it that taught *him?*" He replied, "Well, he became a Buddha through the teachings of the First Buddha." I asked, "And what sort of Buddha was that First Buddha, the one that first taught how to become a Buddha?" At this point my father said, "I suppose he must have fallen down from the sky, or popped up out of the earth," and began to laugh.

Much amused, he said to the people around, "When the kid pressed me for an answer, I didn't have one!"

An Account of a Journey to the East

My age had reached nearly half a century, the frost on my temples growing ever more chill; yet I had lived a profitless life, accomplishing so little that I lacked even a permanent home. I was miserably conscious of my resemblance to the friend of whom Bo Juyi wrote, "He is like a vagrant cloud; his head is as white as frost." It was not that I aspired to seven generations of prosperity such as Jin and Zhang enjoyed; I merely wanted a dwelling like Tao Qian's house by the five willows. But I stayed on in the vicinity of the capital and lived like everyone else, still hesitant about retiring to a brush-thatched hermitage deep in the mountains. As the poet said, my body remained in the profane world while my spirit dwelt in retirement.[22]

Then, quite unexpectedly, I set out from the capital toward the eastern provinces. The season was autumn, toward the middle of the Eighth Month in the third year of Ninji [1242]. My journey was a long one, taking me past countless mountains and rivers, all unfamiliar, but I braved the clouds and cleaved the mists of the endless road. And as a

---

("All those watchful eyes, many as foothills, as wooded hills at Tsukuba Mountain, will not deter one whose heart burns with passionate longing").

22. Probably an allusion to a couplet from a poem in *Wen xuan* by Wang Tangju: "The lesser recluse retires in hills and fields; the greater recluse retires in the profane world." Jin Rishan and Zhang Anshi were powerful nobles during the reign of Emperor Xuandi (r. 73 B.C.–48 B.C.). Tao Qian (365–427) was a reclusive poet.

keepsake for anyone who may remember me with affection, I have set down an account of all that caught my eye or engaged my attention during the dozen or so days before I reached Kamakura—all the sights and points of interest at lodging places and hostelries in mountains and fields, and at lonely seashores and streams.

It was around the time of the full moon, the season for leading horses toward the capital, that I crossed Ōsaka Barrier after setting out from my house near the eastern hills. In the late night, the moon shone dim through a pervasive autumn mist, and the faint crow of a sacred cock brought to mind the Han Valley, where "the traveler pressed on under the lingering moon."[23] Near that barrier in ancient times, the recluse Semimaru had built a straw-thatched hut and lived a melancholy life amid harsh gales, turning constantly to his lute to calm his spirit and to poetry to express his thoughts. There are those who say the vicinity of the barrier is called Shi-no-miya Plain, "Plain of the Fourth Prince," because Semimaru was Emperor Daigo's fourth son.

inishie no	All claims our interest
waraya no toko no	at Ōsaka Barrier,
atari made	even the place
kokoro o tomuru	where the straw-thatched cottage stood,
ōsaka no seki	his dwelling in bygone days.

It is pitiful to imagine the feelings with which the Imperial Lady Higashisanjōin recited these lines, composed when she was about to pass the spring at the barrier, during her return from a pilgrimage to Ishiyama:

amatatabi	How sad that today
yuki ōsaka no	I behold for the last time
sekimizu ni	my face reflected
kyō o kagiri no	in these oft-visited waters
kage zo kanashiki	at Ōsaka Barrier!

After I had passed the barrier mountain, it was still too dark for a good view of Uchide Beach, Awazu Plain, and other well-known places. I was moved by the thought that I must be near the old imperial seat—

23. Anonymous (WKRES 416): "The traveler presses on under the lingering moon; / At Han Valley, a cock crows." Lord Mengchang, imprisoned by King Zhao of Qin, escaped and made his way at night as far as a government checkpoint at Han Valley. When his party learned that the gate would not open until the first cock crowed, one of the men successfully imitated the bird's cry.

the Ōtsu Palace built in the time of Emperor Tenchi, when the capital was moved from Okamoto at Asuka in Yamato Province to Shiga District in Ōmi.

sazanami ya	Now that the palace
ōtsu no miya no	at Ōtsu of rippling waves
areshi yori	has moldered away,
na nomi nokoreru	only the name remains
shiga no furusato	at the Shiga capital.

Dawn approached, revealing Lake Biwa in the distance, as I rode across the Long Bridge at Seta. I recalled the poem Mansei had composed while gazing at the waters of the lake from Mount Hiei.[24] The vanishing white wake of a rowed boat is truly a lonesome sight.

yo no naka o	I gaze in my turn
kogiyuku fune ni	at the self-same waters
yosoetsutsu	where his eyes rested
nagameshi ato o	when he compared this world
mata zo nagamuru	to a boat rowed on its way.

I continued to Noji, where the heavy dew in the grassy fields soon combined with tears to drench the sleeves of my travel robe.

azumaji no	Today seems to mark
noji no asatsuyu	a beginning for sleeves thus drenched:
kyō ya sa wa	morning dewdrops
tamoto ni kakaru	in the fields of Noji
hajime naruran	on the road leading eastward.

At Shinohara, a long dike extended far to the east and west, with the houses of the local folk occupying the area to the north, and the surface of a vast lake stretching away to the south. Deep-green pines lined the opposite shore. The waves, identical in color with the trees, were "green, broad, and deep," even though they did not reflect the Nanshan Mountains.[25] As though in a reed-writing scene, mandarin ducks and mallards flew here and there, or congregated in reeds and water oats where occasional small peninsulas jutted out. According to what I was

24. See footnote 6, p. 389.
25. An allusion to a poem by Bo Juyi about Lake Kunming in springtime: "The green waters reflect the Nanshan Mountains, they are broad and deep." Reed-writing, mentioned in the next sentence, was an eccentric calligraphic style sometimes used for the transcription of poetry. The characters, distorted to resemble natural objects, were incorporated into water-margin scenes depicting birds, reeds, rocks, etc.

told, travelers departing from the capital always used to stop overnight at Shinohara Post Station, but most of them go on past now, and fewer and fewer houses remain. I thought to myself that the pools and shallows of the Asuka River were not the only things subject to change in this world.

yuku hito mo	Having now become
tomaranu sato to	a village where no traveler
narishi yori	stops overnight,
are nomi masaru	it crumbles into ruin—
noji no shinohara	Noji-no-shinohara.

On my arrival at Kagami Post Station, I realized that I must be seeing the mountain memorialized in the poem—the one composed when the seven ancients gathered long ago to lament their aging:[26]

kagamiyama	Before going on,
iza tachiyorite	let me stop by Mirror Mountain
mite yukamu	to look at myself:
toshi henuru mi wa	have I become an old man
oi ya shinuru to	after living all these years?

Much as I would have liked to spend the night there, I went on because there was a place farther ahead where I intended to pay a visit.

tachiyorade	Even though I miss
kyō wa suginan	the old stranger's reflection,
kagamiyama	I must go on today
shiranu okina no	without stopping to behold
kage wa mizu tomo	the Mountain of the Mirror.

Overtaken by darkness on the road, I lodged near a mountain temple called Musadera. As the night advanced, the autumn wind from Tokonoyama chilled me to the bone in the makeshift bed, and I suddenly felt worlds removed from the capital. Toward dawn, the boom of the temple bell evoked a surge of emotion when it resounded near my pillow. Might it have been the same when the poet awakened in the grass-thatched hut beside Yiaisi Temple?[27] My mind dwelt forlornly on the length of the journey ahead.

26. The poem (anonymous, KKS 899) was composed at a literary gathering held in 1172 by the poet-scholar Fujiwara no Kiyosuke (1104–77).
27. Bo Juyi: "Propping up my pillow, I listen to the bell of Yiaisi Temple; / Rolling up the blind, I gaze at the snow on Incense Burner Peak."

miyako idete	Even tonight,
ikuka mo aranu	when I have scarcely set forth
koyoi dani	from the capital,
katashiki wabinu	I pine in a lonely bed:
toko no akikaze	autumn wind from Mount Toko.

While crossing Kasahara Plain from that night's lodging place, I came to the cryptomeria woods at Oiso-no-mori. It would not be long, I thought, before time's swift flight would make frost of the heavy morning dew on the undergrowth.

kawaraji na	No difference, alas—
wa ga motoyui ni	frost falling on my hair-cord
oku shimo mo	and on undergrowth
na ni shi oiso no	at famed Oiso-no-mori,
mori no shitakusa	the Forest of Old Age.

The renowned Samegai Well proved to be a limpid stream flowing from the base of a rock in dense shade, its unblemished purity so cold that it chilled my flesh. Large numbers of travelers had stopped in search of relief from the lingering summer heat. Reluctant to leave despite the long journey ahead, I found myself dawdling, Ban Jieyu's round, snow-white fan forgotten temporarily in the autumn breeze.[28] I wondered if it might have been in just such a place that Saigyō composed his celebrated poem:

michi no be ni	"Only a moment,"
shimizu nagaruru	I thought when I halted,
yanagikage	drawn by willow shade
shibashi tote koso	where fresh spring water
tachitomaritsure	flowed limpid at the roadside.

[I composed:]

michi no be no	Not a wayfarer
kokage no shimizu	but pauses here a moment—
musubu tote	tarries to scoop up
shibashi susumanu	a handful of limpid water
tabibito zo naki	in the shade of roadside trees.

From Kashiwabara, I went to the barrier mountain in Mino Prov-

---

28. Ban Jieyu, an imperial favorite discarded for a rival, was compared by the literatus Ōe no Masahira to a fan, as round as the full moon and as white as snow, which was cast aside in autumn despite its beauty (WKRES 162).

ince. It was a lonely journey along a sunless, tree-shadowed trail, with a valley stream brawling at the bottom of the mist and a mountain wind rustling like rain in the pine boughs. Once across the summit, I arrived at the Fuwa Barrier Post. The seeming antiquity of the thatched building's wooden eaves called to mind the Go-Kyōgoku Regent Yoshitsune's lines, "After the fall into decay, only the autumn wind."[29] It was impossible to improve on his conception. I passed the spot in silence, feeling that it would be worse to produce an inferior poem than to preserve no memento of the occasion at all.

At Kuizegawa, where I spent the night, I strolled out to the riverbank in the dark. The cloudless sky of mid-autumn was reflected in the transparent shallows, which were so clear that I could count the ripples shining in the moonlight. Unable to keep from imagining what must be in the minds of old friends 2,000 leagues away, I found it harder than ever to suppress the loneliness of travel.[30] I inked my brush in the moonlight and scribbled something on a sliding door at the house: "Three days after my departure from the brilliant capital, I am spending the night at Kuizegawa. From time to time, I murmur a mournful verse while gazing at the moon on the Fifteenth of the mid-autumn month; with difficulty, I send my thoughts to the clouds above the 1,000-league road ahead." I added:

shirazariki	Little did I know
aki no nakaba no	that tonight in mid-autumn
koyoi shi mo	I would behold
kakaru tabine no	so magnificent a moon
tsuki o min to wa	at such a travel lodging.

At East Post Station in Kayatsu, I came upon a big crowd of people who were shouting and yelling in strident voices. It was a market day. The passersby were all carrying souvenirs that bore small resemblance to the flowery mementos of the poem, "Were we merely to gaze, could we describe to others."[31]

29. Fujiwara no Yoshitsune (SKKS 1599): hito sumanu / fuwa no sekiya no / itabisashi / arenishi nochi wa / tada aki no kaze ("Eaves fashioned of wood at the Fuwa Barrier Post where no human dwells: after the fall into decay, only the autumn wind").

30. Bo Juyi, on seeing the harvest moon from the imperial palace: "The Fifteenth-night moon, new risen in beauty: / What is in the heart of my old friend, two thousand leagues away?"

31. Monk Sosei (KKS 55): mite nomi ya / hito ni kataramu / sakurabana / te goto ni orite / iezuto ni semu ("Were we merely to gaze, could we describe to others those cherry trees in bloom? Let each of us pick clusters to take home as souvenirs").

hana naranu	Hardly like blossoms—
iro ka mo shiranu	these souvenirs carried home
ichibito no	by market-goers
itazura narade	devoid of elegance,
kaeru iezuto	ignorant of color and scent.

Upon reaching Atsuta in Owari Province, I lost no time in paying my respects at the shrine nearby. The precincts seemed very holy: the rays of the setting sun glimmered in the ancient groves, burnishing the sacred red fences, and the offering strips tangled in the wind. On the near and distant trees, countless herons in search of roosts had settled like patches of white snow, and a feeling of loneliness stole over me as their quarrelsome voices gradually fell silent in the deepening night.

Someone said that the divinity of the shrine was Susanoo-no-mikoto. The god's original shrine was in Izumo Province; his composition there, "A manifold fence," was the first Japanese poem.[32] It was later that he moved to this site, during the reign of Emperor Keikō. I was also told that the object of worship at the shrine was the sacred sword Kusanagi. When Emperor Keikō's son, Yamatotakeru-no-mikoto, was journeying homeward after his subjugation of the barbarians, he assumed the guise of a white bird and departed, but his sword remained at Atsuta.

Ōe no Masahira, a learned doctor in the reign of Emperor Ichijō, went to Owari Province as Governor late in the Chōhō era [999–1003], and while in office, he made a copy of the *Great Wisdom Sutra* to present at this shrine. Most affectingly, he wrote in the Supplication, "My petition has already been granted. My term of duty has expired and I shall go home soon."

omoide no	Had he not offered
nakute ya hito no	a memento of the Law,
kaeramashi	he might have returned
nori no katami o	with nothing to evoke
tamukeokazuba	fond memories of the past.

A forlorn plover cried now and again as I started off from Atsuta, bound toward the shore road under a bleak late moon. Overwhelmed by the loneliness of travel, I felt unutterably depressed.

32. Yakumo tatsu / izumo yaegaki / tsumagome ni / yaegaki tsukuru / sono yaegaki o ("A manifold fence I build, a manifold fence to shut in a wife; Izumo manifold fence, where manifold clouds rise high").

furusato wa	With each passing day,
hi o hete tōku	my old home grows more distant:
narumigata	a trying journey,
isogu shiohi no	rushing when the tide recedes
michi zo kurushiki	on the shore at Narumi.

I reached the Futamura Mountains while it was still dark. The east finally brightened after I passed Yamanaka, disclosing the distant surface of the ocean. The merging waves and sky seemed a continuation of the mountain road.

tamakushige	Faintly, faintly,
futamurayama no	the first light of dawn appears
honobono to	over Futamura,
akeyuku sue wa	hills of jeweled comb boxes—
namiji narikeri	with a wave path at the end.

In time, I came to Yatsuhashi in Mikawa Province, the very spot where Ariwara no Narihira's poem about the irises had made all his companions weep into their parched rice.[33] I looked around, but saw nothing resembling irises—only quantities of rice plants.

hana yue ni	Are they intended
ochishi namida no	as mementos of tears
katami to ya	evoked by flowers—
inaba no tsuyu o	those dewdrops deposited
nokoshiokuran	on the leaves of paddy rice?

It was sad to recall the poem Minamoto no Yoshitane sent to the daughter he left behind when he went to serve as Governor of Mikawa:

morotomo ni	Will you forever
yukanu mikawa no	be thinking wistfully
yatsuhashi o	of the Eight Bridges
koishi to nomi ya	in the province to which
omoiwataran	you do not accompany me?

I arrived at Akasaka Post Station after crossing Mount Miyaji from Yahagi. It was a place difficult to pass, so poignant was the memory of how Ōe no Sadamoto had pronounced religious vows because of the woman who lived there. Many different causes may lead us to the path of enlightenment, but it is admirable that Sadamoto, when he entered the

33. See *Tales of Ise*, Sec. 9.

Travelers pause near irises at Yatsuhashi (*An Account of a Journey to the East*)

true Way, should have taken as guide a heart racked with sorrow over the
death of a beloved mistress.

wakareji ni	How did it happen
shigeri mo hatede	that kudzu leaves, still flourishing
kuzu no ha no	on the road of parting,
ika de ka aranu	should yet have turned away
kata ni kaerishi	to a different path? [34]

34. "How did it happen that this man, who had not yet ceased to mourn the premature
death of his mistress, should nevertheless have turned to the quest for enlightenment?"

At Hon-no-gawara Plain, a hazy landscape extended in all directions, unbroken by mountains or hills. It was like surveying the 1,000 leagues of the Qin domain to see the green plants and earth recede into the distance. I wondered how it would look on a moonlit night. Paths ran through the dense bamboo grass in confusing numbers, but travelers could guide their steps to some extent by following the willow trees. Those trees, still too small to yield shade, were a touching reminder of the late Former Musashi Governor Yasutoki, by whose order the local folk had planted them.

In China, Duke Shi of Shao, the younger brother of King Wu of Zhou, governed the state of Yan as one of King Cheng's Three Ministers. While administering the area west of Shan, the Duke conducted official business under a sweet-pear tree. No official or commoner lost his means of livelihood; moreover, the Duke made fair settlement of all suits and dealt leniently even with serious crimes. After his departure, the people of the region venerated and preserved the tree and wrote poetry in his honor, grateful for his benevolent rule. One thinks with deep respect of the future Emperor Go-Sanjō, who must have been moved by the same spirit when he presented a Chinese poem to his tutor, Sanemasa, as Sanemasa was about to leave for a provincial post:

> Even if the people in that province sing of the sweet-pear tree,
> Do not forget our many years of pleasure with wind and moon . . .

Because the willows were planted through the thoughtfulness of the Former Governor, and because he was a man who followed in the Duke of Shao's footsteps, treating others with a degree of sympathy and compassion that extended even to roadside shade for travelers, all who see them will take great care of them, feeling toward them just as the local folk did toward the Duke. And the day will come when travelers rely on their shade, exactly as he hoped.

ueokishi	Willows on the plain,
nushi naki ato no	left behind by a planter
yanagihara	who no longer lives:
nao sono kage o	men will yet trust to their shade
hito ya tanoman	as to the bounty of that lord.

Kudzu leaves are white underneath. As here—where "flourishing kudzu leaves," a metaphor for intense grief, occurs in conjunction with *kaeru* ("return," translated as "turned away")—they often appear in poems containing wordplays suggested by *ura* ("reverse side") and *hirugaeru* ("turn over").

As I passed Toyokawa Post Station, someone said, "This always used to be the only possible road, but recently all the travelers have suddenly begun to use a new route through Watōzu. Even the local people are moving away." It is society's custom to abandon the old for the new—but why? That is the mystery. Although Toyokawa was not the Sugawara Fushimi of the famous poem, it seemed a pity that the settled inhabitants should drift away, leaving it to "decay into ruins."[35]

obotsukana	Hard to understand:
isa toyokawa no	who might have been the first men
kawaru se o	to decide to cross
ika naru hito no	at a different shallows
watarisomeken	in the Toyokawa River?

The well-known Takashi Hills rise on the border between Mikawa and Tōtōmi provinces. As I made my way through them, I could hear the clamorous waters of a valley stream descending over rocky rapids. It was called the Border River.

iwazutai	I have reached Takashi,
koma uchiwatasu	the mountains where travelers
tanigawa no	make their way past crags,
oto mo takashi no	spurring their horses across
yama ni kinikeri	a noisy valley stream.

The breathtaking beauty of Hashimoto more than justifies its high reputation. To the south stretches the open sea, its waters dotted with fishing boats; to the north lies the lake, its banks edged with houses. A long spit separates the two, thickly wooded with pine trees where the wail of the wind never ceases. The murmur of the pines merges with the sound of the waves. Those who pass feel their spirits sink; those who spend the night always suffer from broken dreams. Hamana Bridge, the span that crosses the lake, has been famous for a long time. Nowhere else is it so depressing to watch clouds rise and dissipate in the morning.[36]

yukitomaru	Leaving a lodging
tabine wa itsu mo	is never an easy task
kawaranedo	for a traveler,

35. Anonymous (KKS 981): iza koko ni / wa ga yo wa henamu / sugawara ya / fushimi no sato no / aremaku mo oshi ("I, at least, will live in no other place than this. How sad that old homes at Sugawara Fushimi must decay into ruins").

36. The departing traveler is especially reluctant to leave so beautiful a scene.

| wakite hamana no | but passing Hamana Bridge |
| hashi zo sugiuki | is especially hard to bear. |

As it happened, there was a hostelry at the station where I had spent the night once before. The moonlight had streamed in through gaps in the old eaves of the straw-thatched building, and one of the group of harlots who had appeared—a woman who seemed a bit more mature than the others—had recited in a quiet voice, "All night, from my bed, I behold the blue heavens."[37] It seemed an elegant gesture.

koto no ha no	The deep refinement
fukaki nasake wa	infusing her utterance
nokiba moru	became visible
tsuki no katsura no	in light from the cinnamon tree
iro ni mieniki	filtering through the eaves.

Despite many twinges of regret, I left that station, too. I continued on to Maisawa Plain, which stretched far and wide to the north and south, with the seashore adjacent on the west. No brocades of flowers or embroideries of plants met the eye—nothing but snowy white sand. Pine trees grew here and there, the sea wind sighing in their branches, and occasional wretched grass-thatched huts came into view, which were doubtless the abodes of fishermen and anglers. As I progressed across the unending flatlands, gazing far into the distance, a fellow wayfarer told me of a wooden statue of Kannon on the plain, erected nobody knew when. Perhaps because the original shelter had fallen into ruins, the image stood inside a temporary thatched shack, exposed to the rains and dews, until a man from Tsukushi came along one year on his way to Kamakura with a petition. The man went before the image and uttered a silent vow to build it a hall if his mission succeeded. The petition was granted at Kamakura, and he built the hall. Since then, my informant concluded, many people have visited the statue.

I hurried off to the hall. The fragrant smoke from ever-burning incense drifted out on the breeze; the altar flowers were fresh and dewy. Papers that looked like petitions were fastened to the curtain cords. I composed this verse, thinking with a trustful heart of the "vast vow as deep as the sea."[38]

37. A line from a poem in Chinese attributed to Miyoshi no Yoshimune (WKRES 536).
38. A phrase from a long passage in the *Lotus Sutra* describing the kinds of protection Śākyamuni has vowed to extend to believers. Here the author attributes the same vow to

tanomoshi na	Fervent is our faith
irie ni tatsuru	when we hear of a response
miotsukushi	as profound as the depths
fukaki shirushi no	measured by channel markers
ari to kiku ni mo	set in an estuary.

At Tenryū Crossing, the river was deep, and the current was frightfully swift. "Autumn rivers bear swollen waters; boats go off quickly." [39] It was difficult for a traveler to reach the opposite shore. To my great alarm, I heard people saying that boats often capsized during spells of high water, and that many passengers ended as refuse on the bottom. I could not help thinking of the current in the Wu Gorge. [40] But then I reflected that this river was placid in comparison with the human heart. Nothing matches the dangers of the road through life.

kono kawa no	Not even the flow
hayaki nagare mo	of this river's swift current
yo no naka no	is as frightening
hito no kokoro no	as the things that lie within
tagui to wa mizu	the hearts of humankind.

Upon arriving at the Tōtōmi provincial seat, Ima-no-ura, I stayed in lodgings for a day or two so that I might go about in a small boat and view the coast. A long spit separates the sea from the lake. To the south, the waves of a remote shore wet the traveler's sleeve; to the north, the wind in the tall pines oppresses the spirit. Indeed, the spot much resembled Hashimoto Post Station of pleasant memory. Had I not been so enthralled yesterday, I thought, Ima-no-ura would have been hard to forget too.

nami no oto mo	The sound of the waves
matsu no arashi mo	and the gale in the pine trees
ima no ura ni	at Ima-no-ura—
kinō no sato no	both evoke fond memories
nagori o zo kiku	of yesterday's lodging place.

A trifling poem occurred to me when I passed in front of the shrine called Koto-no-mama [Just As One Desires]:

Kannon. The "response" in the poem below is Kannon's answer to the prayers of the man from Tsukushi.

39. A line from a poem by Ying Zhan (WKRES 253).
40. A dangerous stretch on the upper Yangzi River near Wu Mountain.

yūdasuki	After prayer, I trust
kakete zo tanomu	to the god's divine response
ima omou	at Koto-no-mama,
koto no mama naru	hoping to gain what I want,
kami no shirushi o	"just as I desire it."

I had often heard that Sayo-no-nakayama was famous because of the *Kokinshū* poem, "stretching itself between us,"[41] but the place itself was a depressing sight. On the north, mountains ranged into the distance, their pines and cryptomerias agitated by a strong wind; on the south, there were mountain fields where dew lay thick on autumn flowers. Journeying from valley to peak, I felt as though I were cleaving a path through clouds. A stag's call drew tears from my eyes, and the plaints of insects sounded deeply moving.

fumikayou	The cliffside pathway
mine no kakehashi	we follow to the peak
todae shite	has come to an end,
kumo ni ato tou	leaving us with clouds as guides
sayo no nakayama	at Sayo-no-nakayama.

After pressing on across those mountains as well, I arrived at Kikugawa. I remembered having been told that the Naka-no-mikado Middle Counselor Muneyuki, when on his way east to answer for an offense, had stopped at the post station during the autumn of the third year of Jōkyū {1221}, and that he had written these words on a pillar at one of the houses:

> In the past, at Chrysanthemum River in Nanyang-xian,
> One might dip water from the lower reaches to prolong one's life;
> Now, at Chrysanthemum River on the Eastern Sea Road,
> I lodge on the west bank and lose my life.[42]

Moved, I inquired about the house, but someone said that a fire had destroyed everything, poem and all. It was depressing to realize that such is the way of the transitory world. Even this memento, set down to record a dying man's last words, had disappeared without a trace.

41. A song from Kai Province (KKS 1097): kai ga ne o / saya ni mo mi shi ga / kekere naku / yokohori fuseru / saya no nakayama ("I wish I might see the mountain peaks of Kai clear before my eyes. Oh! That heartless Saya [Sayo] Pass stretching itself between us!").

42. According to a Chinese legend, in what is now Henan Province there was once a valley, Nanyang-xian, where people lived for as long as 120 years by drinking the waters of a

kakitsukuru	Even the writing
katami mo ima wa	set down as a memento
nakarikeri	has now come to naught.
ato wa chitose to	Who said, "The traces of a brush
tare ka iikemu	endure for a thousand years"?

Soon after crossing the Kikugawa River, I arrived at a village called Kohama. From a point slightly upstream, near the eastern edge of the settlement, I looked out over the Ōi River upon great numbers of shallow rivulets, which crisscrossed a wide bed in a stylized design. It was more interesting to view the river from the shore than to see it while crossing. I could not help lingering, even though it was not the Tatsuta, where "colored autumn leaves float in random patterns."[43]

hikazu furu	Long days of travel
tabi no aware wa	evoke many sad feelings:
ōigawa	my heart overflows
wataranu mizu mo	even before the crossing
fukaki iro ka na	of the Ōi River.

Passing through the vicinity of the new Okabe Post Station after my departure from Maejima, I stopped under a pine tree on a wayside hill and took out something to eat. A chilly storm wind swept through the branches, its bite piercing the thin sleeves of my summer travel robe.

kore zo kono	This is a tree
tanomu ko no moto	where I have sought shelter.
okabe naru	You gale in the pines
matsu no arashi yo	on the Okabe hillside:
kokoro shite fuke	keep that in mind as you blow.

Just as in antiquity, there were dense growths of ivy and maple at Utsu-no-yama. I traveled with a watchful eye, wondering where Narihira might have given the ascetic his message, until I came to a wayside placard announcing the presence of a recluse. The hermitage was near the road, so I went in. A lone monk sat in a tiny grass-thatched hut,

---

river containing petals from miraculous chrysanthemums growing upstream. Muneyuki was executed for having supported Retired Emperor Go-Toba's attempt to overthrow the Kamakura shogunate. See also footnote 72, p. 355.

43. Anonymous (KKS 283): tatsutagawa / momiji midarete / nagarumeri / wataraba nishiki / naka ya taenamu ("Were we to cross it, the brocade might break in two—colored autumn leaves floating in random patterns on the Tatsuta River").

Above: Travelers encounter a wandering ascetic at Mount Utsu. Below: Travelers at Mount Fuji. (*An Account of a Journey to the East.*)

completely unfurnished except for a picture of Amida Buddha and some Pure Land teachings. When I asked about his reason for forsaking the world, he replied that he had been an inhabitant of the province. He had felt no particular revulsion against worldly things, no urge toward religion, nor could he claim any special abilities. Thus, he was too dull to attain the truth through meditation and too indolent to recite

Buddha-invocations. But although he lacked the qualities to pursue either the hard path or the easy one, he had spent many years in a hut on this mountain, inspired by the words of someone who had told him that the mere act of living in the mountains was more efficacious than the performance of austerities in the outside world.

In the past, we are told, Shu Qi plucked spring bracken in the Shouyang clouds, and Xu You purified himself at the Ying River and hung up a gourd. I observed no special cooking facilities near the hut: the hermit had apparently relinquished even the comfort of a fire. Despite his silence, it was clear that this man, a sojourner amid the gales of isolated mountains, was purifying his spirit in a holy place remote from mankind, and I felt more deeply moved and impressed than if he had been a more orthodox seeker after enlightenment.

yo o itou	Unless a man dwells
kokoro no oku ya	on just such a mountainside,
nigoramashi	defilement may reach
kakaru yamabe no	into the innermost recesses
sumai narade wa	of the heart that rejects the world.

Not far from the hermitage, I came to a pass where someone had erected a large, venerable-looking stupa. This poem was among the many verses inscribed on it:

azumaji wa	I deem this the best
koko o se ni sen	of scenes on the eastland road:
utsu no yama	the ivy-lined track
aware mo fukashi	winding its picturesque way
tsuta no shitamichi	into the Utsu Mountains.

Intrigued, I wrote a poem of my own beside it:

ware mo mata	I, too, deem it the best:
koko o se ni sen	there is uncommon beauty
utsu no yama	in the dewdrops
wakete iro aru	where red ivy trails on the path
tsuta no shitatsuyu	through the Utsu Mountains.

Going on, I saw a conspicuous mound of stones under a tree. I asked about it, and someone replied that it was Kajiwara's grave. So Kajiwara had become dust by this roadside! I remembered a poem Middle Counselor Akimoto is said to have liked to recite: "Year after year, the spring grasses come up." It was moving to think that Kajiwara's very name might be forgotten when this grave had grown old in its turn. Even though the mound does not memorialize Yang Hu, travelers with feelings must certainly shed tears.[44]

Kajiwara enjoyed the patronage of two shoguns, won renown for his valor and military prowess, and seemed paramount among men. But he also became an object of hatred, for reasons I do not fully understand. He galloped toward the capital, his life at stake, in the apparent hope of escaping, and was killed at a place in Suruga Province called Kikawa. It was moving to realize that I had reached the spot where he fell.

After the Sanuki Retired Emperor died in exile at Shido, Saigyō visited his grave on a pilgrimage. He composed this poem:

yoshi ya kimi	Ah, Your Majesty!
mukashi no tama no	Now that it has come to this,
yuka tote mo	what good would it do
kakaramu nochi wa	to lie in the ornate bed
nani ni ka wa sen	where you reclined in bygone days?

Of course, what Saigyō says is even more applicable to a man of Kajiwara's inferior status, but it was deeply saddening to see the grave with my own eyes.

aware ni mo	Ah, how moving to think
sora ni ukareshi	that his spirit has risen
tamaboko no	into the heavens,
michi no he ni shi mo	leaving only a name
na o todomekeri	beside the jewel-spear road!

I rested awhile at Kiyomi Barrier, reluctant to leave so beautiful a view. The tide was out, revealing clusters of offshore rocks, misty with spray; and occasional smoke plumes rose from salt-burners' beachside huts to trail away in the wind. It was a scene worthy of rank among anyone's memories of the Eastern Sea Road.

Long ago in the time of Emperor Suzaku, Masakado raised a revolt in the east. The general sent by the court to subjugate him, Popular Affairs

44. Kajiwara no Kagetoki was one of the principal Genji commanders in the campaigns of the 1180's. The author recalls a short poem by Bo Juyi: "An old grave from an unknown age; / We do not know the surname or given name of the deceased. / He has been transformed into dust by the roadside; / Year after year, the spring grasses come up." The local peasants erected a memorial stone on a mountain beloved of Yang Hu (A.D. 221–78), a Chinese official of the Jin dynasty (265–402).

Minister Tadafun, halted when he reached this barrier, and Kiyowara no Shigefuji, a military aide, chanted two lines from a Chinese ballad:

> Reflections of fishing-boat fires: cold, they kindle the waves;
> Sounds of post-road bells: by night, someone crosses the mountains.

It is affecting to learn that Tadafun wept as he listened.

kiyomigata	Even those who pass
seki to wa shirade	unaware that on this site
yuku hito mo	a barrier stood
kokoro bakari wa	will find their hearts given pause
todomeokuramu	at Kiyomigata Beach.

The Okitsu coast is not far from the barrier. Lodged there in a house facing the ocean, I was kept awake all night by the waves, which pounded on the rocky shore as though eager to invade my room.

kiyomigata	A travel lodging
isobe ni chikaki	near Kiyomigata Beach:
tabimakura	even the waves
kakenu nami ni mo	falling short of my pillow
sode wa nurekeri	have brought moisture to my sleeve.

After having spent the night fully clad and sleepless, I had no need to awaken before setting out with the approach of dawn. A ceaseless succession of waves rolled in, driven shoreward by a strong wind, as I attempted to thread my way among the rocks on the wild Kuki-ga-saki coast. It seemed to do no good to dash ahead when the water ebbed; there was never a chance for my sleeves to dry. In dismal spirits, I told myself that I had never expected travel to be like this.

okitsukaze	Following the rocks
kesa araiso no	on a wild coast where the sea wind
iwazutai	blows strong this morning,
namiwakegoromo	I push ahead, breasting waves,
nurenure zo yuku	my robes wet through and through.

At Kanbara Post Station, I went into a house to wait for a companion who had fallen behind. Someone had written a poem on a sliding door:

tabigoromo	On a narrow mat
susono no io no	in this hut on the plain
samushiro ni	below the mountains,

| tsumoru mo shiruki | a traveler understands: |
| fuji no shirayuki | snow is massing on Mount Fuji. |

It must have been composed by a traveler with refined sensibilities.

In the past, a recluse in a cottage at the foot of Incense Burner Peak had opened his blinds on a winter morning and seen snow on the mountaintop; now, a traveler lodging near Mount Fuji had spread the single sleeve of a travel robe in the cold night and thought of snow on the mountain. I felt that both were pure-hearted men.

sayuru yo ni	Who might he have been—
tare koko ni shi mo	the one who imagined
fushiwabite	snow on a high peak
takane no yuki o	while lying here sleepless
omoiyariken	in the chill of the night?

I saw Mount Fuji's lofty summit from the beach at Tago-no-ura. Although its snows are supposed to ignore the seasons, the peak was not white anywhere yet. It rose blue into the heavens, its beauty even greater than in pictures. In the winter of the seventeenth year of Jōgan [875], so Miyako no Yoshika's *Account of Mount Fuji* tells us, two fair maidens in white raiment danced together on the summit for reasons that remain obscure.

fuji no ne no	Might they be the sleeves
kaze ni tadayou	of maidens from the heavens—
shirakumo o	those fleecy white clouds
amatsuotome no	set afloat by the breezes
sode ka to zo miru	where Mount Fuji soars on high?

Ukishima Plain is an incomparable sight. To the north, the plain adjoins the base of Mount Fuji; to the east and west, there is a tremendously long marsh resembling cloth spread to bleach. Sky and water merge, suffused with the reflected green of the mountains. Reed-cutters pole small boats here and there, and huge flocks of waterfowl utter raucous cries. On the south, the surface of the sea is visible far into the distance, an immense expanse of clouded, hazy waves with no island to obstruct the view. There is nothing to be seen but a line of sails on the horizon. Wherever the eye ranges, the scene is lonely. Wavering columns of smoke rise from salt-burners' huts on the plain, and a shore wind moans in the pine trees. I felt even more impressed by the elegance of the spectacle when I learned that the plain was called Ukishima, "Floating Island," because it had once floated on the sea like the three Isles of the Immortals. Perhaps the dwellings I saw belonged to gods or immortals!

kage hitasu	Casting reflections
numa no irie ni	on the waters of the marsh,
fuji no ne no	the smoke plume and clouds
kemuri mo kumo mo	above the peak of Fuji
ukishima ga hara	float on Floating Island Plain.

At Senbon-no-matsubara, just beyond Ukishima Plain, the seashore is not far away. A long line of pine trees casts green reflections far into the distance, and boats in the offing resemble floating leaves as they ply the waters. Both the pine trees and the boats are exactly like the ones in the poem: "Under a thousand pines, a twin-peak temple; In a leaf-small boat, someone a myriad leagues from home."[45] The prospect has no equal anywhere.

miwataseba	How distant the last
chimoto no matsu no	of the thousand pine trees
sue tōmi	when we gaze afar:
midori ni tsuzuku	the surface of the waves
nami no ue ka na	seems to continue their green!

At Kurumagaeshi Village, I lodged in a house that may have been the abode of a net fisherman, an angler, or some other humble fellow of similar occupation. The stench was overpowering, and the straw bed-matting was too narrow. The midnight quarters of Bo Juyi's fettered barbarians must have been similar.[46]

kore zo kono	This is indeed
tsuri suru ama no	the woven-thatched dwelling
tomabisashi	of a fisherman:
itou arika ya	its abominable smell
sode ni nokoran	will linger in my sleeves.

I worshipped at the Mishima Shrine sanctuary after I reached the Izu provincial seat. A gale blew through the dusky pine groves, and an aura of sanctity pervaded the compound. People say its god was brought from

45. From a poem by Zhao Gu (WKRES 578).
46. See *The Journal of the Sixteenth-Night Moon*, entry of Twenty-sixth Day.

Mishima in Iyo Province. It seems presumptuous even to mention the shrine's name, because it is the second home of a miracle-working deity. When the Novice Nōin addressed that god in verse by command of the Iyo Governor Sanetsuna, a sudden rain fell from the parched skies, and the withered rice plants regained their green color in an instant.

seki kakeshi	This is the very god
nawashiromizu no	who dammed the heavenly stream
nagarekite	for the seedling beds:
mata amakudaru	deigning to come to this place,
kami zo kono kami	he descends from the heights again.

Pressed for time, I left that place, too, and journeyed onward to the Hakone Mountains. Rocks on rocks made the going hard, even for horses. Once into the mountains, I came to a wide lake brimming with water. It is called Lake Hakone—or, by some, the Lake of Reeds. The holy site where the god has manifested himself is majestic and awe-inspiring. The magnificent buildings soaring into the clouds make the spectator feel as though he is beholding the Lishan Palace of Tang; the reflections of the grottoes and stone stupas facing the waves might be compared to the scene at Xinshuisi Temple on the Qiantang River. I took the opportunity to pray for future guidance, accompanying my offering with this poem:

ima yori wa	Placing all my faith
omoimidareji	in divine compassion as deep
ashi no umi no	as the Lake of Reeds,
fukaki megumi o	I shall live from this time forth
kami ni makasete	with a mind undistracted.

I lodged at Yumoto after the descent. A shower was falling, borne on a violent wind from the heights, and the flooding valley stream, its tumultuous waves crashing against the rocks, seemed even noisier than the waters audible at night from Wenzhang's dwelling.[47] With a rush of

47. The subject of one of Bo Juyi's poems is a night spent with Wenzhang, the Abbot of a temple near Bo's retreat under Incense Burner Peak. The poem mentioned in the next sentence was addressed by Prince Genji to a Bishop at a mountain temple where the young Murasaki was staying with her grandmother: fukimayou / miyamaoroshi ni / yume samete / namida moyōsu / taki no oto ka na ("My dreams are dispelled by voices borne on the gale gusting from the hills; my eyes overflow with tears at the sound of the cascade"). The author is moved because Genji's words can be given a Buddhist interpretation: "My dreams

emotion, I recalled a poem from *The Tale of Genji*: "My eyes overflow with tears at the sound of the cascade."

sore naranu	There is nothing else
tanomi wa naki o	to which I can turn for solace,
furusato no	yet it bars the way
yumeji yurusanu	to dreams of my old home:
taki no oto ka na	ah, the sound of the cascade!

Toward evening on the day when I went from Yumoto to Kamakura, it began to rain so suddenly that there was not even time to don a hat. I was in too great a hurry to sightsee as I would have liked at Ōiso, Enoshima, Morokoshi Plain, and other famous places.

When I arrived in Kamakura at nightfall, I found lodgings in a commoner's cottage, situated in a locality with "Valley" in its name. People and horses traveled back and forth outside the blinds of the house, which gave immediately onto the road without a gate. The mountains rose just behind, visible from the window, and the incessant cries of deer and insects carried over the fence. It was all so different from the capital that I could not repress a forlorn feeling.

To alleviate the boredom of days spent in such surroundings, I visited Wakae-no-tsukijima, Miura-no-saki, and other coastal areas. The ocean views were quite as moving as the ones at the famous places I had seen on the way.

sabishisa wa	The lonely feeling
sugikoshikata no	of fishing boats at sea:
uraura mo	the scene is the same
hitotsunagame no	as at the many beaches
oki no tsuribune	traversed on my journey here.

tama yosuru	Ah, the clarity
miura ga saki no	of moonlight emerging
namima yori	from between the waves,
idetaru tsuki no	bringers of precious gems,
kage no sayakesa	at Miura-ga-saki!

To speak of the origins of Kamakura: the late Major Captain of the Right Yoritomo, a ninth-generation warrior descendant of Emperor

---

are dispelled" can mean, "I have been awakened from illusion," and "Sound of the Waterfall" was the name of a chant used for the recitation of repentance rites.

Seiwa, raised loyal troops toward the end of the Jishō era [1177–80], subdued the court's enemies, received rewards as ample as Li Guang's, and became shogun.[48] He fixed upon this site for his military headquarters, and the establishment of shrines and temples has ensured its continued prosperity.

At Tsurugaoka Lower Shrine, in particular, the green of the pines and oaks grows ever more luxuriant, and there is never a deficiency in the offerings. Musicians are designated and the seasonal dances are performed punctiliously; officials are charged with the Release of Living Things Service in the Eighth Month. People say that the divine benevolence is the same as at the parent shrine.

Nikaidō is an especially splendid temple. The phoenix tiles gleam in the sun, the bell booms in the frosty air, and everything captures the imagination, from the tall, stately buildings to the groves and ponds.

Zen monks have built rows of cells at Ōmidō, a new Buddhist seat excavated from a sheer rock face. The moon shines on their meditations in front of paper windows; the repetitions of their rituals accumulate; the wind carries constant echoes of their golden chimes.

There are also many more shrines and temples in the various sectors, added by successive shoguns and others.

Someone mentioned that there was a huge image of Amida Buddha at Yui-no-ura. I hastened to pay my respects, accompanied by my informant, and found it a most holy and marvelous sight. Upon inquiry, I learned that a certain saintly Jōkō, a man from Tōtōmi, had been soliciting help from high and low in the Kantō ever since the En'ō era [1239–40], with the design of creating that image and erecting temple buildings. His work is now two-thirds accomplished. The *uṣnīṣa* on the statue's head towers high, penetrating the clouds in midair; the newly polished white curl between the eyebrows glitters in the light of the full moon. The image will be completed in a mere two or three years; the Twelve Towers will soon soar high.[49] Even in India or China, so we are told, there has been nothing to equal the principal image at Tōdaiji

48. Li Guang was a Chinese general who won victories against the Xiongnu barbarians.

49. The *uṣnīṣa* (a protuberance on the skull) and the curl between the eyebrows were two of the distinguishing physical characteristics of a Buddha. "Twelve Towers" is an image derived from a fanciful description by Miyako no Yoshika of the splendors of the palaces on the Isles of the Immortals (WKRES 543).

Temple, the Vairocana Buddha raised by Emperor Shōmu to a height of more than 100 feet, but this 80-foot Amida is more than half as tall. To be sure, the Kamakura Amida is made of wood, not of gilt bronze like the Vairocana, but posterity is certain to consider it remarkable too. Overcome with awe, I wondered whether divine powers in human form might be lending assistance in these days when the dharma is moving eastward.

All such sights and bits of information were fascinating, but I was a person of no significance—unlettered, deficient in the military arts, and lacking the connections that might have allowed me to establish permanent residence in Kamakura. I grew more homesick for the capital every day. The time when I had planned to leave for home slipped by, and autumn gave way to winter. I felt that I could understand the misery of Su Wu, nineteen years absent from Han, and the sorrow of Li Ling, 3,000 leagues distant among the barbarians. The familiar insect sounds faded; the gales from the peaks blew through the pines with ever greater violence. A line of geese, disappearing into the west, evoked deep emotion as I sat with nostalgic eyes fixed on the direction of the capital.

kaerubeki	Geese from the rice fields:
haru o tanomu no	have they too set out weeping
karigane mo	through travel skies,
nakite ya tabi no	hoping that when springtime comes
sora ni idenishi	they may return to their homes?

Shortly after the Twentieth of the Tenth Month, while things were continuing in this manner, a sudden turn of events made it possible for me to go back to the capital. No brush could do justice to my feelings! Of course, I could not hope to wear brocade, but I felt that my joy in returning home was similar to Zhu Maizhen's.

furusato e	Unexpectedly,
kaeru yamaji no	I may don robes of brocade
kogarashi ni	in the autumn wind
omowanu hoka no	on the mountain roads I follow,
nishiki o ya kimu	pursuing my way toward home.

Just before dawn on the Twenty-third of the Tenth Month, when I was on the point of leaving Kamakura for the capital, I wrote this on a sliding door at my lodgings:

narenureba
miyako o isogu
kesa naredo
sasuga nagori no
oshiki yado ka na

This is the morning
when I hasten toward the city,
but despite my joy,
it is sad to bid farewell
to now-familiar lodgings.

A Historian-Biographer of the Fourteenth Century

This selection is excerpted from the last of the six historical tales, *The Clear Mirror* (Masukagami), which was probably written between 1338 and 1376. Like *The Great Mirror*, it purports to be a record of the oral reminiscences of an aged narrator—in this case, a nun more than 100 years old whom the author encounters at a temple near the capital. The nun's tale begins in 1180, with the birth of the future Emperor Go-Toba (1180–1239; r. 1183–97), and ends in 1333, with the return to the capital of Emperor Go-Daigo (1288–1339; r. 1318–39), whom the shogunate had exiled to Oki Island in 1332. In a sense, therefore, it is a chronological history of the period during which the Kamakura government was the seat of political power. But its chief concern is with the court, which it attempts to portray as maintaining its vitality and relevance in an era of political eclipse. Extensive attention is devoted to Go-Toba and Go-Daigo, the two sovereigns who asserted the legitimacy of imperial rule by challenging the shogunate, and to descriptions of official functions, poetic composition, and other symbolic affirmations of the court's role as the center of civilization. The author stresses the continuity of court culture by alluding to *The Tale of Genji* at least twenty times, and by endowing Go-Toba, his most fully realized character, with all the taste, elegance, sensitivity, and accomplishments of the Shining Prince. The selections below, from the first three of the work's seventeen books, trace Go-Toba's life from his birth to his death.

Translation by George Perkins.

PRINCIPAL CHARACTERS

Chūkyō (1218–34; r. 1221). 85th Emperor. Son of Juntoku; grandson of Yoshitsune

Go-Toba (1180–1239; r. 1183–97). 82nd Emperor. Son of Takakura. Controlled court as Retired Emperor, 1198–1221; in exile at Oki, 1221–39

Juntoku (1197–1242; r. 1210–21). 84th Emperor. Son of Go-Toba and Shumeimon'in; exiled to Sado in 1221

Shichijōin (1157–1228). Fujiwara Shokushi; mother of Go-Toba

Shōmeimon'in (1171–1257). Consort of Go-Toba; mother of Tsuchimikado

Shumeimon'in (1182–1264). Consort of Go-Toba; mother of Juntoku

Tsuchimikado (1195–1231; r. 1198–1209). 83rd Emperor. First son of Go-Toba

Yoshitoki, Hōjō (1163–1224). Kamakura Regent

Yoshitsune, Fujiwara (1169–1206). Imperial Regent (1202), Chancellor (1204). Known as a poet

The Clear Mirror

[1]

The eighty-second sovereign after the founding of the imperial line was Emperor Go-Toba, whose personal name was Takahira. He was Retired Emperor Takakura's fourth son. His mother was Shichijōin, a daughter of Master of the Palace Repairs Office Nobutaka. Shichijōin seems to have been something of a secret imperial favorite during Emperor Takakura's reign (a time when she served the Empress as Lady Hyōe-no-kami), for the future Emperor was born to her on the Fifteenth Day of the Seventh Month in the fourth year of Jishō [1180]. Emperor Takakura had abdicated in favor of Empress Kenreimon'in's three-year-old son around the spring of that same year, and the consequent ascendancy of the Heike prevented the younger Prince from receiving any special attention.[1] Retired Emperor Takakura died on the Fourteenth of

---

1. Kenreimon'in was the daughter of the Heike chieftain, Kiyomori.

the First Month of the following year, which made it seem even less likely that the boy might succeed to the throne.

After the Heike carried off the new Emperor Antoku to wander the distant western seas, Priestly Retired Emperor Go-Shirakawa summoned his remaining grandsons. It was in his mind to elevate the oldest, the Third Prince, to the imperial dignity, but the Third Prince took a dislike to him and burst into tears. He dismissed the child in a huff and called for the Fourth Prince, who went straight to his arms and settled happily onto his knee. "This is my true grandson," he said. "He looks just like his father when he was a little boy. He is delightful!" He placed the four-year-old Prince on the throne on the Twentieth of the Eighth Month in the fourth year of Juei {1183}.

The Sacred Mirror, the Necklace, and the Sword are always transmitted to a new Emperor when his predecessor steps down, but now, for the first time, the Three Treasures were missing, carried off to Tsukushi by Emperor Antoku. It was an extraordinary accession. (The Mirror and the Necklace were returned later. Most regrettably, the Sword sank with Emperor Antoku when he entered the sea.)

Emperor Go-Toba's Accession Audience took place on the Twenty-eighth Day of the Seventh Month in the first year of Genryaku {1184}. The ceremonies seem to have been performed in the customary manner. It is awesome to imagine the feelings of his older brother, the former Emperor, and of all the others, high and low, when the news reached the Heike, who were still wandering in Tsukushi.

The Purification ceremony was held on the Twenty-fifth of the Tenth Month in that same year, and the Great Thanksgiving Festival followed on the Eighteenth of the Eleventh Month. This poem by Middle Counselor Kanemitsu was inscribed on a folding screen in the Hall of the West. (I think the subject was a place in Tanba Province called Nagata Village.)

kamiyo yori	Have they been waiting
kyō no tame to ya	since the age of the gods
yatsukaho ni	for today's events—
nagata no ine no	Nagata's long, rich rice heads,
shinai someken	bent low with ripening grain?

The young sovereign was very grown up and bright, and the Retired Emperor was well pleased with him.

The First Reading took place on the First of the Twelfth Month in the second year of Bunji [1187], when His Majesty was seven.[2] A Junior Consort entered the palace in the sixth year of the same era. A daughter of the Tsukinowa Chancellor, she progressed to the status of Empress and later came to be called Gishūmon'in. Her only child was Shunkamon'in.

The Emperor performed the coming-of-age ceremony on the Third of the First Month in the first year of Kenkyū [1190], when he was eleven. He began to rule alone after the death of Priestly Retired Emperor Go-Shirakawa, which occurred on the Thirteenth of the Third Month in the third year of the same era. No billows rose on the seas in the four directions; no winds disturbed the branches. The realm was peaceful; the populace was tranquil. The waves of the sovereign's all-encompassing mercy overflowed the confines of our Isles of Rich Harvests; his benevolence was deeper than the shadows on Mount Tsukuba. Because he was skilled in every pursuit, many men of talent appeared in the provinces, and the age was in no way inferior to earlier times.

His Majesty exhibited particular talent as a poet. People quoted any number of his verses, including this noble composition, which was a clear indication of his concern for proper government:

okuyama no	Through tangled thickets
odoro no shita o	deep, deep in the mountain's heart
fumiwakete	I would push my way,
michi aru yo zo to	that I might show to others,
hito ni shirasen	"Even there lies the right path!"

In the First Month of the ninth year of Kenkyū [1198], the Emperor ceded the throne to his oldest son, who had just turned four. He had reigned for fifteen years. He was barely twenty, not yet of an age to retire, but he may have preferred the freedom of movement and the peace and quiet of a former sovereign's life to the ever-present constraints imposed on a reigning Emperor. Happily, he continued to govern as before.

The newly retired sovereign's customary residences were the Toba

2. The First Reading (*fumihajime*) was performed when the son of a high-ranking family reached the age of seven or eight. Ostensibly designed to show the child how to read, it was a purely symbolic event, during which the elaborately dressed young principal sat in silence while others repeated a few words from the *Classic of Filial Piety* or another suitable text.

and Shirakawa mansions, both of which he had refurbished. He also built an indescribably elegant villa at Minase, where, during his fre-² quent visits, he celebrated the beauties of spring blossoms and autumn leaves with entertainments so elaborate that they became the talk of society.³ The view of the distant Minase River from the villa was especially striking. The Retired Emperor composed these lines for a Chinese-Japanese poetry competition held around the Genkyū era [1204–5]:

miwataseba	The Minase River,
yamamoto kasumu	flowing where haze dims the base
minasegawa	of the distant hills!
yūbe wa aki to	Why did I think of autumn
nani omoikemu	as the time for evening scenes?⁴

There were beautiful long thatched galleries at the villa, designed with the utmost taste. The arrangement of the rocks where the artificial waterfall cascaded from the hill in front, and the small garden pines, intermingled with mossy forest patriarchs, made the dwelling seem a veritable immortal's grotto, its occupant destined to flourish for a thousand years.

The Retired Emperor summoned a large party of gentlemen for a musical entertainment when the garden was first laid out, and Middle Counselor Teika, who was still a minor official at the time, presented two poems after the end of the festivities:

arihekemu	Still young despite
moto no chitose ni	the thousand years they have seen,
furi mo sede	the pines on the peak
wa ga kimi chigiru	pledge to live a thousand more,
chiyo no wakamatsu	together with His Majesty.

kimi ga yo ni	In our sovereign's reign,
sekiiruru niwa o	a thousand years seem presaged
yuku mizu no	by countless droplets
iwa kosu kazu wa	spraying where the garden stream
chiyo mo miekeri	follows its rocky course.

The personal name of the new ruler, Emperor Tsuchimikado, was Tamehito. His mother, the daughter of Dharma Seal Nōen, gave birth to

3. Minase was an area in Settsu Province just south of the Yamashiro border, across the Yodo River from Iwashimizu Hachiman Shrine. The Minase River was a short tributary of the Yodo.

4. The mention of haze identifies the season as spring.

him while she was a court attendant known as Lady Saishō. She was later adopted by Palace Minister Michichika, and in the end came to be called Shōmeimon'in. Michichika was actually her stepfather, but he treated her like his own child after she was blessed with an imperial Prince. He reared the Prince in his Tsuchimikado Mansion.

Emperor Tsuchimikado's Accession Audience took place on the Third of the Third Month in the ninth year of Kenkyū [1198], his Purification on the Twenty-seventh of the Tenth Month, and the customary Great Thanksgiving Festival in the Eleventh Month. His coming-of-age ceremony was celebrated on the Third of the First Month in the second year of Genkyū [1205]. He was a handsome, appealing lad. His character was not quite as firm as his father's, but he was deeply sympathetic to the feelings of others.

The new Regent, Motomichi, had served Emperor Go-Toba in the same capacity. He was succeeded later by the Go-Kyōgoku Lord Yoshitsune, who held the post for a long time. Yoshitsune was a veritable sage of poetry, and Retired Emperor Go-Toba shared his interest in the art and encouraged its practice. An anthology of verse, *Collection for a Thousand Years*, had been compiled during the Bunji era [1185–89], but none of His Majesty's compositions had been included, probably because he was still a child at the time. Now, during this new reign, the Retired Emperor commissioned a new anthology. He instructed Commander of the Gate Guards of the Left Michitomo (Palace Minister Michichika's second son), Ariie of Third Rank, Middle Captain Teika, Ietaka, Masatsune, and others to collect a wide variety of verses, composed from the earliest times to the present, and then he personally joined them in sifting and choosing among their individual preliminary selections, a most unusual and interesting procedure. His Lordship the Regent, whom I have just mentioned, assisted with the project.

Here is a history of the imperial anthologies, beginning with *Collection for a Myriad Ages*, which was commissioned in antiquity from the Tachibana Minister of the Right during a Nara Emperor's reign:

Collection of Early and Modern Poetry was compiled by Tomonori, Tsurayuki, Mitsune, and Tadamine during the reign of the saintly Engi Emperor.

I think I have heard that the Five Pear-Court Poets were instructed to compile *Later Collection* after the Ichijō Regent, Lord Kentoku, was appointed head of the Poetry Office while he was still a Chamberlain–

Lesser Captain during the reign of the wise Tenryaku sovereign. Or am I mistaken about that?

Later, there was *Collection of Gleanings* in ten books, compiled by Priestly Retired Emperor Kazan himself.

Then *Later Collection of Gleanings* was commissioned from Civil Affairs Minister Michitoshi during the reign of Emperor Shirakawa.

The selections for *Collection of Verbal Flowers*, compiled by order of Retired Emperor Sutoku, were made by Akisuke.

After Emperor Shirakawa abdicated, he ordered Toshiyori to compile another anthology, *Collection of Golden Leaves*. He rejected the work when it was first submitted, displeased because Prince Sukehito was identified by his personal name, and he also found something amiss when it was resubmitted. Only on the third trial did it meet with his approval. That was an unusual case, because the judgment of the compilers had usually been accepted without question.

It was splendid indeed that Retired Emperor Go-Toba should have shared personally in the process of selection.

Before the compilation of the new anthology, the Retired Emperor held a poetry contest in 1,500 rounds. The best authors were chosen as participants; the foremost practitioners of the art were named as judges. His Majesty included himself among the judges, but refrained from committing his criticisms to writing, remarking modestly that he could not hope to function at the same high level as the others, and merely indicating which poems he considered superior, and which inferior. It was an impressively elegant way of handling things.

It may be true that when a man of stature masters an accomplishment, his inferiors wish to follow in his footsteps. Perhaps that is why there were so many excellent poets of both sexes in Retired Emperor Go-Toba's day. One of them was a certain Lady Kunaikyō. A descendant of Emperor Murakami through Minister of the Left Toshifusa, she sprang from a house that had once enjoyed great prestige, but her father had died as a mere gentleman of Fourth Rank, after holding a succession of minor offices. Although she was very young, she wrote poetry of almost unfathomable depth—an extraordinary thing. Before the Fifteen-Hundred-Round Poetry Contest, the Retired Emperor said to her, "The other participants in this contest are all famous, experienced poets. You may not quite fit into the same category yet, but I thought it would do no harm to include you. Try your best to compose verses that will be a credit to me." The blush that suffused the lady's face and the tears that filled her eyes were moving evidence of her devotion to the art. Among the 100 poems she submitted, each one of special interest, there was this:

usuku koki	Pale here, deeper there—
nobe no midori no	the green of the young grasses
wakakusa ni	on the wild meadow
ato made miyuru	where can be seen the traces
yuki no muragie	of the snow's uneven melt.

Who would have expected a beginner to think of gauging the rate of last winter's snowmelt by the color of the grasses? She would have "stirred the invisible spirits and gods" deeply if she had lived to a ripe old age![5] We can only regret her premature death.

The anthology of which I have been speaking was called *New Collection of Early and Modern Poetry*. On the Twenty-sixth of the Third Month in the second year of Genkyū [1205], Retired Emperor Go-Toba held a banquet at the Kasuga Hall to mark its completion—an affair that created a great stir. The former sovereign composed this poem in allusion to the collection compiled in the Engi era [901–22]:[6]

isonokami	Again we follow
furuki o ima ni	the old pattern transmitted
narabekoshi	from the ancient age
mukashi no ato o	when songs of the past were placed
mata tazunetsutsu	alongside those of the present.

Regent Yoshitsune:

shikishima ya	Well have they been polished—
yamatokoto no ha	the precious jewels gathered
umi ni shite	from the vast ocean
hiroishi tama wa	of poetry composed
migakarenikeri	in this land of Yamato.

The other guests seem to have presented poems by turns, but it would be too much trouble to include them all.

Uneventful days passed until the second year of Jōgen [1208]. Then,

5. An allusion to the preface to *Collection of Early and Modern Poetry*: "Poetry . . . stirs emotions in the invisible spirits and gods."
6. I.e., *Collection of Early and Modern Poetry*.

on the Twenty-fifth of the Twelfth Month, there was a coming-of-age ceremony for Retired Emperor Go-Toba's second son, a Prince born of Shumeimon'in. The Retired Emperor doted on the boy. He provided him with incomparably beautiful costumes and furniture, paid close attention to his upbringing, and finally put him on the throne in the Eleventh Month of the fourth year of the same era.

Emperor Tsuchimikado, who had just turned sixteen, ought to have been able to look forward to many prosperous years. It was a terrible blow to be deposed. Back in the Eiji era [1141], Emperor Sutoku had not wanted to step down when Priestly Retired Emperor Toba forced him to abdicate in favor of Emperor Konoe. He had sent pleading messages to the Priestly Retired Emperor until the very night of his successor's elevation, and had turned over the imperial regalia with great reluctance, nursing an anger that led ultimately to the Hōgen Disturbance. But Emperor Tsuchimikado was noble and magnanimous by nature. Although he could scarcely have been happy about the state of affairs, he never allowed his feelings to show. People considered him ill treated, and his mother, Shōmeimon'in, was heartbroken.

In the Twelfth Month of that year, the former Emperor Tsuchimikado was given the honorific title of Retired Emperor. He was called the New Retired Emperor. Retired Emperor Go-Toba, now the Senior Retired Emperor, continued to control the government.

The new Emperor Juntoku, whose name, I believe, was Morinari, turned fourteen. His Great Thanksgiving Festival took place on the Thirteenth of the Eleventh Month in the second year of Kenryaku [1212]. Middle Counselor Sukezane, who had performed the same function for Emperor Tsuchimikado, composed poems for a ceremonial screen in the Hall of the East. On Nagarayama:

suga no ne no	Even the pine wind
nagara no yama no	on the peak of Nagara,
mine no matsu	timeless as its name,
fukikuru kaze mo	seems a voice portending
yorozuyo no koe	a reign for endless ages.

But you probably know all this. It seems to be a failing of the aged to retell familiar tales as though they were new.

Emperor Juntoku's reign was pleasant, a period of gaiety and frequent imperial travel. Particularly interesting was the visit to Kasuga

Shrine in the second year of Kenpō [1214], when all the members of the entourage went to remarkable lengths to outdo one another in the splendor of their attire. The Emperor recalled the occasion when he composed a 100-poem sequence in the following year:

kasugayama	Last spring at Kasuga
kozo no yayoi no	the scent of cherry blossoms
hana no ka ni	sank deep in my soul:
someshi kokoro wa	the gods will have understood
kami zo shiruran	the fervor of my prayers.

Somewhat more talented and lively than his predecessor, Emperor Juntoku excelled in both Japanese and Chinese learning. He composed poetry morning and evening, and it was he who wrote *Revered Notes on the Art of the Eightfold Clouds* [Yakumo mishō] in his later years.

Regent Yoshitsune's daughter was installed as an imperial consort, a brilliant and splendid match. She gave birth to Emperor Juntoku's first son on the Tenth of the Tenth Month in the sixth year of Kenpō [1218]. Everyone was happy and excited, satisfied that now, at last, things were as they should be. The child was made an Imperial Prince very soon, on the Twenty-first of the Eleventh Month, and was installed in the Crown Prince's residence on the Twenty-sixth of the same month. It was probably because the Emperor was concerned about his son's future that those steps were taken with such unusual haste, even before the ceremony marking the fiftieth day after the birth. Once the succession was firmly settled, all seemed even more right with the world. Retired Emperor Tsuchimikado appeared to have resigned himself to the situation.

Retired Emperor Go-Toba lived just as he pleased. Almost all his time was spent at the Minase villa, where he filled the hours with agreeable occupations, listening to the strains of zither and flute and enjoying the blossoms in springtime and the colored leaves in autumn. The boundless prosperity of his era seemed destined to endure forever.

While playing a game of *go* one day, the Retired Emperor called in his younger courtiers, told them to engage in competitions of their own choosing, and watched with amusement as they strove vigorously to outdo one another at everything from small-bow archery to backgammon. In the thought of obtaining a variety of interesting prizes to bestow, he dispatched a certain Middle Captain with a message to Shumeimon'in. "Please send me some things I can use as prizes. Anything will do." The Imperial Lady promptly produced a small, metal-fitted Chinese chest that seemed remarkably heavy. When the Middle Captain cracked open one end of the chest, afraid that something was amiss, he was astonished to discover that it contained coins.

The Retired Emperor smiled at the sight of his envoy's flushed, dismayed face. "Poor fellow! Don't you really know a thing like that? Coins have been used as stakes in courtiers' archery contests since ancient times. When you asked the Imperial Lady for some things to be used as prizes, she gave you these because she knows the old customs. It was an admirable response." The Middle Captain must have been embarrassed when he realized his mistake.

Retired Emperor Go-Toba was adept at virtually all pursuits, cheerful in disposition, and thoroughly knowledgeable in customs and practices. One summer day at the Minase lakeside pavilion, he drank iced water and presented the young senior nobles and courtiers with chilled rice and other such dishes. Sipping a bowl of wine, he said, "What a marvelous writer Murasaki Shikibu was! People are especially warm in their praise of the passage in *The Tale of Genji* that runs, 'They dressed trout from the nearby river and bullheads from the western river in his presence.'[7] I wonder if anyone can perform a culinary feat for us now."

An Escort from the Hata clan, in attendance near the balustrade, washed some white rice in cold water and offered it on a few leaves plucked from the bamboo grass at the water's edge.

"He must want us to remember, 'They look as though they would melt if anyone tried to pick them up.'[8] A clever conceit!" His Majesty removed a robe to bestow as a reward.

A master in the art of drinking as in all else, the Retired Emperor used to drain his bowl time after time. Whatever the circumstances, his personal charm made others feel as though they could never weary of his august presence, not if a thousand years were to pass.

I think it was also at the Minase villa that His Majesty held the so-called "Competition Between Selected Poems," a contest for which he chose the entries with scrupulous care. The judging was done on the spot by the participants, which must have caused the authors keen anxiety.

7. From the beginning of the chapter called "Wild Carnations," describing a picnic at which some of Prince Genji's young friends amuse themselves and him by acting as chefs.

8. In *The Tale of Genji*, a young gentleman compares untrustworthy women to hailstones on bamboo grass.

The event took place in the Ninth Month of the second year of Kenpō [1214]. All the compositions were outstanding, especially the poem of the Left in Round Seven, from the Retired Emperor's own brush:

akashigata	In the quiet dawn,
uraji hareyuku	when clearing skies reveal
asanagi ni	Akashi's shoreline,
kiri ni kogiiru	fishing boats row out of sight
ama no tsuribune	into the lingering mist.

One of the Retired Emperor's North Guards, a certain Fujiwara no Hideyoshi, was always commanded to participate in literary events because he was known to be a superior poet. Although some gentlemen of high rank were represented in this "Competition Between Selected Poems" by no more than one or two poems apiece, nine of Hideyoshi's were accepted. Moreover, it was he who became the Retired Emperor's opponent in the seventh round, which matched this poem against the one about the fishing boats:

chigiriokishi	Though we vowed to meet
yama no ko no ha no	when the mountain trees turned gold,
shitamomiji	the wind of autumn,
someshi koromo ni	symbol of satiety,
akikaze zo fuku	blows through my leaf-colored robes.

I have heard that it was considered the honor of a lifetime for a man of his status.

It has always been regarded as most impressive that Emperor Daigo should have given Mitsune an imperial robe when he summoned him to the foot of the Seiryōden stairs to explain in verse why the crescent moon is called a "drawn bow." And a diary pronounces it a signal honor for poetry that the Biwa Minister of State paid a visit to Tsurayuki's house to request a poem of thanks for the loan of a fish box.[9] More recently, the monk Saigyō, another North Guard, has been looked upon as a great poet. But I wonder if Hideyoshi did not surpass them all.

9. Mitsune's poem punned on *ireba*, a form of *iru* ("shoot"; "set"): teru tsuki o / yumihari to shi mo / iu koto wa / yamabe o sashite / ireba narikeri ("That people name the shining moon *yumihari* ['drawn bow'] must be because it shoots toward the rim of the hills when it sets"). It was actually Fujiwara no Morosuke, the nephew of the Biwa Minister Nakahira, who was loaned a prized fish box on an important occasion by his father, Chancellor Tadahira. A fish box (*gyotai*) was a ceremonial belt ornament decorated with gold or silver fish.

For that particular contest, His Majesty mixed the poems together, regardless of authorship, and selected only the best. Thus, different poets had different numbers of poems chosen. Even the Yoshimizu Archbishop Jien, a peerless master, was represented by a mere four compositions. But my tale will grow too long if I run on like this, so I shall say no more about the event. . . .

The New Retired Emperor Tsuchimikado spent his ample free time in the composition of poetry, but he was withdrawn by nature and disliked assembling people for literary gatherings. Sometime around the Kenpō era [1213–18], he secretly composed a 100-poem sequence, which he sent to Ietaka and Teika as "the work of an insignificant youth." The verses, all of them outstanding, touched on many themes. There was this one recalling the past:

aki no iro o	O familiar moon
okurimukaete	I came to know so well
kumo no ue ni	through all those autumns
narekoshi tsuki mo	in the realm above the clouds:
mono wasure su na	you, like me, must not forget!

Realizing with awe that the Retired Emperor must have written it himself, Teika jotted down a note on the back. "I was completely deceived by Your Majesty's ruse." This was his poem:

akazarishi	Loath to part with you,
tsuki mo sa koso wa	the moon too must surely feel
omourame	just as you do:
furuki namida mo	unforgettable the tears
wasurarenu yo o	shed on that melancholy day!

Retired Emperor Go-Toba probably had occasion to see the former sovereign's poem too. How could he have remained unmoved? The abdication must have been a bitter experience. Most unfortunately for the New Retired Emperor, relations between him and his father were still strained. . . .

[2]

[This section is preceded by a brief history of the Kamakura shogunate, ending with Hōjō Yoshitoki's assumption of power after the assassination of Yoritomo's son Sanetomo, the third shogun.]

The whole realm had fallen under the sway of Yoshitoki, a man whose power all but surpassed that of Yoritomo in the old days. Naturally enough, Yoshitoki's shocking excesses inspired secret thoughts of opposition in Retired Emperor Go-Toba's mind. The senior nobles and courtiers close to the Retired Emperor, the junior North Guards, the West Guards, and all the other private sympathizers with the imperial plans engaged in military pursuits day and night. I do not know how he might have learned, but the Retired Emperor excelled even the experts in the art of appraising swords, and he passed personal judgment on the quality of his men's blades.

The third year of Jōkyū [1221] began in the midst of this activity. On the Twentieth Day of the Fourth Month, Emperor Juntoku abdicated in favor of the Crown Prince, who had turned four. All recent sovereigns had ascended the throne at that age, so the new Emperor Chūkyō could be expected to have a bright future. On the Twenty-third of the same month, there was an imperial proclamation regarding titles. Emperor Juntoku, who had just abdicated, was given the title New Retired Emperor, and his older brother, Tsuchimikado, was to be called Middle Retired Emperor. Their father, Go-Toba, retained the title of Senior Retired Emperor. Minister of State Iezane, who had been Regent, was replaced after the abdication by Minister of the Left Michiie, the father of the young shogun in Kamakura.

Meanwhile, news of Retired Emperor Go-Toba's plans leaked out in spite of every effort at secrecy, and the authorities at Kamakura probably adopted countermeasures.

As an initial step, the Retired Emperor ordered an attack on the shogunal deputy in the capital, Iga no Hangan Mitsusue. The imperial adherents bore down on the deputy's residence, and Mitsusue disemboweled himself when he saw that he could not escape. His Majesty considered it a good beginning.

There was great agitation in Kamakura. At first, Yoshitoki thought, "Karma has ordained my death," but then he reconsidered. "If a punitive force attacks, I don't intend to die like a coward and have my remains shamefully displayed. The army may be labeled imperial, but it isn't as though the Retired Emperor will be leading it in person. Besides, I'll simply be testing my own fate by resisting." He ordered a mighty host, a veritable cloud of warriors, to march against the capital under the command of his younger brother, Tokifusa, and his oldest son, Yasutoki.

When the army was ready to leave, Yoshitoki seated Yasutoki in front of him. "I have a number of reasons for sending you on this campaign. If you die, let it be like a true warrior. If you show your back to anyone, don't look on my face again. Think of this parting as our last. I may not be worth much, but I am a loyal subject. I have done nothing to deserve a miserable end. Take heart! You will recross the Ashigara and Hakone mountains if you win the battle." He wept as he spoke.

"He's right. I may never see my father's face again." The thought made Yasutoki weep into his shoulder-guard. It was heart-rending for both of them to feel that this might be their final farewell.

On the day after the army's departure, Yasutoki suddenly came galloping back alone, whipping his horse. "What's the meaning of this?" Yoshitoki asked, his heart beating faster.

"I am quite clear about the battle tactics and the general strategy you told us to use," Yasutoki said. "But what shall we do if we meet a solemn imperial expedition on the way, a force flying battle banners and led augustly by His Majesty's own palanquin? I galloped back to ask about this."

Yoshitoki considered briefly. "Well put, son. A good point! It would never do to draw your bow against the imperial palanquin. If you meet such an expedition, you must remove your helmet, sever your bowstring, and place yourself respectfully in His Majesty's hands. But if His Majesty stays in the capital while deploying troops against you, fight at the risk of your life until only one man in a thousand remains." Yasutoki dashed off before his father had finished speaking.

In the capital, the shogunate's actions had been anticipated. Retired Emperor Go-Toba had mobilized warriors, destroyed the bridges at Uji and Seta, and taken other exceptional precautions against the approach of enemy forces. The only captain who failed to answer his call was Kintsune, a man who held the shogunate in high esteem because his grandson was the shogun, and also because his wife was a daughter of the Ichijō Middle Counselor Yoshiyasu and because his wife's mother, Yoshiyasu's wife, was Yoritomo's sister. Kintsune considered the imperial plans ill-advised and dangerous.

Among those who were said to have joined His Majesty's forces were Shichijōin's kinsmen (the Bōmon Major Counselor Tadanobu, the Owari Middle Captain Kiyotsune, and the Nakamikado Major Counselor

Muneie), Shumeimon'in's brother (the Kai Consultant–Middle Captain Norishige), and others too numerous to mention. The army also included many senior nobles and courtiers less closely connected to the Retired Emperor.

Countless esoteric rituals were performed. The support of holy prelates from the exoteric and esoteric sects is a great comfort at such critical junctures. All the officiants prayed fervently, and the Retired Emperor himself offered heartfelt petitions.

His Majesty made a secret pilgrimage to Hiyoshi to offer nightlong prayers and solemn private vows before the Ōmiya god. As the night began to deepen, an eerie hush pervaded the dimly lit shrine precincts. A young page rose trembling from his resting place, ran straight to the Retired Emperor, and delivered a divine message in a ringing voice:

> It is difficult to ignore your pleas when you pay a gracious visit to my shrine. But you showed no mercy when my sacred palanquin was brought to you a few years ago. Because of your men's resistance, the soldier-monks lost faith in me and abandoned the palanquin beside the guard headquarters, where it was exposed to the hoofs of horses and oxen. I can hardly take your part while I harbor a grievance against you. I would not accept your petitions even if you promised to rebuild the halls of the seven shrines in gold and silver!

The boy lapsed into silence and lay scarcely breathing.

The dismayed Retired Emperor shed floods of tears. If only he might have relived the past! He begged forgiveness over and over. The decision to repel the sacred palanquin was not necessarily his, but no such consideration could alleviate his wretchedness. As the saying goes, "All blame resides with the sovereign."

Although he had never spoken of it, Retired Emperor Tsuchimikado had continued to resent the way in which he had been forced off the throne. He does not appear to have become particularly involved in the Senior Retired Emperor's activities. Retired Emperor Juntoku, who shared his father's views, directed military and other operations.

Unusually persistent summer rains had caused extreme flooding and turbulence in the Fuji and Tenryū rivers, and the advancing eastern army was greatly hampered by the waters, which were all but impassable for even the best horses. But news came at last that the shogunal forces were approaching the capital, and the imperial warriors rode out to meet them. I believe I have heard that His Majesty's army numbered over

60,000 horsemen. They were divided into two groups, the one sent to Uji and the other to Seta.[10]

Words cannot describe the turmoil in the city. Some people fled deep into the mountains, others traveled far into outlying areas, and all were anxious and distraught. Retired Emperor Go-Toba himself felt apprehensive and ill at ease.

When a crucial moment arrives, even men who have previously seemed strong and brave may lose their composure, turn pale, and show themselves to be unreliable. I believe it was just past the Twentieth of the Sixth Month when the imperial army went down to defeat after a poor show of resistance. Yasutoki and Tokifusa burst into the capital like a huge tidal wave on a rocky shore, creating indescribable dismay and confusion among people of all ranks.

As one of the measures adopted on orders from the east, the two commanders announced their intention of sending Retired Emperor Go-Toba away from the capital—a decision that may have been influenced by the precedent set in the Hōgen era.[11] Needless to say, the Imperial Ladies, the Princes, and the Princesses were frantic with grief.

It was decided that His Majesty would live in Oki Province. On the Sixth of the Seventh Month, as a preliminary step, he traveled to the Toba Mansion in a crude wickerwork carriage, a sad final outing from the city. Much as he would have liked to return things to their former state, it was not to be: he cut off his hair and pronounced religious vows on that very day. He must have been only a year or two past forty, pitifully young for such a step. He summoned Nobuzane to paint his portrait as a gift for his mother, Shichijōin.[12]

The Retired Emperor embarked on the Thirteenth. Journeying over the interminable waves, he found it hard to believe that he was still the same person. He speculated bitterly about the misdeeds in a previous existence for which he was suffering retribution now.

Retired Emperor Juntoku was banished to Sado Province. Furthermore, Emperor Chūkyō himself was deposed on the Ninth of the Sev-

10. The two main approaches to the capital from the east.
11. In the first year of Hōgen (1156), Retired Emperor Sutoku (1119–64, r. 1123–41) was exiled to Sanuki Province after his unsuccessful attempt to regain the throne by force of arms.
12. Fujiwara no Nobuzane (1176–1265?) was the leading portrait painter of the day.

enth Month. His splendid succession in the Fourth Month seemed a dream. He must have been the first Emperor to step down after a mere seventy days in office. But I think I recall having been told by a scholar about a Chinese monarch who held the throne for only forty-nine days. Might there have been a similar disturbance then?

Retired Emperor Tsuchimikado escaped the shogunate's censure because he had never had anything to do with the affair, but he departed voluntarily for Hata in Tosa Province on the Tenth Day of the intercalary Tenth Month, holding that it would be very wrong to lead a peaceful life in the capital while his father languished in distant exile. I think it was around the Second Month of the previous year that he had become the father of a young Prince, the offspring of a daughter of Shōmei-non'in's prematurely deceased elder brother, Consultant–Middle Captain Michimune. He left the child at the house of Michimune's younger brother, Michikata, and set out, all alone except for some servants and a junior North Guard who was a close attendant. His conveyance was a crude hand-held palanquin. A fierce snowstorm blew up on the way, darkening the sky and obscuring the road in both directions. He expressed his despair in verse, his sleeves icy with frozen tears:

ukiyo ni wa	I was doubtless born
kakare tote koso	fated to suffer like this
mumarekeme	in the fleeting world.
kotowari shiranu	Can it be that my tears
wa ga namida ka na	have failed to grasp the truth?

He moved to Awa Province later, after a suggestion from Kamakura that he at least live nearer the capital.

The country was in a lamentable state. We are told that the Buddha spoke of 18,000 sovereigns who actually killed their own fathers for the throne. Furthermore, there have been countless struggles for hegemony in Japan and China ever since the world entered the age of degeneracy. No doubt there has been a cause for every one: sometimes ministers of a different lineage or even persons of royal blood have been denied influence by some small unexpected development, and the consequent resentment has led to strife. But very, very seldom in our country have subjects of no status crushed an Emperor, as happened in this case. Masakado in Shōhei [931–38], Sumitomo in Tengyō [938–46], and Yoshichika in Kōwa [1099–1103] were all courageous men, but not one of them was able to prevail against an imperial edict. Furthermore, when Retired Emperor Sutoku attempted a coup in the Hōgen era, the reigning Emperor Go-Shirakawa brought him down to defeat, for which reason the men of old said that even though a rebel might belong to the imperial family, the Sun Goddess would apparently protect the occupant of the throne. Although Commander of the Gate Guards Nobuyori presumed to threaten Emperor Nijō, his lifeless corpse lay abandoned by the roadside in the end. With those incidents in mind, people considered it out of the question that anyone might destroy a court consisting of three Retired Emperors and a reigning sovereign. We must look beyond this world for an explanation of what happened—a truth incomprehensible to those too benighted to understand karmic law.

Retired Emperor Go-Toba ascended the throne at the age of four and reigned for fifteen years. Even after his abdication, he continued to rule during the twelve-year reign of Emperor Tsuchimikado and the eleven-year reign of Emperor Juntoku. As master of the realm for thirty-eight years, he governed just as he pleased, controlling all officialdom and exercising a dominion more absolute than that of the wind that bows trees and grasses to its will. With compassion more abundant than showering raindrops, he pitied the distant folk and cherished those near at hand; though affairs of state permitted him spare moments no more frequent than gaps in the well-thatched roof of a Settsu cottage, he remained ever alert to prevent the nation from becoming as disordered as tangled reeds at Naniwa. The pines on the peak at his lofty dwelling ought to have added branch to branch and flourished through 1,000 and 8,000 years; he ought to have resided in his immortal's grotto through countless springs, enjoying peace and tranquility as endless as the rising and setting of the sun and moon. But now, because of a single trifling incident, he and his kin were forced to leave the brilliant capital and scatter, each to his own place of exile, condemned to dwell under eaves jostled by the crude thatches of fishing shacks on rocky shores. Visited only by small boats coming to fish in the waters of the bays, they spent their time gazing at smoke plumes from salt-refiners' fires, wondering if the drifting columns pointed the way toward home. Even if there had been fixed terms to their sentences, they would still have suffered from the uncertainty of life in this world. But what words can describe the wretchedness of men doomed to spend their lives on distant isles, separated from home by misty leagues of waves, with no inkling of when they might meet again in the capital, their lonely exile finally at an end?

Retired Emperor Go-Toba settled into an isolated island dwelling far from human habitations. The house stood against a towering rock in the shade of the mountains, somewhat inland from the shore. It was of very simple construction, with pine pillars and thatched galleries—a residence in form only, although possessed of a certain elegance and taste, despite its resemblance to Saigyō's "temporary brushwood hut." [13] The memory of the Minase villa was like a dream. The vast sea view, which seemed to stretch into infinity, brought home anew the meaning of Bo Juyi's line, "two thousand leagues away." The former sovereign composed these lines with the blast of the violent sea wind loud in his ears:

ware koso wa	The new island guard
niishimamori yo	is none other than myself.
oki no umi no	Ye wild winds raising waves
araki namikaze	on the seas around Oki:
kokoro shite fuke	be forewarned and blow with care!

onaji yo ni	Will I return
mata suminoe no	to view again in this world
tsuki ya min	Suminoe's moon?
kyō koso yoso ni	Today I am cast aside,
oki no shimamori	the keeper of Oki Island.

The new year [1222] began. The imperial exiles lived in the depths of despair on their separate islands. At Sado, Retired Emperor Juntoku devoted himself to Buddhist discipline day and night, hoping against hope for a change in his fortunes. At Oki, Retired Emperor Go-Toba fixed his gaze on the misty skies stretching far into the distance across the bay, shedding irrepressible tears as he recalled the happenings of the past.

urayamashi	How I envy them!
nagaki hikage no	The fisherfolk who scoop
haru ni aite	the briny waters
shio kumu ama mo	can doubtless dry their sleeves
sode ya hosuran	in the sunshine of long spring days.

13. Saigyō (SKKS 1778): izuku ni mo / sumarezuba tada / sumade aran / shiba no iori no / shibashi aru yo ni ("If there be no place where I can live, I'll not stay long in a single spot. This world is brief and fleeting—a temporary brushwood hut"). "Two thousand leagues away," below, is a reference to a poem by Bo Juyi, composed on seeing the harvest moon from

Summer came, and with it the incessant downpours of the rainy season onto the thatched eaves. Unaccustomed to such sights, the Retired Emperor found them novel and intriguing.

ayame fuku	A rushing wind blows
kaya ga nokiba ni	across miscanthus-thatched eaves
kaze sugite	adorned with sweet flag,
shidoro ni otsuru	and the torrential rain
murasame no tsuyu	veers and swirls as it descends. [14]

Life seemed sadder than ever when the winds of early autumn began to blow. His Majesty's tears increased with the increasing dew, and his misery was beyond words.

furusato o	No return for me—
wakareji ni ouru	not though autumn has arrived,
kuzu no ha no	the season when leaves
aki wa kuredomo	turn back on the kudzu vines
kaeru yo mo nashi	along the road that led from home. [15]

In a particularly despondent mood one evening, he saw what seemed a distant fishing boat, drifting shoreward like a tiny leaf. It proved to be a vessel carrying a message from the city. In the cold of the nights there, Shichijōin had thought of him far away, and had dispatched black clerical robes and bedding. A lump rose in his throat as he opened her letter, and he was forced to calm himself before reading it.

"These have been miserable months and days for me. If only I might see you just once more before this uncertain old life of mine draws to its close! I don't see how I can even get across the Shide Mountains with things as they are." So she rambled on. He pressed the paper to his face.

tarachine no	Mother clings to life,
kieyarade matsu	her body fragile as dew,
tsuyu no mi o	awaiting my return.
kaze yori saki ni	If only I might visit her
ika de towamashi	before the death wind blows!

---

the imperial palace: "The Fifteenth-night moon, new risen in beauty: / What is in the heart of my old friend, two thousand leagues away?"

14. In the Fifth Month, the aromatic leaves of the sweet flag, or calamus, a plant regarded as healthful, were stuffed under eaves as a precaution against hot-weather diseases.

15. Kudzu leaves, which are white underneath, are associated in classical poetry with wordplays suggested by *ura* ("reverse side") and *hirugaeru* ("turn over"). The play here is on *kaeru* ("return").

yaoyorozu	O great host of gods,
kami mo awareme	take pity on my mother
tarachine no	and let me return:
ware machimin to	she merely clings to life
taenu tama no o	that she may see me again.

A succession of melancholy letters from various quarters arrived on the wings of autumn's first wild geese.[16] The Retired Emperor wept without restraint as he read them. One message, so voluminous that it must have resembled the epistle sent from Ise to Suma, came from Lord Ietaka of Second Rank. Ietaka, a compiler of the *New Collection* and an imperial intimate in matters having to do with poetry, had continued to mourn the absence of his master night and day. "I shall never forget the old times in the Poetry Office," he wrote. He went on to speak of his regret that his unhappy life still dragged on, and added many other inexpressibly sad remarks. At the end, there was this poem:

nezame shite	Awakening by chance,
kikanu o kikite	I seem to hear a sound
wabishiki wa	I do not hear—
araisonami no	the voice of the waves at daybreak
akatsuki no koe	crashing on a rocky shore.

Deeply moved, the Retired Emperor wept until his sleeves were drenched. His poems:

namima naki	Long have I remained
oki no kojima no	distant from the capital,
hamabisashi	my home a seaside hut
hisashiku narinu	on tiny Oki Island,
miyako hedatete	where the waves beat endlessly.

kogarashi no	As cold autumn blasts
oki no somayama	bend trees in the forests
fukishiori	on the hills of Oki,
araku shiorete	I too bow down, overcome
mono omou koro	by the burden of my thoughts.

The Retired Emperor assembled the poems he had written on various occasions and sent them to Shumeimon'in. Among them, there were these:

16. It was a literary convention, based on a Chinese legend, to treat migrating wild geese as couriers. The author compares Ietaka's message, described below, to a long letter in *The Tale of Genji* sent from Lady Rokujō at Ise to Prince Genji at Suma.

minaseyama	My Minase home
wa ga furusato wa	must be in ruins by now,
arenuramu	its rustic fence destroyed,
magaki wa nora to	leaving only a wild plain
hito mo kayowade	where no one comes to visit.

kagiri areba	Unable to change
sate mo taekeru	the destined span of my days,
mi no usa yo	I live in misery,
tami no waraya ni	eaves aligned side by side
noki o narabete	with the thatched roofs of common folk.

kazashi oru	Would that in this place
hito mo arabaya	there were those who might pluck
koto towan	cedar sprigs to deck caps—
oki no miyama ni	people with whom to converse.
sugi wa miyuredo	The Oki hills bear cedars, but . . .

Although there were many more such compositions, my aging memory has failed me for the moment. I will try to insert others in appropriate places if I recall them.

[3]

The Retired Emperor on Oki heard vague rumors of happy and sad events in the capital. His own island existence seemed to him a mere accumulation of wretched years. Sources of inexhaustible grief multiplied as he aged, and he found relief only in the poetry he had loved so long. When an opportunity presented itself, he called for poems on topics he sent to the capital. His devoted former associates responded with eagerness, unable to forget the past, and he filled his lonely leisure hours by judging their compositions in the manner of a contest. (Moved by the imperial request, Lord Ietaka assembled and sent off poems composed by himself and others, a small remembrance from someone now far advanced in years. Hideyoshi, another former attendant whom I have had occasion to mention, had taken Buddhist vows after the Jōkyū disorders and become a recluse with the religious name Nyogan. The invitation to participate in this competition must have evoked poignant memories of an earlier event.)

As before, I could not possibly include all the poems that were submitted, but I shall recite at least a few of them.

Retired Emperor Go-Toba (Left):

hitogokoro	Now that men's hearts have changed
utsurihatenuru	like fading cherry blossoms,
hana no iro ni	it is distressing
mukashi nagara no	even to hear the name
yama no na mo ushi	of Nagara, Changeless Mountain.

Ietaka (Right):

nazo mo kaku	How did it happen
omoisomeken	that I began to utter sighs
sakurabana	over cherry blossoms—
yama to shi takaku	sighs that have accumulated
narihatsuru made	to the height of a mountain?

Hideyoshi:

wata no hara	O companion ship
yasoshima kakete	bound for the land of Oki
shirube se yo	far in the distance,
haruka ni kayou	guide me past the myriad isles
oki no tomobune	on the vast expanse of the sea.

On the topic "Mountain Home," Retired Emperor Go-Toba (Left):

nokiba arete	Who beholds the moon
tare ka minase no	on Minase's ruined eaves?
yado no tsuki	It shines as clear
sumikoshi mama no	as in the days when I dwelt there,
iro ya sabishiki	but how lonely its color now!

Ietaka (Right):

sabishisa wa	Here is loneliness:
mada minu shima no	merely through imagination,
yamazato o	to know the feel of life
omoiyaru ni mo	in a mountain dwelling
sumu kokochi shite	on an island yet unseen.

In judging the last two poems, His Majesty assigned the victory to his own composition, with the touchingly gentle remark, "Perhaps there is slightly more depth of emotion in remembering a place where one lived for many years than in imagining an island one has never seen."

It was with such trifling pursuits, as well as with prayers to Amida

Buddha, that His Majesty whiled away the time. Two practice compositions:

ware nagara	I have come to feel
u to mihatenuru	quite out of patience
mi no ue ni	with my misery—
namida bakari zo	it is only that these tears
omogawari senu	refuse to cease their falling.

furusato wa	Little more hope have I
irinuru iso no	of seeing my old home
kusa yo tada	than if the city
yūshio michite	were grasses on a rock
miraku sukunaki	submerged by the evening tide.

Retired Emperor Go-Toba died at the age of sixty on the Twenty-second Day of the Second Month in the first year of En'ō [1239]—the seventeenth year, I believe, of his life on the island. Most awesomely, he breathed his last without realizing his cherished ambition to return to the capital. We can but deplore the heartlessness of the world.

The usual cremation ceremonies took place on a mountain near the former sovereign's abode at Oki, the scant attendance heightening the pathos and melancholy of the occasion. The North Guard Yoshimochi, who had accompanied his master to Oki as a monk, took the ashes to the capital in a box suspended from a cord around his neck. The remains were deposited in the Hokkedō Hall at Ōhara, and revenues from several of the Retired Emperor's old estates were set aside to cover the cost of meditations on the *Lotus Sutra*, which continue there to this day. The Retired Emperor's beloved buildings at Minase were removed to Hokkedō at Shumeimon'in's behest. Even the paulownia prayer beads His Majesty held at the last still remain in the temple, a most awesome and moving circumstance. I myself have had occasion to pay my respects to them.

A Military Tale

The selections below are drawn from *The Great Peace* (Taiheiki, 40 books). The longest of the military tales, except for a forty-eight-book variant text of *The Tale of the Heike*, this work has traditionally been ranked with *The Tale of the Heike* as one of the two best examples of the genre. According to a contemporary source, its author was the otherwise unidentified "Kojima Monk Enjaku," who died in 1374, but a number of people seem to have had a hand in its composition, which probably extended over two or more decades, from around 1340 to the 1360's or 1370's. In spite of its name, its general topic is the political and military strife of the fourteenth century. The first twelve books deal with Emperor Go-Daigo's struggle against the Kamakura shogunate, one of the main concerns of *The Clear Mirror* as well. Books 13–21 cover the years between the restoration of imperial power in 1333 and Go-Daigo's death in 1339, a period in which the Emperor tried without success to control the military, quarreled with the powerful warrior Ashikaga Takauji, and presided over a Southern Court in the Yoshino Mountains while a rival sovereign reigned in Kyōto with Takauji's backing. Books 22–40 describe in minute detail the endless fighting that plagued the land after Go-Daigo's death. The narrative breaks off inconclusively around 1368, with the two courts still in competition and no resolution in sight.

Despite internal evidence pointing to multiple authorship, the work as a whole emphasizes a single theme, the inevitability of civil turmoil when virtue is absent in high places. Hōjō Takatoki's unseemly conduct, symbolized by the two anecdotes in the fourth selection below, is seen as responsible for the downfall of the Kamakura shogunate, Ashikaga Takauji's greed and disrespect for the throne as responsible for the refusal of other warriors to accept his hegemony, and government based on Confucian principles as the only avenue to the peace of the title.

The reader confronted with the insistent moralizing of *The Great Peace*, its lengthy retelling of edifying stories from Chinese history, its attention to military tactics, and the formlessness of its last books may feel inclined to say of it what F. R. Leavis remarked of George Eliot's *Romola*: "Few will want to read [it] a second time, and few can ever have got through it once without some groans."[1] Nevertheless, it has enjoyed centuries of respect and popularity in Japan. Quite aside from the practical considerations that have recommended it to historians, politicians, and military students, it contains substantial attractions for the general reader—notably, a wealth of interesting, skillfully narrated anecdotes on a wide variety of subjects, some of particular interest to fanciers of heroic literature, others romantic in the old courtly fashion, and still others possessing the universal appeal of the odd and humorous. Its style, which is frequently ornate, imposing, and majestic, has also been widely admired.

The selections below have been chosen to illustrate some of the work's main characteristics and, in the case of the first three, to permit comparison with the treatment of a similar subject in *The Clear Mirror*. The first, "The Empress's Grief," relies for its effectiveness on the evocation of *mono no aware* (the "sadness of things") and the use of poetry. The next three, "The Exile of the Former Sovereign," "Bingo no Saburō Takanori," and "The Sagami Novice's Enjoyment of Field Music; Also, the Dogfights," leaven Confucian elements with *mono no aware* or, in the third, with lively, fantastic tales in the setsuwa vein. The last three, "The Attack on Rokuhara," "Nagasaki Takashige's Last Battle," and "Takatoki, His Kinsmen, and the Others Kill Themselves at Tōshōji," center on the warrior class and its ethos.

PRINCIPAL CHARACTERS

Akamatsu Enshin (1277–1350). An imperialist captain from western Japan

1. *The Great Tradition* (New York, 1973), p. 50.

Ashikaga Takauji (1304–58). A powerful eastern Genji who joined the anti-Hōjō movement, made a major contribution to its success, and eventually established the Muromachi shogunate

Chigusa Tadaaki (d. 1336). An imperialist captain

Genji. Warriors under the command of Ashikaga or Nitta; also called imperial forces

Go-Daigo, Emperor (1288–1339; r. 1318–39). Deposed by the Kamakura shogunate in 1331 and exiled to Oki in 1332 for attempting to restore power to the throne; escaped from Oki early in 1333

Heike. Shogunal warriors, so called because the Hōjō Regents belonged to the Taira clan; also called Rokuhara forces

Hōjō Takatoki, see Sagami Novice

Kōno Michiharu. A shogunate captain

Kusunoki Masashige (1294–1336). An imperialist captain from western Japan

Nagasaki Novice Enki (d. 1333). See under Sagami Novice

Nagasaki Takashige (d. 1333). A shogunate captain

Nitta Yoshisada (1301–38). An eastern Genji, leader of the imperialist force that captured Kamakura in 1333

Sagami Novice. Hōjō Takatoki (1303–33). The head of the Kamakura shogunate until 1326, when he resigned and took Buddhist vows. He continued to exercise authority in conjunction with three vassals who were the real powers behind the shogunate: Adachi Tokiaki, his maternal grandfather; Nagasaki Enki, the Hōjō family steward; and Nagasaki Takasuke, Enki's son

Stronghold Novice. Adachi Tokiaki (d. 1333). See under Sagami Novice

Suyama. A shogunate captain

The Great Peace

The Empress's Grief (4.5)

[*This and the following two episodes describe events associated with the exile of Emperor Go-Daigo in 1332.*]

It became known that the Seventh of the Third Month had been chosen as the date of the former sovereign's departure for Oki, his place of exile. On the night before, the Empress went to visit him at Rokuhara under cover of darkness. Her attendants brought the carriage to the middle gate, and she raised the blinds when he came out.

The Emperor could think of nothing but the future, of the time when he must leave his consort in the capital and wander where waves would disturb his travel sleep and the moon would shine on interminable stretches of beach. The Empress, for her part, imagined him far away and felt that life held no more hope for her—that she must remain lost in the darkness of eternal night, never to know happiness again. Dawn would have overtaken them too soon if they had tried to express everything that was in their hearts, even if the night had been as long as 1,000 autumn nights rolled into one. But their sorrow was beyond the power of words to convey, and they sat together in silence, blinded by tears, until the cold, pale moon sank toward the horizon.

At daybreak, the carriage was faced around for the journey home. The weeping Empress said only this:

kono ue no	Never shall I feel
omoi wa araji	sharper anguish than this.
tsurenasa no	Life is too cruel:
inochi yo sareba	how much time must elapse
itsu o kagiri zo	before the end arrives?

As the carriage bore her away, prostrate with grief, she was pitifully certain that they would never meet again.

The Exile of the Former Sovereign (4.6)

On the morning of the Seventh of the Third Month, Chiba no Suke Sadatane, Oyama no Gorō Saemon, and the Buddhist Novice Sasaki Dōyo secured the streets with 500 horsemen and started off with the former Emperor toward Oki Province. His Majesty's only attendants were the Ichijō Head Chamberlain Yukifusa, the Rokujō Lesser Captain Tadaaki, and Lady Sanmi to see to his personal needs. All the other members of the party were helmeted and armored warriors, equipped with bows and arrows, who kept the carriage surrounded as it creaked westward along Shichijō Avenue, then south along Higashi-no-tōin. Men and women of all classes lined the city streets, their fearless voices audible everywhere. "Imagine a lawful Emperor's subjects sending him into exile! This means the end for the military!" they said. People sobbed like motherless children, and even the warriors in the escort pressed their shoulder-guards to their eyes and wept, moved by the spectators' grief.

When the Emperor passed Sakura Post Station, he commanded the bearers to set down his palanquin while he prayed to Hachiman for a safe return. "The Great Bodhisattva Hachiman, a manifestation of Emperor Ōjin, has sworn to protect all Emperors. He is certain to keep a watchful eye on any sovereign, even one in the most remote of temporary abodes," he thought with deep faith. Again, when he saw the Fukuhara capital after passing the Minato River, he comforted himself with the memory of how Taira no Kiyomori had seized control of the state and moved the imperial seat to that damp, low site, and of how the Taira had suffered swift destruction as a consequence. "That was what happened when arrogant men tried to overthrow their superiors. It was a punishment from Heaven."

As he passed the beach at Suma, with Inano Plain visible far in the distance, he thought, "Long ago, Prince Genji spent three years in exile on this shore after people learned about his affair with Lady Oborozukiyo. No wonder he lamented those autumns away from home, 'feeling as though the waves were breaking at his very ear, and almost setting his pillow afloat with tears that he scarcely knew he shed.'"

At Akashi-no-ura, Awaji Island was dimly visible through the morning mist; at Takasago, high waves rolled shoreward, and the wind swept through the summit pines.

With many mountains and rivers behind them, the party traversed Sugisaka Slope into Mimasaka Province. It was not the season for snow, but at Sarayama in Kume they saw a white peak towering through distant clouds. The Emperor summoned a warrior guard to ask its name. "That is the Grand Mountain of Hōki Province," came the reply. He halted the palanquin briefly and intoned a reverent prayer.

Day after day, they hastened onward, now rising at cockcrow and passing through the moonlight in front of thatched tea-houses, now grinding the frost of wooden bridges under their horses' feet. It was on the thirteenth day after the departure from the capital that His Majesty reached Mio Harbor in Izumo Province. A boat was made ready, and they awaited a favorable wind for the crossing.

Bingo no Saburō Takanori (4.7)

In those days, there was a man in Bizen Province called Kojima Bingo no Saburō Takanori. This Takanori joined the imperial cause and mustered followers while the Emperor was still at Kasagi Stronghold.

News of the premature fall of Kasagi and rumors of Kusunoki's suicide forced him to bide his time in silence, but he reassembled his trustworthy kinsmen in council when he heard of the sovereign's exile to Oki Province.

"It is written, 'The man who seeks righteousness and the man of virtue do not sacrifice virtue to save their lives. There are some, indeed, who sacrifice their lives in the cause of virtue,'"[2] he said. "When the northern barbarians killed Duke Yi of Wei in olden times, the Duke's minister Hong Yan was unable to bear the sight. Yan cut open his own belly, put Duke Yi's liver inside, and died to repay his master's favors. 'To see what ought to be done and not to do it is unmanly.' Let's intercept the imperial party, take away His Majesty, raise an army, and win fame for the sake of our descendants, even if it means leaving our corpses on the battlefield!" All his right-minded kinsmen agreed. "We'll lie in wait at a steep place on the road and strike when the time is ripe," they decided.

Poised for action, Takanori and the others waited in hiding at the summit of Mount Funasaka, on the border between Bizen and Harima provinces. But the imperial party was very slow to appear, and a scout brought word that the escort had not followed the Mountain Sun Road, but instead had taken the Mountain Shade Road at Imajuku in Harima. So Takanori's plan failed.

"All right, we'll wait at Sugisaka in Mimasaka Province. The mountains are wild enough there," Takanori said. But when they reached Sugisaka, after making a shortcut from Mitsuishi-no-yama through the clouds of trackless mountains, it was only to discover that the Emperor had already entered Innoshō. There was nothing for them to do but disband.

"I wish I could let His Majesty know what's in my mind, at least," Takanori said to himself. He stole in disguise to the Emperor's lodgings, hoping to speak to him, but no opportunity arose. Finally, he cut away some bark from a big cherry tree in the garden at the inn, and wrote two lines of Chinese poetry in bold graphs:

> O Heaven, do not let Goujian perish;
> A Fan Li will appear in time.

The warriors were baffled when they found the verse in the morning. "Who wrote that? What's he talking about?" they asked. But the Em-

2. From the *Analects* of Confucius, as is the quotation that follows.

peror understood as soon as he heard the lines repeated, and a broad smile spread over his face.

Because the warriors were still in the dark, they did not bother to strengthen their guard.

[*A long digression, omitted here, relates the famous Chinese story of King Goujian of Yue and his loyal minister Fan Li, who destroyed the King's enemy, King Fuchai of Wu.*]

The former sovereign spent about a fortnight at Mio Harbor in Izumo Province. Then the boatmen pronounced the wind favorable. They untied the ropes, readied the imperial craft for departure, and rowed away toward the clouds a myriad leagues ahead, surrounded by 300 military craft. The blue waters lay hushed as the sun sank beneath the northwestern waves; the distant clouds and mountains loomed high as the moon rose in the southeastern heavens. A single light, the lure on a fishing boat returning for the night, glowed faintly through the willows beside a riverbank.

Day after day, the party journeyed over the waves, mooring their vessels among the reeds of misty shores in the evening and hoisting their sails in the breeze from pine-bordered inlets in the morning. And at last, on the twenty-sixth day after the departure from the capital, the imperial boat reached Oki Province. Sasaki Oki no Hōgan Sadakiyo had built the Emperor a house of unpeeled logs, situated in a place called Kofu-no-shima. Tadaaki and Yukifusa were the only attendants stationed beside His Majesty's chair, and Lady Sanmi was the only lady-in-waiting. Instead of the splendid halls to which the sovereign had been accustomed, there were bamboo rafters with joints as numerous as manifold sorrows, and pine-brush hedges as thick as falling tears. He felt that he could not bear to spend a single night in such a place.

The shouts of the functionary announcing the dawn and the voices of the warrior guards reporting their names echoed close to the Emperor's pillow, frustrating his efforts to sleep at night in the imperial bed-chamber. The coming of day no longer heralded the conduct of affairs of state, but he never neglected his dawn prayers or his obeisances to the gods, not even when Wushan's clouds and rain had entered his dreams.[3]

---

3. "Wushan's clouds and rain" is a euphemism for love-making, derived from a story about a romantic encounter between a Chinese King and the goddess of Wu Mountain in the Yangzi gorges. The goddess told the King that she manifested herself as clouds in the morning and as rain in the evening.

What are we to make of a year in which guiltless officials shed tears of despair beneath the moon of exile, a year in which the Emperor himself fretted and worried amid the winds of an alien land, despoiled of his throne? Not since the beginning of heaven and earth had anyone heard of such extraordinary things! Must not even the celestial sun and moon have felt embarrassed when they were bereft of the monarch for whose sake they were meant to shine? Even the insentient shrubs and trees must have felt too grieved to bear blossoms.

The Sagami Novice's Enjoyment of Field Music; Also, the Dogfights (5.4)

[*In this episode, the head of the Kamakura shogunate is depicted as endangering the country through his disregard of Confucian moral standards.*]

Around that time, field music was immensely popular in the capital among people of all classes. The Sagami Novice Takatoki heard about the vogue, summoned the original and new troupes to Kamakura, and dropped everything so that he could watch their presentations day and night. So excessive was his enthusiasm that he assigned a performer to each of the great landholders, with instructions to costume him in splendid style. The members of the troupes thus became known as "Lord So-and-so's dancer" or "Lord Thus-and-so's dancer," and they wore robes of damask, gauze, brocade, and embroidered silk, lavishly decorated with gold, silver, and gems. When they performed at a feast, the Sagami Novice and all his powerful kinsmen made a great point of removing their *hitatare* and divided skirts and tossing them out as gratuities. It would be impossible to calculate the thousands and tens of thousands of coins represented by the mountains of garments they gave away.

After drinking several rounds at a small party one night, the Sagami Novice stood up, flushed with wine, and favored the company with a lengthy dance. It was not a handsome youth's performance to entertain fellow guests, nor was it a clown's amusing jest; it was merely the besotted posturing of an old Buddhist Novice past the age of forty, an exhibition unlikely to appeal to cultivated tastes.[4] As it was going on, more than ten members of the new and old field-music troupes appeared out of nowhere to dance and sing. Their performance was dazzling, extraordinary in every respect. Presently, the tempo changed, and the

4. Takatoki was actually about thirty.

Goblins perform field music (5.4)

accompanists began to chant, "Oh! To see a Weird Star, a Weird Star at
Tennōji!" A serving woman, attracted by the sound of their voices,
peeped through a crack between two sliding doors and saw not a single
human being among the so-called field-music performers. They were
specters who had taken human form—some with curved beaks like
kites, others with wings and a general resemblance to mountain ascetics.

The astonished woman sent a messenger posthaste to tell the Stronghold Novice, who rushed toward the scene, sword in hand, and the
spirits vanished without a trace at the sound of his footsteps thundering
through the middle gate. Meanwhile, the Sagami Novice had collapsed
in a drunken stupor, dead to the world.

After the Stronghold Novice called for more light in the chamber,
there seemed little doubt that the intruders had been goblins, for the
soiled mats were found to be covered with bird and animal tracks. The
Stronghold Novice stayed awhile, glowering at the empty room, but
there was nothing for him to see. The Sagami Novice woke up a little
later, dazed and unaware of what had happened.

Junior Assistant Minister of Punishments Nakanori, a Confucian scholar from the Southern House of the Fujiwara clan, heard of the affair afterward. "A sinister heavenly body called a Weird Star is said to descend to earth with calamitous results when disorder threatens the realm," he said. "Tennōji Temple is the holy site where Buddhism was first propagated, as well as the place where Prince Shōtoku personally deposited his *Forecast of the Future of Japan.* I find it most odd that the specters should have linked it to a Weird Star in their song. Apparently, a civil disturbance will break out near the temple and bring the country to ruin. Alas! If only the court and the military would forestall disaster by adopting policies of virtuous rule and benevolent government!" In the end, things turned out as he had warned. His ability to foresee calamitous events was a mark of impressive erudition.

Unintimidated by the apparitions, the Sagami Novice went to greater and greater lengths in his pursuit of bizarre pastimes. Amused on one occasion by a pack of dogs fighting in the courtyard, he conceived a passion for such spectacles that penetrated to the marrow of his bones. He rushed off orders to the provinces for dogs to be paid as taxes, and for powerful and illustrious families to provide him with animals. The Constables, the Governors, the Hōjō kinsmen, and the other great landholders in various localities all reared ten or twenty dogs apiece and took them for presentation to Kamakura; and the Novice's people fed them fish and fowl and decorated their leashes with gold and silver, all at tremendous expense. Whenever a dog was taken abroad in his palanquin, busy passersby dismounted to kneel, and peasants at work in the fields were impressed as bearers. Thanks to the Novice's extravagant fancy, Kamakura overflowed with 4,000 or 5,000 strange canines surfeited with meat and robed in brocade.

On the twelve days set aside every month as dogfight days, the Hōjō kinsmen, the great landholders, the hereditary retainers, and the other vassals sat in rows to watch, some of them in the hall and others in the courtyard. One hundred or 200 dogs were released to do battle from each of two camps. They mingled in combat, chased each other down, fought on top of one another, and struggled underneath, their barks resounding in the heavens and shaking the earth.

The less discerning among the spectators were delighted. "Fascinating! They look exactly like men contesting for victory on the battlefield," they said. The wiser ones grieved. "Nothing could be more inauspicious! They sound like they're fighting over corpses in a field."

But although different people interpreted the scene in different ways, all perceived it as suggesting future warfare and death in battle. It was shocking that the Sagami Novice sponsored such events.

The Attack on Rokuhara (9.6)

[*An army led by an eastern warrior, Ashikaga Takauji, proclaims its loyalty to the exiled Emperor Go-Daigo and threatens the western headquarters of the Kamakura shogunate at Rokuhara, across the Kamo River from the capital. The time is early in the Fifth Month of 1333.*]

The authorities at Rokuhara divided their 60,000 horsemen into three forces. One was stationed in front of the Department of Shrines to defend against Lord Ashikaga, one was dispatched to Tōji Temple to defend against Akamatsu, and one was sent north of Fushimi to secure Takeda and Fushimi, which were menaced by the advance of the Chigusa Lord Tadaaki. All three attacked simultaneously at the beginning of the Hour of the Snake [9:00 A.M. – 11:00 A.M.]. Dust from their horses' hoofs veiled the sky to the north and south; heaven and earth echoed to the sound of their battle cries.

Suyama and Kōno had been sent to Uchino at the head of 20,000 valiant chieftains. The imperial forces could not penetrate the enemy ranks easily, nor could the enemy gallop out easily. The two sides assumed defiant stances and passed the time with arrow exchanges.

Presently, a single imperial warrior appeared, wearing a lavender cape and a suit of armor with reddish-yellow braid shaded to pale yellow at the bottom. He galloped forward, halted in front of the enemy, and announced his name in a mighty voice: "I am not a man of high status, so none of you will know my name. I am Shidara Gorō Saemon-no-jō, a hereditary retainer of Lord Ashikaga. If any retainer of the Rokuhara lords considers himself my equal, let him meet me and see how well I can fight!" He drew a sword three and a half feet long, brandished it in front of his helmet, and sat his horse, presenting small target for an arrow. The combatants on both sides stopped fighting and fixed their attention on this one man, whose martial spirit seemed to single him out as a warrior worth 1,000.

Then from the Rokuhara ranks there emerged a veteran warrior about fifty years old, wearing armor with black lacing and a helmet with a five-plate neckguard. He advanced at a deliberate pace on a light chestnut horse, its crupper decorated with green tassels, and announced his name in a mighty voice: "Although I am not a learned man, my family has held a humble position on the Board of Coadjuters for many years. You will doubtless scorn me for a clerk, an unworthy foe. But my ancestors were kinsmen of General Toshihito; my house has been a warrior house for generations. I am Saitō Iyo-no-bō Genki, a seventeenth-generation member of that house! Today's battle will decide the fates of these opposing forces. Why should I try to live? If anyone survives, let him describe my exploits for my descendants!"

The two men galloped together, gripped each other with clashing shoulder-guards, and thudded to the ground. Shidara, the stronger, straddled Saitō and hacked off his head; Saitō, the nimbler, stabbed Shidara three times from underneath. Equally valiant, they maintained their holds to the death and perished on the same spot, the blade of each in the body of the other.

Another man, attired in armor with thick blue Chinese damask lacing and a horned helmet, and with a five-foot sword slung over his shoulder, emerged from the Genji ranks to gallop to within about 150 feet of the enemy. He announced his name in a mighty voice: "Ever since the time of Lord Hachiman, many generations of my kinsmen have won fame as samurai in the Genji service, but my name is unknown nowadays. It won't be easy for me to find a worthy opponent. I am Daikō no Jirō Shigenari, a retainer of Lord Ashikaga. I hear that the Bitchū Governor Suyama and the Tsushima Governor Kōno have displayed great prowess in several recent battles. Is either of them here? Come out and meet me! Join me in a display of dueling!" He waited with taut reins, his horse champing at the bit.

Suyama was absent because he had hurried off to Hachijō after hearing that the enemies at Tōji were proving to be formidable adversaries. Only the Tsushima Governor Kōno Michiharu was there in the front ranks. Kōno was impetuous by nature, not the kind of warrior to hesitate an instant in the face of a challenge.

"Michiharu is here!" He started toward Daikō to grapple with him.

Kōno's adopted son Shichirō Michitō, a young warrior of sixteen, must have resolved not to let his father be killed, for he galloped in front of Kōno, pulled alongside Daikō, and gripped him with all his strength.

Daikō seized him by the cord bow and dangled him in midair.[5] "I'm not going to wrestle with a stripling like you!" he said.

As Daikō thrust Michitō aside, he noticed an armor badge, three horizontal bars inside a double lozenge, which showed that the boy must be Kōno's son or nephew. With a one-handed downward slash, he cut off both of Michitō's legs at the knees. Then he tossed the torso three bow-lengths away.

Life meant nothing to Kōno after he saw his beloved son die in front of his eyes. He galloped forward to grapple with Daikō, his stirrups flapping. When Daikō's retainers saw the enemy advancing, they charged yelling, more than 300 strong, to save their master from death. The Genji, in turn, charged yelling, more than 1,000 strong, to save Daikō from death. Genji and Heike mingled and fought in clouds of dust.

The imperial forces fell back abruptly to Uchino, weakened by the loss of many men. Then they attacked again with fresh men, and the Rokuhara forces fell back quickly to the Kamo riverbed, weakened by heavy losses. Again, the Rokuhara forces sent in fresh men who attacked with grim determination. Locked in furious battle, the opposing sides surged eastward and westward on Ichijō and Nijō avenues, advancing and retreating seven or eight times. Both Genji and Heike fought with no regard for life, neither side more or less brave than the other. But the Genji numbers were greater, and at last the Heike withdrew to Roku-hara in defeat.

The Akamatsu Novice Enshin advanced on Tōji Temple with 3,000 horsemen. When the army reached the two-storied gate, the Shinano Governor Norisuke stood in his stirrups, looked behind him to his left and right, and issued an order. "Some of you men break up the barricade in front of that gate!" Three hundred hot-blooded young warriors dismounted to run forward, members of forces under the leadership of Uno, Kashiwabara, Sayo, and Mashima. The temple was protected by a solid wall made of excellent timbers five to nine inches square in size, some from Yasu District and others of the quality used by lute-makers, and extending from the Rashōmon foundation on the west to the Hachijō riverbed on the east. In front of the wall there was a network of stakes,

---

5. The cord bow (*agemaki*) was a stout cord tied in a bow and attached as an ornament to a ring on the back of the armor.

ropes, and branch barricades, as well as a moat more than thirty feet wide, filled with water diverted from the river.

The attackers hesitated to leap into the water without knowing its depth, nor could they cross on the bridge, which had been stripped of planks. But as they stood perplexed, Mega no Magosaburō Nagamune, a resident of Harima Province, sprang from his horse and lowered his bow into the water to test the depth. The upper end of the weapon just cleared the surface. At that rate, Nagamune thought, the water could not possibly be over his head. He drew his five-foot sword, slung it over his shoulder, discarded his fur boots, and plunged in. The water did not even reach the top of his upper breastplate.

"The moat is shallow!" exclaimed Takebe no Shichirō, who was following Nagamune. A short man only about five feet tall, Takebe jumped in blithely, and the water closed over the front of his helmet. Nagamune threw him a hasty backward glance. "Take hold of my cord bow and climb up," he said. Takebe no Shichirō secured a foothold in Nagamune's armor sash, climbed onto his shoulders, steadied himself, and leaped to the opposite bank.

Nagamune burst out laughing. "You used me for a bridge! Come on, let's break down the wall!" He leaped up from the bank, seized a support jutting out four or five inches from the wall, and gave it a mighty wrench. The wall collapsed, bringing down with it the dirt from the moat, which had been piled on top to mountainous heights of ten or twenty feet, and the moat was transformed abruptly into a flat surface.

Upon seeing what had happened, the defenders released a fast and furious flight of arrows, thicker than falling raindrops, from more than 300 lookouts on top of the tile-capped earthen wall. Nagamune bent back the arrows lodged in his helmet wings and armor skirts, dashed under the main gate, and stood wrathfully gnawing his upper lip in front of the two guardian deities, his swordtip touching the ground. It was hard to tell which of the three figures was Nagamune and which were the Two Kings.

"The main gate is endangered!" clamored the 10,000 Rokuhara warriors stationed at Tōji, Nishihachijō, Hari-no-kōji, and Karahashi. Like rain-swollen clouds descending from the hills at dusk, they joined forces and swooped down from the vicinity of the Tōji eastern gate.

Since Mega and Takebe seemed doomed, Sayo Hyōgo-no-suke,

Tokuhira no Genda, Bessho no Rokurō Saemon, and Bessho no Gorō Saemon attacked with furious determination, eyes straight ahead.

"Don't let them be killed, men!" Akamatsu Enshin; Akamatsu's heir, the Shinano Governor Norisuke; his second son, the Chikuzen Governor Sadanori; his third son, Master of Discipline Sokuyū; and the more than 3,000 warriors led by Majima, Kōzuki, Kanke, and Kinugasa drew their swords and attacked in unison. The 10,000 Rokuhara horsemen were chased back toward the Shichijō riverbed in disarray.

The rear of an army cannot hold when the vanguard has been beaten. Routed after defeats at Takeda, Kohata, and Fushimi, the Hōjō adherents took refuge in the Rokuhara stronghold. The victorious pursuers from various quarters, a total of more than 50,000 horsemen, consolidated their forces and besieged the stronghold with untold thousands and myriads of men, their front extending from the Gojō bridge to the Shichijō riverbed. They left the exit to the east open, in the hope of defeating the enemy more easily by sowing division in their ranks.

The Chigusa Middle Captain Tadaaki issued a command to his warriors. "If we adopt the usual tactics and take our time about reducing this stronghold, the attackers at Chihaya will lift their siege and hit us from the rear. All together, now! Hurry up and bring it down!"

Warriors from Izumo and Hōki provinces assembled 200 or 300 carts, tied the shafts together, and heaped them mountain high with debris from demolished houses. Then they drew them up under the lookouts and burned out the stronghold entrance.

Three hundred armored and helmeted monks from Mount Hiei, cloister mates of the Tendai Abbot's disciples Jōrinbō and Shōgyōbō, emerged from the north gate of the Jizō Hall and dashed forward to the Gojō bridge. Despite their inferior numbers, they routed 3,000 imperial warriors—men under the command of the Bōmon Lesser Captain and Dharma Seal Ryōchū—and chased them along the riverbed for three blocks. Then they went back inside the stronghold, afraid that a determined pursuit might prove disastrous to so small a force.

Although the army inside Rokuhara was relatively small, it numbered more than 50,000 horsemen. The besiegers, who were beginning to waver, would probably not have stood their ground if all its members had united in a simultaneous sortie. But perhaps the hour of the shogunate had struck, for even famous men of valor seemed devoid of martial spirit; even those renowned as peerless archers let their bows hang idle.

They milled around in a daze, gathering here and there and showing no interest in anything except preparations for flight. When warriors who were jealous of their personal reputations and family honor were acting like that, what could have been expected of the Emperor, the former sovereigns, the Imperial Lady, the Empress, the Regent's consort, the senior nobles, the courtiers, the page boys and page girls, and the court ladies, none of whom had ever had any experience of warfare?[6] Terrified by the battle cries and archers' shouts, they were utterly distraught. And as the two Rokuhara lords gazed at the pathetic scene, which they considered entirely natural, they lost their own courage and sank into apathy.

When darkness fell, warriors who had never shown evidence of untrustworthiness opened the gate, scaled the obstacles, and took to their heels, each man for himself. (They may have thought victory was impossible with morale inside the stronghold so low.) Fewer than 1,000 defenders remained, men who preferred death to disloyalty.

Nagasaki Takashige's Last Battle (10.14)

[*The scene shifts to Kamakura as the final defeat of the shogunate approaches. The time is late in the Fifth Month of 1333.*]

In more than eighty battles, waged by day and by night since the initial engagement at Musashino, Nagasaki no Jirō Takashige had always fought in the vanguard; on innumerable occasions, he had broken encirclements to challenge the foe. Except for a mere 150 riders, his subordinates and young retainers had all met their ends, one by one. On the Twenty-second of the Fifth Month, he learned that the Genji had already stormed the valleys and killed almost all the Hōjō commanders. Without bothering to choose his adversaries any longer, he galloped against enemy warriors wherever they approached, disrupting their lines and scattering them in every direction. When his horse tired, he mounted another; when his sword snapped, he fastened another at his waist. Single-handed, he struck down thirty-two men and broke through eight enemy positions. Then he went back to the Sagami Novice's residence in Kasai Valley. He made obeisance at the middle gate and spoke with tears streaming from his eyes.

---

6. The Emperor was the founder of the Northern Court, Kōgon (1313–64), who had been placed on the throne in 1331 to replace the deposed Go-Daigo.

"Generations of my family have enjoyed the honor of serving yours, and I have had the personal privilege of seeing you morning and night. But we shall meet no more in this life after today. I scattered five or six concentrations of the enemy and won several battles, but all of the gateways are breached now. Kamakura overflows with enemy warriors. No matter how hard I might fight, it would do no good.

"Make up your mind not to let yourself fall into enemy hands, but please don't take your life until I come back to tell you it's time. I'll charge into the enemy ranks and fight one last glorious battle while you're still alive. It will be a tale to tell while we go to the nether regions together." He left Tōshōji.[7]

With tears in his eyes, the Novice stood looking sadly at his retreating figure until it receded into the distance. There seemed little chance that they would meet again.

Discarding his heavy armor, Takashige donned an unlined striped robe with an embossed sun-and-moon design, a wide-mouthed divided skirt of the finest silk, and a red-braided corselet. He did not put on armored sleeves. He mounted his horse Tōkei, the best steed in eastern Japan, on which he had placed a gold-flecked lacquered saddle and a short-fringed crupper.

Because that day was to be his last, he began by going to the Sōjuji Abbot Nanzan's residence to request an audience. The Abbot received him with a degree of formality befitting the solemn nature of the occasion.

Takashige stood in the courtyard, compelled to remain in battle array because of the fighting everywhere. He saluted those present on the left and right. Then he addressed a question to the Abbot. "How is a man of valor supposed to behave at a time like this?"

"The greatest valor is to advance, keen blade in hand," the Abbot replied.

One sentence was enough for Takashige. He went back outside the gate, led up his horse, sprang onto its back, and ordered his 150 mounted warriors to fall in to the front and rear. Then he wrenched off his helmet badge and walked his horse quietly into the enemy ranks, bent on approaching Nitta Yoshisada and grappling with him to the death.

7. The temple where Takatoki was staying.

The Genji warriors must have been misled because Takashige and his men carried no standard and kept their swords sheathed. They moved aside indifferently to let them through, and the party managed to reach a spot about fifty yards away from Yoshisada. But fate must have sided with the Genji. Just as the crucial moment approached, Takashige was recognized by Yura no Shinzaemon, a warrior who happened to be directly in front of Yoshisada.

"That's Nagasaki no Jirō—the one coming in without a standard! He's a famous warrior. He wouldn't be here unless he was up to something. Cut them all down! Don't let any of them get away!" Shinzaemon shouted.

Three thousand members of the Seven Leagues of Musashi, men who had been awaiting developments in the front ranks, swept forward from the east and west, surrounded Takashige's band, and began to compete with one another for the glory of killing the adversary. Takashige, his scheme in ruins, concentrated his 150 riders in a tight group. Then he and his men shouted a single mighty battle cry and charged pell-mell into the heart of the 3,000. They appeared here, vanished there, and fought until the sparks flew. They converged and dispersed with bewildering speed, never in the same place for more than a few seconds. When the enemy warriors thought they were in front, they suddenly appeared to the rear; when the enemy thought they were looking at friends, they found themselves facing foes. Takashige's men seemed to be attacking everywhere. Unable to locate Takashige, many of Yoshisada's warriors fell upon their own comrades.

"Stop killing each other, you fools!" Nagahama no Rokurō ordered. "It looks like all the enemy have thrown away their helmet badges. If you see anybody without one, wrestle him down and kill him."

Warriors from Kai, Shinano, Musashi, and Sagami forced their way alongside Takashige's men and seized them in iron grips. When adversaries crashed to the ground, some men took heads and some had their heads taken. Dust hung in the air; sweat and blood muddied the ground. It seemed that the carnage could have been no worse when Xiang Yu humbled the three Han generals, or when the Duke of Luyang battled on after making the sun retreat through three constellations.[8]

8. When darkness began to fall while the Duke was fighting a battle, he prevailed on the sun to move backward by gesturing at it with a spear.

Takashige was still alive, fighting alongside his seven remaining men. Still hoping to grapple with Yoshisada, he rode around in search of the Nitta brothers, parrying or evading enemy advances. Yokoyama no Tarō Shigezane, a resident of Musashi Province, cut him off from Yoshisada and rode ahead to grapple with him.

"If that man is a worthy foe, I'll wrestle him," Takashige decided. He spurred forward, looked at the oncoming rider, and saw that it was Shigezane. "He's no adversary for me!" he said. Getting to Shigezane's right, he dealt him a blow that split his helmet all the way to the cross-stitched bottom plate. Shigezane died, cut in two, and his horse crashed over backwards with a gashed knee.

Another Musashi warrior, Shō no Saburō Tamehisa, was the next to see Takashige as a desirable opponent and try to grapple with him. Shō galloped forward with outstretched arms. Takashige burst out laughing when he saw him from a distance. "If I'd been willing to wrestle someone from the leagues, what was wrong with Yokoyama?" he said. "All right, I'll show you how I kill a man I don't recognize as a real opponent." He grabbed Tamehisa by the cord bow of his armor, dangled him in the air, and sent him flying five bow-lengths away with an easy toss. Two warriors tumbled headfirst from their horses and died spitting blood, struck by the human projectile.

Since he had already been recognized, Takashige thought that he might as well proclaim his identity. He halted his galloping horse and announced his name in a mighty voice: "I intend to die in battle to repay the favors I have received from my lord—I, Jirō Takashige, a grandson in direct line of descent from the Nagasaki Novice Enki, principal adviser to the Former Sagami Governor Takatoki and a descendant in the thirteenth generation from the Taira General Sadamori, a descendant in the third generation from Prince Katsurahara, the fifth son of Emperor Kanmu. If any among you seeks fame, let him come forward! I'll wrestle him!" He got rid of his shoulder-guards, cut away most of his skirts, and resheathed his sword. Then he stretched his arms wide, sent his horse charging in one direction after another, and scattered enemies with his hair flying.

His retainers galloped in front of him to bar the way. "What are you doing? Huge armies are already bursting into the valleys to burn and pillage while you gallop around alone like this. Go back now! Tell His Lordship to commit suicide!"

"It was fun watching those men run away; I forgot my promise to His Lordship. All right, I'll go back," Takashige said.

As the eight horsemen headed back from Yamanouchi, 500 members of the Kodama League came racing after them with contemptuous yells, probably imagining that they were trying to flee. "Come back, cowards!"

"We don't need to worry about their big mouths," Takashige said. They galloped on, ignoring the taunts, until the pursuers got too close. Then the eight glanced behind them, wheeled their mounts, and attacked. Seventeen times between Yamanouchi and Kasai Valley, they turned to give battle, put the 500 enemies to flight, and proceeded calmly on their way.

When Takashige reached Kasai Valley, twenty-three broken arrows were hanging from his armor like strands in a straw raincoat. His grandfather, the Novice Enki, was waiting for him. "What took you so long? Is everything over now?" Enki asked.

Takashige bowed. "I galloped into the enemy ranks twenty times trying to close on Yoshisada and wrestle with him, but I could never reach him. There was nobody else who looked like an opponent of the right status, but I must have cut down four or five hundred ordinary league members. If I hadn't had to remember that killing is a sin, I'd have liked to chase those fellows to the beach, lay into them on both sides, and slice them up. But I was worried about His Lordship, so I came back." His gallant words brought a small measure of comfort to those who were about to die.

Takatoki, His Kinsmen, and the Others Kill Themselves at Tōshōji (10.15)

Takashige ran around to one place after another. "Hurry up! Kill yourselves! I'll go first to set the example!" He cast off his armor, of which only the cuirass remained, drank three times from the wine bowl in front of His Lordship the Sagami Novice Takatoki, with his brother Shin'uemon pouring, and set the bowl in front of the Settsu Novice Dōjun.

"This is especially for you. And here's the relish!" He plunged his dagger into his left side, cut a long gash extending all the way to his right flank, pulled out his guts, and fell prostrate in front of Dōjun.

Dōjun picked up the bowl and drained half its contents. "What a relish! Not even the most abstemious man could refuse this," he jested. He placed the bowl in front of the Suwa Novice Jikishō and killed himself with his dagger.

Jikishō drank calmly three times and set the bowl in front of His Lordship the Sagami Novice. "Now that the young warriors have put on such a show, we can't make our age an excuse for doing nothing. Each of us must provide a relish for the next man," he said. He cut his belly crosswise, withdrew his dagger, and placed the weapon in front of the Sagami Novice.

Apparently uncertain about how the Sagami Novice might behave, the Nagasaki Novice Enki had delayed his own suicide. His fifteen-year-old grandson Nagasaki Shin'uemon bowed in front of him. "A filial descendant brings honor to his ancestors' names. I know the gods and Buddhas will forgive this deed." He stabbed his aged grandfather twice, once at the crook of each arm. Then he pierced his own belly with the dagger, pulled Enki down, and fell on top of him.

The Sagami Novice cut open his belly, shown the way by this young warrior, and then the Stronghold Novice did the same.

Upon witnessing those deaths, the warriors seated in rows inside the hall—the Hōjō kinsmen and all the others—bared their snowy skin and died as they saw fit, some by cutting their bellies and others by striking off their own heads. It was a magnificent spectacle. These were some of the ones who perished, a total of 283 Hōjō kinsmen, each striving to meet death first:

Kanazawa Tayū, the Novice Sōken
Sasuke Ōmi-no-zenji Munenao
Amanō Suruga-no-kami Muneaki
    His son Suruga no Sakon-tayū-shōgen Tokiaki
Komachi Nakatsukasa-no-tayū Tomozane
Tokiwa Suruga-no-kami Norisada
Nagoya Tosa-no-zenji Tokimoto
Settsu no Gyōbu-no-tayū, a Buddhist Novice
Igu Echizen-no-zenji Muneari
Jō no Kaga-no-zenji Moroaki
Aita no Jō-no-suke Morotoki
Jō no Echizen-no-kami Aritoki

Nanbu Uma-no-kami Shigetoki
Mutsu no Uma-no-suke Ietoki
Sagami no Uma-no-suke Takamoto
Musashi no Sakon-no-tayū-shōgen Tokina
Mutsu no Sakon-no-shōgen Tokifusa
Sakurada Jibu-no-tayū Sadakuni
Ema Tōtōmi-no-kami Kin'atsu
Aso no Danjō-shōhitsu Harutoki
Katta Shikibu-no-tayū Atsutoki
Tōtōmi Hyōgo-no-suke Akikatsu
Bizen no Sakon-no-tayū-shōgen Masao
Sakanoue Tōtōmi-no-kami Sadatomo
Mutsu no Shikibu-no-tayū Takatomo
Jō no Suke Takakazu
Jō no Shikibu-no-tayū Akitaka
Jō no Mino-no-kami Takashige
Aita no Jō-no-suke, the Novice Enmyō
Akashi Nagato-no-suke, the Novice Nin'a
Nagasaki no Saburōzaemon, the Novice Shigen
Suda Jirōzaemon
Settsu no Kunai-no-tayū Takachika
Settsu no Sakon-no-tayū-shōgen Chikasada
Thirty-four members of the Nagoya family
Forty-six members of the Shioda, Akahashi,
  Tokiwa, and Sasuke families

The building was put to the torch. Fierce flames shot up and black smoke darkened the air. When the fire became visible to the warriors seated in rows inside the courtyard and in front of the gate, some of them cut open their bellies and dashed into the blaze. Others who were closely related—fathers, sons, older brothers, and younger brothers—exchanged mortal stabs and fell on top of one another. Streams of blood inundated the ground like a river in spate; corpses lay piled in the roads as though on a burial field. Many bodies disappeared in the flames, but later inquiry disclosed that more than 870 men had perished there. In addition, and quite aside from the unknown numbers in remote provinces, there were more than 6,000 people in Kamakura—Hōjō kinsmen and the beneficiaries of Hōjō patronage, monks and laymen, men and women—who died to requite past favors or lived on in sorrow after they heard the news.

Ah, what a day was that! On the Twenty-second of the Fifth Month in the third year of Genkō [1333], the prosperity of the Heike, unblemished for nine generations, was swept away in an hour; the discontent of the Genji, nursed for many years, was dispelled in a morning.

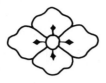

Two Companion Booklets

Like other companion booklets (*otogi zōshi*), the two short tales below are of unknown authorship and date. The first, "Little One-Inch," is usually assigned to the fifteenth or sixteenth century; the second, "Akimichi," to the late sixteenth or early seventeenth century. "Little One-Inch" follows the familiar folktale pattern of the peculiar person who performs remarkable feats; "Akimichi" is a story of revenge and feminine loyalty in the warrior class.

Little One-Inch

In the not too distant past, an old man and an old woman lived at Naniwa Village in Settsu Province. The old woman went to Sumiyoshi Shrine to pray for offspring, grieved because she was still childless at the age of forty. The god took pity on her, and she conceived at the age of forty-one, much to the old man's delight. When her time came in the tenth month, she gave birth to a pretty little boy. But the child never grew more than an inch tall, and so he came to be called Little One-Inch.

As the months and years passed, Little One-Inch reached the age of twelve or thirteen, but he was still not as big as a grown-up. His parents thought and thought about it. "This child is no ordinary human being; he's like some kind of monster. What was the sin the Sumiyoshi god was punishing us for when he gave him to us? It's a miserable piece of luck," they said. It was pitiful just to look at them. "If only we could send this wretched Little One-Inch off somewhere," they thought.

When Little One-Inch heard them talking, he understood the situation at once. "Alas! Nobody has any use for me, not even my parents. I'll have to go away somewhere," he thought. It seemed to him that he would need a sword, so he asked the old woman for a needle. She got one for him, and he made a hilt and scabbard out of barley straw. Then he thought, "I'd like to go to the capital, but how could I get there without a boat?" This time, he asked the old woman for a bowl and a pair of chopsticks, and she gave them to him. Saddened by the parting, the old couple tried to detain him, but he set out anyway. He got into the bowl at Sumiyoshi Beach and rowed toward the capital.

suminareshi	With what emotions
naniwa no ura o	do I set forth from the shore
tachiidete	at Naniwa,
miyako e isogu	where I have lived so long,
wa ga kokoro ka na	to hasten toward the capital!

He disembarked at Toba Harbor and proceeded to the capital to take in the sights. He was speechless with astonishment when he saw Shijō and Gojō avenues. At Sanjō Avenue, he approached the house of a certain Consultant.

"Excuse me!" he said.

"What an interesting voice!" the Consultant thought. He went to the front edge of the veranda and looked around, but nobody seemed to be there.

"At this rate, I could get trampled to death," Little One-Inch thought. He took shelter under a pair of high clogs nearby. "Excuse me!" he said.

"This is very odd," the Consultant thought. "I can't see anybody, but I hear somebody shouting in an interesting voice. I think I'll just go out and look around." To a servant, he said, "I want to put on those clogs."

A voice spoke up from under the clogs. "Please don't step on me."

Looking down in surprise, the Consultant discovered an extraordinary person. "You're certainly an interesting fellow," he said with a laugh.

Time passed and Little One-Inch turned sixteen, but he stayed the same height. Now it happened that the Consultant had a daughter who had reached the age of thirteen. The moment Little One-Inch saw that young lady, he was captivated by her beauty. "If only I could find a way to make her my wife!" he thought.

One day, Little One-Inch put some rice in a paper tea-leaf bag, smeared it on the daughter's lips as she lay sleeping, and sat wailing with the empty bag in his hand. He had his reasons for what he did.

The Consultant saw him and wanted to know what was the matter.

"Her Ladyship took away the rice I had been saving, and she ate it all up," Little One-Inch said.

The Consultant flew into a rage. Sure enough, there was rice on his daughter's lips. "It's just the way you said it was; you weren't telling a lie. We can't keep a creature like this in the capital. Find some way to get rid of her," he told Little One-Inch.

"You took what was mine, so your father has told me to do whatever I please with you," Little One-Inch said to the daughter. Inside, he was immeasurably elated.

For the young lady, it was just like a dream. She was absolutely dumbfounded. With Little One-Inch prodding her to hurry, she got ready to go from the capital wherever her feet might lead, feeling like someone beginning a long journey into the dark. We can imagine her emotions. Ah, how pitiful she was! Little One-Inch started off behind her. The Consultant had hoped that his wife would stop her, but the woman was her stepmother, so she made only a token effort. None of the ladies-in-waiting went with her.

"Now that it's come to this, it doesn't matter where I go," the daughter thought in despair. "I might as well go to Naniwa." She boarded a boat at Toba Harbor.

Just then, a violent gale blew up. It carried the boat to a queer-looking island, which seemed to be uninhabited when they disembarked and looked around. It was an ill wind that had blown them there! What were they going to do?

As Little One-Inch stood looking around, racking his brains, two demons came out of nowhere. One of them carried a wish-granting mallet. The other one said, "I'm going to eat this fellow up and take the girl."

But no sooner had the demon got Little One-Inch into his mouth than Little One-Inch came out of his eye.

"What a weird fellow! If I shut my mouth on him, he comes out of my eye," the demon said. He and his companion were terrified because Little One-Inch had come out and danced around after being swallowed.

"This is no ordinary mortal. A fight must be going on in hell," the two said. "Let's get out of here." They ran off to a very black place in the northeast, abandoning their wish-granting mallet, their staffs, their whips, and everything else.

Little One-Inch's first act was to take possession of the wish-granting mallet. "Make me big," he said, giving it a bang. In no time, he grew tall. Then, faint with hunger, he tried to produce something to eat, and a delicious repast immediately appeared. What amazing good fortune!

After that, Little One-Inch produced gold and silver, went to the capital with the daughter, took lodgings in the Gojō area, and stayed there about ten days. Because such things could not remain unknown, the news reached the imperial palace, and the Emperor made haste to summon him. When he arrived at the palace, the Emperor said, "A lad that handsome can't be of base origin." He made inquiries about Little One-Inch's parentage, and it became known that the old man was the son of a person called the Horikawa Middle Counselor—a child born in the countryside after someone's slanders had driven the Middle Counselor into exile. The old woman was the daughter of a man called the Fushimi Lesser Captain. Her parents had died when she was small.

Once it was clear that Little One-Inch was not of ignoble birth, the Emperor summoned him to the Courtiers' Hall and named him the Horikawa Lesser Captain—a most splendid thing. Little One-Inch brought his parents to the capital and entertained and waited on them with extraordinary solicitude.

In time, Little One-Inch became a Middle Counselor. He had always been outstanding in feeling, appearance, and every other respect, and the reputation of his house was of the very highest. The Consultant was delighted to hear of his good fortune.

Later on, Little One-Inch fathered three children and prospered in splendid fashion. His descendants also throve, just as the Sumiyoshi god had promised. People said there could be no more remarkable example of worldly success.

Akimichi

There was once a prodigiously wealthy man, Yamaguchi no Akihiro by name, who lived in the vicinity of Kamakura. He had a son, Akimichi, who was his oldest male child. Around the middle of the Third Month in the first year of Juei [1182], Akimichi went to the capital to represent Akihiro in a lawsuit, accompanied by a large party of young retainers. During his absence, a certain Kanayama no Hachirō-zaemon staged a night attack on Akihiro's dwelling at Yamaguchi and seized vast quantities of valuables. Furthermore, he killed Akihiro and many other members of the household. It was impossible to be certain of the bandit's identity, but there was no other obvious suspect, and people everywhere blamed Hachirōzaemon.

This Hachirōzaemon was the cleverest night robber in Japan, a man who had made a fortune from the lawless exploits that were his main occupation. With more than fifty young retainers inside his moat, and famous for his own immense strength, he treated other people as less than human and perpetrated outrageous villainies. On three separate occasions, the Kamakura Lord Yoritomo ordered his men to kill him because of the evil deeds he committed year after year. But far from being killed, Hachirōzaemon fought back furiously, struck down many assailants, and disappeared into some unknown place. People marveled at his ability to vanish from sight for five and ten days at a time, just as though he had gone to the bottom of the sea or penetrated to the innermost recesses of the mountains.

While Hachirōzaemon was going on like this, Akihiro suffered the night attack that claimed his life. Rampant mugwort and weeds rose to the eaves of the rich man's former residence, now abandoned and falling into ruin, and his wife became a nun at the age of forty-two.

Around the spring of the following year, Akimichi returned from the capital, victorious in the lawsuit. When the nun saw him, she burst into tears and told him the whole long story. No words could describe the humiliation and anger that consumed him from that time on. The very sight of his mother in Buddhist garb seemed to paralyze his brain. He consulted others about an attack to avenge the family, but there seemed little chance that so notorious a strong man would let himself be overpowered. He also considered a night attack, but he lacked the means to bring it off. Then, too, the bandit had struck at night, so nobody had seen him very well. A long time slipped by while he tried to think of what to do.

Just the same, this Akimichi was someone who had entered a temple at the age of eleven for a thorough education. Thanks to his rich father, he had also been able to indulge a fondness for the martial arts, and furthermore, he was incomparably handsome. At the age of twenty-five, he shut himself inside his bedchamber and stayed there for seven days and seven nights, pondering ways of killing his enemy.

Akimichi had married his wife, Kitamuki, when she was sixteen. She was now twenty-one. Her formerly affluent father, Nagae no Saitō of Echigo Province, had lost his property and sunk into poverty, and she seldom heard from him. Her beauty was beyond comparison. She played the zither and lute with exceptional skill, painted, made artificial flowers from silk thread, wrote an excellent hand, and composed better poems than anyone else. In short, she was a mistress of all the arts. She stood next to the bedchamber and addressed Akimichi in a sorrowful voice. "Why do you keep grieving in there?" But there was no answer from inside.

On the seventh day, Akimichi emerged. He seated himself opposite his wife and spoke to her in confidence. "I spent seven days in seclusion to try to think of a way to kill Father's enemy. In the end, I made a decision that would ask a lot of you. Are you willing to help?"

Her answer was reassuring. "Do you really need to ask? It's more than five years since I came to this house as a bride. Haven't you seen into my heart yet? I couldn't refuse you anything, no matter what. Even if it cost me my life, I'd do whatever you said." She went on, "We were terrified by what happened that night while you were away in the capital. I never expected to live to see you again. Do I need to say how much I want to pay that man back?"

"That's just why I want to rely on you," he said. He continued in a firm voice, "Go to Kanayama's house and spend the night with him. It will be easy for me to kill him then; I have a plan."

His wife was astounded. "What a mad thing to say! I never heard of such an idea! What possesses you to talk that way? It's unthinkable! I can't consider it, not even if it means I'll be punished for my disobedience by never seeing you again. Even the most virtuous woman is a sinful creature, subject to the Five Hindrances and Three Subordinations. I'd be sure to lose my home in this life and be reborn as a snake in the next. Everyone says a woman will have three-foot iron spikes driven into her body through her mouth if she touches the flesh of two men. I simply can't bring myself to agree."

Akimichi had to admit that she was right, but he hardened his heart and resumed the argument. "What you say is true enough. But unless I kill my father's enemy, I'm bound to get a bad name in the province, lose my lord's confidence, and alienate all my friends. And the horse-headed and ox-headed jailers in hell will keep torturing me and saying, 'Kill your enemy!,' in my next life. The bond between husband and wife lasts for two existences." To this dismal utterance, he added, "It's a graver sin for a woman to know two men than for a man to draw his bow in the service of two masters, but I feel sure the Buddhas will grant forgiveness in our case. Tell me right now that you have no objection." He continued, "If you still refuse, you must have been lying when you said you would do anything I asked, even if it cost you your life. I said what I did because you swore I meant more to you than your own life."

Talked into a corner, his wife bowed to his will. "All right," she said, "think of the very best plan you can. I won't object. But tell me— how are you going to get close to the man and deceive him long enough to kill him?"

"You must go to the place where Kanayama lives and let it be known that you are a courtesan from the capital. Once you're there, he's going to summon you. Question the proprietor at your lodgings to be sure you've got the right man, and then go to his house one night if there's no mistake. Serve him wine; don't serve anyone else. I say this because he won't be suspicious once he's got a good look at you. He's a wild rascal; he'll arrange for you to come and amuse him the next night, too. Then you send me a note by a fast messenger. I'll sneak inside in the dark and kill him just like that. It will be a pious offering to Father's spirit. What's more, it'll make me famous."

"That's foolish talk. A man's heart is like the course of a stream; it can change overnight. Even if I call myself a courtesan from the capital, he certainly won't summon me two nights in a row. It would just be a second humiliation for you," she said.

"No, no. Kanayama is a wild rascal. Once he's set eyes on you, he won't drop you after a night or two. Your beauty would fascinate any man," Akimichi said.

Kitamuki wanted to go off and drown herself in a river or sea. But then, reconsidering, the faithful wife conceived a plan of her own. Even if Hachirōzaemon summoned her for 100 nights running, she would not falter; she would await her opportunity, and she, not her husband, would be the one to kill him.

It was late in the Third Month. Kitamuki composed this poem on the eve of her departure:

kono haru no	It had seemed to me
hana no sakari to	that these springtime blossoms
omoishi ni	had reached their prime,
asu chiriyukan	but tomorrow, alas,
koto zo kanashiki	they are fated to scatter.

Akimichi's reply was prompt:

oroka nari	That is foolishness!
mata mo aubeki	We shall surely see them again.
haru goto no	Though someone may break
eda wa oru tomo	the branch where they bloom each spring,
kokoro kawaraji	our love of the blossoms endures.

Akimichi put his wife into a palanquin with a maid to attend her, and Kitamuki hurried away toward the place where Hachirōzaemon lived. Once inside the province, she took lodgings. The next day, just as Akimichi had foreseen, someone at the inn saw her and thought she would make Hachirōzaemon a fine mistress. In the hope of currying favor with the bandit, that person went off and told him, without a word to anyone else. The delighted Hachirōzaemon hurried to the inn to see her. Needless to say, she was as fair as a green willow swaying in the breeze or a spray of delicately drooping chokeberry blossoms. Her bewitching painted brows hinted at a hundred coquetries; her skin might have been mistaken for white jade. Swept off his feet, Hachirōzaemon arranged with the proprietor to send her right off to his house, where he brought out wine and enjoyed himself with her. But despite his infatuation, this formidable man did not lower his guard at all. Instead of spending the whole night with her, he drank just a little and left early in the evening.

Kitamuki waited until the next night, but the same thing happened again. Hachirōzaemon did not lower his guard at all. He kept ten or twenty young armed retainers around him, and he wore a stout cuirass and armored sleeves and held a spear. He never stretched out flat to sleep, and if he did lie down, he used a silver hair stick for a pillow and kept a sword in his hand.[1] Such were the precautions he took. There was no vulnerable point whatever for Kitamuki to report to Akimichi.

Meanwhile, time passed. A whole year slipped by, and still there was no chance to tell Akimichi of a vulnerable point. Kitamuki conceived late in the year and gave birth to an adorable child, but Hachirōzaemon stayed on his guard as much as ever. He drank a little wine in the evening, dallied with Kitamuki awhile, and then went off some place for the rest of the night. To her great distress, Kitamuki had no idea where he slept.

Back home, Akimichi heard about the child. Matters had taken a disturbing turn, indeed! He had expected Kitamuki's stay to be very brief, but his unorthodox scheme had produced no message, and now, to his infinite chagrin, he learned that his wife had given birth to a child. Seething with anger, he told himself that he had two scores to settle with Hachirōzaemon, one for his father and one for his wife.

Meanwhile, Kitamuki brooded over the state of affairs. "Alas! Akimichi must be furious with me. I thought I would be able to trick the bandit, but he never relaxes his vigilance, and so much time has elapsed that Akimichi must suspect me of a change of heart. Somehow or other, I have to find a way to help him get what he wants," she thought. She pretended to fall ill, refused food for five or ten days, and gave every appearance of being about to succumb.

Hachirōzaemon was worried to death. One day, he went to Kitamuki's side. "What kind of illness can this be? How do you feel? I'll get whatever medicine you need, even if it costs 50,000 or 100,000 coins. You look like you're dying. Your home is in the capital; you must have parents there. Do you want to see them? Are you fretting about them? Speak up. I'll send someone to fetch them. I can have any woman, but I don't want to live without you. Please speak up right now," he said.

"I'm so happy to hear you talk like that," Kitamuki said in response to his entreaties. "The capital isn't on my mind at all. I won't hide the truth any longer. You and I have been intimate ever since last year, but you've never been relaxed enough to spend a whole night with me. You

---

1. Hair sticks (*kōgai*), used as hairdressing aids by both sexes, were long, narrow objects resembling flattened chopsticks, usually made of ivory or silver. Their exact function is not known.

always go away to your own quarters. If you really loved me, you'd tell me where you sleep, but you never do. I've been afraid you were just visiting me in spare moments when you weren't busy with a much prettier woman. That's why I've fallen ill like this."

"I don't blame you for thinking so, but that isn't it at all. If you have any such suspicions, I'll take whatever oath you like that they're false. Why should I hide anything now? I'm a man with lots of dangerous enemies; I don't let anyone see where I sleep. I can understand your resentment; it's only natural. Besides, you're my son's mother. Why should I hide anything from you now? If you get well, I'll show you where I sleep."

Kitamuki was delighted. Little by little, she regained her health, and one day Hachirōzaemon took her by the hand and showed her all over the main building in his compound. After they passed the place where he spent most of his time, they came to a handsome apartment, which seemed to be a place where he diverted himself with a group of young companions. A little distance away, he led her into a small room containing a stout-walled inner bedchamber. Judging from the bordered matting, quilts, rattan pillow, and other furnishings inside, a visitor might have concluded that he slept there, but that was not true. It merely looked as though he did. He went to the rear, opened a small door, and led the way outside.

After walking eight or ten yards, they came to a brimming valley stream with a small craft floating on its clear waters. Hachirōzaemon took Kitamuki by the hand to help her in. Then he rowed for about 100 yards, moored the boat to the cliffside, and began to climb a path leading to the mountain above. Very soon, they arrived at a cave about eighteen feet square. Inside, there were mats with elegant black-and-white borders, fine articles of furniture, tea utensils, and so forth, just as though someone lived there.

"I spend my nights here," Hachirōzaemon said. "This is a first-rate hideout that nobody knows about. One time, Yoritomo ordered my execution for no real reason, and a huge force marched against me, but I took refuge here. It's a fine place; nobody knows about it. I'm showing it to you because I think so much of you. I'll never forgive you if you tell anybody."

"Of course, I won't. If only I had realized how prudent you are, I wouldn't have minded the way you acted. I'm truly sorry about that.

Anyway, I feel perfectly at ease now," Kitamuki said. She continued, "You couldn't have made a cave like this without help. The people who worked for you must know about it, don't they?"

"That's a good question. It took more than three hundred men to build it. Once it was finished, I didn't want anyone told, so I tricked and killed the whole three hundred. Not a living soul knows about it now."

Kitamuki thought things over. "What a terrible criminal this man is! But even though I know about the cave, I can't get Akimichi here to kill him. We'd need a boat. It would be all right if there were two boats, but there's only one, and Hachirōzaemon takes it away at night and uses it when he comes back in the morning. Besides, the bedchamber at the house is protected by all kinds of latches and bolts. Akimichi could never get in and make his way through the secret places without a guide. Whatever am I to do?"

After a little time had passed, Hachirōzaemon said to Kitamuki, "My young retainers have told me about a rich man who lives in Shinano Province, and I need to go to his house. I won't be away more than four or five days. Call in some women and amuse yourself with games—backgammon, shell contests, picture contests, things like that." He added a strict injunction. "Be very, very sure not to mention the cave to anyone." Then he left for Shinano.

During his absence, Kitamuki wrote a carefully considered letter and sent it off by a woman who had served her for years. The messenger soon reached Akimichi back home, and Akimichi read the letter. "Come tomorrow by palanquin, disguised as a woman. We need to confer here," it said. It also said, "I've had to stay a long time, little as I wanted to. When we meet, I'll tell you how sorry I am that I haven't written before. Please come as soon as you can." Nobody, whether of high degree or low, could fail to praise Kitamuki's loyalty.

Although Akimichi was glad to get the letter, his wife had been living with another man for more than a year—and, according to report, had recently given birth to a child. He did not see how he could trust her enough to go off tamely to the other man's house. But then he reconsidered. Whatever the circumstances, he could make it the basis of an appeal in the afterworld if he perished in a mortal foe's house. Such was the course of honor for a man. And only by steeling his will and risking his life could he accomplish the cherished aim of slaying his father's enemy. Thus he set out with a few attendants.

In accordance with his wife's plan, Akimichi pretended to be a woman visitor from the capital. He had his palanquin taken all the way to the blinds; then he slipped inside the building. Kitamuki received him promptly, and later behaved in such a way as to make it seem that the guest had departed. Meanwhile, she hid him in the bedchamber. The two talked for a long time that night.

"I worried day and night about how angry you must be with me, but no brush could do justice to the man's vigilance. There was absolutely no way of bringing you here to kill him," Kitamuki said. She showed Akimichi all of Hachirōzaemon's defenses. Then the two went in the boat to the cave, and she showed him the whole interior. Akimichi scrutinized the surroundings. What a bizarre place! The bandit had taken such elaborate precautions that it scarcely resembled a human habitation. The sight was indescribably fearful, enough to make a person's blood run cold. The husband and wife forgot their mutual grievances.

Kitamuki left Akimichi hidden in the cave. "He's certain to come back from Shinano tomorrow," she said. "When he does, kill him in here just as you please. I'll help you, even if it costs me my life." It would be foolish merely to call her trustworthy. Akimichi waited in joyous anticipation.

Hachirōzaemon returned from Shinano after nightfall. He entered the main hall, called Kitamuki in, and, as expected, produced innumerable treasures for her to see. That night, he also amused himself by providing wine for a large group of young retainers. After the party, he retired with Kitamuki to his bedchamber and took out a metal hair stick to use as a pillow. It did not seem at all likely that he would go to the cave.

"Are you drunk? Why don't you go and rest from the trip in the place where you always sleep? There must be some among your men who covet all those treasures. This isn't the way to be careful," Kitamuki said.

Hachirōzaemon probably thought that she was right. Even though he had been drinking on an empty stomach, he put on his cuirass and armored sleeves, picked up his spear, and left the bedchamber by way of a narrow door. As he was about to get into the boat, he raised his candle. "There's something odd here. I'm not going to use this boat," he said.

"What's the matter?" Kitamuki said.

"It isn't tied the way it is when I leave it. Besides, it's wet too high; it looks like it's carried more than one person. That's odd too."

Kitamuki must have felt that the plan would fail if he became suspicious, for she answered with a lie. "Oh, yes," she said. "I was so lonely that I took the baby and went for a ride around noon, just to amuse myself. That's all that's odd about it."

Prudent though Hachirōzaemon was, he did a foolish thing. Like many another man, he trusted a woman's word. "All right," he said. The two of them got into the boat, moored it on the opposite side of the stream, and disembarked. When they started up the mountain, Hachirōzaemon said, "You take the candle and go first."

Kitamuki agreed because she did not want to arouse his suspicions by demurring. She climbed in front of him with the light. But she changed her mind on the way. Pretending to stumble, she dropped the candle, which went out.

When Hachirōzaemon saw that the candle had been extinguished, he drew sulfur and a bamboo spill from his tinder pouch, relighted it, and handed it back to Kitamuki, who had no choice but to take it.

"I have to get rid of this light somehow," Kitamuki thought. "If I go up first with it, Hachirōzaemon will get a good look inside the cave from behind me; he'll kill Akimichi and me both." Before she reached the top, she dropped the candle again and tumbled down headfirst, injuring herself slightly. Foolishly off guard and concerned, Hachirōzaemon picked her up and made a new light. "Did you stumble? Are you hurt? Are you all right?" he asked. He produced some medication, gave it to her, and resumed the ascent, leading her by the hand and holding the candle himself.

Just as they were about to go into the cave, Hachirōzaemon hesitated at the entrance. He would go no farther, he announced; there seemed to be somebody inside. Kitamuki feigned anger. "Why do you keep suspecting me like this? I don't understand it. What's so suspicious?" she asked.

"It's just that there's a pattern of moisture where the rock juts out over the portal. I'm sure someone's breathing hard inside," he said.

Kitamuki explained it away. "What a silly thing to say! There usually isn't any moisture because you come and go alone. It's gathering now because you've brought me along."

Hachirōzaemon was foolish enough to let himself be convinced. "All
right," he said. (He may have thought that he ought not to insist.) But
he was a frighteningly cautious man. A small structure about eighteen
feet square stood a short distance from the side of the cave. He went
there, fashioned a dummy, dressed it in armor, and put a spear in its
hand so that it looked exactly like himself. Then he opened the door of
the cave and thrust it in.

Akimichi mistook it for the enemy. "Aha!" he thought. He drew his
weapon, brought it forward, and got ready to strike as hard as he could.
But a strange thing happened. More than 300 voices echoed through the
cave from some unknown place. "Wait, Akimichi! Don't strike!" they
shouted. In astonished gratitude for what seemed a warning from
Heaven, he put away the sword and waited.

After thrusting the dummy inside, Hachirōzaemon relaxed and
entered, confident that nobody was there. To the waiting Akimichi, it
seemed that Heaven had delivered his enemy into his hands. He lopped
off Hachirōzaemon's head with a single blow, and he and his wife both
rejoiced beyond measure. Hachirōzaemon was thirty-one years old.

The reason Akimichi had heard 200 or 300 voices telling him to wait
was this. For no fault of their own, more than 300 men had been killed
when the cave was dug; and their angry spirits, acting in unison, had
seized the opportunity to avenge themselves by uttering the warning.

Akimichi and Kitamuki stole away together hastily. Satisfied of his
wife's devotion, Akimichi wanted to pledge that they would stay together all their lives and come to rest in the same grave. But Kitamuki
refused. "I'm going to become a nun and spend my time reciting
Amida's name and praying for good fortune in the life to come," she said.

Tears streamed down Akimichi's face. "What's this! Are you angry
with me? Why do you talk like that?" he asked.

"I managed to arrange for you to do what you wanted. I didn't love
Hachirōzaemon, but I bore his child, and now I have to offer prayers to
help my child's father win forgiveness for his evil past. That's one thing.
Another is that it would embarrass me to be intimate with you after this.
My love for you, my husband for all these years, made me plan a man's
death. That was a terrible thing for a woman to do, and it will keep on
seeming terrible. It's also embarrassing to think of what other people
will say.

"I'd like to drown myself, but nothing is as precious as life; humiliated or not, I can't help clinging to my wretched existence. When I think about it, it seems to me that I am the most unfortunate person in the world. I married you when I was very young. Then I had to part from you, even before the time when spouses usually have to say farewell in this fleeting world. For love of you, too, I lived a long time with a man I didn't care about, and I suffered the humiliation and unhappiness of conceiving and bearing his child. But even though he was your enemy, I realize that it was horrible to do what I did to my child's father. I simply can't cope with my misery. The only thing I can do is think of this as a chance to achieve enlightenment. I'm going to find a religious mentor and try for rebirth in paradise. Nothing you say will move me." She cut her hair at the age of twenty-two, changed into the black robes of a holy nun, and lived the pure life of a recluse deep in the mountains. Everyone who saw or heard about her admired her character.

The child was sent to serve Yoritomo, provided with a fine fortune, and given his stepfather's name. He was called Yamaguchi no Jirōzaemon.

Akimichi had no desire to remain in society alone. With his mother's permission, he became a monk, ascended Mount Kōya, and lived a pious life.

Whether in the past or in the present, there have been few tales of devious plots to compare with this. Those who read it should take it to heart.

Travel Accounts by Matsuo Bashō

The *haikai* (haiku) poet Bashō (1644–94) was the son of Matsuo Yozae-
mon, a minor samurai who lived at Ueno in Iga Province, about thirty
miles from Kyōto. His given name was Munefusa. In his boyhood, he
became friendly with Tōdō Yoshitada, the youthful heir of a branch of
the local daimyo family, and received instruction from Yoshitada's haikai
teacher, the famous Kyōto master Kitamura Kigin (1624–1705). By
1664, he was already gaining recognition as a poet. In 1666, Yoshitada's
death at the age of twenty-four deprived him of companionship and
patronage and, in the view of some scholars, caused him to leave Ueno to
study poetry, Chinese learning, Zen Buddhism, and calligraphy with
masters in the capital. Whether by that means or another, he acquired a
good knowledge of Chinese and Japanese literature and history during
his early years. He also led an active life as a poet, contributing to haikai
anthologies and compiling an anthology of his own in 1672.

Around the spring of 1672, he left Ueno for Edo (Tōkyō), apparently
in the hope of setting up as a haikai teacher, and by 1677 he was on the
way to establishing a school. In the winter of 1680, he moved from Edo
proper to Fukagawa, an outlying area near the Sumida River, where, a
few months later, a disciple presented him with a banana plant (*bashō*)
for his garden. Before long, his dwelling came to be known as the
Banana-Plant Cottage, and by around 1682 he had taken the pen name
Bashō.

In the winter of 1682, the Banana-Plant Cottage was destroyed in
one of Edo's periodic conflagrations, and Bashō took refuge with friends
in Kai Province. He returned in the following winter, after his disciples

had raised the money to build him a new Banana-Plant Cottage, complete with banana plant, on the approximate site of the old one. In the Eighth Month of 1684, he left Edo again, this time on the first of a series of trips that were to loom large in his life and writings. His main purpose was to visit Ueno and pay his respects at the grave of his mother, who had died in mid-1683, but he also spent time with disciples in various places. During a stay in Nagoya, he and some local disciples composed five linked-verse sequences that became the basis of *Winter Sun* (Fuyu no hi), a collection regarded as the first product of his school's mature style.

Bashō led a quiet life in Edo from his return in the summer of 1685 until the winter of 1687, except for a brief excursion in the Eighth Month of 1687 to view the autumn moon at Kashima Shrine, about fifty miles east of the city. Then, in the Tenth Month of 1687, he embarked on a long western trip that took him first to Ueno and then to Yoshino, Waka-no-ura, Nara, Suma, and Akashi. In the summer of 1688, he reached Nagoya on his homeward journey; in the Eighth Month, he made a side trip to see the moon at Sarashina; and in late autumn he finally reached Edo, after an absence of almost a year.

By the spring of 1689, only a few months later, he had sold the Banana-Plant Cottage and embarked on the most ambitious of his trips. He spent over three months traveling up the Pacific coast to Hiraizumi and down the Japan Sea coast to Ōgaki, and then stayed in and around Ueno, Kyōto, and towns on the south shore of Lake Biwa until the winter of 1691, when he returned to Edo and moved into a new Banana-Plant Cottage with five banana plants.

His health, never robust, had deteriorated badly around 1690, and he remained frail after his return. Because of the renown of his school, which had attracted disciples all over Japan, he was inundated with callers and requests for visits. He was also burdened with the care of a shadowy group of dependents—an ailing man, possibly a nephew, whom he nursed to the end of a last illness, and an indigent nun, thought by some to have been a one-time mistress, with a family of small children. In the autumn of 1693, harried beyond endurance, he closed his gate and refused to see anyone for a month.

In the summer of 1694, much enfeebled, he set out on his last journey to the west, impelled by a desire to mediate between quarreling disciples in Nagoya and Ōsaka and to disseminate a new poetic style that he called *karumi* ("lightness"). He fell ill in Ōsaka and died there on the Twelfth Day of the Tenth Month.

Although Bashō is probably best known today as the author of a distinguished body of poetry and as the founder of Japan's most important haikai school, he was also a prose writer of distinction. In addition to many short miscellaneous pieces, he produced five travel memoirs. One, *The Journey of 1684* (Kasshi kikō, ca. 1687; also called *Exposure in the Fields* [Nozarashi kikō]), recorded his initial trip in 1684 to Ueno and elsewhere in western Japan; another, *A Journey to Kashima Shrine* (Kashima kikō, 1687), the moon-viewing excursion of 1687; a third, *Backpack Notes* (Oi no kobumi, ca. 1690), the trip of 1687–88 as far as Akashi; a fourth, *A Journey to Sarashina* (Sarashina kikō, ca. 1689), the moon-viewing excursion of 1688; and the last, *The Narrow Road of the Interior* (Oku no hosomichi, ca. 1694), the eastward journey of 1689 and the return as far as Ōgaki. *A Journey to Kashima Shrine* and *A Journey to Sarashina* consist of brief prose accounts followed by groups of poems; the other three mingle poetry and prose in the manner of Heian and medieval travel memoirs.

In all of the memoirs, but especially in the longest and most highly regarded, *The Narrow Road of the Interior*, the narrator is an unworldly, physically weak old man, determined to identify with the wandering poets of the past by experiencing hardships and dangers, immersing himself in nature, and seeking inspiration from places famous in literature and history. He is a literary creation, not to be confused with the real Bashō, whose reasons for travel included the practical objectives of propagating his school's principles and working with disciples, and whose provincial admirers seem to have smoothed his path in more ways than the reader is led to believe. Bashō conceived of himself not as a reporter but as an artist, and in *The Narrow Road of the Interior* he did not scruple to omit anything that might have weakened the characterization of his protagonist or diminished the effect he sought to create. Nor did he hesitate to adapt, abridge, or invent for the sake of balance or dramatic effect, as we know from a diary kept during the trip by Sora, his companion. If he had done so, he would almost certainly have produced a less remarkable work.

The Journey of 1684, the first of the two memoirs presented here, is worth attention both as Bashō's initial essay in the genre and as a point of reference from which to approach the second, *The Narrow Road of the Interior*. Although it trails off into a poetry collection, its lyrical descriptions and deft occasional verses foreshadow the greater achievement that lay ahead.

Both translations are complete. Poems marked with asterisks have been translated in whole or in part by Steven D. Carter.

The Journey of 1684

I left my dilapidated riverside house in the Eighth Month of the first year of Jōkyō [1684], trusting to a staff and guided by the words of the man of old: "I pack no provisions for the distant journey; I enter nothingness under the midnight moon."[1] The voice of the wind seemed unaccountably cold.

nozarashi o	Ready in spirit
kokoro ni kaze no	to leave my skull in a field—
shimu mi ka na	the bite of the wind!

aki totose	After ten autumns,
kaette edo o	it is Edo I mean
sasu kokyō	when I speak of home.

Rain fell during the day on which I passed Hakone Barrier; all the mountains were hidden behind clouds.

kirishigure	Mist drizzling down—
fuji o minu hi zo	delightful, also, a day
omoshiroki	with Fuji unseen.

A person named Chiri served as a source of strength on the journey and did everything imaginable for my comfort. We had been on close terms for a long time; he was indeed a man "sincere in intercourse with friends."[2]

fukagawa ya	We set off, leaving
bashō o fuji ni	the *bashō* at Fukagawa
azukeyuku	to Mount Fuji's care.
—Chiri	—Chiri

1. From a verse by the Chan (Zen) monk Guangwen: "Wrapping no provisions for the road, I laugh and sing; / Under the midnight moon, I enter nothingness."
2. From the *Analects* of Confucius.

Near the Fuji River, we found an abandoned child about three years old sobbing in a piteous voice. "Assailed by the autumn wind, the blossoms on the little bush-clover plant will surely scatter tonight or wither in the morning," I thought. "The child's parents, unable to withstand the waves of the floating world, must have brought him to this swift river to await the end of his dewlike life." I left him some food from my sleeve.

saru o kiku hito	You who hear the monkey's cries:
sutego ni aki no	what of an abandoned child
kaze ika ni	in the autumn wind?[3]

How could it have happened? Were you the object of your father's hatred? Of your mother's neglect? I can't believe your father hated you or your mother neglected you. No, this is Heaven's doing; you must simply lament the fact that you were born unlucky.

A steady rain fell on the day when we were to cross the Ōi River:

aki no hi no ame	Fingers will bend at Edo
edo ni yubi oran	on this day of autumn rain:
ōigawa	the Ōi River![4]
—Chiri	—Chiri

Before my eyes:

michi no be no	On the roadside,
mukuge wa uma ni	a rose-of-sharon blossom
kuwarekeri	eaten by my horse.*

It was very dark near the base of the hills, the late moon all but invisible. I rode along with dangling whip, journeying league after league without hearing a cock crow, and started awake at Sayo-no-nakayama as though from the lingering dream in Du Mu's "Setting Out in Early Morning":[5]

uma ni nete	Drowsing on horseback,
zanmu tsuki tōshi	lingering dream and distant moon:
cha no keburi	smoke from a tea fire.

3. Especially in China, it was a poetic convention to interpret the cries of monkeys as sad and touching.

4. The Ōi River was dangerous when its broad channel was full. Chiri imagines Bashō's worried friends as using their fingers to count the days since his departure.

5. "Dangling my whip, I go trusting the horse; / After several leagues, still no cockcrow. / In the woods, I dream a drowsing dream; / When leaves go flying, I start awake."

I went to visit Matsubaya Fūbaku in Ise and stayed about ten days.

I worshipped at the Outer Shrine in the early evening. Twilight shadows veiled the First Torii, lamplight shone here and there, and the wind in the pine trees, blowing from the highest peak of all, seemed to pierce the flesh. Deeply moved:

misoka tsuki nashi	The end of the month, no moon:
chitose no sugi o	ancient cryptomerias
daku arashi	in the storm's embrace.

I wear no sword at my waist but carry a bag around my neck and an eighteen-bead rosary in my hands. I resemble a monk but have the look of a layman; I resemble a layman but my pate is shaven. Even though I am not a monk, a man without hair on his head is treated here as a member of the Buddhist fraternity and barred from entering the divine presence.[6]

There is a stream at the lower end of Saigyō Valley. Upon observing some women washing potatoes:

imo arau onna	Women washing potatoes:
saigyō naraba	if I were Saigyō,
uta yoman	I'd write an *uta*.

On the way back that day, I stopped at a teahouse. A woman named Chō [Butterfly] brought out a piece of white silk with a request to compose a haiku about her name. I wrote this:

ran no ka ya	An orchid's perfume
chō no tsubasa ni	transfers incense to the wings
takimono su	of the butterfly.

Visiting a recluse in his hermitage:

tsuta uete	Ivy planted;
take shigomoto no	a storm wind rustling bamboo,
arashi ka na	four or five stalks.

I arrived at my old home early in the Ninth Month. The forgetting-grass beside the North Hall had withered in the frost until not a trace of it remained. Nothing was the same as before. My brothers' heads were

6. The ban was presumably associated with a rule, dating from at least the ninth century, that prohibited the use of certain common Buddhist words in the presence of the Ise Virgin, the shrine's chief priestess. (As with other Shinto shrines, however, there was already Buddhist ideological influence at Ise long before Bashō's day.)

gray at the temples and there were wrinkles above their eyebrows. "At least, we're still alive." There was no more to say.

My older brother opened an amulet case. "Pay your respects to Mother's white hair. This case is like Urashima Tarō's jeweled casket; your eyebrows have turned quite gray."[7] After we had wept for a time, I composed this:

te ni toraba kien	Were I to pick it up,
namida zo atsuki	it would melt in my hot tears—
aki no shimo	this frost of autumn!

We traveled on foot across Yamato Province to a place called Take-no-uchi in Katsuge District. It was Chiri's home, so we stopped and rested for a number of days.

There was a house far back beyond a bamboo grove:

watayumi ya	Cotton-beating bow:
biwa ni nagusamu	beyond the bamboo grove,
take no oku	solace with a lute.[8]

On a visit to Taimadera Temple on Mount Futagami, I saw in the courtyard a pine tree that must have been 1,000 years old. It could have been called "big enough to hide oxen."[9] Nonsentient though it was, its connection with the Buddhas had preserved it from the ax—a most fortunate and awesome circumstance.

sō asagao	Through generations
ikushinikaeru	of monks and morning glories—
nori no matsu	the pine of the Law.

I made my way alone into the interior of Yoshino, a region of truly vast mountains, where white clouds rested on the peaks and misty rain buried the valleys. Woodcutters' dwellings were visible here and there, looking very tiny. Timber-felling in the west echoed in the east; temple bells struck an answering chord in the listener's heart. Of the men who have entered those mountains to live as recluses, the greater number

7. Urashima Tarō was a fisherman who returned to his native village after spending 300 years with a sea goddess. He aged suddenly when he looked inside a casket, a gift from the goddess, despite her warning not to open it.

8. The sound of the bow suggests a lute (*biwa*).

9. The *Zhuangzi* tells of a serrate oak, "vast enough to shelter several thousand oxen," that has been allowed to grow old because its wood is useless.

have found an escape in Chinese poetry and a refuge in Japanese poetry. Indeed, would it not be fitting to compare the environs to Mount Lu in China?

Borrowing a night's lodging at a pilgrim hostel:

kinuta uchite	Wife of the temple:
ware ni kikase yo ya	let me hear you pounding
bō ga tsuma	on the fulling block.

The onetime site of Saigyō's thatched hut was about 250 yards to the right of the Inner Cloister, its only access a woodcutters' faint path. It faced the opposite hillside across a steep valley, an awesome prospect. The famous "dripping clear water" was still trickling down, apparently unchanged from the past.[10]

tsuyu tokutoku	I would like to try
kokoromi ni ukiyo	washing away worldly dust
susugabaya	with this trickling dew.

If Bo Yi had lived in Japan, he would surely have washed his mouth there; if Xu You had heard about it, he would have washed his ears there.

The autumn sun had already begun to set while I was climbing the mountains and descending the slopes, so I went to pay my respects at Emperor Go-Daigo's tomb without viewing the other famous places.

gobyō toshi o hete	Long years at the royal tomb!
shinobu wa nani o	What is it remembering—
shinobugusa	that "remembrance plant"?

I entered the Ōmi road from Yamato by way of Yamashiro and went on to Mino. Lady Tokiwa's old gravesite was there beyond Imasu and Yamanaka. When Moritake of Ise said, "Autumn wind resembling Lord Yoshitomo," what exactly did he take the resemblance to be?[11] I composed this:

yoshitomo no	The wind of autumn:
kokoro ni nitari	it is Yoshitomo's heart
aki no kaze	that it resembles.

10. A poem attributed to Saigyō: tokutoku to / otsuru iwama no / kokeshimizu / kumihosu hodo mo / naki sumai ka na ("My sleeves never dry in this dwelling where I scoop up clear moss water, trickling in hesitant descent, drop by drop, between the rocks").

11. Yoshitomo (1123–60), a leader of the victorious faction in the Hōgen Disturbance of 1156, fought against his father, Tameyoshi, the head of the Minamoto warrior clan, and

At Fuwa:

akikaze ya	The wind of autumn:
yabu mo hatake mo	bamboo thickets and farm plots
fuwa no seki	at Fuwa Barrier.

I was a guest at Bokuin's house during the night I spent in Ōgaki. At the time of my departure from Musashino, I had been determined to make the trip even if it meant ending as a skull in a field. Thus:

shini mo senu	This autumn evening:
tabine no hate yo	still alive, I come to the end
aki no kure	of travel sleep.

At Hontōji Temple in Kuwana:

fuyubotan	Winter peonies:
chidori yo yuki no	shall we call the plovers
hototogisu	cuckoos of the snow? [12]

Weary of my travel pillow, I went out to the beach in the brightening dark before dawn:

akebono ya	Just before daybreak:
shirauo shiroki	gleaming icefish, of whiteness
koto issun	a single inch.

I made a pious visit to Atsuta Shrine. The precincts were in a sad state of neglect, the collapsed walls hidden by clumps of bushes. Here and there a stretched rope marked the former site of a branch shrine, or a stone bore the name of a god no longer worshipped. Overgrown as they were with mugwort and ferns, the grounds seemed more appealing than if they had been maintained to perfection.

shinobu sae	This lodging: rice cakes bought
karete mochi kau	where even the remembrance plants
yadori ka na	have withered away.

---

was subsequently forced to order Tameyoshi's execution. A few years later, he was killed by a traitor in Owari Province, where he had fled, virtually alone, after suffering defeat in the Heiji Disturbance of the Twelfth Month of 1159 (January 1160). Bashō imagines him as feeling the sadness and loneliness of which the autumn wind was a symbol. Tokiwa was Yoshitomo's concubine, Arakida Moritake (1473–1549) an early haikai poet.

12. Plovers and snow were winter images, peonies and cuckoos summer images. The poem plays on the name of the *fuyubotan*, a type of peony that blooms twice a year.

I chanted poetry on the Nagoya road. A jesting verse:

kogarashi no	A strong resemblance
mi wa chikusai ni	to Chikusai—this figure
nitaru ka na	braving the wintry blast![13]

kusamakura	Travel sleep and showers:
inu mo shigururu ka	is he also moved to tears—
yoru no koe	that dog howling at night?

I walked out to look at the snow:

ichibito yo	People of the town:
kono kasa urō	I'll sell you this elegant
yuki no kasa	snow-covered hat.

On seeing a traveler:

uma o sae	Even a horse
nagamuru yuki no	draws the eye on a morning
ashita ka na	when snow has fallen.

Spending a day at the beach:

umi kurete	Faint cries of wild ducks
kamo no koe	over darkening seas—
honoka ni shiroshi	indistinct splashes of white.

The year drew to a close as I journeyed on, untying my straw sandals here and casting aside my staff there. Thus:

toshi kurenu	While I still put on
kasa kite waraji	hat and straw sandals, the year
haki nagara	has drawn to a close.

Composing such verses, I saw the year out at my mountain dwelling:

ta ga muko zo	The Year of the Ox:
shida ni mochi ou	whose son-in-law leads the beast
ushi no toshi	bearing rice cakes and ferns?[14]

13. Chikusai, the quack-doctor hero of a popular story, wandered the provinces reciting comic verses and meeting with amusing adventures. He stopped for a time in Nagoya.

14. A son-in-law brought his wife's family a special kind of rice cakes during the New Year season.

On the way to Nara:

haru nare ya	Ah, springtime is here:
na mo naki yama no	The morning haze envelops
asagasumi	even nameless hills.

In retreat at the Nigatsudō Hall:

mizutori ya	The water-dipping:
kōri no sō no	clear and cold as ice the sound
kutsu no oto	of monkish footgear.[15]

I went to the capital and visited Mitsui Shūfū's mountain villa. In the plum grove:

ume shiroshi	The plums are pure white.
kinō ya tsuru o	It must be that yesterday
nusumareshi	someone stole the cranes.[16]

kashi no ki no	Ah, what dignity
hana ni kamawanu	in the aspect of the oak
sugata ka na	indifferent to flowers!

On meeting the reverend Ninkō at Saiganji Temple in Fushimi:

wa ga kinu ni	Please sprinkle my robe
fushimi no momo no	with dewdrops from Fushimi's
shizuku se yo	blossoming peach trees.

Crossing the mountains on the Ōtsu Road:

yamaji kite	The wild violets—
naniyara yukashi	somehow strangely appealing
sumiregusa	on the mountain track.

A view of the lake:

karasaki no	Even less distinct
matsu wa hana yori	than cherry blossoms—the pine
oboro nite	of Karasaki.

15. Water-dipping (*mizutori*) is a general term for a series of nighttime austerities still performed by monks at the Nigatsudō, a hall of Tōdaiji Temple in Nara, during the first fourteen days of the Second Month. In one of the rituals, the participants circumambulate the inner sanctuary repeatedly, increasing their speed each time.

16. Bashō politely compares his host to a Song recluse, Lin Hejing, whose name was associated with plum blossoms and cranes.

As a noontime rest, sitting at an inn:

tsutsuji ikete	Azaleas arranged,
sono kage ni hidara	and behind them a woman
saku onna	slicing dried codfish.

Composed as I journeyed:

nabatake ni	As though flower-viewing:
hanamigao naru	sparrows flitting in a field
suzume ka na	of rapeseed blossoms.*

I met an old friend at Minakuchi, someone I had not seen for twenty years:

inochi futatsu	While we two lived on,
naka ni ikitaru	they survived—these cherry trees
sakura ka na	in glorious bloom.

A monk from Hiru-ga-kojima in Izu Province had also been on pilgrimage since last autumn. He heard about me and followed me to Owari in the hope of joining me as a traveling companion. Thus:

iza tomo ni	Well, then, together
homugi kurawan	let us journey, though we must eat
kusamakura	ears from barley fields.

The same monk told me that the Engakuji Abbot, Daiten, had died early in the First Month. Although I could scarcely believe it, I hastened to send Kikaku a message from the road:[17]

ume koite	Longing for the plum,
unohana ogamu	I bow my head and shed tears
namida ka na	before the deutzia.*

Sent to Tokoku:

shirageshi ni	As a memento,
hane mogu chō no	the butterfly leaves a torn wing
katami ka na	in the white poppy.

I stayed with Tōyō again. On the point of setting out toward the east:

17. Kikaku was one of Bashō's disciples. The deutzia (*unohana*) was blooming when Bashō composed this poem (in the Fourth Month); the plum, which blooms in the First Month, is a metaphor for the Abbot.

botan shibe fukaku	The bee that had burrowed deep
wakeizuru hachi no	into the peony's stamens
nagori ka na	sadly takes his leave.

Visiting a mountain house in Kai Province:

yuku koma no	Ah, this shelter
mugi ni nagusamu	where the journeying horse finds
yadori ka na	solace in barley!

At the end of the Fourth Month, I returned to my hermitage and rested from the trip.

natsukoromo	Summer attire—
imada shirami o	before I have even finished
toritsukusazu	picking out the lice.

The Narrow Road of the Interior

The sun and the moon are eternal voyagers; the years that come and go are travelers too. For those whose lives float away on boats, for those who greet old age with hands clasping the lead ropes of horses, travel is life, travel is home. And many are the men of old who have perished as they journeyed.

I myself fell prey to wanderlust some years ago, desiring nothing better than to be a vagrant cloud scudding before the wind. Only last autumn, after having drifted along the seashore for a time, had I swept away the old cobwebs from my dilapidated riverside hermitage. But the year ended before I knew it, and I found myself looking at hazy spring skies and thinking of crossing Shirakawa Barrier. Bewitched by the god of restlessness, I lost my peace of mind; summoned by the spirits of the road, I felt unable to settle down to anything. By the time I had mended my torn trousers, put a new cord on my hat, and cauterized my legs with moxa, I was thinking only of the moon at Matsushima. I turned over my dwelling to others, moved to a house belonging to Sanpū, and affixed the initial page of a linked-verse sequence to one of the pillars at my cottage.

kusa no to mo	Even my grass-thatched hut
sumikawaru yo zo	will have new occupants now:
hana no ie	a display of dolls.*

It was the Twenty-seventh Day, almost the end of the Third Month. The wan morning moon retained little of its brilliance, but the silhouette of Mount Fuji was dimly visible in the first pale light of dawn. With a twinge of sadness, I wondered when I might see the flowering branches at Ueno and Yanaka again. My intimate friends, who had all assembled the night before, got on the boat to see me off.

We disembarked at Senju. Transitory though I know this world to be, I shed tears when I came to the parting of the ways, overwhelmed by the prospect of the long journey ahead.

yuku haru ya	Departing springtime:
tori naki uo no	birds lament and fishes too
me wa namida	have tears in their eyes.*

With that as the initial entry in my journal, we started off, hard though it was to stride out in earnest. The others lined up part way along the road, apparently wanting to watch us out of sight.

That year was, I believe, the second of the Genroku era [1689]. I had taken a sudden fancy to make the long pilgrimage on foot to Mutsu and Dewa—to view places I had heard about but never seen, even at the cost of hardships severe enough to "whiten a man's hair under the skies of Wu." [18] The outlook was not reassuring, but I resolved to hope for the best and be content merely to return alive.

We barely managed to reach Sōka Post Station that night. My greatest trial was the pack I bore on my thin, bony shoulders. I had planned to set out with no baggage at all, but had ended by taking along a paper coat for cold nights, a cotton bath garment, rain gear, and ink and brushes, as well as certain farewell presents, impossible to discard, which simply had to be accepted as burdens on the way.

We went to pay our respects at Muro-no-yashima. Sora, my fellow pilgrim, said, "This shrine honors Ko-no-hana-sakuya-hime, the goddess worshipped at Mount Fuji. The name Muro-no-yashima is an allusion to the birth of Hohodemi-no-mikoto inside the sealed chamber the goddess entered and set ablaze in fulfillment of her vow. It is because of that same incident that poems about the shrine usually mention smoke. The passage in the shrine history telling of the prohibition against *konoshiro* fish is also well known."

18. An allusion to a poem written by someone seeing off a Song monk on his travels: "Your hat will be heavy with the snows of Wu; / Your boots will be fragrant with the fallen blossoms of Chu." Snow on a traveler's hat was associated with hardships and with whitening hair.

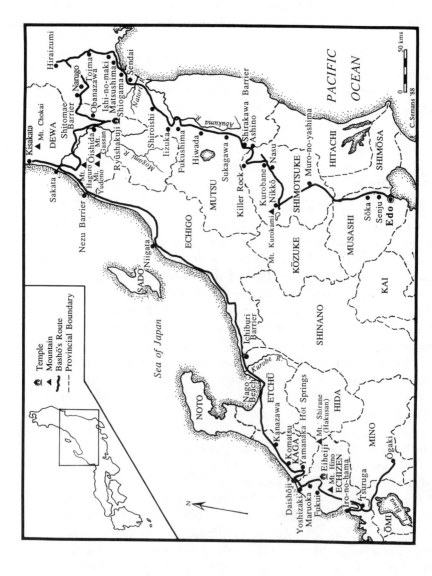

Route of Bashō's journey along *The Narrow Road of the Interior* in 1689

Legend:
- 卍 Temple
- ▲ Mountain
- Bashō's Route
- --- Provincial Boundary

PACIFIC OCEAN

Sea of Japan

0   50 kms

C. Semans '88

Provinces and places (as labeled on map):
Hiraizumi, Narugo, Toima, Mt. Chokai, Shitomae Barrier, DEWA, Obanazawa, Ishi-no-maki, Matsushima, Shiogama, Sendai, Kisakata, Sakata, Haguro, Oishida, Mt. Haguro, Mt. Gassan, Mt. Yudono, Ryūshakuji, Shiroishi, Iizuka, Fukushima, Hiwada, Shirakawa Barrier, Ashino, Nezu Barrier, Niigata, SADO, MUTSU, Sukagawa, Killer Rock, Kurobane, Nasu, Nikkō, Mt. Kurokami, SHIMOTSUKE, Muro-no-yashima, HITACHI, SHIMOSA, KŌZUKE, MUSASHI, Sōka, Senju, Edo, KAI, ECHIGO, SHINANO, Ichiburi Barrier, Kurobe R., Nago Beach, ETCHŪ, NOTO, Kanazawa, Komatsu, KAGA, Yamanaka Hot Springs, Mt. Shirane (Hakusan), HIDA, Eiheiji, Mt. Hino, ECHIZEN, Daishōji, Yoshizaki, Maruoka, Fukui, Iro-no-hama, Tsuruga, MINO, Ōgaki, ŌMI

Rivers: Natori, Mogami R., Abukuma R.

On the Thirtieth, we lodged at the foot of the Nikkō Mountains. "I am called Buddha Gozaemon," the master of the house informed us. "People have given me that title because I make it a point to be honest in all my dealings. You may rest here tonight with your minds at ease."

"What kind of Buddha is it who has manifested himself in this impure world to help humble travelers like us—mendicant monks, as it were, on a pious pilgrimage?" I wondered. By paying close attention to his behavior, I satisfied myself that he was indeed a man of stubborn integrity, devoid of shrewdness and calculation. He was one of those, "firm, resolute, simple, and modest, who are near virtue," [19] and I found his honorable, unassuming nature wholly admirable.

On the First of the Fourth Month, we went to worship at the shrine. In antiquity, the name of that holy mountain was written Nikōsan [Two-Storm Mountain], but the Great Teacher Kūkai changed it to Nikkō [Sunlight] when he founded the temple. It is almost as though the Great Teacher had been able to see 1,000 years into the future, for today the shrine's radiance extends throughout the realm, its beneficence overflows in the eight directions, and the four classes of people dwell in security and peace. This is an awesome subject of which I shall write no more.

ara tōto	Ah, awesome sight!
aoba wakaba no	on summer leaves and spring leaves,
hi no hikari	the radiance of the sun! *

Kurokamiyama was veiled in haze, dotted with lingering patches of white snow. Sora composed this poem:

sori sutete	Black hair shaved off,
kurokamiyama ni	at Kurokamiyama
koromogae	I change to new robes. *

Sora is of the Kawai family; he was formerly called Sōgorō. He lived in a house adjoining mine, almost under the leaves of the banana plant, and used to help me with the chores of hauling wood and drawing water. Delighted by the thought of seeing Matsushima and Kisakata with me on this trip, and eager also to spare me some of the hardships of the road, he shaved his head at dawn on the day of our departure, put on a monk's

19. From the *Analects* of Confucius. Translation after James Legge, *The Chinese Classics*, vol. 1 (Hong Kong, 1960), p. 274.

black robe, and changed his name to Sōgo. That is why he composed the
Kurokamiyama [Black Hair Mountain] poem. The word *koromogae* ["I
change to new robes"] was most effective.[20]

There is a waterfall half a league or so up the mountain. The stream
leaps with tremendous force over outthrust rocks at the top and descends
100 feet into a dark green pool strewn with 1,000 rocks. Visitors squeeze
into the space between the rocks and the cascade to view it from the rear,
which is why it is called Urami-no-take [Rearview Falls].

shibaraku wa	In brief seclusion
taki ni komoru ya	at a waterfall—the start
ge no hajime	of a summer retreat.

I knew someone at Kurobane in Nasu, so we decided to head
straight across the plain from there. It began to rain as we walked along,
taking our bearings on a distant village, and the sun soon sank below the
horizon. After borrowing accommodations for the night at a farmhouse,
we started out across the plain again in the morning. A horse was
grazing nearby. We appealed for help to a man who was cutting grass
and found him by no means incapable of understanding other people's
feelings, rustic though he was.

"What's the best thing to do, I wonder?" he said. "I can't leave my
work. Still, inexperienced travelers are bound to get lost on this plain,
what with all the trails branching off in every direction. Rather than see
you go on alone, I'll let you take the horse. Send him back when he won't
go any farther." With that, he lent us the animal.

Two small children came running behind the horse. One of them, a
little girl, was called Kasane. Sora composed this poem:

kasane to wa	Kasane must be
yaenadeshiko no	a name for a wild pink
na narubeshi	with double petals![21]

Before long, we arrived at a hamlet and turned the horse back with some
money tied to the saddle.

We called on Jōbōji, the warden at Kurobane. Surprised and de-

20. The First of the Fourth Month was the date for changing from winter to summer
clothing.

21. *Kasane* can mean "double," *nadeshiko* both "beloved child" and "wild pink." There
is no such flower as a *yaenadeshiko* ("double wild pink").

lighted to see us, he kept us in conversation day and night; and his younger brother, Tōsui, came morning and evening. We went with Tōsui to his own house and were also invited to the homes of various other relatives. So the time passed.

One day, we strolled into the outskirts of the town for a brief visit to the site of the old dog shoots, then pressed through the Nasu bamboo fields to Lady Tamamo's tumulus, and went on to pay our respects at Hachiman Shrine.[22] Someone told me that when Yoichi shot down the fan target, it was to this very shrine that he prayed, "and especially Shōhachiman, the tutelary deity of my province." The thought of the divine response evoked deep emotion. We returned to Tōsui's house as darkness fell.

There was a mountain-cult temple, Kōmyōji, in the vicinity. We visited it by invitation and worshipped at the Ascetic's Hall.[23]

natsuyama ni	Toward summer mountains
ashida o ogamu	we set off after prayers
kadode ka na	before the master's clogs. *

The site of the Venerable Butchō's hermitage was behind Unganji Temple in that province. Butchō once told me that he had used pine charcoal to inscribe a poem on a rock there:

tateyoko no	Ah, how I detest
goshaku ni taranu	building any shelter at all,
kusa no iori	even a grass-thatched
musubu mo kuyashi	hovel less than five feet square!
ame nakariseba	Were it not for the rainstorms. . .*

Staff in hand, I prepared to set out for the temple to see what was left of the hermitage. A number of people encouraged one another to accompany me, and I acquired a group of young companions who kept up a lively chatter along the way. We reached the lower limits of the temple grounds in no time. The mountains created an impression of great

22. According to legend, Lady Tamamo was a fox-woman with whom an Emperor fell in love. After having been unmasked by a diviner, she fled to Nasu, where local warriors shot her down. Her vindictive spirit survived as Killer Rock, a large boulder releasing poisonous fumes.

23. The hall was dedicated to En no Ozuna (fl. 8th c.), a miracle-working mountain ascetic. The image there is believed to have shown the holy man wearing high clogs and garments of leaves, holding a staff, and leaning against a rock.

depth. The valley road stretched far into the distance, pines and cryptomerias rose in dark masses, the moss dripped with moisture, and there
was a bite to the air, even though it was the Fourth Month. We viewed
all of the Ten Sights and entered the main gate by way of a bridge.[24]

Eager to locate the hermitage, I scrambled up the hill behind the
temple to a tiny thatched structure on a rock, a lean-to built against a
cave. It was like seeing the holy Yuanmiao's Death Gate or the monk
Fayun's rock chamber. I left an impromptu verse on a pillar:

kitsutsuki mo	Even woodpeckers
io wa yaburazu	seem to spare the hermitage
natsu kodachi	in the summer grove.*

From Kurobane, I headed toward Killer Rock astride a horse lent us
by the warden. When the groom asked if I would write a poem for him, I
gave him this, surprised and impressed that he should exhibit such
cultivated taste:

no o yoko ni	A cuckoo song:
uma hikimuke yo	please make the horse angle off
hototogisu	across the field.

Killer Rock stands in the shadow of a mountain near a hot spring. It still
emits poisonous vapors: dead bees, butterflies, and other insects lie in
heaps near it, hiding the color of the sand.

The willow "where fresh spring water flowed" survives on a ridge
between two ricefields in Ashino Village.[25] The district officer there, a
man called Kohō, had often expressed a desire to show me the tree, and I
had wondered each time about its exact location—but on this day I
rested in its shade.

ta ichimai	Ah, the willow tree:
uete tachisaru	a whole rice paddy planted
yanagi ka na	before I set out.

So the days of impatient travel had accumulated, until at last I had
reached Shirakawa Barrier. It was there, for the first time, that I felt

24. The Ten Sights were various rocks, peaks, buildings, etc., within the temple
precincts.
    25. Saigyō (SKKS 262): michi no be ni / shimizu nagaruru / yanagikage / shibashi tote
koso / tachidomaritsure ("'Only a moment,' I thought when I halted, drawn by willow shade
where fresh spring water flowed limpid at the roadside").

truly on the way. I could understand why Kanemori had been moved to say, "Would that there were a means somehow to send people word in the capital!"[26]

As one of the Three Barriers, Shirakawa has always attracted the notice of poets and other writers. An autumn wind seemed to sound in my ears, colored leaves seemed to appear before my eyes—but even the leafy summer branches were delightful in their own way. Wild roses bloomed alongside the whiteness of the deutzia, making us feel as though we were crossing snow. I believe one of Kiyosuke's writings preserves a story about a man of the past who straightened his hat and adjusted his dress there.[27] Sora composed this poem:

unohana o	With deutzia flowers
kazashi ni seki no	we adorn our hats—formal garb
haregi ka na	for the barrier.*

We passed beyond the barrier and crossed the Abukuma River. To the left, the peak of Aizu soared; to the right, the districts of Iwaki, Sōma, and Mihara lay extended; to the rear, mountains formed boundaries with Hitachi and Shimotsuke provinces. We passed Kagenuma Pond, but the sky happened to be overcast that day, so there were no reflections.

At the post town of Sukagawa, we visited a man called Tōkyū, who persuaded us to stay four or five days. His first act was to inquire, "How did you feel when you crossed Shirakawa Barrier?"

"What with the fatigue of the long, hard trip, the distractions of the scenery, and the stress of so many nostalgic associations, I couldn't manage to think of a decent poem," I said. "Still, it seemed a pity to cross with nothing to show for it . . .":

furyū no	A start for connoisseurs
hajime ya oku no	of poetry—rice-planting song
taueuta	of Michinoku.

We added a second verse and then a third, and continued until we had completed three sequences.

26. Taira no Kanemori (SIS 339): tayori araba / ika de miyako e / tsugeyaramu / kyō shirakawa no / seki wa koenu to ("Would that there were a means somehow to send people word in the capital: 'Today I have passed beyond Shirakawa Barrier'").

27. To show respect to Nōin, who established Shirakawa Barrier as a poem pillow (*utamakura*).

Under a great chestnut tree in the corner of the town, there lived a hermit monk. It seemed to me that his cottage, with its aura of lonely tranquility, must resemble that other place deep in the mountains where someone had gathered horse chestnuts.[28] I set down a few words:

To form the character "chestnut," we write "tree of the west."[29] I have heard, I believe, that the bodhisattva Gyōgi perceived an affinity between this tree and the Western Paradise, and that he used its wood for staffs and pillars throughout his life:

yo no hito no	Chestnut at the eaves—
mitsukenu hana ya	here are blossoms unremarked
noki no kuri	by ordinary folk.

Asakayama is just beyond Hiwada Post Station, about five leagues from Tōkyū's house. It is close to the road, and there are numerous marshes in the vicinity. It was almost the season for reaping *katsumi*. We kept asking, "Which plant is the flowering *katsumi*?" But nobody knew. We wandered about, scrutinizing marshes, questioning people, and seeking "*katsumi, katsumi*" until the sun sank to the rim of the hills.

We turned off to the right at Nihonmatsu, took a brief look at Kurozuka Cave, and stopped for the night at Fukushima.

On the following day, we went to Shinobu in search of the Fernprint Rock, which proved to be half buried under the soil of a remote hamlet in the shadow of a mountain.[30] Some village urchins came up and told us, "In the old days, the rock used to be on top of that mountain, but the farmers got upset because the people who passed would destroy the young grain so they could test it. They shoved it off into this valley; that's why it's lying upside down." A likely story, perhaps.

sanae toru	Hands planting seedlings
tamoto ya mukashi	evoke Shinobu patterns
shinobuzuri	of the distant past.*

We crossed the river at Tsukinowa Ford and emerged at Senoue Post Station. Satō Shōji's old home was about a league and a half away, near

28. Saigyō: yama fukami / iwa ni shitataru / mizu tomen / katsukatsu otsuru / tochi hirou hodo ("In these remote hills, I try to trap water dripping onto the rocks; I gather horse chestnuts dropping to the ground").

29. The character for "chestnut" consists of the character for "tree" surmounted by an element resembling the character for "west."

30. The rock was said to have been used to imprint cloth with a moss-fern design, a specialty of the area.

the mountains to the left. Told that we would find the site at Sabano in
Iizuka Village, we went along, asking directions, until we came upon it
at a place called Maruyama. That was where Shōji had had his house. I
wept as someone explained that the front gate had been at the foot of the
hill. Still standing at an old temple nearby were a number of stone
monuments erected in memory of the family. It was especially moving
to see the memorials to the two young wives. "Women though they
were, all the world knows of their bravery." The thought made me
drench my sleeve. The Tablet of Tears was not far to seek![31]

We entered the temple to ask for tea, and there we saw Yoshitsune's
sword and Benkei's pannier, preserved as treasures.

oi mo tachi mo	Paper carp flying!
satsuki ni kazare	Display pannier and sword, too,
kaminobori	in the Fifth Month.

It was the First Day of the Fifth Month.

We lodged that night at Iizuka, taking advantage of the hot springs
in the town to bathe before engaging a room. The hostelry turned out to
be a wretched hovel, its straw mats spread over dirt floors. In the absence
of a lamp, we prepared our beds and stretched out by the light from a
fire-pit. Thunder rumbled during the night, and rain fell in torrents.
What with the roof leaking right over my head and the fleas and mos-
quitoes biting, I got no sleep at all. To make matters worse, my old
complaint flared up, causing me such agony that I almost fainted.

At long last, the short night ended and we set out again. Still feeling
the effects of the night, I rode a rented horse to Kōri Post Station. It was
unsettling to fall prey to an infirmity while so great a distance remained
ahead. But I told myself that I had deliberately planned this long
pilgrimage to remote areas, a decision that meant renouncing worldly
concerns and facing the fact of life's uncertainty. If I were to die on the
road—very well, that would be Heaven's decree. Such reflections helped
to restore my spirits a bit, and it was with a jaunty step that I passed
through the Great Gate into the Date domain.

We entered Kasajima District by way of Abumizuri and Shiraishi
Castle. I asked someone about the Fujiwara Middle Captain Sanekata's
grave and was told, "Those two villages far off to the right at the edge of

---

31. The tablet was a memorial to a good provincial official, Yang Hu (221–78),
erected by the grateful local folk. All who saw it wept.

the hills are Minowa and Kasajima. The Road Goddess's shrine and the 'memento miscanthus' are still there." [32] The road was in a dreadful state from the recent early-summer rains, and I was exhausted, so we contented ourselves with looking in that direction as we trudged on. Because the names Minowa and Kasajima suggested the rainy season, I composed this verse. [33]

kasajima wa	Where is Rain Hat Isle?
izuko satsuki no	Somewhere down the muddy roads
nukarimichi	of the Fifth Month!*

We lodged at Iwanuma. It was exciting to see the Takekuma Pine. The trunk forks a bit above the ground, and one knows instantly that this is just how the old tree must have looked. My first thought was of Nōin. Did he compose the poem, "Not a trace this time of the pine" because a certain man, appointed long ago to serve as Governor of Mutsu, had felled the tree to get pilings for a bridge to span the Natori River? Someone told me that generations of people have been alternately cutting down the existing tree and planting a replacement. The present one is a magnificent specimen—quite capable, I should imagine, of living 1,000 years.

Kyohaku had given me a poem as a farewell present:

takekuma no	Late cherry blossoms:
matsu misemōse	please show my friend the pine tree
osozakura	at Takekuma.

Thus:

sakura yori	After three months:
matsu wa futaki o	the twin-trunked pine awaited
mitsukigoshi	since the cherry trees bloomed.

We crossed the Natori River into Sendai on the day when people thatch their roofs with sweet-flag leaves. We sought out a lodging and stayed four or five days.

I made the acquaintance of a local painter, Kaemon by name, who

32. Someone had planted a clump of miscanthus at Sanekata's grave in allusion to a memorial poem composed there by Saigyō (SKKS 793): kuchi mo senu / sono na bakari o / todomeokite / kareno no susuki / katami ni zo miru ("Only his name, eternally unwithered, has escaped decay: we see, as a memento, miscanthus on a sere plain").

33. *Mino* can mean "straw raincoat," *kasa* "rain hat."

had been described to me as a man of cultivated taste. He told us he had devoted several years to locating famous old places that had become hard to identify, and took us to see some of them one day. The bush clover grew thick at Miyagino; I could imagine the sight in autumn. It was the season when the pieris bloomed at Tamada, Yokono, and Tsutsuji-ga-oka. We entered a pine grove where no sunlight penetrated—a place called Konoshita, according to Kaemon—and I thought it must have been the same kind of heavy moisture, dripping from those very trees long ago, that inspired the poem, "Suggest to your lord, attendants, that he wear his hat."[34] We paid our respects at the Yakushidō Hall and at Tenjin Shrine before the day ended.

Kaemon sent us off with a map on which he had drawn famous scenes of Shiogama and Matsushima. He also gave us two pairs of straw sandals, bound with dark blue cords, as a farewell present. The gifts showed him to be quite as cultivated as I had surmised.

ayamegusa	Let us bind sweet flags
ashi ni musuban	to our feet, making of them
waraji no o	cords for straw sandals.

Continuing on our way with the help of the map, we came to the *tofu* [ten-strand] sedge, growing at the base of the mountains where the "narrow road of the interior" runs.[35] I am told that the local people still make ten-strand mats every year for presentation to the provincial Governor.

We saw the Courtyard Monument Stone at Tagajō in Ichikawa Village. It was a little more than six feet tall and perhaps three feet wide. Some characters, faintly visible as depressions in the moss, listed distances to the provincial boundaries in the four directions. There was also an inscription: "This castle was erected in the first year of Jinki [724] by the Inspector–Garrison Commander Ōno no Ason Azumabito. It was rebuilt in the sixth year of Tenpyō Hōji [762] by the Consultant–Garrison Commander Emi no Ason Asakari. First Day, Twelfth Month." That was in the reign of Emperor Shōmu.

34. A Michinoku song (KKS 1091): misaburai / mikasa to mōse / miyagino no / ko no shitatsuyu wa / ame ni masareri ("Suggest to your lord, attendants, that he wear his hat, for beneath the trees of Miyagino the dew comes down harder than rain").

35. The narrow road of the interior, the source of Bashō's title, extended from what is now northeastern Sendai to Tagajō City.

Although we hear about many places celebrated in verse since antiquity, most of them have vanished with the passing of time. Mountains have crumbled, rivers have entered unaccustomed channels, roads have followed new routes, stones have been buried and hidden underground, aged trees have given way to saplings. But this monument was a genuine souvenir from 1,000 years ago, and to see it before my eyes was to feel that I could understand the sentiments of the old poets. "This is a traveler's reward," I thought. "This is the joy of having survived into old age." Moved to tears, I forgot the hardships of the road.

From there, we went to see Noda-no-tamagawa and Oki-no-ishi. A temple, Masshōzan, had been built at Sue-no-matsuyama, and there were graves everywhere among the pine trees, saddening reminders that such must be the end of all vows to "interchange wings and link branches."[36] The evening bell was tolling as we entered Shiogama.

The perpetual overcast of the rainy season had lifted enough to reveal Magaki Island close at hand, faintly illuminated by the evening moon. A line of small fishing boats came rowing in. As I listened to the voices of the men dividing the catch, I felt that I understood the poet who sang, "There is deep pathos in a boat pulled by a rope," and my own emotion deepened.[37] That night, a blind singer recited a Michinoku ballad to the accompaniment of his lute. He performed not far from where I was trying to sleep, and I found his loud, countrified falsetto rather noisy—a chanting style quite different from either *Heike* recitation or the *kōwaka-mai* ballad drama. But then I realized how admirable it was that the fine old customs were still preserved in that distant land.

Early the next day, we visited Shiogama Shrine, which had been restored by the provincial Governor. Its pillars stood firm and majestic, its painted rafters sparkled, its stone steps rose in flight after flight, and its sacred red fences gleamed in the morning sunlight. With profound reverence, I reflected that it is the way of our land for the miraculous powers of the gods to manifest themselves even in such remote, out-of-the-way places as this.

In front of the sanctuary, there was a splendid old lantern with an

36. An allusion to the pledge exchanged by Emperor Xuan Zong and Yang Guifei in Bo Juyi's "Song of Everlasting Sorrow": "In heaven, may we be birds with shared wings; / On earth, may we be trees with linked branches."

37. A Michinoku song (KKS 1088): michinoku wa / izuku wa aredo / shiogama no / ura kogu fune no / tsunade kanashi mo ("However it may be elsewhere in Michinoku, there is deep pathos in a boat pulled by a rope along Shiogama shore").

inscription on its iron door: "Presented as an offering by Izumi no Saburō in the third year of Bunji [1187]." It was rare, indeed, to see before one's eyes an object that had remained unchanged for 500 years. Izumi no Saburō was a brave, honorable, loyal, and filial warrior. His fame endures even today; there is no one who does not admire him. How true it is that men must strive to walk in the Way and uphold the right! "Fame will follow of itself."

Noon was already approaching when we engaged a boat for the crossing to Matsushima, a distance of a little more than two leagues. We landed at Ojima Beach.

Trite though it may seem to say so, Matsushima is the most beautiful spot in Japan, by no means inferior to Dongting Lake or West Lake. The sea enters from the southeast into a bay extending for three leagues, its waters as ample as the flow of the Zhejiang Bore. There are more islands than anyone could count. The tall ones rear up as though straining toward the sky; the flat ones crawl on their bellies over the waves. Some seem made of two layers, others of three folds. To the left, they appear separate; to the right, linked. Here and there, one carries another on its back or cradles it in its arms, as though caring for a beloved child or grandchild. The pines are deep green in color, and their branches, twisted by the salt gales, have assumed natural shapes so dramatic that they seem the work of human hands. The tranquil charm of the scene suggests a beautiful woman who has just completed her toilette. Truly, Matsushima might have been made by Ōyamazumi in the ancient age of the mighty gods! What painter can reproduce, what author can describe the wonder of the creator's divine handiwork?

Ojima Island projects into the sea just offshore from the mainland. It is the site of the Venerable Ungo's dwelling, and of the rock on which that holy man used to practice meditation. There also seemed to be a few recluses living among the pine trees. Upon seeing smoke rising from a fire of twigs and pine cones at one peaceful thatched hut, we could not help approaching the spot, even though we had no way of knowing what kind of man the occupant might be. Meanwhile, the moon began to shine on the water, transforming the scene from its daytime appearance.

We returned to the Matsushima shore to engage lodgings—a second-story room with a window on the sea. What marvelous exhilaration to spend the night so close to the winds and clouds! Sora recited this:

matsushima ya	Ah, Matsushima!
tsuru ni mi o kare	Cuckoo, you ought to borrow
hototogisu	the guise of the crane.[38]

I remained silent, trying without success to compose myself for sleep. At the time of my departure from the old hermitage, Sodō and Hara Anteki had given me poems about Matsushima and Matsu-ga-urashima (the one in Chinese and the other in Japanese), and I got them out of my bag now to serve as companions for the evening. I also had some *hokku*, compositions by Sanpū and Jokushi.

On the Eleventh, we visited Zuiganji. Thirty-two generations ago, Makabe no Heishirō entered holy orders, went to China, and returned to found that temple. Later, through the virtuous influence of the Venerable Ungo, the seven old structures were transformed into a great religious center, a veritable earthly paradise, with dazzling golden walls and resplendent furnishings. I thought with respectful admiration of the holy Kenbutsu and wondered where his place of worship might have been.

On the Twelfth, we left for Hiraizumi, choosing a little-frequented track used by hunters, grass-cutters, and woodchoppers, which was supposed to take us past the Aneha Pine and Odae Bridge. Blundering along, we lost our way and finally emerged at the port town of Ishi-no-maki. Kinkazan, the mountain of which the poet wrote, "Golden flowers have blossomed," was visible across the water.[39] Hundreds of coastal vessels rode together in the harbor, and smoke ascended everywhere from the cooking fires of houses jostling for space. Astonished to have stumbled on such a place, we looked for lodgings, but nobody seemed to have a room for rent, and we spent the night in a wretched shack.

The next morning, we set out again on an uncertain journey over strange roads, plodding along an interminable dike from which we could see Sode-no-watari, Obuchi-no-maki, and Mano-no-kayahara in

38. "Your song is appealing, cuckoo, but the stately white crane is the bird we expect to see at Matsushima [Pine Isles]." Pines and cranes were a conventional pair. Sora's poem alludes to an old poem of uncertain provenance and unstable wording, one version of which reads in part: chidori mo karu ya / tsuru no kegoromo ("[When snow falls] does the plover borrow the crane's [white] plumage?").

39. Ōtomo no Yakamochi, on the presentation of gold from Michinoku in 749 (MYS 4097): sumerogi no / miyo sakaemu to / azuma naru / michinokuyama ni / kugane hana saku ("For our sovereign's reign, an auspicious augury: among the mountains of Michinoku in the east, golden flowers have blossomed").

the distance. We walked beside a long, dismal marsh to a place called Toima, where we stopped overnight, and finally arrived in Hiraizumi. I think the distance was something over twenty leagues.

The glory of three generations was but a dozing dream. Paddies and wild fields have claimed the land where Hidehira's mansion stood, a league beyond the site of the great gate, and only Mount Kinkeizan looks as it did in the past. My first act was to ascend to Takadachi. From there, I could see both the mighty Kitakami River, which flows down from Nanbu, and the Koromo River, which skirts Izumi Castle and empties into the larger stream below Takadachi. Yasuhira's castle, on the near side of Koromo Barrier, seems to have guarded the Nanbu entrance against barbarian encroachments. There at Takadachi, Yoshitsune shut himself up with a chosen band of loyal men—yet their heroic deeds lasted only a moment, and nothing remains but evanescent clumps of grass.

> The nation is destroyed; the mountains and rivers remain.
> Spring comes to the castle; the grasses are green.[40]

Sitting on my sedge hat with those lines running through my head, I wept for a long time.

natsukusa ya	A dream of warriors,
tsuwamonodomo ga	and after dreaming is done,
yume no ato	the summer grasses.

unohana ni	Ah, the white hair:
kanefusa miyuru	vision of Kanefusa
shiraga ka na	in deutzia flowers.
—Sora	—Sora

The two halls of which we had heard so many impressive tales were open to visitors. The images of the three chieftains are preserved in the Sutra Hall, and in the Golden Hall there are the three coffins and the three sacred images.[41] In the past, the Golden Hall's seven precious substances were scattered and lost; gales ravaged the magnificent jewel-studded doors, and the golden pillars rotted in the frosts and snows. But just as it seemed that the whole building must collapse, leaving nothing

40. Du Fu, lamenting the devastation wreaked by the rebellion in 755 of An Lushan (d. 757), who dealt the Tang dynasty a blow from which it never fully recovered.

41. The coffins contained the mummified remains of Hidehira, his father, and his grandfather; the images were those of Amida Buddha and his attendants Kannon and Seishi.

but clumps of grass, new walls were put around it, and a roof was erected against the winds and rains. So it survives for a time, a memento of events that took place 1,000 years ago.

samidare no	Do the Fifth-Month rains
furinokoshite ya	stay away when they fall,
hikaridō	sparing that Hall of Gold?

After journeying on with the Nanbu Road visible in the distance, we spent the night at Iwade-no-sato. From there, we passed Ogurazaki and Mizu-no-ojima and arrived at Shitomae Barrier by way of Narugo Hot Springs, intending to cross into Dewa Province. The road was so little frequented by travelers that we excited the guards' suspicions, and we barely managed to get through the checkpoint. The sun had already begun to set as we toiled upward through the mountains, so we asked for shelter when we saw a border guard's house. Then the wind howled and the rain poured for three days, trapping us in those miserable hills.

nomi shirami	The fleas and the lice—
uma no bari suru	and next to my pillow,
makuramoto	a pissing horse.

The master of the house told us that our route into Dewa was an ill-marked trail through high mountains; we would be wise to engage a guide to help us with the crossing. I took his advice and hired a fine, stalwart young fellow, who strode ahead with a short, curved sword tucked into his belt and an oak staff in his hand. As we followed him, I felt an uncomfortable presentiment that this would be the day on which we would come face to face with danger at last. Just as our host had said, the mountains were high and thickly wooded, their silence unbroken even by the chirp of a bird. It was like traveling at night to walk in the dim light under the dense canopy. Feeling as though dust must be blowing down from the edge of the clouds, we pushed through bamboo, forded streams, and stumbled over rocks, all the time in a cold sweat, until we finally emerged at Mogami-no-shō.[42] Our guide took his leave in high spirits, after having informed us that the path we had followed was one on which unpleasant things were always happening, and that

42. To emphasize the murkiness of the atmosphere, Bashō borrows from a poem in which Du Fu compliments a Princess by implying that she lives in the sky: "When I begin to ascend the breezy stone steps, a dust storm blows down from the edge of the clouds."

it had been a great stroke of luck to bring us through safely. Even though the danger was past, his words made my heart pound.

At Obanazawa, we called on Seifū, a man whose tastes were not vulgar despite his wealth. As a frequent visitor to the capital, he understood what it meant to be a traveler, and he kept us for several days, trying in many kind ways to make us forget the hardships of the long journey.

suzushisa o	I sit at ease,
wa ga yado ni shite	taking this coolness
nemaru nari	as my lodging place.
haiide yo	Come on, show yourself!
kaiya ga shita no	Under the silkworm nursery
hiki no koe	the croak of a toad.*
mayuhaki o	In my mind's eye,
omokage ni shite	a brush for someone's brows:
beni no hana	the safflower blossom.
kogai suru	The silkworm nurses—
hito wa kodai no	figures reminiscent
sugata ka na	of a distant past.*[43]
—Sora	—Sora

In the Yamagata domain, there is a mountain temple called Ryū-shakuji, a serene, quiet seat of religion founded by the Great Teacher Jikaku. Urged by others to see it, we retraced our steps some seven leagues from Obanazawa. We arrived before sundown, reserved accommodations in the pilgrims' hostel at the foot of the hill, and climbed to the halls above. The mountain consists of piles of massive rocks. Its pines and other evergreens bear the marks of many long years; its moss lies like velvet on the ancient rocks and soil. Not a sound emanated from the temple buildings at the summit, which all proved to be closed, but we skirted the cliffs and clambered over the rocks to view the halls. The quiet, lonely beauty of the environs purified the heart.

shizukesa ya	Ah, tranquility!
iwa ni shimiiru	Penetrating the very rock,
semi no koe	a cicada's voice.*

43. Here, as Bashō does elsewhere, Sora expresses nostalgia for a way of life that had disappeared from the cities to the west.

At Ōishida, we awaited fair weather with a view to descending the Mogami River by boat. In that spot where the seeds of the old *haikai* had fallen, some people still cherished the memory of the flowers. With hearts softened by poetry's civilizing touch, those onetime blowers of shrill reed flutes had been groping for the correct way of practicing the art, so they told me, but had found it difficult to choose between the old styles and the new with no one to guide them.[44] I felt myself under an obligation to leave them a sequence. Such was one result of this journey in pursuit of my art.

The Mogami River has its source deep in the northern mountains and its upper reaches in Yamagata. After presenting formidable hazards like Goten and Hayabusa, it skirts Mount Itajiki on the north and finally empties into the sea at Sakata. Our boat descended amid luxuriant foliage, the mountains pressing overhead from the left and the right. It was probably similar craft, loaded with sheaves, that the old song meant when it spoke of rice boats.[45] Travelers can see the cascading waters of Shiraito Falls through gaps in the green leaves. The Sennindō Hall is there too, facing the bank.

The swollen waters made the journey hazardous:

samidare o	Bringing together
atsumete hayashi	the summer rains in swiftness:
mogamigawa	Mogami River!

On the Third of the Sixth Month, we climbed Mount Haguro. We called on Zushi Sakichi and then were received by the Holy Teacher Egaku, the Abbot's deputy, who lodged us at the Minamidani Annex and treated us with great consideration.

On the Fourth, there was a *haikai* gathering at the Abbot's residence:

arigata ya	Ah, what a delight!
yuki o kaorasu	Cooled as by snow, the south wind
minamidani	at Minamidani.*

On the Fifth, we went to worship at Haguro Shrine. Nobody knows when the founder, the Great Teacher Nōjo, lived. The *Engi Canon*

44. Masters from two older haikai schools had spent time in the area. "Blowers of shrill reed flutes" means untutored country folk.

45. A Michinoku song (KKS 1092): mogamigawa / noboreba kudaru / inafune no / ina ni wa arazu / kono tsuki bakari ("I do not say no [*ina*, like *inafune*, rice boats traveling up and down the Mogami]: it is only for this month").

mentions a shrine called "Satoyama in Dewa Province," which leads one to wonder if *sato* might be a copyist's error for *kuro*. Perhaps "Haguro-yama" is a contraction of "Dewa no Kuroyama" [Kuroyama in Dewa Province]. I understand that the official gazetteer says Dewa acquired its name because the province used to present birds' feathers to the throne as tribute.[46]

Hagurosan, Gassan, and Yudono are known collectively as the Three Mountains. At Haguro, a subsidiary of Tōeizan Kan'eiji Temple in Edo, the moon of Tendai enlightenment shines bright, and the lamp of the Law of perfect understanding and all-permeating vision burns high. The temple buildings stand roof to roof; the ascetics vie in the practice of rituals. We can but feel awe and trepidation before the miraculous powers of so holy a place, which may with justice be called a magnificent mountain, destined to flourish forever.

On the Eighth, we made the ascent of Gassan. Donning paper garlands, and with our heads wrapped in white turbans, we toiled upward for eight leagues, led by a porter guide through misty mountains with ice and snow underfoot. We could almost have believed ourselves to be entering the cloud barrier beyond which the sun and the moon traverse the heavens. The sun was setting and the moon had risen when we finally reached the summit, gasping for breath and numb with cold. We stretched out on beds of bamboo grass until dawn, and descended toward Yudono after the rising sun had dispersed the clouds.

Near a valley, we saw a swordsmith's cottage. The Dewa smiths, attracted by the miraculous waters, had purified themselves there before forging their famous blades, which they had identified by the carved signature, "Gassan." I was reminded of the weapons tempered at Dragon Spring.[47] It also seemed to me that I could understand the dedication with which those men had striven to master their art, inspired by the ancient example of Gan Jiang and Moye.

While seated on a rock for a brief rest, I noticed some half-opened buds on a cherry tree about three feet high. How admirable that those

46. The Chinese graphs representing *sato* and *kuro* are similar in appearance, especially when written in cursive script. The *ha* of Haguroyama and the *wa* of Dewa are written with the same kana symbol and were once the same sound.

47. Dragon Spring (Longquan) was a spring in what is now southern Zhejiang Province, China, whose waters were used for tempering sword blades. Gan Jiang, mentioned in the next sentence, was a swordsmith in the Chinese kingdom of Wu. He and his wife, Moye, forged two famous swords.

late blooms had remembered spring, despite the snowdrifts under which they had lain buried! They were like "plum blossoms in summer heat" perfuming the air.[48] The memory of Archbishop Gyōson's touching poem added to the little tree's charm.

It is a rule among ascetics not to give outsiders details about Mount Yudono, so I shall lay aside my brush and write no more.

When we returned to our lodgings, Egaku asked us to inscribe poem cards with verses suggested by our pilgrimage to the Three Mountains:

suzushisa ya	Ah, what coolness!
hono mikazuki no	Under a crescent moon,
hagurosan	Mount Haguro glimpsed.

kumo no mine	Mountain of the Moon:
ikutsu kuzurete	after how many cloud peaks
tsuki no yama	had formed and crumbled?

katararenu	My sleeve was drenched
yudono ni nurasu	at Yudono, the mountain
tamoto ka na	of which none may speak.

yudonoyama	Yudonoyama:
zeni fumu michi no	tears fall as I walk the path
namida ka na	where feet tread on coins.
—Sora	—Sora

After our departure from Haguro, we were invited to the warrior Nagayama Shigeyuki's home, where we composed a sequence. (Sakichi accompanied us that far.) Then we boarded a river boat and traveled downstream to Sakata Harbor. We stayed with a physician, En'an Fugyoku.

atsumiyama ya	Evening cool!
fukuura kakete	A view from Mount Atsumi
yūsuzumi	to Fukuura.

atsuki hi o	Mogami River—
umi ni iretari	it has plunged the hot sun
mogamigawa	into the sea.

48. "Plum blossoms in summer heat" is a Zen metaphor for the rare and unusual and, by extension, for passing beyond this world to enlightenment. The poem to which Bashō refers in the next sentence was composed by the ascetic Gyōson (1055–1135) when he discovered unseasonal cherry blossoms in the Yoshino Mountains (KYS 556): morotomo ni /

I had already enjoyed innumerable splendid views of rivers and mountains, ocean and land; now I set my heart on seeing Kisakata. It was a journey of ten leagues northeast from Sakata, across mountains and along sandy beaches. A wind from the sea stirred the white sand early in the afternoon, and Mount Chōkai disappeared behind misting rain. "Groping in the dark," we found "the view in the rain exceptional too."[49] The surroundings promised to be beautiful once the skies had cleared. We crawled into a fisherman's thatched shanty to await the end of the rain.

The next day was fine, and we launched forth onto the bay in a boat as the bright morning sun rose. First of all, we went to Nōinjima to visit the spot where Saigyō had lived in seclusion for three years. Then we disembarked on the opposite shore and saw a memento of the poet, the old cherry tree that had suggested the verse, "rowing over flowers."[50] Near the water's edge, we noticed a tomb that was said to be the grave of Empress Jingū, together with a temple, Kanmanjuji. I had never heard that the Empress had gone to that place. I wonder how her grave happened to be there.

Seated in the temple's front apartment with the blinds raised, we commanded a panoramic view. To the south, Mount Chōkai propped up the sky, its image reflected in the bay; to the west, Muyamuya Barrier blocked the road; to the east, the Akita Road stretched far into the distance on an embankment; to the north, there loomed the majestic bulk of the sea, its waves entering the bay at a place called Shiogoshi.

The bay measures about a league in length and breadth. It resembles Matsushima in appearance but has a quality of its own: where Matsu-

---

aware to omoe / yamazakura / hana yori hoka ni / shiru hito mo nashi ("Let us sympathize with one another, cherry tree on the mountain: were it not for your blossoms, I would have no friend at all").

49. Bashō compares Kisakata to the famous West Lake in China, of which Su Tongbo (1037–1101) wrote: "The sparkling, brimming waters are beautiful in sunshine; / The view when a misty rain veils the mountains is exceptional too. / West Lake can be compared to Xi Shi: / She is charming whether her makeup is light or elaborate." "Groping in the dark" is probably an allusion to a poem composed at the lake by a visiting Japanese monk, Sakugen (late Muromachi period): "The sun is setting beyond Yuhangmen; / All the sights are indistinct, there is no view. / But I recall the poem, 'Exceptional in rain, beautiful in sunshine'; / Groping in the dark, I feel West Lake's charm."

50. Attributed to Saigyō: kisakata no / sakura wa nami ni / uzumorete / hana no ue kogu / ama no tsuribune ("The cherry blossoms at Kisakata lie buried under the waves: seafolk in their fishing boat go rowing over flowers").

shima seems to smile, Kisakata droops in dejection. The lonely, melancholy scene suggests a troubled human spirit.

kisakata ya	Xi Shi's drooping eyelids:
ame ni sei shi ga	mimosa in falling rain
nebu no hana	at Kisakata.

shiogoshi ya	At Shiogoshi
tsuruhagi nurete	crane legs drenched by high tide—
umi suzushi	and how cool the sea! *

A festival:

kisakata ya	A shrine festival:
ryōri nani kuu	what foods do worshippers eat
kamimatsuri	at Kisakata?
—Sora	—Sora

ama no ya ya	At fishers' houses,
toita o shikite	people lay down rain shutters,
yūsuzumi	seeking evening cool.
—Teiji	—Teiji, a Mino merchant

Seeing an osprey nest on a rock:

nami koenu	Might they have vowed,
chigiri arite ya	"Never shall waves cross here"—
misago no su	those nesting ospreys?[51]
—Sora	—Sora

After several days of reluctant farewells to friends in Sakata, we set out under the clouds of the Northern Land Road, quailing before the prospect of the long journey ahead. It was reported to be 130 leagues to the castle town of the Kaga domain. Once past Nezu Barrier, we made our way on foot through Echigo Province to Ichiburi Barrier in Etchū Province, a tiring journey of nine miserably hot, rainy days. I felt too ill to write anything.

fumitsuki ya	In the Seventh Month,
muika mo tsune no	even the Sixth Day differs
yo ni wa nizu	from ordinary nights.[52]

51. The phrase "never shall waves cross" constitutes a vow of eternal fidelity. See Glossary, Sue-no-matsuyama.

52. Because people were preparing for the Tanabata Festival, which was held annually on the Seventh Day.

araumi ya	Tumultuous seas:
sado ni yokotau	spanning the sky to Sado Isle,
amanogawa	the Milky Way.

That night I drew up a pillow and lay down to sleep, exhausted after having traversed the most difficult stretches of road in all the north country—places with names like "Children Forget Parents," "Parents Forget Children," "Dogs Go Back," and "Horses Sent Back." The voices of young women drifted in from the adjoining room in front—two of them, it appeared, talking to an elderly man, whose voice was also audible. As I listened, I realized that they were prostitutes from Niigata in Echigo, bound on a pilgrimage to the Grand Shrines of Ise. The old man was to be sent home to Niigata in the morning, after having escorted them as far as this barrier, and they seemed to be writing letters and giving him inconsequential messages to take back. Adrift on "the shore where white breakers roll in," these "fishermen's daughters" had fallen low indeed, exchanging fleeting vows with every passerby.[53] How wretched the karma that had doomed them to such an existence! I fell asleep with their voices in my ears.

The next morning, the same two girls spoke to us as we were about to leave. "We're feeling terribly nervous and discouraged about going off on this hard trip over strange roads. Won't you let us join your party, even if we only stay close enough to catch a glimpse of you now and then? You wear the robes of mercy: please let us share the Buddha's compassion and form a bond with the Way," they said, weeping.

"I sympathize with you, but we'll be making frequent stops. Just follow others going to the same place; I'm sure the gods will see you there safely." We walked off without waiting for an answer, but it was some time before I could stop feeling sorry for them.

hitotsuya ni	Ladies of pleasure
yūjo mo netari	sleeping in the same hostel:
hagi to tsuki	bush clover and moon.[54]

I recited those lines to Sora, who wrote them down.

53. Anonymous (SKKS 1701): shiranami no / yosuru nagisa ni / yo o tsukusu / ama no ko nareba / yado mo sadamezu ("I have no abode, for I am but the daughter of a fisherman, spending my life on the shore where white waves roll in"). Port harlots domiciled near the shore went out in small boats to greet incoming vessels.

54. In this much-discussed poem, Bashō is probably not making an invidious comparison between the prostitutes (showy, ephemeral flowers) and himself (the pure, remote

After crossing the "forty-eight channels" of the Kurobe River and innumerable other streams, we reached the coast at Nago. Even though the season was not spring, it seemed a shame to miss the wisteria at Tako in early autumn. We asked someone how to get there, but the answer frightened us off. "Tako is five leagues along the beach from here, in the hollow of those mountains. The only houses are a few ramshackle thatched huts belonging to fishermen; you probably wouldn't find anyone to put you up for the night." Thus we went on into Kaga Province.

wase no ka ya	Scent of ripening ears:
wakeiru migi wa	to the right as I push through,
arisoumi	surf crashing onto rocks.

We arrived at Kanazawa on the Fifteenth of the Seventh Month, after crossing Unohana Mountain and Kurikara Valley. There we met the merchant Kasho, who had come up from Ōsaka, and joined him in his lodgings. A certain Isshō had been living in Kanazawa—a man who had gradually come to be known as a serious student of poetry, and who had gained a reputation among the general public as well. I now learned that he had died last winter, still in the prime of life. At the Buddhist service arranged by his older brother:

tsuka mo ugoke	Stir, burial mound!
wa ga naku koe wa	The voice I raise in lament
aki no kaze	is the autumn wind.

On being invited to a thatched cottage:

aki suzushi	The cool of autumn:
tegoto ni muke ya	let's each of us peel his own
uri nasubi	melons and eggplant.*

Composed on the way:

akaaka to	Despite the red blaze
hi wa tsurenaku mo	of the pitiless sun—
aki no kaze	an autumn breeze.

At Komatsu [Young Pines]:

moon), but simply using aspects of the scene at the inn to comment in amusement on a chance encounter between two very different types of people. It has often been suggested that he may have recorded the meeting at the barrier—or possibly invented it—as a means of including a reference to love, a standard topic in linked verse.

shiorashiki	An appealing name:
na ya komatsu fuku	The wind in Young Pines ruffles
hagi susuki	bush clover and miscanthus.

At Komatsu we visited Tada Shrine, which numbers among its treasures a helmet and a piece of brocade that once belonged to Sanemori. We were told that the helmet was a gift from Lord Yoshitomo in the old days when Sanemori served the Genji—and indeed it was no ordinary warrior's headgear. From visor to earflaps, it was decorated with a gold-filled chrysanthemum arabesque in the Chinese style, and the front was surmounted by a dragon's head and a pair of horns. The shrine history tells in vivid language of how Kiso no Yoshinaka presented a petition there after Sanemori's death in battle, and of how Higuchi no Jirō served as a messenger.

muzan ya	A heartrending sound!
kabuto no shita no	Underneath the helmet,
kirigirisu	the cricket.

We could see Shirane's peaks behind us as we trudged toward Yamanaka Hot Springs. The Kannon Hall stood at the base of the mountains to the left. Someone said the hall was founded by Retired Emperor Kazan, who enshrined an image of the bodhisattva there and named the spot Nata after completing a pious round of the Thirty-three Places. (The name Nata was explained to us as having been coined from Nachi and Tanigumi.[55]) It was a beautiful, impressive site, with many unusual rocks, rows of ancient pine trees, and a small thatched chapel, built on a rock against the cliff.

ishiyama no	Even whiter
ishi yori shiroshi	than the Ishiyama rocks—
aki no kaze	the wind of autumn.

We bathed in the hot springs, which were said to be second only to Ariake in efficacy.

yamanaka ya	At Yamanaka,
kiku wa taoranu	no need to pluck chrysanthemums:
yu no nioi	the scent of the springs.[56]

55. Nachi in Kii and Tanigumi in Mino were the beginning and ending points on an eleven-province tour of 33 places sacred to Kannon.

56. Chrysanthemums were associated with longevity.

The master was a youth called Kumenosuke. His father, an amateur of *haikai*, had embarrassed Teishitsu with his knowledge when the master visited Yamanaka from the capital as a young man. Teishitsu returned to the city, joined Teitoku's school, and built up a reputation, but it is said that he never accepted money for reviewing the work of anyone from this village after he became famous. The story is an old one now.

Sora was suffering from a stomach complaint. Because he had relatives at Nagashima in Ise Province, he set off ahead of me. He wrote a poem as he was about to leave:

yukiyuki shite	Journeying onward:
taorefusu tomo	fall prostrate though I may—
hagi no hara	a bush-clover field!

The sorrow of the one who departed and the unhappiness of the one who remained resembled the feelings of a lapwing wandering lost in the clouds, separated from its friend.

kyō yori ya	From this day forward,
kakitsuke kesan	the legend will be erased:
kasa no tsuyu	dewdrops on the hat.[57]

Still in Kaga, I lodged at Zenshōji, a temple outside the castle town of Daishōji. Sora had stayed there the night before and left this poem:

yomosugara	All through the night,
akikaze kiku ya	listening to the autumn wind—
ura no yama	the mountain in back.

One night's separation is the same as 1,000 leagues. I too listened to the autumn wind as I lay in the guest dormitory. Toward dawn, I heard clear voices chanting a sutra, and then the sound of a gong beckoned me into the dining hall. I left the hall as quickly as possible, eager to reach Echizen Province that day, but a group of young monks pursued me to the foot of the stairs with paper and inkstone. Observing that some willow leaves had scattered in the courtyard, I stood there in my sandals and dashed off these lines:

57. As one of a pair of travelers, Bashō had probably followed the common practice of writing on his hat the four-character phrase *dōgyō ninin*, "Two persons following the same path."

niwa haite	To sweep your courtyard
idebaya tera ni	of willow leaves, and then depart:
chiru yanagi	that would be my wish!*

At the Echizen border, I crossed Lake Yoshizaki by boat for a visit to the Shiogoshi pines.

yomosugara	Inviting the gale
arashi ni nami o	to carry the waves ashore
hakobasete	all through the night,
tsuki o taretaru	they drip moonlight from their boughs—
shiogoshi no matsu	the pines of Shiogoshi!
—Saigyō	—Saigyō

In that single verse, the poet captures the essence of the scene at Shiozaki. For anyone to say more would be like "sprouting a useless digit."

In Maruoka, I called on the Tenryūji Abbot, an old friend.

A certain Hokushi from Kanazawa had planned to see me off a short distance, but had finally come all the way to Maruoka, reluctant to say good-bye. Always intent on conveying the effect of beautiful scenery in verse, he had produced some excellent poems from time to time. Now that we were parting, I composed this:

mono kaite	Hard to say good-bye—
ōgi hikisaku	to tear apart the old fan
nagori ka na	covered with scribbles.

I journeyed about a league and a half into the mountains to worship at Eiheiji, Dōgen's temple. I believe I have heard that Dōgen had an admirable reason for avoiding the vicinity of the capital and founding his temple in those remote mountains.

After the evening meal, I set out for Fukui, three leagues away. It was a tedious, uncertain journey in the twilight.

A man named Tōsai had been living in Fukui as a recluse for a long time. He had come to Edo and visited me once—I was not sure just when, but certainly more than ten years earlier. I thought he must be very old and feeble by now, or perhaps even dead, but someone assured me that he was very much alive. Following my informant's directions into a quiet corner of the town, I came upon a poor cottage, its walls covered with moonflower and snake-gourd vines, and its door hidden by cockscomb and goosefoot. That would be it, I thought. A woman of humble appearance emerged when I rapped on the gate.

"Where are you from, Reverend Sir? The master has gone to see someone in the neighborhood. Please look for him there if you have business with him." She was apparently the housewife.

I hurried off to find Tōsai, feeling as though I had strayed into an old romance, and spent two nights at his house. Then I prepared to leave, hopeful of seeing the full moon at Tsuruga Harbor on the Fifteenth of the Eighth Month. Having volunteered to keep me company, Tōsai set out in high spirits as my guide, his skirts tucked jauntily into his sash.

The peaks of Shirane disappeared as Hina-ga-take came into view. We crossed Azamuzu Bridge, saw ears on the reeds at Taema, journeyed beyond Uguisu Barrier and Yunoo Pass, heard the first wild geese of the season at Hiuchi Stronghold and Mount Kaeru, and took lodgings in Tsuruga at dusk on the Fourteenth. The sky was clear, the moon remarkably fine. When I asked if we might hope for the same weather on the following night, the landlord offered us wine, replying, "In the northern provinces, who knows whether the next night will be cloudy or fair?"

That night, I paid a visit to Kehi Shrine, the place where Emperor Chūai is worshipped. An atmosphere of holiness pervaded the surroundings. Moonlight filtered in between the pine trees, and the white sand in front of the sanctuary glittered like frost. "Long ago, in pursuance of a great vow, the Second Pilgrim himself cut grass and carried dirt and rock to fill a marsh that was a trial to worshippers going back and forth.[58] The precedent is still observed; every new Pilgrim takes sand to the area in front of the shrine. The ceremony is called 'the Pilgrim's Carrying of the Sand,'" my landlord said.

tsuki kiyoshi	Shining on sand
yugyō no moteru	transported by pilgrims—
suna no ue	pure light of the moon.

It rained on the Fifteenth, just as the landlord had warned it might.

meigetsu ya	Night of the full moon:
hokkoku biyori	no predicting the weather
sadame naki	in the northern lands.

58. Pilgrim (*yugyō*) was a title given the patriarch of the Ji sect of Buddhism. The Second Pilgrim was Taa (1237–1319).

The weather was fine on the Sixteenth, so we went in a boat to Iro-no-hama Beach to gather red shells. It was seven leagues by sea. A man named Ten'ya provided us with all kinds of refreshments—compartmented lunch boxes, wine flasks, and the like—and also ordered a number of servants to go along in the boat. A fair wind delivered us to our destination in no time. The beach was deserted except for a few fishermen's shacks and a forlorn Nichiren temple. As we drank tea and warmed wine at the temple, I struggled to control feelings evoked by the loneliness of the evening.

sabishisa ya	Ah, what loneliness!
suma ni kachitaru	More desolate than Suma,
hama no aki	this beach in autumn.

nami no ma ya	Between wave and wave:
kogai ni majiru	mixed with small shells, the remains
hagi no chiri	of bush-clover bloom.

I persuaded Tōsai to write a description of the day's outing to be left at the temple.

Rōtsu came to meet me at Tsuruga and accompanied me to Mino Province. Thus I arrived at Ōgaki, my journey eased by a horse. Sora came from Ise, Etsujin galloped in on horseback, and we all gathered at Jokō's house. Zensenji, Keikō, Keikō's sons, and other close friends called day and night, rejoicing and pampering me as though I had returned from the dead.

Despite my travel fatigue, I set out again by boat on the Sixth of the Ninth Month to witness the relocation of the Ise sanctuaries.[59]

hamaguri no	Off to Futami,
futami ni wakare	loath to part as clam from shell
yuku aki zo	in waning autumn.

59. The two sanctuaries at the Grand Shrines of Ise are still rebuilt in new locations every 20 years.

Reference Material

Appendix A

Offices, Ranks, and the Imperial Palace

The highest court offices for male subjects, in descending order of importance, were Regent (*sesshō* or *kanpaku*), Chancellor (*daijō daijin*), Minister of the Left (*sadaijin*), Minister of the Right (*udaijin*), Palace Minister (*naidaijin*), Major Counselor (*dainagon*), Middle Counselor (*chūnagon*), and Consultant (*sangi*). Other prestigious titles included Major Captain (*taishō*), Middle Captain (*chūjō*), Guards Commander (*hyōe no kami*, *emon no kami*), and Head Chamberlain (*kurōdo no tō*). There were nine major ranks, each with subdivisions, descending from Senior First through Junior Eighth Lower to Lesser Initial Lower. Unofficially, every male aristocrat also belonged to one or more of the following three groups.

1. Senior nobles (*kugyō*). This group, defined partly by rank and partly by office, consisted of the Ministers of State (i.e., the Chancellor, the Ministers of the Left and the Right, and the Palace Minister); the Major and Middle Counselors; the other holders, if any, of the top three ranks; and the Consultants, who sat with the others on the Council of State even though their prescribed rank was only Senior Fourth Lower. Together with members of the imperial clan, this small group constituted the cream of court society.

2. Courtiers (*tenjōbito*). These were men who had been authorized individually by the reigning sovereign to enter the Courtiers' Hall of the Seiryōden. The group ordinarily included all senior nobles, certain hold-

ers of Fourth and Fifth Rank, and one special category of lower-ranking officials, Chamberlains of Sixth Rank, who frequented the Courtiers' Hall in the course of their duties.

3. Non-courtiers (*jige,* "gentlemen of low rank"). This large group consisted mainly of holders of Sixth and lower Rank.

The women at court fell into three main overlapping categories.

1. Imperial consorts and concubines. An official consort bore the title Junior Consort (*nyōgo*) or Empress (*kōgō, chūgū*), and might eventually be named Grand Empress (*kōtaigō*) and Senior Grand Empress (*taikōtaigō*). An unofficial consort was often known as the Lady of the Bedchamber (*miyasudokoro*).

2. Female officials. The most important of these were the Mistress of the Wardrobe (*mikushigedono*), who often served as an imperial concubine, and the members of the Handmaids' Office (*naishi no tsukasa*), who were in constant attendance on the Emperor.

3. Ladies-in-waiting of the Emperor and his consorts. In the case of the Emperor, these included the Mistress of the Wardrobe and the leading members of the Handmaids' Office.

Imperial Lady (*nyōin*) was a title of respect sometimes conferred by an Emperor on his mother, his sister, or a woman of comparable standing.

Women were eligible for appointment to court rank, but few rose above Third Rank.

The center of court activity, the Greater Imperial Palace, occupied an area of about 400 acres in the north central section of the capital. Among its principal buildings were the Great Hall of State (Daigokuden) and the structures inside the Imperial Residential Compound—the Shishinden (also called Nanden), a ceremonial building; the Seiryōden, the imperial residence; and various buildings usually occupied by consorts, concubines, and their attendants, such as the Fujitsubo (also called Higyōsha), the Kokiden, the Sen'yōden, the Shōkyōden, and the Shigeisha (Kiritsubo). After 960, repeated conflagrations forced successive sovereigns to live elsewhere for years at a time. It became increasingly difficult to find the resources to rebuild, and in 1227 the Greater Imperial Palace finally passed into history, its site commemorated only by the name Palace Fields (Uchino).

Mentions of the Emperor's residence and its structures in works written between 960 and 1227 may refer either to the Greater Imperial Palace or to "town palaces" (*sato dairi*) with buildings named for palace buildings. Mentions after 1227 refer to town palaces.

Appendix B

Classical Japanese Poetry

This anthology contains examples of three forms of Japanese lyrical poetry: the *tanka* ("short poem"), the *chōka* ("long poem"), and the *haikai* ("eccentric [poem]"), as well as references to a fourth, the *renga* ("linked verse"). The tanka is a 31-syllable composition in the metric pattern 5-7-5-7-7; the chōka is a longer poem of indeterminate length in 5-7 meter, usually with two seven-syllable lines at the end; the mature haikai has 17 syllables in the pattern 5-7-5; and the renga is a series of alternating 17-syllable and 14-syllable links, each combining with its predecessor to form one tanka and with its successor to form another. The type of renga composed by Bashō and mentioned most frequently herein was *haikai no renga* ("eccentric linked verse"), so called because the authors disregarded many of the limitations imposed on the renga proper, which was bound by preexisting literary conventions and by extremely complicated rules of linkage.

The tanka and the chōka, the oldest of the four, antedate the classical age. Two general terms for them, which are also used of the tanka alone, are *waka* ("Japanese poetry," as contrasted with poetry written in Chinese) and *uta* ("song"). The renga as a significant form dates from the early medieval period; the *haikai no renga*, from the late medieval period. The basic renga sequence consists of 100 links; a *haikai no renga* usually consists of 36, 50, or 100 links. The haikai, or haiku, as it is usually called today, originated as the first link (*hokku*) in a *haikai no renga* sequence.

For an understanding of the poems in the main body of the anthology and an appreciation of the differences between them and Bashō's haikai, which make frequent use of unsanctioned diction, images, and topics, it is useful to have in mind some of the principal waka conventions. Because few chōka were composed after the eighth century, the discussion below will focus on the tanka.

The development of the tanka was shaped by social practice, by evolving guidelines governing composition for folding screens and poetry contests, and, most importantly, by criteria formalized in the first imperially sponsored waka anthology, *Collection of Early and Modern Japanese Poetry* (Kokin wakashū, ca. 905), and ratified in the 20 imperial anthologies that followed. Anthology poems were organized into some ten to twelve subject-matter categories, which usually included Spring, Summer, Autumn, Winter, Love, Miscellaneous, Parting, Travel, and Felicitations, and of which the best represented were the four seasons and Love.

A superior seasonal composition was held to be one that treated an aspect of nature in a manner showing appreciation of beauty and sensitivity to the passing of time, as has been done in the spring poem below (*Tales of Ise*, Sec. 82).

yo no naka ni	If ours were a world
taete sakura no	where blossoming cherry trees
nakariseba	were not to be found,
haru no kokoro wa	what tranquility would bless
nodokekaramashi	the human heart in springtime!

Seasonal images were not chosen at random. Cherry blossoms were regarded as epitomizing the "essential nature" (*hon'i*) of springtime, and consequently as ideal subjects for a spring poem, because they were especially beautiful and, at the same time, especially fragile. Other recognized spring images were lingering snow, haze, young grasses, the bush warbler, plum blossoms, homing geese, spring rain, willow trees, kerria, and wisteria. For summer, appropriate images were heartvine, sweet flags, the cuckoo, orange blossoms, rice seedlings, summer rain, and cormorant boats; for autumn, the autumn wind, dew, mist, miscanthus, reeds, the moon, autumn leaves, wild geese, insects, chrysanthemums, and frost; for winter, fallen leaves, winter rain, the winter moon, frost, plovers, and snow. To reject such images in a search for originality was to risk failure to capture the spirit of a season.

The pleasures of poetic love were even more equivocal than those afforded by the transitory beauties of nature. As unfolded in an imperial anthology, a love affair was a basically unhappy progression through three stages. In the first, the typical persona was a man lamenting his inability to meet a woman with whom he was passionately in love. In the brief second, a man and woman met, became intimate, and exchanged poems in which the man expressed undying devotion, the woman questioned his constancy, and both worried about gossip. In the third, the man's interest waned and the grieving woman gradually came to accept the fact that she had been abandoned.

Other conventional topics were approached in a similar manner. Feelings of homesickness, loneliness, and anxiety were considered the essential aspects of travel. Partings were sad by definition; approximately half of the 21 anthologies included Laments as a category; and a typical Miscellaneous section contained many poems on social failure, taking Buddhist vows, living in lonely seclusion, aging, and ephemerality.

In short, the Heian cultivation of sensitivity to the "sadness of things" (*mono no aware*) meant that the tone of formal poetry tended to be melancholy, even though casual social compositions were often lighthearted. The serious writer also strove for an effect of elegant beauty, paying close attention to aural qualities, avoiding imagery and diction that might strike a fastidious ear as coarse, ugly, stiff, or shocking, and using figurative language and other rhetorical devices to achieve the kind of verbal complexity that could transform a banal statement into one that sparkled with wit or evoked a deep emotional response.

Two venerable resources, the pillow word (*makura kotoba*) and the preface (*jo*) appear fairly often in classical verse, especially in compositions dating from the Nara and early Heian periods. The pillow word is a short formulaic expression, ordinarily five syllables long, preceding one or more specific nouns or verbs. By the classical age, the meanings of many were no longer understood, and they seem to have been used primarily to add an aura of antiquity. In the example below, from *An Account of a Journey to the East*, "jewel-spear" merely represents what might be a meaning of *tamaboko no*.

> aware ni mo   Ah, how moving to think
> sora ni ukareshi   that his spirit has risen
> tamaboko no   into the heavens,

michi no he ni shi mo	leaving only a name
na o todomekeri	beside the jewel-spear road!

The preface is a longer, nonformulaic expression that decorates or reinforces the main statement of a poem, to which it is joined by metaphorical association, wordplay, or homophony. It often establishes a link between man and nature, as in the example below, a composition by Ki no Tsurayuki from *Collection of Early and Modern Japanese Poetry* (KKS 471).

yoshinogawa	Swift indeed has been
iwanami takaku	the birth of my love for you—
yuku mizu no	swift [as] the current
hayaku zo hito o	where waves break high over rocks
omoisometeshi	in the Yoshino River.

More common during most of the classical age was the pivot word (*kaketotoba*), so called because it was used in two senses, one applying to the preceding phrase and the other to the following, and both contributing to the meaning of the poem. In the example below, from *The Journal of the Sixteenth-Night Moon*, the pivot word is *nami*, which means both "since they are no more" and "waves." A literal translation of the last two lines might read, "The people I used to know are no more; thus [of] the waves I will inquire about the past."

hamamatsu no	I hoped to find friends
kawaranu kage o	unchanged as the shore-pine shade,
tazunekite	but they are no more:
mishi hito nami ni	I can but question the waves
mukashi o zo tou	for tidings of days gone by.

Common kakekotoba, many of which appear in this anthology, are *aki* ("autumn"; "satiety"), *ama* ("nun"; "fisher"), *furu* ("age"; "fall"; a form of *fu* ["go through life," "spend time"]), *haru* ("spring"; "swell"; "stretch"), *iro* ("color"; "situation"; "beauty"; "sexual passion"), *kai* ("efficacy"; "shellfish"; "valley"), *kaku* ("rake"; "write"), *karu* ("reap"; "hunt"), *kiru* ("cut"; "wear"), *matsu* ("wait"; "pine-tree"), *mirume* ("seeing eye"; a type of seaweed), *moru* ("guard"; "leak"), *nagame* ("grief"; "revery"; "long rain"), *tatsu* ("cut out [cloth]"; "leave"; "stand"; "hover" [as of mist or haze]), and *utsurou* ("change"; "fade").

Classical poets also made extensive use of the "associative word," or *engo*. An engo has two meanings: a primary one contributing to the main statement and a secondary one establishing a tonal relationship with something in the statement. In the example below, from *The Journal of the Sixteenth-Night Moon*, the proper noun Utsu echoes the reference to traveler's garments (*tabigoromo*) because it is homophonous with a verb meaning "to full cloth."

tabigoromo	Even between showers
namida o soete	at Utsu-no-yama Mountain,
utsu no yama	showers must have fallen,
shigurenu hima mo	for tears added their moisture
sazo shigururan	to the traveler's garments.

Another kind of overtone was produced by the inclusion of a "poem pillow" (*utamakura*), the name of a place made famous by earlier writers. Each such geographic locale had one or more recognized associations on which a poet might build. Because the associations constituted the place's "essential nature," it was usually considered a mark of ignorance, obtuseness, or eccentricity to substitute others. Thus, no resonance with earlier poems could have been achieved by speaking of the cuckoo, a summer bird, in connection with the Yoshino Mountains, which were associated with cherry blossoms, snow, and reclusion. Some other familiar poem pillows were the Asuka River (impermanence, changeability), Mount Fuji (smoke, snow), Fuwa Barrier (barrier post), Ise (shells, fisherfolk), Kasuga (young greens), Oiso-no-mori (old age), Ōsaka Barrier (parting, meeting, Semimaru), Saya-no-nakayama (old age, Saigyō), Shirakawa Barrier (autumn wind), Sue-no-matsuyama (constant love), Suma (salt-making, exile), Tatsuta (autumn leaves), Utsu-no-yama (ivy, maple, wandering ascetics, Narihira), Waka-no-ura (poetry), and Yatsuhashi (irises, Narihira).

Sometimes the use of a poem pillow constituted a reference to one particular poem, rather than to a body of literature. It then resembled a technique known as allusive variation (*honkadori*, "taking a base poem"). An allusive variation comments in some way on a statement by an earlier writer, who is usually but not always a poet. In *The Clear Mirror*, for example, Retired Emperor Go-Toba's poem in praise of the Minase River takes issue with Sei Shōnagon's famous dictum in Section 1 of her *Pillow Book*, "In autumn, the evening [is most beautiful]." The Retired Emperor's reference to haze indicates that the season of his poem is spring.

miwataseba	The Minase River,
yamamoto kasumu	flowing where haze dims the base
minasegawa	of the distant hills!
yūbe wa aki to	Why did I think of autumn
nani omoikemu	as the time for evening scenes?

In this poem from *Tales of Ise* (Sec. 59), the speaker longs to become a recluse in order to achieve peace of mind:

sumiwabinu	Tired of my life,
ima wa kagiri to	I would abandon it now
yamazato ni	to seek shelter
mi o kakusubeki	in a mountain dwelling
yado motometen	where I can sink out of sight.

At the end of the Heian period, Fujiwara no Shunzei (1114–1204) composed an allusive variation on the *Ise* poem, in which he presented himself as someone who had taken the decisive step of retirement, only to find that the anticipated tranquility had eluded him. His choice of language makes it clear that his poem (SZS 985) is to be considered in conjunction with the earlier one.

sumiwabite	Tired of my life,
mi o kakusubeki	I had thought to seek shelter
yamazato ni	in a mountain dwelling—
amari kuma naki	and now the midnight moon
yowa no tsuki ka na	floods every corner with light.

Shunzei's last two lines contain intentional ambiguities. He may be saying that the beauty of the scene evokes nostalgia for the brilliant court life he has rejected, or that he misses his old quiet association with a few friends during the moon-viewing season, or that he regards the moon as a symbol of the coming of autumn and (by conventional connection) of human aging and his own mortality. If we know something about him, we may favor the last interpretation or a combination of the last two, but we cannot be certain that we are correct. Perhaps the speaker is simply depressed by the slowness of his progress toward enlightenment, the state symbolized by the full moon in Buddhist doctrine. Or we may be intended to pity the solitary figure in his tiny hut, alone in a vast, indifferent natural world symbolized by the moon's cold beauty.

Shunzei rewards attention because he says much in little, even when translated. In this anthology, Bashō is a poet of the same kind. Others—for instance, Abutsu, the author of *The Journal of the Sixteenth-Night Moon*—are harder to appreciate because they often aim to divert and impress through skillful wordplay, rather than to convey unspoken meanings or to elicit an emotional response. Theirs are the compositions that often sound bafflingly trivial in English. For readers who are so inclined, it should be possible to see below the surface of many of their poems by looking at the transliterations with these notes in mind. For others, it may be of some interest to know that more is going on than meets the eye.

Glossary

Terms and names that are listed separately are given in small capital letters.

Amida (Skt. Amitābha). A Buddha. Lord of the Pure Land (Western Paradise), into which believers in him were reborn.

Asuka River. A swift, winding stream in the southern part of the Nara basin, known for its changeable course. Associated especially with an anonymous old poem (KKS 933): yo no naka wa / nani ka tsune naru / asukagawa / kinō no fuchi zo / kyō wa se ni naru ("In this world of ours, what is there of constancy? Yesterday's deep pool in the River of Tomorrow [Asuka River] today becomes a rapid").

Atsuta Shrine. An important old religious center in Owari Province (now within Nagoya City). Said to have been founded by the semi-legendary Prince Yamato-takeru (4th c. A.D.?).

Benkei. Semi-mythical monk-retainer of YOSHITSUNE.

Bo Yi. With his brother, Shu Qi, retired to Shouyang Mountain to live on bracken rather than serve King Wu of Zhou (12th c. B.C.?). The two died of starvation.

Chihaya[jō]. A mountain stronghold in what is now Ōsaka Prefecture. Defended against the Kamakura shogunate by the imperialist warrior Kusunoki Masashige in 1333.

Cinnamon tree. According to Chinese legend, there is a cinnamon tree in the moon. Since the Chinese cinnamon, or cassia (*Cinnamomum cassia*), was unknown in Japan and there was no native word for it, poets regularly referred instead to the *katsura* (*Cercidiphyllum japonicum*), which was usually written with the Chinese character for *gui*, "cassia."

Dengaku ("field music"). A dance form that seems to have begun as a planting ritual in the Heian period. It became a theatrical entertainment for medieval city-dwellers and aristocrats and later formed one of the elements that went to make up the noh drama.

Eight Expositions. Eight ceremonious events, held twice daily over a four-day period, at which each of the eight books of the LOTUS SUTRA was expounded and praised in turn.

End of the Law (*mappō*). A 10,000-year period of decline presaging the final disappearance of the Buddhist religion. It was believed that the period would begin 2,000 years after Śākyamuni's death—i.e., around 1050, according to one theory.

Enryakuji, *see* HIEI

Escort. When capitalized, this word translates *zuijin*, an armed guard assigned by the court to an important member of the aristocracy. A Retired Emperor was entitled to fourteen, a Regent to ten, and so forth.

Fayun (467–529). One of the Three Great Monks of Liang. In his last years, he preached from a hut built on a high rock.

Field music, *see* DENGAKU

Five Hindrances. For a woman, the inability to become a Brahma-king, an Indra, a Māra-king, a chakravartin, or a Buddha.

Forgetting-grass. *Wasuregusa*, a kind of day lily. The first two syllables are homophonous with a form of the verb *wasuru*, "forget."

Forgetting-shell. A literal translation of *wasuregai*, either an unidentified mollusk or a word for an empty shell.

Forty-ninth-day services. Especially in the Heian period, it was believed that the soul of the dead entered a brief intermediate existence before being reborn. On every seventh day until the forty-ninth, the soul had a chance at rebirth, and its fate could be influenced by the acts of the living. Wealthy aristocrats usually arranged for elaborate Buddhist rituals on each of the seven days, culminating in a grand event on the forty-ninth, and for offerings of many kinds.

Fukuhara. Site of Taira no KIYOMORI's villa in what is now part of Kōbe City; became the capital briefly in 1180.

Genji (or Minamoto). A clan of imperial descent. Some of its members, like the protagonist of *The Tale of Genji*, were high court nobles; others were warriors. The warrior branch known as the Seiwa Genji founded the Kamakura and Ashikaga shogunates.

Godless Month (*kaminazuki*). The Tenth Month, so called because it was held to be the time when all the gods left their home shrines to assemble at the Grand Shrine of Izumo.

Gosechi. Dances performed by young girls at the TOYO-NO-AKARI, the final banquet of the GREAT THANKSGIVING services in the Eleventh Month.

Grand Shrine(s). The complex of shrines at Ise centering around the sanctuary dedicated to the Sun Goddess, Amaterasu, revered as the ancestor of the imperial clan.

Great Peaks (*ōmine*). Mount Kinpu and other heights frequented by ascetics in the rugged YOSHINO MOUNTAINS of Yamato Province.

Great Thanksgiving. An elaborate harvest thanksgiving ceremony performed in the Eleventh Month of the first year of a new reign. *See also* GOSECHI; PURIFICATION; TOYO-NO-AKARI.

Hare sticks, hare wands. Presented by members of the nobility to the Emperor and to one another as magical protectors and decorations on the first Day of the Hare in a new year. The sticks, some three to five inches long, were perforated at the paper-wrapped top, from which colored streamers and other adornments were suspended. The wands were slender five-foot rods, covered with paper at the top and tied together in small bundles.

Hasedera, Hatsuse. Two names for a temple dedicated to KANNON in the present Shiki-gun, Nara Prefecture (Yamato Province). Relatively far from the capital but deeply venerated by the aristocracy.

Heartvine (*aoi*). *Asarum caulescens* Maxim, a creeping, ivy-like plant with pairs of heart-shaped leaves growing directly from rooted horizontal stems. Associated in literature with the KAMO Festival, for which it was used as a decoration.

Heiji Disturbance. An abortive coup d'état staged in late 1159 by the court noble Fujiwara no NOBUYORI and the (Seiwa) GENJI clan chieftain YOSHITOMO. It was put down by the HEIKE. Nobuyori was executed, Yoshitomo was murdered as he fled eastward, and the Genji were temporarily eliminated as a military force.

Heike (or Taira). A predominantly warrior clan of imperial descent. One of its chieftains, KIYOMORI, dominated the court toward the end of the twelfth century, and one of its branches, the Hōjō family, held ultimate political power during most of the Kamakura period.

Hidehira, Fujiwara (d. 1187). Last of three successive local Fujiwara chieftains who made Michinoku (Mutsu Province) a quasi-independent power and Hiraizumi a cultural center.

Hiei, Mount. On the Yamashiro-Ōmi border; site of Enryakuji Temple, the headquarters of the Tendai sect of Buddhism. The leading religious institution of the Heian period in terms of wealth, political influence, and military strength.

Hitatare. An amply cut two-piece costume, worn originally by commoners but taken up by warriors and, for private use, by aristocrats. Also an abbreviation for *yoroi hitatare* ("armor hitatare"), a tighter costume worn under armor.

Hiyoshi, seven shrines of. An influential group of shrines at the eastern foot of

Mount HIEI, regarded as protectors of the doctrines expounded in the
LOTUS SUTRA: Ōmiya, Ni-no-miya, Shōshinji, Hachiōji, Marōto, Jūzenji,
and San-no-miya.

Hōgen Disturbance. A failed coup d'état by Retired Emperor Sutoku in 1156.
Sutoku, angered at having been forced off the throne by his father, Retired
Emperor Toba, joined forces with the court noble Fujiwara no Yorinaga
in an attempt to dethrone Emperor Go-Shirakawa after Toba's death, but
was defeated in a single battle by the imperial adherents, prominent
among whom were the warriors Taira no KIYOMORI and Minamoto no
YOSHITOMO. Yorinaga was killed by an arrow as he fled toward Uji, and
Sutoku was exiled to Shikoku, where he died.

Hōjōji. A great temple built by Fujiwara no Michinaga east of his principal
residence, the Tsuchimikado Mansion. It has been regarded as an attempt
to recreate the Western Paradise of AMIDA Buddha.

Isles of the Immortals, *see* PENGLAI

Isles of Rich Harvests (*akitsushima*). A name for Japan.

Iwashimizu Hachiman Shrine. A major shrine on Mount Otokoyama near the
capital. Also called Yawata.

Izumi no Saburō (1167–89). Son of Fujiwara HIDEHIRA. Died a suicide in
defense of YOSHITSUNE's Takadachi stronghold.

Kamo. General term for the Upper and Lower Kamo Shrines outside the capital
near the Kamo River (now a part of Kyōto). Its main festival in the Fourth
Month was a series of colorful events, including the Virgin's Purification,
the Virgin's procession from her residence to the shrines, and the Virgin's
return. There was also a Kamo Special Festival in the Eleventh Month,
another important court event, although the Virgin did not participate.

Kanefusa, Masuo. Elderly guardian of YOSHITSUNE's wife; a hero at the defense
of Takadachi.

Kannon (Skt. Avalokiteśvara). The bodhisattva of compassion; an attendant of
AMIDA especially revered in Heian and medieval Japan.

Kasagi. A mountain (289 m) bordering the Kizu River in what is now Kyōto
Prefecture. Emperor Go-Daigo fled there in mid-1331 after the discovery
of his anti-shogunate plot, trusting to the terrain and the support of
friendly soldier-monks, but was soon defeated and captured by shogunate
forces.

Kasuga. A plain at the western edge of the Kasuga hills, between the present
Tōdaiji Temple in Nara and the Kōfukuji Great Eastern Torii. Site of
Kasuga Shrine, the main tutelary shrine of the Fujiwara clan.

Kinbusen, *see* GREAT PEAKS

Kiyomori, Taira (1118–81). De facto ruler of Japan after 1160. Died shortly
after the start of the war with the Minamoto that brought down his clan
and led to the establishment of the Kamakura shogunate.

Ko-no-hana-sakuya-hime. A goddess who conceived on the first and only night she slept with Ninigi-no-mikoto, the grandson of the Sun Goddess. Vowing that the child would survive if it was legitimate, she entered a parturition chamber, sealed it, set fire to it, and gave birth safely to Hohodemi-no-mikoto. Her shrine banned *konoshiro*, a fish that was thought to smell like burning human flesh when it was broiled.

Kumano. General term for three shrines in Kii Province: Hongū, Shingū, and Nachi. Though widely separated, the three were unified by the Kumano faith, a form of Buddhism devoted especially to the prolongation of life and rebirth in paradise. Kumano was one of the great religious institutions of the Heian and early medieval periods, frequently visited by retired sovereigns and other notables, as well as by wandering ascetics and ordinary pilgrims.

Li Ling (Shaoqing). A Chinese general defeated and captured by the Xiongnu nomads.

Lotus Sutra (Skt. Saddharmapuṇḍarīka-sūtra, J. Hokekyō). A statement of Mahayana Buddhist doctrine revered by the Heian aristocracy. It contains dramatic scenes, anecdotes, and parables, and promises many benefits to those who believe in it and extol it.

Lu, Mount (1,474 m). In northern Jiangxi Province, China. Famous for its beauty and as a Buddhist center; many literary associations.

Masakado, Taira (d. 940). Eastern warrior who revolted and seized control of the main eastern provinces in 939. Killed in 940 by forces under his cousin Taira no Sadamori and Fujiwara Hidesato.

Matsushima. A general term for the 260-odd islands in and around Matsushima Bay and the surrounding scenic area in Mutsu Province.

Meeting Hill Barrier. A literal translation of Ōsaka-no-seki (ŌSAKA BARRIER).

Michinoku. Another name for Mutsu Province.

Mimosuso River goddess. Amaterasu, the principal object of worship at the GRAND SHRINES of Ise. Mimosuso is another name for the Isuzu River, the stream that flows through the shrine precincts.

Minamoto, *see* GENJI

Mirror cakes (*mochii kagami*). An old name for the round, flat rice cakes still displayed in Japan during the New Year season.

Naniwa. The present Ōsaka and its environs.

Ninnaji. A major center of the Shingon sect of Buddhism, situated at what is now Omuro, Kyōto.

Nobuyori, Fujiwara (1133–59). The principal court noble involved in the plot that led to the HEIJI DISTURBANCE in late 1159. He was seized and executed.

Nōin, monk (b. 988). An early wandering monk-poet, known especially for his poem about SHIRAKAWA BARRIER.

North Guards. Warriors who guarded the residence of a retired sovereign, so called because they were stationed in the northern part of the grounds.

Ōsaka Barrier. A checkpoint south of the present city of Ōtsu, on the main road leading eastward from the capital. Poets punned frequently on its first syllable and the then homophonous *au* ("meet").

Ox-Driver, *see* TANABATA

Ōyamazumi. A mountain god. Son of Izanami and Izanagi, the divine brother and sister who created the Japanese islands and begot numerous gods and goddesses.

Penglai (J. Hōrai). The best known of three fabulous island-mountains in the eastern sea, said in Chinese legend to be the dwelling places of immortals.

Purification. A Shinto practice that frequently involved ceremonial cleansing with water. One of the most important such rituals was a preliminary to the GREAT THANKSGIVING, usually performed by the Emperor on the west bank of the Kamo River. Its main feature was an elaborate procession marked by the presence of the Acting Consort (*nyōgodai*), a lady whose function was purely decorative but who nevertheless was the queen of the occasion.

Remembrance plant. *Shinobugusa*, a type of fern commonly found on eaves. The first two syllables are homophonous with a verb meaning "remember," "yearn."

River of Heaven. The Milky Way.

Rokuhara. A region in the vicinity of Rokuhara Mitsuji Temple, east of the Kamo River. It contained the residences and administrative offices of the Taira clan and later became the headquarters of the two deputies the Kamakura shogunate stationed in the capital.

Sacred Spirit Services. A rite to appease pestilence gods and angry spirits, performed annually at Gion Shrine east of the capital. It included a comic dance by "thin men" wearing rectangular cloth masks.

Saigyō (1118–90). Satō Yoshikiyo, a minor aristocrat who became a monk in 1140. Traveled to Mutsu when he was about 30 and again at 68; traveled to Shikoku at 50; spent many years in areas of Mount Kōya and Ise. Departed from current literary practice by writing poetry based on personal experience rather than on prescribed topics. Best known and most influential of the wandering monk-poets.

Śākyamuni. The historical Buddha.

Samurai. This word represents *saburai* ("one who serves"), the earlier form that appears in the texts. In the classical age, some saburai were armed retainers; others served in a general capacity.

Sanekata, Fujiwara (d. 998). A young man of high birth, known as a poet, who was posted to Mutsu Province as Governor. According to legend, he was struck dead for failing to dismount when he passed the road goddess's shrine at Kasajima.

Sanemori, Saitō (1111–82). A onetime GENJI warrior who served the HEIKE. Killed in battle by YOSHINAKA's forces.

Sanuki Retired Emperor. Emperor Sutoku, so called from the name of the province to which he was exiled after the HŌGEN DISTURBANCE.

Sarugaku. A type of popular entertainment involving skits, juggling, miming, and the like. One of the antecedents of the noh drama.

Satō Shōji. Father of Tsuginobu and Tadanobu, two heroes who lost their lives in western Japan while serving Minamoto no YOSHITSUNE. According to legend, their wives tried to cheer their mother-in-law by putting on armor and impersonating their husbands.

Sayo [Saya]-no-nakayama. A steep, dangerous mountain pass in what is now Kakegawa City, Shizuoka Prefecture. Associated especially with a poem composed by SAIGYŌ when he traveled to Mutsu Province as an old man (SKKS 987): toshi takete / mata koyubeshi to / omoiki ya / inochi nari-keri / saya no nakayama ("Never had I dreamed of crossing the Pass of Saya a second time in ripe old age—this is the span of life I have been vouchsafed!").

Shide Mountains. Crossed by the spirits of the dead as they made their way through the nether regions to Enma's court for judgment.

Shikishima. A name for Japan. *Shikishima no michi* ("the Way of Shikishima"): the art of poetry.

Shirakawa Barrier. An old official checkpoint where travelers entered Mutsu Province. Associated especially with the monk NŌIN's autumn poem (GSIS 518): miyako o ba / kasumi to tomo ni / tachishikado / akikaze zo fuku / shirakawa no seki ("Though I left the city with the hovering haze as companion, an autumn wind is blowing at Shirakawa Barrier").

Shōtoku, Prince (574–622). Son of Emperor Yōmei; regent of his aunt, Empress Suiko (r. 592–628). Considered a paragon of good government; also an early sponsor of Buddhism.

Shu Qi, *see* BO YI

Śuddhipanthaka. A disciple of Śākyamuni, the historical Buddha. He is said to have been too stupid to remember his own name, but to have attained enlightenment through his boundless energy.

Sue-no-matsuyama. A mountain not far from Sagajō in Mutsu Province. Associated with an anonymous old song (KKS 1093): kimi o okite / adashigo-koro o / wa ga motaba / sue no matsuyama / nami mo koenamu ("Would I be the sort to cast you aside and turn to someone new? Sooner would the waves traverse Sue-no-matsu Mountain").

Sumeru, Mount. In Buddhist doctrine, a lofty peak towering at the center of every world.

Sumitomo, Fujiwara (d. 941). Military figure in the Inland Sea area. He rebelled against the central government in 939 and was put down in 941.

Sumiyoshi. Also Suminoe. A coastal area in what is now Ōsaka; site of Sumiyoshi Shrine. Associated with poetry and pine trees.

Su Wu (d. 60 B.C.). A general sent by the Chinese Emperor Han Wudi to fight the nomadic Xiongnu people. When conquered, he refused to submit to the Xiongnu chieftain, who exiled him to uninhabited territory. According to legend, he was repatriated nineteen years later, during a period of peace, when a message carried by a wild goose informed Wudi's successor that the general was still alive.

Sweet Flag Festival. Held on the Fifth of the Fifth Month to ward off summer illnesses. It embraced a variety of ceremonies and customs, most of them involving the aromatic leaves and roots of the sweet flag, or calamus.

Taira, *see* HEIKE

Takadachi, *see* YOSHITSUNE

Takasago. Said to have been near the mouth of the Kako River in Harima Province. Associated in poetry with deer.

Tanabata. A festival held on the Seventh of the Seventh Month to celebrate the reunion of two stars, the Weaver Maid (Vega) and the Ox-Driver (Altair), who are separated by the River of Heaven (Milky Way) and can meet only once a year.

Three Crossings, River of (*sanzu no kawa*). A stream that was believed to flow through the nether regions on the far side of the SHIDE MOUNTAINS. It was to be crossed on the seventh day after death by one of three ways: a bridge for the good, shallows for minor sinners, and deep waters for major sinners.

Three Evil Paths (*sanzu*). The three evil paths of transmigration; also called the Three Hells. A person's karma determined which one he would enter after death.

Three Subordinations. For women, subordination to father, husband, and son.

Toshihito, Fujiwara. Famous early-tenth-century court general.

Toyo-no-akari. Flushed Faces Banquet. The grand final banquet of the GREAT THANKSGIVING.

Tsukushi. An old name for Kyūshū.

Two Kings (*niō*). Fierce deities whose statues guard the gates of Buddhist temples.

Uchino ("Palace Fields"). The medieval name for the site of the old imperial palace.

Ungo (1581–1658). A monk who restored Zuiganji Temple; teacher of Butchō, Bashō's Zen master.

Utsu, Mount (279 m). A hill on the mountainous border between Shida and Abe districts in the present Shizuoka Prefecture (Suruga Province). Literary associations derive primarily from *Tales of Ise*, Sec. 9.

Waka-no-ura. A coastal area in Kii Province celebrated for its beauty. Often associated with poetry because the first two syllables of its name are homophonous with *waka* ("Japanese poem").

Weaver Maid, *see* TANABATA

West Guards. Warriors stationed in the western sector of a retired sovereign's residential estate. First appointed by Retired Emperor Go-Toba.

Xi Shi (5th c. B.C.). A Chinese beauty. Originally the consort of the King of Yue, she was later forced to wed his conqueror, the King of Wu.

Xu You. A recluse who washed his ears in the Ying River to cleanse them after hearing that Emperor Yao wanted to abdicate in his favor. Someone gave him a drinking gourd, but he threw it away because he disliked the sound of its rustling in the wind.

Yamato. A name for Japan.

Yawata, *see* IWASHIMIZU HACHIMAN SHRINE

Yoichi, Nasu no. A GENJI warrior who won fame by shooting down a fan displayed on a HEIKE boat as a challenge to enemy archers during the battle of Yashima in 1185.

Yokawa. The northern of the three main compounds in the vast Enryakuji complex on Mount HIEI.

Yoritomo, Minamoto (1147–99). Son of YOSHITOMO; victorious leader of the war against the Taira (HEIKE) in the 1180's; founder of the Kamakura shogunate.

Yoshichika, Minamoto (d. 1108). Son of the famous warrior Yoshiie (1039–1106). Revolted in western Japan in 1101; was put down by official forces under Taira no Masamori in 1108.

Yoshinaka, Minamoto (1154–84). Called Kiso. Cousin of YORITOMO. Leader of northern forces in the war against the Taira (HEIKE).

Yoshino Mountains. A range of high, wild mountains in Yamato Province. Associated with snow, reclusion, and cherry blossoms.

Yoshitomo, Minamoto (1123–60). GENJI clan chieftain killed in the aftermath of the HEIJI DISTURBANCE of late 1159.

Yoshitsune, Minamoto (1159–89). Half-brother of YORITOMO, for whom he fought and won the main battles of the war against the Taira. The two fell out shortly after the final victory, and in 1187 Yoshitsune fled eastward from the capital area to Hiraizumi, where an old friend, the powerful

Fujiwara HIDEHIRA, installed him in a fortress residence, Takadachi. After Hidehira's death, his son Yasuhira attacked Takadachi, overwhelmed its handful of defenders, and forced Yoshitsune to commit suicide.

Yuanmiao (1238–95). A Chinese monk who sequestered himself for fifteen years in a cave he called Death Gate.

Yuima (Skt. Vimalakīrti). A wealthy lay disciple of the Buddha who lived in a small hut.

Zhu Maizhen. A poor man who left home, became rich in the service of the Chinese Emperor Han Wudi (r. 141 B.C.–87 B.C.) and returned home in triumph, "wearing brocade."

Selected Bibliography of Works in English Translation

I. Tales

Anecdotes, Folktales, etc. (setsuwa)

Brower, Robert Hopkins. "The *Konzyaku monogatarishū*: An Historical and Critical Introduction, with Annotated Translations of Seventy-Eight Tales." Ph.D. dissertation. University of Michigan, Ann Arbor, 1952.

Mills, Douglas E. *A Collection of Tales from Uji: A Study and Translation of Uji Shūi Monogatari*. Cambridge, Eng., 1970.

Morrell, Robert E. *Sand and Pebbles: The Tales of Mujū Ichien, A Voice for Pluralism in Kamakura Buddhism*. Albany, N.Y., 1985.

Ury, Marian. "Recluses and Eccentric Monks: Tales from the *Hosshinshū* by Kamo no Chōmei," *Monumenta Nipponica* 27 (1972), pp. 149–73.

———. *Tales of Times Now Past: Sixty-Two Stories from a Medieval Japanese Collection*. Berkeley, Calif., 1979.

Poem Tales (uta monogatari)

McCullough, Helen Craig. *Tales of Ise: Lyrical Episodes from Tenth-Century Japan*. Stanford, Calif., 1968.

Tahara, Mildred. *Tales of Yamato: A Tenth-Century Poem Tale*. Honolulu, 1980.

Romances ([tsukuri] monogatari)

Backus, Robert L. *The Riverside Counselor's Stories: Vernacular Fiction of Late Heian Japan*. Stanford, Calif., 1985.

Cranston, Edwin A. "*Atemiya*: A Translation from the *Utsubo Monogatari*," *Monumenta Nipponica* 24 (1969), pp. 289–314.

Hochstedler, Carol. *The Tale of Nezame*: *Part Three of Yowa no Nezame Monogatari*. Cornell University East Asia Papers 22. Ithaca, N.Y., 1979.

Keene, Donald. "The Tale of the Bamboo Cutter," in Thomas Rimer, *Modern Japanese Fiction and Its Traditions: An Introduction*. Princeton, N.J., 1978.

Lammers, Wayne P. "The Succession (*Kuniyuzuri*): A Translation from *Utsubo Monogatari*," *Monumenta Nipponica* 37 (1982), pp. 139–78.

Rohlich, Thomas H. *A Tale of Eleventh-Century Japan: Hamamatsu Chūnagon Monogatari*. Princeton, N.J., 1983.

Seidensticker, Edward G. *The Tale of Genji*. 2 vols. New York, 1976. Also in paperback.

Uraki, Ziro. *The Tale of the Cavern* (Utsuho Monogatari). Tokyo, 1984.

Waley, Arthur. *The Tale of Genji: A Novel in Six Parts*. New York, 1976.

Whitehouse, Wilfred, and Eizo Yanagisawa. *The Tale of the Lady Ochikubo: A Tenth Century Japanese Novel*. Tokyo, 1965.

Willig, Rosette E. *The Changelings: A Classical Japanese Court Tale*. Stanford, Calif., 1983.

Historical Tales (rekishi monogatari)

McCullough, Helen Craig. *Ōkagami, The Great Mirror: Fujiwara Michinaga and His Times*. Princeton, N.J., 1980.

McCullough, William H., and Helen Craig McCullough. *A Tale of Flowering Fortunes: Annals of Japanese Aristocratic Life in the Heian Period*. 2 vols. Stanford, Calif., 1980.

Military Tales (gunki)

Cogan, Thomas J. *The Tale of the Soga Brothers*. Tokyo, 1987.

Kitagawa, Hiroshi, and Bruce T. Tsuchida. *The Tale of the Heike*. Tokyo, 1975. Also in paperback.

McCullough, Helen Craig. *The Taiheiki: A Chronicle of Medieval Japan*. New York, 1959.

———. *The Tale of the Heike*. Stanford, Calif., 1988. Also in paperback.

———. "A Tale of Mutsu," *Harvard Journal of Asiatic Studies* 25 (1964–65), pp. 178–211.

———. *Yoshitsune: A Fifteenth-Century Japanese Chronicle*. Stanford, Calif., 1966.

Rabinovitch, Judith N. *Shōmonki: The Story of Masakado's Rebellion*. Tokyo, 1988.

Sadler, Arthur L. "The Heike Monogatari," *Transactions of the Asiatic Society of Japan*, Ser. 1, 46 (1918), 1–278; 49 (1921), 1–354. Abridged version in *The Ten Foot Square Hut and Tales of the Heike*. Rutledge, Vt., 1972.

Companion Booklets (otogi zōshi)

Araki, James T. "Bunshō Sōshi: The Tale of Bunshō, the Saltmaker," *Monumenta Nipponica* 38 (1983), pp. 221–49.

Childs, Margaret H. "Chigo Monogatari: Love Stories or Buddhist Sermons?," *Monumenta Nipponica* 35 (1980), pp. 127–51.

———. "Didacticism in Medieval Short Stories: *Hatsuse Monogatari* and *Akimichi*," *Monumenta Nipponica* 42 (1987), pp. 253–88.

Mills, D. E. "The Tale of the Mouse: Nezumi no sōshi," *Monumenta Nipponica* 34 (1979), pp. 155–68.

Steven, Chigusa. "Hachikazuki: A Muromachi Short Story," *Monumenta Nipponica* 32 (1977), pp. 303–31.

II. Memoirs

General

Bowring, Richard. *Murasaki Shikibu: Her Diary and Poetic Memoirs*. Princeton, N.J., 1982.

Brazell, Karen. *The Confessions of Lady Nijō*. Stanford, Calif., 1982.

Brewster, Jennifer. *The Emperor Horikawa Diary: Sanuki no Suke Nikki by Fujiwara no Nagako*. Honolulu, 1977.

Cranston, Edwin A. *The Izumi Shikibu Diary: A Romance of the Heian Court*. Cambridge, Mass., 1969.

Harries, Phillip Tudor. *The Poetic Memoirs of Lady Daibu*. Stanford, Calif., 1980.

Keene, Donald. "An Account of My Hut," in Keene, *Anthology of Japanese Literature*. New York, 1955.

———. *Essays in Idleness: The Tsurezuregusa of Kenkō*. New York, 1967.

Miner, Earl. *Japanese Poetic Diaries*. Berkeley, Calif., 1969.

Morris, Ivan. *As I Crossed a Bridge of Dreams: Recollections of a Woman in Eleventh-Century Japan*. New York, 1971.

———. *The Pillow Book of Sei Shōnagon*. 2 vols. New York, 1967.

Seidensticker, Edward G. *The Gossamer Years: The Diary of a Noblewoman of Heian Japan*. Rutland, Vt., 1964.

Terasaki, Etsuko. "The Saga Diary," *Literature East and West* 15: 4–16: 1–2 (Dec. 1971–Mar.-June 1972), pp. 701–18.
Whitehouse, Wilfrid, and Eizo Yanagisawa. *Lady Nijō's Own Story*. Rutland, Vt., 1974.

Travel Accounts

Britton, Dorothy. *A Haiku Journey*. Kodansha International: Tokyo and Palo Alto, Calif., 1980.
Carter, Steven D. "Sōgi in the East Country: *Shirakawa kikō*," *Monumenta Nipponica* 42 (1987), pp. 167–209.
Corman, Cid, and Kamaike Susumu. *Back Roads to Far Towns*. New York, 1968.
Katō, Eileen. "Pilgrimage to Dazaifu: Sōgi's *Tsukushi no Michi no Ki*," *Monumenta Nipponica* 34 (1979), pp. 333–67.
Keene, Donald. "Bashō's Journey to Sarashina," in Keene, *Landscapes and Portraits: Appreciations of Japanese Culture*. Kodansha International: Tokyo and Palo Alto, Calif., 1971.
———. "Bashō's Journey of 1684," in Keene, *Landscapes and Portraits: Appreciations of Japanese Culture*. Kodansha International: Tokyo and Palo Alto, Calif., 1971.
McCullough, Helen Craig. "A Tosa Journal," in McCullough, tr., *Kokin Wakashū: The First Imperial Anthology of Japanese Poetry*. Stanford, Calif., 1985.
Plutschow, Herbert, and Hideichi Fukuda. *Four Japanese Travel Diaries of the Middle Ages*. Cornell University East Asia Papers 25. Ithaca, N.Y., 1981.
Yuasa, Nobuyuki. *Bashō: The Narrow Road to the Deep North and Other Travel Sketches*. Baltimore, 1966. Paperback.

Library of Congress Cataloging-in-Publication Data

Classical Japanese prose: an anthology / compiled and edited
  by Helen Craig McCullough.
    p.   cm.
  Includes bibliographical references.
  ISBN 0-8047-1628-5 (hbk.): ISBN 0-8047-1960-8 (pbk.)
  I. Japanese prose literature—Heian period, 794–1185.
  2. Japanese prose literature—1185–1600.
  PL777.115.C57   1990
  895.6'808—dc20   89-78331
                                                   CIP

⊗ This book is printed on acid-free paper

7321